Landscapes and Artefacts:

Studies in East Anglian Archaeology Presented to Andrew Rogerson

Edited by

Steven Ashley and Adrian Marsden

Archaeopress Archaeology

Archaeopress
Gordon House
276 Banbury Road
Oxford OX2 7ED

www.archaeopress.com

ISBN 978 1 905739 75 2

© Archaeopress and the individual authors 2014

Cover images: Silver fish from East Walton, Norfolk (© Norwich Castle Museum and Art Gallery)
Badeslade's pocket-sized map of Norfolk from *Chorographia Britanniae* published in 1742
Back cover image: Photograph of Andrew Rogerson at Wicken Bonhunt 1972 (Bob Carr)

All rights reserved. No part of this book may be reproduced, stored in retrieval system,
or transmitted, in any form or by any means, electronic, mechanical, photocopying or otherwise,
without the prior written permission of the copyright owners.

Printed in England by CMP (UK) Ltd

This book is available direct from Archaeopress or from our website www.archaeopress.com

Contents

LIST OF CONTRIBUTORS iii

ACKNOWLEDGEMENTS v

INTRODUCTION vii
Tom Williamson, Steven Ashley and Adrian Marsden

LIST OF PUBLICATIONS BY ANDREW ROGERSON xi
Compiled by Steven Ashley

DIGGING A SAXON CEMETERY 1
Anthony Thwaite

LATE BRONZE AGE FINDS FROM BANYARD'S HALL, BUNWELL, NORFOLK 3
Andrew J. Lawson

A LATE BRONZE AGE HOARD FROM FELTWELL 11
Alan West

THE BOUDICA CODE: RECOGNISING A 'SYMBOLIC LOGIC'
WITHIN IRON AGE MATERIAL CULTURE 27
John Davies

SOME ROMAN BROOCHES FROM SCOLE AND ELSEWHERE 35
Jude Plouviez

SATYRS, LEOPARDS, RIDERS AND RAVENS 45
Adrian Marsden

ICKLINGHAM: A PROVOCATIVE VIEW OF A CENTRE OF WEALTH AND POWER
IN WESTERN EAST ANGLIA 73
Stanley West

'SPONG MAN' IN CONTEXT 79
Catherine Hills

THE ANGLO-SAXON CEMETERY AT MORNING THORPE: FURTHER THOUGHTS 89
Kenneth Penn

THE COMPLEAT ANGLO-SAXONIST: SOME NEW AND
NEGLECTED EARLY ANGLO-SAXON FISH
FOR ANDREW ROGERSON 113
Helen Geake

THE WICKHAM SKEITH, THWAITE OR CAMPSEY ASH COIN HOARD................................. 123
Edward Martin

NORWICH BEFORE NORWICH: AN EXPLORATION OF THE PRE-URBAN
LANDSCAPE OF THE MEDIEVAL CITY 129
Brian Ayers

BAWSEY – A 'PRODUCTIVE' SITE IN WEST NORFOLK... 139
Tim Pestell

THE FRANSHAMS IN CONTEXT: ISOLATED CHURCHES AND COMMON EDGE DRIFT 167
Tom Williamson

THE ELMHAMS RE-VISITED 181
Stephen Heywood

GREAT DUNHAM CHURCH AND ITS ELEVENTH-CENTURY CONTEXT 189
T.A. Heslop

RECENT FINDS OF LATE TWELFTH OR EARLY THIRTEENTH-CENTURY SWORD AND DAGGER POMMELS ASSOCIATED WITH THE CRUSADES 199
Steven Ashley and Martin Biddle

TOO MANY CHURCHES: THE ENIGMA OF A NORWICH CHAPEL OF ST ANN 211
Elizabeth Rutledge

THOMAS BADESLADE: HIS LIFE AND CAREER FROM
EASTERN ENGLAND TO NORTH WALES 217
Bob Silvester

NEW BUCKENHAM IN 1820 231
Paul Rutledge

AN EXPERIMENT IN CONSERVATION:
THE EARLY YEARS OF THE NORFOLK ARCHAEOLOGICAL TRUST 235
Peter Wade-Martins

List of Contributors

Steven Ashley DipHS, FSA,
Norfolk Historic Environment Service, Union House, Gressenhall, East Dereham, Norfolk NR20 4DR
steven.ashley@norfolk.gov.uk

Brian Ayers BA, FSA, FRSA, MIfA,
Former Norfolk County Archaeologist, now Honorary Senior Lecturer, University of East Anglia
b.ayers@uea.ac.uk

Martin Biddle OBE, FBA, FSA,
19 Hamilton Road,
Oxford OX2 4BY
martin.biddle@hertford.ox.ac.uk

John A. Davies PhD, FSA,
Chief Curator, Norfolk Museums Service, Shirehall, Market Avenue, Norwich NR1 3JQ
john.davies@norfolk.gov.uk

Helen Geake PhD, FSA,
White Cottage, Mill Lane, Woolpit, Bury St Edmunds, Suffolk IP30 9QX
hg260@cam.ac.uk

T.A. Heslop FSA,
Professor of Visual Arts, Sainsbury Institute for Art, University of East Anglia
t.heslop@uea.ac.uk

Stephen Heywood MA, FSA,
Pitt's Hill Farmhouse, Pitt's Hill, Saxlingham Nethergate, Norfolk NR15 1PB
stephen.heywood@btinternet.com

Catherine Hills PhD, FSA,
Newnham College, Cambridge, Sidgwick Avenue, CB3 9DF
ch35@cam.ac.uk

Andrew J. Lawson MSc, FSA, MIfA,
29 St Ann St, Salisbury, Wiltshire SP1 2DP
andrew.lawson@tiscali.co.uk.

Adrian Marsden D.Phil,
Norfolk Historic Environment Service, Shirehall, Market Avenue, Norwich NR1 3JQ
adrian.marsden@norfolk.gov.uk

Edward Martin BA,
Oak Tree Farm, Finborough Road, Hitcham, Ipswich, Suffolk IP7 7LS
edwardmartin8@btinternet.com

Kenneth Penn FSA,
19 Tillett Close, Ormesby St Margaret, Great Yarmouth, Norfolk NR29 3PW
kennethpenn@hotmail.co.uk

Tim Pestell PhD, FSA,
Curator, Norfolk Museums Service, Shirehall, Market Avenue, Norwich NR1 3JQ
tim.pestell@norfolk.gov.uk

Jude Plouviez BA, FSA,
Archaeological Service, Suffolk County Council, IP33 1RX
jude.plouviez@suffolk.gov.uk

Elizabeth Rutledge LLB,
Research Associate, School of History, University of East Anglia
member@erutledge.fsnet.co.uk

Paul Rutledge MA,
Research Associate, School of History, University of East Anglia
member@erutledge.fsnet.co.uk

R.J. Silvester BA, PhD, FSA, MIfA,
Deputy Director & Head of Field Services Clwyd-Powys Archaeological Trust, 41 Broad Street, Welshpool, Powys SY21 7RR
bobsilvester@cpat.org.uk

Anthony Thwaite OBE, MA, Hon DLitt., FSA,
The Mill House, Low Tharston, Norfolk NR15 2YN
athwaite@me.com

Peter Wade-Martins PhD, FSA,
The Longhouse, 46, Eastgate Street, North Elmham, Dereham, Norfolk, NR20 5HD
peterwm@hotmail.com

Alan E. West BA,
Curator, Norfolk Museums Service, Shirehall, Market Avenue, Norwich NR1 3JQ
alan.west@norfolk.gov.uk

Stanley E. West MA, PhD, FSA,
The Paddocks, Upthorpe, Cam, Dursley, Gloucestershire, GL11 5HR
sandiwest1@btinternet.com

Tom Williamson,
Professor of History, University of East Anglia
T.Williamson@uea.ac.uk

Acknowledgements

We are most grateful to Jenny Glazebrook for assistance with copy editing the papers in this volume and for many helpful suggestions; and to Andrew Hall, who, at very short notice, gave much of his time to edit and prepare many of the figures included herein. Thanks are also due to Bob Carr who kindly provided some of the photographs of Andrew used in the Introduction and on the back cover.

Introduction

Tom Williamson, Steven Ashley and Adrian Marsden

Andrew Rogerson is widely recognised as one of the most important and influential archaeologists in East Anglia, but he was born on the other side of the country, at Whitchurch in Shropshire, on 30 May 1949. He comes from a long line of doctors and clergymen: his English father and Welsh mother were both GPs. He attended prep school in Staffordshire before going on to Ampleforth College and then to Liverpool University to read Archaeology and History. Andrew moved to Norfolk in 1970 to join Peter Wade-Martins' excavations at North Elmham Park. It was while working on the excavations at nearby Spong Hill in 1972 that he met his wife Julia (Peckham), on holiday from her sculpture course at Camberwell. Andrew also worked on a number of sites in a variety of places outside Norfolk around this time, including Oxford, Grantham, Wallingford and Wicken Bonhunt, returning to his home town in 1973 and 1976 to conduct solo excavations in advance of a bypass, where he rescued evidence of Roman burials: the complete Roman mirror he discovered remains on display in the town museum. Andrew was one of the founder members of the Norfolk Archaeological Unit in 1973 (along with Peter Wade-Martins, Keith Wade, Bob Carr and Derek Edwards) and in the same year directed the organisation's first major excavation, at Scole, on the Norfolk-Suffolk border. He has worked for the NAU, and its various subsequent non-contracting incarnations (now Norfolk Historic Environment Service), ever since. He was elected a Fellow of the Society of Antiquaries in 1990.

The essays assembled in this volume represent a particularly fitting tribute to Andrew Rogerson's work in East Anglia over many decades, closely reflecting his principal interests in archaeology and history. In part this happy correspondence simply arises from the fact that those invited to contribute to a *festschrift* of necessity feel an obligation to address some issue of interest to the recipient. But it is in addition a sign of the profound influence that Andrew himself has exercised upon those with whom he was worked, to an extent which he would himself, almost certainly, fail to recognise. This influence has been exercised not only though his many publications and lectures but also though years of informal contacts and a number of the contributors, especially Brian Ayers, recollect the impact made on their own ideas by one of Andrew's throw-away lines or off-the-cuff, often half-humorous comments. What binds these essays together, more than with most such volumes, is thus the character of Andrew himself. Yet at the same time the contributions mirror what might be called the wider archaeological culture of East Anglia; having been involved in the region's archaeology for so many decades, Andrew has served to shape, in critical ways, a number of its distinctive elements.

Therefore, while the essays range widely, they focus on a number of key areas. A substantial proportion deal with 'small finds' of various kinds, and especially with artefacts or groups of artefacts recovered accidentally, rather than through excavation or survey work. Metalwork finds loom particularly large. Such an emphasis reflects Andrew's role, in recent years, as head of the Identification and Recording Service for archaeological finds and portable antiquities within Norfolk Historic Environment Service. But it also arises from his close association, over many decades, with amateur metal detectorists. Norfolk, as many readers will know, pioneered – initially with the activities of the late Tony Gregory – the policy of dealing sympathetically with and working alongside this active group of volunteers, rather than vilifying and alienating them, then the customary practise of 'establishment' archaeology. Andrew has accordingly spent innumerable long evenings in cold village halls, attending meetings where finds are identified, and their location carefully recorded. It is thus particularly fitting that many of the essays deal with objects, or groups of objects, recovered by metal detecting.

A number of contributions attempt to understand the meaning and significance of particular artefacts, or of the symbols they carry. Helen Geake's stimulating analysis of Anglo-Saxon representations of fish, for example, beginning with the silver model discovered by a metal-detectorist at East Walton in 2008 (perhaps derived from a hanging bowl like that recovered from Mound 1 at Sutton Hoo), argues that the artists responsible generally intended to render the specific likeness of a pike, symbol of strength and aggression, rather than some generic 'fish' – thus casting doubt on the traditional interpretations of such items as having a specifically Christian significance. Geake's contribution, like that by Jude Plouviez on Roman brooches from Scole, focuses on the intrinsic significance of a small group of artefacts. But Andrew's interests in small finds are more spatial in character: his perspective is that of the landscape archaeologist, as much as of the finds specialist, in that he is concerned with the distribution of different types of artefact, and with where they occur within the landscape. A number of the chapters accordingly embrace such a perspective, including some which – like Geake's – are particularly concerned with iconography and meaning. The contributions by John Davies and Adrian Marsden complement each other perfectly, the one dealing with Iron Age artefacts and the other with examples from the Roman period, but both examining the *distribution* of styles and types in order to throw light on the specific beliefs held by the inhabitants of the land of the Iceni. The meaning of artefact distributions looms large in other chapters devoted to metalwork finds; Steven Ashley and Martin Biddle's joint piece on medieval sword pommels; and those by Andrew Lawson and Alan West, on Norfolk Bronze Age hoards. But the interpretation of distributions, as Rogerson has often pointed out, is a tricky business, a matter which Alan West's intelligent but accessible discussion, of the extent to which recorded patterning in the data reflect processes of survival and discovery, addresses directly. The awareness that patterning can result from processes of discovery – including the processes of 'official' discovery represented by the logging of finds in the Historic Environment Record – underlies, of course the original desire of Tony Gregory and Andrew Rogerson to liaise so closely with detectorists. And the kinds of confusions that can arise from poor recording of findspots in the past is neatly dealt with in Edward Martin's examination of the hoard discovered in the nineteenth century at Thwaite – or Campsey Ash – or Wickham Skeith – in Suffolk.

Andrew's archaeological enthusiasms, of course, extend far beyond metalwork, and far beyond stray finds. His interests are catholic, but in period terms his main concern has always been with the early Middle Ages. This focus is likewise reflected in a number of the contributions to this volume, including Stanley West's thoughtful piece on the long-term significance, from the Roman into the Anglo-Saxon period, of the area around Icklingham in Suffolk. Andrew's critical involvement in the excavations of the Anglo-Saxon cemeteries at Morning Thorpe and Spong Hill are recognized in two chapters (as well as in a poem by Anthony Thwaite). Catherine Hill's discussion of the cremation urn lid, in the form of a seated man, recovered from Spong Hill throws important new light on an unusual artefact, while Kenneth Penn offers interesting new interpretations of badly eroded burials at Morning Thorpe. Andrew's interests also extend into the middle and later Saxon periods, and especially to questions of exchange, social change and urbanism. Tim Pestell presents the first detailed account of the 1998 excavations undertaken by the *Time Team* at Bawsey – a site with which Rogerson has, once again, been closely involved over many years. Pestell not only describes the various discoveries made during the excavation of the site – an atmospheric ruined and isolated church in west Norfolk which is associated with the most prolific of the county's 'productive sites'. He also, using his particularly detailed knowledge of these dense, enigmatic collections of middle Saxon coinage and other metalwork, places the site within a wider social and economic context, drawing parallels between the pairing of productive sites at Caistor and Bawsey with the towns at Norwich and King's Lynn, and raising important questions about the genesis of late Saxon urbanism.

Medieval towns are another subject which has long interested Andrew, in part through his involvement in excavations at Fullers Hill in Great Yarmouth. Urban studies rely not only on the evidence of excavations, however, but also on topographic analysis, and Brian Ayers' discussion of Norwich is full of originality and surprises – including the observation that aspects of the city's medieval topography may have been influenced by the survival, into the twelfth century, of upstanding prehistoric monuments. Later urban matters are addressed in Paul Rutledge's essay, which shows dramatically how far a single new source can transform our understanding of a place – in this case a nineteenth-century illustration of New Buckenham; while Elizabeth Rutledge usefully, and elegantly, explodes the myth of the missing chapel of St Ann in Norwich, and in passing illustrates how easily false information can become orthodoxy unless challenged by rigorous analysis.

Medieval churches, their origins and place in the landscape are other areas in which Andrew has made major contributions to our knowledge, especially through his excavation at Barton Bendish. A number of contributions reflect this interest. Stephen Heywood revisits the private chapels erected by Herbert de Losinga at North and South Elmham, in Norfolk and Suffolk respectively, showing how the bishop consciously employed architectural references to the early church, and to the ecclesiastical buildings of the western Empire, to associate himself and his position with the ancient origins of his diocese. Williamson's contribution attempts to place Norfolk's isolated churches within a wider national context, while Sandy Heslop presents intriguing thoughts on the cluster of late eleventh-century churches around Great Dunham. This is a particularly fitting tribute, not only in terms of subject matter but also in its intellectual perspective, for Heslop emphasises the importance, in the archaeological analysis of standing structures, of 'such apparently prosaic matters as the materials used, and their availability and likely cost' as ways of understanding origins, meaning and chronology. Such an approach accords well with Andrew's own intellectual approach to the past, which – while by no means eschewing archaeological theory – has always treated its wilder shores with some scepticism and caution, and is always firmly grounded in the practical. To Rogerson, moreover, theory is only as good as the evidence upon which it is based, and much of his most important work has indeed been based on the meticulous analysis of vast amounts of data – archaeological and documentary – at a landscape scale, especially in his research at Barton Bendish and at Great and Little Fransham. The latter project, pursued over many decades, represents one of the most detailed fieldwalking surveys and documentary studies of any parish in England, and formed the basis of both his PhD and of an imminent and long-awaited monograph. Indeed, it is worth noting in passing that while most people know Andrew as an archaeologist, he is also an accomplished historian, able to use, and interpret in novel ways, a wide range of documentary evidence, and well versed in the wider debates in medieval history, as much as in medieval archaeology. Hence the contributions in this volume by individuals, like the Rutledges, better known for their documentary than for their archaeological research; and that by his old colleague Bob Silvester, archaeologist and historian, on the maps of Thomas Badeslade.

Although, as the contributions by Stanley West and Edward Martin indicate, Andrew's interests and influence extend beyond the county boundary, into Suffolk – he served for many years on the Scole Committee, and has liaised extensively with Suffolk colleagues in the wider study of the Anglo-Saxon kingdom of East Anglia – he is above all a *Norfolk* archaeologist, deeply familiar with the geography of this very special county, his adopted home. Indeed, this volume arguably testifies to his role as the *paramount* Norfolk archaeologist of the later twentieth and early twenty-first century. Andrew's vast knowledge is, in particular although not exclusively, knowledge of the archaeology and history of one particular area of England. This does not imply, in any sense, an inward-looking antiquarianism, but rather an awareness and acceptance of the fact that England was, and to an extent still is, composed of a number of distinct regions, each with its own particular past, and with its own particular kinds of evidence through which that past can be studied. He is part of a long and proud tradition of both amateur and professional engagement with archaeology and history in the county (aspects of which are admirably dealt with in Wade-Martins' piece on the history of the Norfolk Archaeological Trust); albeit one which, during the course of his own professional career, was to an extent eroded by changes in the organisation of public archaeology, especially the enforced division between curatorial and field teams, and the emergence of competitive tendering for archaeological projects. This, by encouraging units from anywhere to dig anywhere, ensured the excavations have on occasions been undertaken by people largely unfamiliar with local issues, and local evidence, something rather different than the old model of county-based field archaeology within which Andrew began his career.

This volume – embracing studies in small finds, landscape history, and urban and ecclesiastical archaeology – thus reflects better than most *festschrifts* the sheer scale of the contribution which its recipient has made, and the influence he has had over a region's archaeology through many decades. That influence will doubtless continue, if not increase, over the decades to come. We haven't seen the last of Andrew Rogerson yet: indeed, the best is probably yet to come.

Clockwise from centre left: AR shovelling at Wallingford; on scaffolding; at Wicken Bonhunt (all 1972); examining Thetford-ware pottery from Group Captain Knocker's excavations at Thetford (1979) and recording a section with S. Ashley at Guestwick Church (1983)

List of Publications by Andrew Rogerson

Compiled by Steven Ashley

1973

J. Musty, K. Wade and AR, 'A Viking pin and inlaid knife from Bonhunt Farm, Wicken Bonhunt, Essex' *Antiquaries Journal* 53, p. 287

1976

'Excavations on Fuller's Hill, Great Yarmouth' *East Anglian Archaeology* 2, pp. 131-245

1977

'Excavations at Scole, 1973' *East Anglian Archaeology* 5, pp. 97-224

1978

B. Green, and AR, *The Anglo-Saxon Cemetery at Bergh Apton, Norfolk* East Anglian Archaeology 7

AR and N. Adams, 'A Saxo-Norman Pottery Kiln at Bircham' *East Anglian Archaeology* 8, pp. 33-44

AR and N. Adams, 'A Moated Site at Hempstead, near Holt' *East Anglian Archaeology* 8, pp. 55-72

1982

AR and S.J. Ashley, 'An Unfinished Well and its Contents at Bowthorpe' *Norfolk Archaeology* 38, pp. 215-18

1983

AR, S.J. Ashley, and P.J. Drury, 'Medieval floor tiles from St. John the Baptist's Church, Reedham' *Norfolk Archaeology* 38, pp. 380-3

1984

AR and C. Dallas, *Excavations in Thetford, Norfolk, 1948-59 and 1973-80* East Anglian Archaeology 22

T. Gregory, and AR, 'Metal-detecting in archaeological excavation' *Antiquity* 58, pp. 179–84

B. Hooper, S. Rickett, AR, and S. Yaxley, 'The Grave of Sir Hugh de Hastyngs', *Norfolk Archaeology* 39, pp. 88-9

1985

'Saxon Brooch' in J. Hinchliffe with C. Sparey Green, *Excavations at Brancaster 1974 and 1977* East Anglian Archaeology 23, p. 205

AR and S.J. Ashley, 'A Medieval Pottery Production Site at Blackborough End, Middleton' *Norfolk Archaeology* 39, pp. 181-9

S.J. Ashley and AR, 'A Medieval Wooden Coffin Lid from Guestwick' *Norfolk Archaeology* 39, pp. 216-7

1986

AR and R.J. Silvester, 'Middle Saxon Occupation at Hay Green, Terrington St Clement' *Norfolk Archaeology*, 39, pp. 320-22

1987

B. Green, AR, and S. White, *The Anglo-Saxon Cemetery at Morning Thorpe, Norfolk* East Anglian Archaeology 36 (2 vols.)

'A Medieval Pottery Production Site at Barton Bendish' *Norfolk Archaeology*, 40, pp. 127-130

AR and S.J. Ashley, 'The Parish Churches of Barton Bendish: The Excavation of All Saints and the Architecture of St. Andrew's and St. Mary's' in AR, S.J. Ashley, D. Williams and A. Harris, *Three Norman Churches in Norfolk* East Anglian Archaeology 32, pp. 1-66

AR and P. Williams, 'The Late Eleventh Century Church of St Peter, Guestwick' in AR, S.J. Ashley, D. Williams and A. Harris, *Three Norman Churches in Norfolk* East Anglian Archaeology 32, pp. 67-80

1988

'Appendix I: The medieval pottery' in R.J. Silvester, *The Fenland Project Number 3: Marshland and the Nar Valley, Norfolk* East Anglian Archaeology 45, pp. 174-5

1989

K. Penn and AR, 'An Anglo-Saxon brooch fragment from Shelfhanger, near Diss' *Norfolk Archaeology*, 40, p. 324

1990

R. Bond, K. Penn and AR, *Norfolk Origins 4: The North Folk; Angles, Saxons & Danes* (North Walsham)

S.J. Ashley, K. Penn, and AR, 'Four Continental Objects of Early Saxon Date' *Norfolk Archaeology*, 41, pp. 92-3

1991

S. Ashley, K. Penn and AR, 'A Further Group of Late Saxon Mounts from Norfolk' *Norfolk Archaeology* 41, pp. 225-9

'Tony Gregory, 1948-1991: An Appreciation' in *Excavations in Thetford, 1980-1982, Fison Way* East Anglian Archaeology 53 (2 vols.), vol.1, xi-xii

1992

S. Ashley and AR, 'Three radiate brooches and a small-long brooch from Norfolk' *Norfolk Archaeology* 41, pp. 361-2

AR and A.J. Lawson, 'The Earthwork Enclosure of Tasburgh' in J.A. Davies, T. Gregory, A.J. Lawson, R. Rickett and AR, *The Iron Age Forts of Norfolk* East Anglian Archaeology 54, pp. 31–58

1993

'The Middle Saxon period' in P. Wade-Martins (ed.), *An Historic Atlas of Norfolk* (Norwich), pp. 38-9

'Moated sites' in P. Wade-Martins (ed.), *An Historic Atlas of Norfolk* (Norwich), pp. 66-7

'Castles' in P. Wade-Martins (ed.), *An Historic Atlas of Norfolk* (Norwich), pp. 68-9

B. Ager, S. Ashley and AR, 'Two Norfolk finds of imported Continental brooches' *Norfolk Archaeology* 41, pp. 510-2

M.A.S. Blackburn and AR, 'Two Viking-age Silver Ingots from Ditchingham and Hindringham, Norfolk: the first East Anglian Ingot Finds' *Medieval Archaeology* 37, pp. 222-4

1994

S. Ashley and AR, 'An Enamelled Late Saxon Disc Brooch from Walpole St Peter' *Norfolk Archaeology* 42, pp. 102-4

M. Leah, AR, and P. Andrews, 'Excavations at Sites 22954, 24054 and 24054 (Vong Lane)' in M. Leah *Grimston, Norfolk. The Late Saxon and Medieval Pottery Industry: Excavations 1962-92* East Anglian Archaeology 64, pp. 21-66

S. Jennings and AR, 'The Distribution of Grimston Ware in East Anglia and Beyond' in M. Leah *Grimston, Norfolk. The Late Saxon and Medieval Pottery Industry: Excavations 1962-92* East Anglian Archaeology 64, pp. 116-119

1995

A Late Neolithic, Saxon and Medieval Site at Middle Harling, Norfolk East Anglian Archaeology 74

S. Ashley and AR, 'Further examples of radiate and related brooches from Norfolk' *Norfolk Archaeology* 42, pp. 219-20

1996

S. Ashley and AR, 'A Seventeenth-century mourning ring found in Postwick' *Norfolk Archaeology* 42, pp. 385-6

'Rural Settlement *c.*400-1200' in S. Margeson, B. Ayers, and S. Heywood, *A Festival of Norfolk Archaeology* (Norwich), pp. 58-64

1997

AR with A. Davison, 'An Archaeological and Historical Survey of the Parish of Barton Bendish' in AR, A. Davison, D. Pritchard and R. Silvester, *Barton Bendish and Caldecote: fieldwork in south-west Norfolk* East Anglian Archaeology 80, pp. 1-42

S. Ashley and AR, 'Sir Robert Wynde's Hawk-Ring' *Norfolk Archaeology* 42, p. 538

AR and S. Ashley, 'Bloodgate Hill, South Creake: a newly rediscovered early seventeenth-century map' *Norfolk Archaeology* 42, pp. 535-7

'Saxon and Early Medieval Archaeology' in N. Pevsner and B. Wilson, *The Buildings of England. Norfolk 1: Norwich and North-East* 2nd Edition (London), pp. 36-8

1998

S. Ashley and AR, 'A Norfolk Hundred Seal Matrix Recently Found in Kent' *Norfolk Archaeology* 43, pp. 180-1

1999

'Arable and Pasture on Two Norfolk Parishes: Barton Bendish and Fransham in the Iron Age' in J. Davies and T. Williamson (eds.), *Land of the Iceni: The Iron Age in Northern East Anglia* (Norwich), pp. 125-31

'Saxon and Early Medieval Archaeology' in N. Pevsner and B. Wilson, *The Buildings of England. Norfolk 2: Norwich and North-East* 2nd Edition (London), pp. 36-8

1999-2001

H. Geake, AR, and S. Ashley, 'Medieval Seal Matrices from Norfolk (1996-8, 1999 and 2000)' *Norfolk Archaeology* 43, pp. 353-8, 508-12 and 683-8

2000

S. Ashley, AR, and H. Geake, 'A Reclining medieval knight as a sleeping Roman soldier, from Shingham' *Norfolk Archaeology* 43, pp. 507-8

2001

'Thetford' in P.J. Crabtree (ed.), *Medieval Archaeology An Encyclopedia* (New York and London) pp. 339-40

'Thetford-Type Ware' in P.J. Crabtree (ed.), *Medieval Archaeology An Encyclopedia* (New York and London) pp. 340-1

2002-2013

AR, and S. Ashley 'Medieval Seal Matrices from Norfolk (2001-2012)', *Norfolk Archaeology* 44; pp. 133-7, 348-53, 558-63 and 732-6, 45; pp. 108-112, 244-9, 422-8 and 551-5, 46; pp. 115-120, 243-7, 402-6, 549-54

2003

'Six Middle Anglo-Saxon Sites in West Norfolk' in T. Pestell and K. Ulmschneider, *Markets in Early Medieval Europe* (Macclesfield), pp. 110-21

2005

'Middle Saxon Norfolk (*c.*AD 650-850)' in T. Ashwin, and A. Davison (eds.), *An Historic Atlas of Norfolk* (Third edition, Chichester), pp. 32-3

'Moated Sites' in T. Ashwin and A. Davison (eds.), *An Historic Atlas of Norfolk* (Third edition, Chichester), pp. 68-9

2006

Book Review: G. Barnes and T. Williamson, *Hedgerow History. Ecology, history and landscape character* (Macclesfield, 2006), in *Landscape History* 28, p. 91

2007

The late A. Davison with an introduction by AR, 'Investigations at Godwick and Beeston St Andrew' *Norfolk Archaeology* 45, pp. 141-154

2008

AR and S. Ashley, 'A Selection of Finds from Norfolk Recorded Between 2006 and 2008' *Norfolk Archaeology* 45, pp. 428-41

2008/9

Book Review: C. Loveluck, *Rural Settlement, Lifestyles and Social Change in the Later First Millennium AD. Anglo-Saxon Flixborough in its wider context* (Oxford, 2007), in *Landscape History* 30, pp. 99-100

2009

AR and S. Ashley, 'A Selection of Finds from Norfolk Recorded in 2009 and Earlier' *Norfolk Archaeology* 46, pp. 556-70

2010

Book Review: C. Scull, *Early Medieval (Late 5th-Early 8th Centuries AD) Cemeteries at Boss Hall and Buttermarket, Ipswich, Suffolk* Society for Medieval Archaeology Monograph 27 (2009), in *Norfolk Archaeology* 46, pp. 99-100

AR and S. Ashley, 'A Selection of Finds from Norfolk Recorded in 2010 and Earlier' *Norfolk Archaeology* 46, pp. 121-135

N. Crummy with contributions by M. Blackburn, AR, and P. Wise, 'Coins' in R. Atkins and A. Connor, *Farmers and Ironsmiths: Prehistoric, Roman and Anglo-Saxon Settlement beside Brandon Road, Thetford, Norfolk* East Anglian Archaeology 134, pp. 40-42

2011

'Grantham Friary and the excavation of 1972 and 1973' in D. Start and D. Stocker (eds), *The Making of Grantham: The Medieval Town* (Sleaford, 2011), pp. 137-50

S. Ashley, AR and K. Penn, 'Rhineland Lava in Norfolk Churches' *Church Archaeology* 13, pp. 27-33

AR and S. Ashley, 'Some medieval gaping-mouth beast buckles from Norfolk and elsewhere' *Medieval Archaeology* 55, pp. 299-302

AR and S. Ashley, 'A Selection of Finds from Norfolk Recorded in 2011 and Earlier' *Norfolk Archaeology* 46, pp. 248-262

Book Review: R. Hoggett, '*The Archaeology of the Anglo-Saxon Conversion*' (Woodbridge, 2010), in *Landscape History* 32, pp. 88-9

2012

AR and S. Ashley, 'Jet Seal Matrix' in M. Hinman, and E. Popescu, *Extraordinary Inundations of the Sea: Excavations at Market Mews, Wisbech, Cambridgeshire* East Anglian Archaeology 142, p. 55

AR and S. Ashley, 'A distinctive group of keys: a Norfolk speciality?' *Medieval Archaeology* 56, pp. 317-9

AR and S. Ashley, 'A Selection of Finds from Norfolk Recorded in 2012 and Earlier' *Norfolk Archaeology* 46, pp. 406-21

2013

Book Review: R. Gilchrist, *Medieval Life: Archaeology and the Life Course* (2013), in *History* vol. 98, pp. 428-9

'Oxborough dirk' and 'Pentney Hoard' in I. Collins (ed.) *Masterpieces: Art and East Anglia*, (Norwich, 2013), pp. 52 and 70-1

AR and S. Ashley, 'An aberrant form of 10th-century strap-end' *Medieval Archaeology* 57, pp. 278-80

J. Rogerson and AR 'Brandon Parva: The Old Rectory', 'Litcham: Licham Hall' and 'North Elmham: Silverstone Farm' in P. Dallas, R. Last and T. Williamson *Norfolk Gardens and Designed Landscapes*. (Oxford, 2013), pp. 92-3, 261 and 293-5

AR and S. Ashley, 'A Selection of Finds from Norfolk Recorded in 2013 and Earlier' *Norfolk Archaeology* 46, pp. 554-68

Forthcoming

Book Review: P. Blinkhorn, *The Ipswich ware project: Ceramics, trade and society in Middle Saxon England* (2012)

AR and S. Ashley, 'Metalwork: The 1930s assemblage' in P. Cope-Faulkner and S. Anderson 'The Archaeology of Binham Priory' *Norfolk Archaeology*

S.D. Bridgford, J.P. Northover, A.R., and A. West, *Three Bronze Age Weapons Assemblages from Norfolk* East Anglian Archaeology

Fransham: people and land in a central Norfolk parish from the Palaeolithic to the eve of Parliamentary Enclosure East Anglian Archaeology

Digging a Saxon cemetery

Anthony Thwaite

We approach you briskly,
Crowded clay-dwellers,
Inhabitants now well
Dispersed in your persons,
And come as callers
On hands and knees
With trowels and rulers.

You would be puzzled
To see us, scavengers
Dressed in our casual
Clothes without ritual,
Turning up ornament,
Weapon, cremation,
Plotting your downfall.

Now dedicated to Andrew Rogerson, remembering Morning Thorpe 1975-6, and many happy sessions of sherd-shuffling since.

Late Bronze Age finds from Banyard's Hall, Bunwell, Norfolk

Andrew J. Lawson

Abstract: In 1981 ten pieces of Late Bronze Age metalwork were found by metal-detectorists on the surface of a ploughed field near Banyard's Hall, Bunwell, Norfolk. The socketed objects, comprising two axes, a hammer, a chisel, a spear and four small items, together with two fragmentary pieces found subsequently, are considered to have been deposited together as a hoard. Prompt reporting of the discovery by the finders, unusual at the time and presaging more recent practice, enabled the dispersal of the pieces to be assessed. The types represented belong to the Ewart Park Tradition of the ninth to tenth centuries BC, but the composition of the hoard is unusual. Subsequent discoveries in south Norfolk complement the finds from Bunwell.

Introduction

Banyard's Hall lies about 1km south-east of the parish church at Bunwell in central Norfolk, and about 17km south-west of the centre of the city of Norwich. Although the current building was probably erected in the seventeenth century, and was faced with brick in the nineteenth, it stands within the remains of an isolated moat which is thought to have once surrounded a pre-Conquest hall.[1] It was therefore one of the many rural moated sites systematically assessed in the early years of the relatively new Norfolk Archaeological Unit (NAU). In 1977, Andrew Rogerson, one of the original field officers of the NAU with particular responsibility for medieval sites, visited the moat and managed to recover medieval and later finds within its precinct, thus providing limited evidence for the date of activity within it.[2]

Some four years after Dr Rogerson's visit, evidence for much earlier activity near the moat was revealed by the discovery of Late Bronze Age metalwork. That find forms the subject of this article. At the time of discovery, few Bronze Age hoards were known in south Norfolk and hence it made an important contribution to an understanding of the period in the region. Subsequently, more hoards have been found to enrich the regional context, many of them conscientiously recorded by Dr Rogerson in his later role as Senior Landscape Archaeologist for Norfolk County Council.

Description of the site and circumstances of discovery

The site of discovery comprises a flat trapezoidal arable field, at the time some 300m long and 150-300m wide, situated immediately south-west of Banyard's Hall. The find spot lies approximately 170m west of the farm complex, 60m south of the track which skirts the north side of the field, and 40m east of the boundary with Bunwell Wood which flanks the western side of the field (at NGR TM 1320 9216). Although the hedge on the east side of the field has been removed subsequently, the other boundaries remain the same. The ground lies at c. 50m above sea level and overlies the chalky Pleistocene till of the Lowestoft Formation of the central Norfolk plateau.

All the objects were found on or near the surface of ploughsoil while using metal-detectors. The first object (No. **1** below, all objects are shown in Fig. 2) was located by Mr Pride James of Norwich late in the evening of 25 April 1981. Further objects (Nos. **2-10**) were detected on 5 May 1981 by Mr James working with Mr Martin and Mr Stewart Smith of Hingham.

On 8 May 1981, the current author visited the find spot on behalf of the NAU. With the permission of the landowners, F.H. Easton & Sons Ltd., and with the guidance of the finders, he created a sketch plan of the distribution of the pieces (Fig. 1). The plan was based on the memories of the finders and hence is only indicative. Nonetheless, most of the objects seem to have been found within a restricted area some 8m by 4m. Two objects, a small flat piece of copper alloy and a short length of iron with a copper-alloy binding were also detected in the general area, but these were considered not to be Bronze Age in date.

Details of the discovery, based on a preliminary report prepared by the current author, were passed by the finders to local newspapers,[3] and subsequently to other local magazines.[4]

Although primary accounts exist of the discovery of all the objects in close proximity to each other, their original association is inferred. The discovery might be regarded as an 'area find', but due to the probable contemporaneity of the objects, it seems reasonable to suggest that all ten items were once buried together as a hoard.[5] Primary sources of information concerning the discovery of the Bunwell Hoard, comprising contemporary field notes, sketches, and photographs are contained in Norfolk County Council Historic Environment Record 17474. All the objects were retained initially by the finders. However, in 1984 they were acquired by the Norwich Castle Museum.[6]

One further object, a fragment of a socketed axe (No **2c**) from the same location as the hoard, was reported to the Norwich Castle Museum in 1985. It had been found

---

[1] Pevsner and Wilson 1999, p. 226
[2] HER 10015
[3] *The Eastern Evening News* 6 May 1981; *The Journal*, 8 May 1981, p. 10
[4] e.g. *East Anglian Monthly*, February 1983, pp. 49-52; Day 1985, pp. 26-31
[5] Needham, Lawson and Green 1985, Category 7
[6] Acc. No. 1984.1-6

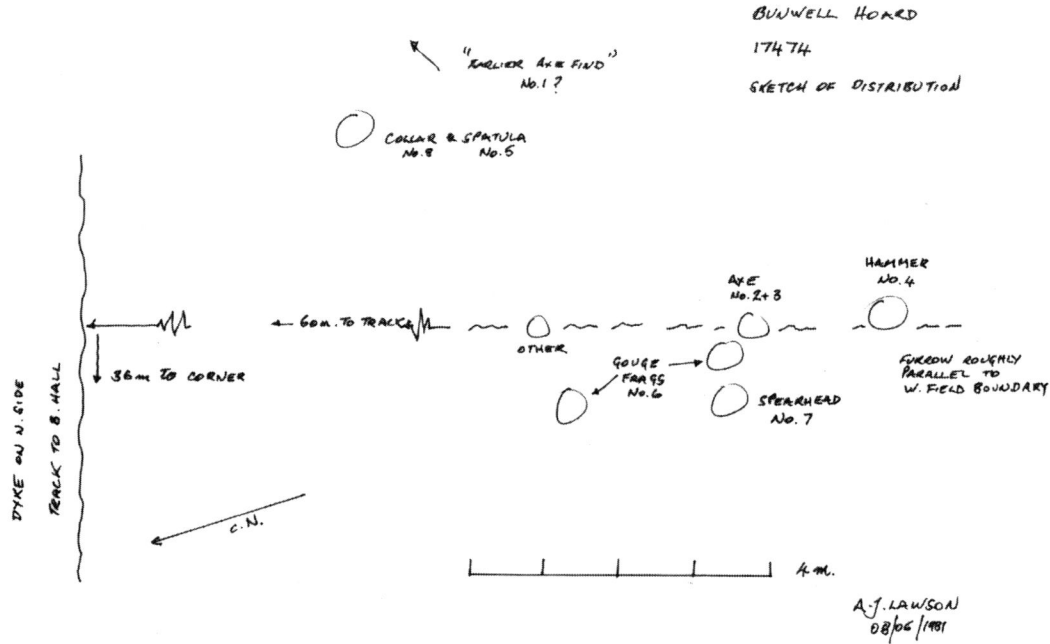

Fig. 1 Sketch plan of the Bunwell hoard

together with other metal objects from the same field, including another small cone (cf. No. **10** below), which were thought to be of Romano-British date. 'Romano-British' and 'medieval' pottery was also reported from the area at this time but none was retained for identification.

Description and comparisons

All the objects are generally in good condition with a very dark green patina. In places, the surfaces are pitted or stained brown (with iron pan). Two objects (Nos. **2** and **6**) are in poorer condition. The metal of objects has not been analysed, but from its colour and patina, it is assumed to comprise copper alloy, probably bronze.

1 FACETED SOCKETED AXE with circular mouth and flaring trumpet collar. Light single loop with vertical rib. Octagonal body widening to flared cutting edge. Two internal deep-set vertical ribs.[7]

L: 10.8cm; Wt: 219.7gm.

Comparisons:

Meldreth Type;[8] Feltwell Fen Hoard, Norfolk;[9] Gorleston I Hoard, Norfolk;[10] Husbands Bosworth Hoard, Leics.[11]

2 FRAGMENTARY FACETED SOCKETED AXE with simple everted rim: two body fragments (**2a** and **2b**) recovered in 1981, and a third, rim fragment (**2c**) found in 1985. Single loop with vertical rib. Distorted octagonal body expanding to flared cutting edge, with facet edges marked by slight ribs. Lower part of body depressed. Most of upper body and mouth missing. Contained No.**3** (and a fragment of wood considered modern: Wendy Carruthers pers. comm.).

L (of fragment **2a**): 8.3cm; Wt (**2a**): 96.6gm; L (**2b**): 3.2cm; Wt 5.7gm: L (**2c**): 3.9cm.

Comparisons:

Similar to No.1; Meldreth Hoard, Cambs.[12]

3 AMORPHOUS LUMP found within No.**2a**.

L: 2.6cm; Wt 15.8gm.

4 SOCKETED HAMMER. Square mouth with angular moulding. Square sectioned body with parallel sides, slightly splayed to asymmetric bevelled striking face with rounded facets. Sides with marked casting flashes ground or filed.

L: 7.9cm; Wt 224.6gm.

Comparisons:

Carleton Rode Hoard, Norfolk;[13] Thorndon Hoard, Suffolk;[14] Reach Fen Hoard, Cambs;[15] Isle of Harty Hoard, Kent.[16]

---

[7] Ehrenberg 1981 Type 1b
[8] Schmidt and Burgess 1981, pp. 204-6
[9] Smith 1958, No. 1
[10] Clough and Green 1978, Nos. 21, 22, 58
[11] Clough 1979, Fig. 55
[12] Hawkes and Smith 1955b, No 3
[13] Norfolk Museums Service 1977, Pl VI, No. 16
[14] Hawkes and Smith 1955a, No. 4
[15] Smith 1956a, No. 34
[16] Smith 1956b, No. 23

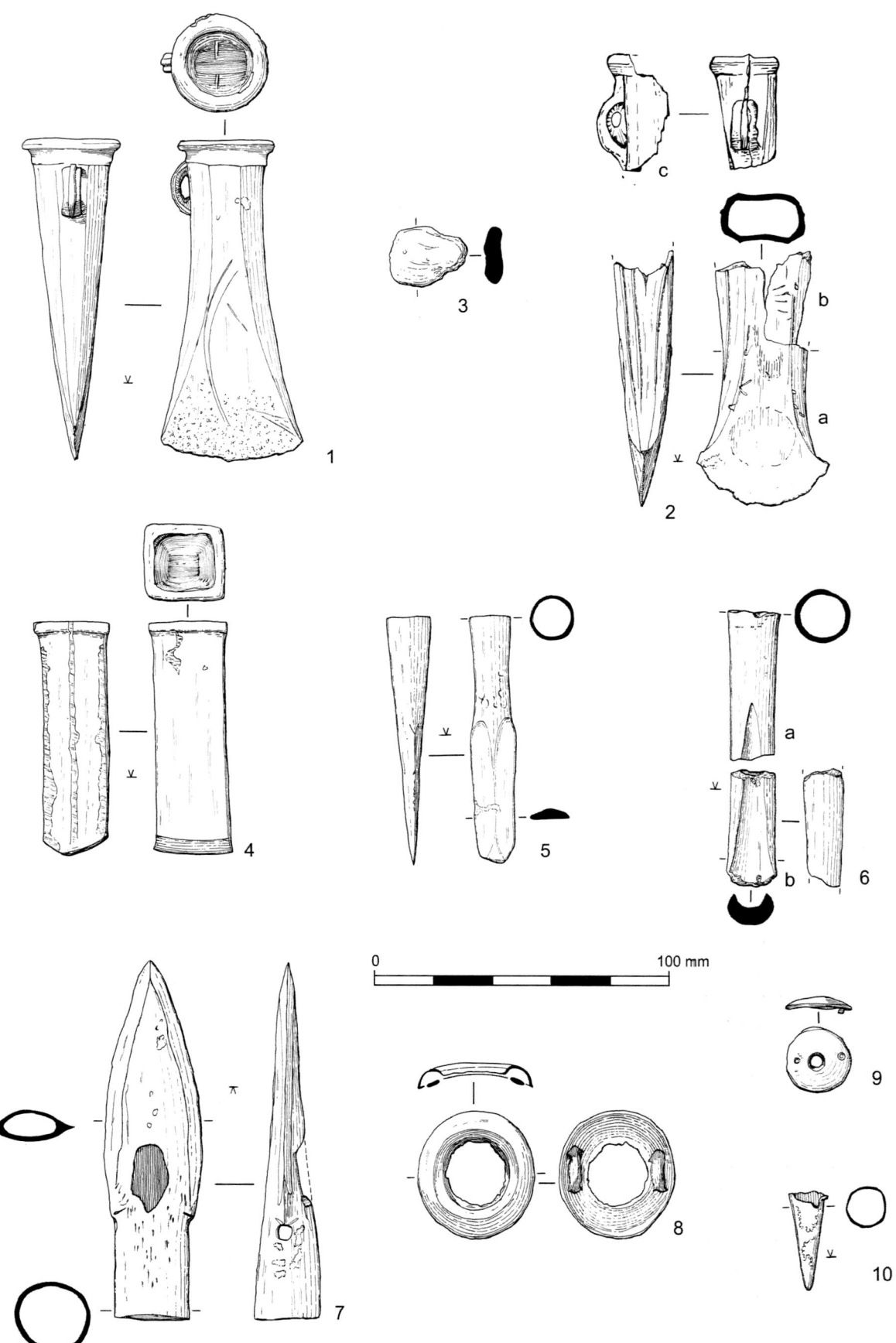

Fig. 2 The Bunwell hoard Scale 1:2

5 SOCKETED CHISEL OR KNIFE with cylindrical socket. Spatulate, parallel-sided blade with low, triangular section, tapering towards rounded end. Edges dull.

L: 8.5cm; Wt 31.6gm.

Comparisons:

Nore Hill, Chelsham, Surrey[17]

6 FRAGMENTARY SOCKETED GOUGE. Two conjoining pieces, one (**6a**) with circular, slightly expanded mouth, and the second (**6b**) with cutting edge in poor condition.

L: c.8.8cm; Wt: 41.0gm (**6a**); 34.1gm (**6b**)

Comparisons:

Carleton Rode Hoard, Norfolk;[18] Thorndon Hoard, Suffolk;[19] Reach Fen Hoard, Cambs.[20]

7 SOCKETED SPEARHEAD with cylindrical socket. Leaf shaped blade with bevelled edges and rudimentary barbs above peg holes. Surface hammered giving a rain drop patterning to part of the socket. Reverse damaged with part of the socket missing.

Comparisons:

Broadward Tradition Type 4[21]

8 HOLLOW CAST RING OR COLLAR with semi-circular cross-section and two diametrically opposed suspension loops beneath. Inner edge rebated as if to receive central setting.

Diam. 4.2cm; Wt 14.8gm.

Comparisons:

Edinburgh Hoard, Scotland;[22] Great Freeman Street Hoard, Nottingham;[23] Welby Hoard, Leics.[24]

9 CIRCULAR CONCAVE BUTTON with irregular edge, as if filed. Countersunk central perforation and two small flanking rivets, one missing.

Diam. 2.1cm; Wt 2.8gm.

10 SMALL HOLLOW CONE with circular, damaged mouth and one possible peg hole beneath.

L 3.4cm; Wt 5.7gm.

Comparisons:

Yattendon Hoard, Berks.[25]

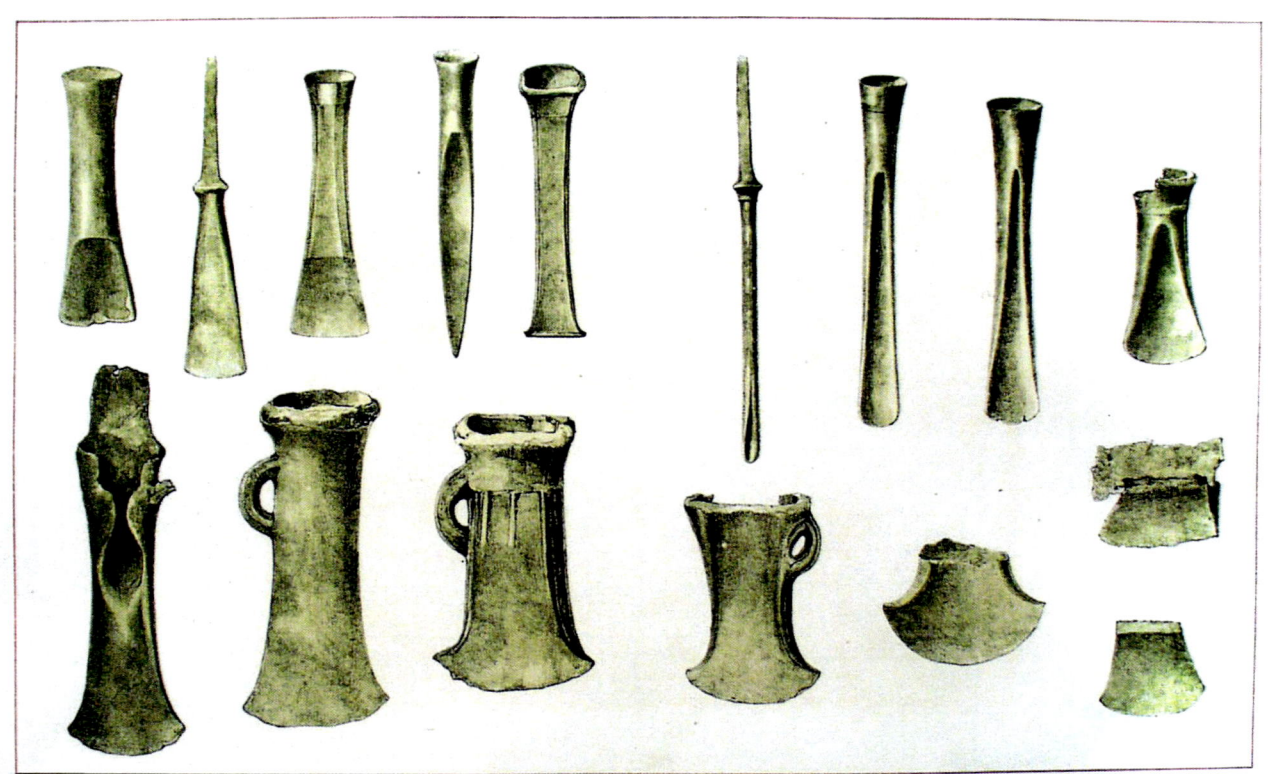

FIG. 3 OBJECTS 'FOUND AT CARLETON RODE...' LITHOGRAPH BY HENRY NINHAM

---

[17] Skelton 1987
[18] Norfolk Museums Service 1977, Pl VI, No. 13
[19] Hawkes and Smith 1955a, No. 3
[20] Smith 1956a, Nos. 32-3
[21] Burgess et al. 1972
[22] Evans 1881, p.290 and fig. 500
[23] Smith and Pitman 1957, No. 16
[24] Smith and Clarke 1957, No. 16
[25] Coghlan 1970, Y55

Interpretation and dating

Although it is not difficult to find parallels for many of the individual items in this assemblage, the overall character of the hoard is noteworthy. The association of tools, weapons, trinkets and casting waste is a hallmark of the Late Bronze Age Ewart Park Tradition. Nonetheless, some of the specific forms in this assemblage are unusual in Norfolk.

The faceted axes (Nos. **1** and **2**) belong to a form which originated in the Wilburton Tradition but is commonly found throughout southern and eastern England in the succeeding Ewart Park Tradition. Of later tradition is the late Sompting-type ribbed axe found in 1964 by Mr T Mickleburgh of Tibbenham while hoeing sugar beet c.600m north-east of Banyard's Hall.[26] Both the reported location and typological date of this find suggest it was not part of the Bunwell Hoard.

Socketed hammers (cf. No. **4**), socketed gouges (cf. No. **6**) and ingot fragments (cf. No. **3**) are also widely found in Ewart Park hoards. The socketed tool, possibly a chisel (No. **7**), would not look out of place in the Carleton Rode Hoard (Fig. 3).[27] The latter, with its incomparable range of at least 22 tools, was discovered in 1844 less than 2.5km west of the Bunwell site. Furthermore, the hollow ring (No. **8**) and button (No. **9**) may reflect the introduction of horse harness, and the need to join and elaborate leather straps, as seen in other hoards of this period. The hollow cone (No. **10**) is more unusual. It is possibly a fragment of a more complex cast object or composite item, or it might be a small pointed ferrule.

However, the most distinctive item is the spearhead (No. **7**), with its short leaf-shaped blade, rudimentary barbs and peg holes. Barbed spearheads are an archetypal component of the Broadward Complex.[28] Although fragments of 'classic' barbed spearheads are present in a few East Anglian hoards, such as the pieces of Type II weapons in the Aylsham and Carleton Rode Hoards,[29] they are generally rare in the region. The Complex is thought to have developed at much the same time, but independently of, the Wilburton Tradition, but fully developed barbed spearheads are considered contemporary with Ewart Park metalwork. Examples certainly occur in the hoards of this tradition in southern East Anglia (such as the Felixstowe Railway Cutting and Levington Hoards in Suffolk, and the Hatfield Broad Oak Hoard in Essex)[30]

Comparison can be made between the socketed chisel from Bunwell (No. **6**) and a tool also found with a socketed gouge (*inter alia*) by metal detector at a ringfort on Nore Hill, Surrey.[31] The similarity is not exact because the latter has a rectangular sectioned blade. Nonetheless, wood, presumably from the contemporary handle of this parallel, has given a radiocarbon date of 2765±45 uncal bp.[32] The calibrated range of this date, 1020-820 cal BC at 95% confidence, reflects not only the date of the Ewart Park Tradition, but also the probable date of the Bunwell Hoard.

Significance

As well as the unusual composition of the Bunwell hoard, several other aspects of its discovery should be noted. First, the prompt reporting by Mr Pride James and his colleagues, and the willingness of the landowner to permit archaeological recording, set an important precedent in the area. Although today such basic requirements underpin the code of practice that accompanies the 1996 Treasure Act, they were frequently avoided in earlier decades. In this case, it was possible to record the approximate dispersal of the objects, so that a start could be made on assessing the effects of ploughing on a (presumed) buried deposit. Now, comparable information from other hoard sites confirms that ploughing can disperse objects over a far greater distance than that witnessed at Bunwell.

Secondly, the find helped to fill a blank in the distribution map of Bronze Age activity in Norfolk. A number of Late Bronze Age hoards were known in the Norwich area (and elsewhere in the county) but few had been revealed in that part of Norfolk south of the city. The important hoard found at Carleton Rode in 1844 has already been mentioned (above). Another had been found about 1828 at Pulham St Mary, a little more than 10km south-east of Bunwell. Manuscript notes compiled by the Norfolk antiquarian, Goddard Johnson, state that '…Eight bronze Celts, some Spear and Arrow Heads and a Sword All of the same sort of metal…' were discovered, but that he was only able to recover one of the 'Celts' which the un-named finder had kept as a memento (NNRO MS16, f.28). The findspot was once thought to be in Pulham Market (HER 1685) but its location was subsequently re-assessed (HER 10765). The description of the find would fit a typical Ewart Park tradition hoard.

However, since the discovery at Bunwell, several additional hoards have come to light in south Norfolk, greatly enriching our knowledge of Late Bronze Age practices in the area. Another collection of metalwork was found at Pulham St Mary between 1986 and 1989. Although much of the material spread across the site hints at the presence of a high status Romano-British site, the finding of fragments of a spearhead, a chape, a hollow ring, a sword hilt and a socketed axe attest Late Bronze Age activity, if not a dispersed hoard.[33]

Two socketed axes had been found in 1966 during the hoeing of sugar beet at Kenninghall, about 11 km south-west of Bunwell, but around 1998 it seems that

---

[26] HER 10033
[27] HER 10022; Norwich Castle Museum 1977, Pl VI
[28] Burgess et al 1972
[29] Clough 1971, pp. 163 and 166, no. 18; Norfolk Museums Service 1977, 30 and 31 resp.
[30] Burgess et al fig. 9 Nos. 3-4, fig. 21 No. 9, and fig. 29, No. 75 resp.
[31] Skelton 1987
[32] Needham et al 1997, DoB 5
[33] HER 22927

about ten more axes were found at the same site by an anonymous detectorist.[34] Although word of the find came to the notice of Andrew Rogerson, the objects had been sold before they could be fully assessed. A second Late Bronze Age hoard, comprising a single palstave and nine socketed axes, one of which was broken, was found with a detector at Kenninghall in 1995, together with Romano-British and medieval coins. The discovery was reported to Norwich Castle Museum where the individual items were recorded.[35] The number of objects is suspiciously similar to that attributed to the first site[36] but without a clearer record it is impossible to clarify the facts. Thus, another important aspect of the Banyard Hall find lies in the fact that the hoard was not dispersed and the bronzes sold individually. The circumstances of their discovery were documented, and later the entire collection was acquired by the Norwich Castle Museum where it is curated enabling this and future study. Because it remains accessible, it can be made available for future analysis, such as metal composition, when pressing new research questions arise.

Four Late Bronze Age hoards have been found in recent years by metal detectors in the Attleborough area, less than 10km north-west of Bunwell, three of them near Great Ellingham. At the first site, near Attleborough, four socketed axes, some fragmentary, were found between 1994 and 1998 in the same area as Saxon and medieval metalwork.[37] Late in 1996 Andrew Rogerson led a small excavation near Great Ellingham, where previously six socketed axes, three fragments of sword and a casting jet had been recovered from a restricted area of ploughsoil, some 11m by 5m. By 2005, the same site had produced a total of at least 18 bronzes, as well as Saxon and medieval material.[38] In September 2007, Dr Rogerson also recorded the excavation of the site of a second hoard from Great Ellingham, comprising a socketed axe and 26 ingot fragments.[39] Between 2007 and 2010, he also recorded the discovery of socketed axes and sword blades found in a 30cm square pit cut 9cm into the clay subsoil at a third Great Ellingham site. Unusually, organic material comprising a fragment of cloth and a wooden board were also recovered from the pit. Later that spring, nine more bronze fragments were recovered from the same site by detectorists.[40]

The Bunwell find can therefore be seen as the first of a wave of new discoveries of Late Bronze Age metalwork hoards in south Norfolk. The popularity of metal-detecting since the 1970s, and the consequent discovery of prehistoric objects, is not restricted to that part of Norfolk: without counting the number of isolated individual bronzes, the number of Late Bronze Age hoards now known in Norfolk alone currently stands at about one hundred. A full analysis of the ever-growing number of finds is beyond the scope of this paper but many of them belong to the Ewart Park tradition and together with the Bunwell find display the diverse range of tools, weapons and smaller objects skilfully created by the consummate smiths of the period. Furthermore, by mapping the spatial distribution of metal types represented in the hoard, it is possible to suggest the range of social and economic contact in the British Late Bronze Age.

Acknowledgements

Knowledge of recent metalwork finds has resulted from a growing respect and trust between detectorists and archaeologists, and in the case of the latter, much of the credit of developing good working relationships is due to Andrew Rogerson. Although his principal interest lies in medieval archaeology, his understanding of other periods is deeper than he might admit, and his dedication to fieldwork is without equal. The current author had the pleasure of working with Andrew and his colleagues of the Norfolk Archaeological Unit between 1973 and 1983, and with fond reminiscences, I have great pleasure in dedicating this short article to him.

The published line drawings, based on the author's original sketches, were prepared by Rob C. Read with the help of a grant from the Society of Antiquaries of London. The author is most grateful for their valuable support. The drawing of No. 2c is based on a sketch by Bill Milligan.

Copy of the lithograph of objects 'Found at Carleton Rode...' by Henry Ninham (NWHCM 1954.138, Todd 1D, Depwade, 2:F) is reproduced with the kind permission of the Norfolk Museums Service (Norwich Castle Museum and Art Gallery)

---

[34] HER 10797
[35] HER 32005
[36] HER 10797
[37] HER 30938
[38] HER 31588
[39] HER 51148
[40] HER 54009

Bibliography

Burgess, C., and Coombs, D. (eds.) 1979, *Bronze Age Hoards: Some Finds Old and New* (Oxford, British Archaeological Report 67)

Burgess, C.B., Coombs, D., and Davies, D.G. 1972, 'The Broadward Complex and Barbed Spearheads' 211-83 in F. Lynch and C.B. Burgess (eds.) *Prehistoric Man in Wales and the West: essays in honour of Lily F Chitty* (Bath, Adams and Dart)

Clough, T.H. Mck 1971, 'A Hoard of Late Bronze Age Metalwork from Aylsham, Norfolk', *Norfolk Archaeology* 35, ii, pp. 159-69

Clough, T.H. McK 1979, 'Bronze Age Metalwork from Rutland' pp. 117-36 in C. Burgess and D. Coombs (eds.)

Clough, T.H. McK, and Green, C. 1978, 'The first Late Bronze Age founder's hoard from Gorleston, Great Yarmouth, Norfolk', *Norfolk Archaeology* 37, i, pp. 1-18

Coghlan, H.H. 1970, *A Report upon the Hoard of Bronze Age Tools and Weapons from Yattendon Near Newbury, Berkshire* (Newbury, The Borough of Newbury Museum)

Day, P.G. 1985, The Archaeology of Bunwell, Ms report (copy NCM 378.985), pp. 26-34

Ehrenberg, M. 1981, 'Inside socketed axes', *Antiquity* 55, (215), pp. 214-8

Evans, J. 1881, *The Ancient Bronze Implements, Weapons and Ornaments of Great Britain and Ireland* (London, Longman and Green, 2nd ed.)

Hawkes, C.F.C., and Smith, M.A. (eds.) 1955a, 'The Thorndon Hoard (Suffolk)', *Inventaria Archaeologica* GB. 11 (London, British Museum)

Hawkes, C.F.C., and Smith, M.A. (eds.) 1955b, 'The Meldreth Hoard (Cambridgeshire)', *Inventaria Archaeologica* GB. 13 (1-3) (London, British Museum)

Needham, S., Bronk Ramsey, C., Coombs, D., Cartwright, C., and Pettitt, P. 1997, 'An Independent Chronology for British Bronze Age Metalwork: The Results of the Oxford Radiocarbon Accelerator Programme' *Archaeological Journal* 154, pp. 55-107

Needham, S.P., Lawson, A.J., and Green, H.S. 1985, 'Context types for Bronze Age metalwork', *British Bronze Age Metalwork A1-6 Early Bronze Age Hoards*, v-vii (London, British Museum)

NNRO (Norfolk and Norwich Record Office) MS: additions to Blomefield vols 1-2 by Goddard Johnson MS16 (formerly Norwich Public Library) c.1840, Vol 1 & 2 (currently bound together in a single volume)

Norfolk Museums Service 1977, *Catalogue of the Bronze Age Metalwork in Norwich Castle Museum*, 2nd ed., (Norwich, Norfolk Museums Service)

Pevsner, N., and Wilson, B. 1999 *The Buildings of England. Norfolk 2; North West and South* 2nd ed. (London, Penguin)

Schmidt, P.K., and Burgess, C.B. 1981, *The Axes of Scotland and Northern England*, Prähistorische Bronzefunde Abt. IX, Bd 7 (Munich, C H Beck)

Skelton, A.C. 1987, 'Nore Hill, Chelsham: a newly discovered prehistoric enclosure', *Surrey Archaeological Collections* 78, pp. 43-54

Smith, M.A. (ed.) 1956a, 'The Reach Fen Hoard, Reach (Cambridgeshire)', *Inventaria Archaeologica* GB. 17 (1-3) (London, British Museum)

Smith, M.A. (ed.) 1956b, 'The Isle of Harty Hoard, Kent', *Inventaria Archaeologica* GB. 18 (1-3) (London, British Museum)

Smith, M.A., and Clarke T.D. 1957, 'The Welby Hoard, Leicestershire', *Inventaria Archaeologica* GB. 24 (London, Garraway)

Smith, M.A., and Pitman, C.F. (eds.) 1957 'The Great Freeman Street Hoard, Nottingham (Nottinghamshire)', *Inventaria Archaeologica* GB. 22 (1-2) (London, Garraway)

Smith, M.A. (ed.) 1958 'The Feltwell Fen Hoard, Feltwell (Norfolk)', *Inventaria Archaeologica* GB. 35 (1-2) (London, Garraway)

A Late Bronze Age hoard from Feltwell

Alan West

Abstract: During the course of writing this article I have spent some time looking through the secondary files of the Historic Environment Record, and time and time again I have come across the phrase 'Ident AR'. That is, 'Identified by Andrew Rogerson.' So much of what we know about the archaeology of Norfolk would not have been possible without 'AR', and this article is no exception.

A Bronze Age hoard was discovered in the West of Norfolk on the Fen Edge in 1992, and was excavated in subsequent years. The hoard consists of 13 complete or fragmentary bronze objects, one stone, one complete bun ingot and 41 ingot fragments, and dates from the Late Bronze Age. It is unusual in that it contains a complete ingot, the first from Norfolk.

The hoard is now in the collections of Norwich Castle Museum, accession number NWHCM: 1993.198.2, and is known as the Feltwell II hoard.

Background to the area

The site lies in the Wissey Embayment, part of the West Norfolk Fen Edge (Fig. 1). The embayment is defined on the south and south-west by the Little Ouse, on the west by the Great Ouse and in the east by the chalk upland.[1] The site of the hoard itself (Norfolk Historic Environment Record (NHER) number 5169/c8, in the parish of Feltwell, see Fig. 1) sits on the edge of one of the rounded spurs of chalk which project into the fen.[2] Other finds which have come from this site include a leaf-shaped flint arrowhead, a flint scraper, Roman and Medieval sherds, several Roman brooches and an iron spur; not an unusual assemblage for this area of Norfolk.

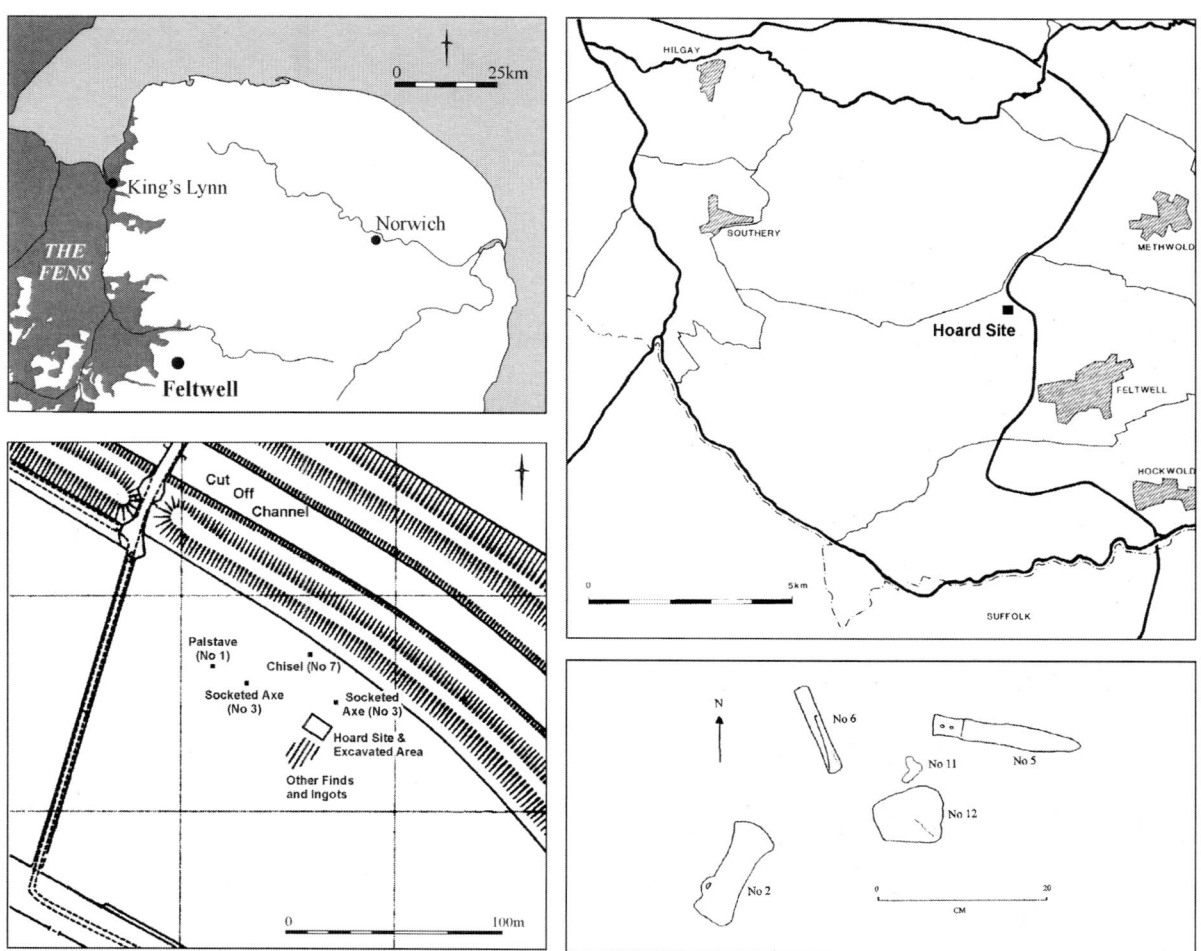

FIG. 1 LOCATION OF THE FELTWELL II HOARD, SHOWING ITS SPREAD AND A PLAN OF THE EXCAVATED PART OF THE HOARD

---

[1] Silvester 1991, p. 1

[2] Silvester 1991, p. 29

It is one of two hoards from the parish of Feltwell, the Feltwell Fen Hoard, part of the Canon William Greenwell collection (NHER 5295, now in the British Museum), which consists of 3 socketed axes plus 2 socketed axe fragments, 2 spearheads, a socketed chisel, socketed gouge fragment, 2 socketed knife fragments, a pair of tweezers, a razor, part of a gold foil hair-ring, an amber bead, a toggle, 2 small fragments of boar's tusk, and a small piece of plano-convex copper-alloy ingot.[3]

A cauldron and a flesh hook were also found in 1961, and could be considered to be a third hoard. The cauldron shows signs of repairs on its base, probably as a result of damage through heating from pot-boiler stones. It is likely that it was primarily a ceremonial cooking vessel, and the presence of the flesh-hook suggests that it was used for cooking meat.[4] It dates from the Penard Phase (1275-1140 BC[5]) and is of the Colchester Type.[6]

The Fen Edge as a whole is very rich in prehistoric sites and finds with 4 other Late Bronze Age hoards from the area, as well as 19 socketed axes, 6 swords, 7 spearheads, 1 spear ferrule, 2 socketed gouges, 1 chisel and 2 fragments of riveted sheet bronze which are stray finds,[7] pot-boiler sites and some of the few Bronze Age settlement sites.

Discovery and Excavation

The initial part of the Whiteplot Hoard was discovered in 1992 by Mr Derek Woollestone, using a metal detector. Found at this time were a socketed axe (No. 4), a socketed chisel (No. 7), a mortising chisel (No. 8), an awl (No. 9) and most of the bronze ingots (No. 13).

A small area was excavated in September 1993 by Mr Woollestone, centred on the finds of bronze ingots. A socketed axe (No. 2), a socketed knife (No. 5), a socketed gouge (No. 6), a fragment of bronze (No. 11), and a stone (No. 12) were all recovered (Fig. 1). They were all lying on the chalk, under 24cm of plough soil and 18cm of marl (probably the remains of post-war deep ploughing) with no signs of a hoard pit. A palstave (No. 1), and another socketed axe (No. 3) were also recovered by metal detector from elsewhere in the field.

There was a further excavation by Mr Woollestone in January 1994, again centred on the main hoard findspot, when an area 9m square was uncovered. Along the North-western side a 63cm wide feature was found with straight sides, which is probably a machine cut land drain. One other feature was found, 235cm x 60cm, with a sandy fill, also with straight sides, which again is probably modern. This was not excavated. Nothing else was found apart from 2 animal bones, a sherd of prehistoric pottery (possibly Iron Age) and a fragment of socketed axe (No. 10). These were located on or near the second feature, all at the plough line. The plans and photographs of both excavations have been deposited with the Castle Museum, Norwich.

As can be seen in Fig. 1, the elements which make up the hoard were not all found at the same spot. Items which can definitely be said to be part of a hoard are the ingots (No. 13), and the objects recovered in the 1993 excavation. The rest, like the palstave (No. 1) which was found over 50m away, are in fairly close proximity, but are not so close that we can say with certainty that they were buried together. Needham *et al*[8] named this context type an Area Find (land): 'finds from close proximity to each other but not all together and not necessarily [found] on the same occasion'.

Catalogue

The finds are in generally good condition, with some having areas of corrosion, the rest being patinated. The objects are not conserved, and they have not been metallurgically analysed. The museum accession number is NWHCM: 1993.198.2.

1 Palstave *NWHCM: 1993.198.2.7* (Fig. 2)

Narrow-bladed looped palstave with trident decoration. Low flanges fall back along 2/3 of hafting slot in a straight line. Blade sides parallel with only moderate splay at cutting edge.

Length: 15.5cm

Blade width: 4.4cm

Weight: 391.06g

2 Socketed Axe *NWHCM: 1993.198.2.14* (Fig. 2)

Looped socketed axe with a sub-square mouth moulding and 2 horizontal ribs below, otherwise no decoration. Sub-rectangular section body ending in flared blade showing signs of wear. There are signs of mineralised organics at collar, which have been identified as grass or *Phragmites* stems (the reed/rush family).[9]

Length: 10.8cm

Blade width: 5.4cm

Weight: 248.85g

3 Socketed Axe *NWHCM: 1993.198.2.6* (Fig. 2)

Looped socketed axe with double mouth-moulded sub-square mouth, otherwise no decoration. Sub-rectangular section body ending in a slightly flared blade showing signs of wear. A hole is visible through the body of the axe underneath the curve of the loop, which may be a casting flaw.

---

[3] Smith 1958a
[4] Gerloff 1986, p. 87
[5] Needham et al 1997, p. 82
[6] Gerloff 1986, p. 89
[7] Healy 1996, p. 43

[8] Needham *et al* 1985, p. iv
[9] Val Fryer *pers comm.*

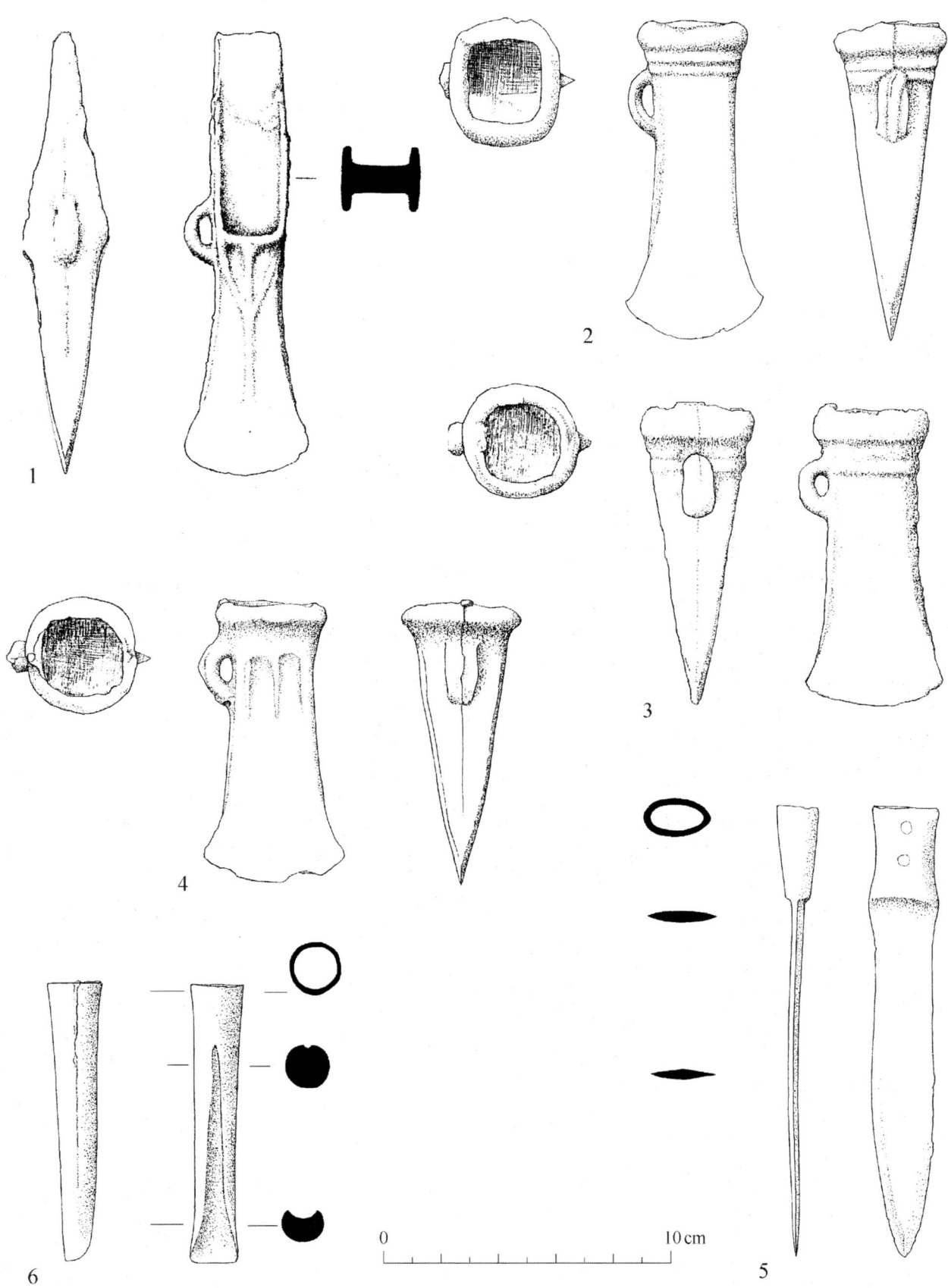

Fig. 2 Palstave, socketed axes, socketed gouge and a socketed knife. Catalogue Nos. 1-6 (1-4 drawn by Jonathan Clark) Scale 1:2

Length: 10.5cm

Blade width: 4.8cm

Weight: 300.08g

4 Socketed Axe *NWHCM: 1993.198.2.3* (Fig. 2)

Looped socketed axe with flared collar at sub-square mouth with 3 parallel vertical ribs on each face extending downward for c. 2cm. Sub-rectangular section body ending in flared blade with 2 large notches and other signs of wear. Casting flash is visible down each side.

Length: 9.9cm

Blade width: 4.9cm

Weight: 217.23g

5 Socketed Knife *NWHCM: 1993.198.2.8* (Fig. 2)

Socketed double-edged knife with leaf-shaped lozenge sectioned blade showing signs of wear. Oval sectioned socket, slightly flared at mouth, with 2 rivet holes one above the other in line with the blade.

Blade length: 12.2cm

Socket length: 3.1cm

Weight: 60.50g

6 Socketed Gouge *NWHCM: 1993.198.2.9* (Fig. 2)

Socketed gouge with very slight flare at circular-section socket mouth, no collar or other decoration. Very slight flare at blade end which shows signs of wear.

Length: 9.6cm

Blade width: 1.8cm

Weight: 73.3g

7 Socketed Chisel *NWHCM: 1993.198.2.4* (Fig. 3)

Socketed chisel with round-sectioned flared-mouth with remains of wood in socket, identified as *Fraxinus excelsior* (ash) less than 10 years old.[10] Straight sides diverge from mouth, making body oval in section, to blade that has corners broken off.

Length: 7.8cm

Blade width: 3cm, nearer 4cm if blade was complete

Weight: 0.21g

8 Mortising Chisel Fragment *NWHCM: 1993.198.2.10* (Fig. 3)

Socketed mortising chisel fragment with circular-section irregular mouth, possibly showing the remains of a collar. There is a 'wall' across the diameter of the socket dividing it in two. The object extends down to a break at the top of the blade where the section begins to flatten out. The socket contained wood, identified as *Fraxinus excelsior* (ash) less than 15 years old.[11] This has been ^{14}C dated to 2620 ± 45 BP (2-sigma calibration: 910-760 BC (92%), 680-660 BC (2%), 630-600 BC (1%)).[12]

Length: 4.5cm

Blade width: not present

Weight: 26.02g

9 Awl *NWHCM: 1993.198.2.5* (Fig 3)

Bronze awl with square-section for about 1/3 of length before becoming circular in section and tapering to a point.

Length: 6.5cm

Weight: 10.89g

10 Socketed Axe Fragment *NWHCM: 1993.198.2.11* (Fig. 3)

Curved piece of bronze, showing casting flash down one side. Probably mid/upper part of axe body below the socket mouth.

Length: unknown

Blade width: unknown

Weight: 31.03g

11 Bronze Fragment *NWHCM: 1993.198.2.12*

Irregular fragment of bronze, with signs of a casting flash on one part. It is possible that this is a fragment of socketed axe that has been flattened out.

Weight: 28.35g

12 Stone *NWHCM: 1993.198.2.13* (Fig. 3)

Igneous stone, not a common type. There are no obvious signs of working.

Length: 7.3cm

Width: 5.7cm

Weight: 181.33g

---

[10] Stuart Needham *pers comm.*

[11] Needham *et al* 1997, p. 65
[12] Needham *et al* 1997, p. 65; OxA-5977.

13 Bronze Ingots *NWHCM: 1993.198.2.1 & .2* (Fig. 3)

The complete ingot is plano-convex in cross-section, and roughly circular in plan. The surface is uneven, showing a 'bubbly' appearance that is probably left from the casting process.

Diameter: 13.2cm

Weight: 1,382g

The remaining 41 pieces of bronze ingot range from 1,109g to 311.68g, with a total weight of 11.27 kg. Five of these other pieces show signs of having come from circular ingots.

Found in later years:

14 Socketed Axe Fragment (Fig 3)

Fragment of socketed axe blade found in 2007.

Length: 40mm

Width: 52mm

Weight: 54.62g

15 Socketed Gouge (Fig 3)

Socketed gouge missing socket mouth found in 2012. Wood was found in the socket, but has not been identified or dated.

Length: 39mm

Weight: 26.53g

Discussion and Dating

The hoard can roughly be divided into three different categories: axes, tools and ingots.

The Axes

The Palstave (1) is of a type distinctly different from Middle Bronze Age types, with the narrow blade and straight low flanges in contrast to the earlier wider blades and more curved convex flanges. It is not common in the earliest hoards of the Late Bronze Age,[13] and is found mainly in later hoards of the Late Bronze Age. The trident decoration is an insular tradition, probably derived from the North French narrow palstave form.[14]

The two plain socketed axes (2, 3) are the most common form of socketed axe in South-Eastern Britain in the Ewart Park phase, with earlier forms of plain axe having multiple collar mouldings.[15] The mineralised organic substance at the collar of axe 2 may be the remains of vegetation or wood present when the material was buried.

The third socketed axe (4), with its three vertical ribs, is a Yorkshire axe type, also dating from the later part of the Late Bronze Age.[16] This type is mainly found either side of the Vale of York, with an Eastern distribution into Lincolnshire, Northumbria, and Northern East Anglia.

The Tools

Objects such as the socketed gouges (6, 15) first occur in the Wilburton phase (LBA 2), but are rare until the Ewart Park Phase when they become current throughout Britain.[17] The socketed chisel (7) which only occurs in Britain in the Ewart Park Phase[18] is an insular design. The chisel, together with the mortising chisel (8) and the gouges (6, 15), form part of the basic carpenters equipment of the Ewart Park period,[19] and can also be seen in the Carleton Rode hoard (NHER: 10022, NWHCM: 1845.70 and NWHCM: 1948.86), see also Andrew Lawson's paper in this volume).

The socketed knife (5) is of a form typical in Britain and Ireland of this period.[20]

The Stone

This is the most enigmatic of the finds from this hoard. Although a rare find, a fragments of stone (3.5g) was found in the West Acre hoard (NHER 31075) that has copper alloy corrosion markings on it. Due to this parallel the Feltwell stone has been tentatively identified as a rubbing stone, used in the post-casting working of bronze objects.

The Ingots

The ingots form the bulk of the hoard, and show the hoard to be that of a bronze founder. It is unusual to have a complete plano-convex ingot; this is the first example to be found in Norfolk. A similar example exists from Worthing, Sussex (now in the British Museum) which, with a diameter of 14cm, is very similar in size to the Whiteplot ingot.[21] Another is from Barnham, Suffolk (at West Stow Anglo-Saxon Village, 1977.698), but otherwise they are very rare. Analysis of the composition of the metal of ingots from other Late Bronze Age founders' hoards reveals that they are nearly pure copper, ranging from 94.27% Cu from the Plymouth, Devon, hoard to 99.9% Cu from the Watford, Hertfordshire, and Stunty Fen, Cambridgeshire, hoards,[22] so it is probable that the Feltwell II hoard ingots are of similar composition. This points towards the copper being alloyed by the founder from refined ingots

---

[13] Smith 1959: p. 176
[14] Rowlands 1976, p. 38
[15] Burgess 1968, fig. 11.3 & fig 13.5
[16] O'Connor 1980, p. 168
[17] Burgess 1968, pp. 39-40
[18] Burgess 1968, pp. 39-40
[19] Coombs 1979, p. 214
[20] O'Connor 1980, p. 178
[21] Tylecote 1986, p. 23, fig. 9: Smith 1958b
[22] Tylecote 1986, p. 18

LANDSCAPES AND ARTEFACTS

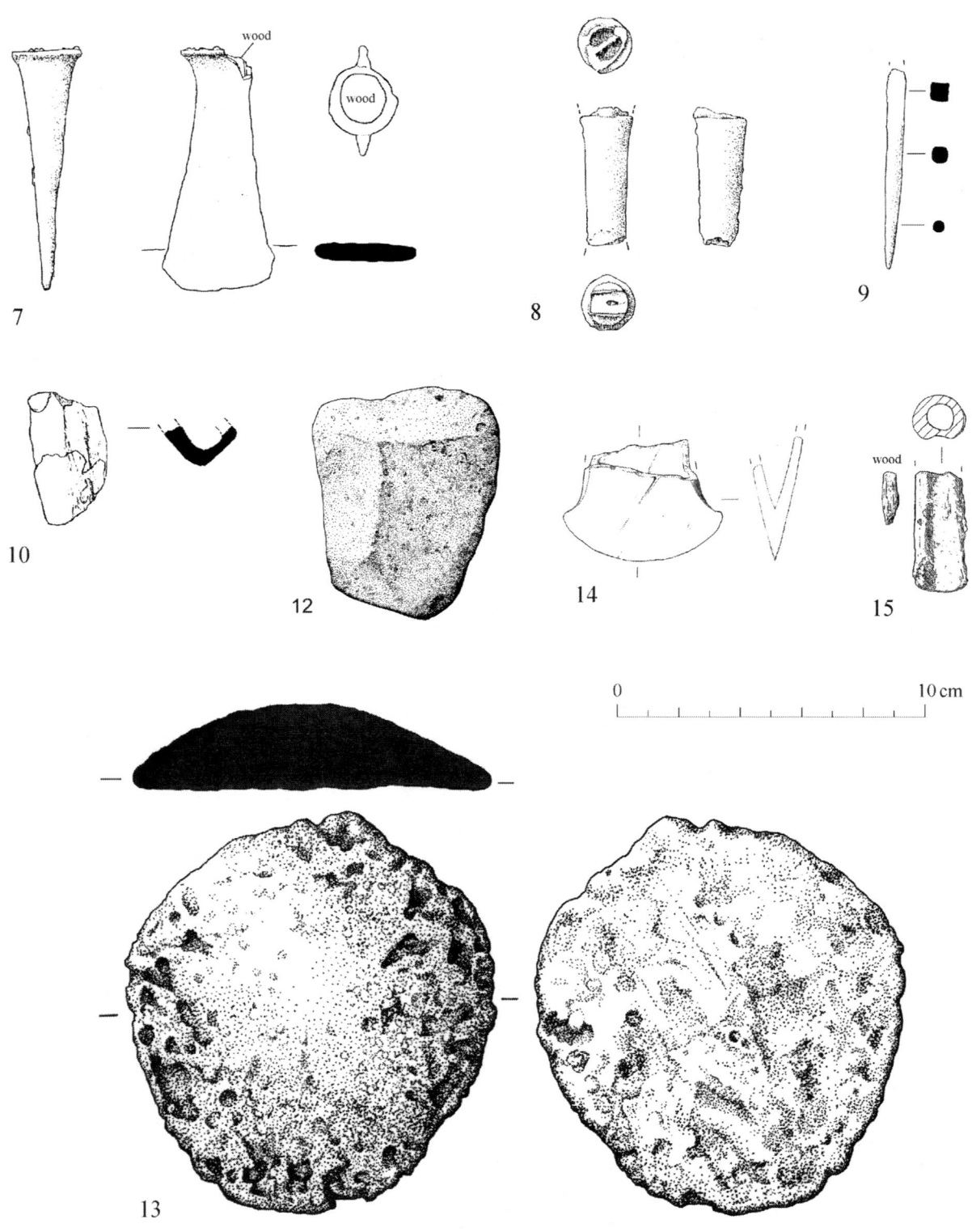

Fig. 3 Socketed chisels, awl, socketed axe fragments, stone, complete ingot and a socketed gouge. Catalogue Nos. 7-15 (12-13 drawn by Jason Gibbons, 14-15 drawn by Jonathan Clark) Scale 1:2

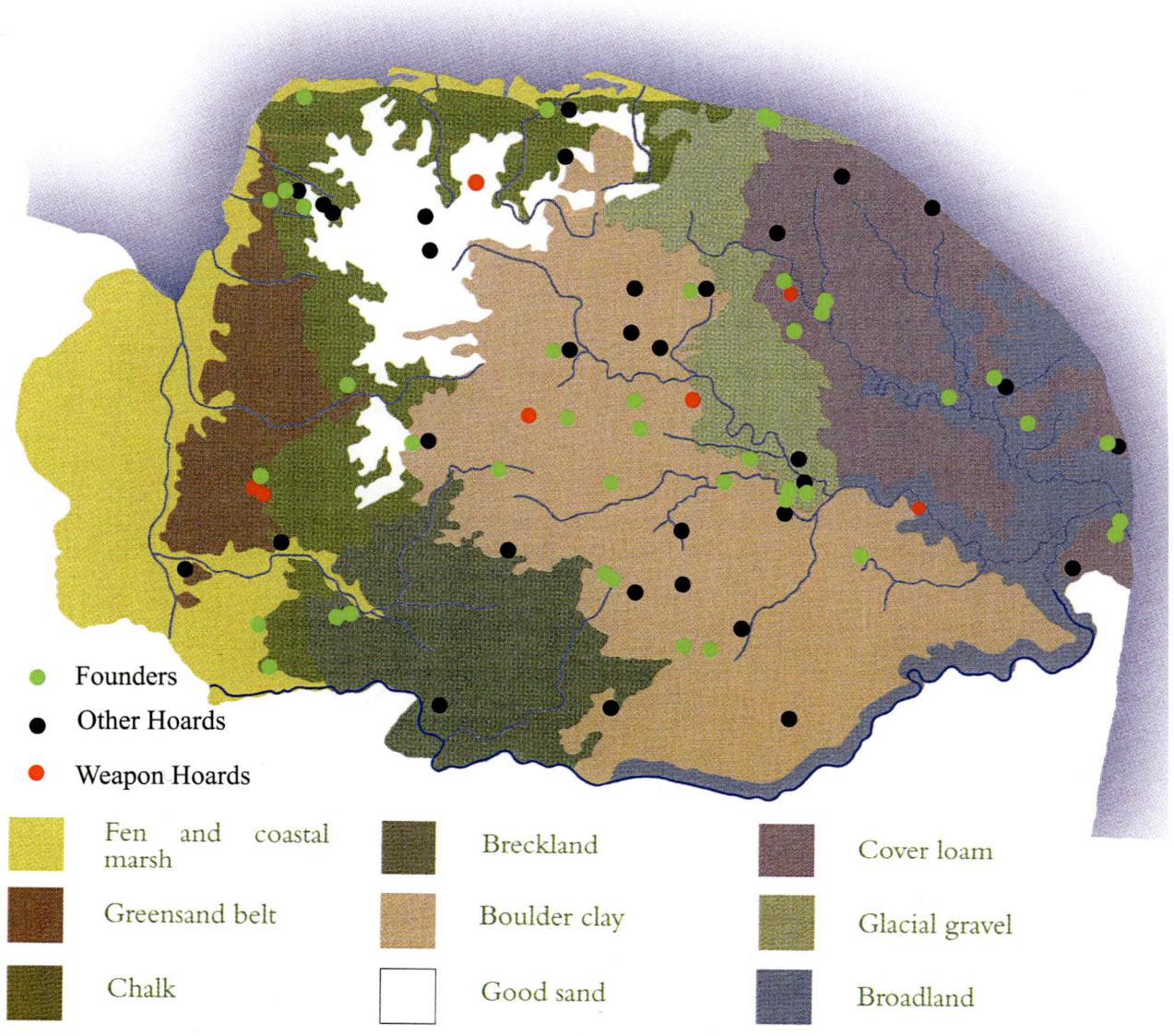

Fig. 4 Distribution map of Late Bronze-Age hoards in Norfolk
(soil and river data from Davies 2008, figs 10 and 11)

of copper and tin, rather than by the smelters at the source of the ore. No tin was found in the hoard, and generally tin ingots are rare finds in Late Bronze Age hoards. One small tin ingot was found as part of a hoard from Grays Thurrock, Essex, discovered in 1906, and the hoard is of very similar composition to the Feltwell II hoard,[23] but very few others have been found. The reason why more tin ingots are not found, especially considering that they should form about a tenth of the total finds of ingots, is that tin is only stable above 13°C. Below that temperature, tin will over time disintegrate to a non-metallic grey-brown powder.[24]

In the Late Bronze Age, lead also formed a part of the bronze alloy, frequently between 4-7% of the total weight, but sometimes as high as 15%.[25] A small block of lead/tin alloy (GRYEH: 1977.368) weighing 158g forms part of the West Caister Hoard,[26] and one of the hoards from Snettisham (NHER 25920) has a lead ingot. A similar lead block as well as other lead objects, were found at the Late Bronze Age settlement site at Runnymede Bridge.[27] Generally however, very little lead has been found associated with Late Bronze Age finds, possibly due to the lead having been overlooked.

Dating

From the composition of the hoard it is possible to date it to the Late Bronze Age as part of the Ewart Park tradition, 900-800 BC.[28] This matches with the ^{14}C date of 910-760 BC from the mortising chisel (8).

---

[23] Butcher 1922, p. 108
[24] Tylecote 1986, p. 49
[25] Brown and Blin-Stoyle 1959, p. 193
[26] Lawson 1979, p. 176
[27] Needham & Hook 1987, p. 260
[28] Needham *et al* 1997, pp. 55-109

Bronze Age Hoards

Bronze Age hoards can consist of a number of different categories of artefacts: tools (including axes), weapons, ornaments and ingots. Traditionally, hoards have been seen as either personal hoards, trader's hoards, founder's hoards or ritual hoards.[29] This hoard contains tools and ingots, and because of this it probably represents a bronze founder's hoard, a category that can be defined by the presence of bronze ingots. Broken tools and swords on their own may also indicate a bronze founder's hoard, with the bronze having been broken up for recycling.

However, there are some aspects to the hoard that might suggest a ritual or votive explanation. Characteristics for votive hoards are: deposition in a specialised location (often wet places), a restricted range of items (often only weapons), and a formal arrangement of the objects.[30] It is this last characteristic that can be seen with this hoard. When the core of the hoard was excavated the objects were found in an arrangement round the Rubbing Stone (No. 12 in Fig. 1). Other founder's hoards of similar dates that have been found with a formal arrangement are the Withersfield hoard from Suffolk and the Hollingbourne hoard from Kent. Both these hoards had axes positioned vertically, surrounded by ingot fragments.[31]

Assessing the likelihood of these two explanations is difficult. While there are few other hoards that have been found with this kind of formal arrangement, relatively few hoards of this composition from Norfolk have been fully excavated. It could be chance that the hoard became arranged in this particular pattern. The Gorleston I hoard was buried in some kind of bag.[32] It is possible that if the rubbing stone was placed in the bottom of a similar bag the other objects might sag down in an arrangement around it, with the objects higher up the bag being displaced by later agricultural processes.

There is of course the possibility that both explanations are correct, that it was a founder's hoard, and that on this occasion, at the end of its utilitarian life, that it was deposited in a ritual fashion.

The Feltwell II hoard is one of 99 Late Bronze Age hoards from Norfolk (see Fig. 4). This is in dramatic contrast to the two hoards from the Early Bronze Age and 13 hoards from the Middle Bronze Age. It is also in contrast to the other archaeological evidence from the Late Bronze Age. There is virtually no settlement evidence, little pottery (Bronze Age pottery is made of very friable fabrics[33]), and few recognisable enclosures or land divisions or burials.[34] This makes the hoards (and the many single finds of metalwork, unfortunately beyond the scope of this paper) the only way of interpreting Late Bronze Age Norfolk.

As noted at the beginning, the Fen Edge is rich in metalwork, and it is concentrated in a linear strip of land where the higher ground meets the flat fenland. There are other concentrations of hoards: for instance the five in the parish of Snettisham, and five from west Norwich. It is possible to test the distribution of the hoards using Nearest Neighbour Analysis to determine if these clusters are real, or as a result of random chance. Nearest Neighbour Analysis produces a dimensionless number between zero and 2.15, with zero showing complete clustering, 1 showing randomness and 2.15 showing complete regularity of spacing.[35] The number is derived by averaging the distance between each hoard and its nearest neighbour and dividing this number by the expected average if the distribution is random.

To compensate for the edge effect (where a hoard on the border of Norfolk may actually be nearer a hoard in Suffolk, but is only compared to another in Norfolk, thus skewing the results) the correction (which takes into account the perimeter of the study area) suggested in Bailey and Gatrell[36] will be used.

When this is applied to the 86 hoards that have known grid-references, the Nearest Neighbour result is 0.6, showing that the distribution of the hoards is partly clustered. Comparing the average nearest neighbour distances to the expected average if the distribution was random using a one sample t-test[37] with a null-hypothesis that the distribution is random shows that the null-hypothesis can be rejected as being extremely unlikely (t=3, p=0.004). In other words, the distribution of the hoards shows some clustering and this result is not due to chance.

Parish	Size (Hectares)	Total Number of Find Spots	Density (finds/ha)	Number of Bronze Age Find Spots	Density (finds/ha)
Feltwell	5216	98	0.0188	15	0.00288
Hockwold	3105	260	0.0837	25	0.00805
Methwold	4912	145	0.0295	18	0.00366

TABLE 1

---

[29] Evans 1881, p. 458
[30] Bradley 1990, p. 14
[31] Barber 2003, pp. 59-60
[32] Clough and Green 1978, p. 3
[33] Silvester 1991, p. 87
[34] Lawson 1984, p. 167
[35] Roberts 1996, p. 56
[36] Bailey & Gatrell 1995, p. 100
[37] Drennan 1996, p. 159

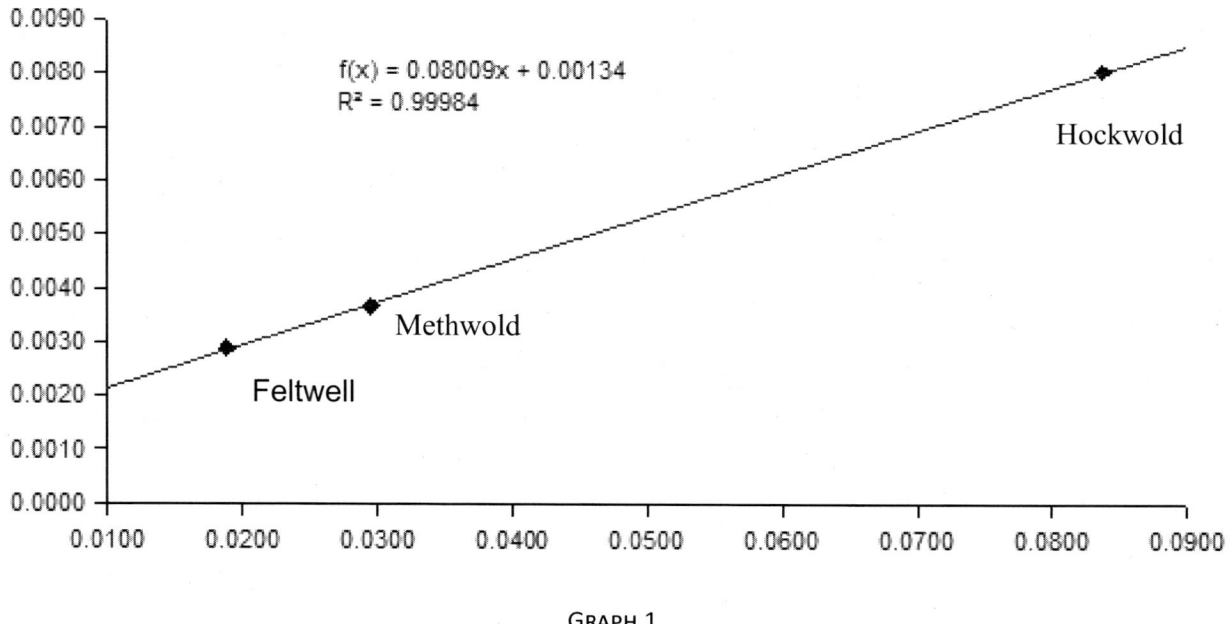

GRAPH 1

It is possible that this result is due to recovery bias. Gurney[38] with his analysis of metal-detecting 'events' (defined by him as being the number of times a parish has been visited by a metal-detectorist and recorded on the Historic Environment Record) shows that the overall distribution of metal-detected finds from all periods (Bronze Age to Post-medieval) is not constant across Norfolk. He identifies the following factors as being important in determining the number of finds: search technique, machine used, expertise of the searcher, time spent, area covered, ground conditions, weather conditions and the soil type, all of which can obscure the underlying distribution.

Confirmation of this can be seen in an analysis of the density of all metal-detected finds from Feltwell and the parishes to the North and South (Methwold and Hockwold respectively) against the density of Bronze Age finds.

As can been seen from the graph above there is a near perfect correlation between the density of all metal-detected finds and Bronze Age metal-detected finds (linear regression test, r=0.999, F=6070, p=0.0082). This suggests that the number and density of metal-detected Bronze Age metalwork objects found may be a function of time spent searching, rather than differences in the distribution 3,000 years ago.

However, not all of the hoards were found by metal-detectorists. As can been seen in Table 2, 47 hoards (54.7%) were found by metal-detectorists, and 38 hoards (44.2%) were casual finds (agriculture, ditch digging etc.). These two groups can each be subjected to separate Nearest Neighbour analysis, and they give figures of 0.64 (casual finds) and 0.68 (metal-detected finds), partly clustered, the same as the figure for all the hoards together. Furthermore, the average nearest neighbour mean distances between the two sets of hoards can be analysed by a two-sample t test,[39] with a null-hypothesis that the difference is nothing more than the vagaries of sampling. The result (t=1.1, p=0.29) shows that the null-hypothesis cannot be rejected. This means that there is no difference in the distribution of the casually found hoards and the metal-detected hoards, a result that is in opposition to the results from Hockwold/ Feltwell/ Methwold above. This may be due to the first test examining all Bronze-Age finds, and the latter test only looking at Late Bronze-Age hoards.

Assuming that the recovery of hoards by casual means is random, and representative of the original Late Bronze Age distribution, both the casually found hoards and metal-detected hoards can be analysed further together (Fig. 4).

A visual examination of the distribution of the hoards looking at the soil types and rivers shows some interesting points (Fig. 4). Firstly there is the paucity of hoards from the very south on the heavier boulder clay soils. This is also mirrored in the distribution of Early Bronze Age barrows, which are also scarce in this area.[40] This may reflect the lack of occupation in this area throughout the Bronze Age as the heavy boulder clay soils would have been unsuitable for the agricultural techniques of the time.

Then there are a number of hoards on the Fen Edge, others dotted along the coast, and, those slightly further inland, but on the edges of the Great Estuary. These are all hoards that are not buried in wet places (one of the signifiers of votive hoard deposition) but are next to wet places. During the Late Bronze-Age the climate became cooler and wetter, seen in other parts of the country by the abandonment of

---

[38] Gurney 1997, p. 529

[39] Drennan 1996, pp. 155-7
[40] Ashwin 2005, p. 20

many upland areas as agriculture there became unviable.[41] This disruption may have caused a change in Norfolk's agriculture and society, and is possible reason for the lack of non-metalwork archaeological evidence mentioned above. This may have generated greater competition for the reduced amount of viable land, and have led to the concept of private ownership of land,[42] with boundaries between owned territory (the dry land) and communal spaces such as the fens and the sea.[43] These hoards may be marking a liminal space in the landscape. The clustering at places such as the Fen Edge, Snettisham, Beeston Regis and Gorleston may represent several groups depositing their own hoards in competition, or the same group repeating the process over time.

Many of the rest of the hoards occupy a loose group in the centre of Norfolk. Looking at these in conjunction with the distribution of rivers it can be seen that there is a possible correlation, with 21 hoards near to rivers. Again, these findspots are not within the wet places, but next to them, and may also be acting as boundary markers. Interestingly, the weapons hoards, often seen as being votive deposits in wet places,[44] seem in Norfolk to be mostly away from rivers or the fens, although an examination of the micro-topography might show that they were buried in localised wet places.

Conclusion

The Feltwell II hoard in many ways can be seen as an archetypal hoard from Norfolk. It is a founder's hoard, as are the majority, discovered by a metal-detectorist and responsibly recovered, reported and recorded before acquisition by a museum. Its place in the landscape, on the boundary between dry and wet, between private and common, is common to many of the other Late Bronze Age hoards in Norfolk.

It remains, of course, to subject these ideas to rigorous spatial analysis, to see if the eye is seeing patterns where none actually exist.

Acknowledgments

For all their help: Jonathan Clark, John Davies, Val Fryer, Andrew Lawson, Adrian Marsden, Bill Milligan, Stuart Needham, Livia Roschdi, and Andrew Hall for preparing the figures.

TABLE 2 LATE BRONZE-AGE HOARDS FROM NORFOLK
(DUE TO THE SENSITIVE NATURE OF SOME LOCATIONS OF THE HOARDS THE GRID-REFERENCES HAVE NOT BEEN LISTED. RESEARCHERS WISHING TO OBTAIN THE GRID-REFERENCES SHOULD CONTACT THE NORFOLK HISTORIC ENVIRONMENT RECORD.)

Late Bronze-Age Hoards from Norfolk with grid-reference

Parish/Hoard Name	NHER Number	Type	No of Objects	Discovery Method	Museum Number (where applicable)	References
Attleborough	30938	Axes	4	metal-detected		
Aylsham	7396	Founder's	26	casual find	NWHCM: 1968.915	Clough 1969, 348-351; Norfolk Museums Service 1977, 30
Beeston Regis I	15534	Founder's	23	metal-detected	NWHCM: 1981.79	Lawson 1980a, 17-219
Beeston Regis II	18037	Founder's	11	casual find		
Bradenham	37104	Founder's	27	excavation		Hinds and Bates 2010, 84-91
Brampton	24343	Founder's	32	metal-detected		
Brampton	52906	Founder's	6	metal-detected		
Bunwell	17474	Founder's	11	metal-detected	NWHCM: 1984.1	
Caister on Sea	12872	Founder's	9	metal-detected		Lawson 1979, 173-180
Carleton Rode	10022	Founder's	26	casual find	NWHCM: 1845.70 & 1948.86	Norfolk Museums Service 1977, 31
Cawston	51514	Weapons	14	metal-detected	NWHCM: 2009.205	
Costessey	16398	Founder's	13	metal-detected	NWHCM: 1999.1.11.1 (part of hoard)	
Costessey	39351	Founder's	8	metal-detected		
Cranwich I	15915	Founder's	12	casual find		

---

[41] Cunliffe 2012, p. 264
[42] Cunliffe 2012, p. 258
[43] Pryor 2004, pp. 287-8
[44] Bradley 1990

Cranwich II	13697	Founder's	16	metal-detected	NWHCM: 1993.198.1	
Cringleford	16229	Axes	3	metal-detected	NWHCM: 1997.708	
Dereham	2853	Founder's	21	casual find	NWHCM: 1952.213	Norfolk Museums Service 1977, 32
Dersingham	1685	Axes	2	casual find		
Earlham	873	Ornament	3	casual find		
East Rudham	35907	Axes	44	casual find, excavation and metal-detecting		
Erpingham	55424	Axes	14	casual find	NWHCM: 2012.114	
Feltwell	5191	Cauldron	2	casual find	NWHCM: 1961.373	
Feltwell II	5169	Founder's	54	metal-detected	NWHCM: 1998.198.2	
Fincham	29491	Founder's	5	metal-detected		
Fincham I	33343	Weapons	15	metal-detected	NWHCM: 2009.52	
Fincham II	36176	Weapons	18	metal-detected	Norwich Castle	
Fleggborough	31130	Founder's	13	metal-detected		
Forncett	31949	Axe & spear	2	metal-detected		
Foulsham	3089	Axes	141	casual find	NWHCM: 1953.40	Norfolk Museums Service 1977, 33
Foxley	42656	Gold Bracelets	7	metal-detected	NWHCM: 2004.34	
Fritton	28338	Spear & Knife	3	metal-detected		
Garvestone	25689	Founder's	3	metal-detected		
Gorleston I	10556	Founder's	110	casual find	NWHCM: 1953.152 & 1961.49	Clough and Green 1978, 1-18; Norfolk Museums Service 1977, 37-8
Gorleston II	10557	Founder's	11	casual find		
Great Ellingham	54009	Axes	186	metal-detected		
Great Ellingham	31588	Founder's	18	metal-detected		
Great Ellingham	51148	Founder's	27	metal-detected	NWHCM: 2008.544	
Great Melton	17472	Founder's	70	metal-detected	NWHCM: 1999.1.32.13	
Great Wichingham	35269	Founder's	6	metal-detected		
Hevingham	36973	Founder's	6	metal-detected	NWHCM: 2003.71	
Hilgay	13891	Axes	3	casual find		Lawson and Ashley 1980, 328-333
Hindringham	2078	Axes	2	casual find		Clough 1969, 348-351
Hockwold	5316	Founder's	24	metal-detected		
Horning	8446	Founder's	5	metal-detected		Lawson 1980b, 333-338
Kenninghall	10797	Axes	12	casual find & metal-detected		
Kenninghall	32005	Axes	10	metal-detected		
Ludham	21440	Axes	5	metal-detected		
Ludham	35617	Founder's	45	metal-detected		
Norwich - Norgate Rd	9551	Founder's	12	casual find	NWHCM: 1952.62	Norfolk Museums Service 1977, 34-5
North Elmham	2925	Axes & Weapons	2	casual find		
North Elmham	1123	Founder's	48	casual find & excavation	NWHCM: L1971.1	Clough and Wade-Martins 1970, 6-18; Norfolk Museums Service 1977, 32-3
North Tuddenham	36081	Founder's	62	metal-detected		
North Tuddenham	16592	Founder's	8	metal-detected		

Location	ID	Type	Count	Find method	Museum ref	Reference
Northrepps	11969	Axes	5	casual find & metal-detected	NWHCM: 2005.351	
Norwich	18149	Axes	15	casual find		Society of Antiquaries. Society of Antiquaries. Vol VIII, pp 159-60
Norwich - Unthank Rd	500	Founder's	16	casual find	NWHCM: 1946.161	Norfolk Museums Service 1977, 34; Evans 1881, 447, 468, Hoard 110.
Norwich – Eaton II	41383	Founder's	145	casual find	NWHCM: 2007.77	
Norwich – Peckover Rd	9552	Founder's	6	casual find	NWHCM: 1953.85	
Paston	6877	Axes	4	casual find	NWHCM: 1947.27 & 1956.60	
Pulham St Mary	10765	Axes & Weapons	11	casual find		
Salle I	41976	Axes	9	metal-detected		
Salle II	42594	Founder's	5	metal-detected		
Shernbourne	1679	2 axes + 1 spear	3	casual find		
Snettisham	25920	Founder's	8	metal-detected		
Snettisham II	1670	Axes & Weapons	6	casual find		
Snettisham III	1671	Founder's	14	casual find		
Snettisham IV	1672	Founder's	41	casual find & metal-detected		
Snettisham V	28136	Founder's	38	metal-detected		
South Creake	1944	Founder's	12	casual find & metal-detected	NWHCM: 1964.87	
South Creake	28817	Weapons	111	metal-detected	NWHCM: 1964.87	Norfolk Museums Service 1977, 31-2
Sparham	56476	Axe & Knife	3	metal-detected		
Sparham	34690	Founder's	36	metal-detected		
Sporle	4137	Gold	3	casual find	NWHCM: 1961.440	Norfolk Museums Service 1977, 35
Stiffkey	1858	2 axes & mount	7	casual find		Clough 1969, 348-351
Stiffkey	22306	Founder's	21	metal-detected		
Stoke Ferry	4726	Ornament	6	casual find	NWHCM: 1920.27	Sainty 1935, 60-71
Stoke Ferry	4725	Weapons	12	casual find		
Syderstone	32820	Axes	2	metal-detected		Brown and Blin-Stoyle 1959, 188-208, 201, 202; Case 1954, 18-27
Thetford	16461	Axes		metal-detected		
Thornham	41091	Founder's	6	metal-detected	NWHCM: 2006.477	
Watton	8777	Axes	7	casual find	NWHCM: 1959.30	Norfolk Museums Service 1977, 37
Wendling	42701	Weapons	3	metal-detected	NWHCM: 2011.345	
West Acre	31075	Founder's	9	metal-detected	NWHCM: 2009.237	
West Caister	8675	Gold	4	casual find	GRYEH: 1977.368 & NWHCM: 1955.210	
Weston Longville	3051	Weapons	2	casual find	NWHCM: 1954.17	
Wymondham	18111	Hoard	9	metal-detected		Pendleton 1999, 207

NWHCM = Norwich Castle Museum, GRYEH = Great Yarmouth Museums

Late Bronze-Age Hoards from Norfolk with no grid-reference

Parish/Hoard Name	NHER Number	Type	No of Objects	Discovery Method	Museum Number (where present)	References
Belton	24660	Founder's	4	unknown		
Burham Thorpe	19368	Hoard?	3	Casual find		
Norwich – Eaton I	9550	Founder's	69	Casual find	NWHCM: 1954.108	Norfolk Museums Service 1977, 33-4; Clark, W.G. 1907, 408
Feltwell Fen Hoard	5295	Founder's	19	Casual find	British Museum	
Hoe	2790	Founder's	14	Casual find	NWHCM: 1898.42	
Horstead	8031	Axes	c.30	Casual find	NWHCM: 1894.27	Rye, W. 1909, 26 no. 281
Ingham	8216	Founder's	19	Casual find	Liverpool	Evans 1881, 319; Nicholson, S.M. 1980,
Oxbourgh	2615	Weapons	19	Casual find	NWHCM: 1829.100	Rye, W. 1909, 19
Pentney	3944	Ornaments	4+	Casual find		Lawson, A J. 1985, 169-175
Reepham	3134	Chisel/Axe/Spear	c.40	Casual find		Clark, W.G. 1907, 408
Shernbourne	25483	Founder's	5	Casual find		
Snettisham I	1504	Axes	4+	Casual find		
Walsingham	2022	Axes	4	Casual find		Pendleton 1999, 204

Bibliography

Ashwin, T, 2005. 'Late Neolithic and Early Bronze-Age Norfolk (c.3000-1700 BC)' in T. Ashwin and A. Davison, (Eds.), *An Historical Atlas of Norfolk*, Chichester, Phillimore

Bailey, T.C., and Gatrell A.C. 1995, *Interactive Spatial Data Analysis*, (Harlow, Longman)

Barber, M. 2003, *Bronze and the Bronze-Age*, (Port Stroud, Tempus)

Bradley, R. 1990, *Passage of Arms*, (Cambridge, Cambridge University Press)

Brown, M.A., and Blin-Stoyle, A.E., 1959, 'A sample analysis of British middle and late bronze age material, using optical spectrometry' *Proceedings of the Prehistoric Society* 25

Burgess, C.B. 1968, 'The later Bronze Age in the British Isles and North-Western France' *Archaeological Journal* 125, pp. 1-45

Butcher, C.H. 1922, 'A hoard of bronze discovered at Grays Thurrock' *Antiquaries Journal* II, pp. 105-108

Clark, W.G. 1907, 'The distribution of flint and bronze implements in Norfolk' *Transactions of the Norfolk and Norwich Naturalists' Society*, 8 (pt 3) (for 1906-1907) pp. 393-409

Clough, T.H. McK. 1969, 'Recent discoveries of Late Bronze Age metalwork in Norfolk' *Norfolk Archaeology* 34, pp. 348-351

Clough, T.H. McK., and Wade-Martins, P. 1970, 'A Late Bronze Age hoard from Foxburrow Farm, North Elmham, Norfolk, 1970' *Norfolk Archaeology* 35, pp. 6-18

Clough, T.H. McK., and Green, C. 1978, 'The first Late Bronze Age founder's hoard from Gorleston, Great Yarmouth, Norfolk' *Norfolk Archaeology* 37, pp. 1-18

Coombs, D. 1979, 'A Late Bronze Age Hoard from Cassiobridge Farm, Watford, Hertfordshire' in C. Burgess and D. Coombs (eds.), *Bronze Age Hoards* BAR 67, (Oxford, BAR)

Cunliffe, B. 2012, *Britain Begins*, Oxford, (Oxford University Press)

Davies, J. 2008, *The Land of Boudica*, (Oxford, Oxbow Books)

Drennan, R.D. 1996, *Statistics for Archaeologists*, (New York, Plenum Press)

Evans, J. 1881, *The Ancient Bronze Implements, Weapons and Ornaments of Great Britain and Ireland*, (London, Longmans)

Gerlof, S. 1986 'Broze Age class A cauldrons: typology, origins and chronology' *J. Roy. Soc. Antiq. Ireland* 116, pp. 84-115

Gurney, D. 1997, A note on the distribution of metal-detecting in Norfolk' *Norfolk Archaeology* 42, pp. 528-531

Healy, F. 1996, *The Fenland Project, Number 11: The Wissey Embayment: Evidence for pre-Iron Age Occupation* EAA 78, (Dereham, Norfolk Archaeological Unit)

Hinds, K., and Bates, S. 2010, 'A Late Bronze Age Hoard from Bradenham. Norfolk' *Norfolk Archaeology* 46, pp. 84-91

Lawson, A.J. 1979, 'A Late Bronze Age hoard from West Caister, Norfolk' in Burgess, C. and Coombs, D. (eds.) *Bronze Age Hoards*, BAR 67

Lawson, A.J. 1980a, 'A Late Bronze Age hoard from Beeston Regis, Norfolk' *Antiquity* 54, No 212, pp. 217-219

Lawson, A.J. 1980b, 'Recent archaeological finds - the Horning hoard' *Norfolk Archaeology* 37, pp. 333-338

Lawson, A.J. 1984, 'The Bronze Age in East Anglia with particular reference to Norfolk' in C. Barringer, (ed.), *Aspects of East Anglian Pre-History*, (Norwich, Geo Books), pp.141-177

Lawson, A J, 1985, 'Bronzes from Brettenham, Boxford, Barton Bendish, Boughton and Bradmoor Common' *Norfolk Archaeology* 39, pp. 169-175

Lawson, A.J., and Ashley, S.J. 1980, 'The Hilgay hoard' *Norfolk Archaeology* 37, pp. 328-333

Needham, S.P., and Hook, D.R. 1987, 'Lead and lead alloys in the Bronze Age - recent finds from Runnymead Bridge' in E.A. Slater, and J.O. Tate (eds.) *Science and Archaeology Glasgow 1987*, BAR 196, (Oxford, BAR)

Needham, S.P., Lawson, A.J., and Green, H.S. 1985, *British Bronze Age Metalwork A1-6 Early Bronze Age Hoards*, (London, British Museum)

Needham, S.P., Bronk-Ramsey, C., Coombs, D., Cartwright, C., and Pettitt, P. 1997, 'An independent chronology of the British Bronze Age metalwork: the results of the Oxford radiocarbon accelerator programme' *Archaeological Journal* 154, pp. 55-109

Nicholson, S.M. 1980, *Catalogue of the Prehistoric Metalwork in Merseyside Museums*

Norfolk Museums Service 1977, *Catalogue of the Bronze Age Metalwork in Norwich Castle Museum*, 2nd ed., (Norwich, Norfolk Museums Service)

O'Connor, B. 1980, *Cross-Channel Relations in the Late Bronze Age* BAR 91, (Oxford, BAR)

Pendleton, C.F. 1999, *Bronze Age Metalwork from Northern East Anglia. A study of its distribution and interpretation.* BAR British Series 279, (Oxford, Archaeopress)

Pryor, F. 2004, *Britain BC*, (London, Harper Perennial)

Roberts, B.K. 1996, *Landscapes of Settlement: Prehistory to the Present* (London, Routledge)

Rowlands, M.J. 1976, *The Organisation of Middle Bronze Age Metalworking* BAR 31, (Oxford, BAR)

Rye, W. 1909, *Catalogue of Antiquities Found Principally in East Anglia*

Sainty, J.E. 1935, 'Norfolk Prehistory. Report of the Annual Meeting, 1935. Norwich, September 4-11' *British Association for the Advancement of Science* Appendix pp. 60-71

Silvester, R.J. 1991, *The Fenland Project Number 4: The Wissey Embayment and Fen Causeway, Norfolk* East Anglian Archaeology 52, (Dereham, Norfolk Archaeological Unit)

Smith, M.A. (ed.) 1958a 'The Feltwell Fen Hoard, Feltwell (Norfolk)', *Inventaria Archaeologica* GB. 35 (1-2) (London, Garraway)

Smith, M.A. (ed.) 1958b 'Forty Acre Brickfield Hoard, Worthing (Sussex)', *Inventaria Archaeologica* GB. 37.3 (1-6) (London, Garraway)

Smith, M.A. 1959, 'Some Somerset hoards and their place in the bronze age of Southern Britain' *Proceedings of the Prehistoric Society* 25, pp. 144-187

Tylecote, R.E. 1986, *The Prehistory of Metallurgy in the British Isles*, (London, Institute of Metals)

The Boudica Code: recognising a 'symbolic logic' within Iron Age material culture

John Davies

Introduction

Andrew Rogerson's contribution to the archaeology of Norfolk and beyond has embraced a readiness to engage with all archaeological periods. He has twice been a key contributor to conferences on the Iron Age of northern East Anglia.[1] My own initial work on the Iron Age of Norfolk was through its coinage. I was intrigued that the major study of Icenian coinage at that time, published in 1970, referred to the complex and diverse range of imagery on the coins as merely *space fillers*.[2] In subsequent years, as I have seen more objects belonging to the Iceni, I have become more convinced that the symbols and depictions on coins and other items of the period have significance far beyond just decoration.

Furthermore, as we come to explore Iron Age society, the importance of not just symbols, but also the relevance of structured behaviour and ritual, to these people becomes more apparent. Throughout the 1990s research increasingly showed how such behaviour permeated all aspects of their daily life.[3] One of the better known sites where structured deposition can be evidenced is Ken Hill, at Snettisham in Norfolk, where very carefully ordered hoard deposits of gold and silver objects were discovered, providing a view of complex behaviour within this late pre-historic society.[4]

During the course of my work in Norfolk, in my own 'shorthand', I have come to refer to my observations of such imagery and structured behaviour within the tribal area of the Iceni as 'The Boudica Code'. In this paper I will attempt to draw attention to a range of activities, as interpreted through studies of their artefacts, which together provide a body of evidence with the potential to throw light on this complex late prehistoric society, in the absence of their own writings. In this paper I will explore the use of symbols, representations and behaviours which appear to reflect the presence of hidden meanings in relation to the Iron Age of Norfolk.

The social structure of Britain during the Iron Age was based on tribal groupings that were territorial. The Iceni are the tribe associated with northern East Anglia and the inhabitants of the area will be referred to accordingly.

The Iconography

The material culture of the Iceni carries a wealth of imagery and symbols. It is apparent that a number of these representations were repeatedly chosen and, by implication, that they carried meaning for the Iceni. The deep significance of symbols and imagery in material culture can be observed in relation to other tribal societies, such as the plains Indians of North America, whose objects of everyday use possessed deep symbolic importance to them.[5] Here I will provide some initial observations and thoughts in relation to Icenian objects.

There is an increasing awareness that the imagery represented on Iron Age coins carries significance. This is a fertile area for ongoing and future research.[6] The Iceni produced a prolific coinage, which is well known to us through the studies of Amanda Chadburn and John Talbot.[7] Icenian coins carry a diverse range of stylised designs which include symbols that have been interpreted as animals and astronomical representations. Although few symbols on Iron Age coins can be said to be unique to specific tribal groups, including the Iceni, it is possible to identify examples which were favoured by individual tribes. One motif commonly used by the Iceni is the *back-to-back crescent*, which is found on both gold and silver issues and is particularly prominent on the prolific *Pattern-horse* and later inscribed series (Fig. 1). It is considered that this motif may have served as a tribal emblem.[8] It is not restricted to coins but is also found elsewhere within Icenian material culture. A bronze bowl or bucket fitting designed around the back-to-back crescent motif was found at Fakenham in 1993.[9] Another example from Tattersett (unpublished), in the form of an enamelled disc, appears to have been purely ornamental and was perhaps worn as a form of badge by its owner.

Symbols which emphasise the number three are commonly encountered on Iron Age objects right across Europe. These include Y-shaped symbols, trefoils and pellet triangles (Fig. 2). These symbols are again found on Icenian coins. The 'triplet' is sometimes positioned below a portrait. As such, could it have served as a stamp of authority or power for the issuer? Another bronze item from the county which echoes this triplet motif is a form of button and loop fastener.[10]

---

[1] Davies and Williamson 1999; Davies 2011
[2] Allen 1970
[3] Hill 1993, 1995; Fitzpatrick 1992, 1994; Hingley 1993; Parker Pearson and Richards 1994
[4] Stead 1991
[5] Carocci 2011
[6] for example, see Nash Briggs 2012
[7] Chadburn 2006; Talbot 2011
[8] Nash-Briggs 2012, p.32; Davies 2009, pp. 110-12
[9] Davies 2009, fig. 78
[10] Davies 2009, fig. 83

Fig. 1 Icenian Pattern-horse type silver unit (Copyright Norfolk Museums Service)

Fig. 2 Triplet symbol, as used on a pair of linch pins from Norfolk (Copyright Norfolk Museums Service)

We may never be in a position to accurately interpret what such individual symbols meant. However, the fact that they were used repeatedly suggests that they did carry meaning of some kind. Through his studies of Icenian coinage, John Talbot has described the choice and positioning of motifs and designs as 'a sort of *symbolic logic*' (*pers comm*).

An additional importance of some symbols may have been to reinforce tribal identity and their use in this way would have been especially important in the absence of writing. The use of recognised symbols and other imagery, such as an association with particular animals, appears to have distinguished the Iceni from their neighbours. The Iceni are the only tribe to have used a depiction of the wolf on their coinage (see below). Peoples living further to the south also used their own distinctive imagery. It is noticeable that the societies who were more regularly exposed to Roman influences, such as the Trinovantes and Atrebates, frequently used symbols from the classical world on their coins, such as the centaur, Pegasus, sphinx and capricorn.[11] In contrast, the Iceni did not employ such classical devices.

The power of symbols

Having considered the intentional use of symbols within Icenian material culture, it is worth emphasising how such images can carry great power and significance within a society. Symbols potentially represent another language. They can communicate a lot in a relatively simple way. They can be used to *inspire*, as with the example of the swastika and also with the poppy; both of which had powerful associations for people of Europe during the 20th century. Symbols can also *represent* things and also be used to *motivate* people. However, at the same time, we must not ignore the fact that symbols can also be used more simply as decorative devices.

If it is accepted that the Icenian material record does carry a wealth of symbolic meanings, this recognition potentially provides a new way of understanding the people of this time, who have not left us any written records. In this way, it may eventually be possible to understand more about the working of their society.

Structure within Icenian society

It is becoming clear just how far the daily regime of people who lived during the Iron Age was highly structured. Archaeology is continuing to identify their ritual behaviour. Much material deposited on Iron Age settlements can now be considered as 'structured deposition' and resulted not from daily refuse maintenance activities but from periodic rituals.[12] The surviving archaeological record contains relatively few casually discarded or lost items of this period. It must be recognised at this point that there were relatively few of the types of object in circulation that were casually lost in subsequent historical periods, such as the prolific brooches and base metal coins of the Roman period. However, it is the case that much of what has survived from the Iron Age was clearly intentionally deposited in what appear to be formal ways.[13] These conclusions from the national picture can broadly be observed in the archaeological record of Norfolk.[14]

People of the Iron Age had a very different concept of religion from that familiar to people living in Britain today.[15] Everyday life was imbued with actions and activities that made reference to spiritual belief and to the gods. They attached significance to sacred places, which could sometimes be natural places in the landscape or even locations within their homes and settlements.[16] Archaeology continues to reveal how selected objects were carefully placed in pits, holes, ditches and watery places, which had a sacred association.[17] Others could be buried in high places in the landscape, such as on the tops of hills; a practice which continued into the Romano-British period.

We may view these special deposits as votive offerings. Objects selected for such purposes were not always finely made items. They could also be parts of people or animals, or even quantities of carefully selected pottery. Representations of human heads are also encountered in such contexts.

Places of significance in the landscape

It is possible to identify some of the places of special significance in the landscape of Iron Age Norfolk. Some of these were natural, while sometimes special places were constructed. For example, people at this time would dig wells and shafts at selected locations, which penetrated deep into the ground, perhaps to serve as an interface with the underworld.

Ritual locations which have been identified in Norfolk include the enclosures at Fison Way, Thetford.[18] The final phase of this settlement was a focus of specialist activities and a grand ceremonial centre. Between the 40s and mid-60s AD the enclosure was surrounded by parallel rows of close timber fencing, which may have formed an artificial oak grove, representing a place of religious importance for the region.

The location of the hoard site at Snettisham,[19] which is a huge carrstone projection, dominates the surrounding landscape of north-west Norfolk. Ken Hill is located 2km inland, on the northern end of the prominent hilltop.

---

[11] Van Arsdell 1989, 443-1; 2089-1; 2099-1; 2057-1
[12] Hill 1993, 1995; Hingley 1990, 1993
[13] Hill 1995
[14] Davies 2009, pp. 112-114
[15] for example, see Fitzpatrick 1992
[16] Bradley 2000
[17] see, for example, Cunliffe 2013, p. 267
[18] Gregory 1991
[19] Stead 1991

This was the highest point in the whole area and provides views right across the Wash, into Lincolnshire, as well as far inland. It was also visible from many miles inland and from the sea. This was clearly selected as a special place.

The ritual shafts were often constructed adjacent to *oppida* sites right across Europe. Such a shaft was discovered at Ashill in Norfolk.[20] Lined with oak timbers, it had been filled with separate layers of pottery vessels, each of which had been placed within a bedding of twigs and leaves.

Other objects of significance

The 'rear-hook' brooch

In addition to the type of symbols and behaviour recognised above, it may be possible to interpret significance in relation to specific types of object. One form of brooch special to the Iceni is known as the 'rear-hook' type. It was introduced in c.AD 40 and continued in production through to c.AD 60-65. This brooch form, which employs a rear-facing hook to hold the spring chord, is commonly found across Norfolk and also spreads into north Suffolk.[21] The rear-hook thus can be associated with the territory of the Iceni during the critical period of the Client Kingdom.[22] The question may be posed as to whether this form of brooch was a local overt expression of Icenian identity, an emblem of the tribe, or whether this was merely a local way of doing things. However the observation is interpreted, this artefact form conforms very tightly to the tribal area of the Iceni and indicates that there was a strong tribal unity and lack of integration with other tribal peoples at that time.

Animal representations on objects

Animals were venerated and sacrificed in rituals across Iron Age Europe. Bulls, boars and other animals played a prominent part in Celtic iconography. Until recently, there has been little recognition of the representation of animals in Iron Age Norfolk. However, there is now growing evidence for Norfolk's own iconographic menagerie, which also includes the duck, swan, wolf, horse and possibly dragon.[23] Animals were considered to have divine powers and attributes.[24] The association of animal representations to objects may be associated with the conferring of symbolic meaning to them.

Chopped-up and re-worked objects

The Snettisham Treasure comprises a series of intentionally buried deposits from the site at Ken Hill, which were recovered between 1948 and 1990.[25] Thirteen individual hoards have been discovered at the site, with spectacular contents of items which are mainly associated with personal adornment, made from gold, silver, electrum and bronze. To date, the literature describing these magnificent discoveries focuses on the beautiful and complete examples of torcs (neck rings), bracelets and coins. Little mention is ever made of the so-called 'scrap', which comprises the majority of pieces from the site. This large body of incomplete and broken objects used to be considered as pieces left over from the process of metal-working. Coupled with the fact that they were considered less important in aesthetic terms, this component has been largely ignored. Only now is the potential significance of this material being recognised.

Between 2003 and 2009 a campaign of metal-detection was undertaken at Ken Hill and a large body of additional scrap material has added substantially to the collection.[26] This included a wide range of material from the hoard site: fragments of torc, beaded and flat bracelet, wires and other metal fragments. They are accompanied by coins from across the Mediterranean, including Gaul, Carthage and the Greek world.[27]

The religious association of the Snettisham deposits can no longer be doubted. The formal and structured nature of the torc deposits has been recognised.[28] It is in this context that the large quantity of incomplete objects, once termed 'scrap', should be considered. This material was intentionally chopped up into smaller pieces in antiquity. There is evidence to show that some of these pieces were originally re-arranged for structured deposition. For example, there are examples of unusual 'composite' rings known from the site. In these cases, fragments of larger torcs and bracelets have been twisted together prior to deposition. One such 'composite' piece from Hoard B is illustrated in R.R. Clarke's original Snettisham publication, showing an intricate group of conjoined ring-shaped fragments. In that example, seven smaller rings, made from torc and bracelet fragments, are depicted as having been carefully linked around a larger ring.[29] A second, similar, piece was discovered during excavations at the site in 1990, in Hoard F. That example is made from a torc, a bracelet and two torc terminals which had all been intentionally linked around a central ring.[30] Recent research has identified additional composite pieces within the more recently discovered scrap material.[31]

The ritual of breaking objects before deposition is, of course, a well-known practice throughout British prehistory. However, the intentional deposition of re-arranged composite rings made from previously broken pieces poses more of a mystery. Examples of conjoined composite rings are also known from Bronze Age contexts, including regionally local examples from Stretham in

---

[20] Gregory 1977
[21] Martin 1999, pp. 86-87
[22] Davies and Robinson 2009
[23] Davies 2011a
[24] Green 1992
[25] Stead 1991

[26] Davies and Seaman forthcoming
[27] Marsden 2011
[28] Stead 1991
[29] Clarke 1954, plate xii
[30] Stead 1991, plate I
[31] Davies and Seaman forthcoming

Cambridgeshire and Gresham in Norfolk.[32] The examples from Snettisham are another puzzle to be answered. Just what was their significance?

Decorated objects

It is becoming clear that only some Iron Age objects were ever chosen for decoration and the reasons for this have been the subject of ongoing studies. Niall Sharples has drawn attention to the significance of decoration on Iron Age objects in relation to individual expression and identity.[33] Jody Joy has looked at decoration across different media and considered how markings applied to chosen objects could subsequently transform their social function.[34] Bradley has argued that once decorated, they possessed a sacred character and the decorated objects became different from those used in daily life.[35] It has also been recognised that such decorated objects tend not to be found on settlements but rather in graves, rivers and sites with specialist functions such as sanctuaries.[36]

A restricted proportion of Iron Age objects from Norfolk carry integral decoration. Among the 400 non-numismatic Iron Age objects held at Norwich Castle Museum, just 17% are decorated. Just why were these specific items selected for decoration and others not? Among the non-Snettisham objects, just 15% were selected for decoration with enamel. Most of these are horse-related objects, such as terret rings and linch pins. These objects are all very small and in order to be aware of the decoration, a person would need to be very close to them. The implication might be that the importance was more symbolic and not necessary for everybody to see it.

Developing a recognition of the 'code'

We can point to specific forms of object that can be associated with the Icenian tribal area and which would have had a significance to the local population.

Horse associated items

A high proportion of Iron Age artefacts found in Norfolk are horse-related, implying that horses were very important to the Iceni. Around one quarter of the county Iron Age collection at Norwich Castle represents horse-related objects, which is higher than that recorded in other parts of Britain. This appears to have been an important horse breeding area.

Rear-hook brooches

The rear-hook form of brooch has been referred to above. It was made within the area and served to identify those who lived in and came from Icenian territory. It may possibly be viewed as a tribal symbol or badge.

Symbols

The use and predominance of the back-to-back crescent and triplet motifs on objects has already been mentioned above. These appear to have had significance to the Iceni.

Animal depictions used on coins

A restricted range of animals were depicted on the coinage of the Iceni. The boar was known as a symbol of strength in Celtic society and they were used to decorate weaponry and armour. The prominence of the boar on the coinage in this part of Britain may signify that the creature had a particular significance in northern East Anglia. It is depicted both in the coinage of the Iceni and that of their western neighbours, the Corieltauvi. The Icenian issue is commonly known as the *boar-horse* (Fig. 3).[37] The creature is stylised, with a body which widens towards the shoulder and with no neck.

Another creature represented within the iconography of the Iceni is the wolf. It appears on their coinage, on an early uninscribed type known as the *Norfolk wolf* (Fig. 4).[38] Use of the wolf on coinage is unique to the Iceni.

It has been stated that the horse was important to the Iceni but it was not represented in the form of figurines like other creatures, such as the boar. Its image was restricted to coins. Horses were present on all but one of their issues; in which the *Norfolk wolf* was used to replace it.

Representations of the natural world

These people were farmers and lived a rural life. Their iconography unsurprisingly also reflected aspects of the natural world around them. Many images can be recognised as astronomical symbols. Representations of the sun, moon and stars can be seen on the majority of Icenian coin types. The back-to-back crescent itself reflects the crescent moon.

Animals depicted on the coinage include boars, wolves and horses, as cited elsewhere in this paper. However, other creatures are less prominent and obvious. They include birds, such as the lapwing, bittern and avocet.[39]

Elsewhere, enigmatic patterns may in fact also be depictions. The latticed square on the Irstead gold quarter stater appears to depict a sheaf of corn.[40]

---

[32] Davies, forthcoming b
[33] Sharples 2010, pp. 301-2
[34] Joy 2011
[35] Bradley 2012, p. 61
[36] Brunaux *et. al.* 1985; Wells 2007

[37] Van Arsdell 1989, 655-1 to 663-1
[38] British JA and JB; Van Arsdell 1989, types 610-1 to 610-5
[39] Cottam *et. al.* p. 78
[40] Van Arsdell 1989, 628

LANDSCAPES AND ARTEFACTS

FIG. 3 ICENIAN BOAR-HORSE TYPE SILVER UNIT (COPYRIGHT NORFOLK MUSEUMS SERVICE)

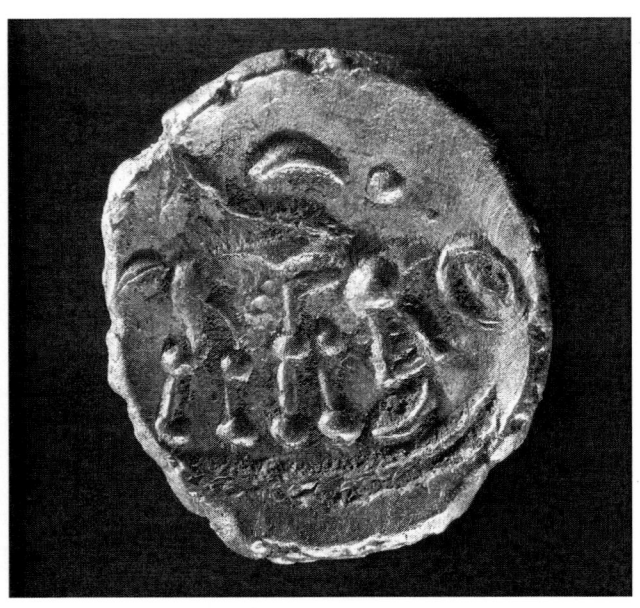

FIG. 4 ICENIAN NORFOLK WOLF TYPE GOLD QUARTER STATER (COPYRIGHT NORFOLK MUSEUMS SERVICE)

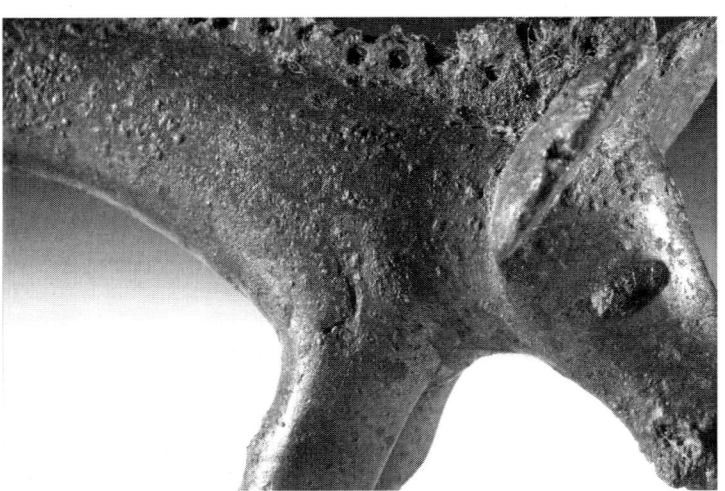

FIG. 5 MARK ON THE RIGHT SHOULDER OF THE BOAR FIGURINE FROM ASHMANHAUGH (COPYRIGHT NORFOLK MUSEUMS SERVICE)

FIG. 6 NOTCH ON THE RIGHT EAR OF THE BOAR FIGURINE FROM ASHMANHAUGH (COPYRIGHT NORFOLK MUSEUMS SERVICE)

FIG. 7 THE ICENIAN BOAR-HORSE SILVER UNIT, WITH A PELLET ON THE RIGHT SHOULDER (COPYRIGHT NORFOLK MUSEUMS SERVICE)

The significance of the boar

In 1997 a beautiful boar figurine was discovered by metal-detection at Ashmanhaugh, 20km north-east of Norwich. It is a three-dimensional representation, made from copper alloy. It is a stylised representation, with a perforated crest running the length of the back. The shape and angle of the feet suggest that this was once attached to a curved surface, which may have been a warrior's helmet. This figurine has previously been more fully described.[41] However, it is relevant to mention two features observed on the figurine here.

The first of two deliberate markings in the casting is located on the right shoulder. This is a symbol in the shape of a 'tick' (Fig. 5). This has no possible function and must have carried a significance that was strong enough to warrant deliberate inclusion on the figurine.

The right ear carries the second unexplained casting feature. There is a clear semi-circular notch which again can have no possible function and must be symbolic (Fig. 6). More intriguingly, this feature is echoed in another boar figurine from beyond Britain. It was discovered in France, at Soulac-sur-Mer, Dep. Gironde, just under 100km north of Bordeaux.[42] That example has a deliberately-placed patch of silver on its ear, which echoes the mark on the Norfolk example.

It has been mentioned above that the boar motif was used on the coinage of the Iceni. A sub-type of this issue[43] depicts a pellet prominently featured on the right shoulder; a feature to which no significance has previously been attributed (Fig. 7). This feature can be seen to refer back to the shoulder mark on the figurine. There is yet more evidence to point to significance in relation to boar shoulders.

At Llanmaes in south Wales, an abundance of pig bones were found in association with an Early Iron Age context.[44] Only the right fore-quarters of the pigs had been incorporated into the site's midden, indicating a specific selection and separation of this portion. Elsewhere, at Hallaton (Leicestershire) excavations at an Iron Age ritual site recovered a large animal bone assemblage. Of these, 97% were pig bones and there was a clear *absence* of right fore-limbs represented.

We are not yet in a position to explain the significance of the right shoulders of boars but the increasing and diverse body of evidence shows that there was such significance and that it was widely recognised at that time. These observations together serve to enrich the growing body of evidence for hidden meaning.

Conclusions

This paper must be viewed very much as the start of a work in progress. A whole range of observations have been outlined, which reflect cultural tradition, collective choices, accepted and agreed forms of decoration and reverence of natural places. Together they show that there was an extensive and structured set of behaviours that would have been familiar to the Iron Age population of Norfolk and beyond. In the absence of written records, archaeology is beginning to show that such meanings were present. So we have an increasing range of clues to the way that they behaved and thought.

Will we ever know the true meaning of these clues? The answer is probably not. It is likely that the people of the Iron Age interpreted images and behaviour very differently from the way we see them today. Wells has referred to a 'visual code' and has considered how recognisable shapes, such as human and animal forms, could be transformed into derivative shapes by different societies.[45] So will it ever be possible for us to determine how they saw and interpreted things? Further consideration is beyond the scope of this short paper and must be pursued elsewhere.

The most important aspect at this stage is to recognise that there is a large body of visual information of potential importance and that this is significant beyond merely the decorative. Although we may not understand the meanings implicit in the decoration and methods of deposition, we are able to recognise the expression of significance and also identity among these people. The way they looked and behaved can be seen to have differed from their neighbours.

In the mean-time, metal-detected objects continue to come through Norfolk's thriving Identification and Recording Service. These new discoveries will continue to provide additional clues which will improve our understanding of this late prehistoric society.

Acknowledgements

I would like to thank Andrew Fitzpatrick and Tim Pestell for supplying useful information. I would also like to thank Adrian Marsden for commenting on an earlier draft of this paper. Finally I must thank Andrew Rogerson for the guidance, support and encouragement he has provided over many years, since my first arrival in Norfolk.

---

[41] Davies 2011a
[42] Moreau, Boudet and Schaaf 1990
[43] Van Arsdell 1989, type 655-1, 657-3, 659-3
[44] *Current Archaeology* 233, p. 32

[45] Wells 2008

Bibliography

Allen, D.F. 1970, 'The coins of the Iceni', *Britannia* I, pp. 1-33

Bradley, R. 2000, *An Archaeology of Natural Places* (Routledge, London)

Bradley, R. 2012, *The Idea of Order: The Circular Archetype in Prehistoric Europe* (Oxford, University Press)

Brunaux, J.-L., Meniel, P. and Poplin, F. 1985, *Gournay 1. Fouilles sue le sanctuaire et l'oppidum*. Revue archeologique de Picardie, numero special

Carocci, M. 2011 *Ritual and Honour, Warriors of the North American Plains* (London, British Museum Press)

Chadburn, A. 2006, *Aspects of the Iron Age coinages of northern East Anglia with especial reference to hoards* (Unpublished PhD thesis, University of Nottingham)

Clarke, R.R. 1954 'The early Iron Age Treasure from Snettisham, Norfolk', *Proceedings of the Prehistoric Society* 20, pp. 27-86.

Cottam, E. de Jersey, P., and Rudd, C. 2010, *Ancient British Coins* (Chris Rudd, Aylsham)

Cunliffe, B. 2013, *Britain Begins* (Oxford, University Press) *Current Archaeology* 233 August 2009, 'The champion's portion? Prehistoric feasting at Llanmaes', pp. 29-35

Davies, J.A. 2009, *The Land of Boudica: Prehistoric and Roman Norfolk* (Heritage/Oxbow, Oxford)

Davies, J.A. (ed.) 2011, *The Iron Age in Northern East Anglia: New Work in the Land of the Iceni* (Oxford, British Archaeological Report 549)

Davies, J.A. 2011a. 'Boars, Bulls and Norfolk's Celtic Menagerie', in J.A. Davies (ed.), pp. 59-68

Davies, J.A. forthcoming a. *Iron Age Artefacts in Norwich Castle Museum*

Davies, J.A. forthcoming b. *A History of Norfolk in 100 Objects* (The History Press)

Davies, J.A. and Seaman, A. forthcoming 'The Snettisham Treasure', in Davies, J.A. forthcoming a

Davies, J.A. and Robinson B. 2009, *Boudica: Her Life, Times and Legacy* (Cromer, Poppyland)

Davies, J.A. and Williamson, T. (eds.) 1999, *Land of the Iceni: The Iron Age in Northern East Anglia* (Centre of East Anglian Studies, Norwich)

Fitzpatrick, A.P. 1992, 'The Snettisham, Norfolk, hoards of Iron Age torques: sacred or profane?' *Antiquity* 66, pp. 395-8

Fitzpatrick, A.P. 1994, 'Outside in: the structure of an Early Iron Age house at Dunston Park, Thatcham, Berkshire', in A. Fitzpatrick and E. Morris (eds.), *The Iron Age in Wessex: Recent Work* (Association Francaise D'Etude de L'Age du Fer/Trust for Wessex Archaeology, Salisbury) pp. 62-67

Green, M. 1992, *Animals in Celtic Life and Myth* (Routledge, London)

Gregory, T. 1977, *The enclosure at Ashill*, in P. Wade-Martins (ed.), East Anglian Archaeology 5, pp. 9-30

Gregory, T. 1991, *Excavations in Thetford, 1980-1982, Fison Way*, East Anglian Archaeology 53

Hill, J.D. 1993, 'Can we recognise a different European past? A contrastive archaeology of later Prehistoric settlements in Southern England', *Journal of European Archaeology* 1, pp. 57-75

Hill, J.D. 1995, *Ritual and Rubbish in the Iron Age of Wessex: A Study in the formation of a specific Archaeological Record*, British Archaeological Report 242

Hingley, R. 1990, 'Domestic organisation and gender relations in Iron Age and Romano-British households', in R. Samson (ed.), *The Social Archaeology of Houses* (University Press, Edinburgh), pp. 125-149

Hingley, R. 1993, 'Society in Scotland from 700 BC to AD 200', *Proceedings of the Society of Antiquaries for Scotland* 122, pp. 7-53

Joy, J. 2011, 'Fancy objects' in the British Iron Age: Why decorate?', *Proceedings of the Prehistoric Society* 77, pp. 205-229

Marsden, A. 2011, 'Iron Age coins from Snettisham', in J.A. Davies (ed.), pp. 49-58

Martin, E. 1999, 'Suffolk in the Iron Age', in Davies and Williamson 1999, pp. 45-99

Moreau, J., Boudet R. and Schaaf, U. 1990, 'Un sanglier-enseigne a Soulac-sur-Mer, Dep. Gironde' *Archaeologisches Korrespondenzblatt* 20, pp. 439-442

Nash Briggs, D. 2012, 'Sacred Image and Regional Identity in Late-Prehistoric Norfolk', in T.A. Heslop, E. Mellings and M. Thofner (eds.) *Art, Faith and Place in East Anglia: From Prehistory to the Present* (Boydell, Woodbridge)

Parker Pearson M. and Richards C. 1994, 'Architecture and order: spatial representation and archaeology', in M. Parker Pearson and C. Richards (eds.), *Architecture and Order: Approaches to Social Space* (Routledge, London, pp. 38-72)

Sharples, N. 2010, *Social Relations in Later Prehistory: Wessex in the First Millennium BC* (OUP, Oxford)

Stead, I.M. 1991, 'The Snettisham treasure: excavations in 1990', *Antiquity* 65, pp. 447-65

Talbot, J. 2011, 'Icenian coin production', in J.A. Davies 2011 (ed.), pp. 69-82

Van Arsdell, R.D. 1989, *Celtic Coinage of Britain* (Spink, London)

Wells, P. 2007, 'Weapons, ritual and commemoration in Late Iron Age Northern Europe', in C. Haselgrove and T. Moore (eds) *The Later Iron Age in Britain and Beyond* (Oxford, Oxbow), pp. 468-77

Wells, P.S. 2008, *Image and Response in Early Europe* (Duckworth, London)

Some Roman brooches from Scole and elsewhere

Jude Plouviez

Abstract: A study of two, relatively unusual, Roman brooches found in Andrew Rogerson's excavation at Scole in 1973 in the light of more recent finds. The chronology and findspots suggest that the 'small towns' in Roman East Anglia played an increasing role in the distribution of locally produced goods during the later first century.

Introduction

The Roman brooch is one of the classes of object that have been recorded in thousands in Norfolk and Suffolk during the last thirty years as a result of working with metal detector users. The various classification systems allow one to study variations in brooch assemblages, differentiating the assemblages chronologically, geographically and perhaps functionally.[1]

In this paper however I am exploring a couple of very specific brooch types that might be produced within a single workshop. Both types were first published in the report by Don Mackreth for Andrew Rogerson's publication of his excavations at Scole in 1973.[2] They are within the broad class of 'Colchester derivatives', which encompasses many of the bow brooches produced in Britain immediately after the Roman conquest in AD 43. Scole brooches 1 and 2 were however noted as unusual by Mackreth because they use 'a variant of the Polden Hill method of securing the spring to the body of the brooch'.

Mackreth's classification of the Colchester derivatives (so-called because their form derives from the pre-Conquest one-piece 'Colchester' brooch) is based on the method of attaching the pin and spring to the main body. He has shown that there is a strong element of regionality in their use, and so by inference in their production; direct evidence for the production of specific copper-alloy objects in early Roman Britain is sparse.

The broad classes of Colchester derivative[3] are (Fig. 1):

1. Harlow spring system (CD Ha). The axis bar and the spring chord pass through pierced holes in a central lug in the back of the wings. Also known as the 'double pierced lug' or 'double lug' and includes Hull's Colchester B and BB types.[4] The core area of use relates to the tribal areas of the Trinovantes and Catuvellauni but the type is common and very widespread.

2. Rear hook spring system (CD RH). The only apparent attachment for the spring is a central hook on the top of

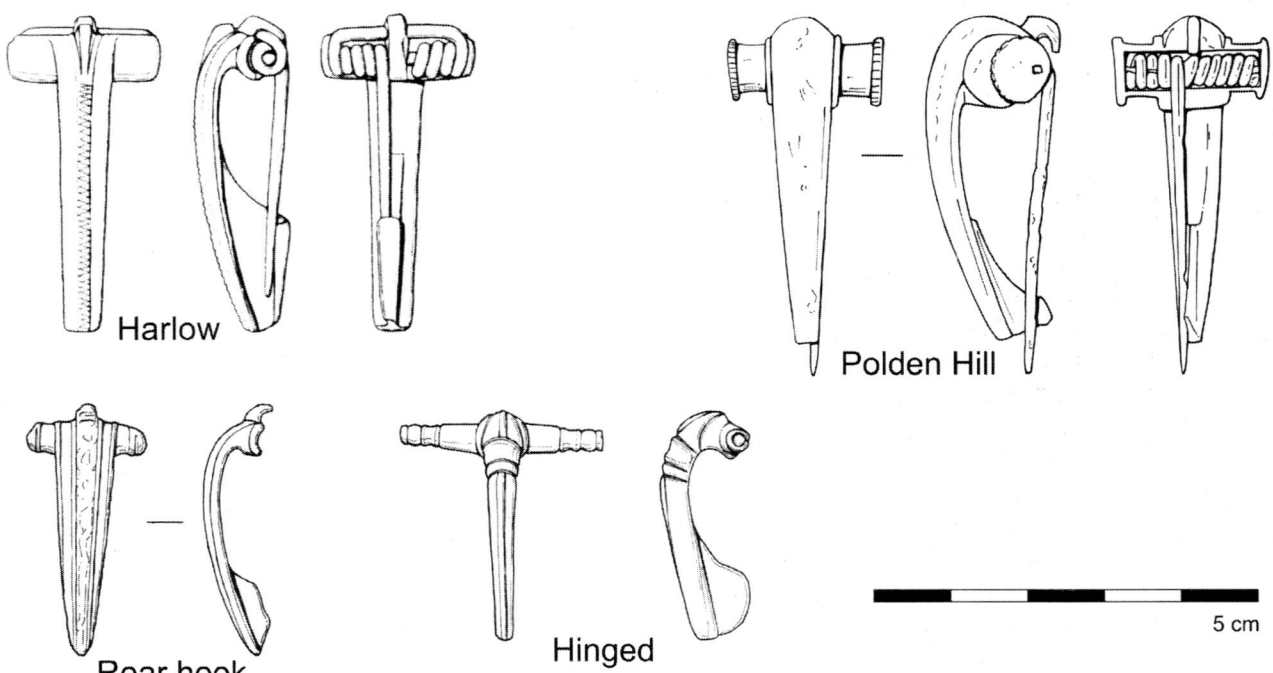

Fig 1 Examples of the different groups of Colchester derivative brooches from Suffolk, scale 1:1

---

[1] for example Plouviez 2008
[2] Mackreth 1977, pp. 129–30, fig. 54, 1–2
[3] Mackreth 2011, chapter 3
[4] Crummy 1983, 12

the wings facing backwards to hold the spring chord. In practice occasional traces of solder indicate that the spring could be stuck to the back of the wings (usually on the left hand wing); even so the majority of the type are found with the spring missing. The type is focussed on the area of the Iceni in Norfolk, Suffolk and Cambridgeshire and the dating tends to suggest that production ceased at the Boudican revolt in AD60/61. The term 'Dolphin' is sometimes used for some of this group.

3. Polden Hill spring system (CD PH). Pierced plates at the ends of the wings hold the axis bar, and the spring chord can be held by either a rear hook or by a pierced lug at the centre top of the wings. The core area for their initial production is the Severn Valley and the main types are commonest in the western half of Britain (including the more typical 'Dolphin' shape).

4. Hinged pin (CD H). This class includes a number of different groups, some clearly related to eastern England and others focussed in the west and south-west.

The 'variant' of the Polden Hill system used on Scole brooches 1 and 2 has extended flaps on the wings folded around the axis bar instead of the pierced flat plate at the end of each wing. Both also have a rear hook to catch the spring chord. In his brooch corpus[5] Mackreth places both within an Eastern Group of Polden Hill brooches, as CD PH 6.a1. (Scole 2) and CD PH 6.a2 (Scole 1). From his knowledge of significant brooch assemblages metal detected in Norfolk in the 1980s and 1990s Mackreth included fourteen further examples of Scole 1 in his 6.a2 group (plus one from the Hattatt corpus[6] and one from Hacheston[7]), stating that they were 'the product of a definite workshop'. Only one other example of Scole 2 was included in group 6.a1, corpus no 12010 from Usk, with the comment that both had lost their sheet metal catchplates and 'should have been made by the same craftsman'. In practice there is another example in the corpus, one from West Stow which Mackreth lists under group 6.b1[8] because the published account does not give full details of the attachment system.[9]

During time spent recording metal detected finds in Suffolk I observed the occurrence of various odd spring attachment systems, and had particularly noted the quirks of the Scole 2 type as being distinctive. The collated data presented here includes examples of both types added to the Suffolk Historic Environment Record (HER) between c 1980 and 1998, Suffolk and Norfolk examples added to the Portable Antiquities Scheme database (PAS) from 1998 to the present, the few published examples and a rapid visual search of all 'Polden Hill' brooches with images on the PAS. Because the Norfolk entries on the PAS are still fewer than Suffolk (1,398 Roman brooches from Norfolk, 2,219 from Suffolk) and the extensive records of metal finds in the Norfolk HER have not been searched, there is a definite imbalance in the results. The search of Polden Hills on the PAS produced three examples from Essex and none from Cambridgeshire; as an extra check all 409 Roman brooches from Cambridgeshire were rapidly examined but no examples of either Scole 1 or Scole 2 were seen.

Characteristics: Scole 1 (Fig. 2)

Fifty-nine examples are identified as probably of this type (some pieces were very fragmentary and corroded). The wings have mouldings (bead and reel) at the terminals, which may occasionally be reduced to vertical lines. The bow has a flat or slightly convex back, flat sides and a rounded front. The junction between wings and bow is quite angular in profile. Along the centre of the bow there is decoration: the typical examples as defined by Mackreth have a sunken ridge which can be beaded with a concave face to each side. However this concave area is not always present and the whole arrangement may also be simplified to four equal grooves along the bow front (particularly noted on examples from Wenhaston, Coddenham (fig. 2, 6–7) and Pettistree in Suffolk). In all cases where it survives the bow tapers to a small foot knob, sometimes upturned, and the catchplate is solid. The smallest example (from Wainford, Norfolk[10]) is exceptional at only 20mm in length whereas the normal range is between 36 and 43mm long. The width across the wings ranges from 20 to 32mm, with most between 28 and 30mm.

Typologically this brooch has quite strong links with the types of hinged Colchester derivative found in East Anglia, such as the example in Fig. 1.

Characteristics: Scole 2 (Fig. 3, 1–5)

Seventy examples of this type have been identified. The wings have a single, occasionally two, three or five, grooves at the ends and often also a diagonal single groove. The bending around the axis bar of the wings sometimes makes them narrower towards the ends. The bow is generally oval in section, may be flattened at the back, and tapers slightly to a blunt point. The commonest form of decoration along the bow is three grooves, defining two central ribs which are often given a wavy outline by using a punch along their edges. An alternative arrangement on the bow is for two grooves to define an extension of the rear hook as a very slight rib with horizontal grooves across it, flattening to a hatched band on the main part of the bow; twenty examples with the two grooves were identified. In all cases where the catchplate survives it is a piece of sheet metal which can be seen to have been made separately and inserted into a slot in the back of the bow; more commonly the slot is visible as a scar where the catchplate has been lost. The length of the bow ranges from 46 to 65mm, most falling within a 49 to 59mm bracket. The width at the wings is between 21 and 36mm plus a single outsize 45mm wide; the majority lie between 26 and 32mm.

---

[5] Mackreth 2011, pp. 78
[6] Hattatt 1989, pp. 71-2, fig. 34, 1513
[7] Plouviez 2004, p. 95, fig. 63, 77
[8] Mackreth 2011, p. 79. pl. 52, 12049
[9] West 1990, p. 71, fig.53, 160, and redrawn below in fig.3, 2

[10] Mackreth 2011, pl. 51, 2107

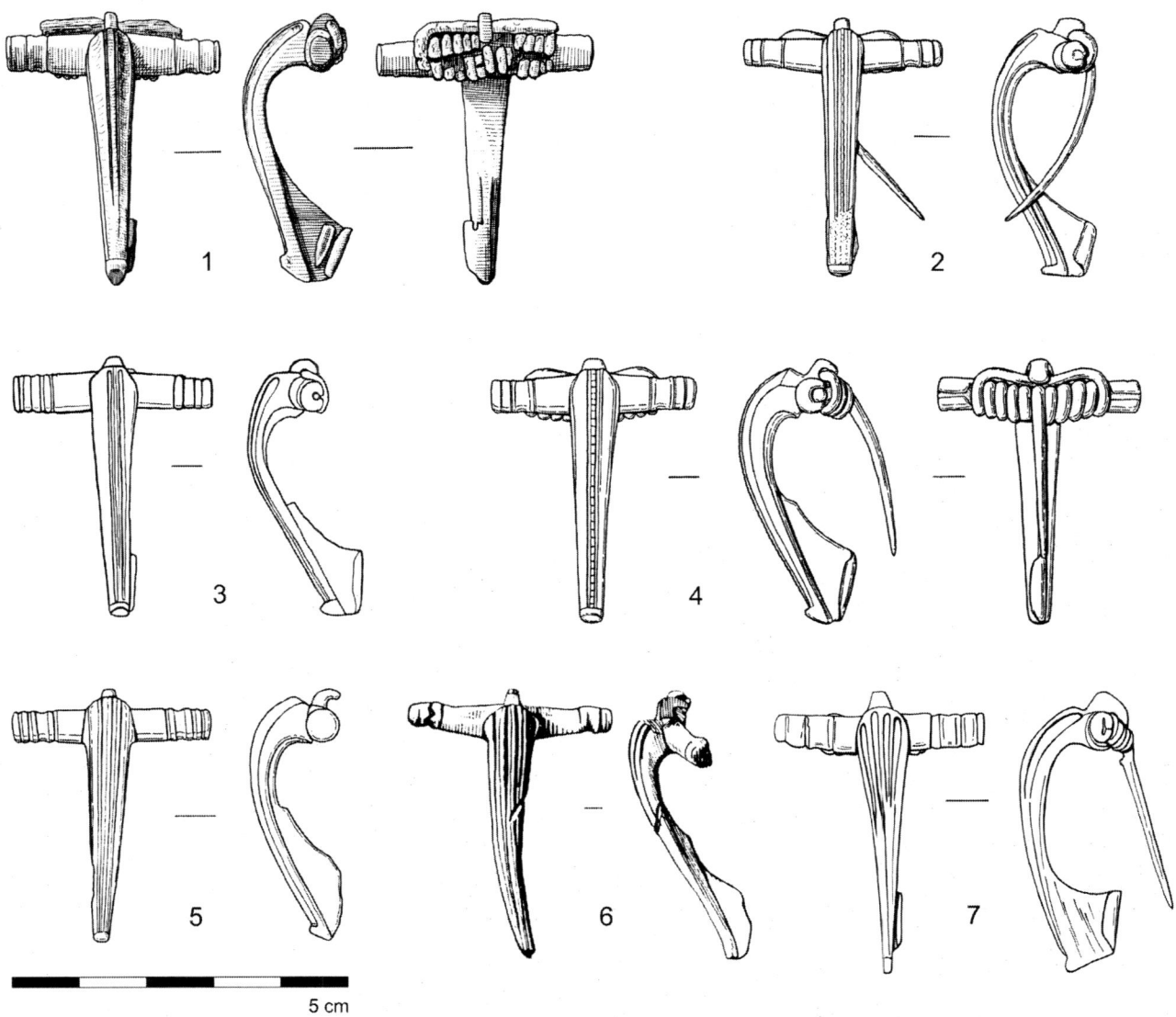

Fig 2 Scole 1 brooches, from Scole, Whitton, Great Walsingham, Hacheston, Wenhaston and Coddenham, scale 1:1

Overall this is not a very complex brooch as the shape is simple and the use of a sheet insert for the catchplate is unusual and perhaps experimental, as is the variant Polden Hill spring attachment system. The decorative elements are also found on rear hook type Colchester derivatives, indeed the notched ribs in a reserved band are first seen on pre-Conquest Colchester types. Occasionally the use of sheet metal catchplates is also identified on rear hook brooches (Fig. 3, 6–7).

Findspots (Fig. 4 and Fig. 5)

There are clear dangers in making distribution maps of single items. Most types of Roman brooch rapidly swamp a map once they cease to reflect patterns of modern collection and recording processes. In this case it seemed worth examining whether these two types, each likely to be products of a single workshop, could answer questions about how goods were being traded in the early Roman period.

The Scole 1 examples are shown mapped in Fig. 4, and were all found in Norfolk and Suffolk. The Suffolk distribution shows a gap in the western half of the county. This is not purely a product of discovery bias, although there probably is still a slightly higher level of finds recorded overall from eastern Suffolk (but not from the north-east of the county) because of the early foundation of the Ipswich detecting club[11]. The pattern is more widespread in Norfolk with a substantial presence in the north-west, strongly suggesting that this is an incomplete sample of the type. Although there are twice as many from Suffolk (39:20) the absence of the Norfolk HER data may be hiding the majority of the type. Both counties show substantial groups from some of the small towns (four from Hacheston and seven from Wenhaston in Suffolk; five each from Ditchingham (including Wainford) and Great Walsingham/Wighton in Norfolk).

---

[11] The Ipswich & District Detecting Club was founded in the 1970s, reporting finds to Suffolk County Council Archaeology from 1978 onwards; it was the only club serving Suffolk up to the 1990s. Many individual detector users based in the west of the county reported their finds directly to SCC at this time

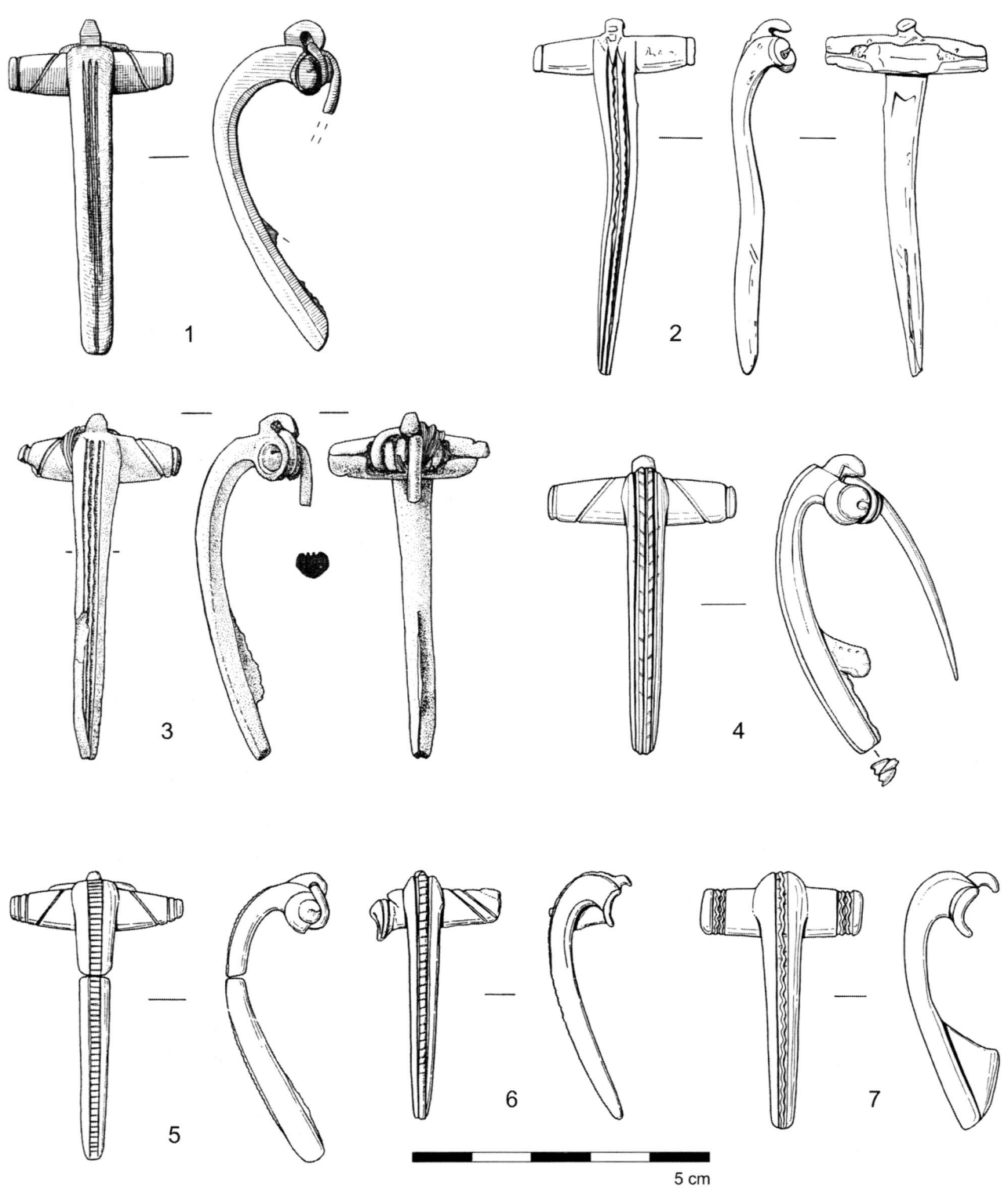

FIG 3 SCOLE 2 BROOCHES FROM SCOLE, WEST STOW, USK, SOMERSHAM, ALDERTON AND (6–7) REAR HOOK BROOCHES FROM FLOWTON AND LAXFIELD IN SUFFOLK, SCALE 1:1

The Scole 2 distribution shown in Fig. 5 is more even across Suffolk but still relatively sparse in the west. It is noteworthy that the assemblage of 153 brooches found in excavations at Pakenham in 1985 did not include either of the Scole types[12]. There are only two examples from Norfolk; although this would undoubtedly be increased by further research, the absence from the groups examined by Mackreth must show a real difference. Within eastern England there are also three examples from Essex, but as discussed above none were seen on the PAS database from Cambridgeshire. A couple of others are very far flung. One is recorded on the PAS database from Arreton on the Isle of

[12] Unpublished archive, PKM 005, held by SCC

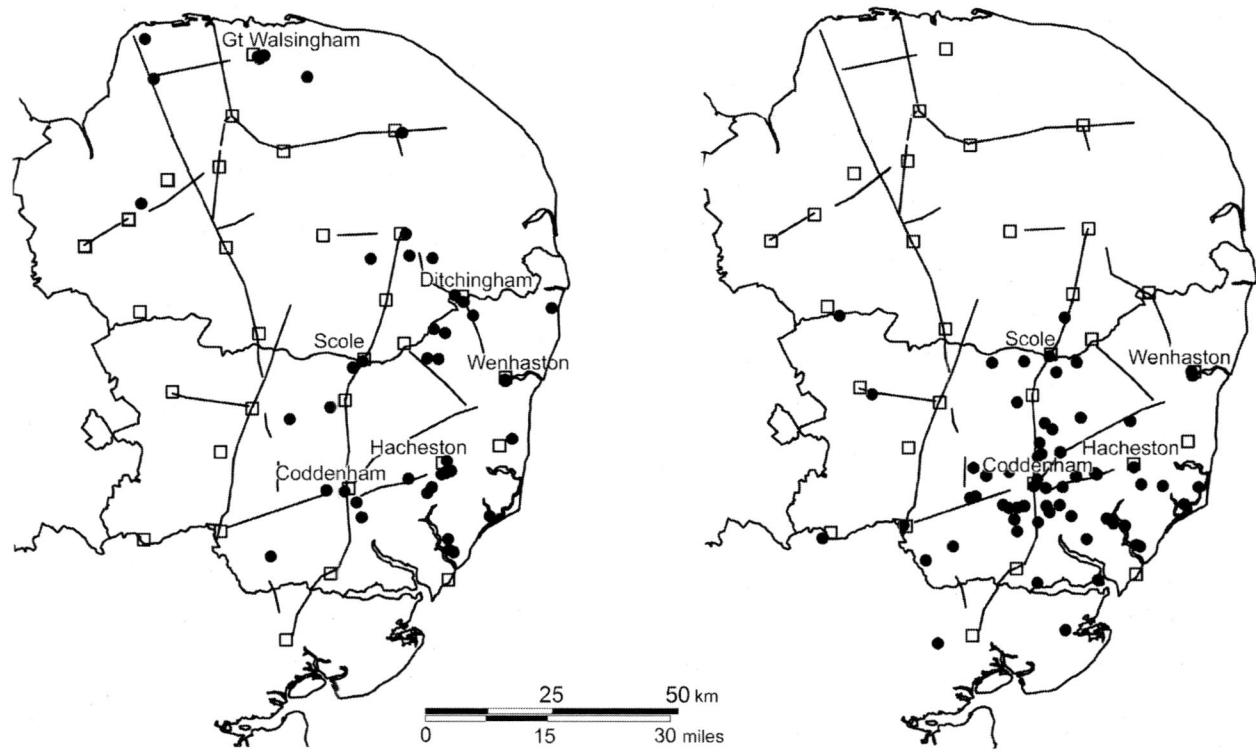

FIG 4 THE DISTRIBUTION OF SCOLE 1 BROOCHES

FIG 5 THE DISTRIBUTION OF SCOLE 2 BROOCHES IN EAST ANGLIA. OPEN SQUARES ARE ROMAN TOWNS, SMALL TOWNS AND SIMILAR LARGE SETTLEMENTS

Wight. Another was found in excavations at the legionary fortress at Usk, South Wales, in 1974.[13]

The Scole 2 is apparently less concentrated at small town sites. The largest group, of four, is from Wenhaston at the north-east extremity of the distribution and only single examples from Coddenham, Hacheston and Scole. A group of three from a site at Otley, between Coddenham and Hacheston, are known only from metal detecting; the finds also include evidence for first to second century cremations. There are pairs from various other rural assemblages. A possible central point of the distribution is Coddenham: thirty-six Scole 2 brooches lie within a 15km radius of this site.

The variation in decoration on the Scole 2 bow (Fig. 3, 4-5) seems to follow exactly the same pattern of distribution: both are present in the Wenhaston group, both are mainly found within the core area around Coddenham, the Isle of Wight find has traces of the horizontal hatching of the smaller group, whereas the Usk example is of the main type.

Chronology

Unfortunately the few examples of each brooch from excavated contexts in East Anglia provide little useful dating evidence. The two brooches from the Scole excavations were found in Period II contexts of the second century. Both are likely to have been in use during Scole period I, c.70–100. The Scole 2 brooch from West Stow was found in an Anglo-Saxon sunken-featured building; the site was in probably continuous use from the late Iron Age into the second century. All four of the Hacheston brooches were unstratified; the settlement almost certainly began in the late Iron Age.

The Scole 2 from Usk (Fig. 3, 3) is in the upper, levelling, fill of a well in a compound outside a *fabrica* in the north-west part of the legionary fortress;[14] the associated pottery is all contemporary with the use of the fortress (c.55-75) and the report suggests that the upper fills may relate to the closing down of the fortress and incorporate a considerable amount of residual material. The brooch had been repaired: the axis bar is missing and a piece of fine wire had been wrapped around the spring and wing for security, so it was far from new by the time it was lost or discarded.

In 1977 Mackreth treated both the Scole brooches on typological grounds as possibly dating to around AD50, noting that Scole 2 had particular similarities in the use of the double wavy line down the bow to the earliest Colchester derivative types in the immediate post-Conquest period. By the time of the Mackreth corpus in 2011 neither type had any context information other than the original Scole data. The Scole 2 example remains his

---

[13] Webster 1995, p. 72, fig. 23, 25

[14] Manning 1989, p. 58

earliest type (6.a1) in the Eastern group of transitional Polden Hill style Colchester derivatives.

The close typological relationship of the Scole 2 to some rear hook Colchester derivatives has been mentioned. Five Suffolk examples of rear hook types are noted as having the same catchplate construction of sheet inserted into a slot. Of these, four also compare well with the decorative elements of the Scole 2, having either a notched centre band (Fig. 3, 7 from Laxfield) or a defined centre band with horizontal grooves (Fig. 3, 6 from Flowton). Dating for the production of rear hook Colchester derivatives falls within the period AD43 to 60.

The Scole 1 is less closely linked to the rear hook group and has proportions similar to many hinged Colchester types. The hinged Colchesters also sometimes have the small foot knob and other more common decorative elements such as mouldings at the wing terminals.[15] If the Scole 1 immediately precedes or is contemporary with the hinged Colchesters it is likely to have been manufactured slightly later in the first century than the Scole 2.

Discussion

Evidence for the manufacture of brooches in early Roman Britain is very sparse, but tends to support the idea that they were the product of itinerant craftsmen rather than permanent workshops.[16] It seems virtually impossible to identify the product of an individual as against a group of people working together, so the term workshop seems more appropriate for groups of brooches with very specific shared characteristics.

Although largely based on typology it seems that the Scole 2 brooch is the earlier, and that the two styles of bow decoration on it are contemporary. The combination of a standard appearance, an uncommon version of the spring attachment and an odd method of attaching the catchplate must be the products of a single workshop. It seems likely that the four rear hook brooches of similar appearance with the same catchplate system can be attributed to the same workshop. The experimental appearance of the brooches and the distribution suggests small scale production and marketing within south and east Suffolk, on the southern edge of the Icenian area where the rear hook type of Colchester derivative is dominant. There is little sign that the small towns played a significant role in distribution. The two that travelled widely, to Arreton and particularly the one to Usk, might instead suggest occasional sales to customers in the army at one of the forts at Coddenham which were probably in use in the mid 40s and in the early 60s.

The Scole 1 brooch is less typologically isolated; there are other brooches with the same body shape and spring system but different bow treatment and there is the general similarity to hinged Colchester derivative types from eastern England. The distribution illustrated in Fig. 4 is clearly incomplete in the key Norfolk area as discussed above. It does seem to show a change to a pattern of distribution via the small towns during the later first century, with those in the west of Suffolk (Pakenham, Icklingham, Wixoe and Long Melford) apparently outside the supply area of this workshop.

Acknowledgements

This piece is for Andrew Rogerson as a long-time friend and a colleague who is always very helpful and entertaining.

The drawings of the Suffolk brooches were done for the county HER by Donna Wreathall, Rebecca Archer and Glenys Wade. The Walsingham brooch is taken from a drawing by Don Mackreth in the Norfolk HER and the two original Scole brooches from Mackreth in Rogerson 1977. My thanks to Bill Manning and Janet Webster for permission to reproduce the brooch from Manning 1995, which was drawn by the late Sabina Thompson.

---

[15] See for example from Scole Mackreth 1977, p. 130, no. 5 and from Hacheston Plouviez 2004, pp. 96–8, nos. 115–35
[16] Mackreth 2011, p. 242

Bibliography

Blagg, T., Plouviez, J., and Tester, A. 2004, *Excavations at a large Romano-Britiish settlement at Hacheston, Suffolk in 1973–4,* East Anglian Archaeology 106 (Suffolk)

Clark, J., Cotton, J., Hall, J., Sherris, R., and Swain, H. 2008, *Londinium and Beyond, Essays on Roman London and its hinterland for Harvey Sheldon,* CBA Res Rep 156, (York)

Crummy, N. 1983, *The Roman small finds from excavations in Colchester, 1971–9,* Colchester Archaeological Report 6, (Colchester)

Hattatt, R. 1989, *Ancient Brooches and other Artefacts,* (Oxbow, Oxford)

Mackreth, D. 1977, 'Brooches' in Rogerson, A, pp. 129–34

Mackreth, D. 2011, *Brooches in Late Iron Age and Roman Britain,* (Oxbow, Oxford and Oakville)

Manning, W.H., with Scott, I.R. 1989, *Report on the excavations at Usk 1965-1976. The fortress excavations 1972-1974 and minor excavations on the fortress and Flavian fort,* (University of Wales Press, Cardiff)

Manning, W.H., Price, J., and Webster, J. 1995, *Report on the excavations at Usk 1965–1976. The Roman small finds,* (University of Wales Press, Cardiff)

Plouviez, J. 2008, 'Counting brooches', in Clark, J., *et al*, pp. 171–6

Plouviez, J. 2004, 'The brooch catalogue' in Blagg, T., Plouviez, J., and Tester, A. pp. 89–108

Rogerson, A. 1977, *Excavations at Scole 1973*, in P. Wade-Martins (ed.), East Anglian Archaeology 5, pp. 97–224

Webster, J. 1995, 'Jewellery and Trinkets' in Manning, W., Price, J., and Webster, J.

West, S. 1990, *West Stow, The Prehistoric and Romano-British Occupations,* East Anglian Archaeology 48, (Suffolk)

Appendix

References in the tables are to PAS numbers (NMS-, SF- etc), Suffolk HER (BRH 016 etc) with additional numbering in parentheses following, and to published sources with object number (Mackreth 2011 12009 etc).

TABLE 1 SCOLE 1 BROOCHES

Parish	Reference
Norfolk	
Briningham	NMS-F561B7
Broke	Hattatt 1989 1513
Buxton with Lammas	NMS-2D7056
Caister st Edmunds	Mackreth 2011 12009
Ditchingham	Mackreth 2011 2110
Ditchingham	Mackreth 2011 2111
Ditchingham	Mackreth 2011 2108
Ditchingham (Wainford)	Mackreth 2011 2112
Ditchingham (Wainford)	Mackreth 2011 2107
Fring	Mackreth 2011 13555
Fring	Mackreth 2011 9841
Marham	NMS-23A982
Scole	Mackreth 1977 1, above Fig 2, 1
Shotesham	Mackreth 2011 11513
Thornham	NMS-7E6572
Walsingham/Wighton	Mackreth 2011 11505
Walsingham/Wighton	Mackreth 2011 11506, above Fig 2, 3
Walsingham/Wighton	Mackreth 2011 11507
Wighton	NMS-6A9DE2
Wighton	Mackreth 2011 13477
Wreningham	Mackreth 2011 13638
Suffolk	
Alderton	SF-6B2DF4
Alderton	SF135
Alderton	SF-1E79B2
Barham	BRH 016 (437)
Barking	SF-233643
Boxford	LVPL-D8FB04
Carlton Colville	SF8128
Charsfield	SF8725
Charsfield	SF8726
Coddenham	CDD 003 (IM954.66.8), above Fig 2, 7
Fressingfield	NMS-C32FE5
Gedgrave	SF-D99713
Great Ashifield	SF-ADA473
Hacheston	SF1780
Hacheston	Plouviez 2004 77, above Fig 2,4
Hacheston	Plouviez 2004 78
Hacheston	Plouviez 2004 79
Homersfield	SF-F65E56
Leiston	SF-191715
Marlesford	SF-4E3C04

Metfield	SF-031D82
Parham	SF-E4A2D6
Pettistree	PTR 009
Ramsholt	SF-8363B7
Shottisham	SF123
St John Ilketshall	SF6910
St Margaret South Elmham	SF10203
Stuston	SF3836
Ufford	SF1325
Wenhaston	WMH 005 (Steadman 47)
Wenhaston	WMH 005 (Allen 9), above Fig 2, 5
Wenhaston	WMH 005 (Catchpole 9), above Fig 2, 6
Wenhaston	WMH 005 (Catchpole 12)
Wenhaston	SF1100
Wenhaston	SF-6F53E0
Whitton	WHI 007, above Fig 2, 2
Wickham Market	SF-E5F801
Wickham Skeith	SF-D79386

TABLE 2 SCOLE 2 BROOCHES

Parish	Reference
Essex	
Beaumont	SF-B7ED53
Birch	ESS-C07014
Steeple Bumpstead	SF-5DCF12
Isle of Wight	
Arreton	IOW-DF5BF2
Norfolk	
Tivetshall St. Mary	SF1980
Scole	Mackreth 1977 2, above Fig 3, 1
Suffolk	
Akenham	SF-8E6C20
Alderton	ADT 038 (48+66), above Fig 3,5
Badingham	SF-0A6785
Badley	SF-649302
Bramford	BRF 037
Brandon	BRD 010
Brantham	SF-219780
Buxhall	SF-6B8A54
Charsfield	SF10587
Charsfield	CHA 011
Claydon	CLY 023
Coddenham	SF-D84F87
Coddenham	CDD 022
Debenham	DBN 014
Edwardstone	EDN Misc
Flowton	SF9247
Hacheston	Plouviez 2004 80
Hemingstone	SF9544
Henley	SF4738
Hinderclay	SF-2DFDF8
Hintlesham	SF-1528C8
Hitcham	HTC
Hoxne	SF-2F3C05

Little Cornard	SF-30A235
Little Finborough	FNL 003
Long Melford	LMD 074
Martlesham	SF6707
Martlesham	MRM 033
Mickfield	SF8272
Monk Soham	SF-4C0125
Nettlestead	SF-482322
Nettlestead	SF-855356
Nettlestead	SF5325
Offton	OFF 006
Orford	SF-2572A1
Otley	SF-3C5417
Otley	SF1218
Otley	SF-E05397
Pettaugh	SF879
Pettaugh	SF-0F9766
Purdis Farm	SF-A6EF17
Ramsholt	RMS 011
Shotley	SF-45D5B4
Somersham	SSH 003, above Fig 3, 4
Stonham Aspal	SF-9EF692
Stonham Aspal	SF1989
Sudbourne	SF-9325B6
Sutton	SF-6F9F07
Syleham	SF-5C85E2
Tuddenham St. Martin	SF-4D6492
Wantisden	SF-74E885
Wattisham	SF-F598A4
Wenhaston	WMH 005 (Barker)
Wenhaston	JP7381
Wenhaston	SF-6F0F71
Wenhaston	SF-D41A62
West Stow	West 1990 160, above Fig 3, 2
Wetheringsett	WCB 048
Wetheringsett	WCB 048
Whitton	WHI 005
Wickham Skeith	SF-61EE72
Wortham	SF-F56536
Wales	
Usk	Webster 1995 25 & Mackreth 2011 12010, above Fig 3, 3

Satyrs, leopards, riders and ravens

Anthropomorphic and Zoomorphic objects from Roman Norfolk: A safari through the county's religious landscape

Adrian Marsden

Abstract: Andrew Rogerson's most recent incarnation has been as head of Norfolk Historic Environment Service's Identification and Recording Service. It has been this writer's pleasure to work alongside Andrew and the co-editor of this volume, Steven Ashley, for a number of years. Our team records several thousand items of metalwork every year; of these, a significant number are of Roman date and, among these, a very few are in some way anthropomorphic or zoomorphic. Most of these are representations of animals but a small number depict deities. Over the years the corpus of these items has become large enough to consider what they might tell us about religious belief in Roman Norfolk.

There are a number of difficulties in a survey of this sort. Considering Norfolk in relative isolation is awkward since the Icenian domains covered a considerably larger area. For example, Rogers in an unpublished MA thesis drew attention to the large amount of Roman religious material from the Fens and, in particular, from the Fen-edge.[1] Much of this corpus was found outside Norfolk but the group is best considered as a whole. Likewise, many objects that relate to beliefs in Roman East Anglia and connect to similar finds in Norfolk have been unearthed south of the county in Suffolk. Troublesome in terms of Norfolk itself is the uneven nature of metal detector survey in the county, some areas being well-searched and others, for various reasons, not being searched at all.

Another problem lies in the difficulty of searching for old finds in the records. Descriptions of many further items probably lurk in the paper files of Norfolk's Historic Environment Record (henceforth HER) but tracking them down would require going through many hundreds of thousands of finds records. There is also the question of different standards of recording. The vast majority of items mentioned here are recorded on the HER and this number, referring to a specific location, is given in brackets in the text. However, some objects discovered before the late 1990s are very basically described and the only images easily accessible are polaroids, often of rather indifferent quality. Many of them are mentioned very briefly in the roundup of recent finds listed in the county journal *Norfolk Archaeology* and, for the sake of completeness, these references are given. Others are recorded to a far higher standard and some are also available online on the Portable Antiquities Scheme (henceforth PAS) database. Where this is the case the PAS reference, usually headed by the prefix NMS, is given after the HER number. A number of items have been acquired by Norwich Castle Museum; in these cases the accession number, beginning NWHCM, is also given.

All in all, however, there is enough material to make an investigation of what has been recovered well worthwhile although it is beyond the scope of this offering to consider finds from further afield than Norfolk in any depth. Nor it is possible to include other items which most probably belong to the realm of religion such as seal boxes. Bagnall Smith makes a compelling argument for these having been part of the process of making a vow to a deity, the act of *nuncupatio*, but there is not space to include them here.[2] They are explored fully in a recent study by Andrews.[3] Small votive tools and weapons comprise another category which is not considered here. Those from Norfolk have been published briefly elsewhere[4] and the group as a whole has been discussed by Kiernan.[5]

Various pieces of research in recent years have increased considerably our knowledge of religious belief in the Eastern counties of Britain. We now know, based on the concentration of the so-called TOT rings in the area of the Corieltauvi, modern-day Lincolnshire, that the god Toutatis was particularly revered in that tribe's territory.[6] The assimilation of the god Faunus with the tribal god of the Iceni has also been explored.[7] Metal detecting near Baldock in Hertfordshire has uncovered votive plaques and a statuette naming Senua, a hitherto unknown deity.[8] She was almost certainly the goddess of a sacred spring that issued up at the site.

The case of Senua is particularly instructive when one considers the lack of surviving monumental inscriptions from Norfolk. This is hardly surprising given the lack of native stone suitable for engraving in the county. Presumably wood and other perishable materials were used that do not survive to embellish the archaeological record. Thus, the epigraphic evidence that survives at other sites in Roman Britain is non-existent in Norfolk. We have none of the names of the more well-known gods and goddesses recorded on stone and we also lack the names of any minor deities that may have been worshipped. Gods and goddesses whose area of influence was local, confined to a spring, stream or grove fall into this category.

---

[1] Rogers 2004 (unpublished)
[2] Bagnall Smith 1999, pp. 48-51
[3] Andrews 2012
[4] Marsden 2012a, pp. 62-3
[5] Kiernan 2009
[6] Daubney 2010
[7] Nash Briggs 2012 and Marsden 2012a, pp. 54-5
[8] Jackson 2002

Other local deities may have had their origins in the deeds of local heroes or the semi-mythical founders of settlements that later came to be tribal centres. We have the writer Pausanius as a source for similar figures in the eastern provinces of the empire but, for the provinces of Britain, non-literate before the Roman conquest, and other parts of the west, we have no such sources. It has been postulated that the stories of the martyrdom of St. Alban at Verulamium have their origin in an older, pre-Roman head cult at the place.[9] One would speculate that important centres in Norfolk had their own tales about how they came into being and what semi-mythical events occurred there.

Sadly, the opportunity to travel through East Anglia in the Roman period and listen to the tales centring on these long-lost heroes and local deities is no longer a possibility. Some of the characters mentioned might be known to us but some would probably be individuals of whom we know nothing.

The lack of any epigraphic evidence that might offer the odd insight renders us truly blind on the subject of Icenian myths and the gods and goddesses who featured therein. Mosaics, on occasion another source of evidence for religious belief, are also rather lacking in Norfolk. Indeed, only one sizeable fragment of a mosaic is known from Norfolk, from the Roman villa at Gayton Thorpe and this carries only geometric patterns.[10] There is nothing significant in the category of wall paintings.[11] In any case, these media do not generally deal with local gods, especially mosaics and wall paintings which tend to reference more well-known and widespread Roman subject matter.

Thus, we are left with a range of items, most of which fall into the category of metalwork. These include only six inscriptions with a religious content and all have been published at some length elsewhere. Five are *defixiones* (curse tablets) in lead, a small fragment from Hockwold (HER 5587) that can offer nothing of use, another from the same site with a few words petitioning a deity's help in retrieving a stolen towel or napkin,[12] and another where Caelianus petitions a deity for help regarding a theft.[13] An example from Weeting with Broomhill is in a similar vein[14] whilst a complete example from Caistor St Edmund (HER 9819, NWHCM 2005.600) asks Neptune for his aid in catching a thief.[15] The other, a *lamella* (a prayer inscribed on a sheet of gold), was found in Billingford (NWHCM 2005.297).[16] It is an interesting item where the appellant, one Tiberius Claudius Similis, asks the god Abrasax for 'Health and Victory'. It was brought into the finder's garden in topsoil, however, and the lack of any firm provenance renders it of limited importance.

All of these objects, moreover, are very standardised, following set formula after a very Roman tradition. In order to look at what was being done differently in Norfolk, if anything was being done differently, it is necessary to consider other material, the items, mainly metalwork, with which this paper is concerned.

Major hoards and site assemblages of religious material

To sketch the background, it is probably most logical to begin with a survey of the major finds of metalwork, both hoards and significant site assemblages, that have been recorded over the years. Some of these have already been published and some are very old finds indeed but it is still useful to mention them in summary here before considering the other material.

The oldest notable find, a hoard of religious objects from Felmingham, offers a good starting point (HER 7533, Fig. 1, no. 1). This group was discovered in 1844 and is now in the British Museum.[17] The hoard was concealed in a pottery vessel imitating in form a bronze cauldron, complete with looped handles. A coin of Valerian II or Saloninus, struck in the mid-250s, suggests a date of burial in the later part of the third century. One is tempted to speculate that the burial of the hoard was connected with raiding on the north Norfolk coast in the years immediately before the British emperor Carausius came to power (AD286-93), the contents of a group of shrines being hastily gathered together and concealed for safety.

The hoard is a rich one and includes bronze heads of Jupiter and Minerva, a mount depicting a male bust with a crescent on his forehead and solar rays erupting from his brows, best interpreted as the head of a god of the heavens (Fig. 1, no. 2), the figurine of a Lar, two statuettes of corvids originally mounted on iron wands, a votive wheel[18], a sceptre handle, a priest's rattle[19] and various other ceremonial items of metalwork. As an introduction to religious assemblages it is particularly instructive since it demonstrates the wide-ranging nature of some Roman religious deposits, containing objects in the image of a number of deities. Clearly, many so-called Roman temple sites comprised a number of shrines, each devoted to the worship of a particular god or goddess.

Felmingham is a very old find. More recently, metal detecting has been responsible for the recovery of enormous amounts of material and some of the resulting assemblages are of great importance. A very productive site, undoubtedly representing a religious centre, is that at Great Walsingham (HER 2024). The objects are numerous (Fig. 2, no. 3) and depict a range of deities. These have been

---

[9] Niblett 2001, 111
[10] Neal and Cosh 2002, pp. 215-6, mosaic 71.2, fig. 185
[11] Ling 2007
[12] Hassall in Gurney 1986, p. 87
[13] Tomlin 2008, pp. 380-1
[14] Hassell and Tomlin 1994, pp. 296-7
[15] Hassell and Tomlin 1982, pp. 408-9
[16] Tomlin 2004, Marsden 2012a, pp. 52-3

[17] Gilbert 1980. British Museum Accession no. 1925, 0160
[18] See Kiernan 2009, 33-9, which places these wheels in the context of the worship of Jupiter assimilated with a Celtic 'Wheel God'
[19] Boon 1983

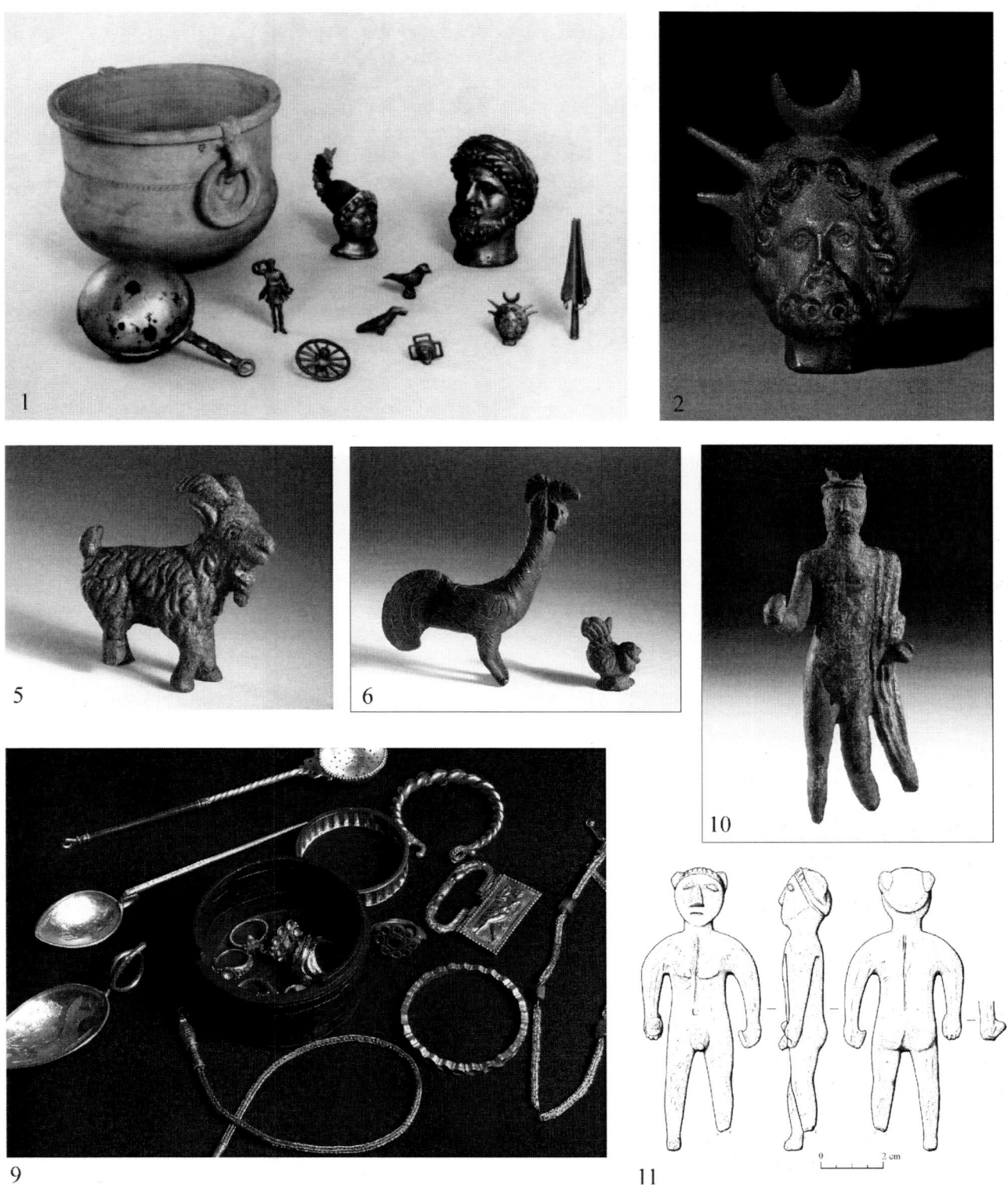

Fig. 1, 1 Felmingham hoard, 2 Head of a deity (Trustees of the British Museum), 5 Goat, Great Walsingham. 6 Cockerels, Great Walsingham (Norfolk Museums Service), 9 Items from the Thetford Treasure (Trustees of the British Museum), 10 Mercury, Wicklewood (NMS), 11 Mercury, Gimingham (Norfolk Historic Environment Service)

comprehensively published and include three Mercury statuettes (NWHCM 1985.379.1, Fig. 2, no. 4) and a Minerva figurine from the nearby site at Wighton (HER 1113).[20] There are many other objects, three-dimensional appliqué busts of Minerva and Jupiter, a number of masks of satyrs and possible cupids, two figurines of goats (Fig. 1, no. 5) and three of cockerels (Fig. 1, no. 6), and many rings with a range of gods and goddesses decorating the bezels, either as intaglio gem settings or in relief. The wide range of the objects which reference different gods and goddesses point to a number of shrines being present at this large so-called Roman temple site. The coins recorded number upwards of 10,000 and many more have probably been illegally recovered by so-called 'night hawks'.

One of the items from this assemblage deserves additional mention because it should probably be discounted as being of Roman date. Described in Jean Bagnall Smith's catalogue as the bust of a three-horned deity, it is true that the piece's lentoid eyes and the apparent torc it wears give it the initial appearance of a Romano-British object.[21] However, in general form it resembles very closely a series of laver mounts in the shape of human heads which date to the fifteenth century. The flat back and circular hollow in the rear of the head, together with the shoulders being represented by two pointed projections, are standard features of these mounts and it is probably wisest to assign this odd object to the medieval period. The curious spherical knops on the end of the horns are rather unusual and would seem to indicate that a jester is intended.

Another large assemblage from Hockwold-cum-Wilton (HER 5587 and others) also clearly defines a temple site. Again, the objects are wide-ranging, including statuettes, vessel mounts, brooches, rings and many other items. It is to be hoped that these will be fully published at a future date. A hoard of late Roman pewter and glass vessels was also discovered at the site. Perhaps the most striking object is a fine figurine of Mercury (Fig. 2, no. 7).[22] The flat back is an unusual feature but finds a parallel of sorts with another depiction of Mercury from Caistor St Edmund (NWHCM 1976.303.1, Fig. 2, no. 8), more accurately described as a mount than a figurine. As at Walsingham, the coin list is extensive.

The Thetford Treasure, discovered in 1979, represents one of the most important assemblages of cult objects from Roman Britain (Fig. 1, no. 9).[23] The contents comprise inscribed silver spoons, items of gold jewellery, including necklaces, bracelets, rings and pendants, and a magnificent golden belt buckle and buckle plate decorated with the figure of a prancing satyr. In particular, the spoons provide important epigraphic evidence for the worship in the area of the god Faunus, perhaps best described as a Roman version of the Greek god Pan. Some are inscribed with personal names, those of the god's worshippers, and others with the various titles applied to Faunus.

It is surely correct to interpret these spoons in the context of a *collegium*, what should probably in modern terms be referred to as a coven, of worshippers. The personal names, Agrestius, Auspicius, Ingenuus, Persevera, Primigenia, Restitutus, Silviola and Vir Bonus, would appear to be the cult names used by the members of this group; certainly they do not seem to be normal, everyday names.[24] Many have rather overt connotations when taken in the context of the worship of Faunus and all may be said to reference aspects that fall within the areas of the god's specific concern.

The various titles applied to Faunus himself on a number of the spoons must also have been of significance. Sadly, the meaning of many of these is now, to say the least, somewhat obscure. The original translations of some style him 'Mighty', 'Mead-begotten', 'Bringer of Blossom', 'Protector' and, most aptly, 'Prick-eared'.[25] Some of the more recent, interpretations are equally interesting.[26]

Other objects from the hoard demonstrate an acquaintance on the part of the Thetford *collegium* with the ancient myths relating to Faunus. For example, a gold ring with shoulders in the form of woodpeckers upholding a bezel set with a piece of glass recalls the fact that Picus, the Woodpecker, was the father of Faunus.[27] Another must surely show the goat-like head of Faunus himself.[28]

The obvious fact that becomes apparent from the Thetford Treasure is that the *collegium* concerned was a group at the top of society. The men and women who worshipped Faunus near Thetford in the late Roman period were members of an elite who could afford items of gold and silver for use in their ceremonies. It is worth considering the possible context in which these precious objects were concealed.

The hoard was deposited in the very last years of Roman authority in Britain. Its burial was almost certainly connected with the two Edicts *De Templis* of Theodosius enacted in 391 and 392, the first of these prohibiting public worship of the old gods, the second their private worship[29]. In this milieu sacred objects such as the spoons, intimately connected with the worship of Faunus and inscribed with his name and epithets and the names of his worshippers, would have implicated their owners most dreadfully. The possibility does remain, however, that the Thetford Treasure was a votive deposit although this author believes its deposition is more convincingly placed within the context of Theodosius' anti-Pagan legislation.

---

[20] Hassall and Tomlin 1994, p. 306 and Bagnall Smith 1999
[21] Bagnall Smith 1999, pp. 26-8
[22] Gurney 2006, p. 117
[23] Johns and Potter 1983
[24] Hassall and Tomlin 1981, pp. 389-93 and Henig 1984, pp. 222-3
[25] Johns and Potter 1983, pp. 84-5
[26] Nash-Briggs forthcoming
[27] Johns and Potter 1983, p. 84, no. 7
[28] Johns and Potter 1983, p. 95, no. 23
[29] Salway 1993, p. 287. The rumour that coins of Magnus Maximus were found with the hoard would, if true, provide further evidence (if any were needed) of this late date; see Johns and Potter 1983, p. 15

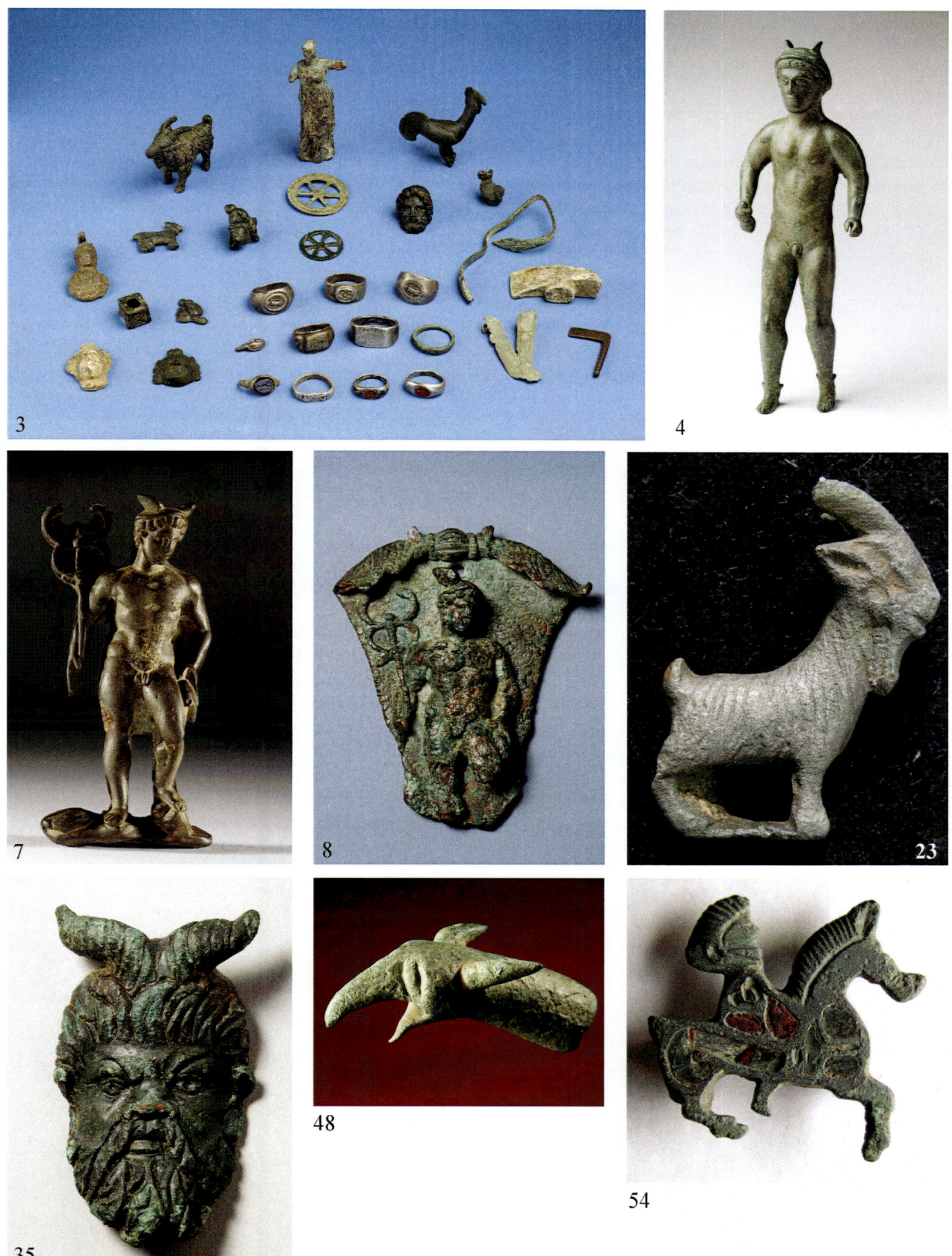

Fig. 2, 3 Religious material from Great Walsingham, 4 Mercury, Great Walsingham, 7 Flat-backed Mercury, Hockwold, 8 Mercury mount, Caistor St Edmund (All NMS), 23 Goat, South Walsham (NHES), 35 Faunus head, Elsing, 48 Griffin head staff terminal, Wickmere (both NMS), 54 Horse and rider brooch, Beeston-with-Bittering (NHES)

It is wise at this point to consider what sort of god was Faunus, to reflect on his main attributes and concerns and why he may have been worshipped in Roman Norfolk. His origins go back to the first days of Rome, to the era of her foundation, and thus he was connected with the festival of the Lupercalia, held in honour of the she-wolf who suckled Romulus and Remus. Befitting this, Faunus was first and foremost a rural god whose main concerns were the protection of fields and flocks. However, he also had the power of prophecy and might vouchsafe oracles to mankind.[30]

The god came to be represented in a plural form by the *Fauni*; just as Faunus is identified with Pan so these creatures are to all extents and purposes satyrs. Hence there was a close connection between Faunus and Bacchus in whose train the satyrs were found.[31] It would not be unreasonable to suggest that, at least in the minds of the men and women who used the Thetford Treasure to celebrate their mysteries, the cults of Faunus and Bacchus were heavily intertwined.

Bacchus was a popular god in Roman Britain[32] and in the Thetford Treasure itself there are a number of objects that are demonstrably Bacchic in the images they carry, such as the large gold buckle decorated with a relief figure of a satyr prancing to the right and the spoon with an invocation to *Dei Fauni Nari* that carries upon the interior of its bowl the figure of a springing panther.

Worship of Bacchus constituted the main opposition to Christianity in fourth-century Roman Britain and it is in this context that we should probably try to understand the Thetford Treasure. Bacchus was also, like Faunus, a god who could vouchsafe oracular utterances. To be sure, the members of the Thetford *collegium* worshipped Faunus but they would also no doubt have been well versed in the myths pertaining to Bacchus. It would be unreasonable to deny some degree of cross-fertilisation between the two cults, a fact strongly implied by some of the objects discussed below.

Probably the worship of Faunus in Norfolk, or rather a native version of the god, goes back much further than the late fourth century and the Thetford spoons should be considered in the context of Roman assimilation of native gods in the period following the conquest. The assimilation of the native deities of Roman Britain with their Roman counterparts is well known. In many areas of Britain, most famously the case of Sulis-Minerva at Bath, a local god or goddess came to be equated with his or her Roman counterpart and worship continued. In Norfolk, part of the territory of the Iceni, the situation may have been governed by the Boudiccan revolt which almost drove the armies of Rome into the ocean. The tribal gods of the Iceni, contaminated by the rebellion of their worshippers, may have been thought beyond assimilation.

Perhaps, in the case of the Icenian dominions in the aftermath of the Boudican revolt, it was felt wise to compel worshippers not to speak the original name of the tribe's chief god at all and simply refer to him as Faunus. Perhaps, by the end of the fourth century, any other names had simply been lost in the mists of time in any case.

Alternatively, in the wealthy and sophisticated milieu of late Roman elite society, it may have seemed rather parochial to dwell on the god's British tribal origins and he was identified instead solely with the ancient deity who was so connected with Rome's beginnings.

It is time to move on from the large assemblages and consider the other anthropomorphic and zoomorphic material that forms the main part of this paper

Anthropomorphic statuettes

Statuettes depicting deities offer a good starting point in any survey of religious material. They are generally instantly recognisable, most gods and goddesses having attributes and adjuncts that make them clearly identifiable. A reasonable, if not large, number of these have been unearthed in Norfolk over the last few decades.

Not surprisingly, a number of statuettes of Mercury have surfaced to stand alongside those already mentioned. They underline the widespread popularity of the god in Norfolk as well as in Britain and the North-Western provinces of the Roman Empire as a whole. They occur across Norfolk as can be seen from the distribution map (Map 1). They are best seen as representing the background of Roman religious belief, a background in which Mercury, being associated with various Celtic gods, was very much revered.

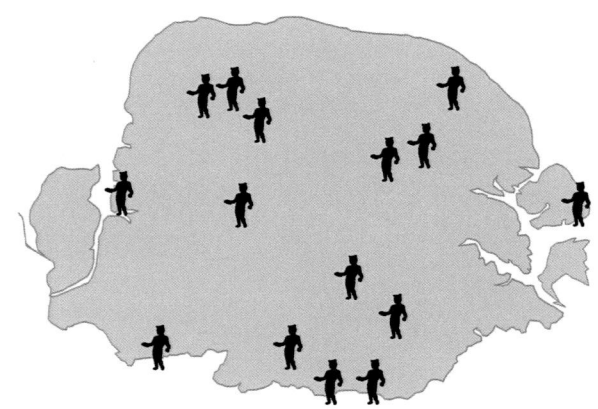

MAP 1 DISTRIBUTION OF MERCURY STATUETTES

---
[30] Johns and Potter 1983, p. 50
[31] Johns and Potter 1983, p. 51
[32] Henig 1984, pp. 200-3 and 221-4

One of the better modelled examples was discovered whilst gardening at Roudham (HER 28205) and figures Mercury holding a purse in his right hand with a cape draped over his left arm.[33] Some of the casting seams are visible and the piece appears unfinished but there is no good reason to doubt that it is of Roman date. A rather elegant and slightly smaller figurine from South Lopham (HER 29680) features the god in an identical posture.[34]

Another figurine from Wicklewood (HER 18111, NWHCM 1993.6.1, Fig. 1, no. 10) depicts a rather non-classical Mercury whilst records of others, of varying sizes and levels of competence, exist for Caistor-by-Yarmouth (NWHCM 1905.50), Diss (no further provenance), Forncett (HER 56704), Hockwold (HER 5351), Sculthorpe (HER 31838)[35], Stanhoe (NWHCM 1966.286), Tuttington (HER 30474)[36], West Winch (HER 28120) and Wicklewood (NWHCM 1985.380.4).

Another Mercury figurine from Gimingham (HER 52909, Fig. 1, no. 11) is surely a native product. The figure is ill-proportioned with short legs and its head, with lentoid eyes and a coarsely-defined nose and mouth falls well outside the parameters of classical art. He holds what is apparently a purse in the palm of his hand whilst the other hand probably once held a caduceus. His identity is confirmed by the winged cap, the *petasos*, which he wears. He is otherwise naked.

A figurine from Great Dunham (HER 4188), in reasonable style, appears to wear a *petasos* but the damaged hands with a consequent lack of adjuncts do not permit a firm attribution to Mercury. From North Creake (HER 1913), a headless, naked statuette whose right hand appears to have gripped the shaft of an uncertain object, perhaps a caduceus, may have been another Mercury but this is also uncertain. The execution is competent but no more, the upper part of the legs appearing rather too long for the trunk.

Mars is represented by two figurines, both relatively recent discoveries. A rather corroded example from Ingoldisthorpe (HER 1553, Fig. 3, no. 12) features the god wearing a cloak and armour, the latter comprising a breastplate, a skirt of scales, greaves and high-crested helmet. His right arm is raised and would most likely have originally held a spear. The left arm hangs by his side, partly covered by the folds of the cloak. Another, from Beighton (HER 51861, NMS-1CFD67, NWHCM 2009.203, Fig. 3, no. 13), is of larger size and substantially complete although it is missing most of its feet and its left arm.[37] The god is armoured, with a tall helmet, breast- and backplate and a skirt of *pteruges* although he does not appear to wear greaves. Mars does not seem to have been very popular in Norfolk, being more worshipped in the Military Zone that occupied the North of Britain although he was frequently venerated as an agricultural deity, as in the Cotswolds.[38]

Worship of Jupiter, king of the gods, was apparently not especially widespread in Roman Britain but three figurines have come to light, at Great Ryburgh (HER 11360), Tacolneston (HER 35831)[39] and Salle (HER 50246, NMS-76AEA1). That from Great Ryburgh is a well-proportioned piece with the god's right arm raised, presumably in the act of casting a thunderbolt. The Salle example has its right arm lowered, perhaps to hold a patera, the left held up, probably to grasp a sceptre. The Tacolneston specimen is headless and missing most of its limbs; the right arm is outstretched and holds an unidentified object, probably a thunderbolt.

Jupiter's son, the demigod Hercules was rather more popular. His legendary *Virtus*, the heroic courage which enabled him to complete his labours and defeat monsters inimical to mankind formed a suitable point of reference for warriors and soldiers. Like Mars, however, he does not appear to have been overly reverenced in Norfolk, although a small figurine from Brampton missing its lower right arm but with the characteristic lionskin draped over the left does depict him (NWHCM 1985.442.1). Presumably, the reasons are the same; with few soldiers based in Norfolk until the later third century there were few men who would naturally look towards Hercules for help and patronage.

An unusual import is a seated figure of Isis suckling the infant Horus from Skeyton (HER 36588, NMS496). It must attest some interest in the Egyptian pantheon and it is difficult to see it as anything other than the property of a traveller although other evidence for the worship of Isis is known from Roman Britain, including a temple to the goddess at London.[40]

Other figurines also portray less well encountered deities. A figurine from Billingford (no HER number, HESH-A1B593) missing head and feet but with exaggerated male genitalia might represent Priapus. Another, from Felbrigg (HER 33827, NWHCM 1999.122.1), most probably does show the god.[41] The male figure's short tunic is pulled back to reveal genitalia. A statuette from Scole, described as being made of lead, has also been identified as a Priapus (HER 30650).

Perhaps the finest substantially complete statuette to be recovered in recent years was found at Ashby-with-Oby (HER 39918, NMS-038224, Fig. 3, no. 14). A youthful satyr, beautifully modelled, is depicted in a prancing pose, his weight balanced on his right leg which is thrust slightly forward. A *nebris* covers part of his chest; he is otherwise naked. His left arm, broken just above the elbow, is raised at a right angle to his body and would probably have held

---

[33] Gurney 1992, p. 367
[34] Gurney 1994, p. 109
[35] Gurney 1997, p. 542
[36] Gurney 1995b, p. 225
[37] Worrell 2009, pp. 304-5

[38] Henig 1984, pp. 50-1
[39] Gurney 2001, p. 700
[40] Henig 1984, pp. 113-6
[41] Gurney 1999, p. 362. Also see Johns and Henig 1991 and Plouviez 2005

Landscapes and Artefacts

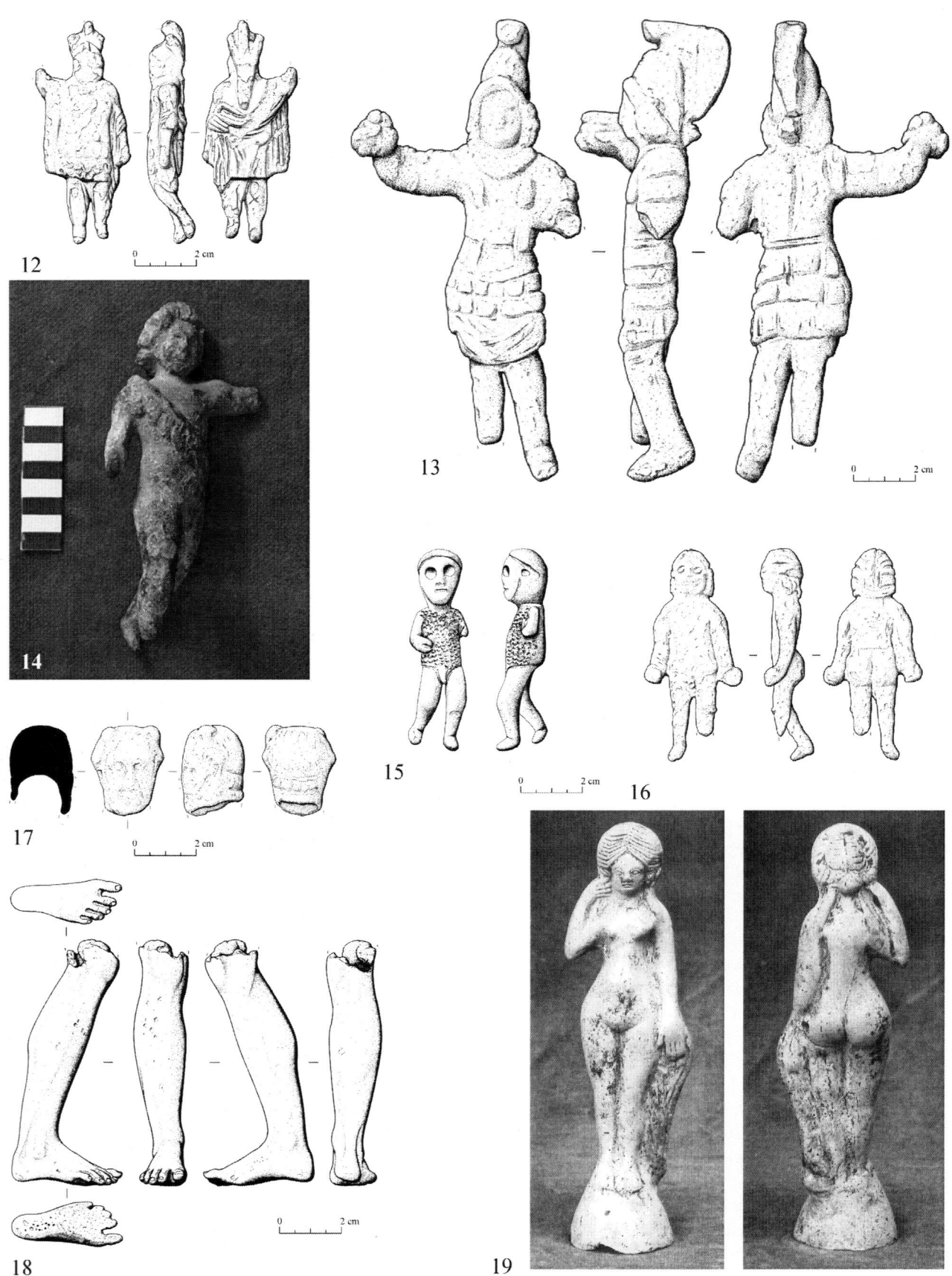

Fig. 3, 12-3 Mars from Ingoldisthorpe and Beighton. 14 Satyr, Ashby-with-Oby, 15 Probable satyr, Banham, 16 Unidentified god, Acle, 17 Head, Brampton, 18 Fragment of leg, Acle (All HES), 19 Pipeclay Venus figurine, Brampton (NMS)

aloft a bunch of grapes whilst the right, broken just below the elbow, trails at his side. This object is almost certainly of first-century Italian manufacture and thus represents a relatively early import into the British provinces.

Satyrs are numbered among the followers of Bacchus and feature on a number of objects from East Anglia, in particular the Mildenhall great dish and the gold buckle plate from the Thetford Treasure mentioned above. Does this object represent an imported luxury item, brought over for a wealthy Icenian eager to demonstrate both his *Romanitas* and his loyalty to the old tribal god of his people? The figurine does not have the goat legs of true *Fauni* but satyrs were analogous to these woodland creatures and would have provided a subtle point of reference for followers of Faunus himself and the Icenian deity with whom he had possibly been identified.

A figurine that is much less Classical in its modelling was found at Banham (HER 32136, Fig. 3, no. 15).[42] Although it has flattened areas at the rear, suggesting that it may have been mounted in some way, the modelling is so three-dimensional that it is best to treat this piece as a figurine and not a mount. The somewhat grotesque statuette is in the form of a male who prances forward, naked except for a figure-hugging piece of clothing perhaps best described as a tank top. His left arm is broken just below the shoulder whilst his right, claw-like, hand is held to his chest. The oversized head has huge eye sockets that would presumably have originally held glass insets as has been noted on a number of other Romano-Celtic statuettes. A groove running transversely across the forehead gives the impression that this rather monstrous little statuette is wearing a spaceman's helmet. The figure's posture, however, prancing forward as it does, echoes that of the Ashby-with-Oby statuette whilst the tank-top is suggestive in some ways of a *nebris*, the fawn skin in which satyrs are clad. This is probably a locally-produced version of a satyr, manufactured by a local artisan who did not quite understand the subject.

Another small figurine found at Matlask (HER 36550) may also depict a satyr.[43] Although badly damaged with the head and most of the arms and legs missing, the pose is consistent with such an attribution. The right arm is raised and the figure seems to be prancing forward with the weight balanced on the left leg and the right lifted up somewhat.

Two odd statuettes defy easy identification. The first, from Acle (HER 50193, Fig. 3, no. 16) is puzzling on account of the fact that it does not really resemble any known deity.[44] The male figure stands with knees slightly bent and arms by its side, and his hairstyle is at odds with anything that might expected from a Roman male figurine. It recalls

---

[42] Gurney 1997, p. 542, fig. 2A
[43] Gurney 2002, p. 155
[44] Marsden 2012a, p. 58, fig. 4.6, Rogerson and Ashley 2008, p. 429, fig. 3.10

somewhat the elaborate hairstyles of early third-century empresses. Nonetheless, the statuette is undoubtedly that of a man. The piece is crude in appearance, the arms being joined to the torso along their entire length and the fists blob-like and undefined. The surfaces are unfinished and one's first impression is of a figurine that was awaiting further treatment.

A second figurine from Hethersett (HER 16870) is remarkably similar in its posture and, if anything, even more crudely produced. The right hand seems to support an object that may have been intended to represent a club and this, together with the suggestion of a lionskin headdress, has led to the piece being described as a Hercules although this identification is far from certain. The piece is as unfinished as the first.

There are a number of fragments, broken arms, legs and so forth. An enormously worn and abraded torso from Leziate (HER 28955) with a head and only the stumps of its limbs is almost certainly Roman in date but is utterly illegible. Other fragments are sometimes more useful.

For example, a hand grasping a purse from Cawston (HER 19522, NMS-82E021) clearly comes from a figurine of Mercury. Given the presence of the purse, it can be nothing else, a demonstration that sometimes the smallest part of a lost whole can be informative. From Methwold (HER 22637) a head from a statue has been described as of Minerva.

A hollow cast head discovered at Brampton (HER 38154, Fig. 3, no. 17), is somewhat enigmatic. It is possible that this object was originally a mount but an identification as the head of a statuette is far more compelling. The modelling appears to have been fine although corrosion has removed the surfaces and obliterated the nature of certain details. In particular, this heavily corroded condition renders interpretation of the knobbly features at the side of the forehead and just below rather difficult. If a laurel wreath was intended then it is possible that this head represents an emperor of the second century, perhaps Antoninus Pius (AD138-61). On the balance of probabilities, however, it seems more likely that the protrusions represent a pair of horns above a pair of goat-like ears. If this is the case then the most likely subject is the god Faunus. The piece is probably relatively early in date, of the first or second century, and, like the satyr statuette discussed above, may have been of Italian manufacture.

Three other heads of uncertain identity have been found. The fragment of what appears to have been the top of the head of a relatively large piece of sculpture from Riddlesworth (HER 30519) seems to have been directly damaged by fire. From Kenninghall a hollow cast head is almost certainly a surviving fragment from a figurine but the damaged and worn state renders further analysis impossible (HER 31412, NMS-2D5AE1). The top of a head from Emneth (HER 31622) lacks horns and wings, eliminating a number of possibilities in terms of its subject.⁴⁵

A left arm bent at the elbow from Hockwold (HER 5587, NMS-23F215) represents a partial survival from another statuette deposited at one of that site's shrines whilst another left arm comprising hand and forearm broken at the elbow from Old Hunstanton (HER 29563) has a tinned or silvered surface and given its large size (about 10cm) must have originally formed part of a large figure. A rather crudely-produced hand wearing a bracelet from Letheringsett-with-Glandford represents all that remains of another figurine (HER 33796, NMS-AOF425).

A hand holding a pine branch that must have originally formed part of a beautifully made statuette of a youth, a *dendropheros* or tree-bearer, was found at Hockwold (NWHCM 1962.396.106). This character was connected to the cult of Attis, consort of Cybele, and suggests the existence of yet another shrine there. There is other evidence that Cybele had a following in Roman Britain.⁴⁶

A very finely rendered fragment of a leg from Acle is a highly impressive piece, so beautifully made that individual toenails are distinguished and the arteries at the back of the calf are visible (HER 42032, NMS-3CECC3, Fig. 3, no. 18).⁴⁷ The leg is broken at the knee but the figurine of which it once formed a part must have been relatively large, around a foot tall, and were it complete would have made this statuette amongst the largest so far discovered from Norfolk. It was found in the field next to that where one of the crude and curious figurines just discussed was discovered (HER 50193), raising interesting questions as to the nature of the site which must surely have had a religious element. However, in terms of its quality it is of a completely different order and must surely have been an import. It is to be hoped that more of this statuette may come to light in the future but the discovery of a large cake of bronze very close by raises the unhappy possibility that metalworking was taking place at the site and the Acle leg represents the only surviving limb of a statuette melted down as scrap.⁴⁸

A fragment representing the lower part of a left leg and foot from Dunton (HER 7112) may be from a figurine or may be a complete votive whilst a foot from Narford (HER 54758, NMS-2173A7) is clearly broken from a statuette, traces of solder surviving on the underside.

Finally, although they are not made of metal, the small number of pipeclay figurines found in Norfolk is deserving of mention. Examples of the most popular type, or parts thereof, depicting Venus, have been noted from Hockwold (HER 5351, NWHCM 1958.380), Brampton (NWHCM 1961.199.54)⁴⁹ and Scole (1962.590.1) with the major part of another example being recovered during excavations at Brancaster.⁵⁰ An abraded example from North Wootton (HER 29076) also almost certainly represents Venus. A fragment, a female posterior that is undoubtedly a portion of a Venus figure was recovered during the recent excavations at Caistor St Edmund in 2012.⁵¹

Another pipeclay figurine of Venus, a fine complete example, is represented by a photograph in the Brampton excavation archive from Dr. Keith Knowles' earlier excavations in the 1960s now held at the Castle Museum (Fig. 3, no. 19). Its present whereabouts are unknown and there seems to be no record of the figurine in the rest of the records although it is to be hoped that more information will come to light when the archive is fully investigated. Another from the same excavations, missing its head and feet, is currently in the Castle Museum archive from the site but has yet to be accessioned.

Figurines (or parts thereof) of a Dea Nutrix have been found at Denver (HER 4235, NWHCM 1967.587) and Brancaster.⁵² The final fragments worth mentioning are two joining pieces representing a shoulder and the lower torso of a male wearing a short cloak discovered during the 2012 Caistor St Edmund excavations; this must have been part of a Mercury.⁵³

Zoomorphic figurines

A number of animal figurines have been recovered in recent years.⁵⁴ The function of these objects is of cardinal importance. Given the fact that so many have been discovered at sites which had a religious dimension, it seems certain that they were votive in nature. Were they, as Green has suggested, intended to represent various gods in an animal guise?⁵⁵ The answer here is probably not. It seems more likely that they were intended to represent living animals and function as offerings in the form of creatures sacred to a particular deity. Thus they might be said to have stood in for the beast in question, providing a less messy alternative to the actual sacrifice of a live animal.

A fragment of the hollow cast head of a lion found at Banham (HER 28766), comprising the ears and part of the mane, may be from a large figurine but is perhaps more likely to have been a portion of a mount.⁵⁶ A lion, from Ashwellthorpe (HER 30205)⁵⁷, this time complete apart from damage to some of the legs, appears to have stood upon a base, now missing, whilst another, from Gunthorpe

---

⁴⁵ Gurney 1996, p. 392
⁴⁶ Henig 1984, pp. 110-3
⁴⁷ Worrell and Pearce 2012, pp. 374-5
⁴⁸ Marsden 2012b, p. 376
⁴⁹ Jenkins in Green 1977, p. 87 (fig. 36, no. 239)
⁵⁰ Hinchliffe and Sparey Green 1985, p. 58, no. 131
⁵¹ Natasha Harlow personal communication
⁵² Jenkins in Green 1977, p. 87
⁵³ Natasha Harlow personal communication
⁵⁴ A boar of lead alloy from Foxley, although recorded on the PAS website (BH-CDA5A2), is most likely of relatively modern date. It does not appear Roman and the presence of a casting seam, must surely count against anything other than a Post-medieval date
⁵⁵ Green 1977, p. 305
⁵⁶ Gurney 1996, p. 391
⁵⁷ Gurney 1994, p. 108

(HER 28847), was also most probably a vessel mount although its three-dimensional rendering also places it in the realm of statuettes. It could have been religious in function, lions being associated with Hercules.[58]

A representation of a leopard or panther from Hainford (HER 42543, NMS-5012F4, Fig. 4, no. 20) was almost certainly a votive connected with the cult of Bacchus.[59] It is incomplete, only the torso, neck and part of the head surviving.

An unusual figurine of what appears to be a cat from Swanton Morley (HER 17486, Fig. 4, no. 21) is unlikely to be related to the worship of Bacchus. It could belong to the secular realm and indeed finds parallels in a range of small animal figures in both copper alloy and jet but the possibility that is was a votive of some kind cannot be discounted.[60]

An object long in Norwich Castle Museum's collection and said to have been found at Caister-on-Sea (NWHCM 1894.76.725) takes the form of a dog-like animal, perhaps a jackal, standing upon a plinth. This probably formed the top of a sceptre or wand and, if this is the case, it is an important cult object. A heavily abraded dog figurine, this time probably a votive, was recovered from North Walsham (HER 34682).[61] The dog was associated with the goddess Nehalennia whose worship is attested in Germany and the Low Countries.[62] If this was a votive, then trading contacts and cultural affinities could explain her worship in Norfolk.[63]

Horse figurines are known, a rather abstract-looking example from Banningham (HER 50376, NMS-DA9D68), one from Bunwell (HER 10007, NWHCM 1985.378.147)[64] and the fragment of another from Hillington (HER 32137, NMS811). Another standing horse is recorded from Bradenham (no HER number available). Given the large amounts of Iron Age horse furniture from the Icenian realms and the probability that this relates to horse-breeding, these figurines may well reflect a continued interest in the raising of horses in the Roman period. They possibly represent votives dedicated to Epona, goddess of Horses although the only sculpture of Epona known from Britain is from Colchester.[65]

A number of figurines of rams and goats have been found in Norfolk in recent years. Sometimes it is difficult to differentiate one species from the other. These horned animals were sacred to Mercury and are invariably said to have been connected with that god. However, as a protector of flocks, goats, rams and lambs would also have been suitable as sacrifices to Faunus, echoing on one level the goatskin *nebris* worn by satyrs.

A charming example of a goat from Great Walsingham has already been mentioned[66]. Another, crude and rather flat, is known from the same site. A well-modelled goat recently found at Quidenham is of a higher artistic standard (HER 58462, NMS-C71211, Fig. 4, no. 22) and another, from South Walsham, is also pleasing to the eye, despite its rather outsized head (HER 39988, Fig. 2, no. 23). A well composed ram with a long coat is known from Newton Flotman (HER 40445, NMS-100220)[67] and another from Hethersett with rather a long neck (HER 25509) squats realistically with its front legs spread out in front. Other caprids and ovids include examples from Wymondham (HER 33069)[68], Caistor St Edmund (HER 9815[69] and HER 12872) and a rather crudely-produced specimen from Postwick with Witton (HER 13603, NMS-419374).

A very stylised figurine of a hare from Stanfield (HER 58543, KENT-9B0EB4) is unusual; its front legs bear a passing resemblance to *phalli* and this suggestion of fertility is very apt given that hares were sacred to Venus. It is an unusual object, however, and stands apart from the normal run of votive figurines.

As we have seen from the Walsingham and Hockwold assemblages, figurines of cockerels were popular and several have been found at other sites. With his cry the cockerel heralds the dawn and so came to be associated with Mercury, herald of the gods. A crudely-made cockerel with an exaggerated wattle and rather large head was recently discovered at Paston (HER 58885, NMS-A07183, Fig. 4, no. 24) whilst others are known from Ashwellthorpe (HER 30205)[70], Binham (HER 24150), Caistor St Edmund (NWHCM 1894.76.725), Costessey (HER 25624), Merton (HER 21484), Quidenham (HER 10792)[71], Quidenham (HER 30382) and Wicklewood (HER 8897)[72], whilst an example missing its head and feet was found at Weybourne (HER 29097). A heavily abraded figurine from Walsingham almost certainly represents another cockerel (HER 17543, NMS-687685). Three small cockerel figures have (or would have had) suspension loops; they may have been pendants, serving an amuletic function, or small steelyard weights. Examples are known from Beeston-with-Bittering (HER 4084)[73], Scole (HER 39960, Fig. 4, no. 25)[74] and Shouldham (No HER number recorded).[75]

---

[58] Rogerson and Ashley 2008, p. 429, fig. 3.12
[59] Gurney 2007, p. 254, fig. 2F
[60] See Toynbee 1964, pp. 126-7, plate XXXIV for a dog from Lydney, Gloucestershire, Crummy 1983, p. 144, fig. 175 for a hare in jet from Colchester and Worrell and Pearce 2011, pp. 407-8, for a mouse from Hayton, East Yorks. Also Crummy 2010 for a series of jet figurines
[61] Gurney 2000, p. 518
[62] Henig 1984, p. 55
[63] Nash-Briggs 2011
[64] Gregory 1986
[65] Huskinson 1994, no. 14
[66] Bagnall Smith 1999, p. 31, no. 13
[67] Gurney 2005, p. 742
[68] Gurney 1998, p. 188
[69] Gurney 1994, p. 108
[70] Gurney 2005, p. 741
[71] Gurney 1995b, p. 225
[72] Gurney 2001, p. 700
[73] Gurney 1999, p. 362, fig. 3
[74] Gurney 2007, p. 254, fig. 3A.
[75] Gurney 2004, p. 568, fig. 2C. Worrell 2004, pp. 326-7, no. 10

LANDSCAPES AND ARTEFACTS

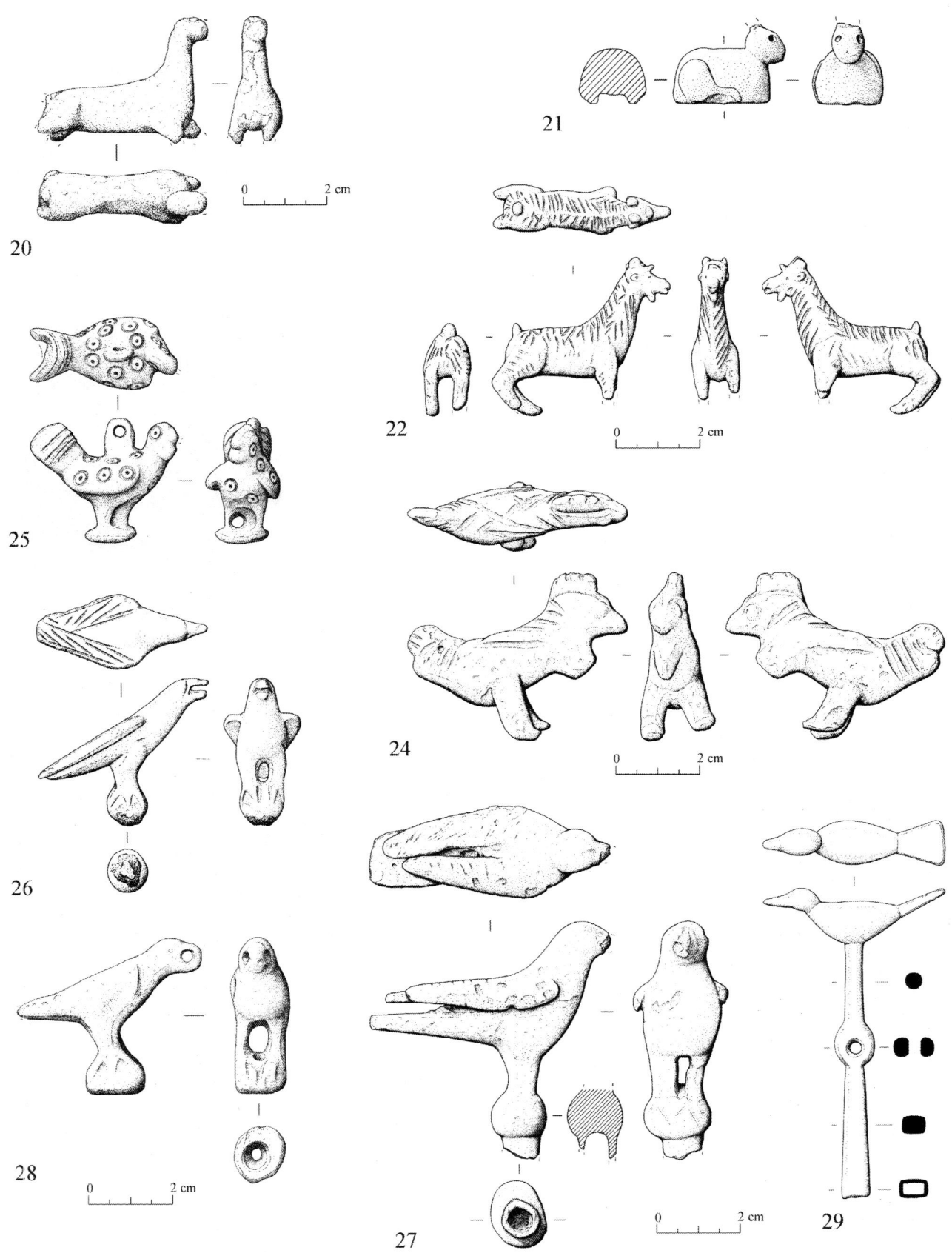

Fig. 4, 20 Panther, Hainford, 21 Cat, Swanton Morley, 22 Goat, Quidenham, 24 Cockerel, Paston, 25 Cockerel with suspension loop, Scole, 26-9 Corvids from Paston, Burgh and Tuttington, Briningham and Letheringsett-with-Glandford (NHES)

Perhaps the most interesting group of zoomorphic figurines is the small number depicting ravens.[76] Those from the Felmingham hoard have already been mentioned; others have appeared from Paston (HER 6893, Fig. 4, no. 26),[77] Burgh and Tuttington (HER 33592, NMS-AE10F0, Fig. 4, no. 27),[78] Briningham (HER 44766, NMS-F46436, Fig. 4, no. 28)[79] and Aylsham (HER 24510).

It is noteworthy that all examples conform to a similar pattern. All are clearly corvids and the majority also sit on a globe and carry a small sphere in their beak. All examples also have traces of an iron attachment inserted into the base; from the Felmingham examples it is clear that these are the remains of the iron sceptres which the birds topped. Thus they are perhaps more correctly described as terminals or mounts.

Another, similar, example has been recorded from Letheringsett-with-Glandford (HER 33796, Fig. 4, no. 29); here the bird perches atop an integral shaft with a pierced circular expansion along its length.[80] In these respects it differs from the other examples but clearly comes from a similar tradition.

Rogerson and Ashley have made the interesting discovery that the findspots of these ravens cluster in north-east Norfolk (Map 2) and have also noted that the Roman name for Brancaster, *Branodunum*, translates as Raven Fort.[81] It is unlikely, especially given the fact that this area of Norfolk is not particularly productive in terms of Roman finds, that this spread is a coincidence.

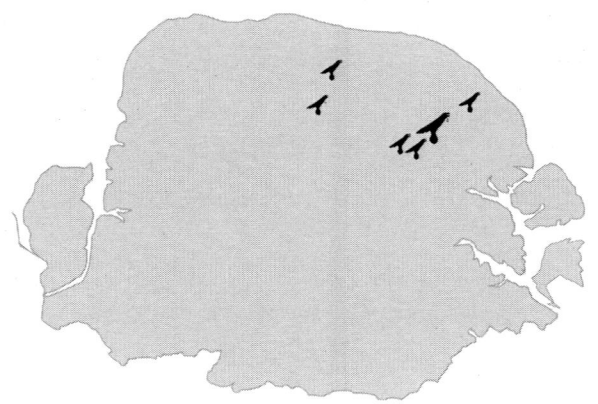

MAP 2 DISTRIBUTION OF RAVEN MOUNTS

Ravens were associated with the sun god Apollo and their flight was reckoned to convey omens.[82] Here the head wearing a radiate crown from Felmingham is interesting. Was Apollo, perhaps equated with a Celtic god of the Sun, worshipped in this area? The head from Felmingham is bearded but the syncretism of the two deities could explain this. The nature of what we might term the Raven Cult in north-east Norfolk must remain uncertain for the time being but a solar nature of some sort for the deity seems likely.

Other anthropomorphic and zoomorphic objects modelled in the round

Within the ambit of the so-called Minor Arts there are a range of objects depicting gods or animals, most notably steelyard weights and key or knife handles, but these have at best a secondary religious function. They may reflect the beliefs of their original owners but it is more likely that they are simply ornamental items of metalwork. Significantly, they are also not often found at sites with any evidence of a religious function, further implying that they belong to a more secular environment. Nonetheless, some of the more important examples should be mentioned since they do, after all, depict anthropomorphic or zoomorphic subjects even if they do not fall within the realm of religious objects.

Steelyard weights frequently depict deities or supernatural creatures. Several examples have been found in Norfolk. The most impressive, the head of a child satyr (NMS-FE90E7, Fig. 5, no. 30) with the distinctive topknot worn by children in the Roman empire, was found in the Burgh Castle area and is probably the largest example of a steelyard weight from Norfolk. A number of Minerva heads have surfaced, notably from Langley-with-Hardley (HER 49581) and Wymondham (HER 40446, NMS-E80FE4) whilst a female head wearing a high diadem, perhaps Venus, was unearthed at Narford (HER 3974).[83] Another in the form of a raven was found in the 19th century at Caistor St Edmund (NWHCM 1894.76.731).

Many key handles and, to a lesser extent, knife handles have also been recorded over the years. A key handle in the shape of a lion mauling a man was recovered during excavations in the 1960s and 1970s at the Roman settlement of Brampton and is now in the Castle Museum, Norwich (Fig. 5, no. 31). From Shouldham (HER 4255) comes a handle depicting a hound springing from a four-petalled flower.[84] A knife handle in the form of a charging boar from Ditchingham (HER 22255, Fig. 5, no. 32) is rendered to striking effect.[85] From Saham Toney (HER 4697, SF-83E2E0) an object probably best interpreted as a handle in the form of a dog who squats on a small pedestal is one of the most charming representations of this animal recorded from Roman Norfolk[86]. There are many more key

---

[76] Rogerson & Ashley 2010, pp. 124-8
[77] Rogerson and Ashley 2010, pp. 125-8, fig. 3.14
[78] Rogerson and Ashley 2010, pp. 125-8, fig. 3.15
[79] Gurney 2007, p. 254, fig. 2B
[80] Rogerson & Ashley 2008, p. 429, fig. 2.7
[81] Rogerson and Ashley 2010, pp. 125-8 and Rivet and Smith 1981, p. 274

[82] Grimal 1986, p. 50
[83] Gurney 2004, p. 567
[84] Rogerson and Ashley 2012, p. 411
[85] Gurney 2005, p. 742, fig. 5A. Worrell 2004, 327, no. 11
[86] Rogerson and Ashley 2010, p. 128, fig. 3.17

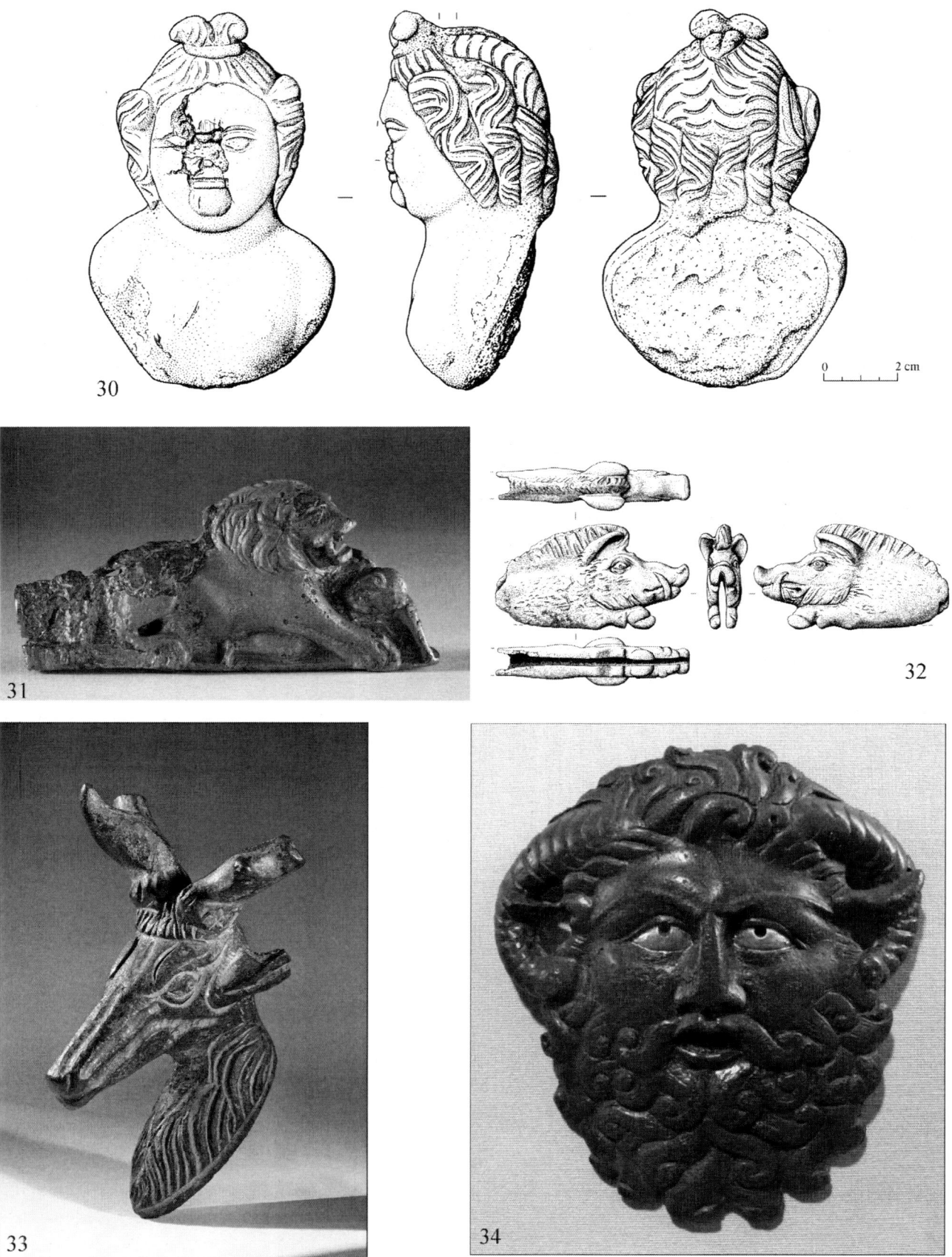

Fig. 5. 30 Child satyr's head steelyard weight, Burgh Castle, 31 Key handle in the form of a lion mauling a man, Brampton (NMS), 32 Folding knife handle in the shape of a boar, Ditchingham (not to scale, length 51mm) (both NHES), 33 Protome of a stag, Brampton, 34 Faunus head mount, Thetford (NMS)

and knife handles featuring animals such as a key handle in the form of confronted dolphins from Brampton (HER 35055, NMS-5B4425).[87]

So-called spatula handles in the form of Minerva busts represent a well-known type of object. The head of the goddess of wisdom would have been an apt item to place atop an object intended for writing. Examples are known from a number of sites, including Beeston-with-Bittering (HER 4084),[88] Fransham (HER 30424), Mileham (HER 30999)[89], Sporle-with-Palgrave (HER 34520) and a piece that was surely the head from another found at Wicklewood (NWHCM 1985.380.3).

Anthropomorphic and zoomorphic mounts

It is profitable to continue by considering the various mounts in bronze depicting deities which have been recovered from sites in Norfolk. To what extent they are religious in function is uncertain – some could simply have served as decorative additions to secular vessels, ewers and the like – but, given the possibility that some at least may have been of a religious nature, a full survey is desirable. Many mounts in the form of animals have been found but, as with the objects just discussed, these most probably do not have a religious dimension and so have in general been excluded. For example, a fine protome of a stag's head from Brampton (NWHCM L1975.16.12, Fig. 5, no. 33), although a striking piece of art, most probably belongs to the secular realm.[90]

Probably the most impressive vessel mount from Norfolk is a large, finely-rendered face from the Thetford area (Fig. 5, no. 34).[91] The full beard is composed of sinuous curls and a pair of ram's horns curve downwards around the goat-like ears. A broad face frames penetrating, silvered eyes. A cast is on display in Norwich Castle Museum; the illustration published here is a photograph of this replica.

Another visually arresting mount from Elsing (HER 30334, NWHCM L1993.7, Fig. 2, no. 35) depicts a facing bust with the sharp, twisted features of a satyr topped with a pair of horns.[92] It is interesting in that it mixes the horns of Faunus with the facial physiognomy of a satyr, demonstrating the way in which the god and the followers of Bacchus were, at least on this piece of art, perhaps understood to be one and the same. Traces of solder show that this mask would have been attached to a vessel, probably a bronze ewer.

A powerful mask forming one of the attachment points of a vessel handle from Feltwell (HER 22920, Fig. 6, no. 36) features the head of Faunus with horns curling outwards from the centre of his forehead and a long, luxuriant beard. This is an evocative piece of work and the fierce stare of the god compels the viewer's attention. It may belong to the secular realm but given its subject matter it is more likely that it furnished part of a vessel used in a ritual capacity.

A vessel mount from Kenninghall (HER 35131, Fig. 6, no. 37), described when originally published as being in the form of a goat's head, appears in fact to be a rather bestial representation of Faunus or Pan.[93] The leering, rather frightening face is topped by a monstrous pair of horns.

Another, rather abraded, mount from Cawston (HER 30455, NMS-57CB72, NWHCM 2008.254, Fig. 6, no. 38) depicts a somewhat more human-looking version of the god.[94] The stubs of horns projecting from his forehead betray his identity.

A very small circular mount from Caistor St Edmund (HER 31803, NMS-48BF58, Fig. 6, no. 39) also appears to depict Faunus[95]. The face is framed by swirling curls which, on the forehead, appear to suggest horns. They certainly do not appear to represent the topknot appropriate to a Cupid or child satyr and the hair at the side of the cheeks, clearly representing a beard, further militate against such an identification.

An interesting object from Ormesby St. Margaret (HER 56260; Fig. 6, no. 40) almost certainly depicts a horned god. The solid, rather square-shaped, head has traces of a rivet on the base, suggesting it was originally a mount from furniture. At first glance the projections on the forehead might appear to represent the wings sprouting from Mercury's *petasos*, his winged cap. However, on closer inspection, it is clear that the rather irregular grooved patterning on the head represents hair and the projections are horns.

A number of other mounts depicts satyrs, including a vessel mount from Mundham (HER 28342) which depicts the facing head of a youthful satyr with the characteristic child's topknot. A solid, flat mount said to be from Caistor St Edmund (NWHCM 1894.76.710) is decorated with a satyr holding a bunch of grapes. A circular mount found at Besthorpe (HER 29171), probably best described as a box mount, has a facing bust in high relief that, with its bald and bearded head, appears to figure Bacchus' elderly companion Silenus. Another from Horsham St Faith (HER 30074) probably also figures the same subject.

Bacchus himself is known from only one vessel mount, an attractive, three-dimensional bust with vine leaves decorating the subject's hair. This is a very old find, said to come from Caister-on-Sea (NWHCM 1894.76.724). It represents the only example known to the author of an item of Roman metalwork from Norfolk that depicts the god.

---

[87] Gurney 2005, p. 741
[88] Gurney 2006, p. 117, fig. 3C
[89] Gurney 1996, p. 392, fig. 3B
[90] Henig 1995, p. 97, fig 62. Bagnall Smith 1999, p. 47, does ascribe this a religious significance
[91] Davies 1996, p. 382
[92] Gurney 1995b, p. 224, Davies 1996, 380 and Marsden 2012a, pp. 54-5
[93] Gurney 2003, p. 360, fig. 3D
[94] Rogerson and Ashley 2008, p. 429, fig. 3.9. Marsden 2012, p. 55
[95] Rogerson and Ashley 2012, pp. 409-11

Fig. 6, 36 Faunus escutcheon, Feltwell, 37 Vessel mount, Kenninghall, 38 Vessel mount, Cawston, 39 Mount, Caistor St Edmund, 40 Head of Faunus, Ormesby, 41 Mercury head, Woodbastwick, 42 Probable Jupiter head mount, Thorpe, 43 Medusa head mount, Beeston-with-Bittering, 44 Mount in the form of a female head, Horningtoft (All NHES)

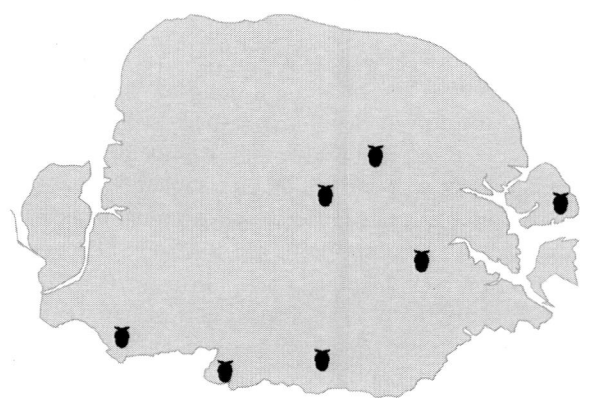

MAP 3 DISTRIBUTION OF FAUNUS MOUNTS

It is remarkable that so many of the mounts that have appeared in recent years depict Faunus. They surely demonstrate that the Thetford *collegium* was not an isolated group and that Faunus was a popular god throughout Norfolk, a supposition strengthened by study of a distribution map of the material relating to the god (Map 3). Davies commented nearly twenty years ago that representations of Pan (or Faunus) were uncommon in Britain and the Western half of the empire and this holds true today, practically nothing relating to the god being recorded on the PAS database.[96] The lack of material featuring Bacchus is equally strange.

Bagnall Smith suggests that Faunus was equated with both Bacchus and Silvanus in Norfolk but the lack of material depicting or naming Bacchus himself seems instead to suggest that Faunus had rather usurped Bacchus' place in the county. The items relating to Silvanus all occur some distance away in Essex, in an area falling within the boundaries of the tribe of the Trinovantes.[97]

Compared to the number of statuettes depicting Mercury, mounts in the form of the god are very few indeed. It is good that the one certain mount, presumably from furniture, and found very recently at Woodbastwick (HER 51187, NMS-800B35, Fig. 6, no. 41), is such a large and splendid example. A youthful-looking Mercury, with eyes carefully defined, wears a *petasos* atop a wreath of what seem to be vine leaves in his hair. The iconography is interesting, surely suggesting a reference to Bacchus. This is an unusual piece of syncretism which seems unparalleled in Romano-British art. It implies a connection was to be sought be in the minds of those viewing it between the very popular Mercury and Bacchus in whose train the satyrs danced. A Hadrianic or perhaps an Antonine date in the second century is almost certain.

A bust and head modelled in the round found at Stoke Holy Cross (HER 9732) also depicts Mercury. A *chlamys* adorns his shoulder and he wears a winged *petasos*. It is likely that it represents a furniture mount although the possibility that it is the surviving, upper portion of a figurine cannot be fully discounted.

The sun god Sol, although very popular in the third century and represented on many coin issues of the period, does not seem to have found much of a following in Britain. Veneration of the god seems to have been more of a State cult promoted by the Danubian emperors of the later third century (who came from an area where worship of Sol was strong) than a religion with a local following. He is, however, represented on a mount from North Creake (HER 1913), a head with what appear to be rays projecting from its top. Another possible head of Sol with what appear to be strange, squared-off solar rays framing his head, was found at Fincham (HER 12595). Given the lack of popularity of the god in Norfolk generally we might suggest that these two pieces were owned by officials or members of the army.

A three-dimensional mount from Thorpe (listed in HER file 40273 but possibly found at HER 57973, NMS-451277, Fig. 6, no. 42) featuring a powerfully-rendered male head with a beaked nose may perhaps depict an emperor, the facial physiognomy being broadly consistent with portraits of Antoninus Pius (AD138-61), but it seems far more likely that Jupiter was the intended subject. The blistered iron shank strongly suggests a mount from some form of furniture.

A large circular furniture mount from Beeston-with-Bittering (HER 4084, Fig. 6, no. 43) originally published as depicting Mercury in fact features a facing head of Medusa.[98] Although probably not strictly belonging to the realm of religion, it is an important piece worthy of mention. A similar object occurred at Hockwold (HER 5587, NWHCM 2007.419.8).[99] The gaze of Medusa was reckoned to avert the evil eye and so the object does have some ritual significance. Medusa heads were also a popular device on cameos, a number being known from Roman Britain, including a number in onyx[100] and one in jet.[101]

A solid, three-dimensional mount from Horningtoft (HER 55326, NMS-4913E0, Fig. 6, no. 44) depicting a female head is difficult to identify with any particular goddess or personage. The style of the portrait is rather strange, indeed almost cat-like, with a narrow face, regressive chin and huge eyes. The hair is plaited into rows of bobbles which sweep back from the forehead. No close parallels can be found for this hairstyle which does not closely replicate any coiffure of Roman imperial date; however, mounts do exist depicting negroid heads which are broadly similar. It could be that this mount was intended to represent an African or it may have been a confused and misunderstood native rendering of one of the elaborate hairstyles of court ladies of the second and third centuries.

---

[96] Davies 1996, p. 380
[97] Bagnall Smith 1999, pp. 47-8
[98] Gurney 2006, p. 117, fig. 3B. Worrell 2006, 448-9
[99] Gurney 2002, p. 155
[100] Henig 2007, pp. 179-80, nos. 725-31
[101] Henig 2007, p. 199, App. 53

Alternatively, the plaits recall the dreadlocked hairstyle found on obverses of the Icenian Iron Age Bury type face-horse coins. These were struck in the late first century BC and feature a female head facing either right or left.[102] The subject of these coins was probably a tribal goddess of the Iceni, offering the possibility that the Horningtoft head was also intended to depict this deity.

From Shouldham (HER 28645), an odd vessel mount is also difficult to interpret as depicting a particular personage. It takes the form of a head wearing what seems to be some sort of hood or hat with bun-like projections over the ears and transverse grooves running across the front of the head. It may have been recognisable as a divinity to those who viewed it but equally may have represented nothing more than a decorative mount.

A flat, facing head from Great Dunham (HER 4188) with a suspension loop above is another unusual piece.[103] It must surely have been attached to the rim of a vessel of some sort. The rather heavy facial physiognomy nonetheless suggests a female subject. The face is framed within a grooved border on each side, suggestive of vertical plaits, and above the forehead, a hairstyle with a central parting occupies the area between the face and the suspension loop. Any attempt at identifying the subject would be little better than guesswork.

There are a number of other mounts recorded but the descriptions leave some room for doubt as to the precise identity of their subjects. One from Thompson (HER 36089), with a top-knot and curling locks, has been suggested as a Cupid but an identification as a boy satyr is perhaps more accurate.[104]

A rather strange lead plaque with a relief bust of Mercury holding a *caduceus* over his shoulder was found at Brampton.[105] Given that it is made of lead, it is unlikely to have functioned as a mount and it is perhaps best regarded as some sort of votive.

A strap slide from Bracon Ash in the form of a satyr's head (HER 29308, NMS-306471, Fig. 7, no. 45) closely parallels another from Great Walsingham except that it faces right and not left.[106] These objects are generally associated with the military but they would still have made suitable votives and the presence of these two at sites which have yielded other material of a religious significance suggests that this may have been their final function. An example from West Dereham (HER 44106) features a facing bust of Silenus, the companion of Bacchus and his satyrs. A similar piece, accompanied by a sketch in the records, is from Hockwold (HER 5351).

Other similar strap slides, one a satyr head example, the other decorated with the head of a large cat, presumably a leopard, have been sold on ebay in recent years. Described as having been found in Norfolk, the fact that they have neither a firm provenance nor have been seen in hand by the author means, sadly, that they cannot meaningfully contribute to this paper.[107] Another, taking the form of the snarling head of a big cat described as having been found in the Norwich area and now in a private collection, is perhaps worth including here (Fig. 7, no. 46). This and the others must originally have formed part of harness suites featuring Silenus, satyr and panther heads.

A rather appealing horse head from the Bracon Ash site mentioned above (HER 29308, NMS-0050A3, Fig. 7, no. 47) almost certainly has a votive significance. The flat back demonstrates that it was originally some kind of mount; it is broken at the neck and so it is uncertain whether it would have formed the head of a horse or a hippocamp. The execution is somewhat naive but forceful, conveying very well the nature of its subject.

A remarkable object, probably best described as the mount from the rim of a vessel although it could perhaps have functioned as a pendant, was recovered from Wicklewood (NWHCM 1983.43.7). This depicts the facing head of an elephant and its significance is difficult to understand. It could belong to the secular realm although it is perhaps more likely that the vessel of which it formed a part was connected to the worship of an Eastern cult. Interestingly, the elephant was associated with Bacchus.

Terminals in the shape of human or animal heads, probably from wands or sceptres, form a particular class of object. Some of these have in the past been assigned to the medieval period but it is far more likely that they are of Roman date. The one example in the form of a god's head, from Carleton Rode (HER 34589)[108], depicts a helmeted bust instantly identifiable as Mars. It is paralleled by a number of similar mounts mainly from the Fenland depicting imperial personages briefly discussed below.

Of the zoomorphic examples, one, with a head best described as resembling a griffin from Wickmere (HER 28524, NWHCM 2002.80, Fig. 2, no. 48) is reasonably closely paralleled by another, more bird-like in that it seems to lack the ears of the first example, from Attleborough (HER 33179). Wickmere, in north-east Norfolk, falls within the area where the corvid figurines discussed above were found. Griffins were associated with Apollo who, in the guise of Sol, was worshipped as a god of the sun. Thus, this object may connect in some way with the mount in the form of a god of the heavens from the Felmingham hoard as well as the corvid figurines themselves, ravens also having been sacred to Apollo.

---

[102] See Talbot 2006 for a corpus of this series
[103] Gurney 1996, p. 391, fig. 2C
[104] Gurney 2002, p. 157
[105] Davies 1996, p. 382, fig. 3
[106] Bagnall Smith 1999, p. 30, no. 12

[107] A number of other objects with Bacchic iconography, including at least one panther figurine, have been noted on ebay, all sold by the same dealer based in South Norfolk. It is unfortunate that they cannot be included here
[108] Rogerson and Ashley 2008, p. 429, fig. 8

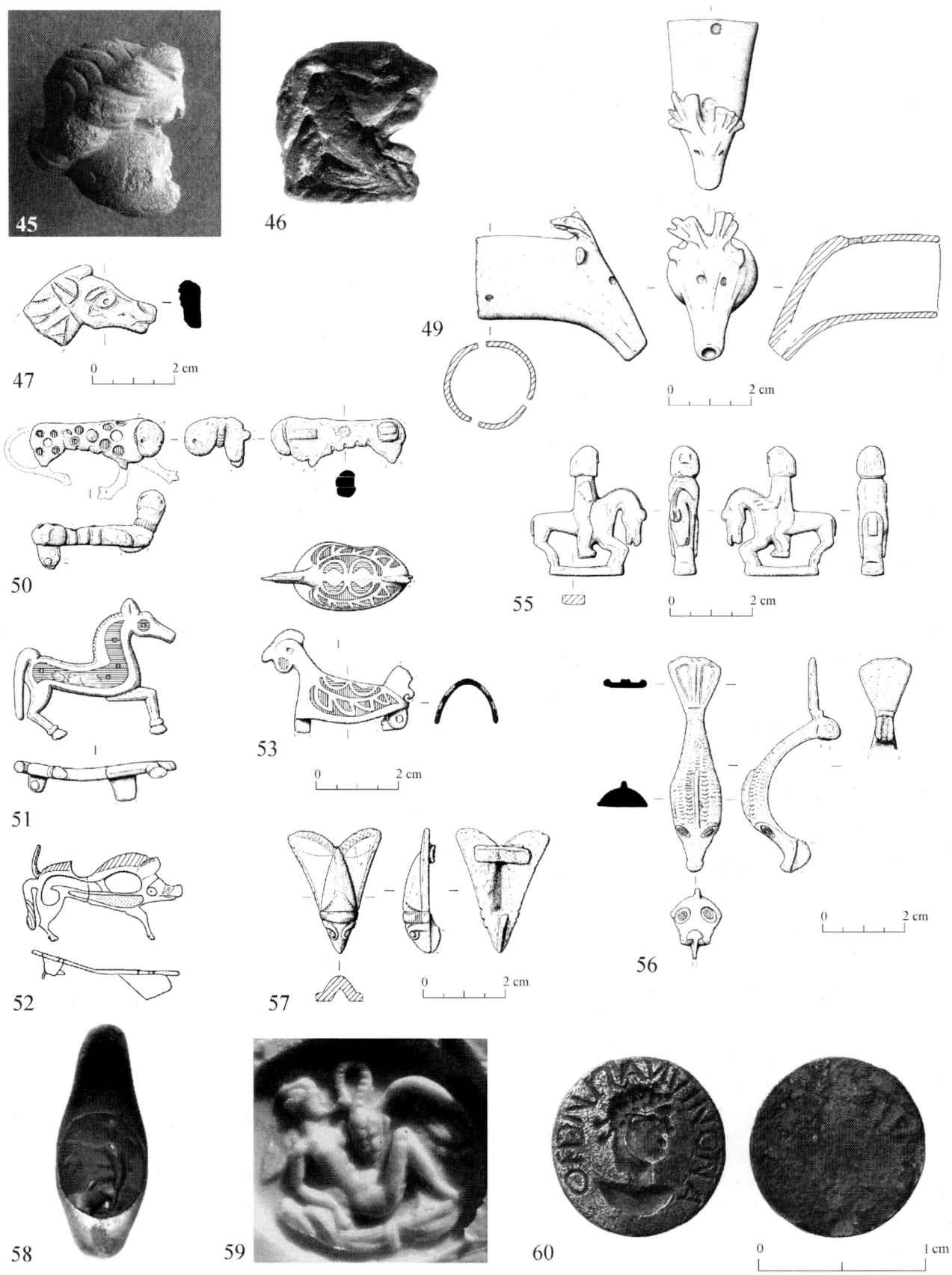

Fig. 7, 45 Satyr's head strap slide, Bracon Ash (length 26mm), 46 leopard head strap slide, Norwich area (length 18mm), 47 Horse head, Bracon Ash, 49 Stag's head staff terminal, Attleborough, 50 Leopard brooch, Bracon Ash, 51 Horse brooch, Hockwold, 52 Boar brooch, Hockwold, 53 Chicken brooch, Hockwold, 55 Horse and rider figurine, Warham, 56 Brooch in the form of a dolphin, Quidenham, 57 Cicada-like brooch, Pulham St. Mary, 58 Silver ring, cornelian intaglio with satyr, Weybourne, 59 Impression of seal ring with Leda and the Swan, Walsingham (length 10mm), 60 Silver ring bezel, Swaffham area (All NHES)

Another terminal also, like the second mount just mentioned, from Attleborough (HER 30102, NMS-6FF7C4, NWHCM 2013.281, Fig. 7, no. 49), but this time in the form of a stag is interesting.[109] The stag was associated with Diana, Silvanus and the Celtic god Cernunnos and it may be that this sceptre was used in the worship of one of those gods. The stag was also used in the later Roman period as the badge of the province of *Britannia Superior* as is attested by a lead sealing from Burgh Castle.[110] Alternatively, as woodland animals, stags may have been connected with Faunus. Attleborough is no great distance from Thetford.

A bull's head with its neck forming a socket for a wooden wand or staff found at Colkirk (HER 30867) most probably comprises another of these animal-headed terminals.[111] The bull had associations with a number of gods and it is probably unwise to try to speculate on the significance of this piece.

A wand or staff terminal from Walsingham (HER 29924, NMS-04B3C5) in the shape of a duck recalls Green's argument that this bird seems to have been associated with a water cult with connections to the sun and healing.[112] Many other small three-dimensional duck mounts are known which may or may not have a connection here such as examples from Dereham (HER 42555)[113], Ditchingham (HER 29457), Little Cressingham (HER 35101, NMS49), Whissonsett (HER 31800) and Wymondham (HER 33031).

Zoomorphic brooches

Zoomorphic brooches, as the name suggests, are a type of plate brooch in the form of birds or animals.[114] Most are three-dimensional with enamelled cells decorating the body. They seem to have appeared in the early second century and production most probably continued well into the third century. Many species are represented and it is likely that these objects had a religious significance, either as marks of affiliation to a particular deity with whom the creature was connected,[115] or as a stand-in for the sacrifice of a living animal.[116] They could be said to have represented a more sophisticated form of votive than the earlier brooches and certainly the bright enamelling apparent on many examples would have made them attractive and eye-catching objects when in their original state. With this emphasis on vivid colours they can be said to belong very much to the aesthetic of the third century and the more elaborate examples, if they do not belong to that period, certainly foreshadow it.

Three brooches are known in the form of leopards, one from Bunwell (HER 24456), one from Wighton (HER 3980) and another from Bracon Ash (HER 29308, NMS-E44886, Fig. 7, no. 50). Mackreth ascribes these a Continental origin which fits with their rarity as British finds.[117] It is interesting that only four others are recorded on the PAS database.[118] As with the figurine from Hainford mentioned above, these probably have Bacchic connections.

An incomplete and corroded brooch from Wreningham (HER 28868, NMS-3E18E5) probably represents a lion. Like the leopards discussed above, its pelt is decorated with small, circular enamelled cells but its more thickset neck suggests a mane and hence a lion. A flatter, more one-dimensional brooch from Long Stratton (HER 34468) is not enamelled. The chariot of Cybele was drawn by lions although the animal was also associated with the demigod Hercules on account of his defeating the Nemean lion.

A plate brooch in the form of a horse from Fincham (HER 33009) carries enamelled cells and is to all extents and purposes identical to a fragmentary specimen from Stanfield (HER 30600).[119] Another example with blue enamelling from Hockwold (HER 52661, Fig. 7, no. 51) is similar. The horse could reference either the Celtic goddess Epona or the Roman god Neptune. The large amount of Iron Age horse furniture from Norfolk might suggest that the association was with Epona or an Icenian version thereof but it should also be remembered that the Caistor *defixio* mentioned above was addressed to Neptune.

Stag brooches are rare and only two are known from Norfolk. One, with incised decoration from Hockering (HER 34934),[120] is probably of Roman rather than Saxon date; the other, an enamelled example from Hockwold (HER 5587, NMS-365796), is certainly Roman and adds to the large number of zoomorphic brooches from this temple site.[121] Stags were associated with Diana, a goddess whose worship is not particularly attested in Roman Britain but could also have been locally connected with other gods, not least Faunus, given his woodland domain. Like the leopards, these brooches were probably manufactured on the Continent.

Another enamelled plate brooch from Hockwold (HER 5351, Fig. 7, no. 52), this time in the form of a boar, may pertain to the worship of Hercules, the defeat of the Erymanthian boar being one of the demigod's labours. Depiction of boars had a long tradition in Iron Age Norfolk, however, with the animal being used on Icenian coins

---

[109] Rogerson and Ashley 2010, p. 128, fig. 16 and Worrell 2010, p. 428
[110] Gurney 1995a
[111] Gurney 1995b, p. 224
[112] Green 1978, p. 24
[113] Gurney 2006, p. 117, fig. 3E
[114] Johns 1996, pp. 173-7
[115] See Crummy 2007, Ferris 2012, p. 35, and Marsden 2012a, pp. 60-1
[116] Marsden 2012a, p. 60

[117] Mackreth 2011, p. 185. It should also be noted that many modern fakes of this type exist, including some rather unconvincing examples in silver. The English provenances ascribed to them should not allow their acceptance
[118] Another, offered for sale on the website Timeline Originals, is also described as having been found in Norfolk
[119] Gurney 2001, p. 700
[120] Gurney 2001, p. 699
[121] See Rogerson and Ashley 2012, p. 411, fig. 22, for an example of Anglo-Saxon date from Sedgeford (HER 1600)

and also represented in the form of several figurines.[122] It appears to have been a totemic animal in the Icenian realms and, given this, could have been connected with Faunus himself in this area. Nonetheless, like many of the other zoomorphic brooches, it is possibly continental in origin and so we should probably be wary of ascribing a local significance to its presence in Norfolk.

Brooches representing hounds comprise a well-known group. As Johns and Mackreth both note, when incomplete they can sometimes be difficult to differentiate from hares but examples that are certainly hounds have been found at Beeston-with-Bittering (HER 4084, NMS-D15192), Howe (HER 15195), and Kirstead (HER 51672, described as a hare, NMS-E94040). Given that almost all examples that may be either hounds or hares have been closely studied by the author this is a small number although hare brooches do seem to have been far more popular than those depicting hounds in the rest of Britain.

Hare (or rabbit) brooches are encountered more frequently in Norfolk. The type most usually encountered in Britain is of a flat form with enamelled cells as represented by examples from Aldeby (HER 41979, NMS-D860D3), Binham (HER 24150), Bracon Ash (HER 28732), Brettenham (no HER number recorded), East Walton (HER 30884)[123], Fincham (HER 25093), Great Walsingham (HER 2024, NMS-6BCFE5), Hindringham (HER 29133), Hockwold (HER 5587), Kenninghall (HER 37284), Narborough (HER 3907), Quidenham (HER 30517, NMS-1DCFC6) and two from Weybourne (HER 29168, NMS-A329A3).[124] Flat mounts of broadly similar form have surfaced at Shipdham (HER 35800)[125] and Tattersett (HER 31569) whilst a rectangular plate brooch with a hare described in enamel was found at Denton (HER 35976).

These examples with enamelled cells are most likely British but tinned examples of what is probably a rabbit rather than a hare, of a more three-dimensional form, with two small rabbits picked out in enamel on the chest are probably Continental; examples of this type have been noted from Beeston-with-Bittering (HER 4085, NMS-011075), Langley with Hardley (HER 24003), and Narford (HER 3974). The group as a whole has a widespread distribution (Map 4). As mentioned above, the hare was sacred to Venus and these items may have had some religious significance. It is easy to see these items not only as colourful dress accessories but as small votives. They may have provided alternatives to the pipeclay Venus figurines discussed above or, given the collapse of that industry in the late second or early third century, they may have replaced them.

An interesting type of brooch depicts a bird best described as some sort of raptor grasping a hare or perhaps a rabbit.[126]

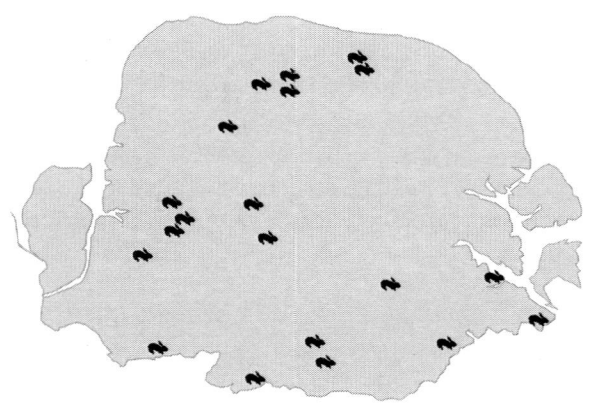

MAP 4 DISTRIBUTION OF HARE BROOCHES

An example excavated from Hockwold HER 5587, NWHCM 1961.199.57) has been supplemented by others from Burgh and Tuttington (HER 28657),[127] Hillington (HER 20467) and Witton (HER 7023, NMS-116425). The device probably alludes to the all-conquering power of death and, as Crummy has suggested for the sandal brooches, these may have had similar significance.[128]

As with cockerel figurines, cockerel or hen brooches have been found in some numbers and their distribution is spread across Britain.[129] These are fully three-dimensional and are best described as representing a broody hen which would have been viewed from above when worn. They are probably a British product since they do not appear to be found in any numbers on the Continent. Indeed, Britain appears to have been a centre for the production of enamelled metalwork in the Roman period, undoubtedly the continuation of an Iron Age tradition.[130]

Like the figurines, the cockerel brooches are undoubtedly connected with Mercury. With their enamelled plumage they may have served simply as colourful brooches but a votive connection cannot be discounted. Two distinct types occur, one with two pairs of tip-to-tip crescents decorating the bird's back and triangular cells forming a border, the other with the wing feathers defined by enamelled cells.[131] In Norfolk examples have been found at Ashwellthorpe (HER 30205), Beeston-with-Bittering (HER 42699, NMS-912690), Brettenham (no HER number recorded), Caistor St Edmund (HER 12575), Cranwich (HER 25479), Forncett (HER 31418), Hockwold (HER 52672, NMS-40D170, Fig. 7, no. 53), Marsham (HER 33240),[132] Shouldham Thorpe (HER 37136, NMS1678), Thetford (no HER number recorded), Warham (HER 55366) and Weybourne (HER 29806).[133] A flat, one-dimensional example was recovered at Warham (HER 1826).

---

[122] Davies 2011, pp. 59-62
[123] Gurney 1995b, p. 225
[124] Johns 1996, pp. 174-5
[125] Gurney 2003, p. 362
[126] Mackreth 2011, p. 184

[127] Gurney 1994, p. 110
[128] Crummy 2007
[129] Mackreth 2011, p. 184
[130] Kunzl 2012, pp. 9-11
[131] The two types are illustrated in Mackreth 2011, plate 126, nos. 14798 and 8012
[132] Gurney 2002, p. 155
[133] Gurney 1994, p. 110

Zoomorphic brooches in the form of ducks swimming on the surface of the water are common and the distribution of the two major types appears to be weighted towards the eastern side of England.[134] Like the cockerels or hens discussed above, they are usually enamelled and these appear to have been a British product. One type has bands of enamel running along the duck's body, the other crescentiform decoration delineating plumage. Examples are known from Besthorpe (HER 29171), East Walton (HER 34888, NMS-007A94), Feltwell (HER 21137), Fincham (HER 41327), Great Walsingham (HER 21106), Keswick (HER 9714), Newton Flotman (HER 32289),[135] Salthouse (HER 6294), Scole (HER 37706) and Great Walsingham (HER 2024). An odd example which also appears to be swimming but with its wings outspread was found at Lynford (HER 40854)[136] whilst another, of rather unusual appearance but still with enamelled plumage came to light at Marham (HER 29262, NMS-E1A9D6).

Their significance is difficult to grasp, since ducks are not obviously sacred to any particular deity. Duck head finials occur on other items from Roman Norfolk, notably on the Crownthorpe cups dated to the earliest years of Roman rule in Britain[137], and, of course, on many of the spoons from the Thetford Treasure. As water birds they would have been very familiar to the denizens of the low-lying counties of Eastern Britain. As we have seen above, Green argued that ducks may be linked to a water cult with associations to the sun and healing.[138] Here the solar association speculated for the ravens mentioned above may be significant. Did this sun and water cult recognise ravens as the agents of the sun god Apollo and also ducks as birds native to water? Another possibility is that the interpretation of their flight may have placed ducks in the category of suitable subjects for augury. Faunus' oracular powers may provide a link here.

In terms of find spots, their distribution is widespread, if weighted slightly towards the south of the county (Map 5). The hen brooches also occur across Norfolk (Map 6).

MAP 5 DISTRIBUTION OF DUCK BROOCHES

As mentioned above, both ducks and hens are known in some numbers from outside Norfolk in any case; within the county the distribution map could well reflect where metal detecting is taking place rather than anything else.

Other brooches depicting birds in flight, perhaps doves, occur from Ashwellthorpe (HER 30205), Heacham (HER 37217, NMS-98DFC5), Hillington (HER 30512), Mattishall (HER 36629, NMS-119B46) and Wicklewood (HER 8897). Unlike the other bird brooches these are generally not enamelled. They are probably of Continental origin but British manufacture for at least some is also possible.

Other zoomorphic bird brooches are rarer, probably a testament to a Continental origin or the relative lack of adherents to the deities which they represented or both. An owl brooch, rare in Britain, was found at Caistor St Edmund (HER 9791).[139] The owl was sacred to Minerva and it would seem likely that this brooch was either worn by an adherent of the goddess or given to her as a gift. Although Minerva was a popular goddess in Roman Britain, her owl is seldom encountered. Interestingly, this brooch is identical to the example illustrated in Hattatt's corpus, also allegedly found in Norfolk.[140]

A flat brooch from Fincham (HER 33343) was probably intended to represent a peacock with its enamelled tail feathers displayed. The peacock was sacred to Juno and the goddess' apparent lack of popularity in Britain is probably a reason why this is so far the only example to have been recovered from Norfolk. It is probably of Continental origin.

Another example from Brettenham (HER 41001), again a flat plate brooch, is inlaid with cells of blue enamel and was probably intended to portray an eagle. A fragment of what may have been a broadly similar specimen but decorated with red and blue enamel was found at Narford (HER 3974, NMS-56BD25). They are without any other parallels from Norfolk and again, appear to be of Continental origin as seems to be the case with most (if not all) of these one-dimensional bird brooches.

The so-called horse and rider brooches form an important sub-category of the zoomorphic group and have recently been the subject of a study by Ruth Fillery-Travis.[141] A large number were recovered from the Hockwold-cum-Wilton site (HER 5587), eight during excavations in 1961[142] and a further two during subsequent metal-detecting (NMS-4B4422 and NMS-36EA72). Two examples of the type have also been found at Beeston-with-Bittering (HER 4084, NMS-9B1C76 and NMS-B9CE17, Fig. 2, no. 54) whilst single specimens have come from Brampton (HER 1124), Brampton (HER 35860, NMS-E66C22), Brettenham (no HER number

---

[134] McReth 2011, pp. 183-4
[135] Gurney 1998, p. 326
[136] Gurney 2005, p. 742
[137] Davies 2011, pp. 64-5
[138] Green 1978, p. 24

[139] Gurney 2003, p. 360
[140] Hattatt 1987, 1154
[141] Fillery-Travis 2012. Also see Mackreth 2011, pp. 181-2 and pp. 241-2
[142] Mackreth in Gurney 1986, pp. 65-7

recorded), Burgh Castle (HER 24659), Caistor St Edmund (HER 9787), Cawston (HER 33889, NMS-B78DC6), Fritton (HER 24463), Great Walsingham (HER 28254)[143], Harling (HER 51752), Langley-with-Hardley (HER 21289), Long Stratton (HER 12513), Mattishall (HER 25729), Quidenham (HER 31405)[144], Stoke Ferry (HER 53725), Stoke Ferry (HER 40006, NMS-C071E3), West Rudham (HER 37209, NMS1024), Wicklewood (HER 18111, NMS-303AE2) and Wighton (HER 1113, NMS-EE0274)).

The significance of these brooches has been debated at some length. It is surely the case, given the large numbers found at temple sites that they were primarily intended as votives. As brooches they may also have served to represent marks of affiliation to the rider god as well as being used as offerings. Guy de la Bedoyere's idea that they might have represented in themselves a pilgrimage or journey is interesting but not very convincing.[145] Johns argues that they may have functioned as souvenirs of a visit to a shrine in the same way as did Medieval pilgrim badges.[146] Their concentration at religious sites must have some bearing on interpreting their function, however, and an interpretation centring on their deposition at these locations as votives is surely the most compelling.

Horse and rider statuettes represent a well known and distinctive group of figurines, being confined in general to an area spreading up from Cambridgeshire into Leicestershire, Northamptonshire and South Lincolnshire. Recent finds have reinforced this distribution and, as far as is known, none have thus far been discovered in Norfolk. The only possible exception is a strange figurine from Warham (HER 55366, NMS-32FEA3, Fig. 7, no. 55) which is, however, so unlike the other statuettes both in size and execution that it is doubtful whether it depicts the same deity. Miranda Green commented on the fact that the horseman cult was centred on the territory of the Catuvellauni and the southern Corieltauvi.[147]

Given the close iconographic relationship between the brooches and statuettes, we may presume that the same deity was the subject of both types of object. The brooches have a far wider distribution but this is most likely due to the fact that they, being smaller, more portable and also functional as dress accessories, travelled far beyond the heartland of the horse and rider cult. The identity of this god has been debated at some length. Green identified the figure as a Celtic form of Mars, a suggestion which Fillery-Travis is wary of accepting although she puts forward no alternatives.[148] Ferris argues that the type represents a celebration of what he terms 'hyper-masculinity' and links it with phallic imagery.[149] The author finds this argument less than compelling.

It is probably best not to try to force too exact an identification on the deity. Celtic gods are often equated with Roman ones but the two figures are rarely exact counterparts. In Roman Britain the equation of one god with another was probably rather loose. His many adherents would have understood who the Rider God was; for us, it is sufficient to conclude that he was a popular deity who must have stood high in the pantheon of the Catuvellauni and Southern Corieltauvi. It is probably best simply to refer to him as the Catuvellaunian Rider God.

The large number of horse and rider brooches from the Roman temple site at Hockwold is illuminating and must point to the existence of a shrine to the god there. Given Hockwold's location, where Icenian territory met that of the Catuvellauni, this would come as no surprise. However, although some brooches travelled into the territory of the Iceni, the lack of any statuettes depicting the Catuvellaunian Rider God implies that the worship of this deity did not gain much favour in Norfolk. Find spots of the brooches are widespread across the county (Map 7).

At least 90 horse and rider brooches, an enormous number, have been recovered from a site near Bosworth in Leicestershire; again, like Hockwold, this must have been a religious centre with a large shrine to the Rider God. Given the vast numbers involved, it would not be unreasonable to speculate that this was probably the major centre of the Rider God cult in Britain.

Brooches in the form of other members of the animal kingdom are reasonably well known but were probably mainly Continental in their manufacture and certainly are not really represented in the Norfolk record at all. A fragmentary frog brooch from Oxborough (HER 33549) is the only one of this type of which the author is currently aware.

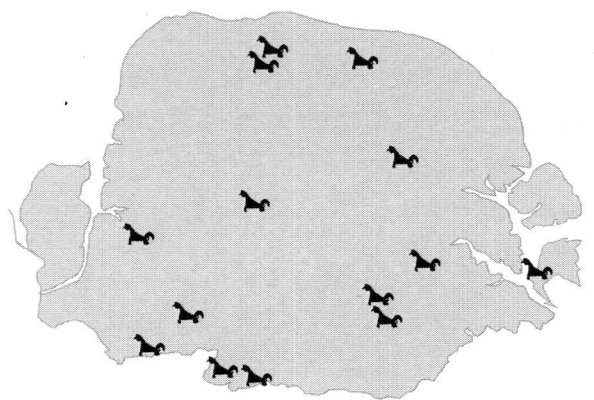

MAP 6 DISTRIBUTION OF COCKEREL BROOCHES

---

[143] Gurney 1994, p. 110
[144] Gurney 2001, p. 699
[145] De la Bedoyere 2002, p. 130
[146] Johns 1996, p. 174
[147] Green 1977, pp. 305-6
[148] Fillery-Travis 2012, pp. 8-9

[149] Ferris 2012, p. 39

As regards the realm of the oceans, a fine example of a dolphin from Quidenham (HER 58452, NMS-C780B3, Fig. 7, no. 56) is another rarity for Britain. Green points out that dolphins could represent the journey of the soul to the Blessed Isles and this may explain their significance.[150] A similar role has been posited for the class of brooches in the form of sandals.[151] Fish brooches have been found at Binham (HER 24150), Little Cressingham (NWHCM 1950.179.6.2), Wacton (HER 30397) and Weybourne (HER 29097)[152]. Another example was uncovered during the excavations at Brancaster.[153] Rectangular plate brooches depicting a fish have been found at Scole (HER 35320)[154] and Spixworth (HER 20914). If these fish brooches had a religious meaning then it is somewhat uncertain but they may have been connected to Neptune.

One category that may have been British is that of the so-called fly brooches. To what extent these are zoomorphic is debateable but some certainly do appear to have been intended to represent the insect. Examples are not numerous but two are known from Seething (HER 40302) and single specimens from Caistor St Edmund (NWHCM 1939.77.1), Narford (HER 3974), and Weeting-with-Broomhill (HER 19722). Wasp-like examples have been found at Hindringham (HER 28470)[155] and Tatterset (HER 31569)[156] and one that is best described as being in the form of a cicada at Pulham St Mary (HER 54885, NMS-0066D6, Fig. 7, no. 57). The significance of the group as a whole (if there was any) is difficult to understand but Crummy may be right in her suggestion that they reference Mercury.[157]

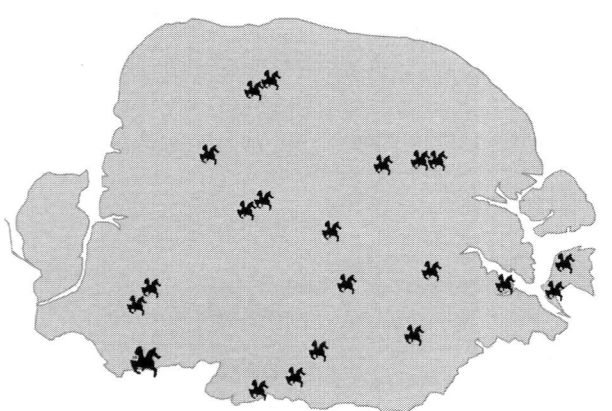

MAP 7 DISTRIBUTION OF HORSE AND RIDER BROOCHES

Other material

Bracelets, and particularly rings, in the form of confronted snake heads were a common item of jewellery in the Roman period. A large number of silver examples, at least 42, were present in the Snettisham jeweller's hoard.[158] Two bracelets and three rings were recovered from the temple site at Great Walsingham (HER 2024).[159] The snake, on account of the fact that it sheds its skin, was regarded as self-renewing and serpents are associated with Salus, the personification of health. These rings (and bracelets) must have been a common sight judging by the number that have appeared over the years. Examples of rings (or fragments thereof) are known from Brettenham (HER 5653), Caistor St Edmund (NWHCM 1976.303.2), East Walton (HER 29273), Fincham (HER 25162), Foxley (HER 50278), Fransham (HER 20508), Hockwold (NWHCM 1962.396.494), Merton (HER 30988)[160], Narford (HER 3974), Quidenham (HER 13700), Scole (HER 21485, two examples, one complete and a fragment), Snettisham (HER 28450)[161], Wreningham (HER 28868) and Yelverton (HER 33109)[162], and bracelets (or fragments) from Bracon Ash (HER 29900)[163], Brettenham (HER 5653), Burnham Market (HER 18496)[164], Hockwold (HER 5587) and Weeting-with-Broomhill (NWHCM 1959.26) but there are probably many more in the records.

Having surveyed and discussed the objects depicting deities in the round (or at least partially in the round) some consideration of other items depicting gods and goddesses is desirable. The most significant category is that of finger rings, both those with engraved bezels and those set with intaglio gems, as well as the large number of unset signet stones from the so-called Snettisham Roman jeweller's hoard that relate to the divinities which have featured above.[165] The Snettisham assemblage contained a large number (127) of rather crudely-engraved cornelians.

It is not surprising, given the religious artefacts we have already seen, that there is a preponderance of rings and ringstones depicting Mercury. A silver ring from the Roman temple site at Great Walsingham[166] is inscribed with the letters MER whilst two other rings from the same site are set with repousse oval plaques depicting the deity.[167] A ring inscribed MERC was found at North Creake (HER 1913), another with the dedication DEO MER at Saham Toney (HER 4697) and a third with DEM at Narford (HER 51245, NMS-DE40B2). Five of the cornelian intaglios from the Snettisham Roman jeweller's hoard, including one set into

---

[150] Green 1977, p. 302
[151] Crummy 2007, pp. 226-7 and Marsden 2012, 61-2
[152] Gurney 1995b, p. 225
[153] Mackreth in Hinchliffe and Sparey Green 1985, p. 203
[154] Gurney 2001, p. 699
[155] Gurney 1992, p. 367
[156] Gurney 2003, p. 362
[157] Crummy 2007, pp. 227-8

[158] Johns 1997, pp. 34-40
[159] Bagnall Smith 1999, pp. 38-9, nos. 38-42
[160] Gurney 2002, p. 155
[161] Gurney 2003, p. 362
[162] Gurney 2005, p. 742
[163] Gurney 1997, p. 542
[164] Gurney 1997, p. 542
[165] See Henig 2007 for a corpus of gems from Romano-British sites and Johns 1996, pp. 79-83 for a useful introduction to the iconography on Roman-British intaglios. Also Marsden 2009 for a corpus of Norfolk finds from 2002-8
[166] Bagnall Smith 1999, p. 32, no. 18
[167] Bagnall Smith 1999, pp. 35-6; nos. 29-30

a silver ring, are engraved with figures of Mercury and demonstrate the god's popularity as a device for signets.[168] Other intaglios from the county also show Mercury, for example a glass example imitating the gemstone nicolo from Grimston (HER 3579).[169]

Mars was represented on two of the Snettisham cornelians, one mounted in a silver ring[170] and one unmounted.[171] One of the two rings from Walsingham described as depicting him in fact shows an armed figure of Minerva.[172] As suggested by the relative lack of figurines of Mars from Norfolk discussed above, he does not seem to have been an overly popular god in the Icenian dominions.

Satyrs occur on five of the intaglios from the Snettisham hoard[173]. Perhaps what is most interesting is that three of these had been mounted into silver rings, implying that they were ready for collection or they were a popular subject for signet stones which would not be long in stock[174]. Only seventeen of the Snettisham cornelians had been mounted; the satyr gems form a relatively high percentage of this total. Other gems, a cornelian from Weybourne (HER 29423, Fig. 7, no. 58) and a nicolo glass from Wacton (HER 42714) also feature satyrs.[175]

A few rings attest what might be termed more esoteric beliefs. A silver ring from Pulham Market (HER 52999, NMS-E3D804), with a depiction in relief of an eagle drinking from a cup proffered by a small figure, references the myth of Jupiter and Ganymede. This has a religious dimension, the themes of metamorphosis and apotheosis being well-known and obvious to anyone with cultural leanings. A similar legend, the seduction of Leda by Jupiter in the form of a swan, is illustrated on an intaglio of nicolo glass set in a silver ring bezel from Pentney (HER 15170, NWHCM 2007.269)[176] and on one of the Walsingham rings (HER 2024, Fig. 7, no. 59).[177]

Two moulded glass intaglios set into third-century gilded oval plate brooches may also feature a tale of metamorphosis, the transformation of either Daphne into a laurel tree whilst attempting to escape Apollo or that of the nymph Ambrosia, turned into a vine that she might attack King Lycurgus. One of these was recovered from Narford (HER 3974)[178], the other from Warham (no HER number recorded). A number of similar examples are known from Britain, including a fine example from Bronington in Wales (NMGW-6A45F5).[179] Interesting as these may be, however, they go beyond the scope of this paper and the light they may cast on religious or quasi-religious beliefs in late Roman Britain will be more fully considered elsewhere.

Conclusions: The Gods of Roman Norfolk

The gods worshipped in the areas neighbouring Roman Norfolk have already been discussed briefly. It is clear from the concentration of TOT rings in Lincolnshire that Toutatis was the principal god of the Corieltauvi. The god we have styled the Rider God dominates the lands of the Catuvellauni with what must have been a significant shrine at Hockwold, a site lying near the border between the lands of that tribe and those of the Iceni.

Looking at the pre-Roman period, analysis by Daphne Nash Briggs of the legends on the inscribed series of Icenian coins and some of the subject matter on the coinage as a whole, suggests that the Iceni's origins lay across the Channel.[180] This might well have implications for the nature of the deities that were worshipped in the area during the Roman period but for the moment it is perhaps better to consider the evidence in hand from the Roman period itself.

Within Norfolk, we have interesting groupings. It must surely be significant that examples of the raven figurines discussed above have only so far been recovered from an area of north-east Norfolk. This suggests a closely defined area in which a particular god held sway. Most likely this was a local cult with its origins quite probably going back to the Iron Age. The god Apollo, or a local version of the god, seems to have been the subject of this worship.

The Faunus mounts are rather scattered and the relatively small number does not make any argument on their distribution very compelling. Nonetheless, none are known from the northern coastal area just as none of the raven figurines are known from the central or southern part of the county. It is interesting that these two groups of material seem to have different distributions and might point to different areas following different deities.

Here Western Norfolk is illuminating. We know that the area was rich in the Roman period, with villas spreading south along the Peddars Way, and much metal detecting has been carried out there but there seems to be a complete lack of anything that can be connected to the worship of Faunus or Bacchus. It may well be that people on the Fen edge and the surrounding area held beliefs which were very different from those of the men and women dwelling in North East Norfolk and those in South Norfolk.

To the west, into the central Fenland, it has been speculated that a large imperial estate occupied much of this area and was centred on Stonea in Cambridgeshire.[181] Interestingly, a number of sceptre terminals in the form of what appear to

---

[168] Johns 1997, p. 90, nos. 174-7 and 95, no. 223 for the mounted example
[169] Marsden 2009, pp. 530-1
[170] Johns 1997, p. 98, no. 234
[171] Johns 1997, p. 91, no. 185
[172] Bagnall Smith 1999, p. 37, no. 35
[173] Johns 1997, p. 91, nos. 181-2
[174] Johns 1997, p. 96, nos. 226-7 and p. 98, no. 233
[175] For the Wacton paste see Marsden 2009, p. 535, and 2012, p. 63
[176] Marsden 2009, pp. 532-4
[177] Bagnall Smith 1999, p. 36, no. 32
[178] Marsden 2009, pp. 531-2
[179] Hattatt 1987, p. 258, fig. 80

[180] Nash-Briggs 2011
[181] Potter 1981, Jackson and Potter 1996 and Davies 2008, p. 194

be imperial busts, including a recently discovered example depicting a late first or early second-century empress[182], may suggest that worship of the imperial cult was strong on this estate. These objects are almost unknown outside this area of Eastern England; nor do they seem to occur in the rest of the Roman Empire.

Snettisham, an enormously important centre in the late Iron Age appears to have become an insignificant backwater in the Roman period. Certainly, the small number of Roman coins from the site compared to the rich deposits of coins and torcs from the time before the conquest suggests that there was a deliberate attempt to deregulate Snettisham as a religious centre. Here the importance of Great Walsingham in the Roman period is probably significant, this centre being promoted at the expense of Snettisham.[183] The setting up of a large Imperial estate encompassing the lands to the south-west of Snettisham may have been a way of ensuring that old beliefs were submerged under the worship of the *Domus Divina*, the Imperial house.[184]

What is interesting in the context of Roman Norfolk is the relative lack of images of Bacchus. Taken in conjunction with the large amount of material depicting Faunus, we should consider the possibility that, in Norfolk, Faunus stood in for Bacchus and it was he who led the procession of satyrs, panthers and maenads who constituted the entourage normally headed by the other god.

There has been practically nothing found in Norfolk to suggest a Christian presence in the Roman period unlike the neighbouring counties of Suffolk and Cambridgeshire. The dearth of explicitly Christian items is remarkable and strongly suggests that the area comprising Norfolk was, on the whole, rather unreceptive to the new religion.

Recently, one find has surfaced near Swaffham has surfaced to show that at least one inhabitant of Roman Norfolk had embraced the faith (HER 30879, NMS-0B5BB1, Fig. 7, no. 60). This is a ring bezel engraved with a male bust and the encircling inscription (*Antonius, may you live in God*) is explicitly Christian. Another ring, in gold from Brancaster, also has a Christian association.[185] Both are very late in date, however, perhaps as late as the early fifth century, and suggest that, even as Roman authority was collapsing in Britain, most of Norfolk's inhabitants stuck stubbornly to the gods of their ancestors. Here, the countryside was still inhabited, at least in the minds of its people, by the cavorting Satyr and the prowling Leopard with Ravens hovering in the skies above.

Acknowledgements

This paper has been a result of the diligent reporting of many objects by many metal detectorists, too numerous to list here by name, and it is they who have made it possible. It has also been a pleasure to discuss objects, both with Andrew Rogerson and Steven Ashley, sometimes over coffee or a meal but more often during trips in a car to one of the detector clubs we all visit every month. Others have also played their part, notably Martin Henig and Natasha Harlow for reading a draft of this paper. Both Martin Henig and Ralph Jackson have always been kind in offering their advice whilst discussions with Daphne Nash-Briggs have always provided a stimulating and original way of considering the role of Faunus in Roman Norfolk. I am also grateful to Natasha Harlow for keeping me informed of the finds from the recent Caistor St Edmund excavations and to Livia Roschdi for doing various tasks, most notably producing the distribution maps. The drawings are by Jason Gibbons with the exception of nos. 15, 32 and 37 by Sue White, no. 21 by Steven Ashley and no. 52 by Tony Gregory. Lastly, enormous thanks are due to Andrew Hall for producing the final figures from a daunting array of source material.

---

[182] Henig and Marsden forthcoming. For the earlier examples, see Toynbee 1963, pp. 124-5, nos. 2-5
[183] Marsden 2011, pp. 49-50
[184] Henig and Marsden forthcoming

[185] Henig 2007, pp. 186-7, no. 790

Bibliography

Allason-Jones, L. 1989, *Women in Roman Britain* (BMP, London)

Andrews, C. 2012, *Roman Seal-Boxes in Britain* (Archaeopress, Oxford)

Bagnall Smith, J. 1999, 'Votive objects and objects of votive significance from Great Walsingham, Norfolk', *Britannia* 30, pp. 21-56

Bird, J. 2011, 'Religion' in L. Allason-Jones (ed.) *Artefacts in Roman Britain. Their Purpose and Use* (Cambridge University Press), pp. 269-92

Boon, G.C. 1983, 'A priest's rattle of the third century A.D. from the Felmingham, Norfolk, find' *Antiquaries Journal* 63, pp. 363-4

Crummy, N. 1983, *The Roman small finds from excavations in Colchester 1971-9.* Colchester Archaeological Report 2

Crummy, N. 2007, 'Brooches and the Cult of Mercury' *Britannia* 38, pp. 225-30

Crummy, N. 2010, 'Bears and Coins: The Iconography of Protection in Late Roman Infant Burials', *Britannia* 41, pp. 37-93

Daubney, A. 2010, 'The Cult of Totatis: evidence for tribal identity in mid Roman Britain', (*BAR* 510 British Series), pp. 105-16

Davies, J.A, 1996, 'Romano-British Cult Objects from Norfolk – Some Recent Finds', *Norfolk Archaeology* 42, pp. 380-4

Davies, J.A, 2008, *The Land of Boudica*. (Oxbow)

Davies, J.A. 2011, 'Boars, Bulls and Norfolk's Celtic Menagerie' in J.A. Davies (ed), *The Iron Age in Northern East Anglia: New Work in the Land of the Iceni* (*BAR* 549 British Series), pp. 59-68

De La Bedoyere, G. 2002, *Gods with Thunderbolts: Religion in Roman Britain* (Tempus)

Ferris, I. 2012, *Roman Britain through its objects* (Amberley)

Fillery-Travis, R. 2012, 'Multidisciplinary analysis of Roman Horse-and-Rider brooches from Bosworth' in I. Schrufer-Kolb (ed.), *More than just numbers? The role of science in Roman archaeology. Journal of Roman Archaeology Supplementary Series* XX (Portsmouth), pp. 1-28

Gilbert, H.M. 1980, 'The Felmingham Hall Hoard, Norfolk', *Bulletin of the Board of Celtic Studies* 28, pp. 160-87

Green, C. 1977, 'Excavations in the Roman Kiln Field at Brampton, 1973-4' in *East Anglian Archaeology Report* 5, pp. 31-95

Green, M. 1977, 'Theriomorphism, and the role of Divine animals in Romano-British Cult Art' in J. Munby, and M. Henig (eds), *Roman Life and Art in Britain* (*BAR* 41 British Series), pp. 297-326

Green, M.J. 1978, *Small Cult Objects from the Military Areas of Roman Britain*. (*BAR* 52 British Series)

Gregory, A. 1986, 'The Bunwell Horse', *Britannia* 17, pp. 330-1

Grimal, P. 1986, *The Dictionary of Classical Mythology* (Blackwell, Oxford)

Gurney, D. 1986, *Settlement, Religion and Industry on the Fen-edge; Three Romano-British Sites in Norfolk*, East Anglian Archaeology 31

Gurney, D. (ed.) 1992, 'Archaeological finds in Norfolk in 1991', *Norfolk Archaeology* 41.iii, pp. 362-70

Gurney, D. (ed.) 1994, 'Archaeological finds in Norfolk in 1993', *Norfolk Archaeology* 42.i, pp. 104-15

Gurney, D. 1995a, 'A Roman Provincial Lead Seal from Burgh Castle', *Norfolk Archaeology* 42.ii, pp. 217-8

Gurney, D. (ed.) 1995b, 'Archaeological finds in Norfolk in 1994', *Norfolk Archaeology* 42.ii, pp. 221-9

Gurney, D. (ed.) 1996, 'Archaeological finds in Norfolk in 1995', *Norfolk Archaeology* 42.iii, pp. 387-96

Gurney, D. (ed.) 1997, 'Archaeological finds in Norfolk in 1996', *Norfolk Archaeology* 42.iv, pp. 539-46

Gurney, D. (ed.) 1998, 'Archaeological finds in Norfolk in 1997', *Norfolk Archaeology* 43.i, pp. 181-92

Gurney, D. (ed.) 1999, 'Archaeological finds in Norfolk in 1998', *Norfolk Archaeology* 43.ii, pp. 358-68

Gurney, D. (ed.) 2000, 'Archaeological finds in Norfolk in 1999', *Norfolk Archaeology* 43.iii, pp. 516-21

Gurney, D. (ed.) 2001, 'Archaeological finds in Norfolk in 2000', *Norfolk Archaeology* 43.iv, pp. 694-707

Gurney, D. (ed.) 2002, 'Archaeological finds in Norfolk in 2001', *Norfolk Archaeology* 44.i, pp. 149-62

Gurney, D. (ed.) 2003, 'Archaeological finds in Norfolk in 2002', *Norfolk Archaeology* 44.ii, pp. 356-68

Gurney, D. (ed.) 2004, 'Archaeological finds in Norfolk in 2003', *Norfolk Archaeology* 44.iii, pp. 563-73

Gurney, D. (ed.) 2005, 'Archaeological finds in Norfolk in 2004', *Norfolk Archaeology* 44.iv, pp. 736-50

Gurney, D. (ed.) 2006, 'Archaeological finds in Norfolk in 2005', *Norfolk Archaeology* 45.i, pp. 112-23

Gurney, D. (ed.) 2007, 'Archaeological finds in Norfolk in 2006', *Norfolk Archaeology* 45.ii, pp. 250-61

Hassall, M.W.C., and Tomlin, R.S.O. 1981, 'Thetford', *Britannia* 12, pp. 389-93

Hassall, M.W.C., and Tomlin, R.S.O. 1982, 'Caistor St Edmund', *Britannia* 13, pp. 408-9

Hassall, M.W.C., and Tomlin, R.S.O. 1994, 'Weeting with Broomhill', *Britannia* 25, pp. 296-7

Hattatt, R. 1987, *Brooches of Antiquity* (Oxford)

Henig, M.E. 1984, *Religion in Roman Britain* (Batsford, London)

Henig, M.E. 1995, *The Art of Roman Britain* (Batsford, London)

Henig, M.E. 2007, *A Corpus of Roman Engraved Gemstones from British Sites.* (*BAR* 8 British Series, 3rd Edition)

Henig, M.E. and Marsden, A.B. (forthcoming), 'A sceptre terminal in the form of a Flavian or Trajanic empress from Stonea, Cambs', *Oxford Journal of Archaeology*

Hinchliffe, J. and Sparey Green, C. 1985, *Excavations at Brancaster 1974 and 1977.* East Anglian Archaeology 23

Huskinson, J. 1994, *Corpus Signorum Imperii Romani 1.8, Roman Sculpture from Eastern England* (Oxford University Press)

Jackson, R.P.J., and Potter, T.W. 1996, *Excavations at Stonea, Cambridgeshire.* (British Museum Press, London)

Jackson, R.P.J. 2002, 'Baldock Area, Hertfordshire' in *Treasure Annual Report*, pp. 38-43

Johns, C. and Henig, M.E. 1991, 'A statuette of a herm of Priapus from Pakenham, Suffolk', *Antiquaries Journal* 71, pp. 236-9

Johns, C., and Potter, T. 1983, *The Thetford Treasure* (BMP, London)

Johns, C. 1996, *The Jewellery of Roman Britain* (London)

Johns, C. 1997, *The Snettisham Roman Jeweller's Hoard* (BMP, London)

Kiernan, P. 2009, *Miniature Votive Offerings in the Roman North-West* (Wiesbaden)

Kunzl, E. 2012, 'Enamelled Vessels of Roman Britain' in D. J. Breeze (ed), *The First Souvenirs. Enamelled Vessels from Hadrian's Wall* (Kendal), pp. 9-22

Laing, J. 1997, *Art and Society in Roman Bitain* (Sutton, Stroud)

Marsden, A.B. 2009, 'Roman Intaglios and Sealings from Norfolk, 2002-08', *Norfolk Archaeology* 45.iv, pp. 529-38

Marsden, A.B. 2011, 'The Iron Age coins from Snettisham' in J.A. Davies, (ed), *The Iron Age in Northern East Anglia: New Work in the Land of the Iceni* (BAR 549 British Series), pp. 49-58

Marsden, A.B. 2012a, 'Piety from the Ploughsoil: Religion in Roman Norfolk through recent metal-detector finds', in T.A. Heslop, E. Mellings, and M. Thofner (eds.), *Art, Faith and Place in East Anglia* (Boydell), pp. 50-65

Marsden, A.B. 2012b, 'Irregular Radiate Production in 3rd-Century Norfolk: An Overview', *Norfolk Archaeology* 46.iii, pp. 370-82

Mackreth, D.F. 1986, 'Brooches' in D. Gurney, *Settlement, Religion and Industry on the Roman Fen-edge, Norfolk*, East Anglian Archaeology 31, pp. 61-7

MackReth, D.F. 2011, *Brooches in Late Iron Age and Roman Britain* (Oxbow, Oxford)

Nash Briggs, D. 2011, 'The language of inscriptions on Icenian coinage' in J.A. Davies (ed.), *The Iron Age in Northern East Anglia: New Work in the Land of the Iceni* (BAR 549 British Series), pp. 83-102

Nash Briggs, D. 2012, 'Sacred Image and Regional Identity in Late Prehistoric Norfolk' in T.A. Heslop, E. Mellings and M. Thofner (eds.), *Art, Faith and Place in East Anglia* (Boydell), pp. 30-49

Neal, D.S. and Cosh, S.R. 2002, *Roman Mosaics of Britain. I. Northern Britain* (Society of Antiquaries of London)

Niblett, R. 2001, *The Roman City of St. Albans* (Tempus)

Plouviez, J. 2005, 'Whose good luck? Roman phallic ornaments from Suffolk' in N. Crummy (ed.), *Image, Craft and the Classical World* (Montagnac), pp. 157-64

Potter, T.W. 1981, 'The Roman Occupation of the Central Fenland. *Britannia* 12, pp. 79-133

Rivet, A.L.F. And Smith, C. 1981, *The Place-Names of Roman Britain* (Book Club Associates, London)

Rogers, A. 2004, *Beyond the Economic in the Roman Fenland. Reconsidering water, land, hoards and religion in the Fenland in Roman times* (unpublished MA thesis)

Rogerson, A., and Ashley, S. 2008, 'A selection of finds from Norfolk recorded between 2006 and 2008', *Norfolk Archaeology* 45.iii, pp. 428-41

Rogerson, A., and Ashley, S. 2010, 'A selection of finds from Norfolk recorded in 2010 and earlier', *Norfolk Archaeology* 46.i, pp. 121-35

Rogerson, A., and Ashley, S. 2012, 'A selection of finds from Norfolk recorded in 2012 and earlier', *Norfolk Archaeology* 46.iii, pp. 406-21

Salway, P. 1993, *The Oxford Illustrated History of Roman Britain.* (Oxford University Press)

Swift, E. 2011, 'Personal ornament' in L. Allason-Jones, (ed.) *Artefacts in Roman Britain. Their Purpose and Use* (Cambridge University Press), pp. 194-218

Talbot, J. 2006, 'The Iceni early face/horse series' in P. De Jersey (ed.) *Celtic Coinage: New Discoveries, New Discussion* (BAR 1532 International Series), pp. 213-41

Tomlin, R.S.O. 2004, 'A Bilingual Roman Charm for Health and Victory', *Zeitschrift fur Papyrologie und Epigraphik* 149, pp. 259-66

Tomlin, R.S.O. 2008, 'Hockwold cum Wilton' in *Britannia* 39, pp. 380-1

Toynbee, J.M.C. 1963, *Art in Roman Britain* (Phaidon, London)

Toynbee, J.M.C. 1964, *Art in Britain under the Romans* (Clarendon, Oxford)

Webster, G. 1986, *The British Celts and their Gods under Rome* (Batsford, London)

Worrell, S. 2004, 'Finds reported under the Portable Antiquities Scheme', *Britannia* 35, pp. 317-34

Worrell, S. 2006, 'Finds reported under the Portable Antiquities Scheme', *Britannia* 37, pp. 429-66

Worrell, S. 2009, 'Finds reported under the Portable Antiquities Scheme', *Britannia* 40, pp. 281-312

Worrell, S. 2010. 'Finds reported under the Portable Antiquities Scheme', *Britannia* 41, pp. 409-39

Worrell, S. and Pearce, J. 2011, 'Roman Britain in 2010. Finds recorded under the Portable Antiquities Scheme', *Britannia* 42, pp. 399-437

Worrell, S. and Pearce, J. 2012. 'Roman Britain in 2011. Finds recorded under the Portable Antiquities Scheme', *Britannia* 43, pp. 355-93

Icklingham: a provocative view of a centre of wealth and power in western East Anglia

Stanley West

Abstract: Amid the welter of erudition and up-to-date research that will characterise this volume, I feel that it might be appropriate for a little old-fashioned speculation. For many years I have been fascinated by the Lark valley and its environs, now I propose to draw together a few threads to consider the possible significance of this remarkable region without an extensive rehearsal of detailed discussions already in print. A little leaven in the lump, perhaps? However, a review of archaeological evidence is provided as the foundation of this article.

The dense occupation of the Fen edge in the Bronze Age as evidenced by metal hoards and scattered finds is a precursor to the importance of this area in centuries of occupation. In the succeeding Iron Age this north-west corner of Suffolk where the Lark valley lies, bounded by the Fens to the west and the heavy soils of central Suffolk to the south, has long been recognised as part of the tribal area of the ICENI who occupied most of Norfolk (Fig. 1).

Two named places are associated with the ICENI, of which VENTA ICENORUM at Caistor by Norwich is clearly identified in the late 2nd century Antonine Itinerary as the primary centre. The second is CAMBORITUM, now accepted as Icklingham, as best fitting the mileages in the Itinerary.[1] Lackford on the opposite bank of the Lark, has been proposed but the open town of Icklingham is more likely than Lackford or Hockwold, a major Roman site

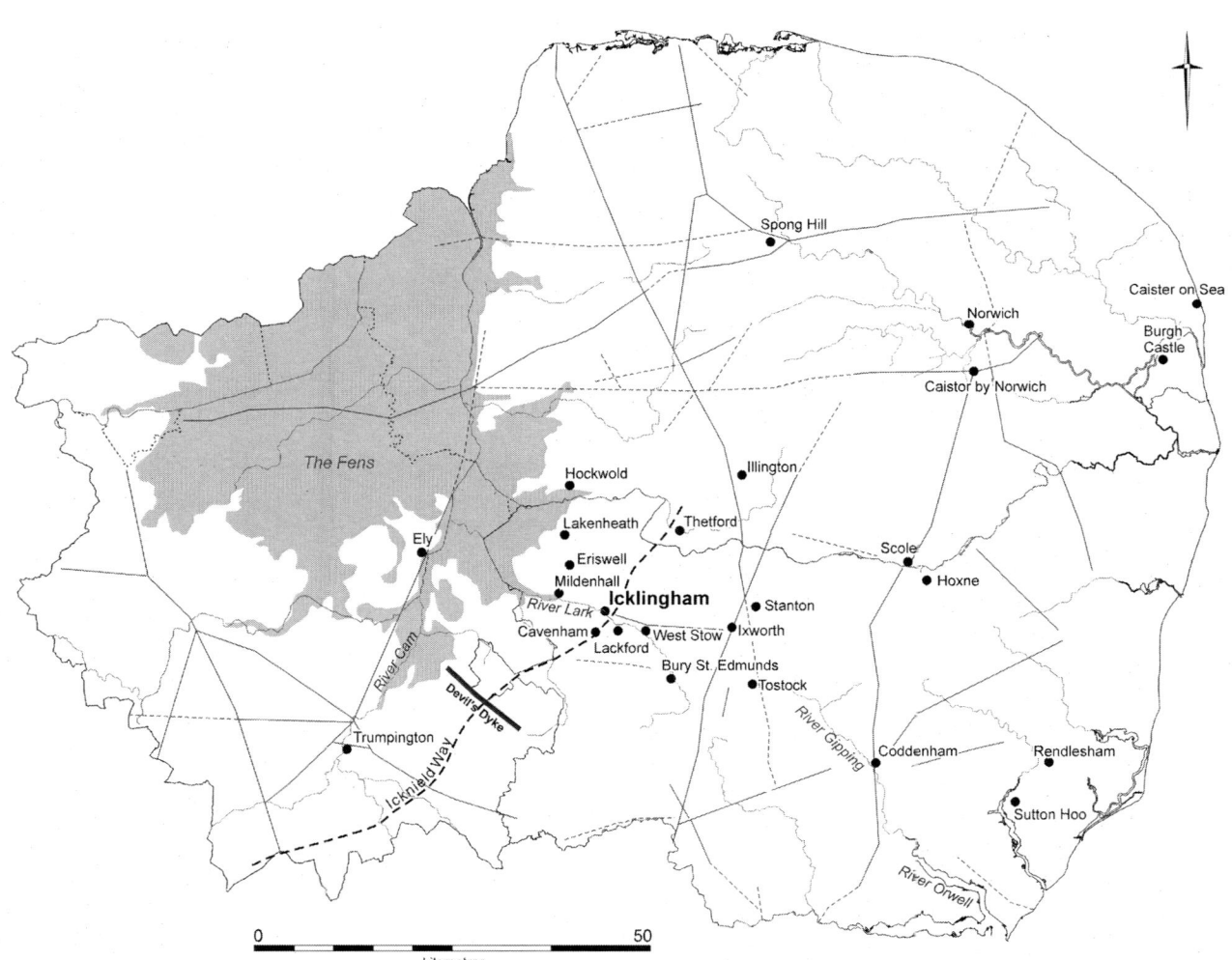

FIG. 1 MAP OF NORFOLK, SUFFOLK AND CAMBRIDGESHIRE SHOWING SITES REFERRED TO IN THE TEXT, ROMAN ROADS, RIVERS AND THE FENS (ANDREW HALL)

---

[1] Davies and Williamson 1999

in south-west Norfolk. The association of Icklingham with the ICENI has been discussed at length by Norman Scarfe, drawing on elements of the Iron Age coinage with variations of ECEN, ECE or EC as representing the tribal name.[2]

If Scarfe is accepted then Icklingham must have been of special significance, such is the rarity of place names on Iron Age coins, although it has to be said that to date, there is no evidence to pin-point a major settlement there. West Stow provides the kind of dispersed Iron Age settlement that spread along the Lark valley and the Fen edge; so far there is no suggestion of consolidated proto-towns at West Stow, or at Caistor by Norwich either. The disturbed hoard of late Iron Age coins from Lords Walk, Eriswell, contained over 400 coins, including 72 Roman Republican issues which provide a date of 55AD.[3] Another hoard from Lakenheath has 415 Iron Age coins and 67 Roman, the latest date being 37AD.[4] Four more inscribed coins are scattered finds from Icklingham, including one with ANTED (or ECEN), a name which is considered to relate to a ruler of the ICENI before Boudicca, rather than a place.

The Icknield Way passes the eastern edge of Icklingham and has long been associated with the site by virtue of its name. A slight variation of the route has been suggested which would take the route through the Roman town but has not yet been proven.

The first recorded discoveries of Roman coins and brooches were noted by Page c.1720[5] which inspired the local interest of Samuel Tymms and Henry Prigg in the latter half of the 19th century. Prigg[6] identified an area of c.800 x 275m as the extent of the 'ancient town' and also states that it 'was at no time walled, but was enclosed by a shallow trench and a slight rampart'. He records that 'there are foundations of buildings, including the hypocaust area of a villa, all in the same area of the site'. Burials recorded by Prigg included a group with two stone coffins and one of lead originally encased in an outer wooden coffin together with two unenclosed burials, one of which was covered with a tile pavement. Three of the burials involved the use of lime.

Other groups of burials are recorded from a sand pit in 1851, possibly the same as the cemetery at Stonepit Hill,[7] mentioning 'fibulae and glass vessels'. Both records are associated with Rampart Field at the east end of the town bordered by the Icknield Way and the east–west road leading to Ixworth.

Prigg also refers to a large cremation cemetery at the west end of the town which included a silver ring, found in 1881. There is little to prove a Roman date for the burials here, the probability is that this cremation cemetery is part of the documented Anglo-Saxon cemetery at Mitchell's Hill, to judge from his description of the urns found there.

Five Roman coin hoards are associated with the Icklingham town, three of which terminate with Honorius and Arcadius issues of the early 5th century. Two more, somewhat earlier, are noted by Moore[8] and include one from the ruinous site of the villa (Prigg).

Evidence for pagan cults is widespread in the Icklingham area, with seven small bronzes from Icklingham itself, of a personal or household nature. More significant is the hoard of bronze animals and human masks looted from the site in the 1980s and currently in the USA. Such a hoard of cult objects may reasonably be coupled with a small weathered stone pillar found in a pit with six human skulls in 1976. The pillar and the skulls were sealed by a layer of chalk which covered the adjacent area and was in turn cut by a later burial in a stone coffin. The weathered pillar and accompanying decorative tiles indicate a high quality of building, possibly a temple, although the precise location is not yet known.[9]

There are four hoards of pewter vessels from the parish. In April 1839 nine were found on heathland of the estate of John Gwilt and subsequently bought by the British Museum in 1841. A further eighteen vessels were acquired by the British Museum from a hoard found in 1853 from an unrecorded site. Four more from that hoard are in the Ipswich Museum. The third hoard, of nine vessels and an iron saw blade, was found in 1956 some 3.5km to the north of the town and the fourth hoard of a bronze bowl, a pewter platter and a pot was found in 1962 on the western edge of the parish. The platter bears a crude drawing of a fish. The total number of pewter vessels stands at 41.[10]

Three large lead 'tanks' have been found in the area of the town; that found in c.1726 has been lost but was well described.[11] The second, from Horselands Field in 1939, is in the British Museum, and the third from the south end of the same field was found in 1971 and contained a fragment of another included with salvaged iron work deposited in the tank.

The subsequent excavation in 1974, on the site of the fourth tank, revealed a small structure of mortared stone with an apsidal end within a few metres of the site of the tank. The foundations of a detached rectangular building lay immediately to the west. A considerable area round that building and to the north of it had a layer of chalk covering earlier features, including the pit containing the stone pillar and six skulls. In an adjoining cemetery, there were forty-one inhumations, including one female in the large stone coffin cutting the filling of the pit to the south.

---

[2] Scarfe 1976
[3] Robertson 2000, p. 11, no. 45
[4] Robertson 2000, p. 3-4, no. 15
[5] Page, 1785
[6] Prigg 1878
[7] Page 1911, p.309

[8] Moore, Plouviez and West 1988
[9] West and Plouviez 1976
[10] Liversidge 1959, pp. 6–10
[11] Salmon 1730, 1, p. 161

Seventeen of the inhumations had evidence of wooden coffins; one had grave goods and one had a coin possibly in the mouth and five others scattered in the grave fill. The concentration of burials in the south-east corner of the field suggests that this is a continuation of the cemetery to the east excavated by Prigg in 1871.

Further afield, the Cavenham bronze crowns from a site opposite the Roman town and a similar group from Hockwold (Norfolk), close to the temple site reported by Phillips,[12] point to a flourishing pagan religion within the region of the presumed temple at Icklingham. This temple with stone pillars and decorative roof tiles can reasonably be associated with the votive figures of animals and human masks from a hoard looted from the site of the Roman town in the 1980s.

Three pottery kilns of 3rd century date were excavated in 1937 just to the east of Prigg's cemetery, probably representing an extension of the earlier industry of the late 1st and 2nd centuries at West Stow.

Four late Roman cross-bow brooches are recorded. One, found in 1849 was bought in 1861 from the Acton collection and noted to have been found with glass vessels from a burial on Stonepit Hill (i.e. Rampart Field) at the east end of the town. This must be from the burials referred to in the *Victoria County History*.[13]

A second high status cross-bow brooch was published by Hattatt as from Icklingham,[14] although there remains some doubt as to the provenance of this piece. The distinctive form of this brooch bears a very close resemblance to that on an ivory diptych of Stillicho (395–408). Two others of lesser status, also in the Moyses Hall museum, are accessed with the same museum number as that from the Acton Collection and labelled 'Icklingham'. They belong with the widespread group of basic cross-bow brooches whose distribution is mainly in northern Europe. There are thirty-nine such cross-bows of the simpler kind in Norfolk with a wide general distribution, particularly in areas of denser settlement, with concentrations around Caistor by Norwich (3), Caister on Sea (5), Burgh Castle (3) and the area south of Norwich towards the major site at Scole (8). On the whole they do not relate closely to the distribution of the late Roman militaria of Hawkes and Dunning, although this may be a variable of collective practice.

Those of gold and silver are generally recognised as symbols of authority, originally awarded for valour. Icklingham has also produced one military type buckle (Type 111A) and one strap end (Type VA), both stray finds.[15] On a smaller scale the cross-bow brooches and late Roman belt furniture are also significant in terms of the social structure of the inhabitants of the town, as are the number of coin and pewter hoards. Unlike the walled cantonal capital of the ICENI at Caistor by Norwich, Icklingham was a linear development at the junction of the Icknield Way and an east–west road from the Fens to Ixworth and thence to Combretovium (Coddenham). As the gateway to the dense Fen edge sites in the west, it was clearly a religious and possibly administrative centre of high status within an area of extraordinary wealth. That area, within easy reach of Icklingham would include Mildenhall, Thetford, Hockwold and Ixworth/Stanton.

Although the Mildenhall treasure is broadly accepted to have come from there, there is still an element of doubt; perhaps the local folk memories that I recall of 'silver bells' being found may have a distorted truth of 'bells'/'bowls'.

To the exceptional wealth of the treasures of Mildenhall, Thetford and possibly Hoxne, can be added the sixteen hoards of coin all within 15km of Icklingham, amounting to some 17,600 coins in all, of which 16,000 are of gold. A further 935 coins, mostly of Ae, in Norfolk but in close proximity to Icklingham, raises the total to c.18,500 (16,774 gold) not including the Hoxne treasure of 14,296.

The three major hoards are all individual in character. Mildenhall is all silver ware with some Christian and some pagan attributes; Thetford is non-Christian with a (damaged) gold buckle without a tongue, indicating exceptional rank, with a strange mixture of silver spoons and personal jewellery. The confused nature of the discovery of the treasure suggests it is incomplete and the rumours of coins are not confirmed.[16]

The complete hoard from Hoxne, at 40km the furthest from Icklingham contained 569 gold, 14,272 silver and 24 bronze coins, 29 items of jewellery, 98 silver spoons and a small number of other items. The coins provide an earliest date for the deposition of 408AD. An important element of this hoard is the large number of personal names on some of the silver ware and gold jewellery together with Christian monograms and inscriptions, which give a Christian background more strongly than either Mildenhall or Thetford. Close to the Hoxne site a hoard of some 600 gold coins was found in 1781, only 4.8km away at Clint Farm, Eye, ending with issues of Arcadius and Honorius.

All hoards are presumably buried with the intention of recovery rather than for ritual reasons so the sites are not necessarily indicative of immediate origins. There are a number of villas for instance, which could have been within a day of the hoard sites, none of which have been completely excavated. There remain intriguing questions as to whether these are all, or in part, 'government' hoards or those of wealthy families, and just how close they are in date, perhaps being a division of an original single treasure?

It remains true that within the compass of the Roman town there was enormous wealth with family connections to

---

[12] Phillips 1970
[13] Page 1911, p. 309
[14] Hattatt 1985, p. 135, fig. 58, no. 507
[15] Hawkes and Dunning 1961

[16] Hobbs 2008

an organised Christian church, all in the general vicinity. The militant church, by actively degrading a pagan temple and ritually cleansing the site, physically suppressed the older, pagan beliefs. Such an open act was presumably undertaken with political assent, if not actual involvement. Once established, the church developed a distinctive missionary district beyond the immediate environs of Icklingham, as far as Huntingdon to the west, as evidenced by the clustering of similar lead tanks, mostly in north Cambridgeshire; the church at Icklingham possibly acting in the role of a minster.

The density of 'sites', hence populations, which is discernible even in the Bronze Age fen-edge sites, continues through the Iron Age and into the Roman era with the establishment of the open township of Icklingham. The Lark valley and surrounding area to the north is well provided with early Anglo-Saxon cemeteries, including one at the west end of the Roman town.

However, there is little so far to suggest a post-Roman occupation of the site itself, apart from a single stamped sherd of Anglo-Saxon pottery, found in the 1974 excavation in top soil in the vicinity of the church. Decorated with a close grouping of circular stamps confined by a double-grooved pendant triangle, it belongs to the sixth century Illington-Lackford workshop.

The Anglo-Saxon cemetery at Mitchell's Hill, found by gravel digging in the 19th century, would appear to be on the edge, if not beyond, the west end of the township. The originating settlement would presumably be within a short distance of the cemetery, to the north or west. A buckle of Hawkes and Dunning Type 111A and a large ornate strap-end of Type VA are among the 19th century finds attributable to the cemetery. Three surviving urns are all decorated; there are no records of associated cremations.

On a hill on the south bank of the Lark, a large Anglo-Saxon cremation cemetery was partially excavated by Lethbridge in 1947.[17] On the lower slopes there is extensive evidence of Roman occupation including two bronze figurines, numerous brooches and coins together with traces of a possible temple. That this is the site of the 'Cavenham Crowns' is strengthened by a sheet of bronze 'leaf' similar to that found with the crowns. Figurines of a horned goddess occur in both Icklingham and Lackford. Within the cemetery area Lethbridge records the foundations of two small rectangular structures, one within a roughly square crop mark, and suggests they were rifled Roman tombs. The incomplete excavation of this cemetery produced c.400 urns; the plan of the excavation would suggest upwards of 1,000 at least.

The similarities to Spong Hill at Elmham, Norfolk are clear. Here, there were 2,000 cremations and an attached enclave of 57 inhumations was excavated and many more were found to have been destroyed in the past. A similar arrangement could well exist on the fringes of the Lackford cemetery. Inhumation is normally the burial rite in the local cemeteries, often with smaller numbers of cremations.

The Lackford cremation cemetery was in operation throughout the early period although end dates for conversion to Christianity are not clearly defined. The diversity of objects and the common use of decorative Illington-Lackford pottery attest the broad spectrum of society that was buried there. The distinctive preference for cremation and the long term use of this cemetery must surely have been based on over-riding religious or ethnographic reasons to draw on a wider catchment area, there being nothing to suggest any particular social structure, apart perhaps from the lack of weapons which normally only occur with inhumations. The dominant long term use of cremation is in parallel with the mixed rite of the local cemeteries.

The hoary old question of the fate of the late Roman population and their possible absorption into the incoming Anglo-Saxon culture is still unresolved. With so few complete excavations of cemeteries or ordered settlements, Lakenheath and West Stow excepted; there seems little point in pursuing population numbers based on the current available information.

The withdrawal and apparently rapid flight of Roman power and the upper echelons at least of personnel inevitably resulted in an immediate collapse of the monetary economy and the economic and social structure. The most obvious result in the archaeological record is the disappearance of the wheel thrown, kiln fired, durable pottery, so clearly recognisable in the settlements and cemeteries of the late Roman period. A dramatic and total change occurred in building technology, with the apparent abandonment of the township. Wooden structures of Anglo-Saxon type appear on nearby sites with no indication of a gradual inter-change.

The impact of the Anglo-Saxon invasion would obviously be clarified by a large scale DNA study of Roman and Anglo-Saxon cemeteries in the same location.

By the time of the Conversion in the 6th century, the Anglo-Saxons had been established for well over 100 years with an aristocratic hierarchy of extreme wealth, sustained and encouraged by diplomatic and economic contact with the Frankish kingdom. The recognition of Redwald as Bretwalda by the Franks gave him an authority that reached back to Constantinople. His burial in Roman style regalia and with diplomatic gifts from Constantinople, albeit second-hand, is indicative of the desire for legitimate recognition.

The superb craftsmanship of the gold and garnet jewellery at Sutton Hoo could not have evolved in East Anglia but surely must have been achieved with imported Frankish technology and probably artisans as well, as shown by

---

[17] Lethbridge 1951

garnet and gold jewellery in Kent. The recent discovery of the Staffordshire hoard carries an important insight into the social structure of the time in East Anglia. Such a wealth of high class weaponry provides an insight into the extent to which the wealth was dispersed among the aristocracy, with all the implications of the ownership of property and the allegiances that pertain to such relationships. The magnificent gold and garnet pendant crosses of Stanton and Wilton, (with enclosed coin of Heraclius, 631)[18] are geographically close to the recent discovery at Trumpington Meadows in Cambridgeshire. Apparently this was attached to clothing by loops on the reverse, and not suspended as a pendant. The design is a simplified version of the Stanton Cross with less use of garnets and none of the complex, often stepped shapes of Stanton and Wilton, perhaps indicative of lower status or a slightly later date.

The close connection of north-west Suffolk with Sutton Hoo can be traced to a series of jewels which spread from Sutton Hoo along the Gipping Valley route to Bury St. Edmunds, via Coddenham (fragment with empty stepped cells), Tostock (buckle and sword pyramid)[19] extended now to Trumpington. High ranking burials with jewellery of this status do not necessarily indicate the settlement site of the deceased, as in the case of Sutton Hoo and Rendlesham.

By virtue of its geographical position and long term standing as a cultural and administrative centre, Icklingham provided access to the north Cambridgeshire route to the midlands. The importance of this route and the immediate hinterland of the Icklingham region were sufficient to be the reasoning behind the construction of the Devil's Dyke and possibly the Black Ditches on the west side of Icklingham as a secondary line of defence.[20] Sigeberht established a monastery at Bedricesworth (Bury St. Edmunds) in 630; the later enlargement of the precinct probably under Abbot Baldwin in c.1065, diverted an existing north–south roadway connecting Bury to Icklingham some 8km away, along the River Lark.[21] Sigeberht and the gold and garnet crosses of Stanton and Wilton (631) must be associated, thus emphasising the importance of that area.

Trumpington extends the range to the west and probably date-wise towards the foundations of Etheldreda's monastery at Ely in 673, some forty-three years after that at Bury and the Stanton and Wilton aristocratic burials whose position in the 'local' society is not yet known.

By drawing together all the evidence for wealth and power in the Icklingham area, a case can be made for the long term strategic and cultural significance of Icklingham and its region through the continuity of folk-lore, belief and administration derived from a continuum of a people whose identity was submerged but not eradicated.

---

[18] West 1998
[19] West 1998

[20] Scarfe 1986, 1987
[21] Stratham 1998

Bibliography

Davies, J. and Williamson, T. (eds.) 1999, 'The Land of the Iceni, the Iron-Age in North-East Anglia', *Studies in East Anglian History*

Hattatt, R. 1985, 'Iron Age and Roman Brooches'. (Oxbow)

Hawkes, S.C. and Dunning, G.C. 1961, 'Soldiers and Settlers in Britain' *Medieval Archaeology* 6, pp. 1–70

Hobbs, R. 2008, 'The Secret History of the Mildenhall Treasure', *Antiquaries Journal* 88, pp. 376–410

Lethbridge, T.L. 1951, 'A Cemetery at Lackford, Suffolk', *Cambridge Antiq. Soc. Quarto Publications new series no. VI*

Liversidge, J. 1959, 'A New Hoard of Romano-British Pewter at Icklingham, Suffolk' *Proceedings of the Cambridge Antiquarian Society* 52, pp. 6–10

Moore, I., Plouviez, J., and West, S.E. 1988, *The Archaeology of Roman Suffolk*, Suffolk County Council

Page, W. 1785, *MS Minutes of the Society of Antiquaries* 1

Page, W. 1911, *Victoria County History of Suffolk* 1.

Phillips, C.W. (Ed.) 1970 'The Fenland in Roman Times' Royal Geographical Society, Series 5 (London)

Prigg, H. 1878, 'The Roman House at Icklingham' *Journal British Archaeological Association* 34, pp. 12-15, reprinted in 'Icklingham Papers', 1901, pp. 72-75, (with inhumation cemetery)

Robertson, A.S. 2000, *An Inventory of Romano-British Coin Hoards* (London)

Salmon, N. 1730, 'A New Survey of England', 1, (London)

Scarfe, N. 1976, 'The Place-Name Icklingham: A preliminary re-examination'; Appendix on the Iclingas by Martin, E.A., East Anglian Archaeology 3, pp. 127-34

West, S.E., and Plouviez, J. 1976, 'The Romano-British site at Icklingham' East Anglian Archaeology 3, pp. 63–125

West, S.E. 1998, *A Corpus of Anglo-Saxon Material from Suffolk*, East Anglian Archaeology 84

Scarfe, N. 1986, *Suffolk in the Middle Ages* (Woodbridge)

Scarfe, N. 1987, *The Suffolk Landscape* (revised) (London)

Statham, M. 1998, 'The Book of Bury St. Edmunds'

'Spong Man' in context

Catherine Hills

Abstract: In this paper the pottery lid in the form of a seated figure, known as Spong Man, will be reconsidered in the context of the recently published analysis and chronology of the Spong Hill cemetery.[1]

Spong man was found in 1979 during the excavation of the early Anglo-Saxon cemetery at Spong Hill, North Elmham, Norfolk. Andrew Rogerson has a close connection with Spong Hill: he worked on site during the initial season in 1972, and directed the final season in 1984 when part of the associated settlement was excavated. He also lived at Spong Farm, just across the road from the site, during the years of its excavation and afterwards, until moving to Great Fransham. For many years since then Andrew has been an invaluable source of information about finds of Anglo-Saxon artefacts in Norfolk, for me as for many other scholars enabling access to the very large quantity of records of objects reported to and recorded by Andrew and by Steven Ashley, one of the editors of this book. Long before the Portable Antiquities scheme made similar records available for the rest of England, Norfolk archaeologists, especially Tony Gregory and Andrew, pioneered this approach.

Spong Man (Fig. 1) was described and illustrated in Part IV of the Spong Hill catalogue of cremations, where it is listed as cremation 3324 although in fact it was not found with an associated cremation urn or bones.[2] It was first published by the author of this paper in *Antiquity*.[3] Since then it has often been illustrated[4] but seldom discussed in detail. An exception is a forthcoming paper by Ruth Nugent. She has examined and photographed the figure in some detail, demonstrating the unevenness of its eyes and interpreting this as deliberate and targeted damage. She presents an interesting interpretation of this, in the context of other examples of uneven or damaged eyes on early medieval artefacts.

FIG. 1 SPONG MAN (NORFOLK HISTORIC ENVIRONMENT SERVICE)

The iconography of the figure is not the main focus of this paper, but there is more to be said on that theme in the light of recent discoveries. The concept of a seated figure carries with it an impression of authority, whether secular or divine, obvious examples being images of Roman emperors or of Christ in majesty. The wooden chair found in association with an inhumation at Fallwerd in North Germany was illustrated with the caption 'Der Thron aus der Marsch', i.e. it was seen as a throne.[5] This chair is possibly contemporary with Spong Man and is further linked to Spong Hill by the drawing of a hunt scene on its associated footstool, very like that on Spong Hill C2594.[6] In recent years there have been several finds in England and Scandinavia of small three-dimensional human figures of early medieval date, but made of metal, not ceramic.[7] There are also tenth century amulets in the form of chairs. A remarkable silver figurine found at Lejre in 2009, also dated to the tenth century, is in the form of a seated figure in a long gown on an elaborately decorated chair with two birds perched on the arm rests.[8] The discussion relating to the interpretation of this figure, whether Odin, Freya or a secular ruler, shows the kind of themes which might be explored in relation to Spong Man, which is also a figure of uncertain gender.

---

[1] Hills and Lucy 2013
[2] Hills, Penn and Rickett 1987, fig. 82, pl IX
[3] Hills 1980
[4] e.g. Higham and Ryan 2013 pl.2a.5, Webster 2012, fig. 20
[5] Schon 1999, p. 81
[6] Hills, Penn and Rickett 1987, fig. 73
[7] Webster 2012, pp. 38-41, Andersson et. al. 2004
[8] Christensen 2013

Comparative contemporary human representations are in many ways the most interesting topic for future research, and more discoveries may throw more light on the iconography of Spong Man. In this paper, however, my aim is to show how analysis of the Spong Hill cemetery itself can provide a clearer picture of its immediate context and suggest a more precise date for its deposition.

Spong Man was not found in association with an urn, but in a shallow irregular pit, context 2383. This was very close to an irregular series of interconnected pits running east–west across the site, immediately to the south of ditch 1177. This ditch corresponds to a field boundary visible in early nineteenth century maps. The pits contained broken urns and scattered cremated bones, very probably representing an urn-digging episode recorded by an antiquary, Peter le Neve, in 1711.[9] Spong Man and its originally associated urn appear to have been the victim of this activity. It cannot therefore be securely associated with any specific surviving urn. It may have belonged to one broken and scattered in 1711, or recovered by the 'persons of more curiosity' who followed the workmen, but lost since. It could instead have been dislodged from an urn buried more deeply which did survive to be excavated and recorded, but most of the pots found in the immediate vicinity of context 2383 are fragmentary and not definitely in situ.

The figure was in several pieces when found, some retrieved from sieving the soil in the pit, but it is almost intact after reconstruction, apart from a piece of the rim of the lid, and one knee of the figure. The older damage might relate to the original disturbance, while the more recent breakage to the more fragile upper body and arms could have resulted from pressure on the fill of the shallow pit caused by the ploughing which was the reason for the 1972-81 rescue excavation. The unusual character of the figure caused initial doubt as to whether it was genuine, but the fabric, colour and surface of the lid are all consistent with that of the rest of the cremation pots at Spong Hill, as are the linear decorative details, and some of the breaks are old. A thermoluminescent (TL) date for the lid was produced by the Research laboratory at Oxford and the Godwin laboratory at Cambridge, giving a date range which covers nearly all of the Anglo-Saxon period, 460-1090 AD.[10] This was useful in confirming it was not a fake, but less so for providing a precise date. The earliest part of the TL date range seems most relevant, because the recent analysis of the Spong Hill cemetery demonstrates that the majority of the cremations were buried in the fifth century AD.[11] It is argued below that the most likely date for the lid and its associated cremation is the early or middle decades of the fifth century AD.

There are several ways of contextualising Spong Man. Lids discovered elsewhere are one starting point, although surviving lids are likely to be a fraction of those which originally existed because the rims and upper parts of the pots were most vulnerable to damage from agriculture, as is shown by the many vessels which have lost all or part of their upper half. Figural lids would have been especially vulnerable, because of their greater height than other surviving lids, and could have broken into unrecognizable lumps of clay. Very few pottery lids have in fact been recorded from Anglo-Saxon cemeteries in England and no other three-dimensional ceramic figures apart from an antiquarian drawing of a lid from Newark with two small birds.[12] The lids which have survived are either the hemispherical 'teapot' form of lid or, in a few cases, a small shallow bowl which has been upturned as a lid on a larger pot.[13] There do not seem to be examples elsewhere in England of the flat lid, which is the most common form at Spong Hill. Myres included only eight pots with lids in his Corpus of Anglo-Saxon pottery, out of a total illustrated of 3470 pots. Three of these are from Lackford, also illustrated by Lethbridge.[14] Two of the Lackford pots are very similar with linear and bossed decoration, the third is smaller, with stamps and linear decoration, with lids made to match their associated pots. Associated finds were iron tweezers, a miniature comb and a sword scabbard mouth. Myres also illustrates a pot from Newark,[15] which is one of a pair of pots with lids forming stamp group 3 at Newark, where again the lids seem to be made for the pots as they have the same stamps.[16] One of these, no.402, contained the cremated bones of a child, glass beads, and fragments of worked antler and bronze sheet.[17] A pot from Baston[18] is identified as belonging to Myres' 'Sancton Baston potter'. This group occurs also at Spong Hill, as stamp group 47, where it includes another pot with a lid, C3078.[19] Detailed examination of the stamp dies and the petrology of this group by Arnold and Russell showed that it should be divided into two or more separate local groups,[20] but the similarity of decorative design across all of Myres' group is noticeable, and the use of lids provides another link. The two remaining examples of lidded pots in Myres' Corpus are both illustrated with upturned bowls as lids. These are from Abingdon, a plain pot with a plain bowl as lid, and Caistor by Norwich A16, shown as the lower half of a pot with linear decoration with the base of another pot upturned as lid.[21] However, the description in the Caistor site report suggests two interpretations for the fragmentary base found mixed with the bones, either as lid or instead as the base of another fragmentary pot buried above A16.[22]

Even fewer lids have so far been recorded in association with cremation urns in Germany. At Issendorf an

---

[9] Hills 1977, pp. 6-7, Rickett 1995, fig. 85, pp. 59-60
[10] Hills 1980, p. 52
[11] Hills and Lucy 2013
[12] Kinsley 1989, fig. 92
[13] e.g. Myres 1977, fig. 30, no. 2030
[14] Myres figs. 127, 137, Lethbridge 1951, fig. 15
[15] Myres fig.112, 3516
[16] Kinsley 1989, fig. 6
[17] Kinsley, p. 73
[18] Myres 1977, fig. 247, no. 3611
[19] Hills, Penn and Rickett 1994 fig. 57
[20] Arnold and Russell 1983
[21] Myres 1977, fig. 30, no. 2030, fig. 275, no. 1556
[22] Myres and Green 1973, p. 124

illustration survives of a pot with a lid carrying the figure of a boar, excavated in the eighteenth century and now lost.[23] From more recent excavations at the same site twenty one lids have been published.[24] The Issendorf lids included examples of flat round lids, and hemispherical or conical lids with in some cases knobs or discs at the apex, and internal rims. Both forms are also found at Spong Hill, adding to the similarities already noted between the two cemeteries of Spong Hill and Issendorf. Several flat lids were also found at Westerwanna.[25]

The scarcity of Migration period lids is in contrast to their frequency amongst earlier Iron Age cremations in North Germany, where both deliberately made lids and upturned bowls were in use.[26] It seems likely that the practice of using lids is a continental tradition, transferred to England with other aspects of the cremation rite in the fifth century AD. The closest parallel to Spong Man is the lost Issendorf lid with a boar. There are also pots which take the form of a boar, at Liebenau, or bird, at Issendorf, paralleling at least the concept of a three-dimensional ceramic figure.[27] Plastic decoration in the form of animal and human figures was applied to pots at Suderbrarup,[28] animals also at Newark.[29]

The remainder of this paper will focus on the context of Spong Man within the cemetery of Spong Hill. Other cremations buried near to context 2383 will be examined first, then pots with necks of an appropriate diameter to fit the Spong Man lid, and finally other lids on cremation urns at Spong Hill.

Many of the burials close to context 2383, which contained Spong Man, are damaged and fragmentary. The closest, all disturbed and scattered, are C2456, C2582 and C2467, all with some decorated sherds, and C2450, which appears to have been plain. None of these can be securely located in their original burial position, or fully reconstructed. Amongst the other burials in that part of the cemetery there are two groups of three in situ near complete cremations which escaped the urn diggers, about 3m to the east of context 2383.[30] One group appears to have been buried together in one pit, defined as Burial Group 178, dated to phase A. This consists of C2494, a wide mouthed plain pot containing the cremated bones of an older adult, C2492, a very small pot with linear decoration and no associated bones, and C2491, a larger pot with linear decoration, also containing the bones of an older adult, which very probably had a neck too wide for the Spong Man lid. None of these had recorded gravegoods, and none is plausible as originally associated with Spong Man.

Three further cremations in the same vicinity were excavated separately and recorded as having adjacent urnpits with undetermined relationships rather than having been deposited at the same time in one pit, but their proximity suggests they could have been contemporary burials. Undecorated pots were often buried with decorated pots in the identifiable contemporary burial groups, and two of these, C2478 and C2534, are plain pots. Both have neck diameters too wide for Spong Man to have been their lid, but the third, C2451, would fit, and is a not impossible candidate although it is perhaps smaller than might be expected.[31] This pot has linear decoration which includes a multiple arm T motif with lines quite similar to the diagonal lines on the outer rim of Spong Man. C2451 is similar to C2504 and both have been grouped with two other pots to form Style Group 27.[32] C2451 contained the bones of a subadult with iron shears and tweezers, antler comb fragment and glass. The rim was damaged, so any lid would have been knocked off, and could then have been moved some distance by plough or diggers. C2478 contained the bones of two adult individuals, a mature probable female and a young possible male. There were also pig bones, but no grave-goods. C2534 included the bones of a juvenile and comb fragments. C2451 is phased to A, the other two were not phased. If these cremations did constitute one burial group it might provide an appropriate context for Spong Man, including a pot with rune or runelike decoration and miniatures.

About five metres to the east from Spong Man was Burial Group 188. This consisted of three pots, C2563, C2564 and C2566, closely linked by position, decoration and the fragments of the same comb found in C2563 and C2564.[33] The smallest of these, C2566, has a neck narrow enough for Spong Man, the others do not. All three were found intact, with complete rims. It seems unlikely that this would have been the case if Spong Man had been knocked off one of them because its deep internal rim would have broken the pot rim when moved.

The cremations discussed above, and Spong Man, lay in the middle of the cemetery, within the distribution zone of burials of both phase A and phase B but outside that of phase C.[34]

Another line of enquiry is the size of the lid, which would have related to the rim diameter of its associated pot. Its diameter measures approximately 7.5cm internally, 10.5cm externally, which would fit a pot with a neck diameter between those two measurements. This means the lid would have been too small for the majority of the complete pots recovered from the site. The size and shape of Anglo-Saxon cremation urns has been analysed by Richards[35] and Lucy.[36] Richards showed that smaller

---

[23] Genrich 1981, Abb. 58
[24] Weber 2000, p. 108, Hassler 2001, Taf. 13
[25] Rohrer-Ertl 1971, Taf. 40
[26] e.g. Wegewitz 1961
[27] Genrich 1981, abb.57, Hassler 1994, farbtafel 7
[28] Bantelmann 1988, Taf. 60
[29] Kinsley 1989, Fig. 67
[30] Hills, Penn and Rickett 1987, fig. 132

[31] Hills, Penn and Rickett 1987, fig. 27
[32] Hills and Lucy 2013, fig. A6.13
[33] Hills, Penn and Rickett 1987, fig. 36, Hills 1994
[34] Hills and Lucy 2013, figs. 3. 20-24
[35] Richards 1987
[36] Hills and Lucy 2013, Chapter 4

vessels tended to be associated with children, while larger narrow necked vessels had an association with adult males. Lucy looked in detail at the relationships between pots, cremated individuals and grave goods at Spong Hill. Richards showed that in absolute terms a rim diameter of less than 10cm was the smallest rim size category for Anglo-Saxon cremation urns,[37] which Lucy confirmed by demonstrating that the average minimum diameter for all categories of burial and all phases at Spong Hill is greater than 10cm.[38] The pot for which Spong Man was made was therefore unusually narrow-necked.

Some of the pots with neck diameters of 10cm or less are small, with proportionately small rim diameters, often containing infants. Spong Man is unlikely to have been made for one of these because it would have been too large and top-heavy for such a pot. There are however some large pots which have narrow necks. These were identified by Richards as associated with adult males and containing many grave-goods especially miniatures.[39] Amongst the pots with complete profiles it is possible to identify nearly fifty with rim diameters of 10.5cm or less and also heights of at least 20cm, the average height for Spong Hill pots, thus average or large pots. Comparing the drawing of Spong Man with the narrow-necked pots at the same scale it was possible to see that some would not fit, bringing the number down to around forty. This includes seven pots which do have lids. While most pots with lids have relatively narrow rim diameters, they range from 10 to 15.5cm, with a couple of lids as wide as 18cm, so Spong Man is at the small end of this range.

The pots identified above as being of the right size to fit Spong Man mostly have bases which could have supported such a lid: with foot rings, pedestals or simply relatively wide and flat. There is a tendency towards a shouldered rather than a globular shape, rounded not biconical: but in that they correspond to the general form of pots at Spong Hill. Nearly all belong to phase A or B, not to the latest phase C of the cemetery's use as defined by Hills and Lucy, and most are decorated, not plain. Bossed and linear decoration is most common, with stamps in combination with bosses on some. They were buried mainly in the eastern half of the cemetery, but not especially close together. They contained cremated bones of both sexes, adults and subadults, also animal bones and a range of grave-goods. More contained male or possible male individuals than female and combs and miniatures were frequent grave goods, which is consistent with the findings of Richards.

Some are elaborately decorated and they include pots belonging to several of the Style Groups defined by Penn.[40] Style Groups 4 and 11 include pots with pedestals, decorated both on the upper and lower half, with bossed and linear designs including slashed cordons. Style Group 4 consists of C1814 C2112, C2286, C2319 and C3052, bossed and stamped pots. It is phased A/B and has a close parallel at Cleatham.[41] Style Group 11, phased B, consists of a pair of pots, C2146 and C3529. If any one pot were to be chosen as most probably like the pot originally associated with Spong Man C2146 is a good candidate (Fig. 2).[42] This is a large pot with a pedestal foot and complex bossed and linear decoration, including diagonally slashed cordons. Spong Man has a diagonally slashed rim, although this is a feature shared by several of the flat lids. C2146 was found some distance to the south of Spong Man, containing the bones of an unsexed adult, glass beads and a fragment of copper alloy, possibly silvered. It has a close parallel with a pot from Suderbrarup in Schleswig Holstein.[43] Also worth noting is Style Group 31, phased B, which consists of two pots with narrow necks, C2009 and C2094, decorated with T-shaped cordons. Style Group 32, also decorated with bossed T motifs, includes only pots with necks too wide for Spong Man. Style Group 20, which does have some narrow-necked pots, includes many of the pots with flat lids, discussed below.[44]

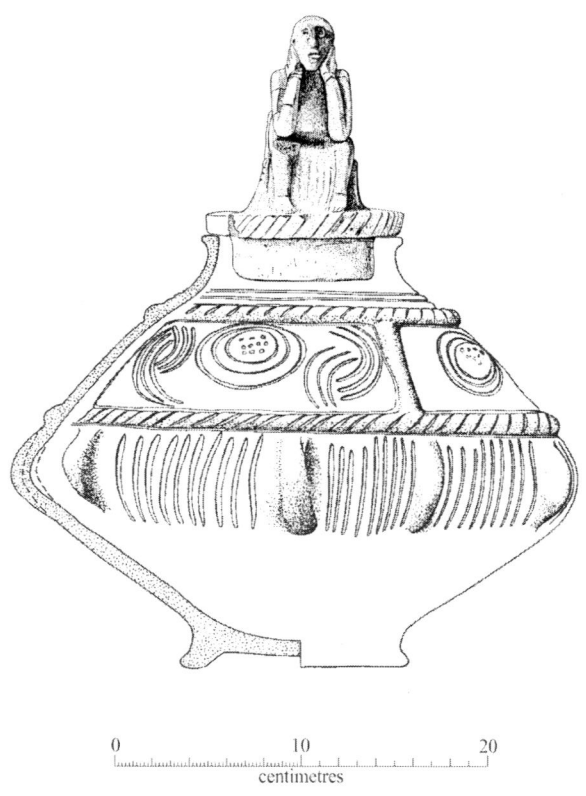

FIG. 2 DRAWING OF C2146 WITH SPONG MAN POSITIONED AS LID (DRAWINGS BY KENNETH PENN, SCANNED AND EDITED BY ANDREW HALL)

---

[37] Richards 1987, tables 36-7
[38] Hills and Lucy 2013, table 4.2
[39] Richards 1987, p. 154.
[40] in Hills and Lucy 2013 Appendix 6
[41] Leahy 2007, fig. 67
[42] Hills and Penn 1981, fig. 67 (or fig.2)
[43] Bantelmann 1988, Taf 158, Hills 1993, fig. 2.2
[44] Penn 2013, fig. A6.9

This analysis gives us a set of probable characteristics for the burial with which Spong Man was originally associated. The pot would have had bossed and linear decoration, less probably stamped, and might have contained the cremated bones of an adult human and some animal bones, also miniatures and a comb. It would have been buried during phase A or B, not phase C, thus before the end of the fifth century.

The other pottery lids from Spong Hill provide another kind of context for Spong Man. Forty-one pottery lids are recorded, which is considerably more than from any other site in England, and in Germany only approached by Issendorf with twenty-eight lids.

The fragmentary lid recorded from C2642B is probably part of the lid from 2642A, leaving forty reliably recorded lids. Some of the lids were found in situ on top of a pot, others were found pushed into the neck of the pot. Most look as if they had been made deliberately to go with the associated pot: they are an appropriate size and the decoration on both pot and lid is similar including use of the same stamp dies. One plain pot, C2022, contained a large piece of a second, small, plain pot which may have been use as a lid. Five lids, including Spong Man, were not found in association with a pot. Very few lid fragments were recorded amongst the many decorated unstratified sherds examined by Stuart and Vera Friedenson to make the 'x series' of stamps,[45] which suggests that a significant proportion of the original lids have been recovered.

The suggestion has been made by Nugent that Spong Man might have been visible above ground.[46] She was following McKinley[47] who outlines alternative possible burial sequences for the cremations deposited in the same pit as a burial group, including leaving the pit open after an initial burial before later depositing others. This scenario cannot be ruled out for some burial groups, although most appear to have been tightly placed together, suggesting burial at one time, and in many cases covered with large flints. The level of the original ground surface is difficult to estimate as it has been subject to ploughing and erosion and clearly much soil had been lost before excavation took place. The excavated depth of the cremation pits varied according to their position on the slope of the hill, and also as ploughing continued cremations excavated in later seasons had a higher degree of damage. Cremations buried in the fill of ditch 146 were buried more deeply than those dug into the sand and gravel subsoil. Spong Man would have required marking in some way if it was left visible. It is clear that it would not have survived intact to the eighteenth century or later if it had not been securely buried before discovery and discard, and burial at the time of original deposition seems most likely, though unprovable. It was found near to the boundary which in 1711 divided the field, described as a hedge and ditch, so it could have been protected from agricultural disturbance by the bank of the hedge.

Other lidded pots were securely buried: in two cases they were found intact, with the lids still in situ: C2531 (Fig. 3) and C2483. In others the pot was crushed with the lid pushed down into the pot. The two intact lidded pots were only partially filled with cremated bones, as were many of the other intact pots whose internal sections were recorded in the individual catalogue reports.[48] Apart from C2531 and C2483 the pots which survived intact were found either full of bones or bones and earth. The latter had either never been lidded, or the lid had been dislodged at a stage when backfilled soil could fill the pot, probably at the time of burial. Many other pots, without surviving lids, were found crushed in situ (Fig. 4), which suggests that these pots had been only partially filled with bones and that pressure from soil on the empty space had crushed the upper half. This means that backfilled soil had not filled the upper half, which suggests that these pots also had been lidded, perhaps with organic covers of wood or textile which have not survived. They could not all have had ceramic lids as the number of fragmentary lids is not very great. To the recorded ceramic lids therefore should be added an unknown, but possibly quite large, number of organic lids. It seems less likely that the pots were wrapped in textile: no visible trace of such textile was recorded on the outer surface of any pot, those in burial groups were tightly packed with little space left for textile in between, and the decoration would have been obscured by such wrappings.

FIG. 3 C2531 WITH LID IN GROUND
(NORFOLK HISTORIC ENVIRONMENT SERVICE)

---

[45] Hills, Penn and Rickett 1994, p. 18
[46] Nugent forthcoming
[47] McKinley 1994, p. 105

[48] e.g. Hills and Penn 1994, figs. 141-144

FIG. 4 C2309 CRUSHED IN SITU
(NORFOLK HISTORIC ENVIRONMENT SERVICE)

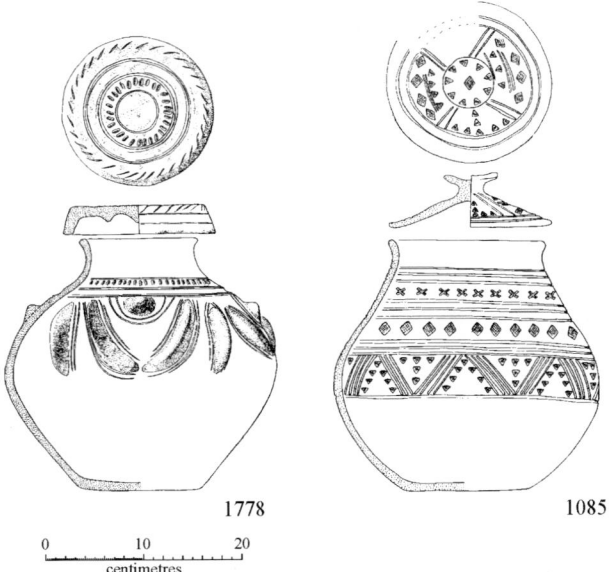

FIG. 5 EXAMPLES OF POTS WITH FLAT (1778) AND 'TEAPOT' (1085) LIDS (DRAWINGS KENNETH PENN, SCANNED AND EDITED BY ANDREW HALL)

The ceramic lids found at Spong Hill include twenty-seven of the same shape, flat round lids, all except two with internal rims, and all except one decorated. There are also eleven 'teapot' lids: hemispherical/conical with flat knobs (Fig. 5). The incomplete lid with C1993 may belong to this group or it could be an upturned bowl. Spong Man does not fit either category. It shares the internal rim of the flat lids, but its height might align it with the 'teapot' lids.

The cremations with lids are:

C3324 (Spong Man);

flat lids: C1310, C1376, C1772, C1778, C1784, C1791, C1806, C1967, C1991, C1992, C2007, C2011, C2016, C2035, C2048, C2056, C2090, C2099, C2111, C2203, C2483, C2531, C2586, C1753B, C1837A, C1837B, C2642A.

Hemispherical 'teapot' lids: C1085, C1360, C1831, C1835, C1857D, C1892B, C1936, C1963, C1993, C2246, C3077, C3078.

Five of the lids, including Spong Man, were found without an associated cremation urn, having been displaced. These are: C1310, C1857D, C2246, C3077 and C3324 (Spong Man). One of these, 1857D, may originally have been associated with the neighbouring cremation C1940A, since both belong to Stamp-linked Group 43 and the rim diameter of the lid is larger than that of the pot, so they could have fitted together. C3077 was associated with cremated bones, part of a copper alloy ring and glass beads, but there was no surviving pot. This lid and bones have been redeposited from a disturbed cremation, but none of the cremations in the immediate vicinity is an obvious candidate for its original context.

Using the recently established phasing for Spong Hill, thirty of the thirty-five lids associated with cremations can be assigned to phase B. Of the remainder one, C1993, is not phased, C2111 is phased B/C and three, C1831, C1835 and C1963, to phase C. Two of the unassociated lids, C2246 and C3077, also belong to pot phase B, while 1857D is B/C and C1310 is unphased. No lids were dated to phase A. The phase C lids are all 'teapot' shape rather than flat. The majority of the ceramic lids from Spong Hill can therefore be dated to phase B, the central decades of the fifth century. This overlaps with the date range suggested above for narrow necked pots, phases A and B.

Considered as a group together the cremations with lids are not obviously distinguished from other cremations, but some patterns do emerge. Most lids are associated with pots of average or slightly above average size, but some are small, for example C1992, C1993 and C2090. All but three of the associated pots were decorated, with a range of linear, stamped and bossed designs. Lids were associated with cremated humans of both sexes and all ages, with a range of animals and grave-goods. Overall most human bones were those of adults, but there were also some subadults and infants both alone and in association with adults. The sexed individuals included six female or possible female burials and five male or possible male: given the imbalance of identified females to males this suggests a bias towards male association. Twenty-one of the lidded pots contained cremated animal bones, twelve with horse. Amongst the grave-goods combs were the most frequent find, found in eight cremations, all of types with a date range mainly in the fifth century.[49] Glass and/or ivory also occurred in eight cremations, copper alloy sheet in five, while miniatures occurred in four, worked bone/

---

[49] Riddler in Hills and Lucy, p. 141

antler in three, glass vessels and earscoops each in two with single examples of copper alloy tweezers, iron knife, copper alloy ring, spindle whorl and large glass bead. These associations are similar to those identified above for narrow-necked pots: male more than female adults, horse and other animal bones, miniatures and combs. Only one brooch fragment was associated with a lidded pot, part of an annular brooch found with C1967. There is a discrepancy here, because C1967 is phased to B on the basis of the pot decoration, whereas annular brooches, which occur in large numbers in inhumations but rarely in cremations, are phased to C at Spong Hill. The pot was complete, with the lid pushed inside and sealing the contents. Perhaps this is an example of a pot which was old when buried.

Three of the associated pots were undecorated: C1376, C1831 and C1993, all with different shapes of lid. Two of these are globular with wide flat bases, the third is C1993, a small wide-mouthed bowl, with a lid which may be another upturned plain bowl.

The 'teapot' lids are distinguished from the flat lids in several ways. Lidded pots were buried across the cemetery, but the flat round lids concentrated on the eastern edge, with a majority in a cluster towards the north-eastern corner of the cremation cemetery (Fig. 6), while the 'teapot' lids were mostly distributed across the northern half of the cemetery. Three of the 'teapot' lids, but only one of the flat lids, were unassociated, dislodged from their pots, as was Spong Man. There are three plain 'teapot' lids, associated with one plain and two decorated pots, as well as the plain bowl/lid with C1993, whereas all but one of the flat lids is decorated. The decorated 'teapot' lids are stamped and, if associated, were with stamped pots from stamp-linked groups. These lids have few securely associated grave-goods.

The flat lids are all decorated, except for the lid with the plain pot C1376. Seventeen of the flat lids belong to Style Group 20, phased B.[50] This Style Group combines two stamp-linked groups, SG31 and SG42, with a number of

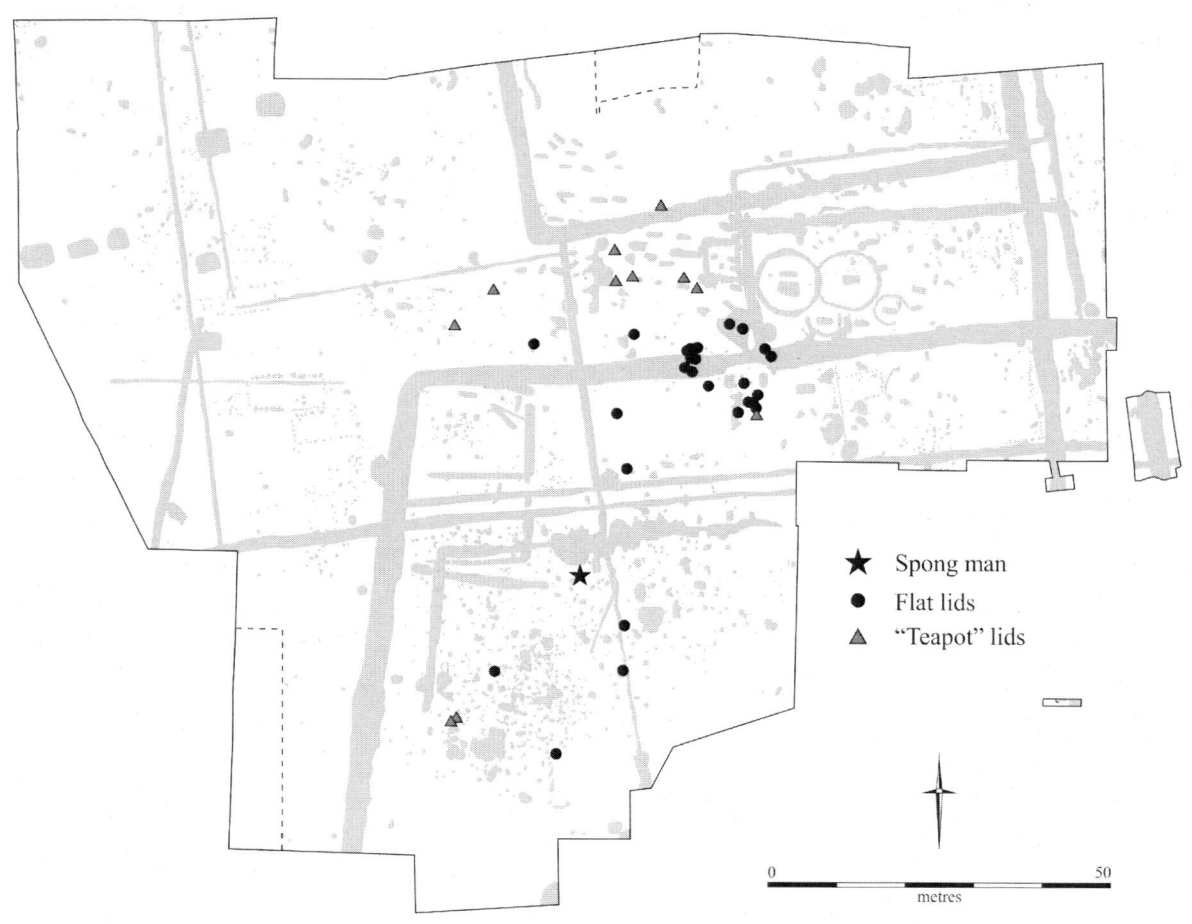

FIG. 6 SITE DISTRIBUTION MAP OF LIDS AT SPONG HILL (DRAWING BY ANDREW HALL)

---

[50] Penn 2013, Fig. A6.9

other pots of similar shape and decorative design. These pots are mostly of average or above average size but there are also small pots, C1992 and C2090. Lids are a linking attribute, but vertical and sloping bosses, together with linear swags, are also recurrent features. Stamps are used sparingly if at all on the pots, but more densely on some of the lids, stamped inside as well as on the top and sides.[51]

Spong Man shares features with both flat and 'teapot' lids, but is not exactly like either.

The height of the 'teapot' lids and the hollow form of Spong Man might suggest a connection, but only the lid with C1360 looks solid enough to support anything more substantial than a terminal knob. The flat lids are structurally more similar because of their internal rims. Some of them share with Spong Man diagonal lines around the outside rim, and the short diagonal lines or nicks around the edge of the chair are also very similar to those on the internal rim of the lid for C1806.[52] Overall the flat lids seem to have more in common with Spong Man but many of them have stamped decoration, which does not occur on Spong Man, and the distribution plot shows Spong Man away from the main flat lid cluster (Fig. 6).

In conclusion, although Spong Man is unique, it can be seen to have a context at Spong Hill, the cemetery where it was buried. Its fabric and some details of form and decoration are shared with other pots from Spong Hill. It would have fitted some of the larger and more elaborate pots from the site. Above all, the use of ceramic lids is well established at the site. The lack of stamped decoration and the location of Spong Man in the middle of the cemetery argue against dating it to the later phase of the cemetery, phase C. The pots of an appropriate shape and size to have had it as a lid belong to phase A/B or B, and the largest group of lids, the flat ones, are also phase B.

A date in phase A or B therefore seems clear for Spong Man.

Two aspects of the associations discussed above might be emphasized. There are links with North Germany indicated by the occurrences of human or animal figural representation in connection with cremation urns, and indeed the phenomenon of lids on pots. Also lids became a distinctive feature at Spong Hill, shared by several of the stamp or style linked groups. An interpretation which might fit both is that Spong Man was created within the framework of ideas brought from north Germany in the early fifth century, and that this was an influential model which was the origin of the later use of lids at Spong Hill. This would suggest a relatively early date for Spong Man, before the middle of the fifth century. Alternatively it could be seen as contemporary with the flat lids, therefore belonging to phase B, the middle decades of the century.

Cambridge, January 2014

---

[51] e.g. C1806, Hills and Penn 1981, fig. 81
[52] Hills and Penn 1981, fig 81

Bibliography

Andersson, G., Beronius Jörpelan, L., Dunér, J., Fritsch, S., and Skyllberg, E. 2004, *Att fora gudarnas talan: figurines from Lunda*, Stockholm Museum archaeological series no. 55

Arnold, C.J, and Russell, A.D. 1983, 'The Sancton Baston Potter' Scottish Archaeological Review, vol. 2, part 1, pp. 17-30

Bantelmann, N. 1988, Suderbrarup: Ein Graberfeld der romischen Kaiserzeit und Volkerwanderungszeit in Angeln, Offa-Bucher Band 63

Christensen, T., 2013, 'A silver figurine from Lejre' Danish Journal of Archaeology, vol.2, Issue 1, pp. 65-78

Genrich, A. 1981, Die Altsachsen, Hannover Museum publications, vol. 25

Hassler, H.J. 1994, 'Neue Ausgrabungen in Issendorf' Studien zur Sachsenforschung 9

Hassler, H.J. 2001, Das Sächsische Gräberfeld von Issendorf, Teil 4 (Studien zur Sachsenforschung 9.4) Oldenburg: Isensee

Higham, N.J., and Ryan, M.J. 2013, The Anglo-Saxon World, Yale University Press

Hills, C.M. 1977, *The Anglo-Saxon Cemetery at Spong Hill, North Elmham, Part 1*, East Anglian Archaeology 6

Hills, C.M. 1980, 'Anglo-Saxon chairperson' *Antiquity* 54, no. 210, pp. 52-54

Hills, C.M. 1993, 'Who were the East Anglians?' in *Flatlands and Wetlands: Current themes in East Anglian Archaeology*, J. Gardiner (ed.), East Anglian Archaeology 50, pp. 14-23

Hills, C.M. 1994, 'The Chronology of the Anglo-Saxon Cemetery at Spong Hill, Norfolk', in B. Stjernquist (ed). *Prehistoric Graves as a Source of Information*, Stockholm, pp. 41-49

Hills, C.M., and Penn, K.J. 1981, *The Anglo-Saxon Cemetery at Spong Hill, North Elmham, Norfolk, Part II*, East Anglian Archaeology 11

Hills, C.M., Penn, K.J., and Rickett, R.J. 1987, *The Anglo-Saxon Cemetery at Spong Hill, North Elmham, Norfolk, Part IV*, East Anglian Archaeology 34

Hills, C.M., Penn, K.J. and Rickett, R.J. 1994, *The Anglo-Saxon Cemetery at Spong Hill, North Elmham, Norfolk, Part V*, East Anglian Archaeology 67

Hills, C.M., and Lucy, S.J. 2013, *Spong Hill Part IX: chronology and synthesis*, McDonald Institute monograph

Kinsley, G.A. 1989, *The Anglo-Saxon Cemetery at Millgate, Newark on Trent*, Nottingham Archaeological Monographs no. 2

Leahy, K. 2007, '*Interrupting the Pots' The Excavation of Cleatham Anglo-Saxon Cemetery, North Lincolnshire*, CBA Research Report 155

Lethbridge, T.C. 1951, *A Cemetery at Lackford Suffolk*, Cambridge Antiquarian Society Quarto publications, New Series no.VI

McKinley, J.I. 1994, *The Anglo-Saxon Cemetery at Spong Hill, North Elmham, Part VIII: The Cremations*, East Anglian Archaeology 69

Myres, J.N.L. 1977, *A Corpus of Anglo-Saxon Pottery of the pagan period*, Cambridge University Press.

Myres, J.N.L., and Green, B. 1973, *The Anglo-Saxon Cemeteries of Caistor-by-Norwich and Markshall, Norfolk*, Society of Antiquaries of London Research Report 30

Nugent, R., forthcoming, *Casting a New Eye on the Spong Hill Chairperson*

Penn, K.J. 2013, *Appendix 6: Catalogue of Style Groups*, in C.M. Hills and S.J. Lucy, pp. 409-437

Richards, J.D. 1987, *The Significance of Form and Decoration of Anglo-Saxon Cremation Urns*, BAR British Series 166

Rickett, R.J. 1995, *The Anglo-Saxon Cemetery at Spong Hill, North Elmham, Part VII: The Iron Age, Roman and Early Saxon Settlement*, East Anglian Archaeology 73

Riddler, I., and Trzaska-Nartowski, N. 2013, 'Artefacts of worked bone and antler' in C.M. Hills and S.J. Lucy, pp. 92-155

Rohrer-Ertl, O. 1971, *Untersuchungen am Material des Urnenfriedhofes von Westerwanna, Kreis Land Hadeln*, Dissertation, University of Hamburg

Schon, M. 1999, *Feddersen Wierde, Fallward, Flogeln*, Museum Burg Bederkesa

Weber, M. 2000, *Das sachsische Graberfeld von Issendorf, Landkreis Stade, Niedersachsen*, Teil 2

Webster, L. 2012, *Anglo-Saxon Art*, British Museum

Wegewitz, W. 1961, *Die Urnenfriedhofe von Dohren und Daensen im Kreise Harburg*

The Anglo-Saxon cemetery at Morning Thorpe: further thoughts

Kenneth Penn

Abstract: Little skeletal evidence survived at the Early Saxon cemetery at Morning Thorpe, Norfolk, and many burials also lacked grave-goods or grave-goods that could be dated or might indicate 'gender'. This note has a focus on these burials, their pattern of accompaniment, and what they add to understanding. The writer identifies two distinct sorts of 'neutral' burials, those characterised as 'knife and buckle', probably males, and 'pot only' burials, all in short graves and presumably young. Subtle changes over time in costume and age ranges may reflect social changes, even the establishment of an elite.

Introduction

The cemetery at Morning Thorpe, south Norfolk, was discovered during gravel quarrying in October 1974. Rescue excavation was carried out under Christopher Sparey-Green, with Andrew Rogerson and Tony Gregory, and for eight weeks in 1975 by Andrew Rogerson. The cemetery lay on higher ground overlooking a tributary of the River Tas; to the north once stood a barrow, recorded on air photographs, but lost in quarrying, which also removed burials to the north; burials to the east lay on unexcavated slopes.[1]

This work recorded over 300 inhumations and nine cremations. The results were published as an illustrated catalogue[2] in the expectation that a discussion would follow. The same policy was adopted for three other Anglo-Saxon cemeteries excavated in that period: Spong Hill and Bergh Apton (Norfolk) and Westgarth Gardens, Bury St Edmunds (Suffolk).

A discussion of the inhumation burials at all four cemeteries was published in *Aspects of Anglo-Saxon Inhumation Burial* in 2007,[3] and cremation burials at Spong Hill were published by Hills and Lucy in 2013.

Aspects adopted a 'top-down' approach to address 'questions about broad-ranging social issues such as ethnic identity and the formation of kingdoms', involving the chronology of furnished and datable burials (weapons and dress fittings). Analysis of the four cemeteries involved correspondence analysis, supported by research on a national sample of weapon graves,[4] and a chronology for glass beads.[5] Absolute dates were derived from continental systems. The result is a chronological model (dating of individual graves is elusive) mapping social structure, through material culture and patterns of individual age and sex.[6] Analysis identified three main phases (A, B and C), although the steps were not the same for males (MA-MC) and females (FA-FC);[7] Morning Thorpe burials belonged to Phases A and B.

Aspects concluded with: 'evidence for children's graves at the four cemeteries suggests that sooner or later the whole range of household members were inhumed, ranging from what appears to be 'unfurnished' burials and graves with a pot as the only grave-good in the archaeological record to those buried with almost the full known range of grave-goods available to their gender'.

Regional differences and variation over time are both integral to historical understanding, but half of burials, the 'neutral' and unfurnished, escape dating. This note explores their character and relationships through grave-good provision and other cultural markers, which may express both social cohesion and competition in uncertain times, and local practices.

Background

Burial at Morning Thorpe began around AD450, continuing into the later 6th century. Burial may have lasted nearly 150 years, with the recorded burials representing a stable population of around 60 individuals at any time.[8] With the 'lost' burials, the final size of the cemetery was possibly around 1000 burials, which could represent a population around 200 at any time, probably from small settlements within a wide area, extending beyond the modern parish of Morning Thorpe. The major rite was inhumation, with cremation a minor rite (at least five burials).

Like other cemeteries on the East Anglian glacial till (Boulder Clay) plateau, bone survival was poor. About a quarter of the inhumations could be assigned an age range, mostly all adult; only a handful could be 'sexed', even tentatively.[9]

The positions of brooches and the existence of 'coffins' sometimes suggests supine burial, and in around twenty burials body positions could be estimated, with more than half probably extended, the others being flexed to some degree. One burial, in Grave 53, could possibly be described as crouched. A few burials lay under a mound, in a coffin or were part of a 'multiple burial' in the longer graves, perhaps reflecting some special status.

---

[1] Green *et al* 1987
[2] Green *et al* 1987
[3] Penn and Brugmann, hereafter *Aspects*
[4] Härke 1989a
[5] Brugmann 2004
[6] *Aspects* pp. 45-7
[7] *Aspects* fig. 5.21

[8] *Aspects* pp. 94-5, 98-100
[9] *Aspects* p. 88

The cemetery was in use for over a century, encompassing changes in material culture and in the way individuals were provided at death. A national study showed that from the early 6th century, there was a marked increase in weapon burials, with a sharp peak in the mid-6th century, followed by a decline and then a slight rise from the later 6th century. Weapon burial became more exclusive, by rank, but with the inclusion of more sub-adults, as the elite included more of its younger members, not given 'adult' burial previously; there were also age thresholds, with younger males accompanied by a spear, then (around 18 years), with shields.[10]

In female burials there was a similar rise in accompanied burial, from the late 5th century (phase A), followed by a lowering of grave-good quality, with lighter annular brooches, and a reduction in amount of metal used, and then a phase (B) with fewer but larger brooches, and lavish objects.[11] As with males, there was possibly wider access to dress accessories for younger individuals in the later phases.

A recent study shows how material culture changed from the mid 6th century and how 'the suite of formal dress accessories…and the highly-visible burial tradition of which they were part, now appear to be a feature of the later 5th and first half of the 6th centuries'.[12]

Nationally, male graves increased in length slightly over time, whilst female graves were fairly stable,[13] but, at Morning Thorpe, there is some evidence of a decrease in average grave lengths for furnished females, possibly reflecting greater age inclusiveness for a new elite.[14] This may be evidenced by increasing proportions of 'dated' burials in the lower half of length range, by phase: FA1 25%, FA2 44%, FB 56%.

Härke's national study of fifty-four cemeteries[15] showed that about 47% of males were buried with weapons (i.e. about 18% of all graves), but this varied regionally from 11% to 90% of adult males, which may suggest social rather than solely biological determinants.

Some 44% of weapon burials had shields, possibly reflecting an age threshold. Juveniles, poorly represented among weapon burials, rarely had shields, but were given spears alone.[16]

National surveys may mask local variations, and this note considers only Morning Thorpe, with reference to other burial places.

TABLE 1. A NATIONAL SAMPLE: AGE AT DEATH: % OF WEAPON BURIALS WITH SHIELDS (AFTER DICKINSON AND HÄRKE 1992)

Age	% with shields
8-14	9%
15-20	17%
20-50	53%

Method

Weapon burials and furnished females have virtually exclusive types of major grave-goods. In cemeteries with poor bone survival, it is 'gendered' grave-goods that create a dichotomy between males in 'weapon burials' and 'furnished females': where sex/gender is unknown, it is usually because of the lack of 'gendered' objects. With rare mixing of 'male' and 'female' objects, burials may be cast into four groups, based on gender-specific items (or absence): weapon burials, furnished females, neutral, and unfurnished burials.

The term 'unfurnished' is used, although organic objects possibly existed and definition of burials as 'gendered' or 'neutral' (on the basis of grave-goods alone) may obscure other patterns, signalled by costume and organic objects.[17]

Burial with 'neutral' items (mostly knives and pots) and unfurnished burials (Group D) have no gender indicators; the neutral burials have been further divided into 'knife and buckle' graves (Group C) and 'pot only' burials, Group E, overwhelmingly corresponding to 'short' graves (see below).

The 'neutral' burials in Group C have a strong 'knife and buckle' pattern, typical of weapon burials. Even without bone, division of the burials into these Groups is supported by their regularity of provision.

Whilst weapon burials and furnished females provide material for correspondence analysis, neutral burials (with few significant grave-goods other than 'knife and buckle' and associated items, mostly vessels) and 'unfurnished' burials are mostly undatable. Only two neutral burials were 'datable': 37 (phase B) and 200 (phase A).

Weapon burials (spears and shields) probably included over 40% of the adult males, and became increasingly linked to status.[18] Furnished females possibly included most females, even the young, who drew from the same range of dress ornament. Neutral burials were mostly 'knife and buckle' burials, with an occasional other item, mostly containers. 'Knife and buckle' burials continued as the main type of furnished burial until this ceased in the late 7th/early 8th century[19], also the case at Flixton, Suffolk, and Saltwood and Buckland in Kent.[20]

---

[10] Härke 1992, p. 182, fig. 36
[11] *Aspects* p. 93
[12] Hines and Bayliss 2013, p. 528
[13] Stoodley 1999, p. 67, fig. 59
[14] *Aspects* pp.76, 93-98
[15] Härke 1989a
[16] Dickinson and Härke 1992
[17] Walton Rogers 2007, p. 249
[18] *Aspects* p. 97
[19] Penn 2000, p. 55; 2011, p. 65
[20] Walton Rogers 2012, p. 178

TABLE 2. GROUPS A-E: % AT MORNING THORPE

Group		Nos (%)
A	weapon burials: defined by a weapon (sword, shield, spear)	65 (21%)
B	Furnished females: with typical female accompaniments of brooches, beads, wristclasps.	106 (34%)
C	Furnished with 'neutral' grave-goods (ie not 'gendered').	60 (18%)
D	Unfurnished burials, that is, with no surviving grave-goods.	48 (15%)
E	'pot only'.	37 (12%)

In some cemeteries, bone survival showed unfurnished burials included all ages, both male and female; at Linton Heath, Cambs, and Portway, Andover, unfurnished burials correlate strongly with burials of children; at Snape, Suffolk, and at Polhill, Kent, they were mostly juveniles, and at Westgarth Gardens, Bury St Edmunds, mostly female (based on a small sample).[21]

It must be noted that although there was widespread lavish investment in the first half of the 6th century, and fewer identifiable burials with grave-goods in the next half-century (*Aspects* pp. 90-1), unfurnished burials 'occur in a consistency of proportions in cemeteries... from the late 5th to 7th centuries'.[22]

Tabulation

'Relic tables' for Groups are organised by grave length (based on the published plans, measured along the axis). Several burials are omitted because of disturbance and truncation: unlikely to be significant since these were from each of the identified groups. Graves varied in size from small pits containing cremation urns to full-size graves around 3m in length, probably reflecting the actual body length of the deceased and therefore their age, with shorter graves for infants and children. Very long graves possibly reflected the social importance of the deceased (and could allow space for e.g. furs and blankets). Grave size and elaboration may reflect investment of resources and energy.

At Wakerley, Northants, many individuals could be given at least an approximate age, and grave length corresponded well with age group (although children and juveniles were occasionally placed in long graves as part of a multiple burial). Children were buried in short-medium length graves, juveniles in graves about 1.30m-1.70m long, whilst adults had graves mostly 1.70m-2.10m long.[23]

The tables reveal a gradual change in burial character around 1.50m in grave lengths, with all Group A and most of the better furnished Group B burials in graves above this length. The longest graves were the most elaborate, occasionally containing a coffin or placed under a barrow, perhaps of more significant individuals, although some 'well-furnished' burials were found in shorter graves.

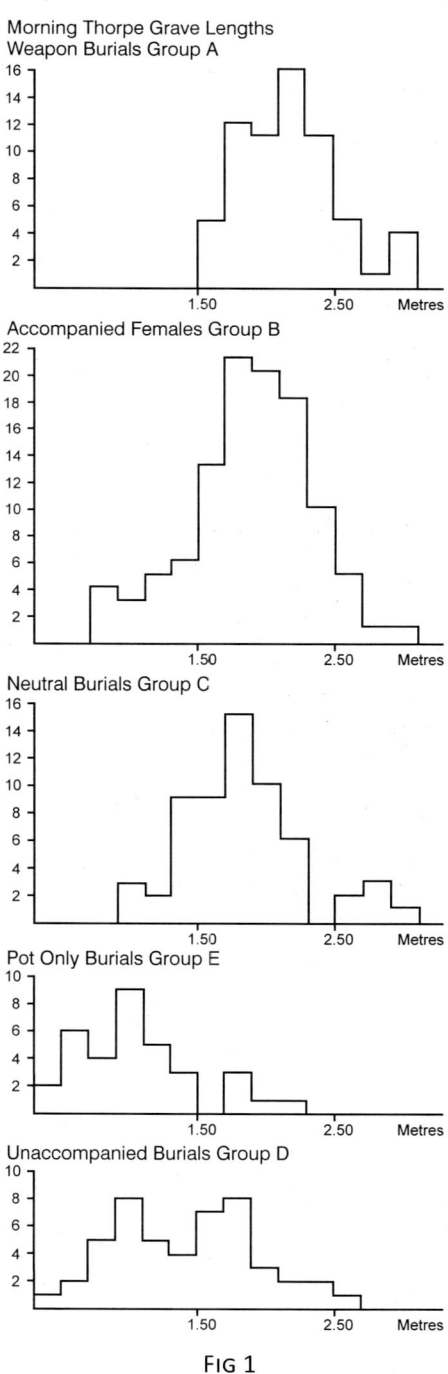

FIG 1

[21] Cook and Dacre 1985; Filmer-Sankey and Pestell 2001; Hawkes 1973; Neville 1854; West 1988
[22] Hines and Bayliss 2013, p. 524
[23] Adams and Jackson 1988-9

TABLE 3. GROUP A: WEAPON BURIALS (LONGEST AT TOP) (K KNIFE, B BUCKLE, TW TWEEZERS, PM PURSEMOUNT)

BC	Individ	Grave	Swrd	Shld	Spr	K	B		pot	other	phase
C		35			1	K	B		?	tub	MA2
				•							
C	ad	1		•	1	K	B				MA1a
BC		157			1	K	B	tw		(gilt belt fittings)	MA2
?B		170			1			tw		?robbed	MA1
		225		•	1	K	B			(?belt fitting)	MA1
		61		•	1	K				(silver shield button)	MA2
C		367		•	1	K	B				MB
	y.ad	351			1						MB
	y.ad	148			1		B	tw	•	glass beaker, Ae sheet frags, ?structure	MA1
?B	y.ad	238			1	K				(double grave), tub, bucket and beads (gold leaf near bucket)	MA2
		356			1	K					
		388		•	1	K	B			+ pot with cremation	MA2
		416			1	K	B	tw, PM			
		333		•	1	K	B	?PM			MB
		304			1		B				MA2
		215		•	1	KK	B				MB
		183		•	?					strapend?	
		129			1	K			•		
	ad	85		•	1	K			•		MA2
		62			1		B			?structure	MA2
?B	ad	126		•	1	K				?bowl	MA2
		370A			1	K	B		?		
	ad	355			1	K		tw	•		
?B	old. ad	218	•	•	1	K	B			bucket (gold leaf near sword)	MA2/MB
		362	axe		1					(disturbed)	MA2
		327			1	K					MA2
		255		•	1	K	B				MB
		132			1	K	B	awl			
		361			1	K					
C	y.ad	297			1	K	B				MA2
		275			1		B				MA2
	y.ad	265		•	1	K	B			(large knife)	MA1
	sub.ad	211		•	1	KK	BB				MA2
		154		•	1	K					
		115		•			B		•	horse tooth	MA2
?B	y.ad	97		•	1	K	B		•	lyre	MA1
		402			1	K			•		MA2
		374		•	1	K	B				MB
C	?ad	178	arrow				B			(belt fittings)	

		389		•	1	K	B			(silver shield button)	MA1a
		341			1	K	B				MA2
		340			1	K					MA2
	y.ad	337			1	K			•		MA2
		332			1	K	B			?box	
		319		•	1	K	B				
	y.ad	296			1	K	B				
		269			1	K	B				
		45		•		K	B	tw			
		42		•	1	K					MB
C	?ad	380		•	1	K					MA2
		330			1	K					
		274			1	K	B	awl		bowl	MA1
		67			1	K	B	tw			MA2
		19			1	K				With cremations 422-4, 427	
		409			1		B			(coiled pin)	MB
	ad	398			1	K	B			(coiled pin)	MB
		381			1	K	B	PM			MA2
		259		•	1	K	B	tool/pin			MA1
	ad	40			1	K	B		•		MA2
		339			1	K	B		•		MA1/S2
		69			1				•	40 sherds	MA2
	ad	142			1	K	B				MA2
		117			1				•		MA2
?B		246		?		K	B				
		68		•	1	K					MA1

TABLE 4. GROUP B: FURNISHED FEMALES (LONGEST GRAVES AT TOP, 'SHORT GRAVES' SHADED) (BROOCHES A ANNULAR, SL SMALL-LONG, C CRUCIFORM, C5 CRUCIFORM GROUP 5, SQ SQUARE-HEAD ; WC WRISTCLASP, K KNIFE, B BUCKLE, O RING, GH GIRDLEHANGER, Ae BRONZE, Ag SILVER)

BC	indiv	grave	pair	centre	beads	pend	WC	girdle gp	Belt	pot	other	phase
		209	AA	C	39		WC	KO key				FA2
		316	SL SL	pin	31		WC		K			FA2a
		253	AA	C	45		WC	O GH tag			iron rods	FA2a
		251	AA	A	8		WC				Ae strip	FA2
C		208	AA	C	34		WC	KO		••		FA1/2
		148	SL SL	pin			WC	O	B tag		tweezers	FA2
		393	AA	C	76			K GH B tag			ring with beads	FA2b
C		392	AA	A	3		WC	KK			Ae sheet, staple	FA1

Landscapes and Artefacts

C		353	CC	C5	90		WC	KOO GH tool	B		?box 2 Ae rings	FA1/2
C		326	AA		14							
		90	CC	C	90		WC	KO		●	Ae rings	FA1
		371A	AA	SQ	18							FB
		371B	AA	C								FA1
		342	AA		46				B		Ae ring	FB
		321	A		10			KO				FA2
		304	AA	A	27			KO				FA2a
		129	A	C	20			K				FA1/2
		370	SL SL	C	12		WC	KO key		●		FA1/2
		153	AAAA	C	8		WC	KO	B		W - E orientation	FA1
C		140	AA	pin	9			KO		●●		FA2
		127	AA		1		WC	KO rod tag		●●		FA2
	y.ad	44	AA	disc	10		WC	K				FA2a
		385	AA		5					●	pot with cremation	FA2
		160	AA	C								FA2
C		362	AA	C	57		WC	KO	B tag		Ae sheet	FA1
		359	AA	SQ	17	pend		KB				FB
		249	AA	pin	1		WC	KB key, tag		●		FA2
		221	AA	pin +K	7		WC	O key				FA2
		141	SL					K				FA1
		133	AA	C	12		WC	K key			bowl, Roman brooch	FA2
		50	AA	pin	11		WC	O		●		FA2
		16	SL SL	C5	49		WC	KO				FA1/2
		131	AA	C							Fe, Ae sheet	FA2
		20	AA		1		WC	KO				FA2
C		396	AA	C	5		WC	KO GH		●		FA2a
		360	AA		40		WC	O tw	B			FA2a
		358A	A	C	19		WC					FA2B
		358B	AA	SL	104		WC	K GH chain tag			?bowl, ? KBB key	FA2B
	y.ad	106	AA		17			KO	B			FA2
?C	y.ad	86	AA	pin	15			KO tag				FA2
		80A	AA	C			WC	KOO				FA1/2
		80B	AA	Ring	20	pend	WC				bracteates, scutiform pendant AE slip-knot	FA2/FB
		51	AA	pin				O	K			FA2
		91	AA	C	90		WC	K			?bowl	FA1/2
		400			46						pin, silver beads	FB

		378	AA	pin	38	pend	WC	KO	B	•	Pair Ag slip-knots	FA2
		375			36	pend		K		•	Ag wire ring	FB
		337	SL SL	pin	42			KKO	B			FA1
		334	AA	Pin	14			K				FA2a
		309			45			KB				FB
		258			14			KB			brooch frag, staple	FB
		231	SL SL		35			K				FA1/FA2a
		173	AA	A	16	pend	WC	KO key			Pendant	FA2a
		407	AA	pin	74		WC	O key	tag			FA2
		146	OO								(2 disc brooches)	FA2A
		373	A									
		369A	A	pin	12	pend	WC	KO bead			?box	FA2a
		369B		Pin	16		WC	KO key	B		Spindlewhorl	FA2a
	subad	322			40	pend		KB			pin + staple	FA2b/FB
		312	AA		2		WC	KO	B tag		iron strip	FA2
		303	AA		24	pend	WC	KB	?			FA2
		286	AA					KKB		•		
B		227			1					•	Ag slip-knot	FB
		124						KO key			sherds on surface	
		64			10					•	PAIR Ag slip-knots	FB
		18	AA	pin	16		WC	KO GH				FA2a
		376	AA		2				?B			
		242	AA		1			K	B			
		30	AA	CCC	140			KO				FA1
		108A	AA		82			KO key			?bowl	FA2
	y.ad	108B	AA	Pin	95		WC	KO GH tag				FA2
		92	A		17	pend					('bucket' beads)	FA2b
		76	AA					K tool				FA2
?B	y.ad	6	AA		32		WC	KO key			?box	FA2
		397	AA	C	18		WC	KO GH B tag				FA2b
		336	AA	Pin							?tools	
		328	SL SL	A	5			K		•		FA1/FA2a
		325			11	pend		K	tw		(pendant, tw, Pair Ae slip-knots at foot)	
		288	SQ		26			KB	tw		(bead at belt)	FB
		284			5			B			Ae sheet	FB
	sub.ad	134	AA	pin				KOB tag				FA2

95

		43						B		Roman brooch	
		96	SL SL	C	16			K			FA1/2
		410	A		17			B			FA2a
		306				3				PAIR Ag slip-knots	FB
	juv	256	AA		15				tag		FA2a
	juv	207	AA		12	pend				•		FA2
	juv	73	A			pend		O		(Roman ring)	FA2
		415	A		6	pend	WC			••		
		387	AA	pin	34		WC	KO tag			FA2
		395								PAIR AG slip-knots	
		368	A		5						
	Inf/juv	276			4						FB
		216B	A		20			KB B tag		Iron rod	FB
		331	AA								
		379			10					PAIR AG slip-knots	FA2
	Inf/juv	384	A	pin	25	pend		KO key B tag		Ag mount ('bell beads')	FB
		323			2					•	PAIR AG slip-knots	
	juv	205			1						
		346	SL SL	C	11				tw	Ae slip-knot(	FA1/FA2a
		338			4						
		149			6					•		FA1
		70			4					•	Pair AE slip-knots	FA2
		318								Cremation (brooch and lace end)	
		383			7					•		
		99		A			WC	K			FA2

TABLE 5. GROUP C: NEUTRAL BURIALS (LONGEST AT TOP, 'SHORT GRAVES' SHADED)

BCM	Indiv	Grave	K	B	other	Pot	
BC		200	K	B			cauldron, bucket, Ae bowl
?B		320	K		strpend	•	(iron pin)
		65	K	B	tw PM	•	(gilt buckle)
		233	K	B			
		266	K	B			
		87			tw		bowl
		174	K	B			
C		78	K	B	tw		?staple
		365	K	B			
		344	K				
		335	K			•	bowl
		93	K	B	steel	•	
		252	K	BB			
		57	KK				
		24	K				
		314	K				
		294	K	B			Iron rod
		281	K		tw		
		245	K				
		229	K				
		77	K	B			
		27	K	B	tw		
		315	K	B			
		254					Ae sheet fragment
		235	KK	B			
		58	K				
		352	K				(charcoal in fill)
		260	K	B			Iron staple
		414		B			coiled head pin
		278	K				?bag
		220	K	B			
		184	K		PM		
		156	K	B	?tool		?box
		147	K	?			
		59	K	B		•	
		350	K	B	?tool		(disturbed). Iron strip, double-tongued buckle
		60	K	B			
?		268	K	B			
		37		B	steel		(triangular buckle)

LANDSCAPES AND ARTEFACTS

		349	K			
		311	KK	B		
		301		?		Ae sheet/staple
		295	K			
		234	KKK	B		
		222	K			
						Ae ring. (cremation in pot)
?		17			●	Ae sheet, burnt
		244	K	B	●	
		182	K	B		
		125	K			
		116			●	iron ring/pin
		53		B		
		239	K	B		
		228	K	B		?bead
		152				?box, potsherds
		46			●	Ae sheet
		7	K	B		
		272	K	B		
		243				?box/bowl
		202	K		●	
		72	K		●	

TABLE 6. GROUP D: UNFURNISHED BURIALS (LONGEST GRAVES AT TOP, 'SHORT GRAVES' SHADED)

Individ	Grave	
	102	
	120	
	54	
	155	coffin
	291	charcoal in pit
	382	
	329	
	305	
	101	
	289	
	277	
	419	
	377	
	345	
	104	
	175	
	237	
	213	
	212	

	391	
	394	
	290	
	279	
	81	
	41	
	308	
	219	
	401	
	49	
	111	
	39	
	180	
	413	
	348	
	166	
	31	
	10	
	271	
	171	
	105	
	399	
	324	
	263	
	267	
	159	
	292	
	162	
	436	

Group A: weapon burials (65) had the longest graves, with none below 1.50m, suggesting weapon burial was restricted to adults. The largest group was Group B: furnished females (106), with graves down to c. 1.00m in length (Fig. 1), the shortest graves being more sparsely furnished, and probably children, and included 'beads only' burials, burials with wire rings, and no brooches (in a late phase).

Amongst Group C: neutral burials [60], a knife and buckle was nearly standard, an occasional extra object at the belt (tool, tweezers, pursemount), and occasional pots. The regular provision of Group A burials (mostly weapons/ knife and buckle/vessel), suggests an homogeneous social group, with few outstanding individuals. Apart from weapons, Group A burials had the same equipment as neutral burials.

Burial provision was age-related, but age thresholds were different between males and females, and would seem to change over time.[24]

Graves under 1.50m in length (conveniently: 'short graves') were mostly sparsely furnished (small brooches, beads, an occasional knife, but no wristclasps), and included many (30/37) 'pot only' graves (Fig. 2). Below around 1.20-1.30m, this pattern was very marked, with almost no grave-goods, except the pots in 'pot only' graves (probably children, based on limited skeletal evidence).

---
[24] Härke 1992, p. 182; Stoodley 1999, p. 105

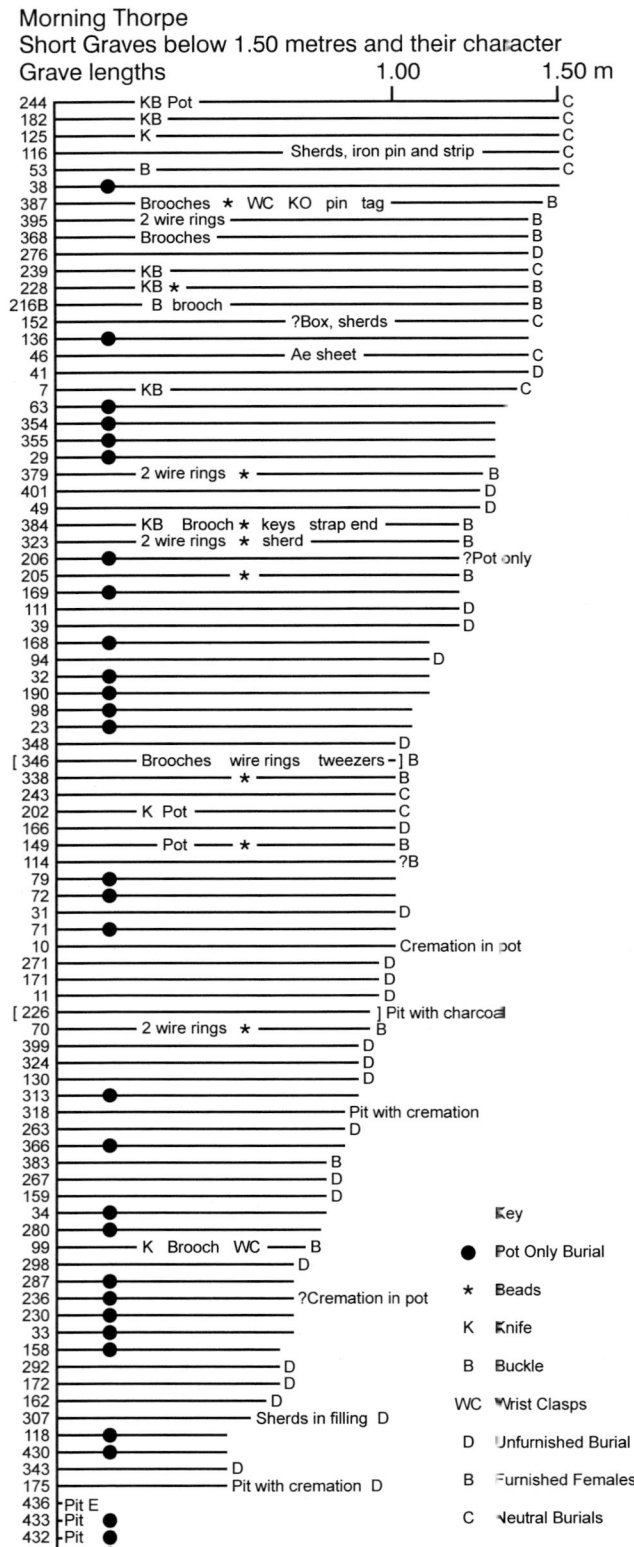

Fig 2

Results

Group A: weapon burials

Group A contained about 21% of all burials, suggesting that 42% of all males at Morning Thorpe had burial with weapons, which suggests no special status; few had any other grave-goods. Härke suggested that burial with weapons was not restricted to those with a place in an active war-band, but was occasionally awarded to older men and children, perhaps evidence that the right to bear weapons was inherited, not achieved, and retained throughout life.[25]

About nineteen could be tentatively 'aged', all young adult/adult, except for 218 (old adult) and 211 (sub-adult).

Weapon combinations were symbolic rather than functional, not reflecting possession of weapons in life. Provision of weapons at death was possibly derived from free-born status, reflected in Group A's greater incidence of longer and wider graves, barrows and coffins, and longer knives. Their limited range (spear and shield) hardly allows stratification, except by age (with youngsters possibly given a spear (and shield around 18 years).[26] But at Morning Thorpe, there was a possible threshold, with all weapon burials in graves over 1.5m, and weapon burials without shields (38/65) were conceivably younger males. (At Lechlade, the threshold for being equipped with a shield in the grave appears to be around 18 years).[27]

Nearly all the weapon burials included a knife, probably suspended from a belt (buckle), occasionally with another small object, like the neutral burials; in contrast, furnished females were often with knife and ring (in phase FA), the ring possibly representing a bag suspended from the belt, or sometimes perhaps a form of girdle-fastener.

At Morning Thorpe, the only burial with a sword (an older adult in Grave 218) was well-provided in other ways: he was buried with his sword, spear and shield, knife and buckle, and a bucket (gold leaf was found close to the sword), and then a barrow raised above him. The dating (MA2/MB) suggests that his was not a 'founder's grave'.

Seven burials had coffins, four in the longest graves, and up to six, across the length range, may have had barrows.

Other hints of individual character in weapon burials come from burials with 'special' objects, mostly vessels (tub; glass beaker; tub, bucket; bucket; lyre: see below). Of notable weapon burials, the longest, in Grave 35, was in a coffin, with weapons and a tub; five had gold/silver items, including two with silver shield buttons (61 and 389), 218 and 157 (with barrow and coffin) with gilt belt fittings, and two (in possible barrows) with gold leaf: a young adult in

---

[25] Härke 1989a
[26] Härke 1989a
[27] Boyle et al. 1998

238 with tub and bucket. Grave 148 held a young adult with spear and glass beaker (under a structure?), and 97 was a young adult with weapons and lyre.

The lyre is an unusual item, famously seen with the 'Prittlewell prince' and the Sutton Hoo ship burial, but also in an otherwise unremarkable grave at Bergh Apton. Perhaps a social taboo regarding personal items prevented their reuse. There was no particular association (or lack of it) between shields and elaborate burial, either coffins, or vessels in the grave; two 'rich' burials in Graves 148 and 238 were without shields.

Group B: furnished females

(Eight disturbed graves (35, 48, 97, 112, 214, 216A, 229 and 293) were not included in the 106 burials tabulated). Grave lengths and proportions of the tabulated burials suggest that Group B included females of all ages, though mostly adults; of 107 burials, 17 were in 'short' graves. The tables set out the dress fittings with each burial, but with no osteological information, associations between age and costume are unclear. Female costume comprised: peplos, dress and cloak/shawl. The fittings may reflect costume, with peplos-wearers having a central brooch or pin fixing a cloak or shawl, whilst wristclasps (not seen in phase FB) represent the inner dress; fittings changed over time (and with age), as seen in the correspondence analysis.[28]

There were few Group B burials under barrows or in coffins, and these were in the longer graves, with, overall, more dress fittings than the others. But there seemed to be no association between brooch types and any other elements of dress fittings, such as numbers of beads, wristclasps, size of girdle group. Wristclasps, characteristic of 'Anglian' costume up to the mid-6th century (phase FA), were found mostly in the longer graves, and worn mostly by adults. Elaborate gilded wristclasps came from Grave 153 (fully furnished) and Grave 353 (a coffined burial).

Nonetheless, some burials in longer graves were also poorly furnished, perhaps older women who had passed on their major dress fittings or girdle groups.[29] At Lechlade, Glos, women with brooches were buried supine, whilst older women (with fewer brooches) were sometimes buried slightly flexed.[30]

Sixteen Group B burials belonged to a late phase (FB), four in 'short' graves; they wore pairs of annular brooches, three also had a square-head brooch. Unlike the females in phase FA, most had a knife and buckle, almost standard in weapon burials, and a characteristic of neutral burials (presumably also mostly males). Amongst furnished females, knives and girdle-groups were strongly associated with the longer graves, over 1.60m (probably the adults). Slip-knots - possibly to hold bead strings or a veil - were found with ten burials in shorter graves (all in the late phase).

Other objects could be associated with a knife, such as pursemounts, tweezers, or a girdle-hanger/iron key, sometimes carried in a bag (see below). Keys and girdle-hangers were probably symbolic, part of the costume of a married woman ('mistress of the house'), since girdle-hangers had no practical function. Both belong to FA2, but keys went on into FB. Although keys appear to be functional objects, unlike girdle-hangers, at Morning Thorpe, girdle-hangers and iron keys did not occur together, suggesting that here they might be alternatives for the same function.

Except for the shorter graves, most furnished females had a girdle group, which usually included a knife, but with suspension rings in phase FA1-2, not a buckle, suggesting that male/female costumes differed in how the knife was worn or carried. Amongst the shortest was an infant/juvenile in Grave 384, with a brooch and pin, beads, pendant and girdle group besides a silver mount. Except for Grave 384, the age range with girdle-hangers and keys was young adult/adult where identifiable. Females in phase FB seem to drop wristclasps, and adopt buckles instead of rings. As noted, the only FB burial with a ring (384) was in other ways exceptional.

There was a gradation rather than clear 'cut-off point' between well-furnished burials and those with no brooches, few beads, and little in the way of girdle groups. The shorter graves are assumed to be mostly minors, and include several late burials with wire rings or slip-knots (and few brooches) probably worn by children (Graves 64, 70, 80B, 227, 306, 323, 325, 375, 378, 379 and 395).

Twenty-one furnished females had no brooch, and eleven had slip-knots (eight with no shoulder brooches). There were no girdle groups amongst these burials, but five with knife and buckle.

Burials with no brooches, burials with wire rings

Amongst the furnished females could be discerned a group of twenty-four burials, all in the lower part of the table, and probably all of a late phase. This group comprises burials with no brooches (22) and burials with wire rings or slip-knots (11), nine of which belong to both sets, the other two had brooches: 80B and 378.

Amongst the shorter burials were twenty-two that were, in effect, 'beads only', with no brooches, wristclasps, or girdle group, and with beads as the sole dress fitting: 'beads only' and slip-knots seem to be children's accompaniments.

Of the seventeen Group B 'Short Graves', ten were 'beads only' or slip-knots (four), and two others had neither brooches or beads. Whilst children may not have been given 'adult' objects such as large brooches, wristclasps or girdle groups, their bronze or silver slip-knots (possibly all late) may have indicated family wealth.

---

[28] *Aspects*; Walton Rogers 2007, pp. 144-80
[29] Stoodley 1999, p. 105; Halsall 1995
[30] Boyle *et al* 1998

TABLE 7. GROUP B: FURNISHED FEMALES: BURIALS WITH SLIP-KNOTS, AND 'BEADS ONLY' BURIALS (LONGEST GRAVES AT TOP, 'SHORT GRAVES' SHADED)

					beads	pend	WC	girdlegp	belt	pot		
		80B	AA	Ring	20	pend	WC				Ae slip-knot, bracteates, scutiform pendant	FA2 /FB
		400			46						pin, silver beads	FB
		378	AA	pin	38	pend	WC	KO	B	•	Pair Ag slip-knots	FA2
		375			36	pend		K		•	Ag slip-knot	FB
		309			45			KB				FB
		258			14			KB			brooch frag, staple	FB
	subad	322			40	pend		KB			pin + staple	FA2b/FB
B		227			1					•	Ag slip-knot	FB
		124						KO key			sherds on surface	
		64			10					•	Pair Ag slip-knots	FB
		325			11	pend		K	tw		Pair Ae slip-knots, pendant, tw, at foot	
		284			5			B			Ae sheet	FB
		43							B		Roman brooch	
		306			3						Pair Ag slip-knots	FB
		395									Pair Ag slip-knots	
	Inf/juv	276			4							FB
		379			10						Pair Ag slip-knots	FA2
		323			2					•	Pair Ag slip-knots	
	juv	205			1							
		338			4							
		149			6					•		FA1
		70			4					•	Pair Ae slip-knots	FA2
		318									Cremation (brooch and lace end)	
		383			7					•		

There was some correspondence too, with date: of the 35 dated burials assigned to a late phase (FA2b/FB), only eleven were not in the group of twenty-four (92, 216B, 288, 342, 358A, 358B, 359, 371A, 371B, 384 and 397). If we accept that slip-knots were part of a bead string, then within the 'no brooch' set, one could identify another group which were in effect, 'beads only'.

Thus, in the later phase, we find either (?) adults with annular brooches, or greater inclusion of younger individuals with no brooches and their beads fastened with slip-knots.

Burials with 'beads only'

Of the 107 furnished females, eighty-five were provided with beads, the numbers of these varying from one to 111 (Grave 30). Of the individuals with beads, about 90% had fewer than fifty beads, and of these, most were well below twenty beads. Amongst the beads were a few metal beads and pendants, mostly associated with burials in the shorter graves, and usually with quite modest dress fittings (dates run from FA1/2 to FB). At Great Chesterford, furnished females consisted of thirty-three adults and three juveniles, whilst the 'beads only' burials were of two adults, one juvenile and eleven infants, evidence for an age threshold in provision.[31]

Burial 80B was part of a double burial (two Group B burials) and had bracteates and a scutiform pendant, as did 322, 359 and 369A (part of another double Group B burial).

---

[31] Evison 1994

Group C: neutral burials

Sixty 'neutral burials' were found, including nine (15%) in 'Short Graves'. The gender-neutral burials were some 19% of the total, possibly the imbalance between the Group A and Group B burials (65:106) suggesting that these were mostly males, Group D (48) of both sexes, and Group E 'pot only' (37), in 'Short Graves', of children. Group D, with no grave-goods, is unidentified to sex, but grave lengths point to a significant proportion of children: 50% regular graves, 50% 'Short Graves'.

Some 80% of Group A burials had a knife, against 55% of Group B. A knife on a belt (buckle) is a feature of Group A burials (54%) but a minor feature of Group B burials (10.6%), where the knife was part of a girdle group, and usually associated with a suspension ring (in phase FA).

A 'knife and ring' was seen in 29% of Group B burials, but none of the sixty Group C burials had a 'knife and ring', although twenty-six had a 'knife and buckle', and seventeen had a knife only, all suggesting that they were males.

In neutral burials, the knife at the belt was sometimes accompanied by another item (pursemount, tweezers, steel) suspended therefrom, rather than carried in a bag, as was often the female fashion. In other cases, an unaccompanied knife lay in the waist area. Possibly neutral burials included females in later phases, when they had adopted buckles.

Of the fifty-nine Group C burials above 1.50m in length, probably adults, forty-six had 'knife and/or buckle'; eight had no 'knife and/or buckle', but other modest items. Of the nine burials in 'Short Graves', six had knife and/or buckle, and four contained items besides the knife and buckle.

Their regularity, mostly just 'knife and buckle', suggests that 'neutral' burials, equal in numbers to weapon burials, had some formal status, but without the right to bear or be buried with arms. They are seen in similar proportions at other cemeteries, and were perhaps a recognised social group, 'possibly the dependent and poor'.[32]

TABLE 8. PROVISION OF KNIFE, BUCKLE AND RING (K, B AND O): PROPORTIONS IN EACH GROUP

	K&B	K&O	K	B	O
Group A	54%	-	21%	12.3%	26%
Group B	10.6%	29%	11%	4%	15.4%
Group C	42-48%	-	34%	3%	28%

[32] *Aspects* p. 94

Nonetheless, there were some exceptional neutral burials. In Groups A and B, the more elaborate burials (barrows, coffins) were associated with the longer graves. The lengths of Group C graves were similar to Group B, with a peak between 1.70m and 2.30m: their grave-goods, essentially 'knife and buckle', suggests 'unweaponed' males; only five stood out (65, 78, 200, 233, 320), and just two or three, in the longer graves (78, 200, 320) were much elaborated.

Grave 65 (2.90m) possibly under a barrow, had typical grave-goods (knife, buckle, pursemount, tweezers, and a gilded belt fitting): Graves 233 and 320 were also possibly barrow burials, and Grave 78, a coffin burial.

Grave 200 was the longest of the Group C graves, at 3.10m, and the most elaborate. It was possibly under a barrow and coffined, with a knife and buckle, and a set of elaborate vessels: cauldron, bucket and bowl. It belonged to phase A, and could be a 'founder's grave'. This individual was unweaponed, when other unweaponed males were apparently mostly just 'knife and buckle' burials. Grave 78 held a coffined individual, but modestly accompanied.

Neutral burials with elaborate vessels are known from Grave 103 at Sleaford with bucket and bowl (and tweezers), and perhaps signalled some special identity, perhaps even priestly, or some connection with feasting.

Group D: unfurnished burials

Unfurnished burials (48) include Grave 10, a pit c. 1.00m long which contained a pot with cremated bone (sub-adult/adult). Pits 8, 94, 226, 298 and 343 could also be graves. Several cut or disturbed graves were not included in table 6 (Graves 113, 201, 250, 264, 270, 300, 310 and 406).

Unfurnished burials included very short graves to those over 2.50m, suggesting a full range of ages. At Westgarth Gardens they were possibly female, adults and children, whilst at Barrington, Cambs, they were mostly young.[33] At Flixton, Suffolk, most unfurnished burials were in 'short' graves, suggested to be children, whilst those in larger graves were possibly servile.[34]

The proportion of 'Short Graves' (50%) must indicate that some were children and juveniles, whilst demographic balance could suggest they were females.

The absence of surviving grave-goods may point to a lower status for these individuals, yet Grave 155 had a coffin, mostly seen with more elaborate burials.

Group E: 'pot only' burials

When the gender-neutral burials (97) were first tabulated, another group of burials stood out, those with 'pot only'

[33] Malim and Hines 1998; West 1988
[34] Walton Rogers 2012, p. 185

LANDSCAPES AND ARTEFACTS

(37), strongly associated with graves below 1.5m (the lower limit for weapon burials), and, therefore, the probable accompaniment of children and/or juveniles. These burials were treated as a separate group, E: 'pot only' burials (Fig. 3).

Pots could be part of burial in all furnished Groups, but their number and character varied in a systematic way, a clue to their possible significance. It was not always clear if sherds in grave fills represent a disturbed but complete pot or residual fragments, even a graveside meal.[35]

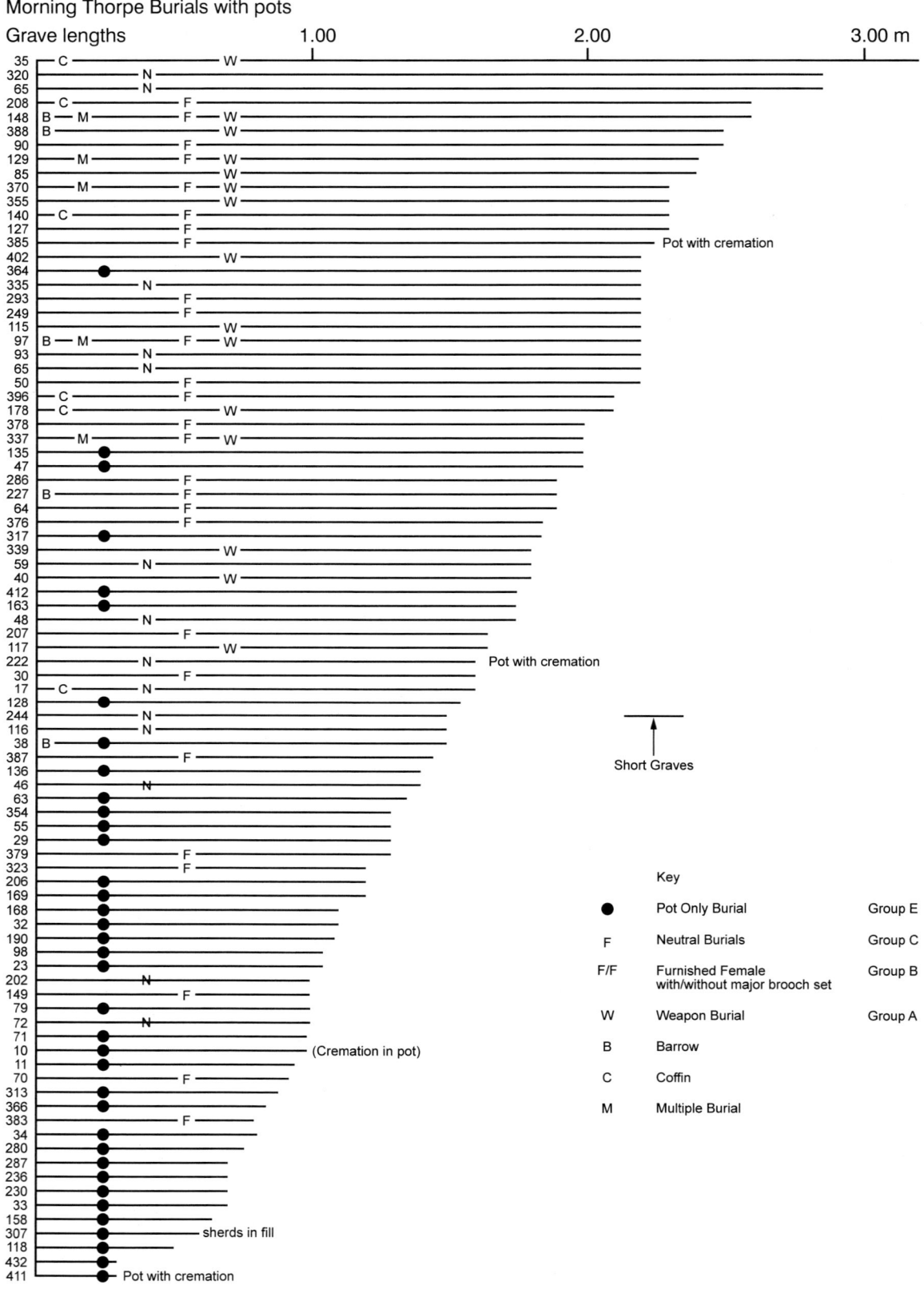

FIG 3

---

[35] Lee 2007, pp. 88–90; Walton Rogers 2012, p. 94

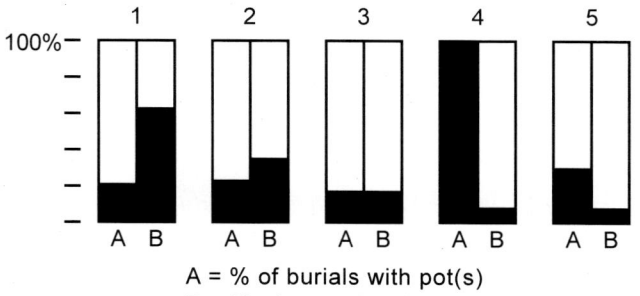

Morning Thorpe Pot Decoration

A = % of burials with pot(s)
B = % of pots with decoration

1 Weapon Burials
2 Furnished Females
3 Neutral Burials
4 Pot Only Burials
5 'Small Graves'

Fig 4

The provision of pots in Groups A, B and C was similar (18%-24%), but with notable differences in their elaboration (Fig. 4). The pots in Group E: 'pot only' graves were mostly plain and coarse pots; only three of the thirty-eight pots (8%) were decorated (two stamped, the other oddly 'rusticated'). 'Pot only' burials, and burials in 'Short Graves' were deliberately less elaborate, even in their pots.

The association of more elaborate burials with decorated pots is emphasized by the plainness of pots in the eighty-seven 'Short Graves' (below 1.50m) which includes pits 114, 175, 226, 318, 343, 346, 411, 432, 433, and 436. Of these, forty (46%) contained pottery, the majority as 'pot only' burials, and a further twenty-six (30%) as neutral burials.

Of the forty-one pots in 'Short Graves', just four (10%) were decorated. Even in the plain pots with furnished burials, there appear to have been deliberate differences in their character: the pots in Groups A and B burials were mostly well-made, the pots in 'neutral' and 'pot only' burials were usually coarser and more shapeless.

'Short Graves'

Grave lengths ranged from below 1.00m to above 3.00m, with a change of character and accompaniment around 1.50m, perhaps a little lower for female burials; the shorter graves probably mostly children and juveniles, not furnished with weapons or major brooch sets.

There were about eighty 'Short Graves', besides seven doubtful examples: 114, 226 and 346, and four possible pit graves (411, 432, 433 and 436), scattered across the excavated area.

The 'Short Graves' contained mostly unfurnished or poorly furnished burials, with twenty-four unfurnished burials and thirty 'pot only' burials (overwhelmingly at the lower length range); enough bone survived in seven 'Short Graves' to suggest a younger age group. The longer graves held most of the grave-goods and gender-specific items in this set of burials.

The 'Short Graves' included Grave 387 (possibly Group B), pits 411 and 432, and 33, 55, 71, 307, and 383 (where sherds represent a disturbed pot). Thirty-seven of these (46%) contained a pot, and twenty-seven (35%) were 'pot only' burials. A pot, but not of distinctive character, was therefore a consistent part of 'Short Grave' burials.

As noted, pots in 'Short Graves', and in 'pot only' burials, were rarely decorated, their plainness contrasting with the association of decoration and completeness with longer and elaborate graves; of the forty pots in 'Short Graves', just four were decorated and most were plain and coarse vessels; about twelve to fifteen (30%-38%) were complete (Fig. 4). 'Short Graves' did include some 'elaborate burials', and amongst these (but only just, at 1.50m), Grave 38, a 'pot only' burial, lay under a barrow. This exception may hint at some specific correspondence between age and 'pot only' graves.

Table 9. 'Short Graves' (below 1.5m): in each Group (%)

Group		%
A	0/65	0
B	17/106	16
C	9/60	15
D	24/48	50
E	30/37	81

Table 10. 'Short Graves': identified skeletal remains

Grave	Type	Individual
10	Cremation	Sub-adult/adult
53	Group C	Sub-adult/adult
175	Cremation	Sub-adult/adult
205	Group B?	Juvenile/sub-adult
236	Cremation	Infant?
276	Group D	Older infant/juvenile
384	Group B	Older infant/younger juvenile

LANDSCAPES AND ARTEFACTS

Knives and buckles

The pattern of knife and buckle in Groups A and C, and grave lengths, suggests that these were males, mostly children/juveniles in Group C. Up to the mid-6th century (phase FA1-2), association with either buckle or ring may reflect the male/female dichotomy. There may be a chronological factor, with fewer knives in the early phases and a greater proportion of unfurnished burials.

Härke has shown that lengths of knives (blades) may be related to age and status (and date), with the longest belonging to adult males.[36] There is a slight difference in the length of knife blades in the three groups, with blades in Group A having the longest knives on average, followed by Group B and then C (Fig. 5). At Sewerby and West Heslerton, Yorks, it was mostly the over-25s in neutral burials with knife and buckle[37], whilst at Barrington, Cambs, 23 burials (22%) were neutral (of all ages), for whom knife and buckle was almost standard, the two exceptions being young children.[38]

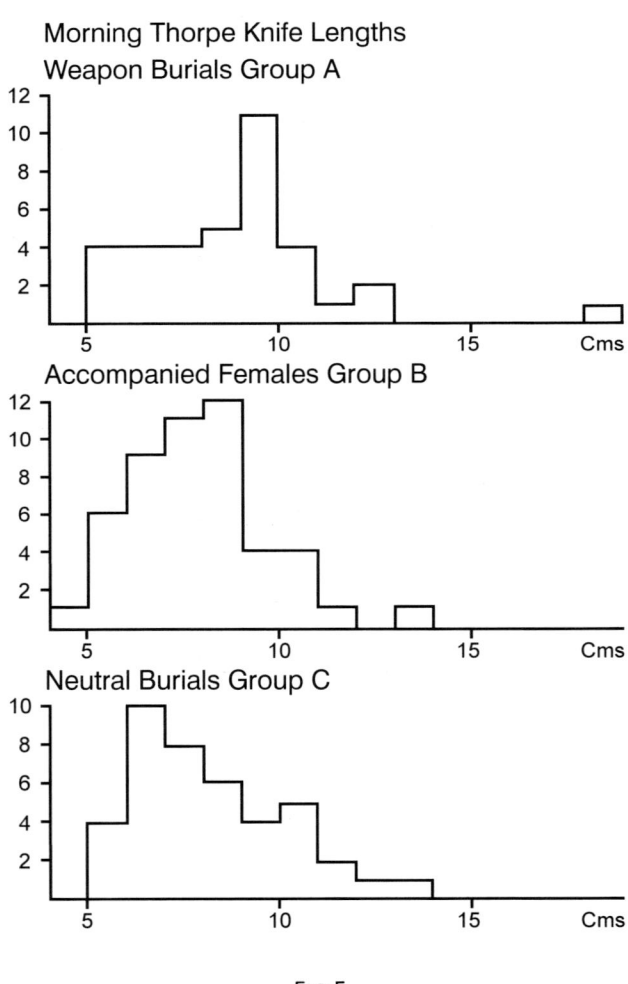

FIG 5

Groups A-C had similar overall ranges, from 50mm to 130mm, with two outliers (some knives were broken and could not be measured). Although the sample sizes were small (36: 41: 49), the observed differences may demonstrate a slight association of knife size and status/sex, although a comparison of knife size with burial provision/grave length was inconclusive.

In fact, the knives were all quite short: a blade of around 8-10cm is a modest instrument. Probably personal equipment for eating, knives may have had an intimate association and taboo against reuse, and continued to be buried until the end of furnished burial. The lack of knives or other objects with Group D burials may indicate a social group lacking basic possessions (at death); some burials in other groups also lacked a knife.

Knives were usually worn suspended at the waist, mostly at the left side; with females (in phase FA1-2) they were often with a ring (presumably part of the suspension), with some evidence of leather sheaths. In phase FA1, and especially FA2, a ring was common amongst girdle-groups, but in phase FB dropped out of use (except Grave 384: see above), that is, there was a shift towards buckles in phase FB.[39] Some women carried a knife loose in a bag, a custom seen when bags/chatelaines were more common, and without a suspension ring.

Use of pots

Of the sixty-five Group A burials, twelve or thirteen (*c.*20%) contained a pot, right across the range of grave lengths and elaboration, and of the sixteen or seventeen pots, nine or ten (60%-63%) were decorated.

Pots probably had a strong association with children and juveniles, but no particular pattern of grave-good association with pots was seen within the weapon burials. However, most pots with weapon burials were complete (10/13=77%), and many stamped, whilst pots with neutral and 'pot only' burials, were mostly very coarse and plain.

In a further contrast, of the 107 furnished females, twenty-four (23%) had pots (with no clear association with grave lengths), but of the thirty-one pots, only eleven (35%) were decorated (Fig. 4), but many were complete (19/31=61%), indicating some deliberate choice in the type of pots placed with burials, in particular, the number of decorated pots. (Apart from pots, well-furnished females at Morning Thorpe had few vessels, compared with weapon burials).

Of the fifty-eight neutral burials, eleven (18%) were buried with pots, of which just two were decorated, the others plain, as were most of the pots in 'pot only' burials (possibly children), in contrast to pots accorded the better-furnished. In this group, the two stamped pots were found in the two longest graves in this Group, Graves 65 and 320. Four of these eleven pots were complete (4/11=36%), in

---

[36] Härke 1989b
[37] Lucy 1998, 76
[38] Malim and Hines 1998

---

[39] *Aspects* p. 31

Table 11. Groups A, B, C and E: pots and decoration

Group	No/% with pot	% decorated	% complete
A	12-14 (20%)	9-10/16-17 (60%)	77%
B	22 (21%)	11/31 (35%)	60%
C	10 (17%)	2/11 (18%)	36%
E	37/37 (100%)	3/38 (8%)	33%-40%

contrast to the pots in weapon burials (77%) and furnished females (60%).

This suggests that completeness, seen at Spong Hill and Westgarth Gardens, is not solely a product of post-depositional factors, but part of the burial rite.

The occurrence of pots varied between cemeteries, and their occurrence as sherds at Bergh Apton, Snape and Wakerley, may be deliberate. At Wakerley, Northants, of eighty-five graves, eight had complete pots, another forty-two had sherds only (and usually just one or two sherds, with no set position for their placing).[40] Deliberate deposition of sherds has been suggested as a 'ritual killing'.[41]

'Elaborate' vessels

Evidence for vessels of wood and metal came from around twenty-three graves, mostly the more elaborate and better-equipped burials (barrows, coffins, long graves, settings); some connection with drinking and eating seems plausible, most likely personal accoutrements connected with social status, signalling control over their household or table, or presence in the lord's hall. Food and hospitality are likely to have had great social significance, with an intimate connection to individuals as hosts and providers.

Possibly a pot represented some aspect of personal equipment (and like the knife) perhaps connected with domestic or even ritual meals: the greater elaboration of pots with Group A and B burials may be some reflection of this.

Besides the glass cone beaker in Grave 148, the most lavish vessels were the iron-bound wooden buckets and tubs. Iron-bound vessels were found with three Group A burials, in Graves 35, 218 and 238, and one Group C burial, Grave 200 (conceivably an individual banned from carrying weapons). Grave 218 and 238 were under barrows, both with gold leaf, and 218 with a sword.

Table 12. Graves with 'elaborate' vessels (selected)

Grave	Group		Vessels	Phase
35	A	3.3M, coffin	Iron-bound tub	MA2
148	A	2.60m, double burial, posthole setting	Glass cone beaker, inside a pot	MA1
238	A	2.50m, double burial?inbarrow?gold leaf on shield, beads by waist	Iron-bound tub and bucket, and remains of another tub?	MA2
126	A	2.30m, coffin? Barrow?	Wooden bowl	MA2
218	A	2.30m, under barrow-grave227,sword, gold leaf on shield	Iron-bound bucket	MA2/MB
274	A	1.90m	Wooden bowl	MA1
108A	B	1.80m, multiple burial	Wooden vessel/bowl	FA2
133	B	2.20m, multiple burial	Wooden vessel/bowl	FA2
358B	B	2.10m	Wooden vessel/bowl	FA2B
200	C	3.10m	Cauldron, bucket, bronze perlrandbecker, wooden bowl	MA1

---

[40] Adams and Jackson 1988-89
[41] Filmer-Sankey and Pestell 2001, p. 245; Hills et al. 1984, p. 7

Iron-bound vessels in the neutral burial in Grave 200 seem to place it with the more elaborate Group A burials, and suggests that male burials might be further divided in terms of burial elaboration, using swords/vessels and coffin/barrow as signifiers. Grave 200 was also outstanding for its position, the space around the grave, in an otherwise crowded area, suggesting the former existence of a barrow above the grave, and supports a date early in the use of this part of the cemetery.

Most recently, Hines and Bayliss[42] have identified an increasing desire over time to place items of practical, domestic equipment with the dead, but this was not evident at Morning Thorpe: here, the incidence of pots varied a little: neutral burials and accompanied females in phases A and B included 20% with a pot, whilst for weapon burials this was 25% in phase A and none in phase B (with just eight 'dated' burials).

Discussion and conclusions

Dressed burial and regular patterns of accompaniment in early Anglo-Saxon cemeteries help fuel 'a consensus that consistencies in the provision of grave-goods and other aspects of mortuary practice...demonstrate a concern to express or assert aspects of the identity of the deceased, both as an individual and as a member of family, kin, household or lineage'.[43] These are thought to involve expressions of status, ideas of sex, age and ethnic identity, and more lately, gender roles, transformations and creation of memory, but little of 'religious' character.

The early Anglo-Saxons were not Christian, but followed pagan practices – in all likelihood – but whether these reached into the grave is another matter. And, beyond respect for the recent dead and the proper burial, whether any burial has a religious message is doubtful.

Nevertheless, Filmer-Sankey argued for ritual as the main force behind burial practice at Snape: 'first and foremost a statement of religious belief':[44] but beyond the great variety of containers (boats, coffins, bier) the familiar pattern of provision had little to suggest a religious dimension, and the same seems to be true at Morning Thorpe.

A religious dimension might be advanced for the choice of cremation. There were five cremation burials, perhaps survivors of many more, besides twenty-five collections of burnt or cremated bone, and evidence of burning in other graves: burnt objects, charcoal, perhaps the remains of grave-side meals.[45] Some of the associations between grave and scatter on the surface or in the fill were deliberate. Grave 19 was a pit with a pot containing the cremated bone of a 'sub-adult/adult'. The surface of Grave 19 was scattered with fragments of pot and human bone, whilst the adjacent Grave 1 had fragments of burnt bronze and bone in the fill, and to the immediate south, pit 8 contained ashy soil with burnt bone and flint, suggesting some deliberate link between the two types of burial.

Burials at Morning Thorpe and other East Anglian cemeteries were quite regularly west-to-east, but the positions of brooches in adjacent Graves 153 (FA1) and 207 (FA2) indicate females with heads to the east (rather like adjacent Graves 5 and 6 at Bergh Apton). Discussion of a similar 'reversed' grave (17) at Flixton, identified this as 'primarily a Norfolk practice' and 'only applied to women',[46] and a religious dimension is attractive, but seems speculative.

Besides vessels, some graves had items which speculation might identify as amulets, keepsakes or charms, for magical or medicinal purposes.[47] These items were odd bits of bronze sheet, 'found objects' and evidence for boxes, but little convincingly to do with belief: it seems

TABLE 13. CREMATIONS

Grave	Group		
10	E	Sub-ad/adult	Pit with pot and cremated bone
175	Crem	Sub-ad/adult	Pit with human and cow bone
236	Crem	?infant	
222	B	Inf/juv	Grave with pot containing cremated bone
385	B	-	Cremated bone at base of grave and in pot
411	Crem	-	Urned cremation with part of burnt comb, on surface
318	Crem	-	Pit with cremation and fragment of burnt brooch

---

[42] 2013, p. 520
[43] Scull 2011, p. 851
[44] Filmer-Sankey and Pestell 2001, p. 263
[45] Lee 2007, pp. 88-90
[46] Walton Rogers 2012, p. 89
[47] Meaney 1981, p. 3

unlikely that the horse tooth in Grave 115 could bear this interpretation, nor a possible bag in Grave 278 and a possible box in Grave 152 (both neutral burials). Amongst furnished females, Graves 43, 73 and 133 held Roman objects, whilst Grave 369B had a spindlewhorl, any of which may have been 'found objects' and no more than keepsakes and personal possessions.

At Morning Thorpe, weapon burials (65) were outnumbered by furnished females (107), who included juveniles/children. Whilst the neutral 'pot only' burials were probably of children, unfurnished burials cannot be 'sexed', but with 50% 'Short Graves' may be adult and child, perhaps mostly of children. Assuming a strong normative pattern, neutral burials were possibly male, unfurnished burials were female and 'pot only' burials were perhaps young males.

At several Cambridgeshire cemeteries, unfurnished burials can be seen as mostly children (Barrington: mostly young; Holywell Row: possibly infants/children; Linton Heath: mostly infants/children).[48] But the equation of unfurnished burials with children is not universal, and at Portway, Andover and Sleaford, Lincs, unfurnished burials were mostly adults, whilst at Westgarth Gardens, Bury St Edmunds, they comprised five adult females and two juveniles.[49] At Sleaford, the excavator noted that nearly all burials were flexed, with about a dozen not flexed, probably children.[50]

The uneven numbers of identified males/females at East Anglian cemeteries is in part a result of different age ranges of males with weapons and females with dress fittings,[51] but some imbalance between the sexes and adults/children is not unlikely, often more adult females than males (cf. Lechlade and Wakerley (Fig. 6)).

Evidence from cemeteries where bone survives suggests that many children were excluded from cemeteries containing furnished burials, with the apparent demography skewed towards adults.[52] At Buckland, Dover, of the buried population, only 20% died before 15 years.[53] Not every cemetery seems to be as skewed towards the adult groups, and at Great Chesterford, Essex, the whole of the population appears to have been represented, since of 202 burials, 42% were under 15 years at death (7% were foetuses/babies).[54]

At most cemeteries however, at least some children were included (recognised by their skeletal remains, grave sizes and accompaniments). The ratio of regular and 'Short Graves' (75/25) may reflect the adult-child/juvenile ratio at Morning Thorpe. Although only a proportion of

[48] Malim and Hines 1998; Neville 1854
[49] Cook and Dacre 1985; Thomas 1887; West 1988
[50] Thomas 1887
[51] *Aspects* pp. 88-9
[52] Crawford 1991; 1993; Stoodley 1998
[53] Evison 1987, p. 128
[54] Evison 1994, p. 31

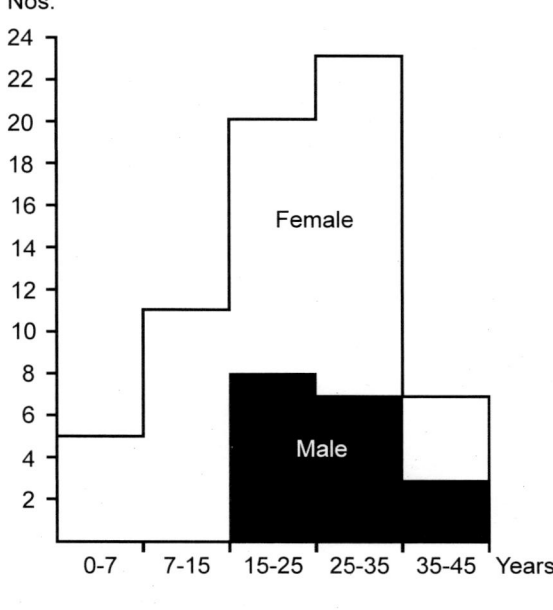

FIG 6

children would appear to have been included, they were accorded distinct treatment, either by position or by accompaniments. Body positions may have marked age, most commonly with children accorded a distinct burial position. This was impossible to discern at Morning Thorpe, but some children, at least, appear to have been given burial with distinctive grave-good ritual; the 'pot only' burials, whilst others, presumably girls, were lacking brooches, but had slip-knots holding beads.

Some selection appears to have operated in admitting individuals to cemeteries. The use of a separate burial or disposal mode for some children seems likely, and may suggest those who were admitted to the cemetery were 'special': and perhaps also warn against assuming that all adults were present? Perhaps the regional variations in proportions of weapon burials could suggest that some males were selectively excluded?

The identified Groups A-E, together with grave lengths, can only allow a very tentative reconstruction of demography.

Evidence from settlements and cemeteries suggests early Anglo-Saxon society was 'flat', with little hierarchy, and it is argued that it was equally-ranked between kinship (or descent) groups, each with internal rankings, possibly with a servile element, or as 'households', again with internal status differences.[55]

Not until the later 6th century do elite groups appear to dominate burial, indicating a widening social structure,

[55] Härke 1997, p. 151; Scull 1993, p. 73; *Aspects* p. 97

TABLE 14. ESTIMATED POPULATION GROUPS

Grave	Male (?)		Female (?)		
Regular grave	Group A	65	Group B	89	
	Group C	51	Group D	24	
	Group E	7			
	TOTAL	123	TOTAL	113	Male and Female (?) 236
'Short Grave'	Group C	9	Group B	17	
	Group E	30	Group D	24	
	TOTAL	39	TOTAL	41	Children (?) 80
	TOTAL MALES	162	TOTAL FEMALES	154	GRAND TOTAL 316

foreshadowing dynastic succession, princely burials and the kingdoms of the early sources.[56]

Migration overseas, however, itself demands leadership and organisation, and 'questions that arise from mass-migration hypotheses are the push- and pull-factors involved, the logistics of the migration itself, its timescale and sustainability at both ends, and settlement patterns created in the process'.[57]

We may think the ability to quit cultivated land, acquire ships, and endure a sea crossing, even before landfall has been made, must imply strong directing forces.[58]

A case has been made for the existence of clearly-defined 'lords' and their semi-free followers at an early date amongst the English,[59] and the pattern of weapon burial may echo the social profile, of small numbers of leaders and groups of men, sometimes armed (for burial at least), although the passage of time might convert functional possession towards symbolism and claim of status.

With an eye on the continental situation, Scull sees the dynamics of 'leaders and retinues' as a factor, even motivation, to migration in the 5th century, embodying arrangements of reciprocity centred on control and access to the most important resource: land – with competition between kin-groups.[60]

And another element might be added: the existence of a servile class, whose labour was an essential part of the wider lord and land nexus, familiar across Europe, integral to ancient society, and featured in the earliest laws in Christian kingdoms.[61]

It is held that 'grave-goods and mortuary ritual were parts of a symbolic vocabulary, in which variations could indicate a social inequality.[62] In this world, the possession of a sword could symbolise a 'free man',[63] possibly defined by his relationship to such a 'leader' and access to land (as is clear in the early laws): diversion of weapons into burials may also have required lordly sanction.

Dickinson and Härke concluded that males of all ages could be furnished with weapons, possibly as an indicator of rank, not just males of fighting age,[64] but, at Morning Thorpe, this was possibly restricted to adults.

However, since about 40%-50% of males in Anglo-Saxon cemeteries in southern England seem to have been buried with weapons[65] it is unlikely that all were part of an elite. Perhaps it was a formal ideal, with little correspondence to reality, used to emphasize social roles and cohesion?

Changing age thresholds too may reflect social evolution and increasing importance of rank, with social restriction for 'furnished' burial.[66] There are hints too of a shift in the balance of power between males and females, seen in a decline in female wealth, and shift of some luxury goods from female to male burials, whilst a greater inclusion of minors may account for smaller graves amongst females in the later phase. Rank is being privileged over age.

This note has identified some local patterns amongst the wider evidence set out in *Aspects*, including a group of individuals, possibly youngsters, buried with a pot alone, that pots were sometimes buried complete, sometimes as sherds, and that decoration mattered to those choosing grave-goods. It can also be seen that there were costume changes over time, and that these went with a greater inclusion of young females in the later phase.

---

[56] cf. *Aspects* pp. 94-6; Geake 1997, pp. 128-9; Härke 1992; Scull 2011; Stoodley 1999, pp. 113, 118
[57] Brugmann 2011, p. 41
[58] cf. Faith 1997, pp. 5-7
[59] Barnswell 1996
[60] Scull 1995, pp. 75-6; 2011
[61] Faith 1997, pp. 60-1
[62] Scull 2011, p. 851
[63] Brooks 1978, p. 83
[64] Dickinson and Härke 1992; Härke 1989a, 1992
[65] Härke 1989a, p. 49
[66] *Aspects* p. 87

Acknowledgements

The writer is grateful to Penelope Walton Rogers for advice and to David Dobson for help with diagrams.

Bibliography

Adams, B., and Jackson, D. 1988-9, 'The Anglo-Saxon cemetery at Wakerley, Northamptonshire; Excavations by Mr D. Jackson', *Northants Archaeol.* 22, pp. 69-83

Barnswell, P.S. 1996, 'Hlafaeta, ceorl, hid and scir: Celtic, Roman or Germanic?' *Anglo-Saxon Studies in Archaeology and History* 9, pp. 53-62

Boyle, A., Dodd, A., Miles, D., and Palmer, S. 1998, *The Anglo-Saxon Cemetery at Butler's Field, Lechlade, Gloucestershire. Volume 1: Prehistoric and Roman activity and Anglo-Saxon Grave Catalogue*, Thames Valley Landscapes Monograph 10 (Oxford Archaeological Unit, Oxford)

Brooks, N.P. 1978, 'Arms, Status and Warfare in Late-Saxon England', in Hill, D. (ed.), *Ethelred the Unready*, British Archaeol. Rep. Brit. Ser. 59, pp. 81-103

Brugmann, B. 2004, *Glass Beads from Early Anglo-Saxon Graves* (Oxbow Books, Oxford)

Brugmann, B. 2011, 'Migration and Endogenous Change', in Hamerow, H., et al. (eds.) *Anglo-Saxon Archaeology* (Oxford University Press, Oxford), pp. 30-45

Cook, J., and Dacre, M.W. 1985, *Excavations at Portway, Andover 1973-1975* (Oxford University Committee for Archaeology Monograph No 4, Oxford)

Crawford, S. 1991, 'When do Anglo-Saxon Children Count?' *Journal of Theoretical Archaeology* 2, pp. 17-24

Crawford, S. 1993, 'Children, life and the after-life in Anglo-Saxon England', *Anglo-Saxon Studies in Archaeology and History* 6, pp. 83-91

Dickinson, T.M., and Härke, H. 1992, 'Early Anglo-Saxon Shields', *Archaeologia* 110 (Society of Antiquaries, London)

Evison, V.I. 1987, *Dover: The Buckland Anglo-Saxon Cemetery*, English Heritage Archaeological Report 3 (London)

Evison, V.I. 1994, *An Anglo-Saxon Cemetery at Great Chesterford, Essex*, Council for British Archaeology Report 91

Faith, R. 1997, *The English Peasantry and the Growth of Lordship* (Leicester University Press)

Filmer-Sankey, W., and Pestell, T. 2001, *Snape Anglo-Saxon cemetery: Excavations and Surveys 1824-1992*, East Anglian Archaeology 95

Geake, H. 1997, *The Use of Grave-Goods in Conversion-Period England, c.600-c.850*, British Archaeological Report, British Series 261

Green, B., Rogerson, A., and White, S. 1987, *The Anglo-Saxon Cemetery at Morning Thorpe, Norfolk*, East Anglian Archaeology 36

Halsall, G. 1995, *Settlement and social organization: The Merovingian region of Metz* (Cambridge University Press, Cambridge)

Härke, H. 1989a, 'Early Saxon Weapon Burials; frequencies, distributions, weapon combinations', in Hawkes, S. C. (ed.) *Weapons and Warfare in Anglo-Saxon England*, Oxford Committee for Archaeology Monograph No 21 (Oxford), pp. 49-61

Härke, H. 1989b, 'Knives in Early Saxon Burials: blade length and age at death', *Medieval Archaeology* 33, pp. 144-148

Härke, H. 1992, 'Changing Symbols in a Changing Society: the Anglo-Saxon Weapon Burial Rite in the Seventh Century', in Carver, M. (ed.), *The Age of Sutton Hoo* (Boydell, Woodbridge), pp. 39-51

Härke, H. 1997, 'Early Anglo-Saxon Social Structure', in Hines, J. (ed.) *The Anglo-Saxons from the Migration Period to the Eighth Century: An Ethnographic Perspective* (Boydell, Woodbidge), pp. 125-70

Hawkes, S.C. 1973, 'The dating and social significance of the burials in the Polhill cemetery', in Philp, B (ed.), *Excavations in West Kent 1960-1970*, Dover, Archaeological Rescue Unit, pp. 186-201

Hills, C., Penn, K., and Rickett, R. 1984, *The Anglo-Saxon Cemetery at Spong Hill, North Elmham, Part III, Catalogue of Inhumations*, East Anglian Archaeology 21

Hills, C., Lucy, S. 2013, *Spong Hill Part IX: chronology and synthesis*, McDonald Institute Monographs (Cambridge)

Hines, J., and Bayliss, A. 2013, *Anglo-Saxon Graves and Grave Goods of the 6th and 7th centuries: A Chronological Framework*, Society for Medieval Archaeology Monograph 33

Lee, C. 2007, *Feasting the Dead: Food and Drink in Anglo-Saxon Burial Rituals*, Anglo-Saxon Studies 9, (Boydell, Woodbridge)

Lucy, S. 1998, *The Early Anglo-Saxon Cemeteries of East Yorkshire: An Analysis and Reinterpretation*, British Archaeological Reports British Series 272 (Oxford)

Malim, T., and Hines, J. 1998, *The Anglo-Saxon Cemetery at Edix Hill, Cambridgeshire (Barrington A)*, Council for British Archaeology Research Report 112

Meaney, A.L. 1981, *Anglo-Saxon amulets and curing stones*, British Archaeological Reports British Series 96 (Oxford)

Neville, R.C. 1854, 'Anglo-Saxon Cemetery on Linton Heath, Cambridgeshire', *Archaeological Journal* 11, pp. 95-115

Penn, K.J. 2000, *Excavations on the Norwich Southern Bypass, 1989-91. Part 2: The Anglo-Saxon Cemetery at Harford Farm, Markshall, Norfolk*, East Anglian Archaeology 92

Penn, K.J. 2011, *The Anglo-Saxon Cemetery at Shrubland Hall Quarry, Coddenham, Suffolk*, East Anglian Archaeology 139

Penn, K.J., and Brugmann, B. 2007, *Aspects of Anglo-Saxon Inhumation Burial: Morning Thorpe, Spong Hill, Bergh Apton and Westgarth Gardens*, East Anglian Archaeology 119

Scull, C.J. 1993, 'Archaeology, early Anglo-Saxon society and the origins of Anglo-Saxon kingdoms', *Anglo-Saxon Studies in Archaeology and History* 6, pp. 65-82

Scull, C. 1995, 'Approaches to material culture and social dynamics in the migration period of eastern England', in Bintliff, J., and Hamerow, H. (eds) *Europe between Late Antiquity and the Middle Ages: Recent Archaeological and Historical Research in Western and Southern Europe*, British Archaeological Reports International Series 617, pp. 71-83

Scull, C. 2011, 'Social Transactions, Gift Exchange, and Power in the Archaeology of the Fifth to Seventh Centuries', in Hamerow, H *et al.*, (eds.), *Anglo-Saxon Archaeology* (Oxford University Press, Oxford), pp. 848-864

Stoodley, N. 1998, 'Post-Migration Age Structures and Age Related Grave Goods in Anglo-Saxon Cemeteries in England', *StudienzurSachsenforschung* 11, pp. 187-195

Stoodley, N. 1999, *The Spindle and the Spear: A Critical Enquiry into the Construction and Meaning of Gender in the early Anglo-Saxon Burial Rite*, British Archaeological Reports British Series 288

Thomas, G. 1887, 'On excavations in an Anglo-Saxon cemetery at Sleaford in Lincs', *Archaeologia* 50, pp. 383-406

Walton Rogers, P. 2007, *Cloth and Clothing in Early Anglo-Saxon England, AD 450-700*, Council for British Archaeology (York)

Walton Rogers, P. 2012, *Circles and Cemeteries: Excavations at Flixton Volume 1*, East Anglian Archaeology 147

West, S.E. 1988, *The Anglo-Saxon Cemetery at Westgarth Gardens, Bury St Edmunds, Suffolk*, East Anglian Archaeology 38

The compleat Anglo-Saxonist: some new and neglected Early Anglo-Saxon fish for Andrew Rogerson

Helen Geake

Abstract: A group of early Anglo-Saxon representations of fish are considered, some three-dimensional, some in high relief and some flat. A new find from Norfolk may be the second known (after Sutton Hoo) from the interior of a hanging bowl. A new find from Northern Ireland is a close parallel to the fish on the Crundale buckle from Kent. The species depicted in both cases is a pike. Some older but neglected finds of fish are also reviewed, and the pike's nature as a predatory animal is considered in the light of other animals in early Anglo-Saxon art.

Some animals are very prominent in the Anglo-Saxon world, whether through art, names or mythology. The boar, the wolf, the eagle are the kind of ferocious animals we associate with this heroic world. This paper is an attempt to add another, this time from a watery dimension to complement those of the land and the air.

The East Walton silver fish

In November 2008 a small model fish made from partly gilded silver was found by Steve Brown, a remarkably expert and prolific metal-detectorist, in the Norfolk parish of East Walton, and reported to Andrew Rogerson (Fig. 1).[1] It was given the PAS number NMS-AA0858 and the Treasure number 2008T693, and in due course was acquired by Norwich Castle Museum (Fig. 10).[2] Other finds from the site, HER number 29273, include objects of Roman, Anglo-Saxon and medieval date, including a girdle-hanger, a wrist-clasp and a cruciform brooch, and also a hanging-bowl escutcheon consisting of a hooked circular frame retaining a small ring (NMS-7CBB46).[3]

A full description of the East Walton fish can be found on the on-line PAS database.[4] It was made from a thick piece of silver sheet folded along the back and hammered together at the tail; a gap or socket runs along the underside as far as the head. The tail and the head were both made by cutting to shape, and are divided from the body by an engraved line on both faces. Niello inlay survives in a short length of the groove at the head. The eyes are punched with an annular stamp and were probably also originally inlaid with niello. The head, tail and fins are gilded, in contrast to the body, and both head and tail are now slightly battered.

The fins are separately made of gilded silver. The dorsal fin is fixed in a slot, probably with solder. The pectoral fins, one of which is incomplete, are hooked in shape, and are held in drilled holes with their inner ends hammered flat to the body. On the underside, behind the pectoral fins, the gap along the body gives the impression that the fish has been gutted. The edges of this slot have a pair of central rounded notches, apparently produced or enlarged by wear.

Most of the surface of the body is covered with the punched impressions of a triangular stamp with concave sides. The upper rows alternate the direction of the triangles to produce a reserved sexfoil effect, but the lowest row on either side has all the triangles arranged apex-down. The impressions were inlaid with niello, much of which is now missing. The fish is 51mm long, 7.2mm deep, and 6.3mm thick; it weighs 5.9g.

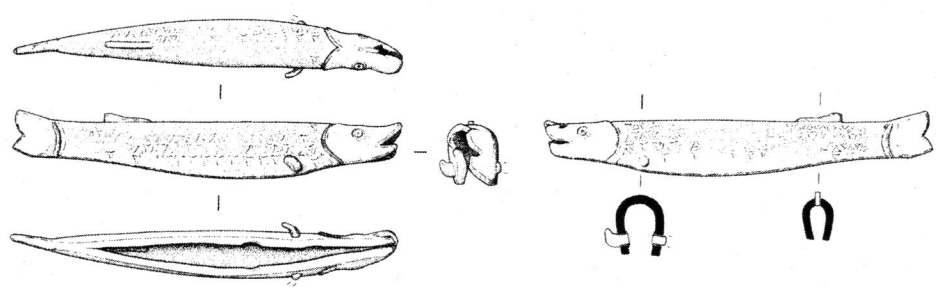

Fig. 1 Partly gilded silver fish from East Walton, Norfolk (NMS-AA0858). Drawn by J. Gibbons (Norfolk Historic Environment Service). Scale 1:1

---

[1] Rogerson and Ashley 2009, pp. 562-3, fig.7, no.31
[2] Accession number NWHCM:2010.8
[3] A drawing of the East Walton hanging-bowl escutcheon can also be found in Rogerson and Ashley 2008, p. 437, fig. 4.28
[4] http://finds.org.uk/database/artefacts/record/id/239154

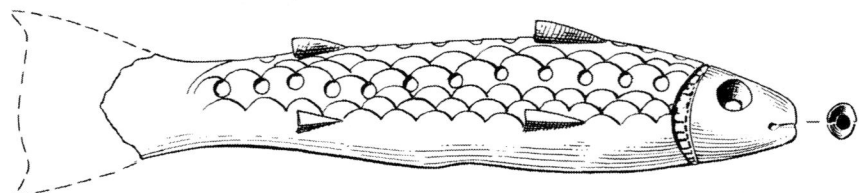

Fig. 2 Tinned copper-alloy fish from the largest hanging bowl in Mound 1, Sutton Hoo, Suffolk (after Bruce-Mitford 1983, fig. 175; © Trustees of the British Museum). Scale 1:1

Other three-dimensional fish in the early Anglo-Saxon world

The East Walton fish's best parallel is the famous hollow free-swivelling fish from the largest hanging bowl in Mound 1 at Sutton Hoo (Fig. 2). This is made from tinned copper alloy and is much larger, with a surviving length of 92mm. It sits on a pedestal which passes through a hole in the base and ends in a rounded tenon. The notches in the base of the East Walton fish, which together form the edges of a rounded hole, could have served to attach it to a pedestal in the same way, and the presence of a hanging-bowl escutcheon from the same site is thought-provoking. The slot in the base of the East Walton fish might have allowed it to tilt on its pedestal, as has been suggested for the Sutton Hoo fish. A row of enamelled spots along each side of the Sutton Hoo fish suggests that it is modelled on a salmon or trout.[5]

Fish appliqués from buckles

The Sutton Hoo fish remains the only other example of a fully three-dimensional fish known from the early Anglo-Saxon world, but there are other high-relief fish known. The most famous of these comes from the buckle found at Crundale, Kent, in 1861, which has recently been joined by another remarkable find from the other end of the British Isles, at Ballyalton in County Down, Northern Ireland (Fig. 11).

The Ballyalton fish was found by metal-detecting in March 2013, and declared Treasure on 30th April 2014 at the Coroner's Court in Northern Ireland. It is in the form of a fish seen from above, measures 59mm long and 10mm wide, and is made from a thin gold foil over a copper-alloy core which is domed above and flat underneath. The gold foil is wrapped around the upper side but is tucked under the edge to a width of only 2mm on the flat underside, where the edge of the foil is neatly cut. The Ballyalton fish is in general well made, but is now very worn in places so that the decoration is smoothed out and difficult to see.

The large head tapers and flattens to a rounded point, around the edge of which is a groove representing the mouth. The eyes are two small circular depressions set at the highest and widest part of the head, one of which can be clearly seen to have a rounded base; it seems unlikely that they were ever embellished with any form of setting. There is no further decoration on the head, which ends in a V-shaped step down to the body. The body is decorated with transverse stripes made from pairs of grooves; no fins or other anatomical details are shown. The tail is shown at right angles to the normal orientation of a fish's tail, and has been formed by flattening the end of the body to give a U-shaped facet decorated with a pair of unworn curving concentric grooves.

The copper-alloy core of this fish is a high-tin leaded bronze. The gold foil was found from surface XRF analysis to be in the region of 85% gold, 12% silver and 2% copper; it is covered with very fine scratches from wear or polishing.

The Ballyalton fish is very like the gold fish appliqué from the Crundale buckle (Fig. 12), now in the British Museum.[6] The Crundale fish is c. 75mm long and is again depicted from above, with a tubular transversely striped body, a head separated from the body, and a tail turned at right angles. The Crundale fish also has a flat underside but, because it is still fixed to the triangular plate of the buckle, there is no information available about its construction (whether solid or made from gold sheet over a separate core). The Crundale fish is more elaborate than the Ballyalton fish, with the stripes rendered in beaded wire and the eyes originally inlaid; it also has tiny pectoral fins near the head.

Two other buckles are known with fish appliqués. The U-shaped plate on the buckle excavated from grave 19 at Eccles in Kent (Fig. 3) had a flat copper-alloy fish riveted to its underside.[7] The Eccles fish measures c. 48mm long, and again the head is clearly distinguished from the long body. The body is decorated with an engraved pattern of scales, and the fish has very small fins and a flaring tail. Both the Crundale and Eccles buckles are thought to date to the mid seventh century, although the triangular plate may suggest a slightly earlier date for the Crundale buckle.[8]

---

[5] Bruce-Mitford 1983, pt. 1, 221-8; 2005, pp. 263-5

[6] Accession number 1893,0601.204; Webster and Backhouse (eds.) 1991, no. 6

[7] Detsicas and Hawkes 1973; Webster and Backhouse (eds.) 1991, no. 7

[8] Webster and Backhouse (eds.) 1991, 24-5; Geake 1997, pp. 76-7

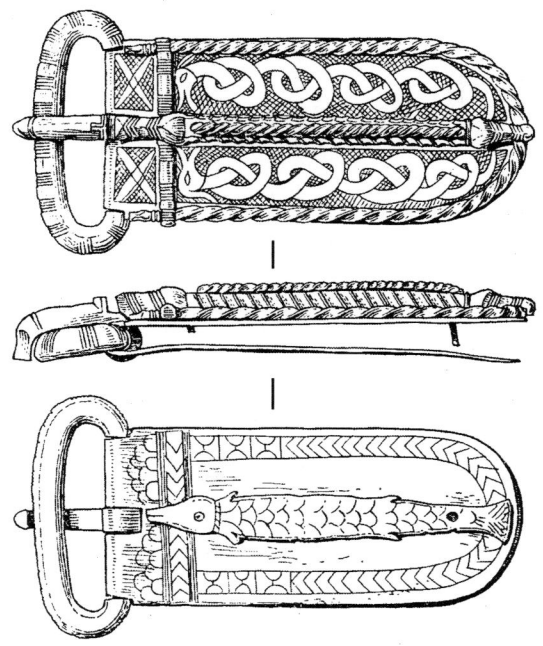

FIG. 3 FRONT, SIDE AND REVERSE OF COPPER-ALLOY BUCKLE FROM GRAVE 19, ECCLES, KENT (AFTER DETSICAS AND HAWKES 1973, REPRODUCED WITH PERMISSION) SCALE 1:1

A tiny three-dimensional fish appliqué, only 24mm long and made from copper alloy, was riveted to the rectangular plate of the Foxton buckle (Fig. 4), found in Cambridgeshire.[9] This has a head which tapers smoothly from the body, larger fins, and a flaring tail; the head has two eyes, but otherwise the fins and tail indicate that a side view is intended. The Foxton buckle is dated by comparison to the Eccles and Crundale buckles to the early or mid seventh century; this is confirmed by the groups of transverse lines on the frame, which are characteristic of several broadly seventh-century artefact types such as annular brooches and silver wire rings.[10]

A fourth buckle plate with a fish motif, but not this time an appliqué, was found at Littlebourne in Kent, recorded on the PAS database at KENT-50B745, and is now in Canterbury Museum (Fig. 13).[11] This has a triangular plate made from gilded silver, with a long thin fish shape engraved along its length. The fish has a flared tail decorated with a V shape, separated from the body by a double line. Two pairs of hooked fins suggest it is seen from above; two pointed-oval shapes are probably eyes, while the end of the head is either rectilinear or disappears beneath the 'shield-shaped' plate at the base of the buckle's pin. This fish is in fact very like the fish stamped on one of the remarkable repair patches on the now-destroyed Gilton bead-rimmed bowl (Fig. 5).[12] The Littlebourne buckle is very similar in shape to the Crundale buckle, and therefore probably also dates to the first half or middle of the seventh century.

Other fish in high-relief

There are four fish-shaped appliqués on the British Museum's hanging bowl from Lullingstone, all semi-circular in cross-section and depicted identically in side view swimming to the right.[13] These fish, like the buckle appliqués, have long, transversely striped tubular bodies and large heads; they have no fins. The bowl has been dated to the late seventh or early eighth century.[14]

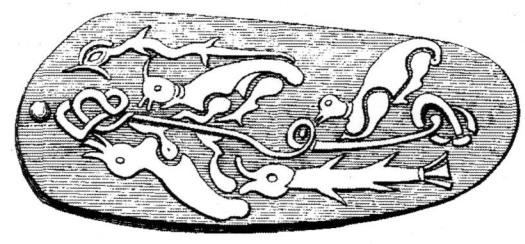

FIG. 5 FISH STAMPED ON A REPAIR PATCH FROM A BEAD-RIMMED BOWL FOUND AT GILTON, KENT, LOST IN THE BOMBING OF LIVERPOOL MUSEUM (AFTER ROACH SMITH 1844). NOT TO SCALE: LENGTH OF FISH C. 20MM

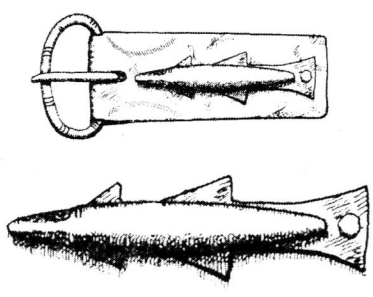

FIG. 4 COPPER-ALLOY BUCKLE FROM FOXTON, CAMBRIDGESHIRE, AND DETAIL OF FISH APPLIQUÉ (AFTER FOX 1924). SCALES 1:1 AND 2:1 RESPECTIVELY

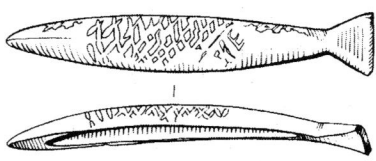

FIG. 6 FISH-SHAPED OBJECT, PERHAPS AN APPLIQUÉ FROM A HANGING BOWL, FOUND AT BARHAM, SUFFOLK (© SUFFOLK COUNTY COUNCIL). SCALE 1:1

---

[9] Fox 1924; Malim and Hines 1998, pp. 323-4
[10] Geake 1997, pp. 48 and 52
[11] Accession number CANCM:2003.389.1-3
[12] Dickinson 2005, p. 155; Roach Smith 1844, pp. 133-4
[13] Accession number 1967,1004.1; Bruce-Mitford 2005, pp. 175-79 and col. pl. 5. More photos of the fish mounts can be found in Brenan 1991, pp. 350-1
[14] Bruce-Mitford 2005, p. 216

A fish from Barham in Suffolk, also now in the British Museum, may also possibly represent an appliqué from a hanging bowl.[15] It is again semi-circular in cross-section, with a hollowed reverse, and its gentle longitudinal curvature would fit a bowl with a diameter of c. 150mm (Fig. 6). Made from tinned copper alloy and 48mm long, it has no obvious eyes or fins to help orientate the viewer, but the distinct carination along its head suggests that it is seen from above (Fig. 14). It has a criss-cross pattern of grooves covering much of the body, perhaps inlaid with enamel, and a small flared tail.

A copper-alloy brooch from Saffron Walden in Essex, recorded on the PAS database (ESS-C4EB33), is similar in appearance to the Barham fish, and may be of similar date. It is 69mm long, rounded on the upper surface with a longitudinal carination, and flat and hollow on the reverse (Fig. 15). It is minimally decorated with ring-and-dot motifs, two forming the eyes and three decorating the flared, round-cornered tail. The eyes show that we are looking at the fish from above, but the tail is turned at right angles as if viewed from the side; there are no fins. The pin fixings on the reverse are unusual in being circular in cross-section. Although a bent-over catchplate survives, the pin lug has been lost, leaving only a circular scar.

The rounded shape of the Saffron Walden brooch is very different to the few certainly Anglo-Saxon fish-shaped brooches known, such as the re-used flat fish-shaped shield mount from Eriswell, Suffolk and the garnet-set flat silver object, apparently a brooch, from the cemetery at Westbere in Kent (Fig. 7).[16] The Westbere brooch bears some resemblance to the dozen or so flat Roman fish-shaped brooches on the PAS database (e.g. NCL-36DF13; Fig. 16).

The species of fish represented

The East Walton fish has a distinctive tubular body, in contrast to most fish species which have a deeper, flatter shape. The definition between the body and the head is very pronounced, the head has a long snout, and the eyes

Fig. 7 Garnet-set silver fish-shaped object, perhaps a brooch, from Westbere, Kent, c. 80mm long (after Jessup 1946, pl. II.6, reproduced with permission)

are placed towards the top of the head. The dorsal fin is small and set close to the tail. From these characteristics, the most obvious candidate is the pike (*Esox lucius*), a very common predatory fish with a long tubular body, small fins and, when older, a large head. The Ballyalton fish, although very differently depicted, could also be a pike, from the tubular shape, the large head with eyes set towards the top, and the striped body; the same follows for the Crundale fish.

Alternatively a sturgeon, the largest fish known from British freshwater, might have been intended; this has a long tubular body and a large head, but has a small round mouth very unlike that of the fish from East Walton, Ballyalton and Crundale. Other candidates are less likely, for a host of different reasons. They might include: the eel, but this has a head and tail hard to distinguish from the body; or the transversely striped perch, but this has a large dorsal fin and a deeper body; or the spotted, not striped, salmon or trout; or perhaps an uncommon long, tubular-bodied bottom-dwelling species such as barbel or burbot. Other fish such as the wels and the zander are superficially similar, but are recent introductions to Britain.

The Lullingstone examples also have long striped bodies and large heads, and are likely also to be pike. The Eccles fish is not striped, but is long and has a large head, as do the Littlebourne and Gilton fish. The Westbere fish can hardly be anything other than a pike, whereas the Foxton, Barham and Saffron Walden fish have fewer species-specific characteristics

Other two-dimensional fish appliqués

Flat fish shapes are often found as appliqués on early Anglo-Saxon shield boards, and in several cases these fish can also be identified as pike. They have been collected and discussed by Dickinson, who dates them broadly to the middle decades of the sixth century.[17]

Fish seen in side view fall within Dickinson's Type ia. The pair of mounts from the shield in grave 31 at Spong Hill also clearly depict long-bodied pike, and it is argued that two other mounts do too.[18] There are no Type ia mounts yet recorded on the PAS database.

Fish seen from above fall within Dickinson's type ib, a group of eleven large (104-145mm long) mounts which have now been joined by two recorded on the PAS database: NMS-E2B508 (gilded and silvered copper alloy, found at Hindringham in Norfolk),[19] and LVPL-E6F3E3 (copper alloy, perhaps found in Hampshire).[20]

A further group of fish appliqués are far smaller, made from gold, and shown from above. SF-1DC2A2 is just

---

[15] Accession number 1984,0103.9; Bruce-Mitford 2005, p. 248; West 1998, p. 8, where it is erroneously stated to be 9.8cm in length, and fig. 6.62
[16] Dickinson 2005, p. 127, fig. 9d; Jessup 1946, pp. 15-16 and pl. II.6; also compare two examples of fish-shaped catchplates from great square-headed brooches in Hines 1997, fig. 49

[17] Dickinson 2005, pp. 127-133 and 141
[18] Dickinson 2005, pp. 127-9
[19] Now fully published as Dickinson, Ashley and Penn 2011
[20] The mount passed into the trade and was only made available for recording subsequently, with the consequent loss of findspot information.

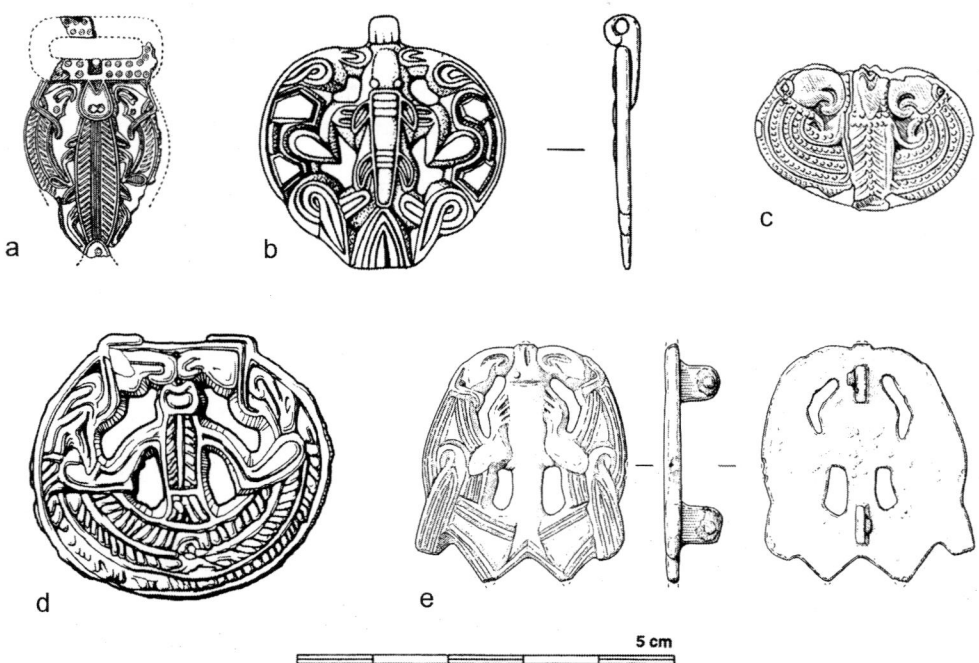

Fig. 8 Fish-between-birds motifs on objects from (a) Faversham (after Smith 1923, fig. 42) (b) Coddenham (drawn by D. Wreathall; © Suffolk County Council) (c) Kingston Down grave 161 (drawn by M. Cox, © Oxford University, Institute of Archaeology) (d) Marlowe Car Park, Canterbury (© Canterbury Archaeological Trust) and (e) Gunthorpe (drawn by J. Gibbons, Norfolk Historic Environment Service). Scale 1:1

44mm long, and has no obvious means of attachment. It was found at Westleton in Suffolk, and is now in the British Museum (Fig. 17).[21] It resembles the Crundale fish in that it has a central spine and transverse stripes made from beaded-wire filigree. Two further small flat gold appliqués were found in the seventh-century Staffordshire Hoard (Fig. 18). K1663 is approximately 30mm in length, and also has a central spine, but the stripes are made from thickly carpeted beaded and plain wires. K0796 is smaller at c. 23mm long, and appears to be shown from the side.

Fish between two birds

Another common instance of fish is in a recurrent motif between two predatory birds (Fig. 8). Depictions of this scene include a gilded copper-alloy buckle plate from Faversham, Kent;[22] a copper-alloy mount from the Marlowe Car Park, Canterbury, Kent;[23] a set of three silver repoussé pendants from grave 161 at Kingston;[24] and a gilded copper-alloy pendant found by metal-detecting at Coddenham, Suffolk.[25] Dickinson lists these and a number of comparanda from England and the Continent;[26] subsequent finds have included a gilded copper-alloy mount from Gunthorpe, Norfolk (NMS-7B86F1);[27] a gilded copper-alloy horse-harness mount from the area of a cemetery at Springhead Park, Northfleet, Kent;[28] and two gold objects from the Staffordshire Hoard, K0042 (c. 22mm long) and K0652 (length of fish from neck to tail c. 50mm) (Fig. 19).

The meaning of the fish motif

As we have seen, the motif of a fish can be found on both sixth- and seventh-century Anglo-Saxon objects, and it seems to have been a standard (if infrequent) part of the design repertoire. Fish modelled in the round, however, appear on present evidence to be an innovation of the seventh century, and so in the past it has been suggested that their use may be linked to the introduction of Christianity.[29] The fish had already become a conventional symbol of Christ by the late second century, when allusions to it appear in the works of Tertullian (c. 160-225) and Clement of Alexandria (c. 150-215 AD). The position of the fish on the Crundale and Eccles buckle plates has been compared with that of the possible symbol of Woden on the otherwise similar Finglesham buckle plate,[30] supporting the suggestion of a direct replacement of pagan by Christian iconography.

---

[21] Accession number 2011,8034.1
[22] Smith 1923, fig.42; Speake 1980, fig. 6n
[23] Webster in Blockley et al. 1995, 1038-40; a residual find in a mid to late Anglo-Saxon context, Blockley et al. 1995, p. 356
[24] Speake 1980, pl. 2c
[25] Martin et al. 2000, p. 500 and fig. 154C
[26] Dickinson 2005, n.112
[27] Rogerson and Ashley 2008, p. 434 and fig. 4.19

[28] *British Archaeology* 100, May/June 2008, 9; Wessex Archaeology 2004, pp. 37, 40, illustrated on front cover and plate 2; http://www.wessexarch.co.uk/system/files/54924-Springhead%20Quarter%20Ebbsfleet%20Kent.pdf, accessed February 2014
[29] On occasion leading to circular reasoning about the date of fish-bearing objects, as with the great square-headed brooch from Alveston 5; Speake 1980, p. 93 n.3
[30] Haith in Webster and Backhouse (eds) 1991, no. 6; Chadwick Hawkes et al. 1965

The remarkably standard appearance of the 'fish-between-birds' motif suggests that it is based on a communally understood and easily recognised mythology involving a fish as prey. It therefore seems likely that the various types of fish had specific meanings within pre-Christian, as well as Christian, art and myth. When looking at fish motifs, we must ask whether our fish is hunter or hunted, in the same way as is acknowledged for birds (Fig. 9).

Like the boar, serpent and predatory bird (the animals considered by Speake in his examination of Style II animal iconography),[31] the pike can, from its appearance on artefacts, be seen as *the* iconic predator fish of the Anglo-Saxon world. Tania Dickinson makes a persuasive case for decorated shields[32] in the sixth and early seventh centuries being connected to a martial masculinity, with a responsibility to exercise protection and an authority to assert power, as well as allegiance to a pagan cult, identified as probably that of Woden/Oðinn.[33] The fish mounts, in the shape of pike or with 'pike-like characteristics', are symbolic of the predatory fish's power and aggression.[34]

As Dickinson points out, the fierce and aggressive nature of the pike does not sit well with a traditional Christian interpretation.[35] The predatory nature of the fish implied by the choice of pike on seventh-century buckle plates and hanging bowls suggests that the standard interpretation (and dating) of the fish as a Christian symbol in the early Anglo-Saxon world should be replaced with one of the fish primarily as a powerful protector, whether or not with a Christian or pagan undertone.

Fig. 9 Predatory bird and prey bird, from the purse lid found in Mound 1 at Sutton Hoo. Scale 1:1

It is unlikely to have escaped notice that all the examples cited in this paper were found either in Kent, in East Anglia broadly defined, or in the Staffordshire Hoard. Distributions of this kind used to be commonplace, but as more and more discoveries are recorded, they are becoming more unusual. The absence of three-dimensional and high-relief fish from Lincolnshire, particularly, is worthy of note.

Conclusion

Three-dimensional fish, whether swimming in hanging bowls like the East Walton example or attached to buckles like the Ballyalton example, have often been seen as symbols of the new Christianity. In fact, because many can be identified as pike, they fit far better into the range fierce predatory animals used as mascots, talismans or familiars in the sixth to seventh centuries. Style II art appears to concentrate on the aggressive aspects of animals more than Style I, and although this may be because Style II includes more details that allow us to identify animal types, such as hooked beaks, tusks and teeth, these specific details do seem to involve precisely the aggressive aspects of the animals concerned. It seems likely in turn that this is linked with contemporary and contested social developments such as state formation, religious change, and the inexorable rise of élites.[36]

We all read these symbols slightly differently, according to our backgrounds and inclinations. An atheist and a cradle Catholic will each bring their own baggage to any study, perhaps especially when considering the art of the seventh century when politics and religion were in such dramatic ferment. It is this that encourages debate and, with luck, new thoughts of the kind Andrew is so good at fostering.

Acknowledgments

I would like to thank Greer Ramsey for details of the Ballyalton fish; Sue Brunning for providing the initial impetus for this article; and Steven Ashley for constant help and unfailing encouragement. Thanks are also due to Jenni Butterworth for preliminary information about items in the Staffordshire Hoard, to Craig Bowen for the image of the Littlebourne buckle, and to Mark Whyman and Catherine Hills for commenting on a version of this article in draft; the deficiencies that remain are entirely mine. My long-term debt to Tania Dickinson's intellect and generosity will be clear from the constant citations within the text, but should also be repeated here.

Andrew Rogerson should above all be thanked, mainly for teaching me all about ancient objects and their landscape contexts, but also for introducing me to the delights and health benefits of Norwich Market's hot mushy peas.

---

[31] Speake 1980, pp. 77-92
[32] Fish-shaped mounts could also have been used on objects other than shields; two mounts from Eastry are argued to have come from saddle harness (Dickinson, Fern and Richardson 2011, p. 47, figs. 23 and 32), where they probably fulfilled the same role as symbols of power and protection
[33] Dickinson 2005, p. 162
[34] Dickinson 2005, pp. 156-7. The word *pike* is Middle English and relates to the fish's shape, with the long, thin connotations of the related words *pike* (weapon) and *spike*. In Old English the fish was called *hacod*, which seems equally to refer to its shape, this word being related to *haca*, a bar or bolt from a door. See Dickinson 2005, n. 115 for more on the words used for this fish
[35] Dickinson 2005, p. 156. While her intuition is no doubt right, it should be pointed out that the idea of Christ as a heroic warrior does also occur, notably in the Dream of the Rood

[36] It is therefore intriguing that the fish in the hanging bowl from Sutton Hoo was clearly intended to represent a species other than a pike, with very different characteristics

FIG. 10 Silver fish from East Walton, Norfolk (NMS-AA0858). (© Norwich Castle Museum and Art Gallery). Not to scale: length of fish, 51mm

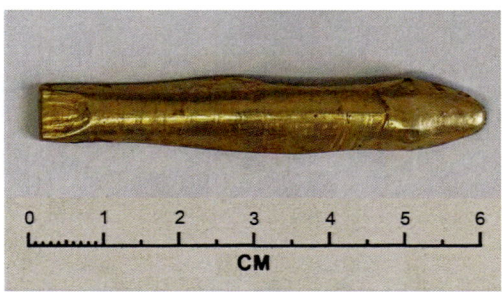

FIG. 11 Fish from Ballyalton, Co. Down, made from gold foil over a copper-alloy core (© National Museums Northern Ireland). Scale 1:1

FIG. 12 Buckle with gold fish appliqué from Crundale, Kent (© Trustees of the British Museum). Scale 1:1

FIG. 13 Buckle of gilded silver from Littlebourne, Kent (KENT-50B745) with engraved fish motif (© Canterbury Museums). Scale approximately 1:1

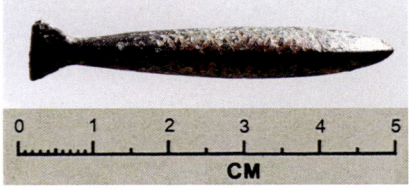

FIG. 14 Fish-shaped object, perhaps an appliqué from a hanging bowl, found at Barham, Suffolk (© Trustees of the British Museum). Scale 1:1

FIG. 15 Fish-shaped brooch from Saffron Walden, Essex (ESS-C4EB33; © Portable Antiquities Scheme). Scale 1:1

Fig. 16 Roman fish-shaped brooch from Piercebridge, Co. Durham (NCL-36DF13; © Portable Antiquities Scheme). Length 41mm, not to scale

Fig. 17 Small gold fish-shaped plaque from Westleton, Suffolk (SF-1DC2A2; © Portable Antiquities Scheme). Scale 1:1

Fig. 18 Gold fish appliqués from the Staffordshire Hoard (© Portable Antiquities Scheme). Not to scale. K1663, c. 30mm long; K0796, c. 23mm long

Fig. 19 Fish-between-birds motifs on objects from the Staffordshire Hoard (© Portable Antiquities Scheme). Not to scale. K42, c. 22mm long; K652, length of fish from neck to tail c. 50mm

Bibliography

Blockley, K., Blockley, M., Blockley, P., Frere, S.S., and Stow, S. 1995, *Excavations in the Marlowe car park and surrounding areas* (The Archaeology of Canterbury vol. V, Canterbury Archaeological Trust, Canterbury)

Brenan, J. 1991, *Hanging Bowls and their Contexts* (British Archaeological Reports 220, Oxford)

Bruce-Mitford, R. 1983, *The Sutton Hoo Ship-Burial, volume 3* (British Museum Publications, London)

Bruce-Mitford, R. 2005, *The Corpus of Late Celtic Hanging-Bowls* (Oxford University Press).

Chadwick Hawkes, S., Ellis Davidson, H.R. and Hawkes, C. 1965, 'The Finglesham Man' *Antiquity* 39, pp. 17-32

Detsicas, A.P. and Hawkes, S.C. 1973, 'Finds from the Anglo-Saxon cemetery at Eccles, Kent' *Antiquaries Journal* 53, pp. 281-6, pls. LVI-LVII.

Dickinson, T.M. 2005, 'Symbols of protection: the significance of animal-ornamented shields in early Anglo-Saxon England' *Medieval Archaeology* 49, pp. 109-163

Dickinson, T.M., Ashley, S., and Penn, K. 2011, 'A zoomorphic shield mount from Hindringham, Norfolk' *Medieval Archaeology* 55, pp. 277-281

Dickinson, T.M., Fern, C. and Richardson, A. 2011, 'Early Anglo-Saxon Eastry: archaeological evidence for the beginnings of a district centre in the kingdom of Kent' *Anglo-Saxon Studies in Archaeology and History* 17, pp. 1-86

Fox, C.F. 1924, 'Excavations at Foxton, Cambridgeshire, in 1922' *Proceedings of the Cambridge Antiquarian Society* 25 (for 1922-23), pp. 37-46

Geake, H. 1997, *The Use of Grave-Goods in Anglo-Saxon Cemeteries c. 600-c. 850* (British Archaeological Reports 261, Oxford)

Hines, J. 1997, *A New Corpus of Anglo-Saxon Great Square-Headed Brooches* (Boydell Press, Woodbridge)

Jessup, R. 1946, 'An Anglo-Saxon cemetery at Westbere, Kent' *Antiquaries Journal* 26, pp. 11-21

Malim, T. and Hines, J. 1998, *The Anglo-Saxon Cemetery at Edix Hill (Barrington A), Cambridgeshire* (CBA Res Rep 112)

Martin, E., Pendleton, C., Plouviez, J., and Thomas, G. 2000, 'Archaeology in Suffolk 1999' *Proceedings of the Suffolk Institute of Archaeology and History* 39.4, pp. 495–531

Roach Smith, C. 1844, 'An account of some antiquities found in the neighbourhood of Sandwich, in the county of Kent' *Archaeologia* 30, pp. 132-6.

Rogerson, A. and Ashley, S. 2008, 'A selection of finds from Norfolk recorded between 2006 and 2008' *Norfolk Archaeology* 45, part iii, pp. 428-441

Rogerson, A., and Ashley, S. 2009, 'A selection of finds from Norfolk recorded in 2009 and earlier' *Norfolk Archaeology* 45, part iv, pp. 556-70

Smith, R.A. 1923, *A Guide to the Anglo-Saxon and Foreign Teutonic Antiquities in the Department of British and Medieval Antiquities* (British Museum, London)

Speake, G. 1980, *Anglo-Saxon Animal Art and Its Germanic Background* (Clarendon Press, Oxford)

Webster, L. and Backhouse, J. (eds.) 1991, *The Making of England: Anglo-Saxon art and culture AD 600-900* (British Museum Press)

Wessex Archaeology 2004, *Springhead Quarter, Northfleet, Kent: archaeological evaluation report ref. 54924.01* (Trust for Wessex Archaeology, Salisbury)

West, S.E. 1998, *A Corpus of Anglo-Saxon Material from Suffolk*, East Anglian Archaeology 84

The Wickham Skeith, Thwaite or Campsey Ash coin hoard – the true location and possible context of a major Late Saxon coin hoard

Edward Martin

Abstract: This paper presents the evidence for the true location of a major Late Saxon coin hoard that was discovered in 1832, together with a discussion of the events that might have led to the deposition of the hoard around AD 1050.

In 1832 a remarkable hoard of late Saxon coins was found in Suffolk at a location that has confused scholars ever since – with Campsey Ash in south-east Suffolk, Thwaite in north-central Suffolk and Thwaite's western neighbour, Wickham Skeith, all having been credited with the discovery (Fig. 1).[1] The discovery was recorded in these words in *The Bury and Norwich Post,* of the 8 February 1832 (p. 2, col. 3):

> A few days since as some labourers were felling an old pollard oak, on the estate of Mrs. Sheppard, at Thwaite, near Eye, they discovered 2 parcels of ancient coins, inclosed in thin lead cases; one of them was quite embedded in the solid part of the root. They are chiefly pennies of Edward the Confessor and Harold the Second, and amounted altogether to nearly 600 pieces. Many of them were divided into halves and quarters, which evidently shew that at that remote period these divided parts were circulated as half-pence and farthings. They were all carefully preserved for Mrs. Sheppard, of Campsey Ash, who is Lady of the Manor of Thwaite.

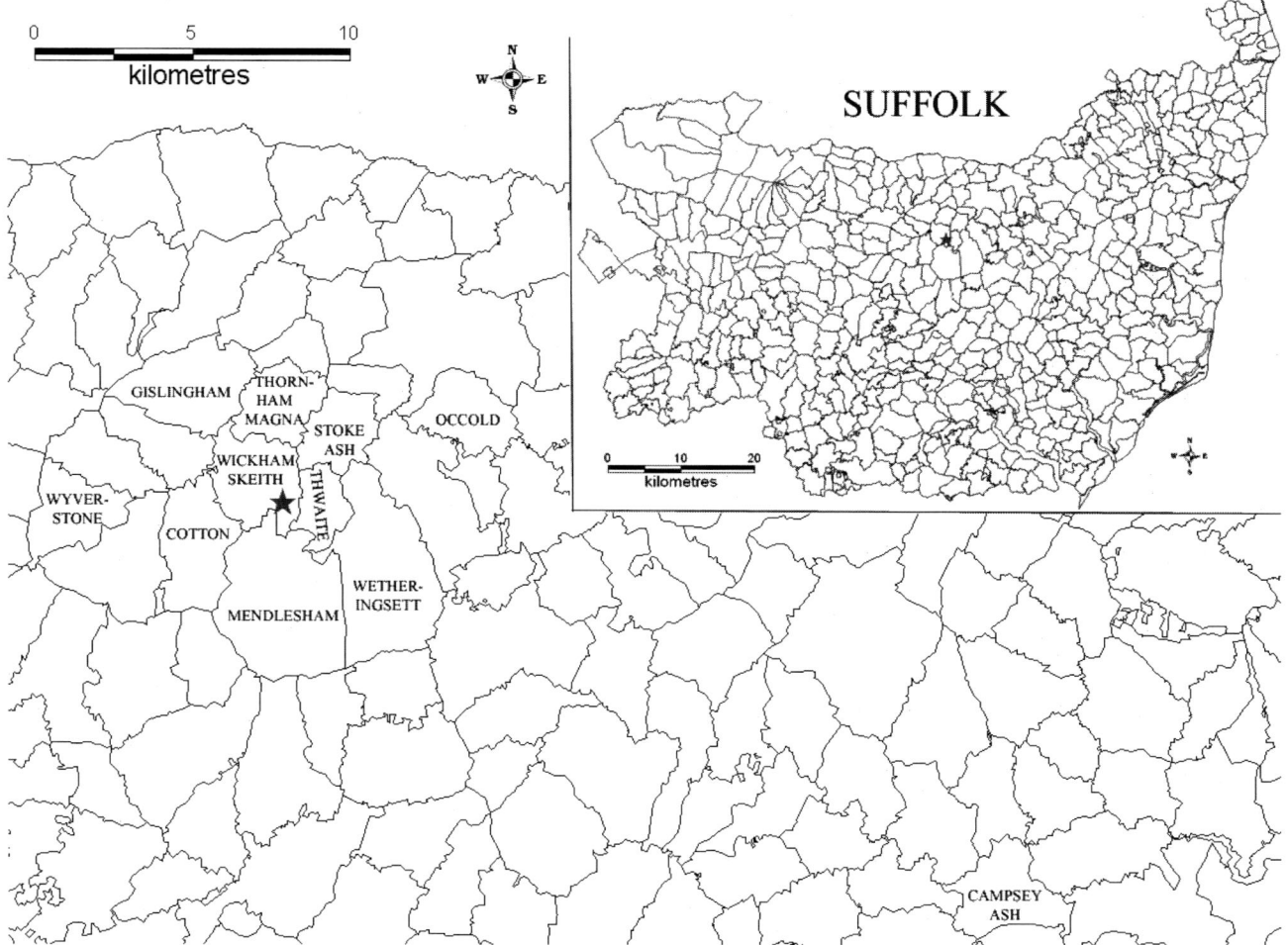

FIG. 1 MAP SHOWING THE LOCATION OF THE MAIN PLACES MENTIONED IN THE TEXT. THE HOARD FINDSPOT IS MARKED BY A STAR.

---

[1] Dolley and Strudwick 1955, p. 36; Thompson 1956, pp. 69, 360; Martin 1956, pp. 414-5; Colman 1992, p. 135; Manville 1993, p. 96; Allen in Cook and Williams (eds.) 2006, no. 37; Fitzwilliam Museum Checklist of Coin Hoards from the British Isles, c.450-1180

The find was also recorded in the *Essex Standard* of the 11 February 1832 (p. 2, col. 5):

> A short time since, a man employed in removing the butt of an oak pollard, recently felled at Wickham Skeith, near Eye, Suffolk, discovered several packages, containing ancient coins of different kinds. In one of the packets there were as many as 500 of these interesting relics of bygone days; and there were several others smaller, making in all about 700. Unacquainted with their value as antiquarian curiosities, the man took them to the chandler's shop; and, finding that they would not purchase any of those necessaries of which he stood most in need, he liberally distributed them by handfuls to any one that would have them. A gentleman of Colchester, being in the neighbourhood shortly after the discovery, procured six of them, all different. An adept in antiquities here, has pronounced them to have been coined previous to the Conquest. One of them bears the effigy and name of *Canute*, who began to reign A.D. 1017; another is supposed to be of the reign of Edred, A.D. 946 and several bear rude but distinct representations of the *fleur-de-lis*. —They are all in an excellent state of preservation.

And in the *Gentleman's Magazine* (vol. 102, part 1, p. 355) under April 1832:

> In the beginning of the present year a large discovery of Saxon coins was made near Eye in Suffolk, by some labourers on the estate of Mrs Sheppard of Campsey Ash. They were felling an old pollard oak, where they discovered two parcels of coins, inclosed in thin lead cases; one of them quite embedded in the solid part of the root. Many of them divided into halves and quarters, which evidently shows that at that remote period these divided parts were circulated as halfpence and farthings. A Correspondent has seen about 200 coins, and is informed that about 600 are in the possession of Mr Page of Woodbridge; perhaps 100 more may have been variously distributed. It would be very desirable to ascertain the exact number of pieces discovered, also a correct list of the types, towns, and moneyers, many of which were probably new.

A little later, *White's Directory of Suffolk* (1844, p. 350), under its entry for the parish of Wickham Skeith, noted that:

> Under an ancient oak on Wizard farm, many Saxon coins, of Harold, Edward the Confessor, &c., were found a few years ago, and are now deposited in the British Museum.

The *Directory* (p. 351) lists a Thomas Tunmer at Wizard Farm – but there is no modern farm of that name in Wickham Skeith. The Ordnance Survey first-edition map 1886 marks, at TM 1021 6794 in Wickham Skeith parish, 'Saxon coins found about here' (Fig. 2). The location is 315m west of the Wickham Skeith/Thwaite parish boundary. This location is recorded in the Suffolk Historic Environment Record as site WKS 001, but with this note derived from an older Ordnance Survey record card (TM16NW6): 'No supporting evidence for this location'. The site is now in an arable field on a high clay plateau (Fig. 3)

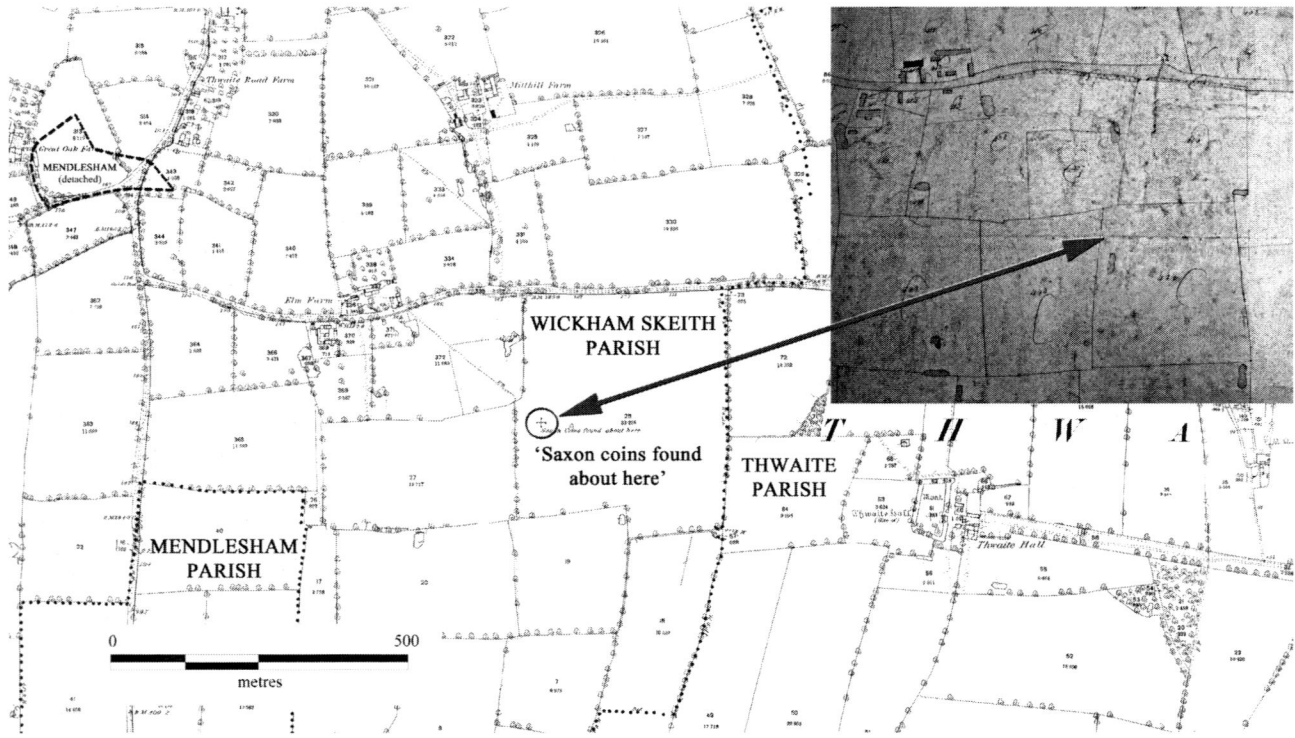

FIG. 2 EXTRACT FROM THE ORDNANCE SURVEY FIRST-EDITION MAP OF 1886 SHOWING THE FINDSPOT OF THE HOARD (RINGED). INSET IS AN EXTRACT FROM THE WICKHAM SKEITH TITHE MAP OF 1838 THAT SHOWS PART OF THE SAME AREA; THE ARROW POINTS TO THE HOARD FINDSPOT ON BOTH MAPS.

FIG. 3 VIEW OF THE FINDSPOT, LOOKING SOUTH, WITH MENDLESHAM CHURCH TOWER IN THE FAR DISTANCE.

The contemporary reports clearly identify the findspot as being on the estate of Mrs Sheppard of Campsey and afterwards the Hon. Mrs Wilson did present a number of the coins to the British Museum. As J.S. Martin has previously worked out, Mrs Sheppard and the Hon. Mrs Wilson were actually the same person.[2] Harriet Sheppard (née Crump), the widow of John Wilson Sheppard of Ash High House, Campsey Ash and Thwaite Hall (he died in 1830) remarried on the 13 Apr. 1832 the Hon. and Rev. Robert Wilson, Rector of Ashwellthorpe in Norfolk – so she was 'Mrs Sheppard' when the coins were found in February 1832, but was the 'Hon. Mrs Wilson' when she presented the coins. The Sheppards had inherited an estate centred on Thwaite Hall in the early 18th century, but lived mainly at their grander estate at Campsey Ash. In 1839 Thwaite Hall itself was tenanted by a William Wilson,[3] but amongst the other farms belonging to the estate was one in Wickham Skeith that was occupied by a Thomas Tunmer – this is now called Elm Farm, but must be the *Wizard Farm* of 1844 – and the Wickham Skeith tithe map of 1838 indicates that the hoard findspot, as recorded by the Ordnance Survey, lies within one of the fields that Tunmer held of the Sheppards.[4] The field, number 444 in the tithe apportionment, was then an arable field but contained an elongated oval pond very close to the findspot recorded by the Ordnance Survey. The oak pollard, the felling of which in 1832 led to the discovery of the hoard, could well have been on the edge of this pond. Unfortunately, the Wickham Skeith tithe apportionment does not give any field names, so there is no confirmatory field name alluding to the treasure find, but there can be little doubt that the 'Thwaite hoard', as it is now almost universally known to numismatists, was actually found in Wickham Skeith.

The composition of the hoard cannot now be fully ascertained, but of the 700 coins referred to in the contemporary accounts, it is known that there are 194 coins in the British Museum ascribed to the 'Thwaite find 1832', plus another 29 gifted by Mrs Wilson in 1877, plus 111 acquired from a Mr Cuff between 1839 and 1854 that are also from the hoard, making 334 in all.[5] There are also 14 coins in the Ashmolean Museum in Oxford;[6] 11 in the Fitzwilliam Museum in Cambridge (presented by Mrs Wilson and the Rev. Greville J. Chester); 2 coins were given to Norwich Museum in 1832 by W.S. Fitch, the Ipswich postmaster, and a further 5 were given in 1835 by the Rev. R. Wilson;[7] and there were 11 coins in the Merseyside County Museum (given by Mrs Wilson in 1878) that were lost through World War II bombing.[8] Altogether, this accounts for 377 coins from the hoard. The vast majority of the coins date from the reign of Edward the Confessor (1042-66), with very small amounts from

---

[2] Martin 1956, pp. 414-5
[3] Thwaite tithe apportionment, SROI FB 153/C3/2-3.
[4] Wickham Skeith tithe apportionment, SROI FDA 288/A1/1a & b
[5] Dolley and Strudwick 1955
[6] Colman 1992, p. 135
[7] Pagan 1980, p. 141.
[8] www-cm.fitzmuseum.cam.ac.uk/dept/coins/projects/hoards/index.list.html.

earlier reigns: Harthacnut (1040-42) 1; Harold I Harefoot (1035-40) 19, Canute (1016-1035) 4. D.M Metcalf has pointed out an oddity in the mint provenances of the coins of Edward the Confessor in this hoard: the early PAXC issue (*c*.1042-44) has 43% of its coins coming from the East Anglian Thetford mint, but the later (and much more numerous) Trefoil (*c*.1046-8) and Short Cross (*c*.1048-50) coins in the hoard are mainly London issues (63% and 75% respectively) with no East Anglian mints being represented. This anomaly has led him to suggest that there may be two 'collections' in the hoard – an earlier locally-sourced group represented by the PAXC coins and a larger and later London assembled group.[9] The deposition date for the hoard is probably *c*.1050.

The deposition of such a large amount of money – and London money too, enough to pay for an army, calls for some explanation. The Anglo-Saxon Chronicle records two events around 1050 that affected East Anglia and could have prompted the hiding of a large hoard. The first concerns a man named OsgodClapa – his byname means 'a coarse or rough person', though the late 11th-century writer, Hermann of Bury, has a vivid (though perhaps imaginary) description of him as dressing in the 'Danish fashion', with golden arm-rings and carrying a gilded axe slung from his shoulder.[10] Osgod is of uncertain origin – either a Danish follower of King Cnut or a descendant of Osgod son of Eadulf, a kinsman of Theodred, bishop of London (d. 951) as both Osgods held land at Pakenham in Suffolk.[11] OsgodClapa first comes to notice in 1042 through the unfortunate occurrence of the sudden death of King Harthacnut 'standing at his drink' at the marriage of Osgod's daughter Gytha to Tovi the Proud 'a staller [royal official] and standard-bearer of the king'.[12] In 1046 Osgod, also described as a staller, was outlawed and expelled.[13] His confiscated estate at Pakenham was given, by King Edward, to the Abbey of Bury St Edmunds.[14] Osgod went to Flanders, from whence he returned in 1049 in a number of ships to *Eadulfesness* [The Naze in Essex] and 'did damage there'.[15] On their return to their ships they were overtaken by a storm and many were lost, but Osgod survived, only to die suddenly in his bed in 1054, possibly in Denmark.[16]

The other important event, or sequence of events, concerned Ælfgar, the son of Earl Leofric of Mercia and his wife Godgifu, better-known as 'Lady Godiva'. In 1051 Eustace, Count of Boulogne (who had married King Edward the Confessor's sister) and his men caused an incident at Dover. Earl Godwine of Wessex and his sons, Earl Swein and Earl Harold of East Anglia, joined him and pursued Eustace who had taken refuge with the king at Gloucester. After a stand-off, Godwine and his sons went into exile, and Ælfgar was given Harold's earldom of East Anglia.[17] But in 1052 Harold returned and was reinstated as earl of East Anglia. A year later there was another redistribution of earldoms when Earl Godwine died and was succeeded in Wessex by his son Harold, and Ælfgar was given, once again, Harold's vacated earldom of East Anglia.[18] Ælfgar's enjoyment of the earldom was, however, short-lived, for in 1055 he was, according to version C of the *Chronicle*, 'outlawed without guilt'; version D says he was 'outlawed, having committed hardly any crime'; but version E says he was 'charged with being a traitor to the king and to all the people of the country', this he admitted 'before all the people who were assembled there, though the words escaped him against his will'.[19] He went into exile in Ireland and Wales, but returned shortly afterwards and joined forces with Gruffuddap Llewelyn, the Welsh king. Together they defeated the English royal army under Earl Ralph at the Battle of Hereford in October 1055. As part of the post-battle settlement, Ælfgar was once more reinstated as earl of East Anglia.[20] In 1057 he succeeded his father Leofric as earl of Mercia, but was outlawed again in 1058. He took refuge once again with King Gruffudd who was now his son-in-law (having married Ælfgar's daughter Ealdgyth) and was yet again reinstated as earl. He finally died *c*.1062-5, being succeeded in his earldom of Mercia by his son Edwin; his daughter Ealdgyth, after the death of King Gruffudd in 1063, became the wife of Harold Godwineson, Earl of Wessex, later to become King Harold II.[21]

Among Ælfgar's other children was a son named Burgheard who died in 1061 in France on his return journey from Rome and was buried in the Abbey of Saint-Rémi at Rheims. In a recent study, Stephen Baxter has drawn attention to the rarity of this name and has suggested that Burgheard son of Ælfgar may be the same man who is mentioned in Domesday Book as Burgheard of Mendlesham (in Suffolk), Burgheard of Shenley (Buckinghamshire) and Burgheard of Fundenhall (Norfolk), whose estates passed in many cases into the hands of Hugh d'Avranches, Earl of Chester, after the Norman Conquest.[22] Burgheard of Shenley is referred to as a 'housecarl of the king' (*huscarleregis*) and as a 'thegn of the king' (*teignusregis*), while Burgheard of Fundenhall is referred to as a thegn. Baxter accepts that there is a potential serious problem in making an equation with a man who

---

[9] Metcalf 1998, pp. 152-56.
[10] Hermann the Archdeacon, 'De miraculis Sancti Eadmundi', *Memorials of St Edmund's Abbey*, ed. T. Arnold, vol. I, Rolls Series 96, 1890, 54: 'Inter quos quidam major domus, Osgodclap cognomine vocitatus, quodam mane pedetenus decoratus mastrugarum decore, armillas quoque bajulans in brachiis ambobus superbe, Danico more deaurata securi in humero dependente, sed postmodum tali suo decore verso in infami dedecore'; Osgod was floored in agony by St Edmund for daring to bring his axe into the saint's shrine. For a discussion of the identity of Hermann see: Licence 2009, pp. 516-544
[11] Whitelock 1930, pp. 3-5: Osgod son of Eadulf was given the estates of Barton, Rougham and Pakenham; Theodred also gave to 'Osgod my sister's son' lands in Mendham, Syleham, Weybread, Chickering. Ashfield, Wortham, Waldringfield and Ipswich.
[12] Whitelock *et al*. 1961, p. 106 n. 8; Wareham 2005, p. 113
[13] Whitelock *et al*. 1961, p. 109
[14] Arnold (ed.) 1890, p. 364; Hart 1966, p. 71
[15] Whitelock *et al*. 1961, p. 113
[16] Whitelock *et al*. 1961, p. 129; Williams 2004a

[17] Whitelock *et al*. 1961, pp. 117-22
[18] Whitelock *et al*. 1961, pp. 128-9
[19] Whitelock *et al*. 1961, p. 130
[20] Whitelock *et al*. 1961, pp. 130-1
[21] Williams 2004b
[22] Baxter 2008, pp. 266-84

died in 1061, five years before the Domesday record, but points out that other long-dead men are cited in Domesday Book, including Burgheard's father Ælfgar. Domesday Book records that Burgheard had held a substantial estate of seven carucates in Mendlesham that was held by the king in 1086.[23] Land belonging to the lordship of Mendlesham or in the assessment of Mendlesham is also mentioned in a number of the surrounding parishes: Cotton, Wetheringsett, Occold, Wyverstone, Stoke Ash, Gislingham and, potentially most significant in terms of the coin hoard, in Wickham Skeith, immediately to the north of Mendlesham (Fig. 2).[24] Domesday Book also records a 61-acre berewick belonging to Mendlesham in Wickham Skeith, and in the 19th century there was still a detached part of Mendlesham in Wickham Skeith only 740m to the west of the hoard find-spot.[25] Burgheard of Mendlesham is specifically mentioned by name as having had two free men under his commendation in Wickham Skeith, and free men belonging to a Burgheard are mentioned in Cotton, Wyverstone, Stoke Ash and Thornham Magna.[26] None of this proves that Burgheard son of Ælfgar and Burgheard of Mendlesham were the same person, but the latter was certainly a person of some wealth which might fit with a kinsman, if not a son, of Earl Ælfgar. Earl Ælfgar's troubles in the 1050s could provide a suitable context for the deposition of the coin hoard and the choice of Wickham Skeith as the hiding place could also be explicable if it lay within the lands of Ælfgar's close family.

---

[23] Rumble 1986, 1.86
[24] Rumble 1986, nos. 1.77-80, 82-87 and 14.146 and 152
[25] Rumble 1986, 1.85. The findspot is only just over 300m from the main part of Mendlesham parish
[26] Rumble 1986, 14.152, and 1.77, 1.84, 1.95, 1.83, 31.36, 1.86, 14.146 and 6.215

Bibliography

Allen, M. 2006, 'The Volume of English Currency, c.973-1158' in B. Cook and G. Williams (eds.) *Coinage and History in the North Sea World: Essays in honour of Marion Archibald* (Leiden)

Arnold, T. (ed.) 1890, *Memorials of St Edmund's Abbey*, vol. I, Rolls Series 96

Baxter, S. 2008, 'The death of Burgheard son of Ælfgar and its context' in F. Fouracre and D. Ganz (eds.) *Frankland. The Franks and the World of the Early Middle Ages, Essays in Honour of Dame Jinty Nelson* (Manchester University Press)

Colman, F. 1992, *Money talks: reconstructing Old English* (Trends in linguistics. Studies and monographs 56) (Berlin and New York)

Dolley, R.H.M. and Strudwick, J.S. 1955, 'The provenances of the Anglo-Saxon coins recorded in the British Museum Catalogue', *British Numismatic Journal* 28(8)1, 26-59

Hart, C.R. 1966, *The Early Charters of Eastern England* (Leicester University Press)

Fitzwilliam Museum Checklist of Coin Hoards from the British Isles, c.450-1180 www-cm.fitzmuseum.cam.ac.uk/dept/coins/projects/hoards/index.list.html

Licence, T. 2009,'History and Hagiography in the Late Eleventh Century: The Life and Work of Herman the Archdeacon, Monk of Bury St Edmunds', *English Historical Review* CXXIV(508), pp.516-44

Manville, H.E. 1993, 'Additions and Corrections to Thompson's *Inventory* and Brown and Dolley's *Coin Hoards* – Part 1', *British Numismatic Journal* 63, pp. 91-113

Martin, J.S. 1956, 'The supposed finds of Thwaite and Campsey Ash 1832', *British Numismatic Journal* 28(8)2, pp. 414-16

Metcalf, D.M. 1998, *An Atlas of Anglo-Saxon and Norman Coin Finds, c.973-1086*, Ashmolean Museum and Royal Numismatic Soc. Special Publication no. 32 (London)

Pagan, H.E. 1980, in a review of T.H.McK. Clough, *Sylloge of Coins of the British Isles 26*, in *British Numismatic Journal* 50, pp. 140-1

Rumble, A. 1986, *Domesday Book – Suffolk* (Phillimore, Chichester)

Thompson, J.D.A. 1956, *An Inventory of British Coin Hoards AD 600-1500* (London)

Wareham, A. 2005, *Lords and Communities in Early Medieval East Anglia*, (Boydell, Woodbridge)

Whitelock, D. 1930, *Anglo-Saxon Wills* (Cambridge University Press)

Whitelock, D., Douglas, D.C., and Tucker, S.I. (eds.) 1961, *The Anglo-Saxon Chronicle* (Eyre and Spottiswode, London)

Williams, A. 2004a, 'OsgodClapa (d. 1054)', *Oxford Dictionary of National Biography* (Oxford University Press) http://www.oxforddnb.com/view/article/20890, accessed 5 Jan 2014

Williams, A. 2004b, 'Ælfgar, earl of Mercia (d. 1062?)', *Oxford Dictionary of National Biography* (Oxford University Press) http://www.oxforddnb.com/view/article/178, accessed 5 Jan 2014

Norwich before Norwich: an exploration of the pre-urban landscape of the medieval city

Brian Ayers

Abstract: This paper is an attempt to explore the pre-urban geography of the medieval core of Norwich, examining the impact of the landscape upon the form of the city. It discusses human exploitation and manipulation of pre-urban features such as the River Wensum and its valley, tributaries to the river, hill slopes and natural deposits.

This paper has its genesis in a chance remark concerning Norwich made to the writer some years ago by Andrew Rogerson. Upon some forgotten matter we happened to discuss the area of the French Borough within the city centre, that part of Norwich almost certainly laid out between 1071 and 1075 at the behest of the Conqueror, King William, and the Earl of East Anglia, the Breton Ralph de Guader. Andrew's eye had alighted upon St Peter's Street, the truncated length of which now runs only in front of City Hall but, until the recent past, extended southward past the church of St Peter Mancroft. He remarked that the slightly sinuous alignment of this street was highly suggestive of the reverse 'S' that one finds in the countryside, marking the distinctive formation of headlands consequent upon medieval agricultural practice.

His observation had the more force given the probable derivation of the name 'Mancroft' from the OE (ge) *mæna* and the Latin *croft* ('common enclosure' or 'common land'), thus indicating open fields predating the early Norman urban development.[1] Subsequent to our conversation, part of the area of Mancroft has been excavated and, while not revealing completely non-urban activity, the work indicated that the area was indeed largely open ground to the west of the pre-Conquest Anglo-Scandinavian borough. Andrew's shrewd observation noted that information concerning the pre-urban landscape was clearly available for study and that the heavily-developed urban townscape itself would hold clues to the subsequent manner in which the city grew and was used.

This paper therefore grows from this premise, that much can be learnt about Norwich from a consideration of the landscape which preceded the city ('Norwich' for the purposes of this paper, largely concerns the medieval core of the city as delimited by the 13th- and 14th-century walls; only rarely will the discussion extend beyond these bounds). Observations, either of early antiquarians discussing, for instance, the numerous streams or cockeys which flow into the Wensum, the principal river through the city or, later, of archaeologists considering pre-occupation deposits, can be combined to shed light on much of this landscape. Furthermore, methodological approaches to urban studies in recent years have developed considerably, no longer considering sites in isolation but seeking to understand their landscape context, as urban entities in their own right, within their hinterlands, and as human-derived expressions imprinted upon the pre-existing geography. This paper, therefore, explores these relationships, specifically seeking to understand how the particular geographical setting of the Wensum valley in central eastern Norfolk influenced subsequent urban development but also exploring the emerging information for pre-urban activity (place- and street-names used within the text are shown on Fig 1).

Norwich is situated on either bank of the River Wensum, a short distance above its confluence with the River Yare. The river enters the city from the north-west, turns eastward before, through a right-angled bend, heading south and exiting the urban area to the south-east. It is a lowland river with extensive water meadows bordering its banks to this day both upstream and downstream of Norwich. Within the medieval city itself, however, the central part of its course is constrained by low hills, to the north-east Mousehold Heath and, to the south, the Ber Street escarpment. These constraining hills aided glacial deposition of sandy gravels which formed terraces some 7m thick in the valley floor, terraces that are relatively narrow south of the river but broader and flatter to the north.

The likely form of much of the prehistoric river within the area of Norwich can be gleaned from the results of recent surveys and excavations. Borehole data and sampling of peat deposits has identified a fairly stable landscape from the Mesolithic period through to the first millennium AD as evidenced by a thick but largely homogeneous peat sampled at Fishergate in 1985. This early Flandrian peat, the earliest levels of which could be dated to 9410±110BP (uncalibrated), contained plant macrofossils of reed swamp plants and aquatics together with insect remains of reed swamp and stagnant water species. There was evidence for occasional flooding from the main river channel[2] so essentially the environment appears to have been a typically sluggish, lowland east Norfolk wetland area, probably similar to modern locations within the Broads.

The impact of such a landscape upon human activity has been observed recently. Excavations at Carrow Road in 2002 uncovered a sand island within the braided river valley of the Wensum (immediately downstream of the site of the later medieval city) upon which were located

---

[1] Sandred and Lindström 1989, p. 71. As an aside, it is also pleasing to note that there is a field name of 'Mancroft' in Beeston-next-Mileham parish, between Andrew's home and his place of work

[2] Murphy 1994, p. 59

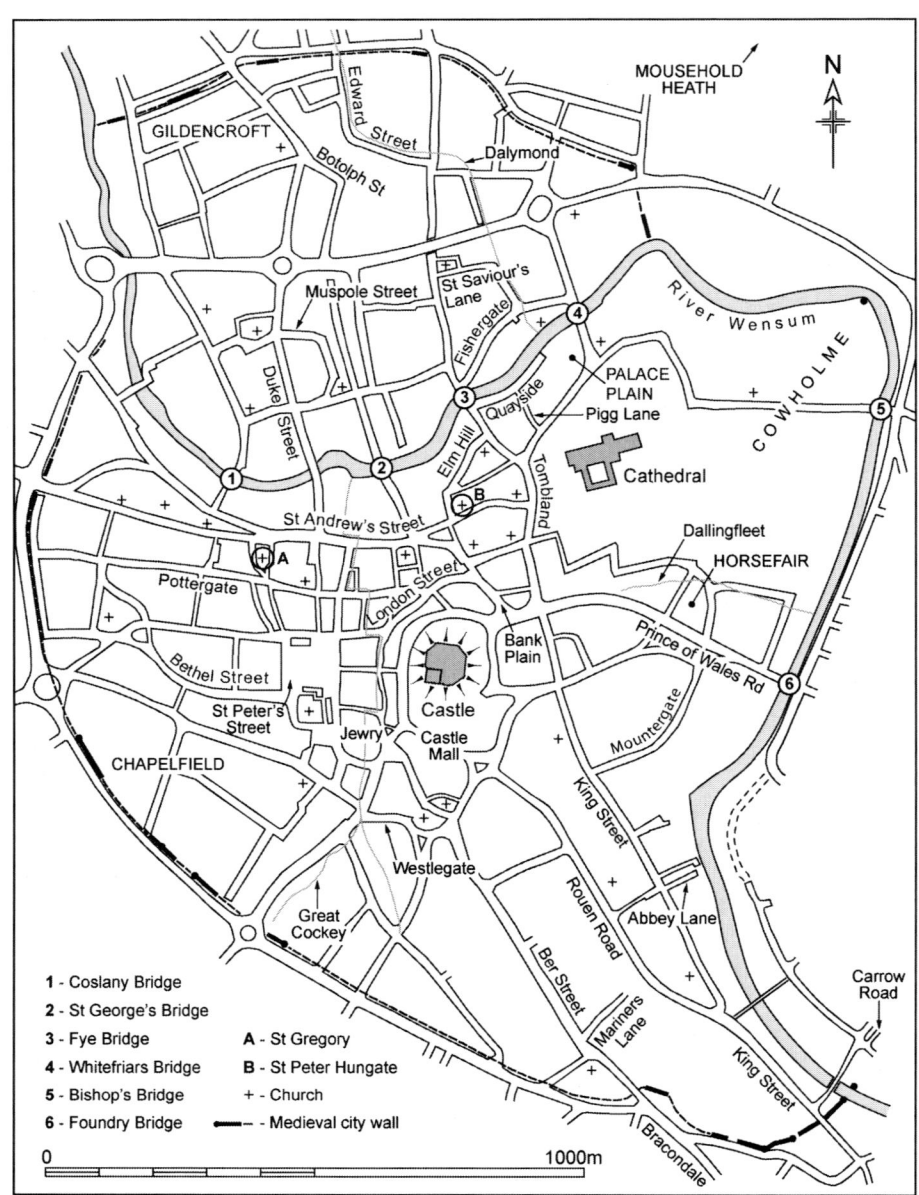

FIG. 1 MAP OF CENTRAL NORWICH WITH PLACE AND STREET-NAMES MENTIONED IN THE TEXT

rough-out waste flints and tools of Upper Palaeolithic date. The excavator surmises that the island provided the ideal position from which to stalk and kill game which entered the marsh and, impeded by the water, became vulnerable to attack.[3]

Slightly later flints have been uncovered even more recently north of the Wensum in the centre of the medieval city. In a discovery similar to that at Carrow Road, flint tools were located in 2011 lying on the western shoulder of a stream called the Dalymond which ran southward across the gravel terrace to a confluence with the river. The site, adjacent to present-day St Saviour's Lane, contained 'dense and consistent collections of worked flints showing potential in situ flint working and site occupation dated to the Upper Palaeolithic/Early Mesolithic, of regional or even national importance.'[4] Again, it is possible to envisage human activity close to watercourses, bringing tools sourced from the surrounding higher ground (such as from flint outcrops at Whitlingham, south-east of the later city) on to the gravel terraces for hunting, fishing and fashioning of clothing and rudimentary shelter.

The river within the urban area was fed by numerous streams (locally called *cockeys*) such as the Dalymond, the alignments of the principal ones being known but others now also known to be lost. As examples, the *Great Cockey* can be traced from a probable source on the western side of the Ber Street escarpment to its outflow into the Wensum immediately upstream of St George's Bridge while the Dallingfleet, also on the south bank, emerged from the eastern slope of the escarpment and entered the river close to the southern boundary of the medieval Cathedral Close. Such cockeys have been observed on a number of occasions, notoriously in 1962 when the culvert of the *Great Cockey* was broken by development on Castle

---

[3] Adams, D. 2002 and *pers. comm.*
[4] House 2012, p. 427

Street causing localised flooding or, in more controlled development activity in 1985, when the *Dalymond* stream was seen flowing through stantion pits east of Peacock Street on the north bank of the river.

The central area of pre-urban Norwich was therefore bisected, as now, by the River Wensum and crossed by numerous streams, most of which are named in early surviving documentation. It is tempting when considering the pre-urban site to explore the evidence of such place-names. An early example of such consideration is that of the Rev William Hudson who, in discussing the cockeys of the city, included an assessment of the name *cockey* itself. Citing unnamed authorities, he felt the term to be derived from 'the Celtic "kok," hollow, a water channel, or Saxon "cuic" or "cuc," living or running water'.[5] Both derivations are doubted in the most recent work on Norwich place-names without offering plausible alternatives save the suggestion that the term may be of Scandinavian origin, the Old Norse 'kók' meaning gullet.[6] This is not helpful but it can be noted that other place-names within the city do suggest something of the pre-urban geography. 'Wensum' itself is from the Old English *wændsum* meaning 'winding' and clearly appropriate to the course of the river both within and beyond Norwich; the fields of Mancroft have already been mentioned; north of the river was *Mereholt* or 'boundary wood', possibly marking an early edge of the borough; and, also to the north, Muspole Street probably refers to a 'muddy pool' although a derivation from the OE *mūs* and thus 'mouse-infested pool' is attractive if probably erroneous.[7]

Such place-name evidence is obviously limited; the winding nature of the river can still be observed and the presence of woods and fields is hardly unexpected. Perhaps it is more instructive to consider the rarity of such place-names within the earliest records of the medieval city. This rarity itself may be indicative of the sheer speed with which the town grew. Norwich has always been something of a puzzle with regard to its early development. There is very little evidence of urban activity before the 9th century and yet, by the 11th century, it was clearly one of the foremost towns of later pre-Conquest England. Its rapid success may well have militated against the survival of distinctive *rus in urbe* elements with attendant place-names; rather, the establishment of a town at such speed and its attendant commercial success brought with it a tendency to create names appropriate to the functions developing within the nascent borough: thus *Tombland*, the empty or open land for the market place, *Fishergate*, the street of the fishermen, *Pottergate*, the street of the potters and, perhaps most tellingly of human impact upon natural features, *Fybriggate* or the street leading to Fye Bridge, a structure most probably in existence by the middle of the 10th century.[8]

The creation of such a town at such a pace may have been undertaken on at least two occasions, before and after the sack of the city in 1004. The 18th-century historian Blomefield, rather endearingly, produced a noble comparable example from his own time for such urban growth: 'why do we wonder at a city repaired and increased so much, in so few years, when we have so late an example as the great city of *Petersburgh* in *Russia*, first founded by *Peter* the great *Czar*, in 1703, who had 30,000 houses erected in one year's time …'.[9] Norwich did not possess 30,000 houses in the 11th century although it may have had 10,000 people.[10] The point stands that a town, densely occupied by contemporary standards, had grown up very quickly indeed, smothering the pre-existing landscape.

Recovering that landscape therefore requires an archaeological approach rather than a toponymic one. It is a task obviously inhibited, not simply by standing buildings but also by clear evidence of massive earthmoving in the past. The extensive excavations at Castle Mall, mainly undertaken between 1989 and 1991, have shown substantial medieval modification of the northern end of the Ber Street escarpment[11] while, in the more recent past, work such as that for the construction of the former Barclays Bank on Bank Plain, led to much removal of earth as, on a much greater scale, did the Castle Mall project itself where, in constructing a largely-subterranean shopping centre, there was mass removal of deposits to a depth in excess of 20m over an area of 2ha (and apparently used to backfill Keswick pit to the south of the city).

Elsewhere the impact of medieval quarrying is still marked within the modern townscape, off Rouen Road within the walls, cutting deeply into the slopes of Mousehold Heath immediately east of the historic core, and off Bracondale to the south. The river itself has been embanked both to the north and south, its floodplain infilled, but it has also been widened in part too, a municipal reaction to bad floods in 1912 (Fig. 2).[12] The cockeys still run in some instances but are now all culverted with only the outflow of the Great Cockey made obvious by its grill in the river wall upstream of St George's Bridge (although there are other, more hidden, outflows such as that of the Muspole beneath Fye Bridge - the Muspole was diverted along Colegate, probably in the 13th century - and the Fresflete beneath Foundry Bridge).[13]

Archaeological investigation is therefore needed to explore the physical geography of the area now occupied by the city. Such work does not necessarily need to be exclusively devoted to excavation; other techniques can also be applied, be they interrogation of antiquarian observation or more modern approaches. One such of the latter is that of borehole 'window-sampling' whereby an appreciation of pre-existing landforms can be obtained

---

[5] Hudson 1889, p. 99
[6] Sandred and Lindström 1989, p. 6
[7] Ayers 2011, pp. 69-70; Sandred and Lindström 1989, p. 120
[8] Sandred and Lindström 1989, *passim* and Ayers 2011, p. 83
[9] Blomefield 1806, p. 9
[10] Campbell 1975
[11] Shepherd Popescu 2009
[12] Ayers 1994, pp. 78 and fig. 37
[13] Andy Shelley, *pers. comm.*

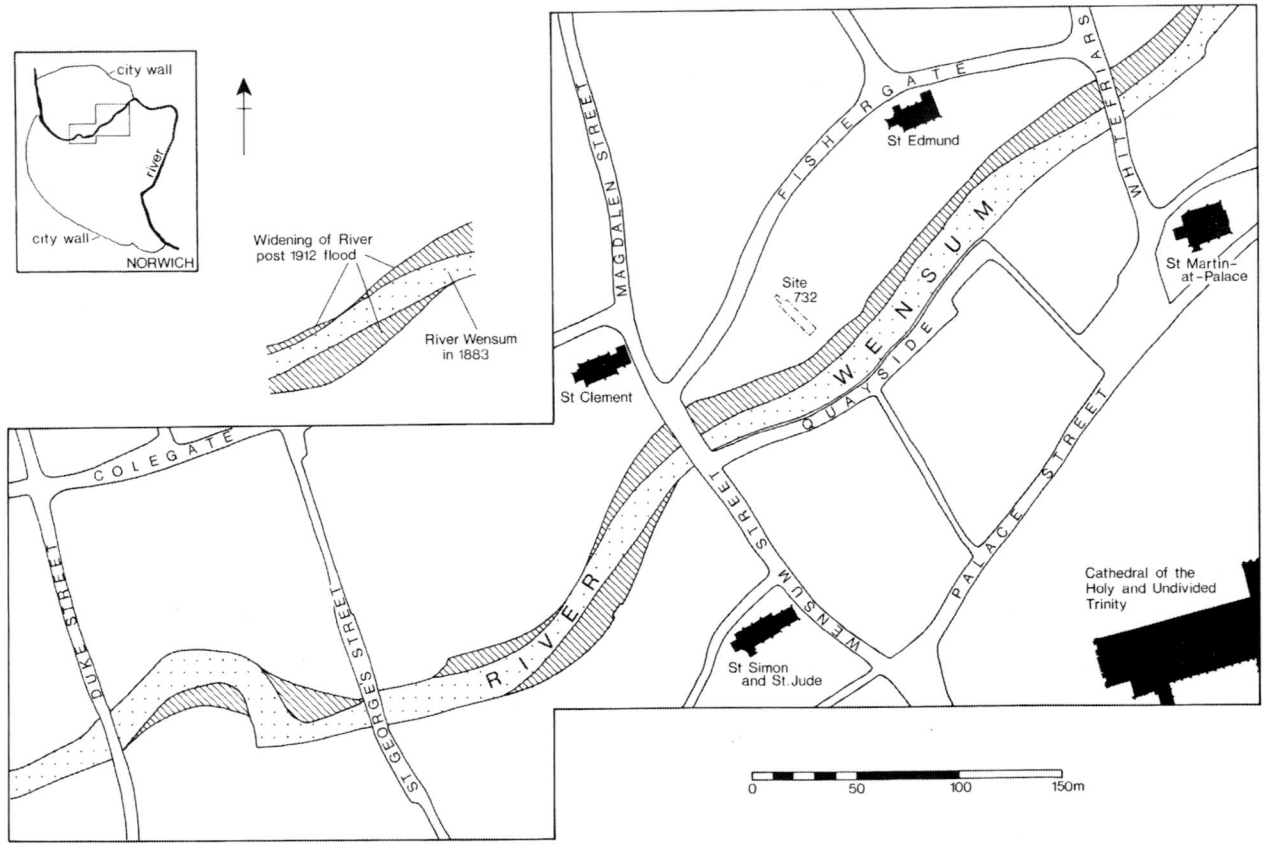

FIG. 2 WIDENING OF THE WENSUM AFTER 1912

even on deeply-stratified sites now surfaced in concrete. Such work at Duke Street adjacent to the south bank of the river, on a development site still awaiting action and at the time of writing a temporary car park, has revealed an embayment of the river which has been modified by infilling over the last millennium. Not only is the form of the embayment visible on the resulting plot but also the angle of the river slope prior to urban activity.[14]

Further east but also adjacent to the south bank of the Wensum, a combination of borehole evidence with an assessment of the results of small-scale trial excavation revealed the existence of a previously unknown - and indeed unsuspected - tributary valley now occupied by Pigg Lane.[15] To the north of the river, the detail recorded in the Ordnance Survey map of 1883 enables the now lost estuarine outflow of the Muspole stream to be identified, its eastern edge marked by the alignment of Water Lane, running from Colegate to the river, and its western edge by the parish boundary south of Colegate between the parishes of St Clement and St George. These cartographically-illustrated alignments are notable for proceeding away from Colegate at right-angles to the street until, nearing the river, they each diverge at an angle of some 45 degrees, Water Lane westward, the parish boundary eastward (Fig. 3).[16] The divergent alignments are still (just) visible in the urban topography; the river end of Water Lane is lost but the post-medieval brick edging of its terminus at the river survives, framing an 18th- and 19th-century horse-watering ramp. The line of the parish boundary is preserved in the rear wall of the former Baptist chapel (currently in use as a covered car park). Both elements could easily be lost in future redevelopment and, with them, minor but telling links with the physical geography beneath.

The Pigg Lane assessment also enabled the suggestion that the lost tributary may have helped to create a mid-channel bar within the Wensum which itself made this part of the river suitable for bridging. Fye Bridge is almost certainly the earliest bridging point of the Wensum, a causeway structure seen in 1896 being one which probably dates to the mid-10th century.[17] However, earlier crossings must have been needed, not least for the two Roman roads which cross the site of the later city. One of these, a road probably running north from Caistor, may well have crossed the river north of St Gregory's church, making use of a known island (now lost) within the Wensum itself (this island is documented in the medieval period and was also used to assist bridging by Coslany Bridge, the 13th-century reference to which is to the *duos pontes de*

---

[14] Ayers 2011, fig. 3
[15] Emery and Ashwin 2001, pp. 670-5
[16] Ayers 1987, p. 10
[17] Ayers 2011, pp. 82-3

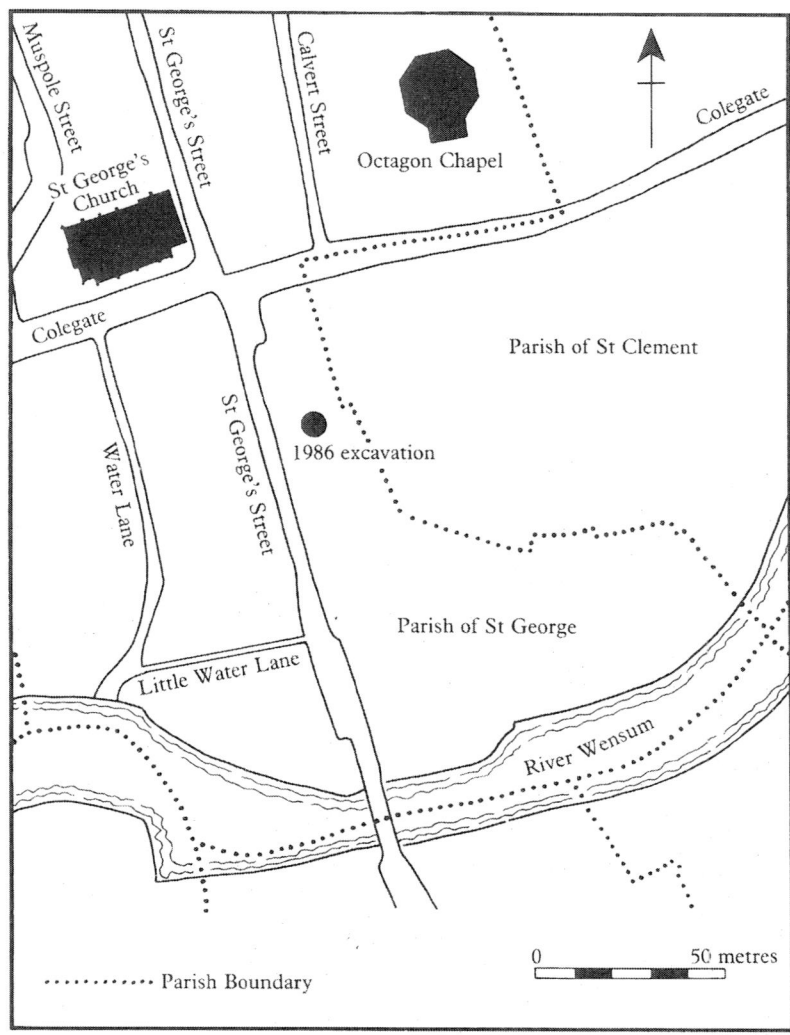

FIG. 3 TOPOGRAPHICAL INDICATORS FOR THE OUTFLOW OF THE MUSPOLE STREAM

Koslanye - the 'two bridges of Coslany', a reference that Sandred and Lindström find 'puzzling' but which clearly refers to bridges on to and off the island).[18] The island has now been joined to the north bank although the narrow remnant of the former northern channel is visible on the First Edition Ordnance Survey map and the course of this channel was observed in excavation undertaken in 1995.[19]

It is possible that, a millennium earlier than the 13th-century *duos pontes*, any Roman crossing at Coslany was via a ford, as may also have been the case at Bishop's Bridge, another medieval crossing (and still marked by the only surviving medieval river bridge in the city) and which is also on the alignment of an (east-to-west) Roman road. The river crossing here is, geomorphologically, at the lowest possible fording point on the Wensum/Yare river system (and may well be the 'ford' referenced in the early place-name *Conesford* - 'the king's ford', from the ODan *kunung*).[20]

Access to, and crossing of, the river was clearly assisted by the gravel terraces underlying the riparian areas of the later city and the location of those terraces and the likely river crossings were significant factors in both pre-urban and urban use of the site. However, the cockeys also impacted upon early development, both in terms of movement around the area and, later, in the social organisation of Norwich itself. Thus, the northern Leet of the *Ultra Aquam* area ('over the water') of the medieval city was subdivided by the Dalymond stream while, to the south of the river, the Dallingfleet stream was crossed by means of a stone bridge (still visible and drawn in 1888 and, quite probably, existing yet beneath Horsefair off Prince of Wales Road).[21] A further such bridge can be suggested as a likely necessity across the Great Cockey on St Andrew's Street while a bridge over this stream further south on London Street is documented in a deed of 1365/6 as *Kokeiebrigg*.[22] The constraining nature of the cockeys or, rather, their influence as determining factors in settlement often, like the streams themselves in the 21st century, lies beneath the

---

[18] Sandred and Lindström 1989, p. 15
[19] Oakey 1996, pp. 405-6
[20] Barbara Green, *pers. comm.*; Sandred and Lindström, p. 114
[21] Hudson 1888, pp. 117-42
[22] Hudson (ed.) 1889, p. 44

surface. As an example, recent analytical work on King Street by Andy Shelley highlights a previously unregarded small cockey which flowed into the Wensum beside what is now Abbey Lane. The location of this particular cockey has enabled Shelley, with other evidence, to suggest a model for early settlement within this part of the nascent city that has implications for increasing understanding of early state administration as well as urban growth.[23]

The Dalymond stream was the only one of the cockeys to have its source outside the walled boundary of the later medieval city (even the Great Cockey was sourced from a spring called *Jack's Pit* close to Ber Street on the southern escarpment). The line of the Dalymond remains evident in the modern topography of northern Norwich, its shallow valley bordered by Waterloo Road to the west and Sprowston Road to the east when it nears the city walls. Within the walls, a strong north-to-south property boundary east of Edward Street probably marks its western edge and eventually curves eastward, mirrored by the street itself. Evaluation excavation in 2013 picked up a likely trace of the eastward original course of the cockey before it was diverted southward and thereafter formed an abuttal for a property off Botolph Street excavated in the 1970s by the Norwich Survey.[24] The incidence of properties noted in early deeds as being bounded by cockeys was remarked upon by Hudson in the 19th century, particularly with regard to the Great Cockey.[25] Such abuttals are indeed fairly common, a geographic feature such as a watercourse forming an obvious boundary between properties (in the case of the Jewry prior to the end of the 13th century, the Great Cockey formed the eastern boundary of several properties[26]).

The cockeys gave access to the growing city from the river and here too their impact can be noted in the modern topography. The Dalymond crosses the line of Fishergate, a curving street north of the river which runs between Fye Bridge and Whitefriars Bridge, meeting both these structures at the edge of the Wensum. However, the street bows markedly and, in the central part of its course, is over 100m north of the river. Excavation in 1985 indicated that this bowed effect was probably not as a result of a river embayment; rather, it seems likely that early use of the Dalymond estuary as a haven for small fishing vessels, must have led to a crossing place further inland so as not to impede the berthing of river traffic.[27]

While it can be demonstrated therefore that the river and its tributaries had a significant impact both on the location of the medieval city and its subsequent internal organisation, the wetlands bordering the river were also influential. Elements of these survived well into the medieval period, notably in the area of the Lower Close (largely open land to this day). Here the location was known as *Cowholme* (from ON *holmr*, technically 'a piece of dry land in a fen, a piece of land partly surrounded by streams or by a stream'[28] but here probably meaning 'cattle summer pasture', the low-lying ground being too wet for such stock in winter). The practice of placing cattle upon the area probably accounts for the name given to the surviving late 14th-century artillery Cow Tower which was originally called *le Dungeon* (or *donjon*, literally 'great tower').[29] *Cowholme* clearly inhibited early settlement and it and other river margins south of the river were bounded by a curving road which, fragmented, survives as Elm Hill, Palace Plain, part of Bishopgate, Horsefair and Mountergate.

The low-lying ground close to the river meant that either measures had to be taken to raise land levels in order to enable settlement or that any moderately-elevated areas attained an importance that they might not otherwise have had. An example of the latter is Palace Plain, a tongue of gravel standing a mere 4m above sea level and yet not only graced with the early name of *Bichil* (either 'bitch's hill' or 'beak-like hill') but also with an early and clearly important church dedicated to St Martin and one suffixed *del Hill* in 1288, *ad Montem* in 1290, and even *super montem* as late as 1627.[30] As for the requirement to raise land levels, it is probable that a causeway of rammed gravel was constructed from the river crossing at Bishop's Bridge, possibly in the Roman period, across the marshy area of *Cowholme*, perhaps similar to the substantial construction seen by excavation of the Roman road at Nordelph in the Fens.[31] Elsewhere, infilling of the river margins, normally to gain better access to deeper water, led to the river becoming constrained between walls initially of timber and subsequently of flint and brick along much of its reach in the central part of the city. Excavation at Quayside in 1993 uncovered the probable remains of a timber revetment at a depth of nearly 4m which was dated dendrochronologically and which demonstrated that the marshy foreshore here had been infilled as far as its modern alignment as early as 1146.[32] The consequence of such urban activity is that much of the river within the central area of the city bears little relationship to its natural form.

Open land survives elsewhere within central Norwich although its use for most of the last millennium has almost certainly been radically different from any pre-urban function. An exception is probably the pasturing of cattle on *Cowholme* together with similar pasturing at Chapelfield in the south-western part of the city. Cattle are shown at Chapelfield both on Cuningham's prospect of 1558 and on the more famous prospect of Braun and Hogenburg in 1581 (which was copied from Cuningham's work). The cows seem to have been replaced by a horse

---

[23] Shelley forthcoming. I am grateful to Andy Shelley for sharing his ideas with me prior to publication
[24] David Adams, *pers. comm*; Evans 1985, 90-1 and figs. 3-5
[25] Hudson 1889, p. 101
[26] Davis 1888 *passim*; Lipman 1967, p. 23 n.1
[27] Ayers 1994, p. 80

[28] Ekwall 1960, p. 246
[29] Ayers, Smith and Tillyard 1988, p. 191ff
[30] Sandred and Lindström 1989, pp. 138 and 45-6
[31] Wallis 2002, pp. 12 - 18
[32] Ayers and Leah 1994, pp. 120-

and at least one sheep on Thomas Cleer's plan of *c.* 1696[33] but the point stands; the rural practice of the grazing of animals persisted here even though the area was also known as the tenting grounds and used for the drying of freshly-fulled and dyed cloth. The extensive area bounded by the walls of the later medieval city meant that there was considerable open space, as is evident on Cleer's plan, and Norwich was famously characterised by Thomas Fuller in 1662 as 'either a city in an orchard or an orchard in a city'. However, while this perhaps summarises well the 17th-century use of open space such as the site of the former Augustinian Friary (a garden of Henry Howard, Duke of Norfolk - 'My Lord's Gardens'), it does not describe the industrial slopes of quarries, lime-kilns and flint-gathering adits along the lower slopes of the Ber Street escarpment, nor the former 'jousting acre' of Gildencroft north of the river. Retrieving the pre-urban landscape here is as difficult as in more intensively-developed parts of the urban townscape.

While therefore the isolation of pre-urban landforms, even in areas such as the river foreshore and its immediate environment, is difficult save in broad geographic terms, the very geographic features can nevertheless be investigated in order to assist understanding of the terrain upon which Norwich now stands. Although there has been much levelling and infilling, the rise and fall of land can still be marked, with vistas often surprising. The view north-eastward from the churchyard of St Peter Hungate is a case in point. The church here is elevated above substantial buildings near the river, occupying a prime hillside site as also does the church of St Gregory which, viewed from the roof of a nearby multi-storey car-park, can be seen to be sailing over neighbouring properties, again because of its particular geographic location. The effect was much more marked in the 18th century when John Kirkpatrick who, as well as writing about streets 'falling' out of those higher up, also noted that the very names of streets evolved due to conditions resulting from the location of the city. Thus he correctly notes that Mariners Lane off Ber Street 'was called Holgate and Hollewent as being a Hollow Way or Lane gulled or washed hollow by the Rain water &c falling down it from Berstreet …'[34]

Archaeological research demonstrates how early land-use can occasionally be seen to have been influential in determining aspects of the later urban settlement. The known and likely locations of prehistoric monuments is a good example. Neolithic and Bronze Age monuments, especially burial mounds or barrows, within the greater Norwich area are now all ploughed out but barrows often survive as 'ring-ditches', that is crop-marks visible under the right conditions from the air. It has been noted that barrow cemetery sites 'are known to have occupied prominent hilltop positions overlooking the valleys of the Wensum, Tas and Yare rivers … part of a wider prehistoric landscape and the presence of settlement sites and ritual sites (for example Eaton Heath and Arminghall Henge)'.[35] Excavation of such features has taken place at a number of locations ahead of modern green-field development, as at Bowthorpe in the west of the city or at Harford Farm on the line of the Norwich Southern Bypass.[36] Occupying hilltop crests, the monuments were sited to be inter-visible with the surrounding landscape. It is clear that the geography of pre-urban central Norwich would have offered similar locations for the placing of such prehistoric monuments but the density of the built environment over the last one-and-a half millennia clearly militates against any survival.

Surprisingly, however, evidence can be found and indeed was located in 2006 when a small ring-ditch indicating a bell barrow was excavated on the west side of Ber Street, on top of the escarpment ridge. The centre of this monument seems to have been bisected by medieval property boundaries, implying that the feature may have still been visible within the landscape as the medieval town was growing. Indeed, its significance may be even greater in that Andy Shelley has noticed that the barrow, opposite Skeygate ('the ridge road') leading downhill towards the river, is at the exact mid-point between the early churches of St John de Sepulchre and All Saints Westlegate.[37] A further possible barrow was also found in 2000 at St Peter's Street/Bethel Street, another elevated site, 'perhaps implying that some prehistoric monuments were visible as late as the eleventh or twelfth centuries in parts of the city' given that the location here was essentially a green-field site before the arrival of the Normans.[38] Possible linkage between the natural landscape, prehistoric monument construction and subsequent medieval urban organisation cannot be overplayed but the possibility certainly exists that elements of the surviving medieval topography took account of pre-existing prehistoric landscape features.

The possible St Peter's Street/Bethel Street barrow would have stood on the crest formed by the western edge of the Great Cockey tributary valley, running northward towards the River Wensum. The gentle slope eastward to the stream was probably an agrarian meadow, its ploughed form being that sensed by Andrew Rogerson and referred to at the start of this *Festschrift* contribution. While it was Andrew's 'rural eye' which thus provided the idea for this 'urban' paper, writing about Norwich is also a tribute to Andrew's contribution to urban studies. His work at Fuller's Hill, Great Yarmouth in the 1970s was an early urban excavation in Norfolk as well as being a formative one for the greater understanding of one of the major ports of medieval England.[39] The pre-urban geography of the Yarmouth sand spit was the major creative factor for the development of settlement there while the volatile nature of that spit, with regular early sand inundations forming interstices between occupation phases, ensured difficult

---

[33] Frostick 2002, pp. 1, 4 and 22-3
[34] Hudson 1889, p. 10
[35] Emery 2009, p. 79
[36] Lawson 1986, pp. 20-49; Ashwin and Bates 2000, p. 52ff and plate XIV
[37] Shelley, forthcoming
[38] Ayers 2011, p. 67
[39] Rogerson 1976, p. 131ff

archaeological excavation conditions. Andrew works with and seeks to understand the natural landscape and the impact of humanity upon that landscape; this paper is a small offering of thanks for the insights that he brings and shares with others.

University of East Anglia, January 2014

Acknowledgements

I am most grateful to Andy Shelley who kindly read a draft of this paper and provided me with helpful comments. I am particularly in his debt for being able to use some of his ideas concerning King Street and Conesford ahead of publication. Thanks are also due to David Adams who continues to update me with new discoveries within Norwich and whose own ideas on the early development of the city are always challenging and thought-provoking.

Bibliography

Adams, D. 2002 (unpublished), *Interim Report of an Archaeological Evaluation at Norwich City Football Club, Carrow Road, Norwich*, Norfolk Archaeological Unit Report 753

Ashwin, T. and Bates, S. 2000, *Norwich Southern Bypass, Part I: Excavations at Bixley, Caistor St Edmund, Trowse*, East Anglian Archaeology 91

Ayers, B. 1987, *Digging Deeper* (Norwich)

Ayers, B. 1994, *Excavations at Fishergate, Norwich, 1985*, East Anglian Archaeology 68

Ayers, B. 2011, 'The growth of an urban landscape: recent research in early medieval Norwich', *Early Medieval Europe* 19(1), pp. 62-90

Ayers, B. and Leah, M. 1994, 'Norwich, Quayside (Site 26406; TG 2335 0905)' in D. Gurney (ed.), 'Excavations and Surveys in Norfolk 1993', *Norfolk Archaeology* 42, pt. 1, pp. 115-123

Ayers, B., Smith, R., and Tillyard, M. 1988, The Cow Tower, Norwich: a detailed survey and partial reinterpretation, *Medieval Archaeology* 32, pp. 184–207

Blomefield, F. 1806, *An Essay towards a Topographical History of Norfolk*, III (Norwich)

Campbell, J. 1975, 'Norwich' in Lobel, M.D. (ed.), *Historic Towns* II (London)

Davis, M.D. (ed.) 1888, *Shetaroth: Hebrew Deeds of English Jews before 1290* (London)

Ekwall, E. 1960, *The Concise Oxford Dictionary of English Place-Names* (Oxford; 4th edition)

Emery, G. 2009, *An Evaluation Excavation and Strip, Map and Sample Excavation at 93-101 Ber Street, Norwich*, NAU Archaeology Report 1393

Emery, P. and Ashwin, T. 2001, 'Prehistoric Occupation Evidence at Busseys Garage, Palace Street, Norwich', *Norfolk Archaeology* 43, pt. 4, pp. 670-675

Evans, D.H. 1985, 'Excavations on 44-56 Botolph Street (Site 170N)' in M.W. Atkin, A. Carter and D.H. Evans, 'Excavations in Norwich, 1971-78, Part II', East Anglian Archaeology 26, pp. 92-112

Frostick, R. 2002, *The Printed Plans of Norwich 1558-1840: A Carto-Bibliography* (Norwich)

House, J. 2012, 'Norwich, St Saviour's Lane, Hi-Tech House (NHER 55576; TG 2328 0925)' in Gurney, D. (ed.), 'Excavations and Surveys in Norfolk in 2011', *Norfolk Archaeology* 46, pt. 3, pp. 421-442

Hudson, W. 1888, 'The Stone Bridge by the Horse Fair in St Faith's Lane, Norwich', *Norfolk Archaeology* 10, pp. 117-142

Hudson, W. 1889, 'On the Ancient "Cockeys" and other Watercourses in the City' in Hudson, W. (ed.) 1889, *The Streets and Lanes of Norwich: a memoir by J. Kirkpatrick* (Norwich), pp. 99-103

Lawson, A.J. 1986, 'The Excavation of a Ring-ditch at Bowthorpe, Norwich, 1979' in Lawson, A.J. *et al.*, *Barrow Excavations in Norfolk, 1950-82*, East Anglian Archaeology 29, pp. 20-49

Lipman, V.D. 1967, *The Jews of Medieval Norwich* (London)

Murphy, P. 1994, 'The Environmental Evidence' in Ayers 1994, pp. 34-61

Oakey, N. 1996, 'Norwich, Coslany Street (Site 26435; TG 227 089)' in Gurney, D. and Ashwin, T. (eds.), 'Excavations and Surveys in Norfolk 1995', *Norfolk Archaeology* 42, pt. 3, pp. 397-412

Rogerson, A. 1976, 'Excavations on Fuller's Hill, Great Yarmouth', in East Anglian Archaeology 2, pp. 131-245

Sandred, K.I. and Lindström, B. 1989, 'The Place-Names of Norfolk: Part One - The Place-Names of the City of Norwich', *English Place-Name Society*, vol. XVI

Shepherd Popescu, E. 2009, *Norwich Castle: Excavations and Historical Survey, 1987-98*, East Anglian Archaeology 132

Shelley, A. forthcoming. 'South Conesford, Norwich: a Danish garrison port?' *Medieval Archaeology*

Wallis, H. 2002, *Roman Routeways across the Fens: Excavations at Morton, Tilney St Lawrence, Nordelph and Downham West*, East Anglian Archaeology Occasional Paper 10

Bawsey – a 'productive' site in west Norfolk

Tim Pestell

Abstract: Among Norfolk's early medieval sites, that at Bawsey in north-west Norfolk is potentially one of the more important, yet it has hitherto led a Cinderella life, half known yet continuing to hide in the shadows. Characteristically, Andrew Rogerson's work has been central to the site being known at all, and fundamental to it being recorded in a manner enabling academic enquiry. This paper aims to bring Bawsey further into the light by providing a first publication of the results of the work undertaken on the site by Time Team *in 1998, and to provide a context to this limited investigation by considering those other finds made on the site through metal-detection, most of which have been recorded by Andrew.*

The site, around the parish church of Bawsey St James, is best known for its concentration of Middle Anglo-Saxon coinage and smallfinds, made through metal-detection, which is exceptional in comparison to the more usual run of material retrieved from many rural sites of a similar date. For this reason it has been considered a 'productive' site of economic significance and exhibiting features of high-status occupation. These indications also led to it being considered promising enough to attract the attention of *Time Team* for one of their earliest live broadcasts.[1] The use of a term such as 'productive' site continues to cause disquiet because it describes sites whose exact nature and function are still unclear. Some have sought to minimise its use, declaring that it conflates a number of distinct site types into an unhelpful single term. Julian Richards has contended that these sites are no wealthier in the numbers of finds than many 'normal'-looking sites.[2] A literature has now developed around the description and the challenges of their interpretation.[3] Although it has become clear that there are profound difficulties in categorising or defining 'productive' sites, more nuanced approaches to interpretation have increasingly come to the fore, not least as the well-excavated settlements of Flixborough and Brandon have proven equally awkward in definition. Such considerations will be revisited later, but I first want to describe in broad terms the nature of the finds made at Bawsey through metal-detection, and then the archaeological narrative revealed through the evaluation work of *Time Team*.

I have so far referred to Bawsey in broad terms. The modern-day parish lies 2km back from the eastern edge of the Fen Basin and 4km from King's Lynn to the west, from which it is separated by the former episcopal manor of Gaywood (Fig. 1). A large portion of the parish has been subjected to quarrying for sand,[4] but the Middle Anglo-Saxon site and parish church sit on a glacial sand promontory jutting out into, and surrounded to the north, west and south by, the Gaywood valley and a tributary stream. The Gay is itself now a minor stream but was once larger and closer to the sea, which has retreated to the west. The church's dramatic position dominates the surrounding area and, with its originally more watery surrounding, is arguably 'the island of *Beaw*' that gives the present-day parish its place-name.[5] The basic geology of the site belies the actual variety in soil types encountered when walking on the ground, the changes occurring quite close together:[6] the sandy top of the hill gives way to a more loamy sand mix with a dense flinty matrix, and as the hill bottoms out to the north-west, rapidly changes to become a friable peat. The peat is effectively devoid of archaeological finds relating to the site, although in 2006 a large Late Bronze Age spearhead was recovered from it by metal-detector.

The visually striking effect of St James's church was certainly a deliberate arrangement from at least the twelfth century when the present building was constructed. However, this was but one manipulation of the landscape setting, as demonstrated by an aerial photograph of the site taken in 1989 (Fig. 2). This clearly shows a substantial linear earthwork once surrounded the entire hilltop and finds possible analogues in Iron Age arrangements. Unfortunately, as we will see, dating this earthwork is still problematic.

That Bawsey certainly did have an ancient significance is emphasised by two gold Iron Age looped-terminal torcs that were found on the hilltop, one in 1941, the other in 1944.[7] Metal-detection close to the church ruins has now revealed further associated material, including a pair of cast silver buffer torc terminals, one of which preserves part of the clay core around which the torc body was constructed, and with 24 gold-alloy wires twisted in pairs. Another

---

[1] The *Time Team* excavation was originally broadcast live over 29-31 August 1998 and was subsequently edited down and repeated as a broadcast in the standard one-hour format in Series 6 on 14 March 1999
[2] Richards 1999
[3] For an overview see the various essays in Pestell and Ulmschneider 2003 and Pestell 2011
[4] White 1836, p. 445 records 'great quantities of grey sand are got, and sent to the glass houses in various parts of the kingdom. For every cart load of this sand, 1*s* 6*d* is paid to the lord of the manor'
[5] Ekwall 1960, p. 31. While Gelling and Cole (2000, p. 42) also see Bawsey as using the OE *ēg* element meaning an 'island' or raised areas of ground in a marshy or watery setting, they compound it with the OE element for 'gadfly'. While possible, Ekwall's rendition of a masculine personal name accords far better with Gelling and Cole's observation that these form 'by far the largest category of qualifiers used with *ēg*' (p. 40)
[6] Soil Survey 1983
[7] The two torcs are now in Norwich Castle Museum and Art Gallery (hereafter NCM), accessioned as 1942.126 and 1944.106. A note by Norwich Castle Museum curator R.R. Clarke states that a few sherds of Iron Age pottery were found in the area of the 1944 torc, although these do not seem to survive. Other Iron Age pottery has been recovered from the field and is now NCM 1998.71.1, .2 and .6

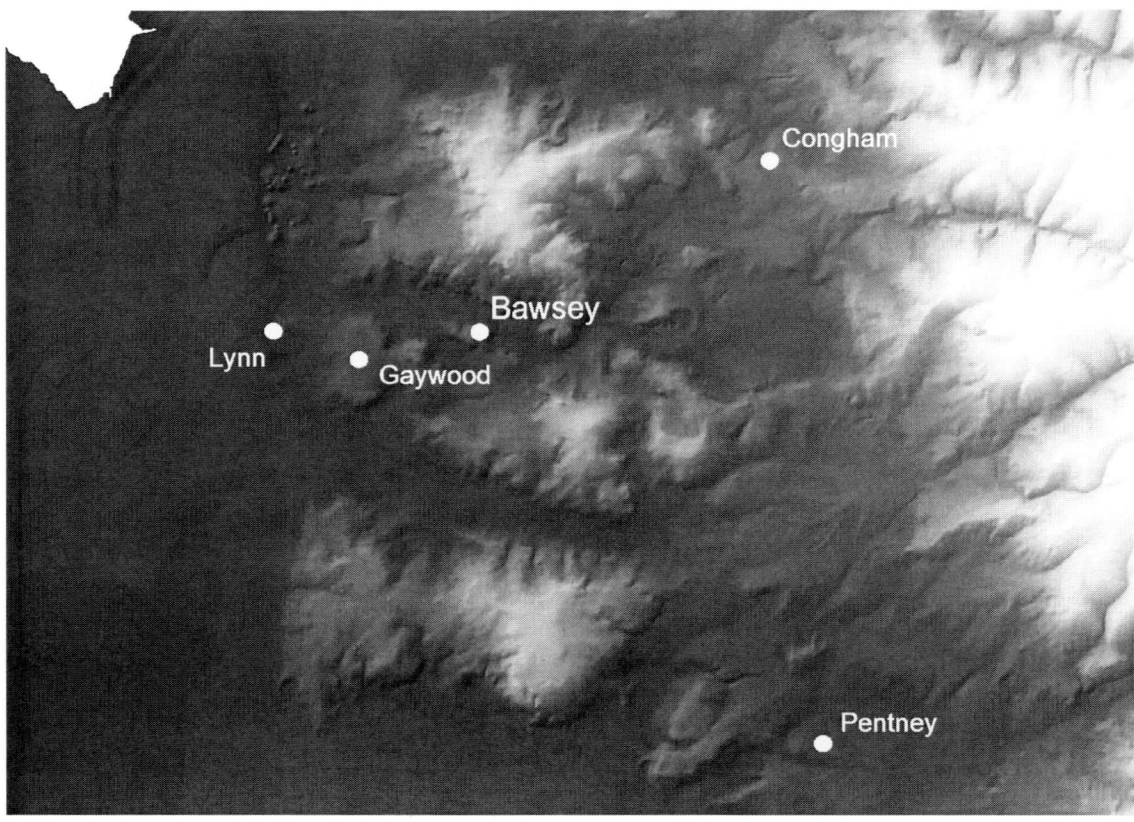

Fig. 1 Contour data showing Bawsey and surrounding land (Pete Watkins)

Fig. 2 The church of Bawsey St James on its hilltop site surrounded by the earthwork enclosure, from the north-west, 17/7/89 (Photograph DA Edwards, courtesy Norfolk Historic Environment Service)

looped torc terminal and over 150 fragments of twisted gold, silver and electrum wire cabling, from the body of torcs, have also been found, weighing some 13.77g.[8] These fragments would appear to have been deliberately broken up, one possibility being that they were cut into small enough pieces to fit into a crucible for remelting. While this implies scrap awaiting reuse, the fragments might equally represent the deliberate destruction of torcs, preparing them for votive burial. This appears to have been the case with the torc debris at Snettisham and probably indicates the same cultural practice occurring at both sites.[9] The places of deposition, on hillsides, are likewise similar and would not contradict this. Intriguingly, another field to the south of the ditched enclosure at Bawsey has yielded two more, matching, torc buffer terminals, made of electrum.[10] Taken together, these finds make Bawsey one of the most 'productive' sites for Iron Age torc material in Norfolk, and indicate its early special nature. The fact that Bawsey is only 9 miles (15km) from Snettisham, reiterates the importance of this whole area in the late Iron Age.

Although these finds are spectacular, the site has yielded only small quantities of Iron Age pottery, and this is true also of the Roman period, little material having been discovered; instead, small and unexceptional Roman occupation evidence lies on the valley edge to the north. There is also little of Early Anglo-Saxon date on the hillside, comprising only a few scattered fragments including florid cruciform brooch fragments, parts of two girdle hangers and a buckle tongue of Frankish type. While these might potentially be disturbed grave-goods from an early Anglo-Saxon cemetery, no other evidence for such burials has emerged and they probably relate to earlier settlement.

Instead, it is the quantity and quality of Middle Anglo-Saxon material found at Bawsey, most specifically the coinage, that is remarkable and which first drew archaeological attention to Bawsey. As with so many archaeological discoveries in Norfolk, the first of the Anglo-Saxon finds from the site were made using metal-detectors. Sadly, a good number of these were made by a man who was subsequently convicted for 'nighthawking', or illicit metal-detecting, and whose finds were never properly reported.[11] Fortunately, since 1984, Mr Steve Brown has conducted a meticulous survey of the site, in recent years with a licence from English Heritage, as the area has been made a Scheduled Ancient Monument. Some 124 coins have now been recovered, of which 109 are pre-900AD, consisting principally of some 80 eighth-century silver *sceattas*. This coinage total makes Bawsey not just a 'productive' site, but by far the most prolific coin-producing Anglo-Saxon site in Norfolk, and one of the largest in England.[12]

This sheer number of coins recovered is exceptional for a Norfolk site. Most have been found in the area surrounding the church, as has most of the metalwork of eighth and ninth-century date. It seems that coin-use at Bawsey possibly began in the second half of the seventh century, a situation paralleled at some other, but by no means all, 'productive' sites. In Suffolk, gold coin-use seems to date from *c.*600 at Rendlesham and possibly also at Coddenham while Heckington in South Lincolnshire and Hollingbourne appear to be more like Bawsey, unlike *Hamwic* or those sites at Tilbury or 'Near Royston'.[13] Sadly, this is not certain despite the claims for the discovery of two gold coins, a *thrymsa* and a Continental *tremissis*, to have been found on the site. Primary and Intermediate-phase *sceattas* found at Bawsey do at least show coin circulation and loss began on the site in the 680s and was more active here in the initial phases.[14] More certainly, a spread of *sceatta* types has been recovered including ten East Anglian Series R coins, three of Series C and three Series Q or R that were minted in either East or Middle Anglia. Series B, D (Continental, runic) and E (Continental 'porcupine') are also represented.

Metalwork from the site

If the quantity of coinage from Bawsey is of interest, the wider metalwork assemblage is no less impressive, and includes a number of interesting find-types. About two-thirds of the dress accessories and other artefacts found date from between the seventh and ninth centuries and include brooches (such as ansate, disc and nummular types), pins (principally facetted and globular-headed), hooked tags, strap-ends and tweezers. Many of the strap-

---

[8] The 154 torc fragments are now held by the British Museum ('BM') as: 1985, 1204.1 and .2 (the two silver torc terminals, of 73g and 61g respectively); 1989, 1201.1 and .2 (two silver wire fragments, total weight 0.9g); 1990, 0304.1-.135 (135 gold wire fragments, total weight 115g); 1991, 0602.1-.7 (seven gold wire fragments, 6.11g in total); 1997, 0901.1-.3 (three gold wire fragments, total weight 1.4g); 2007, 8023.1-.4 (four electrum wire fragments, 4.46g in total). The third looped terminal is now on loan at NCM from the BM, accession L1987.7. A fragment of copper-alloy wire with silvering is NCM 1991.159. The varied nature of the wire fragments is illustrated by two wires found twisted together now in the BM; one is of a silver-copper alloy, the other a copper core with a silver-copper plating as has been observed in a roughly contemporary torc terminal from Hengistbury Head (Treasure Trove report by Dr Peter Northover in Norfolk Historic Environment Record (HER)
[9] Davies 2008, pp. 103-4 and forthcoming; Joy forthcoming
[10] Now NCM 2007.59 and 2008.226
[11] While finds including Roman and later medieval coins were reported by him, the majority of his Anglo-Saxon coins were only reported in 1987 after they had been sold. The descriptions of these coins were therefore vague and only two sceattas were photographed, by Sotheby's, who sold them in July 1984. Another coin subsequently provenanced was a fragmentary example of the eighth-century Kentish king Eadberht Præn (796-8), sold to a London dealer in 1988. Provenancing was possible only when a joining fragment was found in 1989
[12] As will be seen from discussion later on, the numbers are still difficult to use, and this figure is drawn from Blackburn 2003. However the coins recorded on the Corpus of Early Medieval Coins, or 'EMC' (available at http://www.fitzmuseum.cam.ac.uk/coins/emc/), is far smaller, with some 54 sceattas. A final concordance of all coins, using the finds records preserved on the HER, EMC and from the late Mark Blackburn's records, is still in progress
[13] Blackburn 2003, pp. 27-9
[14] The issue is raised because of the second-hand report by the initial, convicted, metal-detectorist about finding two late seventh-century gold coins, apparently a Continental shilling and a Two Emperors *thrymsa*, on the site. These were, however, unexamined by numismatists and while credibility for their Bawsey provenance is strengthened by the presence of primary sceattas, it is interesting that none have been found since Mr Brown began detecting on the site

ends tend to be of typical East Anglian type featuring silver wire inlays, while the overall total of thirty examples, recorded by Thomas, place it alongside other exceptional site assemblages such as Flixborough, Cottam and South Newbald.[15]

Although many of the finds are of 'normal' or average quality, the principal feature is the sheer quantity of such finds, which stands out from many rural sites of Middle Anglo-Saxon date that have been extensively excavated or metal-detected. Nevertheless a few objects are clearly high-status pieces, such as a silver and niello hooked tag with Trewhiddle-style decoration. Equally indicative of the high-status consumption of goods is the number of mounts and fittings, many probably from hanging bowls of seventh or eighth-century date (Fig. 3). Two fragments bearing a red enamel-inlaid design are of particular importance in paralleling designs found on the Lullingstone bowl from Kent. The first is part of a bronze appliqué depicting a walking stag, its legs spread and the interior filled with a

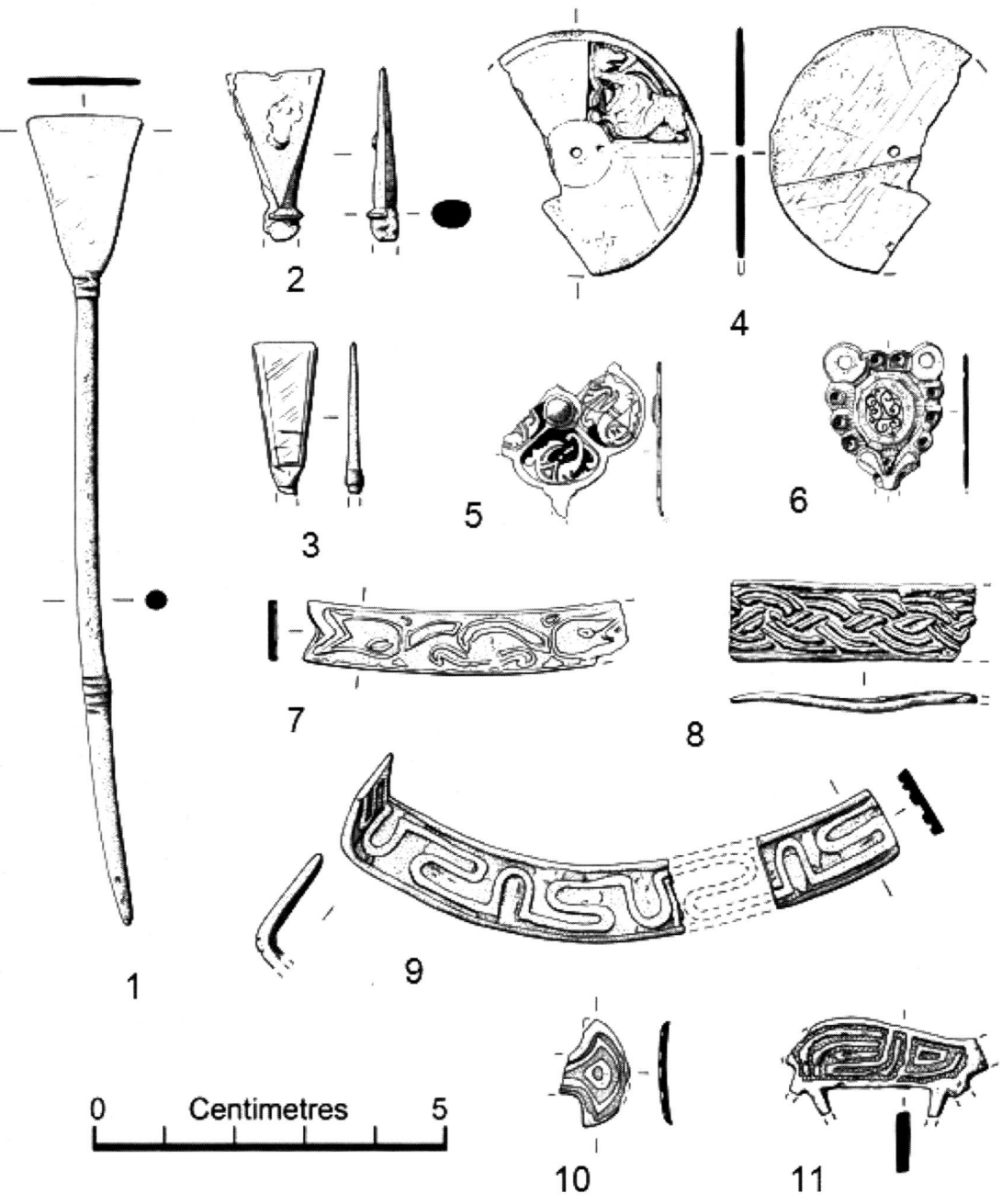

FIG. 3 A SELECTION OF ANGLO-SAXON FINDS FROM BAWSEY (ALL COPPER-ALLOY UNLESS OTHERWISE STATED). 1-3: STYLI, ERASER 3 MADE OF SILVER; 4: TRIAL-PIECE DISC BROOCH; 5-6: HOOKED TAGS, 5 MADE OF SILVER WITH NIELLO INLAY; 7-11: HANGING BOWL FRAGMENTS, 11 THAT OF A STAG. (DRAWN BY STEVEN ASHLEY)

---
[15] Thomas 1996 and 2009, p. 12

linear maze-like design, the surface being tinned against red enamel infill.[16] The slight curvature of the Bawsey stag would seem to derive from a medium to large size bowl. For Bruce-Mitford, the similar infill design, choice of animal and surface silvering, all point to this being a product of the same workshop, and help to confirm the Lullingstone bowl's seventh- or eighth-century date. The second, an axe-shaped mount, is similar if slightly smaller than examples on the Lullingstone bowl, possibly from the base, and also finds parallels in a bowl from Market Rasen in Lincolnshire.[17] Other bowl mount fragments bear similarities to late seventh-century material from Whitby and suggest the former presence and use of several such vessels on the site. Even if the number of the fragments found at Bawsey need not represent a large total number of bowls, this is an uncommon vessel type and shows the design of those represented was more ornate than many of contemporary date.

Another of the specialised find-types recovered are the styli, a class of find indicating literacy on the site. While there is increasing evidence for literacy in eighth- and ninth-century England, it remains uncommonly attested through artefactual evidence and its appearance at Bawsey is yet another indication of the atypical nature of the site.[18]

Given the quantity of Middle Anglo-Saxon coinage and metalwork, its apparent diminution in the tenth and eleventh centuries raises interesting questions about the use and level of occupation on the site. While a decline might be suggested from the quantities of material recovered, more recent analysis of Flixborough, where similar metalwork assemblages were recovered, has led Loveluck to suggest there was instead a change in the types of material culture being used and consumed on site.[19] Occupation certainly continued at Bawsey, as witnessed by a variety of artefacts, including a tenth-century lead model of a Winchester-style strap-end and two Late Anglo-Saxon bronze ingots with their characteristic transverse hammering marks. More common artefact types also occur, such as strap-ends, disc brooches and stirrup-strap mounts. Indeed, occupation continued on the site into the medieval period, as evidenced by a number of post-Conquest hammered silver pennies and an assortment of the usual medieval metalwork assemblages seen from metal-detector finds, including strap-ends and buckles. However, as with the Late Anglo-Saxon metalwork, not only the quantity but the quality of these later finds is unexceptional. Ultimately the site fell into terminal decline, a process which manifested itself in the desertion of Bawsey, like many in this area of West Norfolk, in the medieval and post-medieval period.

Hints of this desertion are made clear as early as 1517 when the village was destroyed by enclosures, while in 1679 a Visitation recorded the church tower as being out of repair.[20] Being a central tower, this must have been a great disadvantage to the church, although baptisms are recorded until 1771 and burials to 1773.[21] By the nineteenth century the church was a roofless ruin, an ignominious end to a fine early Norman building.

Time Team's excavations

The foregoing has provided a brief outline of the unusual material culture which had emerged from Bawsey, making it such an interesting, yet enigmatic, site. With the possibility of uncovering a wealthy Middle Anglo-Saxon settlement, *Time Team* was given permission to investigate the site as part of a large three-day live broadcast in August 1998. The work was undertaken in the established *Time Team* format, essentially of an archaeological evaluation, and was conducted in three principal ways. First, a geophysical survey of much of the hilltop was undertaken; second, a gridded survey was made of a large part of the hilltop by metal-detector and fieldwalking; third, there was selective excavation of features identified through previous aerial photography and the geophysics. Post-excavation work has allowed a further refinement and interpretation of all three elements.

Geophysics

Geophysical survey was undertaken by GSB Prospection as a sub-contractor and covered five areas (A-E) of varying size, using a gradiometer, and also a limited area around the parish church, using a resistivity meter (Fig. 4).[22] The latter technique seems to have been ineffective, the few potential anomalies found apparently relating more to natural variations in the topsoil. By contrast, the gradiometer covered an area of about 6.5 hectares and produced results of more potential interest, although not all the features are easily understood. For instance, Area A to the west of the hill was surveyed, aiming to identify the north-west corner of the enclosure ditch seen on the aerial photographs. A north-south linear feature was found, with an eastward-running extension, which was presumably the enclosure ditch, but this continued north before the signal faded, perhaps as a result of changing soil conditions. Slightly to the east was Area D, a small survey box only some 20×60m, which was positioned to try and locate the postulated northern boundary of the enclosure ditch. In the event it failed to locate this, but it is unclear whether this is a genuine absence of the feature or simply a reflection of poorly enhanced ditch fills; unsurprisingly this area was not chosen for any follow-up trenching in the limited time available, but it would be of interest to evaluate this area as indications of a ditch extending across here are certainly visible on the aerial photograph.

---

[16] Bruce-Mitford 2005, pp. 175-9 and fig. 169
[17] Bruce-Mitford 2005, pp. 207-8 and fig. 236
[18] Pestell 2004, pp. 40-7 and 2009
[19] Loveluck 2001 and 2007, pp. 144-65
[20] Batcock 1991, p. 116 and Norfolk Record Office (NRO) ANW/4/51
[21] *Kelly's Directory* 1883, p. 242
[22] The full report is held in the site archive but a limited version of this report is available online at:
http://hbsmrgateway2.esdm.co.uk/norfolk/DataFiles/Docs/AssocDoc1556.pdf

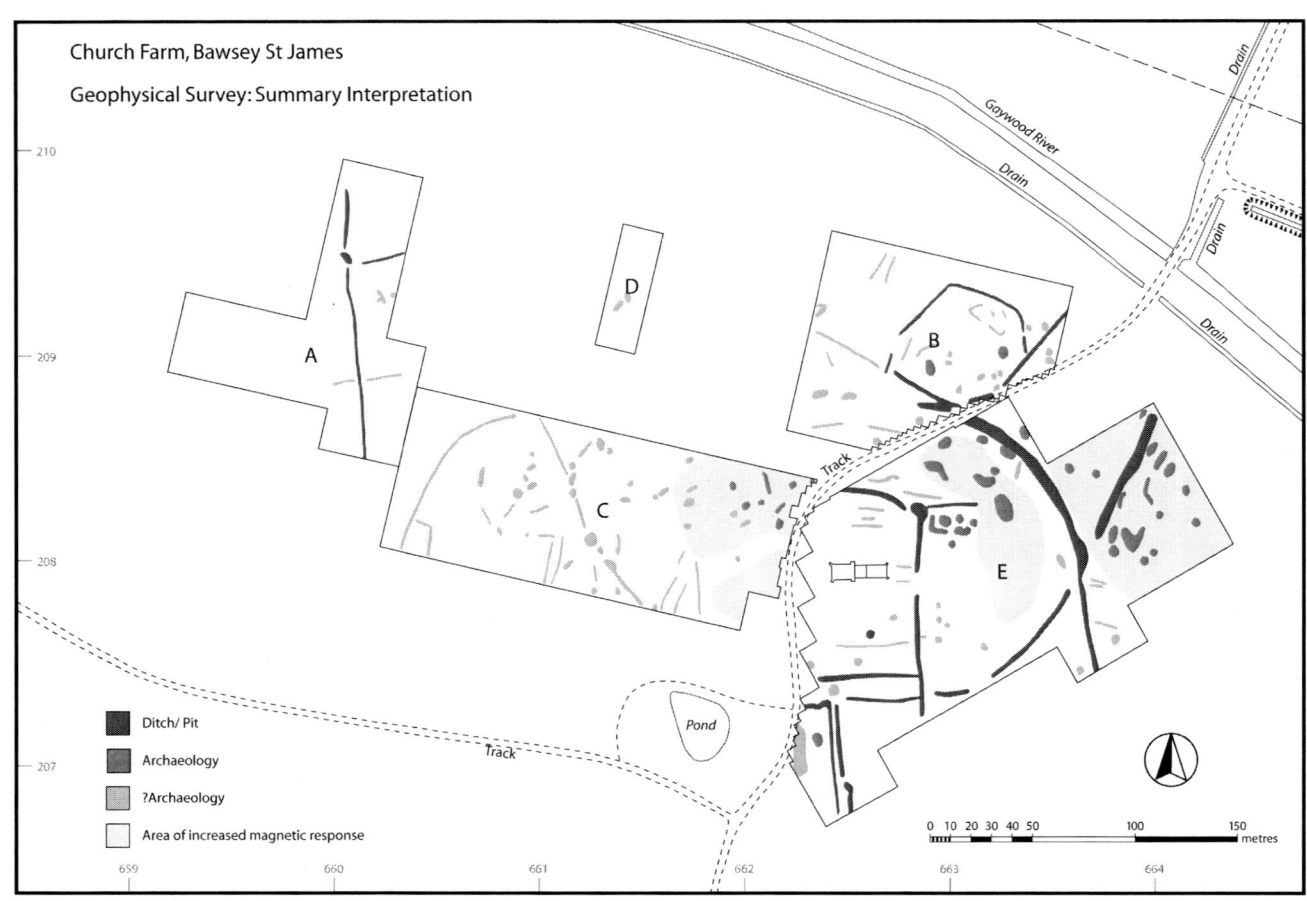

FIG. 4 FEATURES ACROSS THE SITE LOCATED IN GEOPHYSICAL SURVEY CONDUCTED BY *TIME TEAM*, AUGUST 1998 (GSB PROSPECTION/JOHN GATER)

Area B, further east again, was designed to investigate a small enclosure apparently appended to the north of the main ditch circuit, which had been seen originally on aerial photography (Fig. 5). It was thought that this might comprise some form of entrance into the main enclosure, and when located proved to be about 60m by 60m in size, although its exact shape was difficult to ascertain. Several other significant anomalies were also located, potentially indicating rubbish pits or possibly even structures. However, there also appears to have been much recent plough disturbance in this area, and it was noted that the main enclosure ditch continued to the west but as a feature with much reduced signal strength. This may account for why the northern ditch circuit was not seen by geophysics in Area D.

By far the largest areas surveyed were C and E, to the south and south-east of the site. Area C included an area of putative cropmarks on the high ground immediately west of the church, within which area the fragments of gold torc wire have been recovered. Somewhat disappointingly, Area C was in some ways the least productive dataset collected during this project. Although many anomalies were found within the survey, 'few were archaeologically coherent'.[23] Some ditches were identified but these made little sense in terms of an overall site plan, and many of the other features encountered were of uncertain archaeological date. More positively, the excavation of trenches here showed that despite a deep topsoil, archaeological features did still survive.

Finally, another large area, E, proved to yield very good results with a variety of features. The rounded eastern boundary ditch seen so well on the aerial photographs showed up very clearly, as did a series of linear features to the south of the parish church. One reason the eastern ditch may show so well is that it survived relatively late in the landscape, being marked on the 1839 Tithe map of the area.[24] This in turn may indicate that the poor definition of ditches elsewhere is due to their destruction and prolonged attrition by ploughing. Perhaps the other main feature of the area east of the church is the presence of many strong magnetic anomalies characteristic of industrial-type activity. The industrial features appear to have been zoned, for instance within a small area about 20×30m in size lying just inside the boundary ditch. This interpretation was reinforced by metalworking debris subsequently recovered in the metal-detection and fieldwalking survey which clustered on this area. Geophysics also showed odd extensions to the boundary ditch in this area, like that running south from the rounded east end, which is roughly parallel to a north-south ditch east of the parish church (Fig. 6).

---

[23] Report by J. Gater in site archive

[24] NRO, BL 14/31

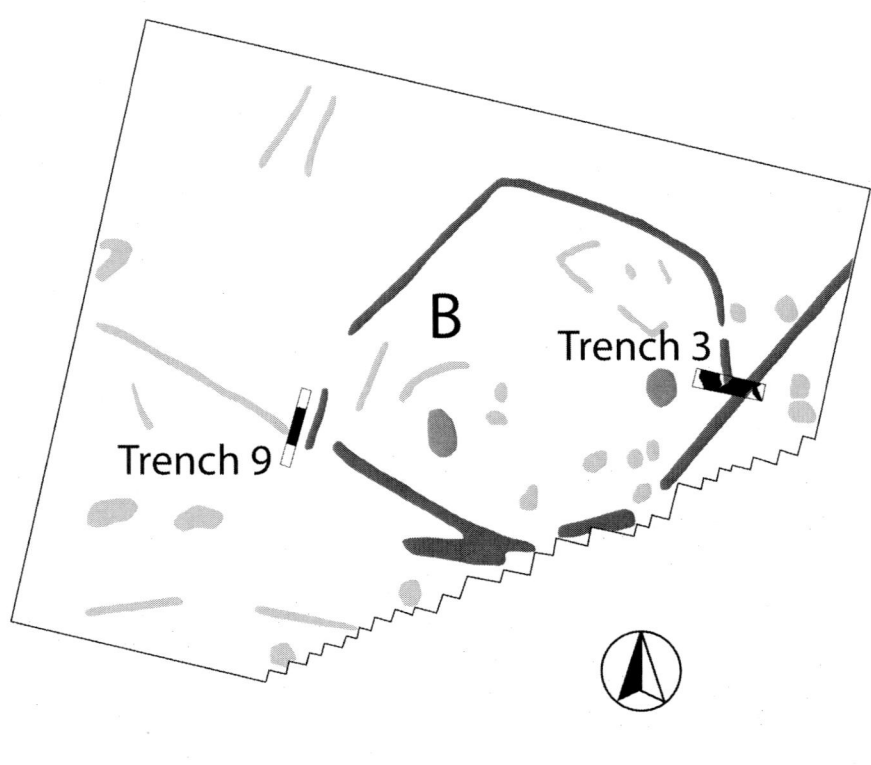

FIG. 5 THE 'ENCLOSURE' APPARENTLY ADDED TO THE NORTH OF THE SURROUNDING EARTHWORK AS REVEALED THROUGH GEOPHYSICS, AREA 'B' (GSB PROSPECTION/JOHN GATER)

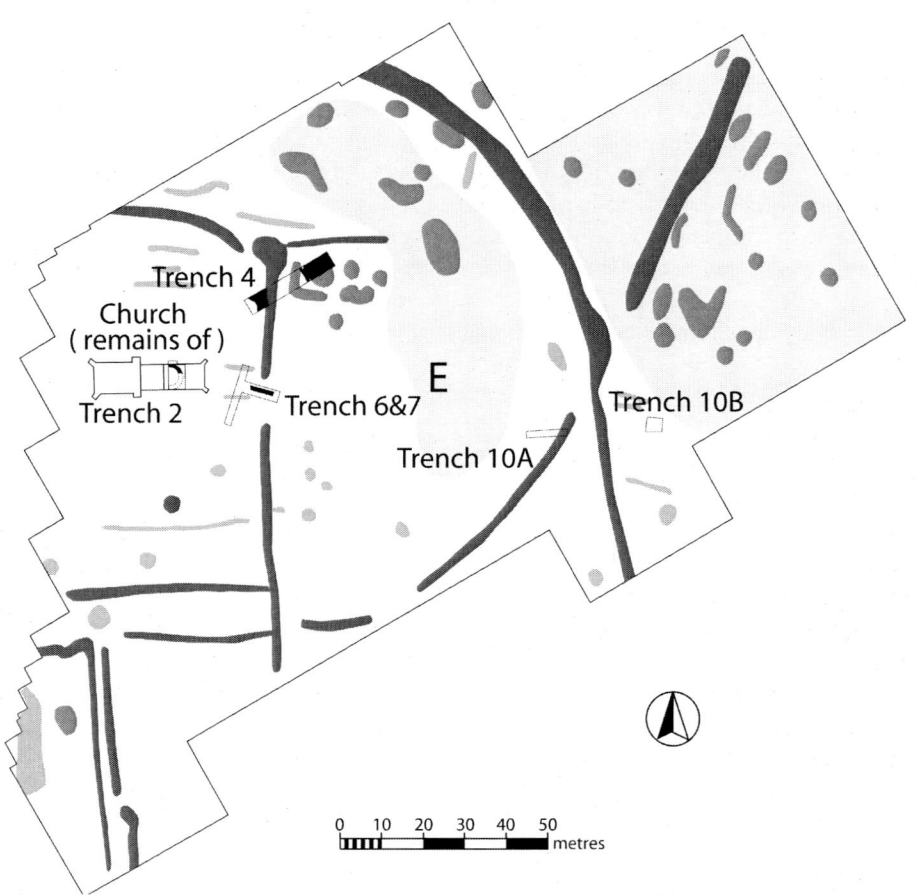

FIG. 6 ARCHAEOLOGICAL FEATURES REVEALED TO THE EAST OF THE PARISH CHURCH BY GEOPHYSICS, AREA 'E' (GSB PROSPECTION/JOHN GATER)

The geophysical survey was therefore of great interest in the investigation of the site and enabled a refinement of the details previously glimpsed only from the air. However, it is also clear that a yet more comprehensive geophysics survey is still desirable. The site at Bawsey is dauntingly large, and the geophysics was undertaken to try to identify potential areas for trial-trenching. However, the results demonstrate there is a real need to map the entire surrounding earthwork.

Fieldwalking

Although the site at Bawsey had been identified by metal-detecting, no systematic fieldwalking had ever been undertaken. As part of the *Time Team* broadcast, an area of 123,750m² was gridded out across the two fields, in 25×25m gridboxes, broadly conforming to the area of the cropmark enclosure. Although the exercise was a valuable one, the survey was conducted in less than ideal conditions as the timing of the broadcast was August. The fields had been lightly cultivated following harvesting of a cereal crop and the soil was dry, while the work was undertaken by largely inexperienced fieldwalkers. There is therefore no doubt that a survey of similar size undertaken on a weathered, ploughed, surface by experienced fieldwalkers would have greatly expanded the amount of material recovered, and probably also the range. Despite this, the light grey fabric of both Anglo-Saxon and several medieval wares can look similar in the soil yet proved to have dissimilar concentrations, making it less likely that there was preferential recovery due to particular fieldwalkers spotting particular types of sherds. A metal-detector survey was also undertaken using the same grid, but the quantity of material recovered was both small and limited, comprising mostly undatable ironwork. Given the amount of metalwork already recorded from the site, this element was therefore unrepresentative and of interest principally in recovering a further three Anglo-Saxon coins: two *sceattas* and a penny of Eadred (946-55).[25]

Plotting of the fieldwalked finds has shown both some interesting distributions and a wide range of pottery, dating from three possible Roman sherds to post-medieval wares. Of most interest with regard to the Anglo-Saxon period of the site's use is the clear concentration of Ipswich ware (dating to *c.*720-850) along the northern edge of the grid, fading fast to the south and east where most of the metal finds of this date have been recovered.[26] Also probably of Middle Anglo-Saxon date are two non-Ipswich ware body sherds that could represent imports, one of these again being discovered along the northern edge of the grid. The later Anglo-Saxon period in East Anglia is marked by the use of Thetford ware pottery and again the fieldwalking revealed a distinct concentration, this time clustering towards the north-east of the site grid, in the region of the Area B geophysics survey. Interestingly, this general distribution was also shared by oyster shell and animal bone from fieldwalking, perhaps indicating they were coterminous in deposition.

Of more interest are the far larger quantities of medieval pottery found across the site, attesting to its continued occupation. These fall into two principal types, Grimston ware, produced locally, and the Local Medieval Unglazed wares made at a variety of sites across Norfolk.[27] A few other imported types such as Livedon ware and Bourne Valley ware were found as single sherds but the overall impression is of locally-sourced pottery being used. The distribution of the medieval pottery was across the site, but with concentrations to the north and east. Perhaps more significant, the sherd size was characteristically small, suggesting that many pieces had been in the ploughsoil for some time, some quite possibly even arriving through manuring. The concentration to the north of the site, predominantly in an area to the north of the enclosure ditch, may represent some underlying distributional focus such as structured deposition like dumping (and it is interesting to note much pottery was recovered in the same area of the site in excavation trenches); through colluvial movement; or alternatively through the influence of an agricultural regime, for instance the dragging of material down the northern hillside by the plough. Perhaps notably, the post-medieval pottery follows a different distribution, concentrating to the west of the grid, outside the hilltop enclosure. The wares then in use, such as Glazed Red Earthenwares (GRE) of the sixteenth to eighteenth centuries are also easier to spot, suggesting this limited pattern of fieldwalked pottery is an accurate one.[28]

Finally, the fieldwalking also recovered some 63.455kg of ceramic building materials (CBM). Again highly visible to even novice fieldwalkers, this showed preferential distribution. While the recovered material included some clearly modern brick and fragments of land drain, much was more generally 'post-medieval'. Most was focused to the north of the site, but the pattern was especially strong when isolated as Roman CBM. Most of those identifiable fragments were of *tegulae* with pronounced square-section side-lips, while a number of fragments with curved edges may represent *imbrices*. The *tegulae* were fairly consistent in their fabric, being well- and evenly-fired reddish-orange sandy fabric with few small inclusions. Their presence, not least with so few other Roman finds from the site, is curious and it is at least possible that they were reused in the Anglo-Saxon period. One final element of CBM of interest were the six pieces or 188g of light whitish-grey daub. Another five pieces (256g) were recovered from the excavation trenches and they seem to reflect the presence of wattle and daub structures on the site, a few pieces preserving the impressions of round-sectioned withies or

---

[25] The *sceattas* were of Series B1b (Type 27b), *c.*685-95, recorded on EMC, as 1998.0095; and of Series D (Type 2c), *c.*700-715, EMC 1998.0094. The Eadred penny is of crowned bust type, moneyer Wilbeorht, probably a Norwich moneyer. It is EMC 1998.0096
[26] For the dating of Ipswich ware see Blinkhorn 2012, pp. 3-8
[27] For a summary of these various medieval wares see Jennings 1981. For the Grimston ware industry see Leah 1994
[28] For the long chronology of Glazed Red Earthenwares see Jennings 1981, pp. 157-8

wicker lining. As so few pieces were found it is hard to known how much can be read into their vague distribution towards the north of the site, and their date is unknown.

Excavation

The Enclosure ditch

Some seventeen trial trenches were opened as part of the *Time Team* survey of Bawsey, many of which were placed to investigate more fully the enclosure ditch or elements associated with it, as revealed through the geophysics survey (Fig. 7). One of the principal difficulties was locating elements of the possible enclosure ditch with certainty through the geophysics, especially to the north of the site, not least as it often seemed to suggest a different pattern of field boundaries to that revealed by the aerial photography. For this reason four trenches were excavated by machine to the west of the site (Trenches 1A-D) in an attempt to define the western end of the enclosure and its return to the north, while another four trenches explored the approximate crest ridge of the hill's southern side and the features that geophysics suggested lay here, apparently within the enclosure.

The results were mixed, largely as a result of the ambitious number of trenches opened: while the general results of the geophysics could be confirmed, qualitative detail was frequently lacking. For instance, the western ditch noted by geophysics in Area A was revealed in trenches 1A, B and D. That part in A was some 5.2m wide, in B 9m wide and in D over 6.5m wide. However, the latter was not excavated, while the section in A was not bottomed. Fortunately, that in B was, but only in a 0.55m wide slot, showing the ditch at that point to be about 1.05m deep. The lower fill, *120*, contained three sherds of unglazed medieval pottery and was sealed by a fill above, *119*, that contained two sherds of Grimston ware and three medieval glazed sherds. The ditch had evidently been recut a number of times as shown in all three trenches but the lack of dating evidence from the first phase ditch, seen most clearly in 1A, makes it uncertain whether it was first laid out in the Anglo-Saxon or medieval periods, although the latter seems most likely. Similarly, a possible ditch – based on geophysics – was located at the southern end of Trench 1C and another possible ditch at its north end. However, the nature and extent of both were left undetermined as there was insufficient time to investigate them further.

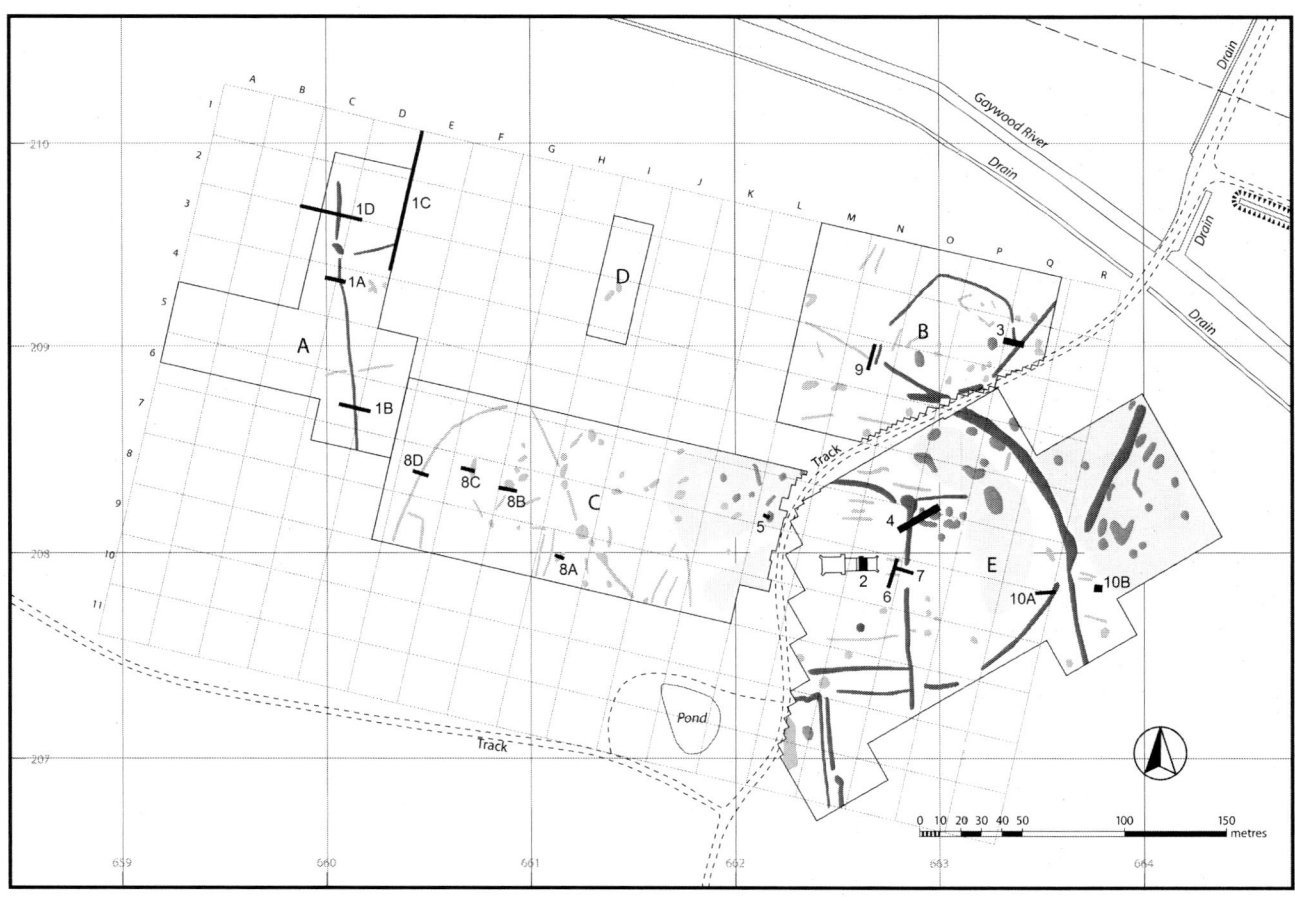

FIG. 7 SUMMARY PLAN SHOWING LOCATION OF WORK BY *TIME TEAM*, AUGUST 1998. THE MAIN ALPHA-NUMERIC SITE GRID USED FOR THE FIELDWALKING AND METAL-DETECTION IS SHOWN, AS ARE THE GEOPHYSICS AREAS AND THE LOCATION OF ALL EVALUATION TRENCHES (PETE BELLAMY)

The southern side of the enclosed area at the west end was similarly inconclusive. Trenches 8A-C were machined and then hand-cleaned, but had only minimal excavation, while 8D was opened by machine but abandoned as there was insufficient time to clean it. Those features that were encountered were sadly uninformative about the Anglo-Saxon element to the site. One of two deposits in 8A, a small 4.1×1.6m trench, apparently contained a concentration of worked flints but this was not excavated, nor were any of these flints apparently recovered. The two contexts were interpreted as a prehistoric occupation deposit but its nature or date remain uncertain.[29] 8B proved to contain a larger sub-circular feature, as indicated on the geophysics plot, all but one of whose edges lay outside the extent of the trench. With a depth of some 0.8m, its bottom layer *823* contained medieval pottery of Early Medieval, Grimston and Cambridge wares. The feature's function remains unclear although one suggestion made at the time of excavation was that it may have been a quarry-pit, perhaps to extract building sand for the church. 8C was similarly undiagnostic. Again investigating a geophysical anomaly, this appears to have been a spread of sand and charcoal, interpreted as the rake-out from some nearby industrial activity. It was sealed by a layer, *832*, that contained a residual sherd of Grimston ware and a sherd of GRE pottery, suggesting a post-medieval date.

More investigation of the possible course of the enclosure's northern ditches was undertaken in Trench 9, but this was blighted first by limited time, meaning that the machine excavation could not be fully recorded, and by waterlogging within the trench (Fig. 8). What could be determined was that a feature probably about 6.8m wide had been cut into the natural sand and filled with deposits containing a large number of animal bones and a highly organic content. A number of medieval sherds including Early Medieval and Grimston wares were found, but there is a suggestion that these were residual because a post-medieval sherd was also apparently found. However, given the difficulties associated with the recording in this trench, undertaken late on the final day, it may yet be that this latter association is erroneous, and the deposit is medieval. This would certainly fit with the picture seen to the west of the site. It also raises the prospect that, in its unbottomed state, this part of the ditch preserves good waterlogged conditions.

Finally, more sampling associated with ditches to the north was carried out in Trench 3, where the possible northern extension to the main enclosure had been seen by geophysics (Fig. 5). Two ditches were encountered, as well as some smaller undated gulley-like features and possible stakeholes. Both ditches had been re-cut and were left unbottomed, but one had medieval pottery (Local Medieval Unglazed and Grimston wares) as well as a few sherds of residual Ipswich and Thetford wares in its upper, recut, fill *303*.

FIG. 8 TRENCH 9 FROM THE SOUTH, SHOWING THE WATERLOGGED BASE (PHOTOGRAPH *TIME TEAM*)

---

[29] It is of interest to note that some sparse evidence of prehistoric occupation was gathered from the fieldwalking, including a Late Neolithic/Early Bronze Age barbed-and-tanged arrowhead and several scrapers, probably of a similar date

The church

As the one certainly-dated feature on the site, the church might have seemed a slightly unnecessary subject for fieldwork, but the ruined building was clearly once a fine Norman structure. Moreover, the discovery of Late Anglo-Saxon grave-slab fragments here, and knowledge of the site's Middle Anglo-Saxon past, made it desirable to try locating any remains of an earlier church underlying the present structure. Although no such traces were found, Trench 2 was able to confirm the presence of an earlier apsidal chancel reported in a brief excavation undertaken at the east end in 1930, but never properly recorded.[30] The apse survived as rough flint and carstone walling about 0.9m wide, with an internal diameter of approximately 4.2m. These wall footings were exposed to a depth of 0.7m but the base was not found.

The square-ended chancel that replaced the original Romanesque apse has now largely collapsed, but elements of its surviving bottom courses were uncovered and within its extent were found remains of a number of floor surfaces. Following demolition of the apse a levelling-up layer of light grey sandy soil, *228*, appears to have been laid down, followed by a crumbly cream-white plaster layer *222*, probably originally a bedding layer for a tiled floor pavement. Another levelling-up layer of orange-yellow sand, *223*, had sealed this before a thick mortar layer was laid down into which were set glazed ceramic floor tiles, several of which remained *in situ* on the south side of the chancel. Of Flemish type, these were laid out in a near-chequerboard pattern of alternating green and buff colours (Fig. 9). Such tiles are very common in East Anglia, having been imported in great quantities from the Low Countries during the fifteenth and sixteenth centuries.[31] They had been poorly laid, and did not align with the chancel south wall to which they abutted, as a result of which tiles had had to be broken to fit the widening gap. A raised step for the altar seems to be indicated by a line of half-bricks running across the width of the chancel, surviving a single course high and revetting a floor make-up of mortar rubble (*218*). The step had evidently been constructed prior to the Flemish tiled floor, which butted up against it.

Excavation of this trench uncovered other material relating to the church, although largely unstratified in surface clearance, or in the backfill of Fairweather's 1930 trenches. This included fragments of relief-decorated 'Bawsey' type floor-tiles; roof-tile and sherds of stained glass. The Bawsey tiles are an unsurprising discovery given the presence of the kiln site producing them within the parish, and their wide distribution attests to their popularity.[32] Eight different designs are represented, including the celebrated pattern erroneously stamped 'Thomas' in reverse.[33] The use of the Bawsey tiles suggests a reflooring within the church was carried out *c.*1350-1400. The ceramic roof-tile recovered is of two principal types: Type I is of rectangular form with a probably single centrally-placed peg-hole. This seems to

FIG. 9 THE FLEMISH FLOORTILE SURFACE EXPOSED IN THE CHANCEL WITH THE BRICK-EDGING FOR A STEP TO ITS EAST. THE REMAINS OF THE CHANCEL SOUTH WALL CAN BE SEEN TO THE RIGHT OF THE PHOTO, WHILE FAIRWEATHER'S RE-OPENED 1930 EXCAVATION TRENCH IS THE DARK CURVED FEATURE TO THE LEFT (PHOTOGRAPH *TIME TEAM*)

---

[30] Fairweather 1931, p. 169

[31] Drury 1993, pp. 165-6
[32] The kiln site is at TF 6812 2051 (HER 1075). For Bawsey tiles see Eames 1955
[33] Eames 1955, cat. no. xviii. The other designs represented are Eames types vi, xxii, xxxvii, xlix, li, liii and lvii

be similar to roof-tiles found in excavations in King's Lynn dating from *c.*1200 onwards.[34] Type II appears to be post-medieval, having a brown glaze similar to Glazed Red Earthenware pottery. Six stone roofing slates, three with drilled nail-holes, were also found. The stained window glass derived principally from Trench 2, thirty-one of the thirty-seven sherds recovered coming from the topsoil clearance here. Examination by David King has led him to conclude that the assemblage very probably dates from at least two glazing campaigns of the thirteenth and fourteenth centuries, although a late twelfth-century date is possible for several pieces and one or two pieces could be later.[35]

Settlement and cemetery

Trenching to the east of the church (Trenches 4, 6, 7 and 10A and B) was again designed to investigate features identified through the geophysical survey, notably the enclosure ditch, but also to investigate the extent of any cemetery associated with the church. Only a single skeleton was encountered, in Trench 6, which was plough-damaged. It suggests that other burials may have been removed, but that the cemetery is unlikely to have extended this far east, at least in any density. Trench 7, which extended east from Trench 6, allowed a section to be partially cut across the large north-south ditch seen to the east of the church. Once again this confirmed the wide upper dimensions seen in the ditches elsewhere, being some 5.8m wide at the upper edges. Unfortunately the ditch section was not bottomed and so the full profile was not revealed, nor was any dating material found for its primary fills. The deepest fill encountered, *703*, contained medieval pottery, including Grimston ware, as well as a sherd of medieval window glass and a high proportion of disarticulated human bone. In Trench 4 to the north of 6 and 7, a continuation of this north-south ditch was again sectioned. While two phases were identified, it was again not bottomed so the primary fill could not be dated. However, the earlier of the two phases identified, *411*, did have medieval pottery within its lowest excavated layer, as well as more disarticulated human bone. The implication is thus that the eastern boundary ditch was of medieval date and that charnel from disturbed burials in its immediate environs had been dumped in the ditch.

Trench 4 and Trenches 10A and B further to the east were also important for investigating strong responses seen in the geophysical survey. That in Trench 4 revealed a series of features that were not fully investigated but which included a small gully and a shallow pit, possibly some form of quarry scoop infilled with refuse including relatively late material such as a sherd of Glazed Red Earthenware. Trenches 10A and B were opened late on the final day of the *Time Team* broadcast and so were only partially excavated. However, they yielded some interesting finds, including a bone needle and bun-shaped loom-weight of Anglo-Saxon type which came from *926*, a dark grey sandy silt, albeit one apparently also containing a sherd of medieval window glass. 10B yielded a clay deposit, *952*, which was left unexcavated but was possibly a large hearth, and which was sealed by layer *951* containing many fragments of metalworking debris. The trenches therefore seem to indicate this was an industrial or craftworking activity area, even if the deposits in these trenches were imperfectly understood, dated or investigated.

Finally, Trench 5 to the west of the church proved to be of considerable interest in containing both Anglo-Saxon and later features. Originally opened to investigate a geophysical anomaly, a series of deposits and features was encountered, most notably nine graves plus a quantity of disarticulated bone. Providing the opportunity to set the churchyard in context, they generally followed the same alignment (WNW-ESE), and did not intercut, suggesting that they were from the same phase of the cemetery's use (Fig. 10). The graves appeared to cut through an occupation layer in which was uncovered the remains of an oven, *502* (Fig. 11) and other postholes. In line with the dating of the ditches, the pottery emerging from this occupation layer was all medieval, the oven being dated by a sherd of Thetford/Grimston pottery recovered from one of the twelve stakeholes associated with it. The disturbed subsoil contained quantities of Early Medieval ware similar to pottery recovered at North Elmham and Castle Acre castle, dating to the eleventh and twelfth centuries, while the actual layer apparently cut by the graves (*537*) contained possible Early Medieval ware and large quantities of Thetford/ Grimston ware pottery; this latter pottery is characterised by large open bowls and dominated west Norfolk pottery types in the period 1050-1150 (Fig. 12).[36] On this basis, the cemetery therefore appears to be of Saxo-Norman date like the present church building, with a similar or slightly earlier phase of activity represented by features such as the oven.

However, a twist to this phasing was added upon the excavation of a sondage in the south-east corner of Trench 5. Removing one grave, *538*, a second was found beneath it containing skeleton *541*, a burial of some palaeopathological interest. A fragment had been sliced off the top of the cranium, but had remained more or less *in situ* and represents a rare example of trephination. Of equal interest to our understanding of the site, the body was radiocarbon dated to 660-900AD (95% confidence), centring on a date of probably 760-880AD.[37] It therefore belongs firmly to the Middle Anglo-Saxon phase of the site and provided the first suggestion that a church may have been present on the site at this date.

The body itself is of some interest. Analysis has shown the person to have been an adult female, aged 30-40, about 5'5" tall. The trepanation appears to have been conducted

---

[34] Richmond *et al.* 1982, p. 122
[35] Unpublished report in the site archive
[36] For Early Medieval ware see Jennings 1981, p. 22 and for that found at Castle Acre see Milligan 1982. For the Thetford/Grimston wares see Clarke 1970 and Leah 1994
[37] WK-7057. At 68.2% probability: 710AD (17.9% probability); 760-880AD (50.3% probability). At 95.4% probability: 660-900AD

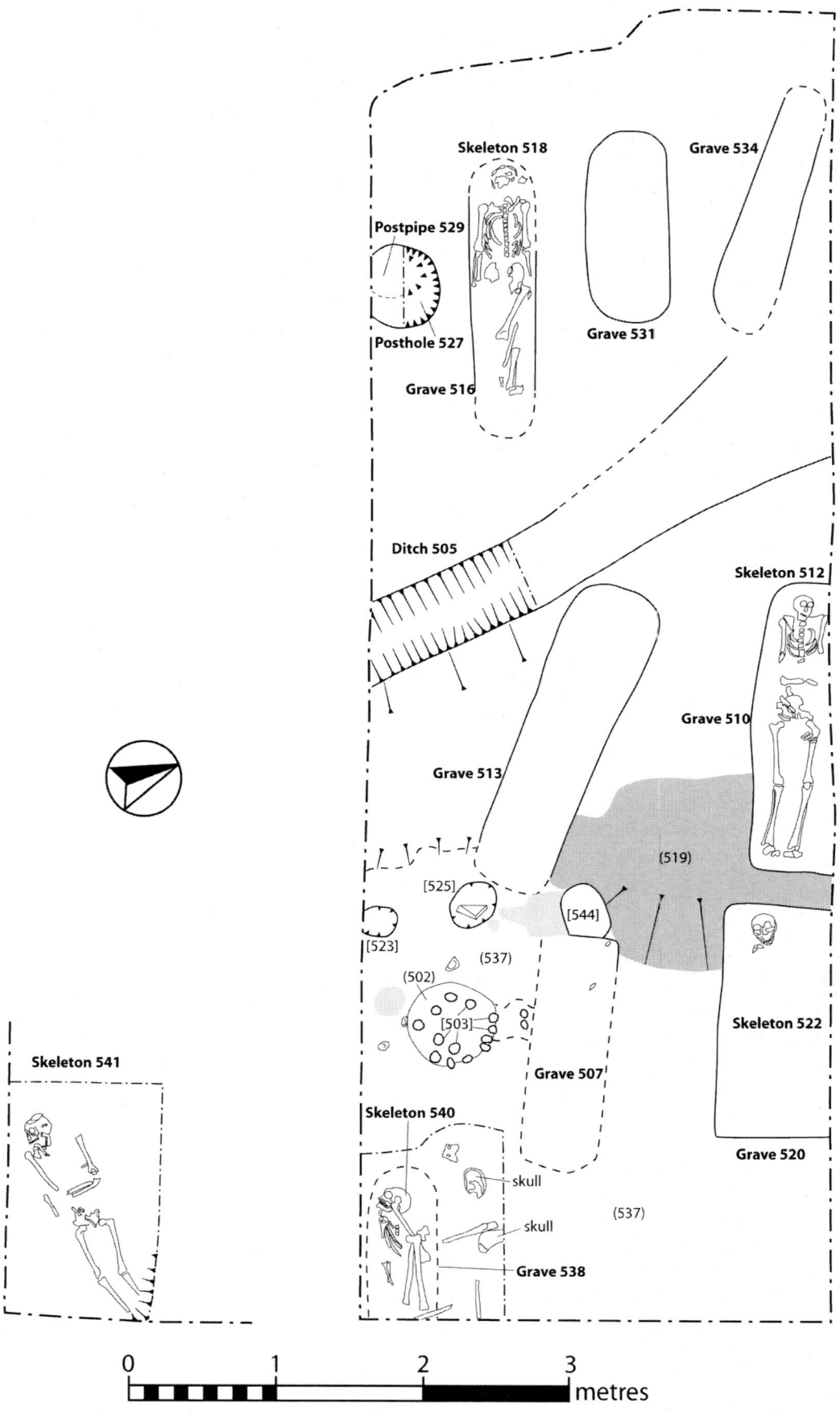

Fig. 10 The graves and settlement evidence revealed in Trench 5. The *sondage* excavated beneath Grave *538*, revealing Skeleton *541*, is shown to the left (Pete Bellamy)

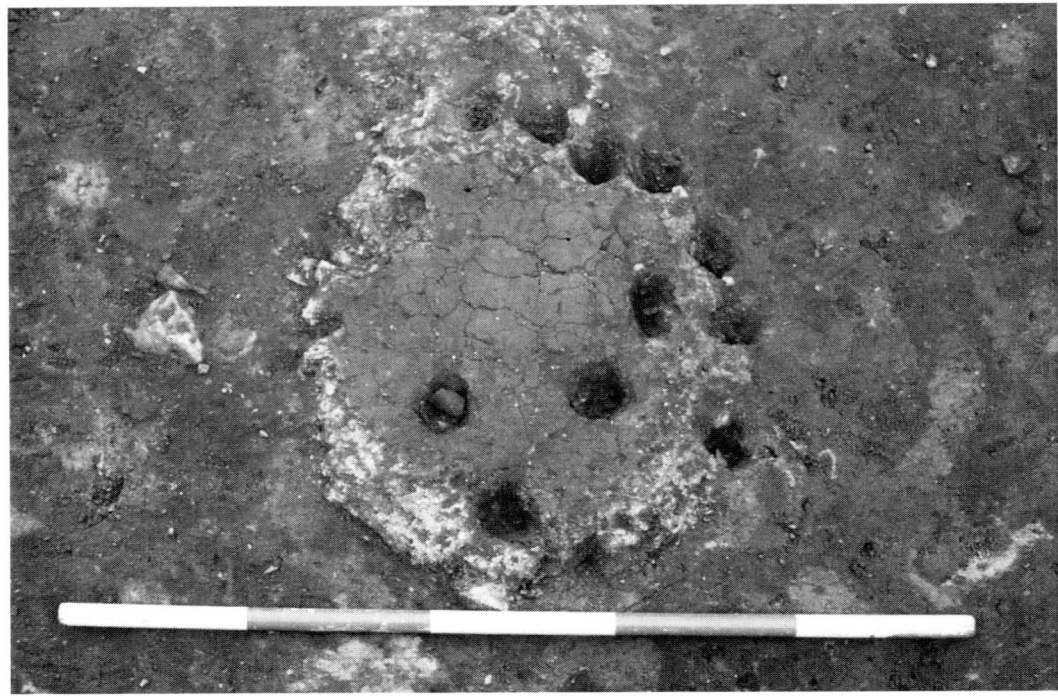

FIG. 11 THE SUGGESTED CLAY-LINED OVEN *503* IN TRENCH 5, FROM THE SOUTH (PHOTOGRAPH *TIME TEAM*)

following a blade wound to the skull from above and behind, probably to relieve an intercranial haemorrhage. Some slight traces of healing suggest that the woman had died at least a week after her original wound but, as if that were not enough, gnaw marks, possibly by a badger, were found on the right femur, that occurred sometime before she was buried.[38] Equally intriguing is that study of the remaining skeletal material has revealed another body, *512*, to have suffered severe trauma, with a series of cuts inflicted by a narrow-bladed weapon such as a sword. Cut marks were found on the rear of the right tibia and two of the right ribs; on the right shoulder blade and what Sue Anderson describes as a 'glancing blow to the side of the left chin, which removed the lower border of the mandible'. Finally, there were two severe chops to the front of the skull and across the back (Fig. 13). The victim was a young to middle-aged adult male, but frustratingly the left arm remains in the ground, unexcavated, so we cannot see fully any possible defence wounds.[39] The occurrence of the two bodies with chop marks within 3m, yet apparently one Middle Anglo-Saxon, the other from a Medieval layer seemed curious. A second radiocarbon determination, of this second body, was therefore sought. The result, of 686-864 at 95.4% probability centred on 686-827AD,[40] demonstrated that the two skeletons both belonged to the Middle Anglo-Saxon period, and that the stratigraphic relationship of the medieval occupation horizon and the grave cuts had been misinterpreted.

Throughout this description of the trial evaluation, perhaps the most surprising and repeated aspect of the *Time Team* excavations is that much of the pottery recovered indicates post-Conquest activity. While sherds of Ipswich and Thetford ware were recovered, these were very much in a minority and residual, a picture reinforced in the limited fieldwalking and seen in the total pottery recovered (Fig. 14). If Bawsey attracted the attention of *Time Team* for its Middle Anglo-Saxon pedigree, excavations essentially stressed its later life. This apparent contradiction between its metal material wealth and archaeological features continues to make the site enigmatic. How, then, might we try to interpret Bawsey's 'productive' site element?

Wider interpretations

Perhaps the most obvious starting point from which to consider the site of Bawsey St James is that which led to its prolonged investigation: the coinage. At the outset it has to be stated that the corpus is less than satisfactory for discussion as it varies according to source. While Blackburn discussed its coin-loss profile on the basis of a sample of 124 coins from 600-1180AD,[41] the *Corpus of Early Medieval Coin Finds* (EMC) lists only 103 for the site. An added complication is that several of these identifications rest on the notes of Mark Blackburn utilising information which is often vague, provided by the convicted metal-detectorist who initially worked at Bawsey. Finally, the Norfolk HER provides a further listing of those coins that were recorded by Mr Steve Brown since he began working on the site. Since our convicted finder found 21 (or 20.4%) of the coins found on the EMC list there is an appreciable margin for possible error.

---

[38] Report by Louise Loe and Margaret Cox in site archive
[39] Report by Sue Anderson in site archive
[40] UB-10588. At 68.2% probability: 694-701AD (4.1%); 707-748AD (43.8%); 766-780AD (14.8%); 794-802AD (5.5%). At 95.4% probability: 686-827AD (89.9%); 839-864AD (5.5%)

[41] Blackburn 2003, pp. 28-32 and 35

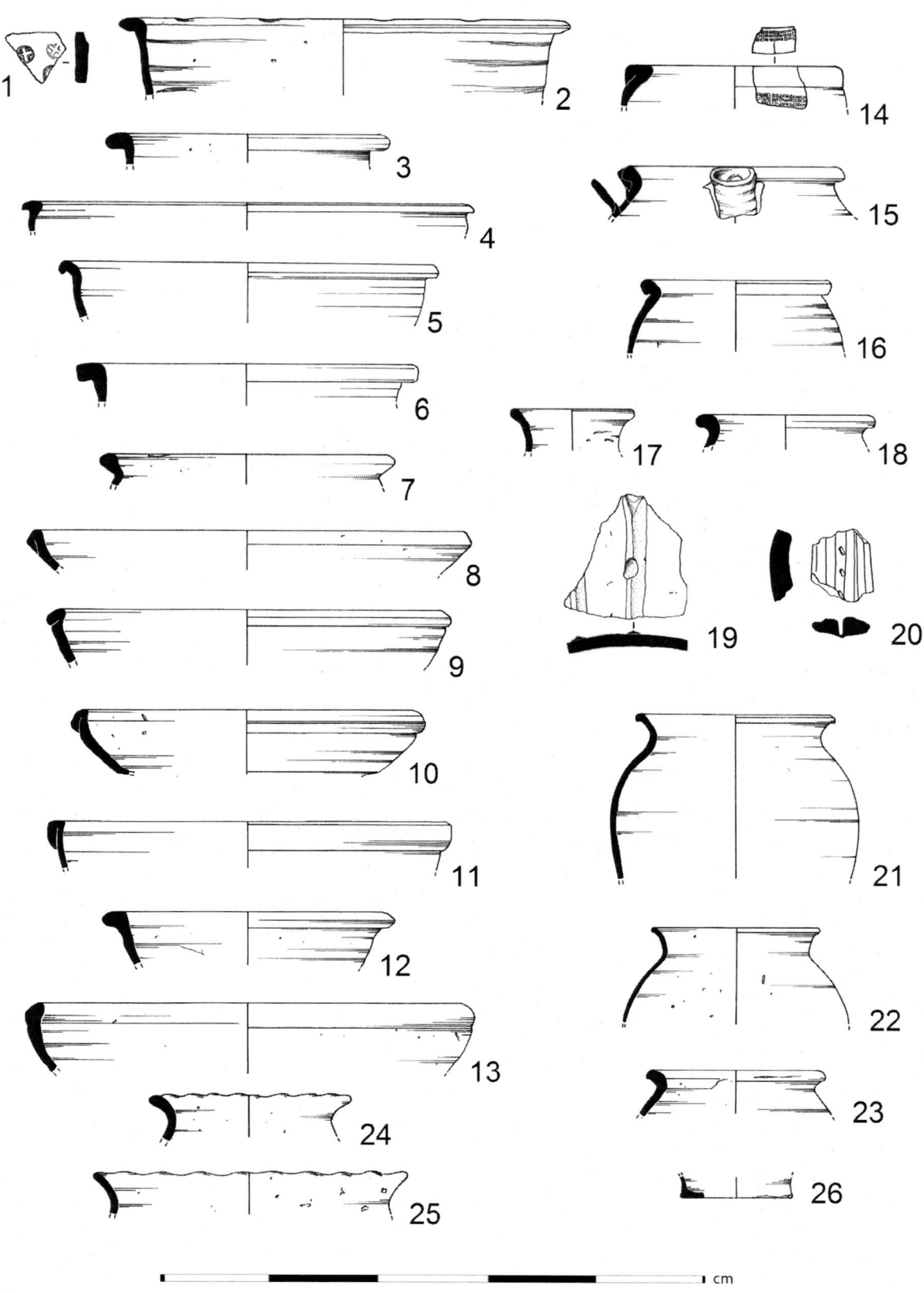

Fig. 12. Pottery from the Time Team excavations and fieldwalking. 1: Stamped Thetford ware; 2-15: Thetford-Grimston type ware jars and bowls. Jar 14 features roulette-stamped decoration on both the rim side and top; 17-19: Unglazed Grimston ware jars; 20: Glazed Grimston ware jug handle; 21-13: Early unglazed Grimston or early Medieval ware jars; 24-25: Early Medieval ware of Castle Acre type; 26: Shelly Fabric St Neot's ware pot base. Scale: 10cm divisions (Drawn by author).

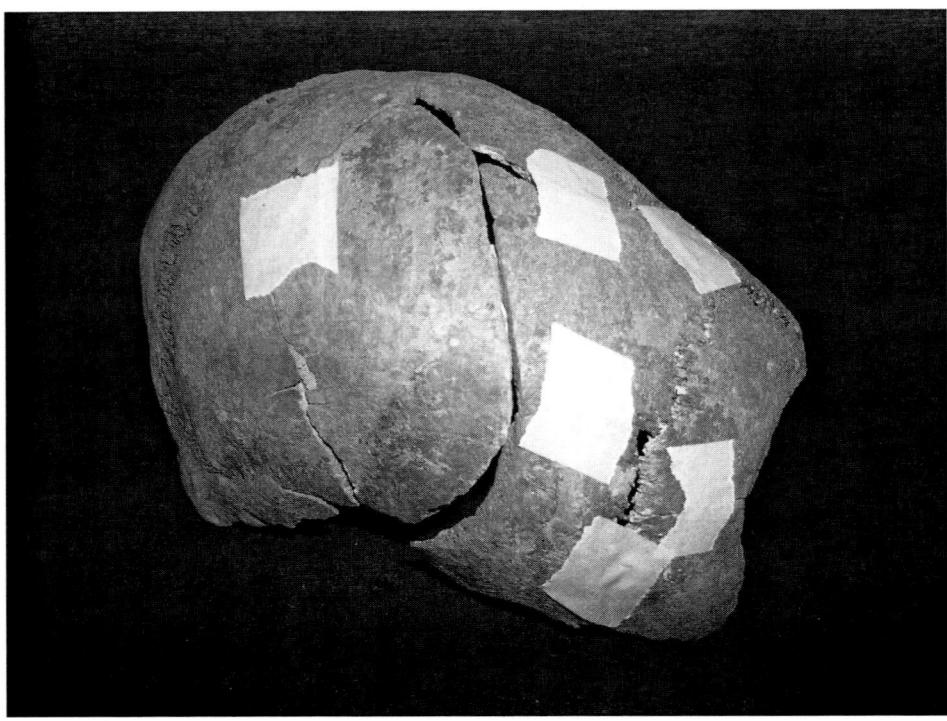

FIG. 13 POSSIBLE SWORD-WOUND CHOP TO THE SKULL OF SKELETON *512*. (PHOTOGRAPH SUE ANDERSON)

Despite this, it is clear that Bawsey may claim to be the most 'productive' site in Norfolk with regard to its Middle Anglo-Saxon coinage, with at least 54 *sceatta*-type pennies. Despite the argument that the site has been heavily disturbed by agricultural activity, freeing a disproportionate number of coins and artefacts into the ploughsoil – Julian Richards' explanation for the presence of 'productive' sites[42] – the trial excavations by *Time Team* have demonstrated that archaeological features do still remain. It is certainly true that much damage has been caused by agricultural activity as demonstrated by the number of damaged or broken broad-flan pennies recovered from the site. At the same time, the sheer number of *sceatta* coins is so unrepresentative of other sites across both Norfolk and England more widely, we are clearly looking at a site acting as a focus of economic exchange within the kingdom of East Anglia. While the number of coins falls off in the post-*sceatta* phase an appreciable presence is clearly maintained into the eighth and early ninth centuries with coinage of the Mercian overlords of East Anglia Offa (in particular) and Coenwulf. Perhaps equally significant, the coinage continues on the site, even in limited numbers through to the twelfth century.[43] This contrasts with several other 'productive' sites such as Heckington (previously known as 'South Lincolnshire'), Hollingbourne and South Newbald.[44] Indeed, it mirrors the peaks and troughs of the generalised circulation of coinage seen through single-finds in southern England and corroborates the picture presented by archaeology, of occupation continuing on the site at Bawsey into the twelfth century. One interesting consideration though, is that by the eleventh century Bawsey's 'single coin' finds are predominantly fractional, comprising pennies cut into halfpennies or farthings (of the 21 coins of Æthelred II to Henry II, 13 (62%) were cut, while the remaining 8 'whole' examples include many fragmentary coins that might also once have been cut). Even if we see a rise in the number of fractional pennies in circulation in this period, it is apparent that the high volume in coinage and sums being exchanged in the late seventh and early eighth centuries had ended and was replaced with a pattern more commensurate with an unexceptional settlement.

The derivation of the coinage is also of interest. The *sceattas* comprise a high proportion (35%) of Continental coins of Series D and E, indicating a considerable integration with international trade and exchange networks. This is unsurprising as a similar picture is present from Norfolk more generally, Continental *sceattas* accounting for 'upwards of fifty percent of *sceattas* recorded as strayfinds' from the county.[45] Indeed, it is interesting to compare the figures from Bawsey with those from Caistor St Edmund (Fig. 15), where metal-detecting has also revealed the presence of a 'productive' site, the second-most prolific in Norfolk in terms of coin-finds, on fields to the south-west of the walled Roman town of *Venta Icenorum*. 43 *sceattas* have now been recorded, of which some 46.5% are of Continental origin (Series D and E), with 16.3% of Series R, that is of local, East Anglian, origin, compared to 24% at Bawsey.[46] Naturally, some variability between sites

---

[42] Richards 1999
[43] Blackburn 2003, pp. 28-9 and fig. 3.4
[44] Daubney 2007; Blackburn 2003, 29-30 and figs. 3.4 and 3.5

[45] Marsden 2013, p. 6
[46] This ignores the possibility that the Series B *sceattas*, conventionally seen as East Saxon products, may in fact also be East Anglian: Metcalf

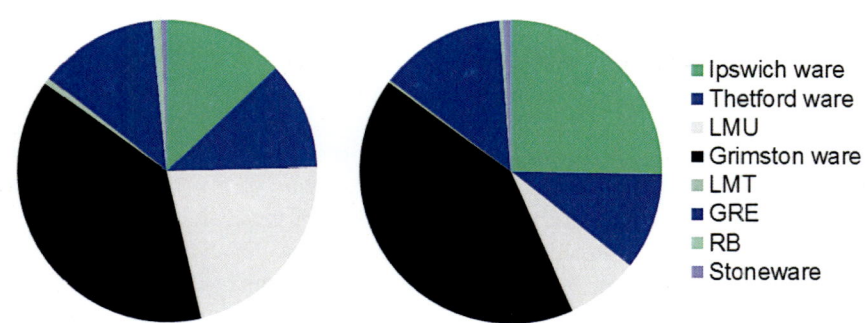

Fig. 14 Proportions of pottery recovered in fieldwalking (a) by sherd count (b) by weight (author)

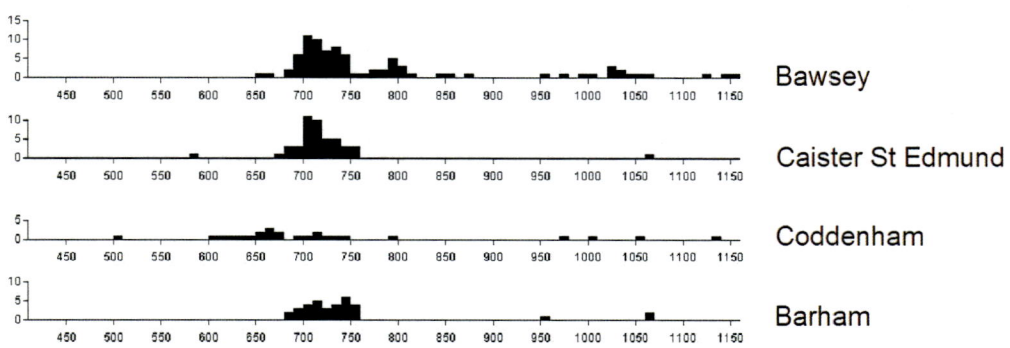

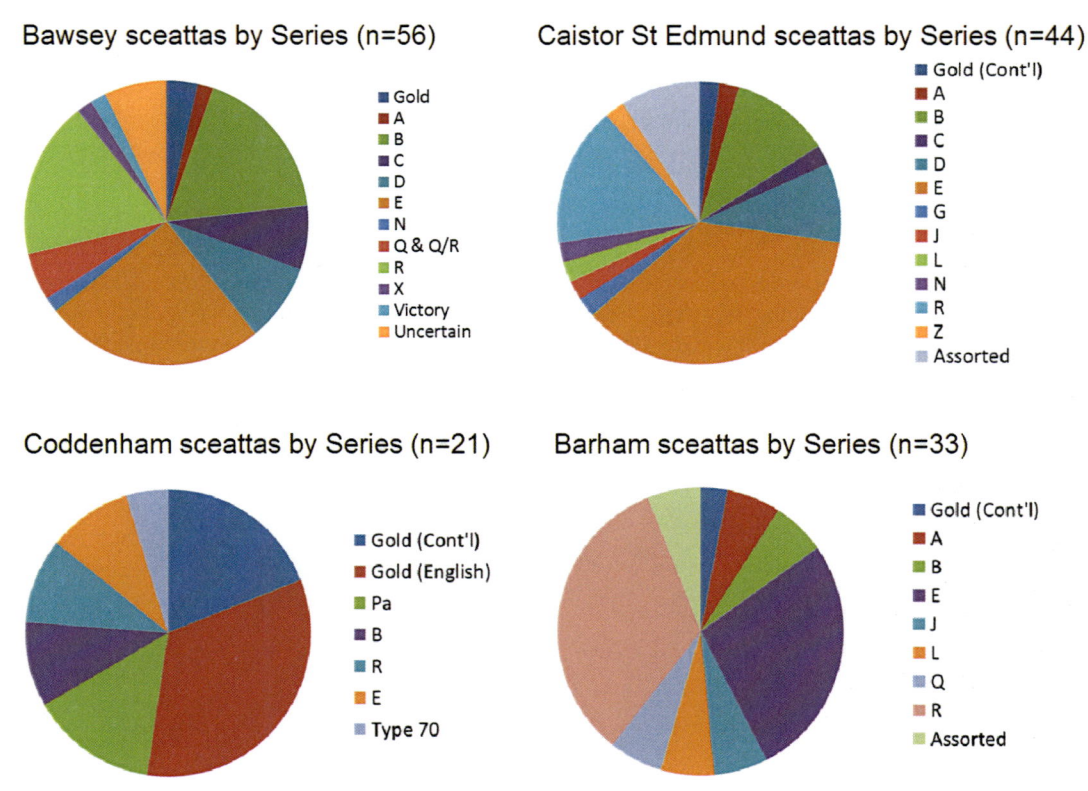

Fig. 15 Comparison of the sceatta finds from Bawsey, Caistor St Edmund, Coddenham and Barham, top as histograms (adapted from EMC plots) and bottom as proportions of sceatta types (author)

is only to be expected and proportions change with each new coin discovered. However, it is potentially instructive that whereas Bawsey may be seen to continue as a trading centre into the eighth and early ninth century with coins of Offa and Coenwulf, at Caistor one single Offa penny of 765-92 and a proto-penny of East Anglian king Beonna (749-60) are the only testament to continued trade here into the second half of the eighth century. At Caistor it may well be that other factors were coming into play in the mid-eighth century, most probably the relocation or drift of commercial activities to the waterfront area of Fishergate in the north *wic* that was to become Norwich.[47] Although both share similar patterns of coinage in the *sceatta* phase, the trajectories of these sites were to differ later on, indicating the continual fluctuation in the fortunes of trading centres. Indeed, as Caistor was replaced by Norwich so, arguably, was Bawsey by King's Lynn.[48]

The relative spheres of interest between these two sites, one on the west coast of the county, the other reached via the river system leading to the east coast, may also have played some role in the coinage recovered at each site. Whereas Caistor has a larger proportion of Continental coins and a smaller one of East Anglian-issue coins, Bawsey's larger number of local coin types may suggest that it was more directly involved in local trade and exchange networks. When detailed quantification and examination of all the known Bawsey coins is at last possible, it may be that die-linkages will also be of interest, my colleague Adrian Marsden having identified a die-linkage between one Series R Bawsey *sceatta* with an example of Fenland provenance now in the Ashmolean Museum. Given Michael Metcalf's work on the regression analysis of East Anglian *sceattas* which has pointed to concentrations of coinage in the north-west and south-east of the East Anglian kingdom, further work may potentially help us to define particular concentrations of linked coinage and perhaps even help point ultimately to mint locations.[49]

Finally, it is of interest to note the preponderance of Kentish coinage at Bawsey even during the late eighth and early ninth century Mercian overlordship.[50] Three pennies of Eadberht Praen and one of Wulfred of Canterbury have been recovered, and of the 13 Mercian coins, 5 were of the Canterbury mint, another 3 possibly London or Canterbury.[51] This is of interest given the wide range of Offa and Coenwulf's overlordship and may again point to a particular set of trade networks in which Bawsey was a part. Clearly this is an area requiring more research and comparison with the coin profiles of other similar sites both close to Bawsey and at some remove from it.

If the coinage from Bawsey made it stand out originally, other aspects of the site's material culture are similarly unusual. Of these, the presence of styli is one of the most eye-catching elements. While styli are familiar enough as writing implements, especially from the Roman world, they remain a rare form of material culture from the Anglo-Saxon period, reflecting an altogether more restricted range of people with literate ability. In the past styli have been seized upon as evidence for the ecclesiastical nature of sites, due to the leading (or at least more obvious) role of clerics in practicing literate abilities. And, since styli indicate the ability of their owners to write rather than simply to possess items like books, their presence clearly suggests an occupying community who required and used the tools of literacy. In this respect it is interesting to note that the broken eraser of one stylus is made from silver, paralleled in Britain only by a complete example from Flixborough and the lower half of a stylus shaft from Little Carlton (Lincs).[52] Such pieces are clearly of high status and had transcended their purely functional aspect. Indeed, while the excavations at Flixborough yielded 22 styli, two-thirds of them were of iron. Because all the Bawsey finds have been recovered by metal-detection, no ironwork has been collected. Potentially, therefore, there are more, iron, styli awaiting discovery at Bawsey.

Of equal importance, however, is the number of styli at Bawsey. Like its coinage, it is the density of examples that makes Bawsey remarkable, having now yielded seven styli, albeit one which is better described as a styliform pin. This is a total which puts it on a par with three other sites, Flixborough with twenty-two examples, Whitby with twelve and Little Carlton with thirteen or fourteen. More importantly, it illustrates that a few sites have particular concentrations. Other examples with clusters of styli are Barking Abbey (Essex) and Ryther (Yorks.) with five and Brandon with three.[53] It therefore seems to be the case that some places acted as particular foci for writing. Blair has seen this as indicative of an ecclesiastical presence, going on to see many 'productive' sites as what he calls 'crypto minsters'.[54] The argument is certainly seductive, but it remains true that we now appreciate there was a far more widespread level of lay literacy, especially in the higher stratum of Anglo-Saxon society – that very level which appears to be represented by the prestige material culture at sites such as Bawsey.[55] While a stylus is not, therefore,

---

1993-4, i, pp. 94-105; Marsden pers. comm.

[47] I hope to expand these arguments in a future paper. I have argued elsewhere that Caistor probably constituted an early Anglo-Saxon estate centre (Pestell 2012, pp. 74-6 and forthcoming) and excavations at Fishergate revealed large quantities of Ipswich ware (Ayers 1994). The number of *sceattas* known from excavations in Norwich remains small, but enough to suggest an origin to trade here too in the late seventh and early eighth centuries

[48] Pestell 2001, pp. 211-16; Hutcheson 2006

[49] Metcalf 2001, and Metcalf 2003 for the geographical variation of different *sceatta* types

[50] For a discussion of the circulation of coinage in this period, actually pointing to the rise in coinage minted at Ipswich 796-c.830, see Naismith 2012, pp. 209-14

[51] Of the 13 coins, three have no mint attribution possible. Two of Offa are by East Anglian moneyers. The only definite London mint coin is a penny of Berhtwulf of Mercia (840-52)

[52] For the Flixborough example see Pestell 2009, pp. 125-6 and 133-4 no. 1006. The Little Carlton example is recorded as PAS LIN-FE9130 (Treasure Case 2011 T677) although the eraser end now appears to have been found (February 2014: G Vickers pers. comm.)

[53] See further Pestell 2004, p. 43 table 1 for a listing of stylus-producing sites, albeit now out of date, and discussion of these sites in Pestell 2009

[54] Blair 2005, p. 209, fn. 116

[55] For the debate about literacy see Kelly 1990 and Lerer 1991. Coatsworth has recently accepted the difficulty in viewing styli as 'adequate evidence

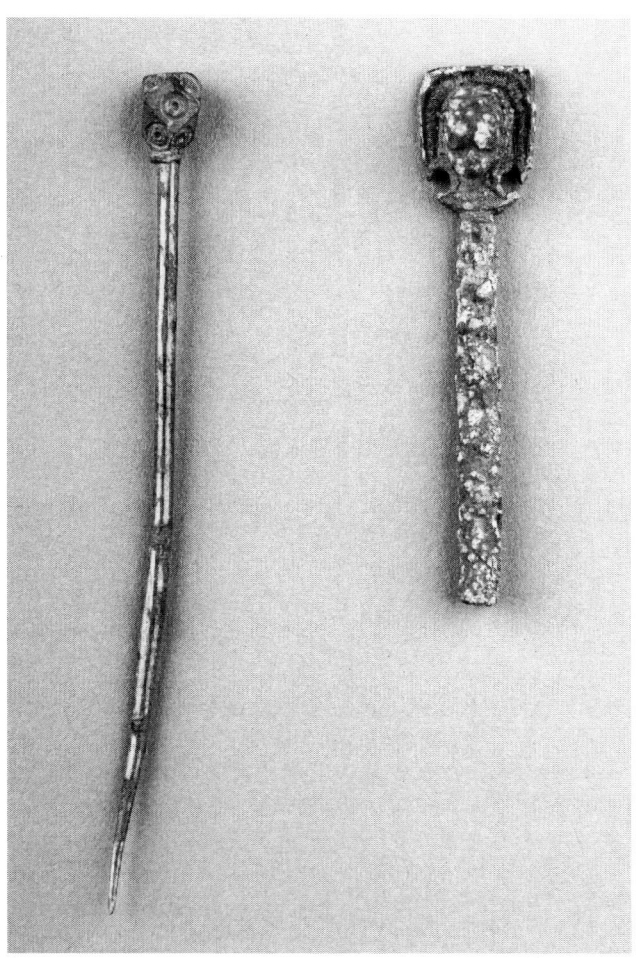

a material correlate of a monk or cleric, their presence in such numbers does suggest a more literate community which might include clerics. Loveluck has refined this argument for Flixborough, arguing that the site may have had different phases of occupation, so that some periods may have had more pronounced ecclesiastical settlement of the site than others.[56]

One final object with potential literate associations has been hitherto described as a pin-head. However, its shaft is very broad and the top end features a ninth-century style animal head, cast in the round, emerging from a square plate (Fig. 16). The reverse has a circular collar, apparently once holding a cabochon stone which would have created a 'double-sided' head quite unlike normal pins of this date. As a pin, the shaft would have been chunky and the double-sided head curiously top-heavy. However, might this have acted as some form of *æstel* or pointer for the reading of text? Although speculative, the form of the object is not dissimilar. While the known corpus of æstels is small, as an emerging artefact category archaeologists have inevitably been making new identifications only on the basis of those well-known from the Alfred and Minster Lovell jewel types.[57] Perhaps it was once far more common to use slightly smaller, more pin-like objects as æstels.

FIG. 16 (A) A POSSIBLE *ÆSTEL* FROM BAWSEY FOUND IN METAL-DETECTION, COMPARED WITH A TYPICAL MIDDLE ANGLO-SAXON POLYHEDRAL-HEADED PIN FROM SEDGEFORD. (B) DETAIL OF SIDE SHOWING THE ANIMAL-HEADED TERMINAL (PHOTOGRAPHS DAVID KIRKHAM, COURTESY NORWICH CASTLE MUSEUM AND ART GALLERY)

---

of monastic status on their own': Coatsworth 2011, pp. 779-80
[56] Loveluck 2001 and 2007, pp. 159-60
[57] Hinton 2008, pp. 32-7

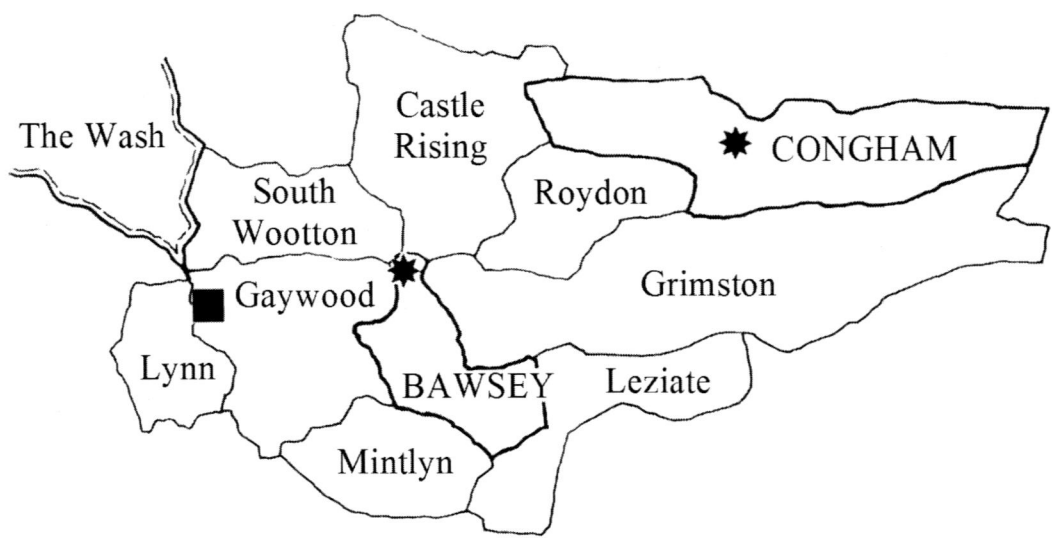

FIG. 17 PARISH BOUNDARIES AROUND BAWSEY (AUTHOR)

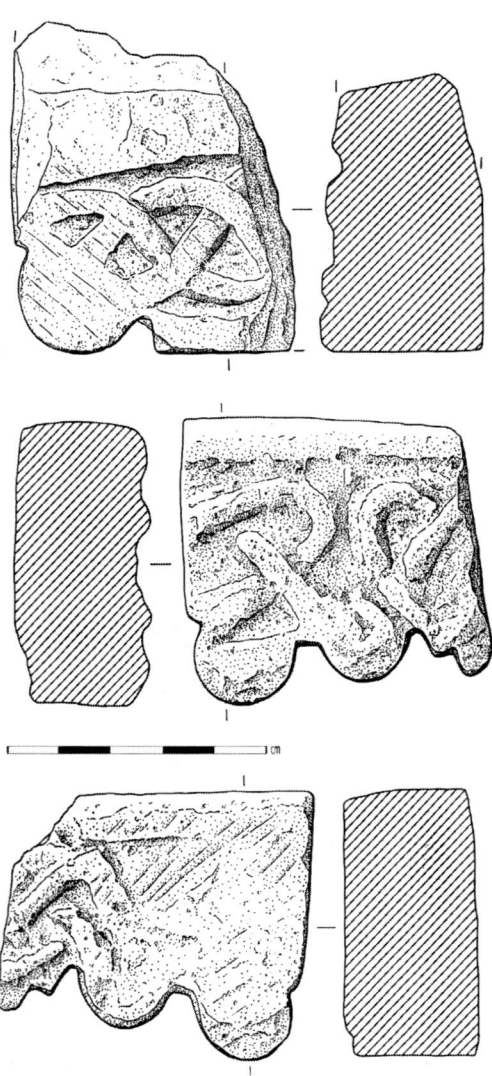

FIG. 18 ANGLO-SAXON GRAVE-COVER FRAGMENTS FROM BAWSEY CHURCH REUSED AS VOUSSOIRS IN THE NORMAN PERIOD. SCALE: 10CM DIVISIONS (DRAWN BY STEVEN ASHLEY)

If the more cerebral world of text is suggested by the styli, evidence for craftworking at Bawsey was strengthened by *Time Team*'s work. As we have seen, geophysics survey suggested a possible industrial area to the east of the church. Although the dating of this appears to be Saxo-Norman, some evidence of earlier craft-working on the site is provided by a bronze motif-piece disc bearing a 'bag-bellied' animal that appears to be a local variant of the Trewhiddle style (Fig. 3). These animals appear in similar form on the Pentney brooches, a collection of silver and silver-gilt jewellery found in 1977 only a few miles away from Bawsey.[58] The trial-piece itself suggests prestige metalworking and it would be unsurprising to see such craft practices being undertaken here.

Perhaps the most obvious feature at Bawsey, dominant on the top of the hill, is the church. That there was some ecclesiastical presence here from the Late Anglo-Saxon period at least is indicated by a number of Anglo-Saxon tomb cover fragments found on the site. One fragment was found by RR Clarke outside the north wall in 1950, while another slab was found in a field to the north of the church in 1960.[59] Further fragments of tomb cover were found when sixteen voussoirs from the outer order of the western tower arch fell between 1975-85: three were found to be reused, preserving Anglo-Saxon interlace decoration on their hidden faces (Fig. 18). Two of these have now been built back into the tower arch.[60] Assuming that the reused

---

[58] Webster and Backhouse 1991, cat. no. 187. Likewise, similarly 'bag-bellied' Trewhiddle animals appear on a new fragmentary silver disc brooch from a site currently called only 'South Norfolk' (Treasure case 2012 T319)

[59] There is no record of the first slab except that it carried interlace decoration and was of Late Anglo-Saxon date (HER 3328 notes). The second fragment is now King's Lynn Museum 1960.58. The HER file says this is complete but from its size it has clearly been cut down

[60] HER 3328 notes, September 1998. One of the voussoirs is retained in English Heritage's stores. The reuse of Late Anglo-Saxon grave covers in Norman work is known elsewhere in Norfolk, for instance a voussoir fragment that was found reused as ashlar in St Mary's Priory, Thetford

voussoirs all derive from the site, at least two funerary monuments may be represented. In design, the interlace plaits of the large fragment are loosely constructed and in their simplicity appear to follow the traits of the Fenland-type grave-covers, which feature interlace bordered by plain rectangular-section border moulding. While the larger piece perhaps represents an example from a sub-group with only a single broad panel on the upper surface, the smaller fragments are of the more usual type forming panels divided by a central cross or rib. They appear to date from *c*.1000-1068AD and are made of the distinctive grey shelly oolite of the Barnack area.[61]

Despite this, there was no physical evidence to suggest there had been an even earlier church on the site until *Time Team*'s discovery of the two Middle Anglo-Saxon burials to the west. In themselves, they need not necessarily have been associated with a church building, as there is increasing evidence for cemeteries existing in the landscape without churches, but in some cases in direct association with settlements. Thus, an example from Bramford in Suffolk was surrounded by a D-shaped enclosure ditch that went out of use in the Late Anglo-Saxon period, as indicated by a structure of that date constructed over the ditch's infill, but which never had a church associated with it.[62] It is perfectly possible that Bawsey's Middle Anglo-Saxon burials later came to have a church established to their east, perhaps in the late tenth or eleventh century, when the tomb cover was also used. Certainly, *Time Team*'s trenching yielded no evidence for an earlier phase of the church.[63]

Even if an early origin to the parish church on the site is still unclear, one curious aspect that does remain is the nature of the building that survives. Its ground-plan, featuring an axial tower, is in contrast to most Early Norman churches in East Anglia which employed a simple two-cell design; their towers, sometimes round, were usually added later at the west end. Furthermore, Ladbrooke's engraving of *c*.1831 suggests that St James' church might once also have had a south transept. An axial arrangement more often appears in churches that were of high status, like minster or mother churches, or of high patronage.[64] For instance, Aldeby in Norfolk was donated as a monastic cell to Norwich Cathedral Priory, while Great Dunham in Norfolk is recorded in a charter from Castle Acre Priory of 1138-1145 as having had a chapel of St Mary subject to it.[65] Ultimately the form dates back to Late Anglo-Saxon minster churches like Breamore.[66] With its axial tower and originally white-rendered external walls, Bawsey church would have been a highly visible landmark in the area, utilising an architectural form indicating prestige.

Batcock has dated the structure to *c*.1120,[67] yet the impressive design is somewhat at variance from the record provided by Domesday Book in 1086. This mentions Bawsey only twice, once as the holding of Wulfgeat, a freeman, who held half a carucate (about 60 acres) here and in nearby Ashwicken, and once as a carucate of land held by Robert Malet which was a *berewick* or subsidiary settlement of nearby Glosthorpe.[68] Ironically Glosthorpe was later absorbed into Bawsey. Because Domesday is arranged by landowner rather than by parish, it is not always easy to see where exact parcels of land lay, but on the face of it the church would hardly appear to belong to a landholder prepared to invest in such an impressive structure in such a visually dominant position.

While the evidence is circumstantial, a more likely owner of the site at Domesday was perhaps the East Anglian bishop whose land surrounded Bawsey to the south and west. A more complex tenurial background is almost certainly disguised by Domesday's laconic entries and one clue to this is arguably the parish boundary, which survives as a curious 'L'-shaped parish that has the appearance of having been cut out of an earlier, larger, land block (Fig. 17). The site of the church is peripheral to the parish, appearing at its northern tip. The more substantial parish of Gaywood to the west was an important manor of the East Anglian bishops prior to 1066 with three carucates of land, while Mintlyn to the south-west was again held solely by the bishops with half a plough. Leziate was held among the annexations of Baynard, but Roger Bigod's predecessor had held the patronage.[69] As Bigod was sheriff of Norfolk and Suffolk, it is at least possible that we see a hint of earlier royal control here. The parish is certainly far larger than the acreage recorded in Domesday, suggesting much of it must have been recorded elsewhere under another landholding. That Gaywood and Mintlyn were certainly key elements of the diocesan's holdings is underlined by Bishop Walter de Raleigh creating a park in Gaywood *c*.1240, apparently incorporating land in Mintlyn.

Is the reason for Bawsey's impressive church therefore a nod to its former status following the bishops' establishment of a new trading settlement at Bishop's Lynn, designed to exploit the newly evolving rivers and shorelines in this part of the Fen-edge? Such an exercise would be paralleled by Bishop Losinga's actions elsewhere in Norfolk, where

---

(now NCM L1995.2.3)

[61] Everson and Stocker 1999, pp. 46-9, who also note Barnack products appear to have been especially successful 'in monopolising the supply of grave-covers to those areas where good stone was scarce' (*ibid.*). I am very grateful to David Stocker for his comments on these fragments

[62] Martin *et al.* 1996, pp. 476-9

[63] For discussion of pre-churchyard burials existing up to *c*.850/900 see Blair 2005, pp. 228-45. His case is that there was an absence of small proprietary churches, whereas churchyard burial was practised earlier at minster sites. This brings us full circle to the issue of whether Bawsey might or might not have been an ecclesiastical centre at this date.

[64] Heywood (1996, p. 1) notes that the central tower makes it one of only 19 such churches in Norfolk

[65] Aldeby Priory was granted to the monks of Norwich 1107-1116, the gift of Hubert de Rye and his wife Agnes de Bellofago (or Beaufour). Hubert was an active supporter of Bishop Herbert de Losinga, being recorded as laying the second foundation stone of Norwich Cathedral, while Agnes was possibly niece of Bishop William de Bellofago, Losinga's predecessor as diocesan: Dodwell 1974, i, no. 2; Saunders 1939, pp. 50-1. For Great Dunham's subject chapel see Harper-Bill 1990, no. 29

[66] Fernie 1983, pp. 112-36

[67] Batcock 1991, pp. 114-16

[68] *LDB* fol. 149a-b and 153b

[69] *LDB* fol. 191a; 197b and 276b

the development of new sites could lead to churches being built, almost as memorials or territorial markers, on the old site. For instance, when St Michael's the principal Anglo-Saxon minster church in Norwich was closed down for the building of the cathedral in 1096, a new chapel was built to the east of the river Wensum and served by a monastic cell of the cathedral, St Leonard's priory. Similarly, when the old Anglo-Saxon cathedral site at North Elmham was closed by the construction over it of a private chapel, the laity were given an impressive new purpose-built parish church to the south.[70] The construction of St James' church may therefore have been no more than a demonstration of Bawsey's ancient status even after the spiritual and economic focus of activity had been relocated to Bishop's Lynn.[71]

Bawsey in its regional setting

How, then, should we seek to interpret the site at Bawsey? It can be looked at from a number of perspectives, including that of its place in a social and settlement hierarchy; as an economic focus; and also, arguably, as a component in wider political processes. As a settlement the material culture recovered clearly places it among a small number of sites that have yielded items of above-average wealth and with unusual find-types. This is most obvious in the appearance of styli and hanging-bowl mounts, objects which for some suggest ecclesiastical use, an interpretation which might agree with the suggested setting of Bawsey into the landholdings of the East Anglia bishops. Equally, the debate over the characterisation of settlements as 'monastic' or 'secular' potentially encourages us to interpret evidence representing only a 'snapshot in time' of a site's longer life.[72] Given the potential for the co-existence of secular and religious communities, or the mutable nature of sites, of more importance to the interpretation of Bawsey is its clear pre-eminence as an economic focus in west Norfolk in the eighth and early ninth century. While rural economic centres become harder to identify in the later Middle and Late Anglo-Saxon periods due to the fall in the number of coins in circulation, Bawsey's continued occupation is at least confirmed by the presence of an appreciable amount of metalwork and Thetford ware pottery. A presumed continuity in some trading activity is implied by the need or desire to maintain an economic focus in this area, necessitating the creation, or stimulation, of a settlement at Bishop's Lynn in the late eleventh century.

If, as seems likely, Bawsey had an economic function later discharged by Bishop's Lynn, its presence in north-west Norfolk may not have been simply fortuitous, or an organic development of exchange networks in the area. Rather, we may perhaps see Bawsey in a geo-political context, fitting into a series of other sites surrounding the wider fen basin. This pattern was remarked upon in a different context by Tom Plunkett when considering the development of Mercian art.[73] He noted similarities in many pieces of sculpture in particular, with important sites or possible centres of production. The findspots of several important objects, for instance the eighth-century whalebone plaque from Larling and the Pentney brooches already mentioned, fit into this geographical spread, indicating a putative cultural zone surrounding the Fenland basin, in which the patronage of monasteries was central.[74] This is not the same as saying all patronage or important sites were monastic, and for this writer the importance of the Church compared to the secular aristocracy has perhaps been over-stressed in the past. It is instructive to note the political implications for much of the patterning we can see.

In particular, the Liberty of Etheldreda is curious in its location in south-east Suffolk. While Ely abbey was refounded c.970, probably as a political move under West Saxon King Edgar to help subjugate Mercia, its extensive Suffolk landholdings are a contrast to the local endowments of the other fenland houses at Thorney, Crowland, Peterborough and Ramsey, all founded at the same time and by the same circle of monastic reformers.[75] The origins of Ely's Liberty might more convincingly predate the tenth century, and quite probably extend back to the seventh or eighth. Ely's earliest saints, Etheldreda and her sisters, were members of the East Anglian royal family, and the abbey was always at the frontier of their kingdom.[76] Many of the landholdings that supported the abbey, however, were in that area that can be most convincingly seen as the East Anglian royal family's heartlands, the Suffolk Sandlings. This area contained royal ship burials at Snape and Sutton Hoo, the royal palace at Rendlesham, the episcopal *sedes* at *Dommoc* (probably Walton Castle) and the *emporium* of Ipswich. As such, the abbey at Ely may well have been maintained as a frontier post funded by lands, as well as symbolically attached to, an area intimately connected with the East Anglian ruling family.

Links between these two areas were also crucial. A geographical view of the kingdom emphasises how this was the strategic gap in the kingdom (Fig. 19), where it was defensively weakest from other rival powers to the south and west, most notably the Mercians. More important, it was the Fenland basin that provided control of access to resources between the Midlands and the Continent. To ensure their economic vibrancy, the royal family with their Sandlings powerbase need to control what John Newman has described as the 'Lark-Gipping corridor', using

---

[70] Pestell 2001, pp. 206-11 and 221-2; Wade-Martins 1980, pp. 188-9 and figs. 10, 12 and 158
[71] Pestell 2001, pp. 211-16; Hutcheson 2006
[72] Loveluck 2001, pp. 120-1; Davies 2010

[73] 'It may, indeed, be possible to understand the development of Anglian art ... as the product of a primarily coastal and fluviatile system of communications ... received and evolved at many centres of high status near the estuarine inlets of that shore': Plunkett 1998, pp. 202-3 and fig. 63
[74] Plunkett 1998, pp. 211-12. For the Larling plaque see Green 1971
[75] For Edgar's use of monasteries see Fisher 1952 and Banton 1982. Ely's Liberty and landholdings are mapped in Pestell 2004, figs 33 and 24 respectively
[76] As described by Bede comprising a region of 600 hides: *HE* iv, 19. The implication is equally that the Fenland to the south around Cambridge was probably not to be associated with the kingdom – see also Hines 1999

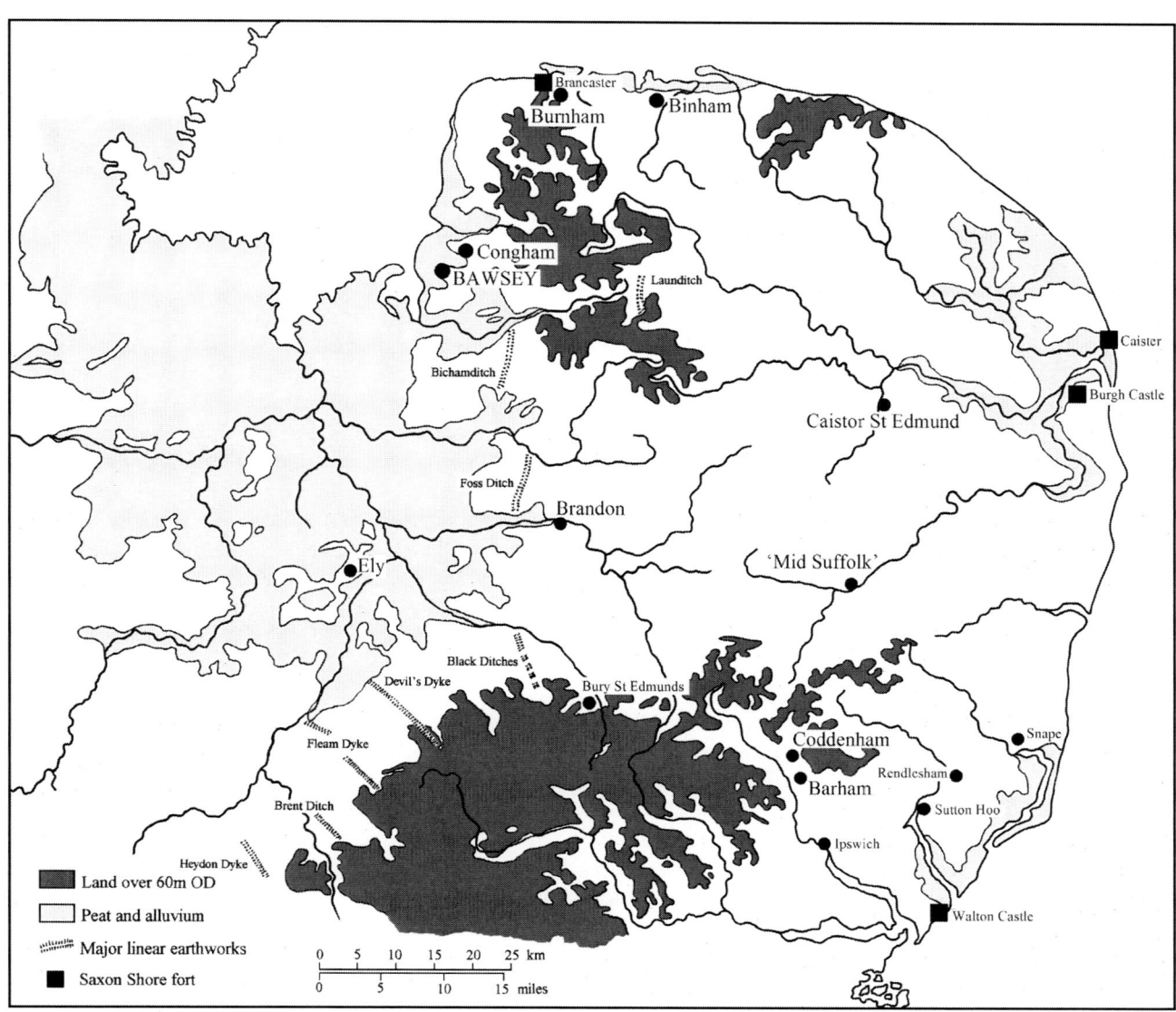

FIG. 19 EAST ANGLIA AND KEY SITES FROM THE SEVENTH AND EIGHTH CENTURIES MENTIONED IN THE TEXT (AUTHOR)

the river system between the two areas.[77] The wealth of a number of sites that may be described as 'productive' illustrates this link, and the importance of this western area of the kingdom is reiterated in Hutcheson's plot of coin-productive sites.[78]

If Ely provided one royally-controlled centre in this nexus of trade, Bawsey arguably provided another, positioned at the margin of the Wash's south-east coast, which together helped control of the trade in the southern Wash basin. Recent research has emphasised the wealth of such coastal (and estuarine) communities, and indeed the importance of the Wash region to trade more generally and the income available to kings through the imposition of tolls.[79] It is probably the case that Fen-edge sites were best placed for trade and exchange occurring at the interface of maritime and riverine routes. The economic importance of Bawsey came as a result of these Continental contacts.

There is, of course, still much debate about the nature and extent of 'control' in trade, not least as the model of a command economy leading to the creation of *emporia* like *Hamwic* and Ipswich under royal patronage has been subject to considerable critique.[80] Nevertheless, royal involvement is arguably the key to the sudden flowering of many 'productive' sites from the second half of the seventh century, just as kingship too became better established with larger, more definite, territories. In these terms, it is also far easier to see the regulation of trade leading directly into the Midlands lying behind the struggle for control of Middle Anglia between the Mercian and East Anglian kings.

Other sites perhaps reflect the development of this control of trade from a less structured, preceding, demand economy. The 'productive' site at Burnham in north-west Norfolk

---

[77] Newman 2003, pp. 107-8
[78] Hutcheson 2006, fig. 1
[79] Thomas 2013; Loveluck and Tys 2006; Kelly 1992

[80] A paradigm adapted from anthropological models and proposed most influentially by Hodges in his *Dark Age Economics* (1982, revised 1989). For critiques see further Moreland 2000, Ulmschneider 2000, Saunders 2001, Naylor 2004 and Pestell 2011

for example has a strong Migration-period assemblage of metalwork including Continental pieces, perhaps indicating cultural exchange networks originating in the seventh century before becoming trading sites with *sceatta* loss in the early eighth.[81] This pattern is possibly seen in other sites with concentrations of early gold coinage, like Coddenham and Rendlesham in Suffolk.[82] So far, Norfolk seems not to have yielded such 'productive' sites with early origins – notwithstanding the debatable evidence from Bawsey discussed above. The exception may be Congham, once again in west Norfolk, which has yielded a linear spread of metal-detected material straddling a western, lowland, branch of the Icknield Way. Three tremisses have now been recorded as well as a number of *sceattas*.[83] The fact that more such early sites have – so far – been found in Suffolk is curious but potentially shows the growing reach of East Anglian kingship, or at least control of the area by one family, lay in south-east Suffolk before extending by the late seventh century into Norfolk, perhaps through the Lark-Gipping corridor.

Interestingly, another recent find may support this hypothesis, namely a hoard of five gold bracteates and two arm-rings or bracelets, one of gold, from Binham in north Norfolk. Not only is this the largest hoard of gold from sixth-century England, it fits within a wider concentration of bracteates, another two sites in Brinton and Blakeney having yielded single examples.[84] That all three sites occur within a six mile radius, yet are the only complete gold bracteates known from Norfolk, is of undoubted significance. On the one hand it might indicate the focus of an early redistributive network in this area. Equally likely at this date, any such contact depended upon the personal contact of high-status individuals with peers in the bracteate-using society of Scandinavia and northern Germany. This perhaps reinforces the nature of bracteates as 'special purpose' money or their use in high-level gift-exchange.[85] It is not only the use of bracteates that is notable, but their designs; these relate them to a shared ideological background, as does the fact that the Binham bracteates had been deposited as a hoard. This is a Scandinavian practice and so far Binham is the only certain case of bracteate deposition known from England. Finally, the concentration of bracteate finds and hoards has often been associated in Scandinavia with high-status settlements or 'central places'. The evidence from Binham is less certain, although if we can see some wealthy family in command of contacts and resources here, it may well provide an explanation for the discovery of a silver-gilt Kentish brooch in a field opposite the bracteate findspot.[86] It therefore seems possible that we may be seeing a very early focus for prestige goods exchange within an emerging territory in north Norfolk, perhaps within the area contained by the Stiffkey and Glaven rivers. So far there is no obvious 'productive' site in this area to signal continued economic success and it may be that whichever aristocratic family was in control of this area came to lose their local powerbase as the East Anglian kingdom became controlled from south-east Suffolk.[87]

If the stimulation and taxation of trade under royal control is accepted, as remains the dominant paradigm for *emporia* like *Hamwic* and Ipswich, then clearly the political as well as purely economic implications of sites like Bawsey need to be more fully explored. As I hope I have shown, Bawsey has an important position within the settlement hierarchy of East Anglia, but also within the political and cultural frameworks of the Middle Anglo-Saxon kingdom. While the exact interpretation of the site remains enigmatic, our current knowledge could place it within both secular and religious worlds. It may also explain why this former importance was later celebrated and memorialised in the twelfth century with the construction of an impressive parish church.

Ultimately, Bawsey's place in the kingdom of East Anglia is likely to be determined by comparison with other sites in the Fen basin, and Eastern England more widely. Its coinage demonstrates that it was economically of front-rank but, much as the twisting river systems of the Fens evolved, our interpretations are likely to shift further with the discovery of new sites – and the better understanding of existing ones.

Acknowledgements

My first debt in the writing of this paper is to Andrew Rogerson himself, who has discussed Bawsey with me for a number of years as I have (too) slowly been writing up the *Time Team* work. I hope seeing an interim statement of the results will provide some satisfaction, as well as whetting the appetite. However, I also apologise for encouraging him to discuss matters (I hope unwittingly) that I have incorporated into the text. I would also like to thank those various authors who have contributed reports to the writing up of the site, and whose work cited as 'in the site archive' here will be presented in full in the forthcoming report: Sue Anderson, Margaret Cox, John Gater, David King, Louise Loe, Adrian Marsden, and perhaps most important Pete Bellamy and Rebecca Montague who began the writing up and who prepared the excavation drawings. The work of the late Mark Blackburn was of course essential in the early years of Bawsey's discovery, and Pete Watkins very kindly provided the contour-data map at the last minute.

---

[81] Rogerson 2003, pp. 114-15
[82] Plunkett 2001, Newman 2003. Rendlesham is now the subject of an archaeological research project for which see Scull forthcoming. A further site producing early gold coinage as well as *sceattas*, called 'mid Suffolk' is still confidential to deter nighthawking
[83] Rogerson 2003, pp. 115-16; Davies 2010
[84] The hoard is published fully in Behr and Pestell forthcoming
[85] Gaimster 1992
[86] The brooch is of Avent's Class 7.1 (Avent 1975) and is now NCM 2006.184

[87] Interestingly, the only gold bracteate from Suffolk was found at Undley, Lakenheath, yet it appears among another cluster of bracteates including four silver examples from cemeteries in Eriswell (Lakenheath) and West Stow (Behr and Pestell forthcoming). Once again, these appear on the Fen-edge and close to the strategically-important river Lark

Bibliography

Avent, R. 1975, *Anglo-Saxon Disc and Composite Brooches*, British Archaeological Reports British Series 11 (Oxford)

Ayers, B.S. 1994, *Excavations at Fishergate, Norwich, 1985* East Anglian Archaeology 68 (Norwich)

Banton, N. 1982, 'Monastic Reform and the Unification of Tenth-Century England' in S. Mews (ed.), *Religion and National Identity* Studies in Church History 8 (Oxford), pp. 71-85

Batcock, N. 1991, *The Ruined and Disused Churches of Norfolk* East Anglian Archaeology 51 (Gressenhall)

Behr, C., and Pestell, T., forthcoming, 'The Bracteate Hoard from Binham – An Early Anglo-Saxon Central Place?' *Medieval Archaeology* 58

Blackburn, M.A.B. 2003, "Productive' Sites and the Pattern of Coin-Loss in England AD 600-1180' in Pestell and Ulmschneider (eds), *Markets in Early Medieval Europe Trading and 'Productive' Sites, 650-850* (Windgather: Macclesfield). pp. 12-36

Blair, J, 2005. *The Church in Anglo-Saxon Society* (Oxford University Press: Oxford)

Blinkhorn, P. 2012, *The Ipswich Ware Project. Ceramics, Trade and Society in Middle Saxon England* Medieval Pottery Research Group Occasional Paper 7 (Dorchester; MPRG)

Bruce-Mitford, R., with Raven, S. 2005, *A Corpus of Late Celtic Hanging Bowls* (Oxford University Press: Oxford)

Clarke, H. 1970, 'Excavations on a Kiln Site at Grimston Pott Row, Norfolk' *Norfolk Archaeology* 35, pp. 79-95

Coatsworth, E. 2011, 'The Material Culture of the Anglo-Saxon Church' in H. Hamerow, D.A. Hinton and S. Crawford (eds.), *The Oxford Handbook of Anglo-Saxon Archaeology* (Oxford), pp. 779-796

Daubney, A. 2007, 'Heckington' in H. Geake 'Portable Antiquities Scheme Report' *Medieval Archaeology* 51, pp. 211-32 at pp. 221-2

Davies, G. 2010, 'Early Medieval "Rural Centres" and West Norfolk: A Growing Picture of Diversity, Complexity and Changing Lifestyles' *Medieval Archaeology* 54, pp. 89-122

Davies, J. 2008, *The Land of Boudica Prehistoric and Roman Norfolk* (Oxford)

Davies, J. forthcoming, *A Corpus of Iron Age Material in Norwich Castle Museum and Art Gallery*

Dodwell, B. (ed.), 1974, *The Charters of Norwich Cathedral Priory I* Pipe Roll Society New Series 40 (London)

Drury, P. 1993, 'Ceramic Building Materials' in S. Margeson *Norwich Households: The Medieval and Post-Medieval Finds from Norwich Survey Excavations 1971-1978* East Anglian Archaeology 58 (Norwich), pp. 163-8

Eames, E. 1955, 'The Products of a Medieval Tile Kiln at Bawsey, King's Lynn' *Antiquaries' Journal* 35, pp. 162-181

Ekwall, E. 1960, *The Concise Oxford Dictionary of English Place-Names*, 4th edn. (Oxford University Press: Oxford)

Everson, P., and Stocker, D. 1999, *Corpus of Anglo-Saxon Stone Sculpture: Lincolnshire* (Oxford)

Fairweather, F.H. 1931, 'Excavations in Norfolk: Summer 1930' *Antiquaries' Journal* 11, pp. 168-9

Fernie, E. 1983, *The Architecture of the Anglo-Saxons* (London)

Fisher, D.J.V. 1952, 'The Anti-Monastic Reaction in the Reign of Edward the Martyr' *Cambridge Historical Journal* 10, pp. 254-70

Gaimster, M. 1992, 'Scandinavian Gold Bracteates in Britain. Money and Media in the Dark Ages' *Medieval Archaeology* 36, pp. 1-28

Gelling, M., and Cole, A. 2000, *The Landscape of Place-Names* (Shaun Tyas: Stamford)

Green, E.B. 1971, 'An Anglo-Saxon Bone Plaque from Larling, Norfolk' *Antiquaries' Journal* 51, pp. 321-3 and Pl. LXVIIb

Harper-Bill, C. 1990, *English Episcopal Acta VI: Norwich 1070-1214* (Oxford)

HE, Colgrave, B., and Mynors, R.A.B. 1969, *Bede's Ecclesiastical History* Oxford Medieval Texts (Oxford)

Heywood, S. 1996, 'The Ruined Church of St Mary, Bawsey St James' Unpublished report in Norfolk HER 3328

Hines, J. 1999, 'The Anglo-Saxon Archaeology of the Cambridgeshire Region and the Middle Anglian Kingdom' *Anglo-Saxon Studies in Archaeology and History* 10, pp. 135-49

Hinton, D.A. 2008, *The Alfred Jewel and Other Late Anglo-Saxon Metalwork* (Oxford)

Hodges, R. 1982, *Dark Age Economics The Origins of Towns and Trade AD 600-1000* (London)

Hutcheson, A. 2006, 'The Origins of King's Lynn? Control of Wealth on the Wash Prior to the Norman Conquest' *Medieval Archaeology* 50, pp. 71-104

Jennings, S. 1981, *Eighteen Centuries of Pottery from Norwich* East Anglian Archaeology 18 (Norwich)

Joy, J. forthcoming, *The Snettisham Treasure* (British Museum Press, London)

Kelly, S. 1990, 'Anglo-Saxon Lay Society and the Written Word' in R. McKitterick (ed.), *The Uses of Literacy in Early Medieval Europe* (Cambridge), pp. 36-62

Kelly, S. 1992, 'Trading Privileges From Eighth Century England' *Early Medieval Europe* 1, pp. 3-28

Kelly's Directory, 1883, *Kelly's Directory for Cambridgeshire, Norfolk and Suffolk* (London)

LDB, Brown, P., (ed.), 1984, *Domesday Book Norfolk*, 2 vols. (Chichester)

Leah, M. 1994, *The Late Saxon and Medieval Pottery Industry of Grimston, Norfolk. Excavations 1962-92* East Anglian Archaeology 64 (Gressenhall)

Lerer, S. 1991, *Literacy and Power in Anglo-Saxon Literature* (Lincoln and London)

Loveluck, C.P. 2001, 'Wealth, Waste and Conspicuous Consumption. Flixborough and its Importance for Mid and Late Saxon Settlement Studies' in H. Hamerow and A. MacGregor (eds.) *Image and Power in the Archaeology of Early Medieval Britain* (Oxbow Books: Oxford), pp. 78-130

Loveluck, C.P. 2007, *Rural Settlement, Lifestyles and Social Change in the Later First Millennium AD: Anglo-Saxon Flixborough in its Wider Context* Excavations at Flixborough 4 (Oxbow Books: Oxford)

Loveluck, C., and Tys, D. 2006, 'Coastal Societies, Exchange and Identity Along the Channel and Southern North Sea Shores of Europe, AD 600-1000' *Journal of Maritime Archaeology* 1:2, pp. 140-69

Marsden, A. 2013, 'The Middle Saxon Coins from the Caistor St Edmund Excavations and Metal-detector Survey 2012' *Norfolk Archaeological Trust Spring Newsletter*, pp. 6-7

Martin, E., Pendleton, C., Plouviez, J., and Wreathall, D. 1996, 'Archaeology in Suffolk 1995' *Proceedings of the Suffolk Institute of Archaeology* 38, pp. 457-85

Metcalf, D.M. 1993-4, *Thrymsas and Sceattas in the Ashmolean Museum Oxford* Royal Numismatic Society Special Publication 27, 3 vols. (London)

Metcalf, M. 2001, 'Determining the Mint-Attribution of East Anglian Sceattas Through Regression Analysis' *British Numismatic Journal* 70, pp. 1-11

Metcalf, M. 2003, 'Variations in the Composition of the Currency at Different Places in England' in T. Pestell and K. Ulmschneider (eds.), *Markets in Early Medieval Europe Trading and 'Productive' Sites, 650-850* (Windgather: Macclesfield). pp. 37-47

Milligan, W.F. 1982, 'The Pottery' in J.G. Coad and A.D.F. Streeten, 'Excavations at Castle Acre Castle, Norfolk 1972-77: Country House and Castle of the Norman Earls of Surrey' *Archaeological Journal* 139, pp. 138-301 at pp. 199-227

Moreland, J. 2000, 'Concepts of the Early Medieval Economy' in I.L. Hansen and C. Wickham (eds.) *The Long Eighth Century* (Leiden), pp. 1-34

Naismith, R. 2012, *Money and Power in Anglo-Saxon England The Southern English Kingdoms, 757-865* Cambridge Studies in Medieval Life and Thought 4th ser (Cambridge)

Naylor, J. 2004, *An Archaeology of Trade in Middle Saxon England* British Archaeological Reports British Series 376 (Oxford)

Newman, J. 2003, 'Exceptional Finds, Exceptional Sites? Barham and Coddenham, Suffolk' in T. Pestell and K. Ulmschneider (eds.), *Markets in Early Medieval Europe Trading and 'Productive' Sites, 650-850* (Windgather: Macclesfield), pp. 97-109

Pestell, T.J. 2001, 'Monastic Foundation Strategies in the Early Norman Diocese of Norwich' Anglo-Norman Studies 21 (Woodbridge), pp. 199-229

Pestell, T.J. 2004, *Landscapes of Monastic Foundation The Establishment of Religious Houses in East Anglia, c.650-1200* Anglo-Saxon Studies 5 (Boydell: Woodbridge)

Pestell, T.J. 2009, 'The Styli' in D.H. Evans and C.P. Loveluck (eds.) *Life and Economy at Early Medieval Flixborough, c.AD 600-1000: The Artefact Evidence* Excavations at Flixborough 2 (Oxbow Books: Oxford), pp. 123-37

Pestell, T. 2011, 'Markets, *Emporia*, *Wics*, and 'Productive' Sites: Pre-Viking Trade Centres in Anglo-Saxon England' in H. Hamerow, D.A. Hinton and S. Crawford (eds.), *The Oxford Handbook of Anglo-Saxon Archaeology* (Oxford), pp. 556-579

Pestell, T. 2012, 'Paganism in Early Anglo-Saxon East Anglia' in T.A. Heslop, E. Mellings and M. Thøfner (eds.) *Art, Faith and Place in East Anglia From Prehistory to the Present* (Woodbridge), pp. 66-87

Pestell, T., forthcoming, 'Runic Finds from the Kingdom of East Anglia and Their Archaeological Contexts' in G. Waxenberger and K. Kazazzi (eds.) *Proceedings of the Eichstatt Symposium on Runes*

Pestell, T., and Ulmschneider, K. (eds.) 2003, *Markets in Early Medieval Europe Trading and 'Productive' Sites, 650-850* (Windgather: Macclesfield)

Plunkett, S.J. 1998, 'The Mercian Perspective' in S.M. Foster (ed.), *The St Andrews Sarcophagus A Pictish Masterpiece and Its International Connections* (Dublin), pp. 202-26

Plunkett, S.J. 2001, 'Some Recent Metalwork Discoveries from the Area of the Gipping Valley, and their Local Context' in P. Binski and W. Noel (eds.) *New Offerings, Ancient Treasures. Studies in Medieval Art For George Henderson* (Stroud), pp. 61-87

Richards, J.D. 1999, 'What's So Special about 'Productive Sites'?' in T. Dickinson and D. Griffiths (eds.) *The Making of Kingdoms* Anglo-Saxon Studies in Archaeology and History 10 (Oxford), pp. 71-80

Richmond, H., Taylor, R., and Wade-Martins, P. 1982, 'Nos. 28-34 Queen Street, King's Lynn' *East Anglian Archaeology* 14 (Gressenhall), pp. 108-24

Rogerson, A. 2003, 'Six Middle Anglo-Saxon Sites in West Norfolk' in T. Pestell and K. Ulmschneider (eds.), *Markets in Early Medieval Europe Trading and 'Productive' Sites, 650-850* (Windgather: Macclesfield), pp. 110-21

Saunders, H.W. (ed. and transl.), 1939, *The First Register of Norwich Cathedral Priory* Norfolk Records Society 11 (Norwich)

Saunders, T. 2001, 'Early Medieval Emporia and the Tributary Social Function' in D. Hill and R. Cowie (eds.), *Wics: The Early Medieval Trading Centres of Northern Europe* (Sheffield), pp. 7-13

Scull, C., forthcoming, 'Archaeology and Geographies of Jurisdiction: evidence from South-East Suffolk in the 7th Century' in J. Caroll, A. Reynolds, and B. Yorke (eds.), *Power and Place in Later Roman and Early Medieval Europe* (London, British Academy)

Soil Survey 1983, *Soils of England and Wales Sheet 4 Eastern England* (Soil Survey of England and Wales)

Thomas, A. 2013, 'Rivers of Gold? The Coastal Zone Between the Humber and the Wash in the Mid Saxon Period' *Anglo-Saxon Studies in Archaeology and History* 18, pp. 97-118

Thomas, G. 1996, 'Silver Wire Strap-Ends from East Anglia' *Anglo-Saxon Studies in Archaeology and History* 9, pp. 81-100

Thomas, G. 2009, 'Strap-ends' in D.H. Evans and C.P. Loveluck (eds.) *Life and Economy at Early Medieval Flixborough, c.AD 600-1000: The Artefact Evidence* Excavations at Flixborough 2 (Oxbow Books: Oxford), pp. 7-16

Ulmschneider, K. 2000, *Markets, Minsters and Metal-Detectors: The Archaeology of Middle Saxon Lincolnshire and Hampshire Compared* British Archaeological Reports British Series 307 (Oxford)

Wade-Martins, P. 1980, *Excavations at North Elmham Park 1967-72* East Anglian Archaeology 9, 2 vols. (Gressenhall)

Webster, L., and Backhouse, J. 1991, *The Making of England Anglo-Saxon Art and Culture AD600-900* (London)

White, W. 1836, *History, Gazetteer and Directory of Norfolk* (Sheffield)

The Franshams in context: isolated churches and common edge drift

Tom Williamson

Introduction

Andrew Rogerson has, over the years, made many notable contributions to our archaeological and historical knowledge. Some of the most important concern the character of Norfolk's medieval landscape, and these arose in part from his systematic fieldwalking surveys of Barton Bendish and, in particular, Great and Little Fransham.[1] In the latter parishes Rogerson was able to demonstrate – as Peter Wade-Martins had previously done in his survey of village sites in the Launditch Hundred, and Alan Davidson at Hales and elsewhere – that the isolated churches which constitute one of the distinctive features of Norfolk's countryside were the consequence of a major adjustment of settlement which occurred in the course of the eleventh and twelfth centuries.[2] Following the stabilisation of settlement in the seventh or eighth century, a single focus in Great Fransham grew *in situ*, and was joined in late Saxon times by another in Little Fransham, both eventually acquiring parish churches. But from the eleventh century farms began to be established on new sites, some distance away: sites which post-medieval maps show were located on the margins of greens and commons. This initial dispersion of settlement was, moreover, followed by the wholesale migration of farmsteads to such locations, creating long lines of common-edge settlement and leaving the two parish churches isolated in the midst of the fields. Rogerson, because of the particularly intensive and systematic character of his fieldwork, was able to add important, additional information to the narrative already outlined by Wade-Martins and Davison. In particular, whereas the former had favoured a post-Conquest date for the movement to the commons, Rogerson was able to demonstrate, with some confidence, that it was already under way by the mid eleventh century.[3]

In general, Norfolk's isolated churches, and the middle and later Saxon settlements with which they are associated, are normally located close to areas of relatively well-drained and fertile soils; the greens and commons to which settlement migrated, in contrast, usually occupy areas of more poorly-draining or acidic ground, difficult or unrewarding to cultivate. Yet it must be emphasised that while isolated churches are a particularly noticeable and characteristic feature of the county's landscape, they are not ubiquitous. Many Norfolk churches are more conventionally sited, within villages; and many others are not truly isolated, but are instead in marginal locations, in the sense that they lie at one end of a settlement which has evidently expanded away from them, usually towards, and partially around, an area of common grazing. Indeed, it is hard to draw a neat conceptual line between the expansion of settlement towards and around the edges of commons, and the drift or migration of settlement away from old sites. The phenomenon might be likened to a blob of mercury: if the main focus of dwellings developed at a sufficient distance from the church, then its 'tail' would seemingly be pulled away after it, leaving the church behind. Nor, in a more general sense, is it possible to distinguish clearly between churches which have been marginalised by the migration of settlement, and those where the growth of settlement in alternative locations has simply suppressed the development of an older site.

To some historians and archaeologists, regional idiosyncrasies in medieval field systems and settlement patterns have ancient roots: they originated in the early and middle Saxon, Roman or even prehistoric periods. They are manifestations of long-term regional cultures, are related to distinct and enduring forms of social organisation, or reflect long-term differences in population density, and in the relative extent of cleared and wooded land.[4] Those who approach medieval landscapes from these kinds of perspectives tend to emphasise the differences, rather than the similarities, between different parts of England. But it is also useful to explore the alternative possibility: that all rural landscapes, in lowland England at least, represent variations on the same essential themes, and that the differences between them are the outcome of the interplay of the same broad range of environmental, economic and perhaps social influences. Landscapes developed over time, in complex ways, rather than simply being, in Homan's famous words, 'the engraving of societies older than written history'.[5]

In this context we should note that churches left isolated by the migration of farms and cottages to the margins of commons, while a particular feature of the Norfolk landscape, are not unique to it. Peter Warner thus highlighted the importance of this phenomenon in north east Suffolk; while sporadic examples can be found in many parts of lowland England.[6] In Hertfordshire, for example, places like Little Gaddesden, Tewin or Sacombe are very reminiscent of Norfolk parishes, with isolated churches located on the edges of clay uplands, and the main focus of settlement strung around one or more large commons on higher and heavier ground.[7] Such patterns of

---

[1] Rogerson 1995; Rogerson *et al.* 1997
[2] Wade-Martins 1980; Davison 1990
[3] Rogerson 1995, p. 161
[4] Roberts and Wrathmell 2000 and 2002; Rippon 2007 and 2008
[5] Homans 1941, p. 13
[6] Warner 1987
[7] Rowe and Williamson 2013, pp. 77-8, 97

movement and expansion are in turn a subset of a more general tendency for late eleventh, twelfth and thirteenth-century settlements to demonstrate a degree of 'mobility', highlighted many years ago by Christopher Taylor.[8] This included, in particular, the growth of settlements along major transport routes, leading to the stagnation or dwindling of older sites or the drift of settlement away from them. Wade-Martins noted how some of the Launditch villages, such as Mileham, expanded towards, or relocated along, major roads.[9] Taylor similarly pointed to the way in which, on its course through Cambridgeshire, the Roman road Ermine Street appears to have sucked neighbouring settlement towards it, so that a whole string of villages, lying along the road, have churches which stand 500 metres or more away, isolated from or only loosely connected to them: notable examples include Arrington, Caxton and Papworth Everard.[10] Villages hugging major roads, separated to varying degrees from their churches, are a particularly frequent feature of counties in the south-east of England like Hertfordshire, which are crossed by numerous major routes heading for London. Churches poorly related to their settlements as a consequence of subsequent growth and/or movement are thus a relatively common feature of the landscapes of lowland England, and the isolated churches of Norfolk, although perhaps an extreme example, are nevertheless part of a wider pattern.

In the pages that follow I will attempt to elucidate the phenomena – sometimes but not always connected – of common-edge settlement, and of marginal or isolated churches. I shall do so by considering not just Norfolk but also two other counties, lying no great distance away, which provide a useful contrast and comparison: Northamptonshire and Hertfordshire (Fig. 1). The former was, in the early Middle Ages, less densely populated and less wealthy than Norfolk. It also differed from it in having a landscape almost entirely 'champion' in character, comprising nucleated villages farming extensive and highly communal open fields. Approximations to such landscapes could, it is true, be found in the north and west of Norfolk but with differences which, while subtle, are enough for many archaeologists to exclude these areas from the true 'heartland' of the 'champion', defined by some as the 'Central Province'.[11] Hertfordshire, except for the far north, similarly lay outside the 'champion'. It was, like much of Norfolk, characterised by a dispersed pattern of settlement, although in this case featuring numerous ring-fence farms and roadside hamlets, in addition to common-edge settlements. It was for the most part a 'woodland' county, to use the term employed by early topographers, characterised by 'irregular' open-field systems and early enclosure. There is no space here to examine in detail the various contrasts in the medieval landscape not only

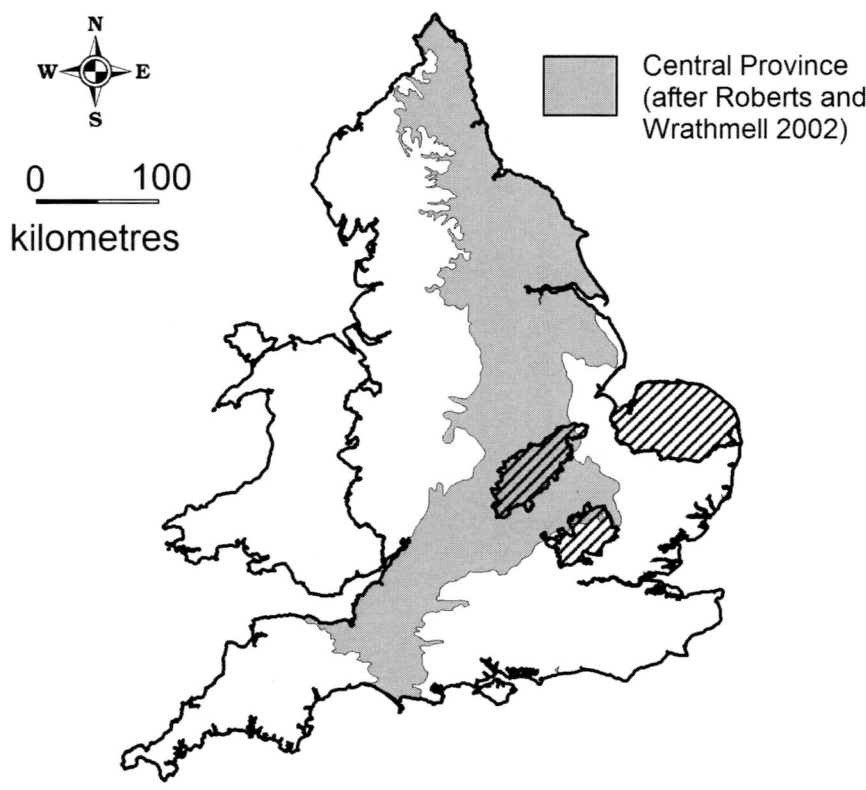

FIG. 1 THE THREE COUNTIES DISCUSSED IN THIS CHAPTER – NORFOLK, HERTFORDSHIRE, AND NORTHAMPTONSHIRE – AND THEIR RELATIONSHIP WITH THE 'CENTRAL PROVINCE'

---

[8] Taylor 1978; Taylor 1983, pp. 151-604
[9] Wade-Martins 1980, p. 47
[10] Taylor 1973, pp. 227-8

[11] Roberts and Wrathmell 2002

between, but also within, these counties. My intention is simply to examine in each of them common-edge settlement, and the relationship between churches and settlement, partly to cast new light on these particular features of the landscape, but partly to learn more about the wider character of regional variation in medieval England.

Common-edge Settlement

Norfolk, before the large-scale enclosures of the late eighteenth and early nineteenth centuries, was characterised by a wide variety of commons, in terms of both ecology and size. In general terms, the largest areas were associated with deposits of acidic, sandy or gravelly drift, and many of these comprised open heathland, or carried wood pastures which, in the course of the medieval and post-medieval periods, degenerated to heath.[12] They generally had margins which were sparsely-settled, relative to their area: houses were clustered along one or two sides, or were thinly scattered around them. In the south and east of the county, on the main mass of boulder clays, commons tended to be smaller – diminutive 'greens' – and had margins which were often, although not always, more densely settled (that is, they had a higher area: marginal dwelling ratio).[13] The concentration of settlement around relatively small greens, rather than larger commons, is a standard feature of the great boulder clay plateau which extends beyond the county, southwards and westwards through the middle of Suffolk and northern Essex, and on into eastern Hertfordshire. This extensive topographic region is bounded on most sides – and not only in Norfolk – by districts featuring more acidic and less fertile soils, often giving rise to more extensive commons. In Hertfordshire, for example, there was a clear contrast before the enclosures of the nineteenth century between the boulder clay districts in the east of the county, with numerous small greens, and the Chiltern dipslope and the London clays in the west and south, where small 'greens' existed but alongside far larger tracts of heath and other kinds of common.[14]

Not surprisingly, the small greens of the East Anglian boulder clays often appear to be the remains of larger and more continuous areas of open ground: they are the fragments left after areas of farmland, usually with roughly oval outlines, had been 'punched', as it were, out of them. The interconnected greens which still survive in the west of the parish of Much Hadham in east Hertfordshire are typical (Fig. 2). Westland Green, the smaller Piggs Green, and a number of tiny triangles of common land, are all

Fig. 2 The development of the landscape around Westland Green, Little Hadham, Hertfordshire. Even a cursory inspection shows that Westland Green and Pig's Green were once a single block of common grazing (a and b), and further intakes into a once much larger area of common land can be identified (c). Together with neighbouring areas of ancient woodland, and Little Hadham Park, this in turn once formed part of a much larger tract of wooded 'waste' (d)

---

[12] Barnes *et al.* 2007
[13] MacNair and Williamson 2010, pp. 113-17
[14] Rowe and Williamson 2013, pp. 159-60

connected, in characteristic fashion, by winding roads. Minor encroachments into these areas of common grazing are easily recognised, but closer inspection shows how the various greens represent the progressive fragmentation of a once much larger and continuous tract by the creation of blocks and ovals of enclosed fields: in the immediate surrounding area, other portions were enclosed to form coppiced woods, and the extensive deer park at Little Hadham. Evidently, as each new farm was established at the expense of the 'waste' a number of broad 'rules' was followed. The new establishment was placed on the edge of the residue of the former common, with its land extending to the rear; the outline of the intake was generally curvilinear in character, presumably to cut down on fencing costs; and – most importantly of all – where an intake was of any serious size a narrow strip of common was left to its rear, running along and fossilising the old common edge. This provided access to remaining areas of common grazing, and to farms already established along the common margins – farms which thus came to stand beside a winding lane. Small greens, and winding lanes, are thus both residual fragments of larger commons. The landscapes in which they occur together represent areas which were colonised after (and often long after) the tenth century, and in which the land was of such value or fertility that most could be brought into cultivation, or at least profitably enclosed. Larger commons, in contrast, constitute areas where eleventh, twelfth and thirteenth-century expansion ground more completely to a halt. They were extensive tracts of land too poor to be enclosed and farmed and also, in some cases, ones on which it was impossible to establish farms because of an absence of accessible water (something which was never a problem on the East Anglian boulder clays, with their complex layers of sand and gravel acting as diminutive aquifers; but which could be a serious barrier to settlement in those areas of more permeable geology where the largest heaths were found). In both types of landscape, however, it was clearly important for farms to be placed on the margins of the remaining tracts of common grazing. Fransham – on the western edge of the Norfolk boulder clays – falls somewhere between these notional extremes, but more towards the 'small green' end of the spectrum – it was a landscape of medium-sized commons – and Rogerson's fieldwalking revealed how the isolated late Saxon farms were nested neatly within ovoid intakes. In such circumstances, at least, 'common edge drift' is perhaps a misleading term: this was colonisation of the wastes, albeit by farmers keen to ensure that their farms, sitting within the new enclosures, nevertheless continued to front on the remaining areas of common pasture.

Before the large-scale enclosures of the eighteenth and nineteenth centuries common and green-edge settlements were a familiar feature of the landscape in the 'woodland' areas of southern and eastern England. It is often assumed that such settlement forms were absent from the 'champion' districts of the country – the 'Central Province' – where houses were clustered in large nucleated villages, outlying farms and hamlets were rare or absent, and the arable was farmed in extensive open fields. But Sue Oosthuizen has pointed to a number of surviving examples of green-focussed villages in Cambridgeshire and Buckinghamshire and has also, more importantly, suggested that many other nucleated settlements in this region were originally laid out or developed around large commons which were subsequently filled with housing, and thus largely or entirely obliterated.[15] More recently, research In Northamptonshire – perhaps the quintessential 'champion' county – has suggested that the majority of villages probably, in the eleventh century, displayed such a form.[16] The adjacent villages of Denton and Yardley Hastings in the south east of that county make an interesting contrast. The former is, unusually for Northamptonshire, still ranged around a long green or common which, flanking a small stream, widens uphill towards an extensive deposit of plateau clay. In Yardley Hastings in contrast there is no single, central common, although once again a stream runs through the middle of the settlement. Instead there are, as in many Midland villages, a number of small, separate greens, connected by curving roads (Fig. 3). There seems little doubt that this plan was formed by the progressive colonisation of what was once a single, large open space, similar to but more extensive than that which has survived at neighbouring Denton. Many other villages in the county with plans characterised by small greens and curving roads likewise appear to have been created through the progressive fragmentation of once much larger areas of common pasture, such as Wappenham, where the common around which the village once clustered is now largely occupied by two large 'ovoids' of housing (Fig. 4). In such villages there is, moreover, often a contrast between the larger tofts and crofts, many of which were still occupied by working farms at the time that the earliest maps were made, which are ranged around the perimeter of the former common; and the smaller, more irregular properties making up the encroachments. Readers will note the broad similarity between these small greens, embedded in village plans, and those which form the focus for hamlet-settlements so common in areas outside the Central Province, and especially on the boulder clays of eastern England. Both were the consequence of the fragmentation of what had once been rather larger tracts of common grazing.

Northamptonshire is a classic 'champion' county with a landscape superficially very different from Norfolk, but closer inspection thus reveals that there were some important similarities in the way that settlement developed in both during the later Saxon period. Settlement stabilised in Northamptonshire, as it did across much of Norfolk, in the seventh and eighth centuries, and as the population expanded during the tenth, eleventh and twelfth centuries farms and cottages spread into, and dispersed around the margins of, tracts of common pasture. Here, however, the kind of extensive dispersal of settlement across the landscape seen in Norfolk did not occur. Limited spread

---

[15] Oosthuizen 2002 and 2006
[16] Williamson *et al.* 2013, pp. 81-7

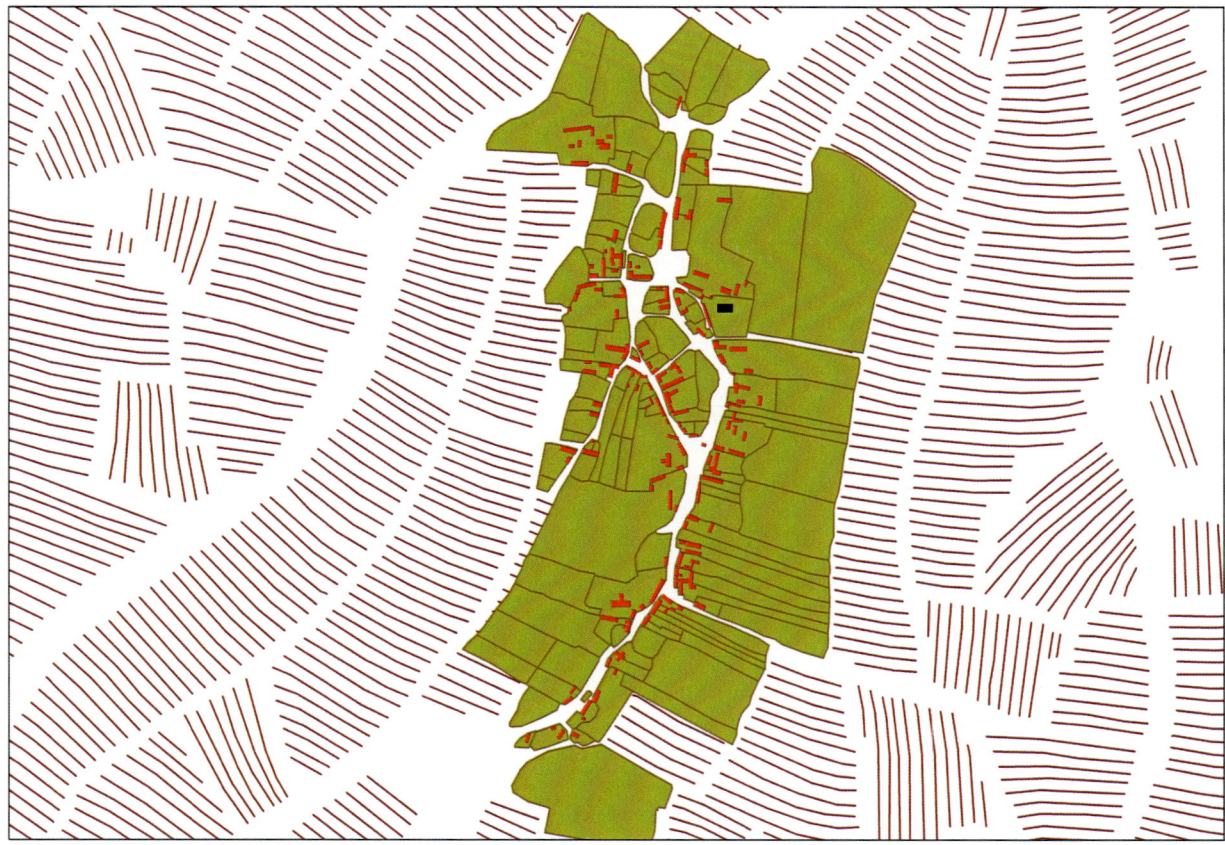

Fig. 3 The morphology of neighbouring villages in Northamptonshire. Denton (top) has a small green, the principal encroachment on which is a chapel-of-ease and associated graveyard. Yardley has a number of small greens, connected by winding roads, which appear to be the fragments of a larger area of common land, like that at Denton, now largely occupied by houses. Key as for Figure 5

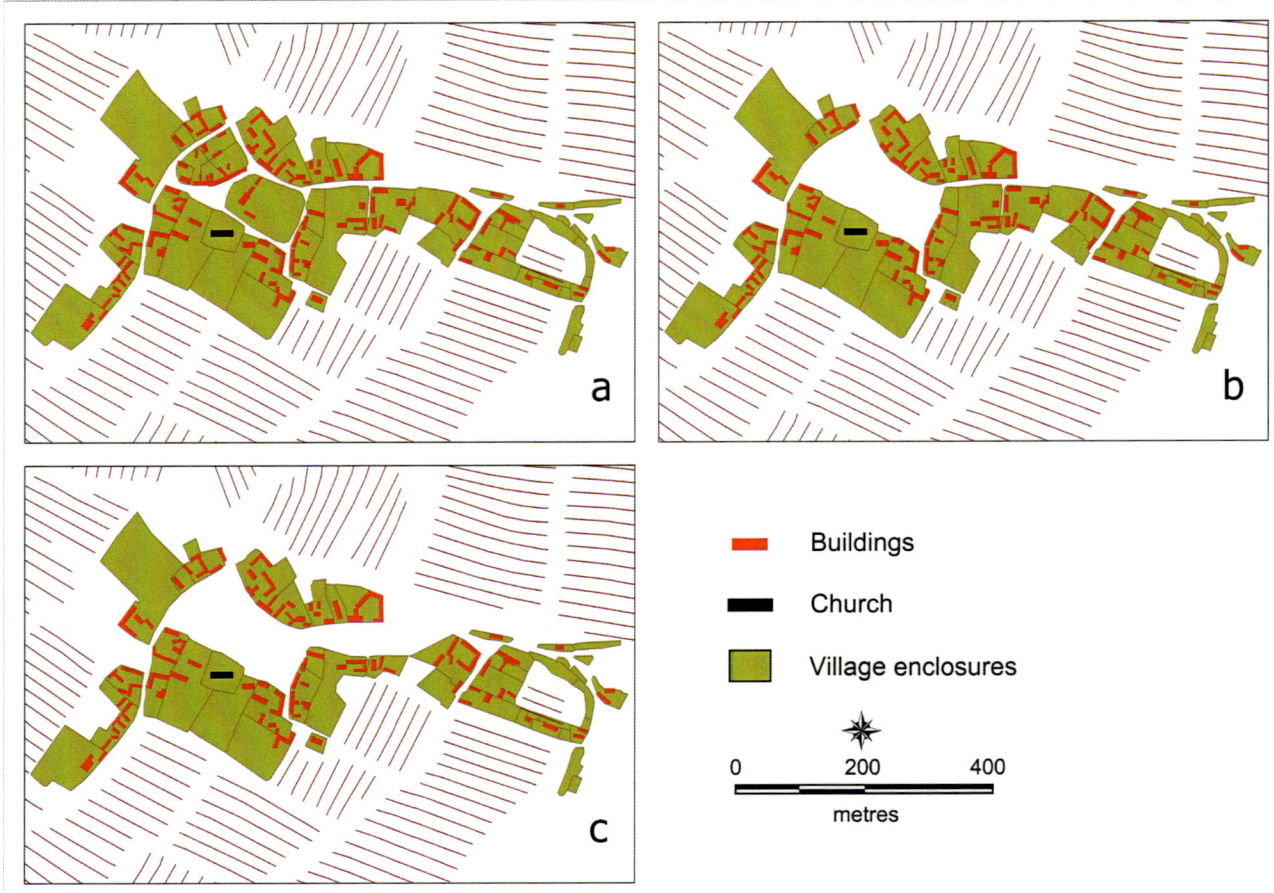

FIG. 4 HYPOTHETICAL REGRESSION OF THE PLAN OF WAPPENHAM, NORTHAMPTONSHIRE. (A), THE VILLAGE IN THE NINETEENTH CENTURY; (B), WITH CENTRAL 'OVOIDS' OF HOUSES REMOVED; (C) WITH FURTHER REMOVALS, BASED ON EXISTENCE OF DOUBLE BUILDING LINES

of farms around the margins of central 'greens' was instead followed, as population continued to build up, by their infilling. In Norfolk in contrast settlement continued to disperse into the common pastures, with many farms coming to stand on the margins of their fragmented remains.[17]

There is no space here to discuss why, in Midland districts, farmers felt obliged to remain in close proximity as settlement expanded, a matter which I have discussed in some detail elsewhere.[18] Suffice it to say that farms may have remained clustered for a variety of – and often a combination of – reasons. These might be agrarian in character – such as the need to facilitate the sharing of ploughs where soils were easily compacted by cultivation when wet, so that a short window of opportunity, for spring cultivations especially, placed a premium on their rapid mobilisation. Or they might relate more to constraints on settlement itself, especially arising from the character of water supply. Many champion landscapes were found in areas of permeable geology, devoid of water except on their margins (where overlain by heavy clay) or at spring lines: it is noteworthy in this context that those areas of

Norfolk conforming – like Barton Bendish, another parish surveyed by Rogerson – most closely to the champion 'norm' are located in the north and west, where chalk is exposed. Large areas of the 'Central Province' also overlie heavy clays, of course, but these generally lack the kinds of aquifers which characterise the East Anglian boulder clays, so that farms were likewise obliged to congregate in particular locations, especially on spring lines. The precise explanation for the difference between 'woodland' and 'champion' areas in general, and between the medieval landscapes of Norfolk and Northamptonshire in particular, are here of less importance than the underlying similarities which are apparent in their development. Rather than deep and ancient differences, we see variations on the same range of themes, and relatively late divergence.

The various common-edge settlements found in Norfolk are thus part of a much wider pattern. As population rose and settlement expanded in late Saxon and early post-Conquest times, and more and more land was brought into cultivation, in all areas of the country many farms and cottages came to stand on the margins of the remnants of the 'wastes' – on the edges of greens and commons. The details of this development displayed much variation, the consequence of differing environmental, demographic, agrarian and perhaps social circumstances. In some areas,

---

[17] Williamson *et al.* 2013, pp. 190-1
[18] Williamson 2013, pp. 184-93

large areas of common land came to form major features of the landscape and these were flanked by scatters of farms and cottages; elsewhere, on more fertile soils, greater fragmentation of the 'wastes' took place, leading to a pattern of settlement which was dispersed around smaller, often pocket-sized greens or commons, as on the boulder clays of East Anglia, Essex and Hertfordshire. In the champion Midlands many settlements which had, by the thirteenth century, become compact villages began as girdles of farmsteads around one or more blocks of common land: but the latter were usually largely built over as population rose, it being difficult or impossible for farms to disperse further from the existing settlement focus. There were, in fact, many variations on these themes. In parts of Hertfordshire, for example, nucleated settlements often appear to have developed – as in Northamptonshire – through the infilling of large central greens, while at the same time outlying pastures were fragmented into numerous small greens, which became the focus for small hamlets.

Of course, we should not overplay the importance of commons and greens in the development of early medieval settlement. In Northamptonshire, for example, villages sometimes expanded, not into and around an area of pasture, but across their own furlongs, thus producing rather regular-looking arrangements of tofts which have often been interpreted as the consequence of 'village planning'.[19] In many 'woodland' districts, as in much of Hertfordshire, a significant proportion of the farms seem always to have stood in the midst of their own fields, some way from other houses, commons or public roads. In addition, as already noted, the spread and movement of dwellings in the course of the eleventh and twelfth centuries – in 'woodland' regions especially – often led to the emergence of other kinds of new settlement, such as ones strung out along major routeways. This said, the development of settlement around the margins of common pastures was a phenomenon evidently shared, to varying extents, by large areas of England.

Churches in the Landscape

The drift or expansion of settlement to new locations in the course of the eleventh, twelfth and thirteenth centuries often appears to have left churches isolated in the landscape, as at Great and Little Fransham: but this of course could only happen if the churches in question had been established before, or at an early stage in, this phase of shift and growth. The date at which churches arrived in the landscape is thus of some importance in understanding their location with respect to settlements. The development of the parochial system has been discussed by a number of scholars, most notably John Blair, Richard Morris and, in an East Anglian context, Rick Hoggett.[20] In middle Saxon times there were, according to conventional wisdom, few churches – *minsters* serving large *parochiae* – and these were mainly located at major estate centres or royal vills. The establishment of local 'field' churches occurred in the course of the later Saxon period, although there may be earlier examples, as Hoggett has cogently argued.[21] It is usually assumed that they were erected by an emerging class of local lords, for whom they served both as a source of profit and as a mark of status, but this argument can be taken too far. Large numbers of churches in England do not appear to be closely related to what, by later medieval times at least, were manorial halls or 'buries'; while in East Anglia, as in Lincolnshire, field churches had been established by the time of the Conquest in places where no manors yet existed. As Warner has argued, many examples in the east of England may have been founded by groups of freemen. The multiple church parishes which are another East Anglian peculiarity – Barton Bendish, with no less than three churches, being a classic example – may reflect the building activities of rival free kindreds, rather than of rival lords.[22] Elsewhere, local churches were clearly established within minster territories by great abbots and bishops, simply to provide for the spiritual needs of distant populations.[23] Local lords doubtless played a major role in the proliferation of churches, but the chronology of church building was perhaps more broadly related to increasing levels of population and, in particular, wealth. After all, where there were no people living, there would be no point in building a church; where little money was available, no church could be built or endowed.

Domesday, as is well known, varies greatly from circuit to circuit, and probably from county to county, both in the way in which it records churches and in the completeness with which they are recorded.[24] In some counties, like Norfolk, large numbers of churches are listed; in others, including Northamptonshire and Hertfordshire, churches are seldom mentioned, although their existence is implied by the presence of priests amongst the recorded population. Elsewhere no indication of their presence is provided. Whatever the number of churches in different parts of the country in 1086, it seems likely that the majority of subsequent additions, to create the medieval pattern of parishes, had been made by the middle of the following century. The later eleventh and earlier twelfth centuries thus saw not only the rebuilding of most existing churches in stone, but also a steady proliferation of new churches, and it is in this context that we need to note the comment of William of Malmesbury, writing around 1125, that 'churches rise in every village'.[25] Churches were thus proliferating at a time when the process of settlement expansion and movement described above was still continuing, and it is thus probable that examples erected at what was, in each district, a relatively early stage of this process were more likely to have become isolated, like those at Fransham, by subsequent settlement change; while those established at a later stage, conversely, were

---

[19] Williamson *et al.* 2013, pp. 83-7
[20] Blair 2005; Morris 1989, pp. 93-167; Hoggett 2010
[21] Hoggett 2010, pp. 146-53
[22] Warner 1986
[23] Williamson 2010, p. 206
[24] Morris 1989, pp. 141-2
[25] Morris 1989, p. 147

more likely to end up standing within the principal concentration of farms in a parish, simply because there was less scope for further migration or growth.

The situation is, of course, a complex one: isolated churches presumably resulted from a subtle balance of circumstances. On the one hand, sufficient wealth must have existed in an area for a church to be erected. But on the other, sufficient land must have remained uncultivated for significant subsequent changes in the pattern of settlement to have taken place; or other stimuli for change in the distribution of dwellings – such as the growth of trade along a major road – must have later arisen. Moreover, a number of factors will have served to complicate and obscure any neat relationship between the location of churches and the chronology of ecclesiastical provision. For example, the important royal manors and estate centres in which the very earliest churches, minsters, were erected often developed into sizeable towns in the course of the Middle Ages, encouraging the growth of settlement *in situ* and discouraging the migration of dwellings elsewhere: many of the earliest churches in England thus stand in the centre of settlements, rather than on the edge of or outside them. In addition, if factors of soil or topography encouraged expansion of settlement to an equal extent in opposing directions, then early field churches might likewise remain at the centre of a settlement which extended away to either side of them. Nevertheless, as a general principal – a broad tendency – it seems likely that churches founded at a time when settlement was still expanding and shifting were more likely to end up marginal to, or isolated from, the main concentration of houses in a parish than those which were established at a later date, in the twelfth century, when scope for further growth or movement had become more limited.

Churches and Settlements

It is difficult to test this hypothesis in Norfolk. Because most medieval parishes already appear as vills in Domesday, it is not possible to compare on any scale the plans of settlements already well-established by the late eleventh century with those of places which were then still coming into existence, as separate tenurial and fiscal entities. Nor, unfortunately, is it possible to compare the settlement morphology of places where churches had appeared by the time of Domesday with those where they had not. This is because the 260 or so churches mentioned in Domesday unquestionably represent only a proportion of those which actually existed, something made clear by a number of pieces of evidence.[26] There are, for example, marked variations in the numbers listed in adjacent hundreds – only one church is thus recorded in the whole of Earsham hundred, and only one in Forehoe, but in the hundred of Depwade lying between them as many as thirteen are noted. No less than 35 churches mentioned in pre-Conquest charters fail to appear in the survey. And, while many large vills do not have churches recorded in Domesday, some are listed in tiny places, such as Thorpe Parva, a parish which never seems to have covered more than 160 acres. When due allowance is made for such omissions it seems likely that the vast majority of parish churches in this particularly wealthy and populous county had already come into existence by the time of Domesday. If most churches already existed, but we cannot be sure which particular examples did not, it follows that any comparison of settlement forms in parishes which had gained a church by late Saxon times, with those that had not, is impossible.

All this said, it is possible – as Imogen Wegman has recently suggested – to compare church location in places which we might consider, on *a priori* grounds, were probably established at a later date than others.[27] Such a procedure is not entirely straightforward: there is, in particular, the problem of defining an 'isolated' church, while some churches may have become isolated through late medieval or post-medieval changes, such as the contraction of settlement following the Black Death. Figure 5 should thus be treated with a measure of caution. It shows the area lying between the rivers Tas and Waveney in south Norfolk, distinguishing not only the light soils in the major valleys from the heavier soils of the intervening uplands, but also identifying the more level parts of the boulder clay plateau, where the soils are particularly poorly-draining. By and large, churches completely isolated by the time the earliest maps were surveyed (more than c.150 metres from other dwellings), or accompanied only by a vicarage or rectory, were more likely to be found on or beside areas of lighter soils, in the major river valleys, or where the plateau is most dissected by tributary streams. Churches located centrally within settlements, or associated with the largest cluster of settlement in a parish, are in contrast found more towards the poorly-draining centres of the main clayland masses, and it seems probable that these represent places which only achieved a significant size and an independent status relatively late in the process of colonisation. Churches in 'peripheral' locations – associated with one small cluster of dwellings out of several in a parish, or standing at one end of a village – tend on the whole to occupy intermediate locations. The pattern is not a strong one, it is true, but it is suggestive, and some of the exceptions are in themselves instructive. The medieval church – in reality, a chapel-of-ease – at Harleston stood in the centre of this large settlement, even though it is located at no great distance from the Waveney valley, and in well-drained, undulating terrain. Yet in spite of its location, Harleston's church was a late arrival in the landscape, for Harleston itself was only established as a market town – cut out of the parish of Redenhall – in the thirteenth century, and does not appear in the pages of Domesday.[28]

Although such patterns are suggestive, the extent to which church location was related to the chronology of settlement, and the chronology of ecclesiastical provision,

---

[26] Cotton 1980; Williamson 1993, pp. 154-57

[27] Wegman 2013
[28] Penn 2005

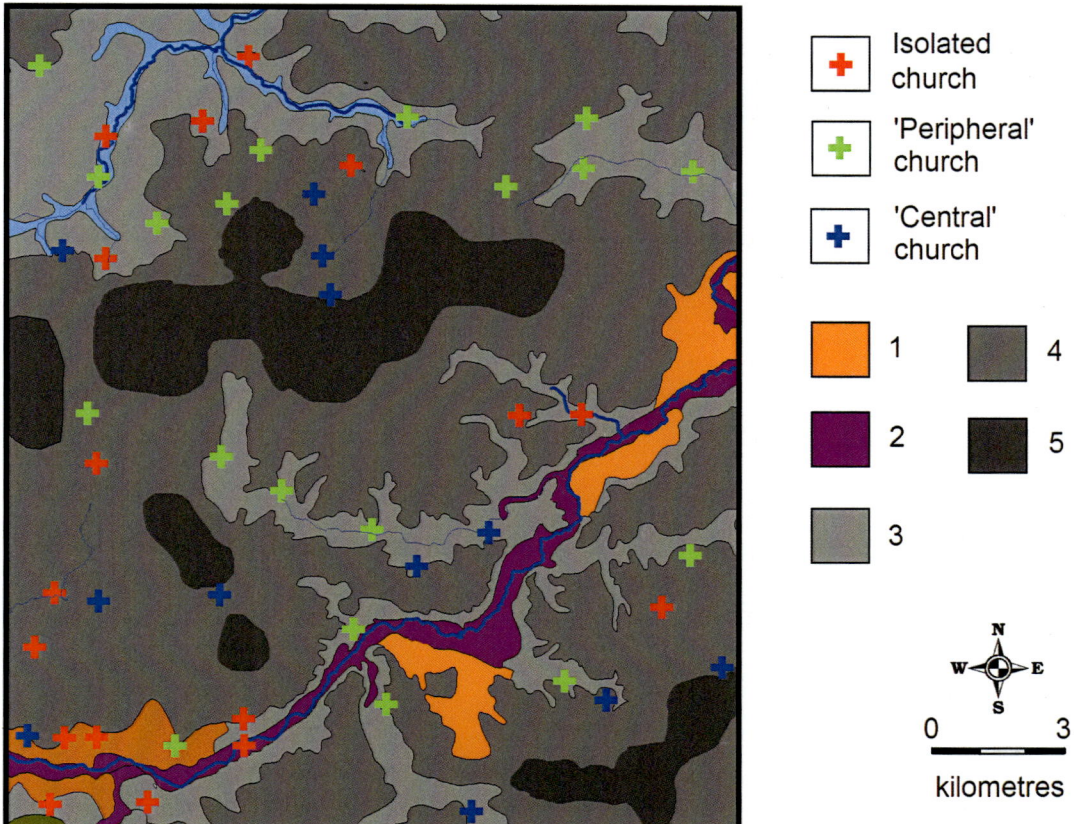

Fig. 5 Church location and soils in south Norfolk. 1. – Newport 3 Association (acid gravels). 2. – Mendham Association (peat). 3. - Burlingham Association (lighter clay soils); 4. – Beccles Association (heavier clays soils). 5. – Beccles soils on level plateau sites

is better addressed in a county like Hertfordshire which, at the time of Domesday, displayed more radical regional contrasts in wealth, demography, and in the extent of cultivation and clearance. The east of the county occupies the south-eastern edge of the East Anglian boulder clay plateau, which is here considerably more dissected by valleys than in Norfolk. In 1086 this district had levels of wealth and population broadly comparable to those found in south Norfolk; but, as in south Norfolk, much land was still to be brought into cultivation, on the clay plateau away from the principal river valleys. Priests are recorded in many of the vills here. The south and west of the county, in contrast, were occupied by much poorer soils, formed in London clay, plateau drift and glacial gravels. These districts were much more sparsely populated in the late eleventh century, were much more extensively wooded, and were above all noticeably poorer – and continued to be so into the fourteenth century.[29] Many places which, by the thirteenth century, had developed into sizeable settlements with their own churches – Ridge, Northaw, Totteridge, Harpenden, Elstree, Barnet, Flaunden, Bovingdon, or Sarrat – are not mentioned at all by Domesday. While they probably existed by this time, they were not considered independent vills and most probably comprised only small collections of farms, farming land of relatively low value.

The far north of Hertfordshire lies within the 'champion' Midlands – forms part of the 'Central Province' – and here settlement took the form, at least by the thirteenth century, of nucleated villages or large hamlets. In the rest of the county most parishes likewise contained, by the thirteenth century, some kind of nucleated village but in addition there were numerous small settlement foci – isolated farms, roadside hamlets, and clusters of dwellings around the margins of commons. The county was mapped, in a schematic but nevertheless broadly accurate manner, by Drury and Andrews in the 1760s and using this, supplemented with other early maps, it is possible to show the varied manner in which the churches within each parish were related to the main focus of settlement. Figure 6 attempts to capture this diversity, this time distinguishing between four different kinds of location. *Central* churches are those found within villages – not necessarily right in the centre of the settlement, but surrounded on at least two sides by houses. *Peripheral* churches in contrast are those which stand at one end of a village, although still effectively attached to it. *Hamlet-churches* are those associated with only a small cluster of dwellings, either because there is no recognisable 'nucleation' within a parish, or because the main settlement lies elsewhere. *Isolated* churches are those which have no other dwellings, or a single one, beside them. Once again, a number of warnings need to be sounded. There is an obvious element of subjectivity in this kind of categorisation; there are a number of problems

---

[29] Darby and Terret 1971; Rowe and Williamson 2013, pp. 18-21

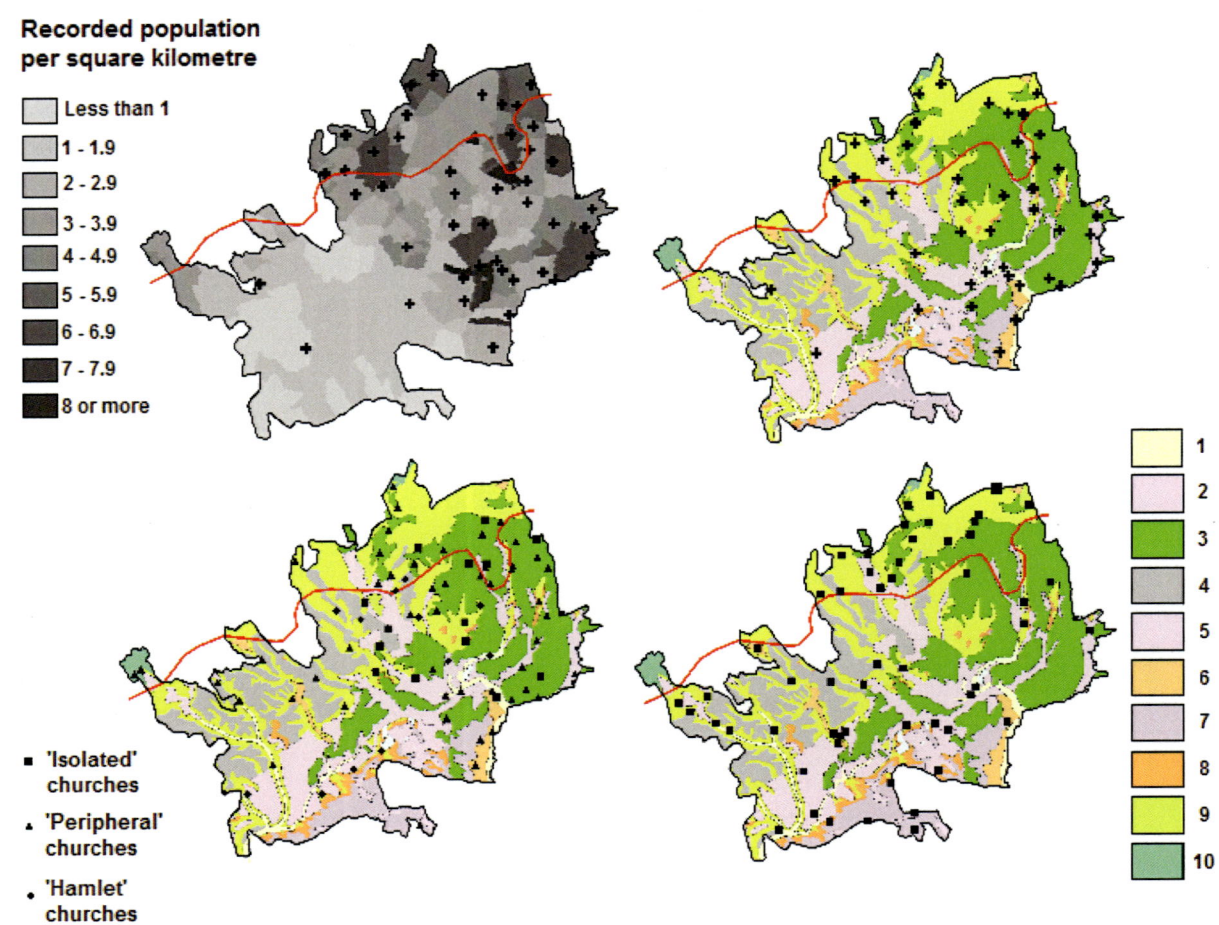

Fig. 6 Churches and settlement in Hertfordshire. Top left – Domesday churches and population density (for method of calculation, see Rowe and Williamson 2013). Top right: Domesday churches and geology. Bottom left - the distribution of 'isolated', 'peripheral' and 'hamlet' churches. Bottom right: distribution of 'central' churches. (Key to surface geology: 1 – Recent alluvium; 2 – Glacial sands and gravels; 3 – Boulder clay; 4 – Plateau Drift; 5 – Pebble Gravels; 6 – River terrace gravels; 7 – London Clay; 8 – Lambeth Group: sands and clays of the Reading and Upnor Formations; 9 – Chalk; 10 – Gault Clay and Upper Greensand).
Red line – boundary of the 'Central Province'

with Drury and Andrews' map itself; and, although it was surveyed at a relatively early date, there had been many changes in the form and disposition of settlement pattern in the period since the Middle Ages. Nevertheless, it is striking how far the relationship between churches and settlements displays a strong pattern of variation across the county. 'Central' churches are characteristic of the 'champion' districts in the north of the county. But they were also dominant in the south and west of the county, where settlement was much more dispersed in character. Churches of this type were, in contrast, comparatively rare in the boulder clay areas in the east of the county, where they were mainly a feature of large villages like Braughing lying within major river valleys, and had often (as here) originated as early minsters.[30] In this part of the county the great majority of churches were of 'peripheral', 'hamlet' or 'isolated' type.

The prominence of 'central' churches in the 'champion' parts of the county is perhaps unsurprising. In districts in which farms and cottages clustered together, and in which there were few if any outlying settlements, most churches inevitably lay at the heart of the villages they served. More intriguing is the contrast between the east of the county, wealthy and populous by the later eleventh century, and the poorer and more sparsely-settled south-west. In the former district it seems likely that most parish churches had been established by the late eleventh century, and were thus likely to be rendered peripheral, or isolated, by subsequent expansion or movement of settlement. In the poorer west of the county there were always fewer churches, a higher proportion of which originated as early 'minster' foundations, like those at Northchurch or Wheathampstead. But more importantly field churches, because they were generally established at a relatively later date than those in the east of the county, were here more likely to be erected within what was becoming, but also remained, the main focus of settlement in each locality.

---

[30] Short 1988

As noted, the north of Hertfordshire forms part of the champion Midlands, and here the failure (for whatever reason) for settlement to disperse far across the landscape as population rose ensured that churches were to some extent bound to be located in 'central' or at least 'peripheral' positions. There are insufficient 'champion' parishes in the county to allow any subtle variations in the position of churches *within* these nucleated settlements to be identified. But Northamptonshire – as noted, an archetypical champion county – provides a better case study. In a few places, such as Milton Malsor, churches stand well outside villages. But the main contrast is between churches in 'central' locations – often fronting on a former green, or erected on what appears to be an intake from it; and those which stand at one end of a village – 'peripheral' churches, including those in what might be described as slightly detached positions.

The degree of subjectivity involved in making such comparatively fine distinctions ensures that a meaningful comparison can only be made between two groups of settlements. The first comprises 58 places where Domesday mentions priests and which by implication possessed churches, 55 of which survived as villages with churches at the time that the earliest maps were surveyed. The second group comprises places which do not appear as vills in Domesday Book, and which only attained an independent existence in the course of the twelfth or thirteenth centuries: these places almost certainly existed by the time of Domesday, but they formed part of some neighbouring territory, had not yet achieved a separate identity, and were thus by implication small and relatively poor. There are 71 such places in the county, all but 27 of which either never became parishes or – being small settlements, vulnerable to late medieval depopulation – had no church by the time the earliest maps were surveyed, or no settlement with which a church's relationship can now be assessed. For all its problems, and there are many, this procedure at least allows us to compare the kinds of relationship between church and settlement displayed at *some* of the places where churches already existed at the time of Domesday, with that found at places which are less likely yet to have gained a church (for the basic data on which this argument is based see the results of the *Agriculture and Landscape in Northamptonshire* project, lodged with the Archaeological Data Service).

Of the 55 places in the first category, 12 (22%) had churches which stood in isolated or near-isolated positions; 23 (42%) were 'peripheral', located at one end of the village or the other; while 20 (36%) lay in the centre of the village, often on what appears to be a former common edge. Of the 27 places in the second category, in contrast, the majority – 17, or 63% – had churches in 'central' positions, with only six (22%) in 'peripheral' locations, and only four (15%) isolated. The figures are no more than suggestive – and a number of other variables may well have skewed them – but they are perhaps enough to indicate that even in 'champion' landscapes, where the extent of settlement movement and dispersion between the eleventh and the thirteenth century was limited, a relationship may exist between the date at which a church was established, and the character of its subsequent spatial relationship with the rest of a settlement. We might also note that those churches in the county which remained chapels-of-ease, and which were therefore presumably relatively late additions to the landscape, not only regularly stand in the middle of settlements but also – as at Abthorpe, or Denton (Fig. 3) – often occupy islands clearly taken out of greens and commons.[31]

Conclusion

The purpose of this short chapter is not to present some coherent, over-reaching argument concerning the development of medieval settlement in Norfolk or indeed elsewhere. It is, instead, more of a meditation on a number of themes and issues raised by Andrew Rogerson's own research in this field. I have suggested that the landscape of Norfolk, like that of other parts of England, is best understood when examined within a wider geographical context, for similar themes and influences informed the development of settlement in all regions of the country, at least within the lowland zone. Looked at in this way it is possible to suggest that isolated churches are particularly common in this county in part because so many had been established here by the middle or later decades of the eleventh century. Had they been founded later they would have been more closely related to the medieval settlement pattern – an argument which also applies to Hertfordshire and, less certainly, Northamptonshire. To put it simply, if the church at Great Fransham had been established in the twelfth century rather than in the tenth or eleventh, it would probably have stood with other buildings in the largest of the common-edge agglomerations in the parish. If the common had subsequently been built over, Fransham would have come to resemble one of the villages in Hertfordshire, with a major settlement focus clustering around the church, and a number of outlying hamlets. Of course, numerous other factors, in addition to the chronology of church building, affected the relationship between church and settlement, in Norfolk as elsewhere. The extent to which settlement and cultivation were able to expand in the course of the eleventh, twelfth and thirteenth centuries, for example – the availability of spare land into which settlement could move, drifting away from existing sites – was also a factor in the generation of isolated churches. This in turn was determined not only by the character of soils and topography but also by social and tenurial circumstances – for where lords were powerful, much of the marginal land was appropriated for demesne farming, the establishment of sub-manors, or the creation of parks and enclosed woods, and was thus unavailable for peasant agriculture. The social peculiarities of Norfolk in the later Saxon period, and to a lesser extent after the Conquest, should be noted here.

---

[31] Williamson *et al.* 2013, pp. 190-193

What I have not addressed in the foregoing discussion is the more basic question of why so many farms in medieval England stood beside common pastures. I have emphasised how greens and commons were created by the fragmentation of larger tracts of common grazing. But it is clear that the movement to their margins, in Norfolk especially, often occurred across very short distances – to nearby valley floors for example – in a way that can have little to do with the expansion of cultivation. The later Saxon and post-Conquest periods appear to have seen a growing desire or necessity for farms to be placed on the edges of commons – at the junction of arable and pasture – in a wide spectrum of contexts, and to a much greater extent – to judge from the locations of churches left isolated by this development – than in previous periods.

Such a change hints at important social and tenurial, as well as demographic and agrarian, developments – perhaps involving the creation of large numbers of fully independent farming entities, each requiring access to its own range of agrarian resources, in place of forms of joint tenure and family landholding. Any discussion of such obscure and intractable matters, however, is beyond the scope of this brief chapter.

Acknowledgements

I would like to thank Andrew MacNair, for supplying a digitised and georectified version of Drury and Andrews map of Hertfordshire of 1766; and Robert Liddiard and Imogen Wegman, for advice and information.

Bibliography

Barnes, G., Dallas, P., Thompson, H, Whyte N., and Williamson, T. 2007, 'Heathland and wood pasture in Norfolk: ecology and landscape history', *British Wildlife* 18, pp. 395-403

Blair, J. 2005, *The Church in Anglo-Saxon Society*, Oxford University Press, (Oxford)

Cotton, S. 1980, 'Domesday Revisited: Where Were the Eleventh-Century Churches', *NAHRG News* 21, pp. 11-17

Darby H.C., and Terrett, I.B. 1971, *The Domesday Geography of Midland* England, 2nd edn. (Cambridge University Press, Cambridge)

Davison, A. 1990, *The Evolution of Settlement in Three Parishes in South East Norfolk*, East Anglian Archaeology 49

Hoggett, R. 2010, *The Archaeology of the East Anglian Conversion*, (Boydell, Woodbridge)

Homans, G.C., 1941, *English Villagers of the Thirteenth Century*, (Harvard University Press, Cambridge (Mass.))

MacNair, A.D.M., and Williamson, T. 2010, *William Faden and Norfolk's Eighteenth-Century Landscape*, (Windgather, Oxford)

Morris, R. 1989, *Churches in the Landscape*, (Dent, London)

Oosthuizen, S. 2002, 'Medieval Greens and Moats in the Central Province: Evidence from the Bourne Valley, Cambridgeshire', *Landscape History* 24, pp. 73-87

Oosthuizen, S. 2006, *Landscapes Decoded: the Origins and Development of Cambridgeshire's Medieval Fields*, (University of Hertfordshire Press, Hatfield)

Penn, K. 2005, 'Medieval Unplanned Towns', in T. Ashwin and A. Davison, *An Historical Atlas of* Norfolk, third edn. (Phillimore, Chichester), pp. 74-5

Rippon, S. 2007, 'Emerging Regional Variation in Historic Landscape Character: the Possible Significance of the 'Long Eighth Century'', in M. Gardiner and S. Rippon (eds.) *Landscape History after Hoskins vol.2: Medieval Landscapes*, (Windgather, Macclesfield), pp. 105-21

Rippon, S. 2008, *Beyond the Medieval Village: the Diversification of Landscape Character in Southern Britain*, (Oxford University Press, Oxford)

Roberts B.K., and Wrathmell, S. 2000, 'Peoples of Wood and Plain: an Exploration of National and Local Regional contrasts', in D. Hooke (ed.) *Landscape: the Richest Historical Record*, Society for Landscape Studies, London, pp. 85-96

Roberts, B.K., and Wrathmell, S. 2002, *Region and Place; a Study of English Rural Settlement,* (English Heritage, London)

Rogerson, A. 1995, 'Fransham: an Archaeological and Historical Study of a Parish on the Norfolk Boulder Clay', unpublished PhD thesis, University of East Anglia, Norwich

Rogerson, A., Davison, A., Pritchard D., and Silvester, R. 1997, *Barton Bendish and Caldecote: fieldwork in south-west Norfolk*, East Anglian Archaeology 80

Rowe A., and Williamson, T. 2013, *Hertfordshire: a landscape history*, (University of Hertfordshire Press, Hatfield)

Short, D. 1988, 'Braughing: a Possible Saxon Estate?', *Hertfordshire's Past* 23, pp. 8-15

Taylor, C. 1973, *The Cambridgeshire Landscape*, (Hodder and Stoughton, London)

Taylor, C. 1978, 'Aspects of Village Mobility in Medieval and Later Times', in S. Limbrey and J.G. Evans (eds.) *The Effects of Man on the Landscape: the Lowland Zone*, Council for British Archaeology Research Report 21, (London), pp. 126-34

Taylor, C. 1983, *Village and Farmstead*, (George Philip, London)

Wade-Martins, P. 1980, *Village Sites in the Launditch Hundred,* East Anglian Archaeology 10

Warner, P. 1986, 'Shared Churchyards, Freemen Church Builders and the Development of Parishes in Eleventh-Century East Anglia', *Landscape History* 8, pp. 39-52

Warner, P. 1987, *Greens, Commons and Clayland Colonization*, (Leicester University Press, Leicester)

Wegman, I. 2013, 'A Study of "Common-Edge Drift" in Norfolk', Unpublished MA Dissertation, University of East Anglia

Williamson, T. 1993, *The Origins of Norfolk*, (Manchester University Press, Manchester)

Williamson, T. 2010, *The Origins of Hertfordshire*, Revised edn. (University of Hertfordshire Press, Hatfield)

Williamson, T. 2013, *Environment, Society and Landscape in Early Medieval England: time and topography*, (Boydell, Ipswich)

Williamson, T., Liddiard R., and Partida, T. 2013, *Champion. The Making and Unmaking of the English Midland Landscapes*, (Exeter University Press, Exeter)

The Elmhams re-visited

Stephen Heywood

Introduction

The status of the ruined chapel at North Elmham has been firmly interpreted as the private episcopal chapel of Bishop Herbert de Losinga to accompany one of his own secondary residences. Another residence, from which the southern part of the diocese of East Anglia was administered, was at South Elmham and an episcopal palace survives there. This site also has a chapel of Norman date. No definitive explanation for both sites having the same name has been forthcoming since North Elmham was given the prize of being the seat of the bishops of East Anglia. As both places were demesne manors belonging to the bishops of East Anglia from before the Norman Conquest until the end of the Middle Ages, it seems likely that the second Elmham, whichever it was, was given the same name in order to strengthen the sense of the perpetuity of the diocese and to maintain its ancient origins with the first bishop of East Anglia – St Felix.

South Elmham

Part of the publication in 1982 of the article[1] which defined North Elmham as the episcopal chapel of Bishop Herbert was devoted to South Elmham which, it was remarked, had the very similar distinctive west tower as at North Elmham. This is the tower having the same external width as the aisleless nave and having a projecting stair leading to an upper chapel. This special characteristic is shared by the church of Brook in Kent which was the private chapel of Prior Ernulf of Canterbury Cathedral (Fig.1b).[2] The latter is not a ruin and has an altar niche at its upper storey. The three churches are, of course, of *circa* 1100. As recorded in a charter of 1101 and copied into the first register of Norwich Cathedral Priory, Herbert de Losinga bought the manor of South Elmham.[3] The charter was understood to say that the manor was to be given to the cathedral priory yet we know that the bishops were holding the manor in demesne at least from the 13th century. This interpretation comes from a misreading of the text.

Herbert bought the manor of South Elmham from Wilelmo Neveris or de Noers or Noyers. The passage in the charter reads after bequeathing manors for his monastery at Norwich ...*et necui successorum meorum gravis videtur minoratio episcopalis, dominumi restitui illus hoc modo. Apud Norwicum reparavi domum viginti libris de Thorp quod retinue in manu mea; in Suthfolchia de Elmham quam emi a Willelmo de Neveris; de Eccles quam redemi*

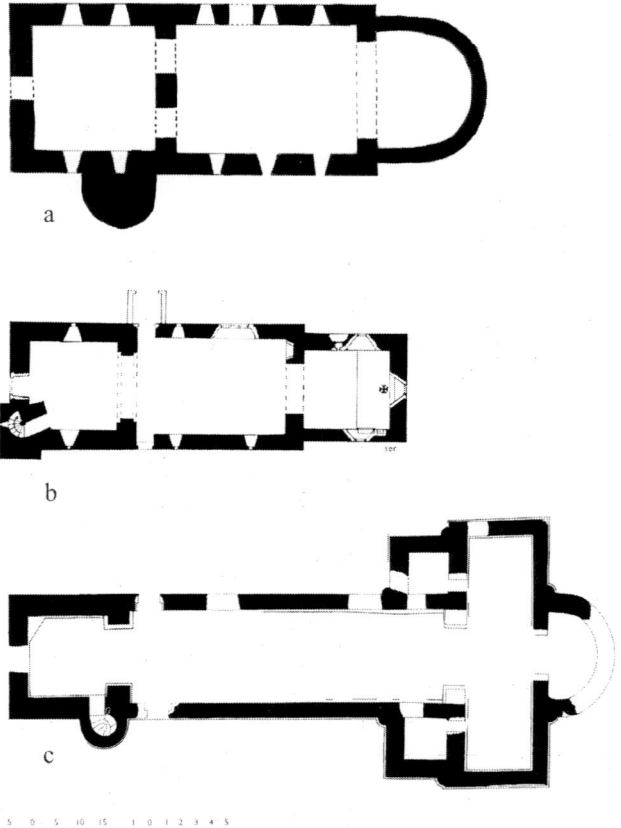

FIG. 1: A. THE MINSTER SOUTH ELMHAM, SUFFOLK (AFTER SMEDLEY AND OWLES 1970), B. BROOK CHURCH, KENT (AFTER RIGOLD 1969), C. BISHOP'S CHAPEL, NORTH ELMHAM, NORFOLK (STEPHEN HEYWOOD)

a Rege Henrico sexaginta libris; manerium de Colkirke. This records the purchase of manors and is translated by Saunders as follows: *and lest this depletion of the episcopal property may seem to any one of my successors a doubtful procedure, I have provided as follows; at Norwich I have restored the house [of the bishops] with £20 from the demesne of Thorp which I retained in my hand. In Suffolk, **I have given also** Elmham which I bought from William Neueris; also Ekles which I bought back from King Henry for £60; also the manor of Colkirk*. In this context it appears that these manors were to belong to the bishopric and indeed Eccles (Quidenham), Colkirk and, of course, South Elmham already were and remained properties of the see. The added explanatory phrase *I have given also Elmham* in Saunders' translation is misleading. *I have **kept** also Elmham* would be a more accurate gloss. However, the interpretation of the charter which sees the purchase

---
[1] Heywood 1982
[2] Rigold 1969
[3] Dodwell 1974, Saunders 1939, folio 4d

of the manors as gifts to the cathedral priory, persists.[4] This may be because earlier in the same charter the bishop gives to his monks at Norwich *Ecclesiam de Elmham cum omnibus appendiciis*. This refers to the parish church which he founded.[5]

There were 10 manors in the South Elmham estate, now nine parishes including Flixton and Homersfield or South Elmham, St Mary. In the Domesday book Bishop Almar of Elmham was one of the overlords of the principal manor in 1066; His successor William de Beaufai or Bello Fago was tenant-in-chief in 1086 and from him the lord was William of Noyers. Bishop Almer of Elmham was overlord of the second manor and his successor William was lord in 1086. In 1101 Bishop Herbert de Losinga inherited the second manor and bought back the principal from William Neveris or of Noyers and consolidated them. The two manors in Homersfield were owned by the bishop in 1066 and 1086. One of the two manors at Flixton was similar. It is clear that before and after the Norman Conquest the bishops of East Anglia had substantial estates in this part of Suffolk.

There is documentary evidence in Bede of episcopal activity in the pre-Danish period in a line of succession from St Felix to Bisi following which the see was divided in two with separate bishops.[6] Elmham itself has no documentary reference until the Council of Clovesho in 803.[7] There is a later document, however, that states that the estate was granted to Felix by King Sigebert.[8]

The association of Hoxne with the martyrdom of St Edmund is ancient and Hoxne is also the location of large manorial holdings of the bishop at the time of the Conquest. The will of Bishop Theodred of London (942-951) shows that he had a 'bishopstool' there and it appears that Suffolk at least was united with the London diocese just before the full re-establishment of the see. Also Domesday refers to it as having been the seat of the bishop at the time of the Conquest.[9] This implies that after the seat of the East Anglian Diocese had been moved to North Elmham a 'bishopstool' was established at Hoxne.

There is plenty of archaeological evidence of activity in St Cross and St Margaret South Elmham with Early and Middle Saxon and Roman pottery.[10] The South Elmham parish of Homersfield immediately north of St Cross is spelt *Humbresfeld* in Domesday and it is thought to mean Hunberht's field. Hunberht was the last of the pre-Danish bishops. Flixton was in the South Elmham estate and there was also another Flixton further east in Lothingland. Both belonged to the bishop at the time of the Conquest and in 1086. Flixton is of course very close to the name of the missionary – Felix-town and may indicate his presence in the area in the 7th century, commemorated later with the parishes being given his name.[11]

The Minster[12]

As to the Norman chapel and its enclosure: it has deliberate archaizing features as does its sister in Norfolk (Figs 1a and 2). At North Elmham it is the continuous transept and the

FIG. 2 SOUTH ELMHAM MINSTER. LOOKING EAST FROM WITHIN TOWER (STEPHEN HEYWOOD)

---

[4] Hoggett 2010, p. 44
[5] Saunders 1939, folio 3d
[6] Hoggett 2010, pp. 40-2
[7] Hoggett 2010, p. 36
[8] Goult 1990 and Stevenson 1926
[9] Carey Evans 1987
[10] Hardy and Martin 1987
[11] Scarfe 1986, p. 25 and Hoggett 2010, pp. 35-44
[12] Smedley and Owles 1970

armpit towers referring to Old St Peter's in Rome and its imperial copies in northern Europe. The flanking towers are a characteristic of the great imperial churches. At South Elmham the reference to early medieval practice is in the plan of the apse and, again as at North Elmham, the apse is formed directly after the chancel arch without having a straight bay beforehand. This early method of forming an apse is used by the 7th century Kentish churches, of which one is at Bradwell-on-Sea in Essex, almost certainly known by the Norman bishops.[13] Normal practice by this date was almost invariably with a straight bay and in the case of the Elmhams it was a deliberate design decision to give the impression of antiquity.

As regards the tower, the comparison with North Elmham is valid owing to it being of the same width as the nave and having a stair turret in the same position. However, there are significant differences primarily owing to the far greater size of the tower at South Elmham – 7.92m internally as opposed to 5.35m at North Elmham (Fig. 1a and c). Furthermore, two arches into the tower from the nave were provided, not because it was too wide a space technically to span with a single arch, as was done for the chancel arch, but because Herbert wished to create a spacious upper storey with two tower arches rising to a much lesser height than a single arch. It is possible that he intended the upper storey to be a tribune in the German manner from which the bishop would participate in the services which were being performed in the nave and chancel from a separate, elevated position. He would be able to see the action and he would be seen to do so from below. Such arrangements are particularly common in northern Europe from the 9th century onwards. Charlemagne's own chapel at Aachen has the emperor's throne at the upper storey[14] and a later version is at the 11th century abbey church of Susteren in the southern Netherlands near Aachen (Fig. 3).[15] This church has two tower arches with a single arched tribune above, very similar to what existed at the minster. The pair of tower arches at Elmham probably had the same function: to provide room for a large tribune arch possibly containing an arcade of three or four smaller arches. The western tribune is not common in Anglo-Norman churches yet discreet examples can be seen at Deerhurst and Brixworth from the Anglo-Saxon period[16] and, from the late 10th century, Jumièges, St Pierre in Normandy.[17]

However the massive tower was not necessary to provide a simple tribune which could easily have been accommodated within a conventional tower. Herbert was seeking to create the impression of something more – most probably a version of the Carolingian westwork such as that at Corvey-on-the-Weser or St Pantaleon in Cologne in miniature.[18] These western *massifs* are characterised by having relatively low vaulted spaces of aisles supporting the principal grander upper floors and are flanked by

[13] Fernie 1983, p. 42
[14] Kreusch 1965-8
[15] Grodecki 1958 pp. 196-8, fig. 73
[16] Fernie 1983
[17] Le Malo and Morganstern 2003
[18] Oswald *et al*. 1966

FIG. 3 SUSTEREN ABBEY, HOLLAND. TOWER ARCHES
(STEPHEN HEYWOOD)

stair turrets sometimes extended upwards to decorate the skyline. The surrounding spaces housed several altars as well being a tribune for the important personage.

The sub-divided low level of the tower at Elmham, the abundance of space in the upper floor and its presence as a massive square block all make references to the Holy Roman Empire. The foundations for a stair turret at the south east corner of the tower are difficult to understand because there is no sign of an entrance to the stair and no sign of steps accommodated in the thickness of the wall which would have been necessary. Therefore it could never have actually functioned as a stair and a possible interpretation is that it was a turret emulating, in form only, one of the flanking towers to westworks in imperial northern Europe (Fig. 4). The turret appears to be an addition as it blocks former windows. This opens the question of how the grander upper storey was gained. An internal or external wooden stair would be possible yet not the only means. Access from the domestic buildings to the north via a bridge should not be wholly discounted given the use of this type of access at Herbert's cathedral at Norwich.

FIG. 4 CHURCH OF HASTIÈRE-PAR-DELA
(STEPHEN HEYWOOD)

The fabric of coursed flint with former ashlar dressings is typical of Norman workmanship. The use of triangular putlog holes is of interest, and most unusual. However, they are also used at the Norman church of St Michael, Oulton to the north east of South Elmham. A lot of the facing flints have been robbed as well as the ashlar dressings. Some quoins escaped from being robbed and they have unmistakeable diagonal tooling indicative of Norman workmanship.

The ditch and banked enclosure within which the chapel stands is undated and could pre-date the church, and provide the ancient status for which Bishop Herbert craved, giving good reason to build his chapel there. Investigation through geophysical survey has yielded indications of walls to the north of the chapel suggesting the possibility of domestic occupation.[19]

There can be little doubt that the author or patron of the building was Bishop Herbert de Losinga who bought back the manor from Wilelmo de Noyers and established an episcopal residence there.

---

[19] GSB Prospection 2000

North Elmham

The ruined church at North Elmham (Fig. 5) has been more fully discussed in the 1982 article mentioned above. Excavations in the park close to the site of the ruined church revealed extensive evidence of middle and late Anglo-Saxon timber-framed buildings and the boundary of a late Anglo-Saxon cemetery which probably related to the site of the ruined church.[20]

It was shown that the fabric of flint with ferruginous conglomerate facing had all dressings and quoins of fine limestone ashlar and some of conglomerate most of which has been robbed. However, the remaining pieces and in particular the jamb of the south doorway have diagonal tooling typical of Norman workmanship. This jamb, surviving quoins and the tower arch responds were discounted as additions and the clear evidence of similar dressings on all the other openings was ignored in previous accounts.[21] A detail which was remarked upon in a footnote to the 1982 article is that when the blocking of the south doorway was unpicked during the excavations the drawing made of the jamb clearly marks a draw bar hole and records its depth at 5 feet (Fig. 6).[22] This further indicates that the doorway with its ashlar dressings was not an addition and the drawbar was necessarily incorporated in the building of the north wall of the tower. The only published disagreement with the conclusion of the 1982 report argues that the ashlar jambs and the ashlar elsewhere were all Norman additions and that the rest of the fabric belongs to an earlier 11th-century date.[23] The draw bar makes this nigh impossible and there is no evidence of the ashlar dressings having been inserted and much evidence of them having been removed.

The method of construction is without doubt of Norman date but the plan is not typical and reflects the personal wishes of the prelate. The continuous transept is a clear reference to Old St Peter's in Rome and the apse, as at South Elmham, is again an early Christian form. The flanking towers refer to the Holy Roman Empire with its predilection for flanking towers and turrets. The churches of the *Hirsauer bauschule* have flanking towers similarly placed in the transept armpits.[24]

A very distinctive feature of the building, apart from its highly personal plan, is the use of quadrant pilasters – rounded filets of masonry filling the re-entrant angles on the exterior (Fig. 7). This is only found on certain early medieval churches of East Anglia and almost exclusively in the angles between a round western tower and the west wall of its nave (Fig. 8). It has not been observed outside the region. The source for its use has been shown to have been the two major Norman churches in the region – the

---

[20] Wade-Martins 1980, 1, p. 164.
[21] Rigold 1962-3
[22] Rigold 1962-3, p. 91, fig. 33 and pl. XI B
[23] Batcock 1991
[24] Hoffman 1950 and Héliot 1965

Fig. 5 Bishop's Chapel, North Elmham. General view from south east (Stephen Heywood)

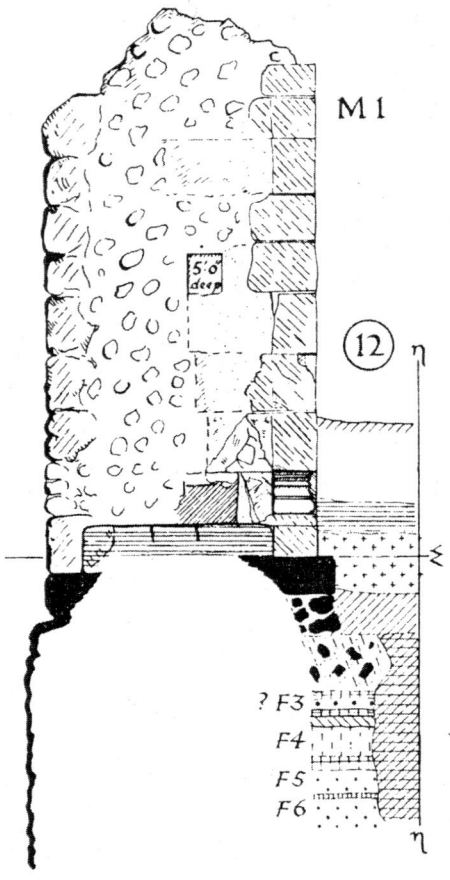

Fig. 6 Bishop's Chapel, North Elmham. West jamb of North doorway. Drawing showing drawbar hole (after Rigold 1962-3)

Fig. 7 Bishop's Chapel, North Elmham. Detail of quadrant pilaster (Stephen Heywood)

Fig. 8 Church of Haddiscoe Thorpe. Quadrant pilaster
(Stephen Heywood)

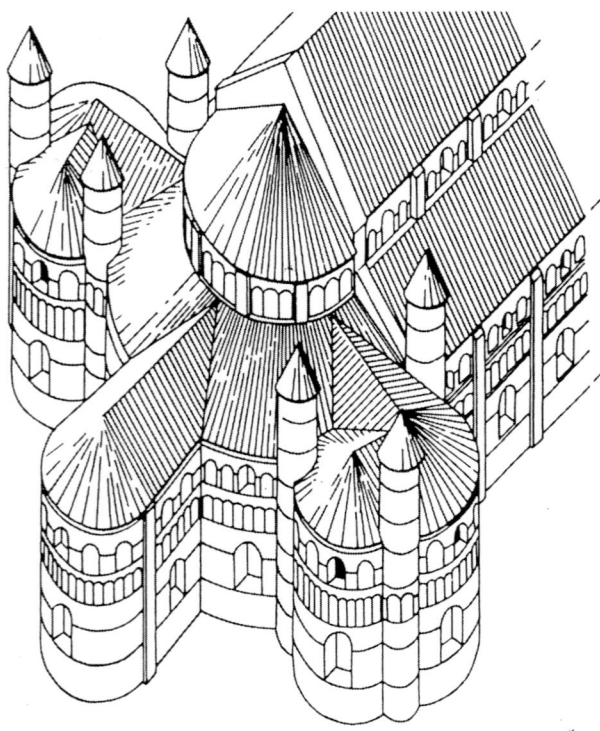

Fig. 9 Norwich Cathedral. Reconstruction drawing of
east end (Steven Ashley)

abbey of Bury St Edmunds and the cathedral at Norwich.[25] Both of these churches used quadrant pilasters in the angles between the radiating chapels and the ambulatory. At Norwich the radiating chapels are more complex (Fig. 9). The important difference is that the quadrant pilasters rose up to form turrets. The early masonry parish churches in the region, as commonly observed elsewhere, wished to emulate the major new foundations. They did this by using round towers and also the accompanying quadrant pilasters but necessarily without the turrets. At the church of St Matthias at Haddiscoe Thorpe an attempt is made to reflect the turrets by topping the pilasters with conical pieces of stone with a carved head above (Fig. 8).[26]

The use of these pilasters, amongst other things, at North Elmham indicates that Bishop Herbert de Losinga, the founder of the cathedral at Norwich, was probably the patron of the chapel. The chapel is the only building where the pilasters are used in angles not associated with round towers apart from the original radiating chapels which were similarly curved. Extending these pilasters into a miniature version of the turrets at Norwich would have been almost impossible to achieve because the eaves heights on the transept in relation to the apse and the towers had to be different. A solution as at Haddiscoe Thorpe could have been employed with a semi-conical stone topping the pilaster. It is of interest that this odd feature was used in miniature at Elmham. Its very distinctiveness immediately refers it to Norwich Cathedral yet its effect and scale would be closer to those examples on round-towered churches.

Bishop Herbert de Losinga's authorship of the chapel at North Elmham is confirmed by the fact that he founded the parish church.[27] The parish would have continued to use the timber cathedral, the timber chapel referred to in the first register[28] after Bishop Herfast had deserted the site for Thetford in c.1071. Herfast hoped Thetford would be the springboard for the acquisition of Bury for his seat with its relics of St Edmund. When Herbert took an interest in the manor he built a palace for himself with a chapel on the site of the former cathedral and he founded a new church built for the needs of the parish and gave it to the cathedral priory whose successors, the dean and chapter of Norwich Cathedral, are still rectors. Two responds of Herbert's church can be seen in the present parish church.

Conclusion

Research over recent years has accumulated evidence from documentary and archaeological sources of Bishop Herbert de Losinga's fervent desire to associate himself and his position with the ancient origins of the Diocese. This is characterised by deliberate archaizing in his cathedral at Norwich with the axial position of the throne, the statue of St Felix and old fashioned decorative

---

[25] Heywood 2012 and 2013
[26] Heywood 2012, pp. 109-10
[27] Saunders 1939, folio 3d
[28] Saunders 1939, folio 1

features. Having lost the prize site for his seat at Bury and suffering the humiliation of not being invited by the abbot to the translation of the relics in 1096 he was determined to equal the prestige gained by the abbey with its ancient foundation around the relics of St Edmund.[29]

One of the ways in which he did this was to use again references to the Early Christian and Imperial architecture in his private chapels at the Elmhams. His choice of site at South Elmham was no doubt owing to the early origins of the place and the pre-Danish existence of bishops of Elmham.[30] He was persuaded perhaps by the enclosure of the site of the chapel that this was the site of the 8th/9th century cathedral or indeed there were remains of it or recorded memories that have since been lost. The minster status with which the building has been associated for a long time suggests that it supported a community of priests such as a bishop would endow.

As suggested by Stevenson in the 1920s and Norman Scarfe in the 1980s,[31] a predecessor of Herbert's at the time of the re-establishment of the see at the new site in Norfolk named it Elmham to reinforce the perpetuity of the see. The use of the same name is an effective way of giving the impression that the running of the diocese and the succession of bishops were continuing as before at a new site called Elmham.

---

[29] Ridgard 1987, p. 198; Fernie 1993, pp. 65-71; Heywood 1996, pp. 90-93; Fernie 1998; Heywood 1998; Gilchrist 2005, p. 74.
[30] Wade-Martins 1980, p. 3; Hoggett 2010, p. 40.

[31] Stevenson 1926; Scarfe 1986, pp. 25-6

Bibliography

Batcock, N. 1991, *The Ruined and Disused Churches of Norfolk*, East Anglian Archaeology 51, microfiche 6:E6

Carey Evans, M. 1987, 'The contribution of Hoxne to the cult of St Edmund King and Martyr in the Middle Ages and later' *Proceedings of the Suffolk Institute of Archaeology and History,* 36, pt.3, pp. 182-195

Dodwell, B. (ed.) 1974, *The Charters of Norwich Cathedral Priory, Pt I*, Pipe Roll Society No.112

Fernie, E.C. 1983, *The Architecture of the Anglo-Saxons* (London)

Fernie, E.C. 1993, *The Architecture of Norwich Cathedral* (Oxford)

Fernie, E.C. 1998, 'The Romanesque Church of Bury St Edmunds Abbey' *British Archaeological Association Conference Transactions for 1994,* 20, pp. 1-15

Genicot, L.F. 1972, *Les églises Mosanes du onzième siècle* (Louvain), pp. 173-4

Gilchrist, R. 2005, *Norwich Cathedral Close* (Woodbridge)

Goult, W. 1990, *A Survey of Suffolk Parish History*, 3 vols (Ipswich)

Grodecki, L. 1958, *Au Seuil de L'art Roman – Architecture Ottonienne* (Collection Henri Focillon)

GSB Prospection 2000, *Geophysical survey report no. 96*

Hardy, M.J., and Martin, E.A. 1987 'Archaeology in Suffolk 1986. Field Surveys', *Proceedings of the Suffolk Institute of Archaeology and History,* 36, pt. 3, pp. 233-235

Héliot, P. 1965, 'Sur les tours de transept dans l'architecture du Moyen Age', *Revue Archéologique,* I, pp. 171-6

Heywood, S. 1982, 'The ruined church at North Elmham' *Journal of the British Archaeological Association*, vol. 135, pp. 1-10

Heywood, S. 1996, 'The Romanesque Building' in I. Atherton, E. Fernie, C. Harper-Bill and Hassell Smith (eds), *Norwich Cathedral: Church, City and Diocese, 1096-1996* (London)

Heywood, S. 1998, 'Aspects of the Romanesque Church of Bury St Edmunds Abbey in their Regional Context', *British Archaeological Association Conference Transactions for 1994,* 20, pp. 16-19

Heywood, S. 2012, 'Towers and Radiating Chapels in Romanesque Architectural Iconography' in J.A. Franklin, T.A. Heslop and C. Stevenson (eds.) *Architecture and Interpretation. Essays for Eric Fernie* (Woodbridge), pp. 99-110

Heywood, S. 2013, 'Stone Building in Romanesque East Anglia' in D. Bates and R. Liddiard (eds.) *East Anglia and its North Sea World in the Middle Ages* (Woodbridge), pp. 230-256

Hoffman, W. 1950, *Hirsau and die 'Hirsauer Bauschule'* (Munich)

Hoggett, R. 2010, *The Archaeology of the East Anglian Conversion* (Woodbridge)

Kreusch, F. 1965-8, 'Kirche, Atrium und Porticus der Aachener Pfalz' in W. Braunfels (ed.) *Karl der Grosse* (Düsseldorf)

Le Maho, J. and Morganstern, J. 2003, 'Jumièges, église Saint-Pierre: les vestiges préromans', *Congrès Archéologique de France,* 161: *Rouen et Pays de Caux,* pp. 97-116.

Oswald, F., Schaefer, L. and Sennhauser, H.R. 1966, *Vorromanische Kirchenbauten* (Munich)

Ridgard, J, 1987, 'References to South Elmham Minster in the Medieval Account Rolls of South Elmham Manor' *Proceedings of the Suffolk Institute of Archaeology and History,* 36, pt. 3, pp. 196-201

Rigold, S.E. 1962-3, 'The Anglian Cathedral of North Elmham, Norfolk' *Medieval Archaeology,* 6-7, pp. 67-108 and pls. IX-XI

Rigold, S.E. 1969, 'The Demesne of Christ Church at Brook', *Archaeological Journal,* 126, pp. 170-1

Saunders, H.W. 1939, *A transcript and translation of The First Register of Norwich Cathedral Priory*, Norfolk Record Society vol. 11

Scarfe, N. 1986, *Suffolk in the Middle Ages* (Bury St Edmunds)

Smedley, N., and Owles, E. 1970, 'Excavations at the Old Minster, South Elmham' *Proceedings of the Suffolk Institute of Archaeology and History,* 32, pt. 1, pp. 1-16 and pls. I-III

Stevenson, F.S. 1926, 'The Present State of the Elmham Controversy' *Proceedings of the Suffolk Institute of Archaeology and History,* 19, pt. 2, pp. 110-116

Wade-Martins, P. 1980, *Excavations in North Elmham Park 1967-1972*, East Anglian Archaeology 9

Great Dunham church and its eleventh-century context

T.A. Heslop

Abstract: Great Dunham church is the most sophisticated building extant in west Norfolk from the two decades following the Norman Conquest. It uses large quantities of Northamptonshire stone, including several with carved geometric decoration, and it follows a coherent proportional system based on the English foot. The patronage of the construction is here attributed to the daughter of the Pre-Conquest landholder, Payne, and Reynold the Priest. From the value of their estate given in Domesday Book, the church must have cost well in excess of one year's revenue.

To judge from the entry in Domesday Book, Great Dunham was a place of substance at the time of the Norman invasion. There were two large estates of four carucates (nearly 500 acres) each.[1] One was part of the valuable honour of Mileham and had been among the very extensive holdings of Stigand, a native of Norfolk who became bishop of Winchester and archbishop of Canterbury but was deposed in 1070. It subsequently passed to the king and then early in the reign of Henry I to Alan fitz Flaad. The other big estate belonged to a man called Payne (Paganus), and subsequently to his son Edmund. Edmund also held land in Hampshire and particularly in Somerset, where his name is entered as one of the king's men. It seems that he had some role in government or in the household of William the Conqueror. Although in 1086 Edmund was clearly still alive, the estate at Dunham was in the hands of his sister, 'with Reynold the Priest' according to Domesday Book. It seems likely that the church of St Andrew, Great Dunham, was a result of the relationship between Edmund's sister and Reynold as that would help to account for its impressive size, distinctive design and (for the period) sophisticated masonry. In what follows, the form and detailing of the church will be analysed in some depth, but first it is worth noting the larger context of landscape and economy in which Dunham belonged.

Dunham means 'settlement on a hill' and by Norfolk standards the hill is quite apparent, especially coming from the north, with the church standing at its highest point about 83m above sea level. Some 500m to the west of the church ran a Roman road, which branched off the Peddars Way at North Pickenham and travelled in a typically Roman straight line up to Shereford[2] where it crossed the upper reaches of the River Wensum and joined another road at Toftrees leading northward to Holkham. The line of the road was clearly significant in the Middle Ages as it constituted the boundaries of several parishes including those between Necton and Sporle, and Wellingham and Tittleshall. Another Roman road, running east-west, lay a mile to the north of Dunham, passing through Kempstone on its way towards the Great Ouse at Denver.[3]

It is no longer possible to identify the location of the two large manors, but it is clear that they fared rather differently in the two decades following the Norman invasion in 1066. Stigand's estate seems to have languished losing ploughing capacity and over a quarter of its manpower (reduced from 38 to 27). By contrast Payne's estate thrived, increasing in population from 23 to 30, in livestock (from 4 to 9 cattle, 4 to 17 pigs, and introducing 100 sheep) and in value, from £5 to £8. As well as the two big estates, there were twelve freemen, holding slightly over 100 acres between them. However, the majority of the land in Dunham was constituted by commons, which lay primarily to the east and south of the church and was part of a great swathe of common land running across from Fransham and Beeston up through to East Lexham.[4]

Great Dunham church is of impressive size, with a tower about 60 feet high, and unusually elaborate in its articulation, for example the blind arcading in the nave (Figs. 1 and 2).[5] It is built of flint, reused Roman brick and Barnack limestone from Northamptonshire. The flint employed in the fabric of the walls was probably locally sourced from field scatters. It is mostly of brownish hue, unlike flint freshly mined from chalk which has a white cortex, and it does not have the oval forms and smooth surface characteristic of 'cobbles' thrown up by the sea. The Roman brick may well come from a site in Dunham itself and was deployed in the church primarily as voussoirs in the window arches, and on the priest's door in the south wall of the chancel.[6] This feature is most unusual in a church of this period and is one reason for supposing that a 'vested' interest was closely involved in the church's design. The limestone elements are predominantly for the quoins (corners) of the west front and tower but several stones bearing geometric decoration were used at key points in the building (see further below).

The measurements of the nave are significant for their proportions, 42'10" long by 17'7" wide. The diagonal of a square of 17'7" is 24'10" which added to 17'7" comes to 42'5". In other words the nave plan is a square plus the diagonal of the same square (the proportion of the side of

---

[1] Brown 1984, I (fol. 137a) 1.212, the king's estate, under Mileham, and II (fol. 264a) 46.1, for Edmund son of Payne
[2] Gurney 2005, pp. 28-29
[3] Gurney 2005, pp. 28-29 and see Margary 1973, pp. 271-73 (roads 38 and 39)
[4] Macnair and Williamson 2010, Ch. 4 and digitised maps 6b and 6g
[5] Taylor and Taylor 1965, I, pp. 217-221 (under Dunham Magna) and Taylor 1978, passim. Other key publications are Carthew 1847 and Williams 1925
[6] Site of Roman building, Norfolk Historic Environment Record 4188

Fig. 1 Great Dunham church, exterior from the south west

Fig. 2 Great Dunham church, interior from the west

any square to its diagonal is 1:1.4142, the square root of 2). Using the diagonal of a square in this way is not unusual in English architecture both before and after the Norman invasion of 1066.[7] It comes about from laying out buildings with ropes and establishing that the corners are reliable 90° angles by checking that both diagonals are identical. Dunham church is indeed set square. But the proportion was also used for its own sake, and it is significant that the length of the nave and tower to the western face of the chancel arch is 59'11". Before the Victorian rebuilding of the chancel, the interior overall was about 85 feet from the west front to the head of the apse (Fig. 3). As 85 feet divided by 1.4142 is 60'1" it seems that the entrance to the chancel was purposefully placed in this position. It may be more than just coincidence that the height of the original fabric of the tower is given by the Taylors as about 60 feet, especially as the present northern boundary of the churchyard lies about 60 feet from the nave and its western boundary is 120 feet away. Quite apart from suggesting that 60 feet was a significant dimension, if the church was located centrally on the site, the original extent of the churchyard would have been almost exactly one acre.[8]

Given an overall original length of about 85 feet, the west face of the tower divided the whole building in half. This is not a unique case, for Newton-by-Castle Acre (see below) uses the same principle and so does the late eleventh century church at Guestwick, excavated by Andrew Rogerson, where the length of the nave was also the distance from the tower arch to the head of the apse, however, in this case the church was smaller, 60 feet internally from east to west.[9] This division of the church into equal halves may have had more than purely geometric significance for above the tower arch at Dunham can be seen a projecting corbel which has plausibly been interpreted as supporting the foot of a crucifix or rood.[10] In this way Christ's sacrifice on the Cross is placed in the exact centre of the structure, facing the congregation in the nave and implying that what lies further to the east behind him is the realm of heaven, the sacred and unknowable place that is the goal of Christian life on earth. Christ's death is thus the fulcrum on which our salvation turns. It seems likely that the top of the crucifix would have been located immediately below a now blocked opening from the tower into the nave, the sill of which is some 21'6" above the floor, close to half

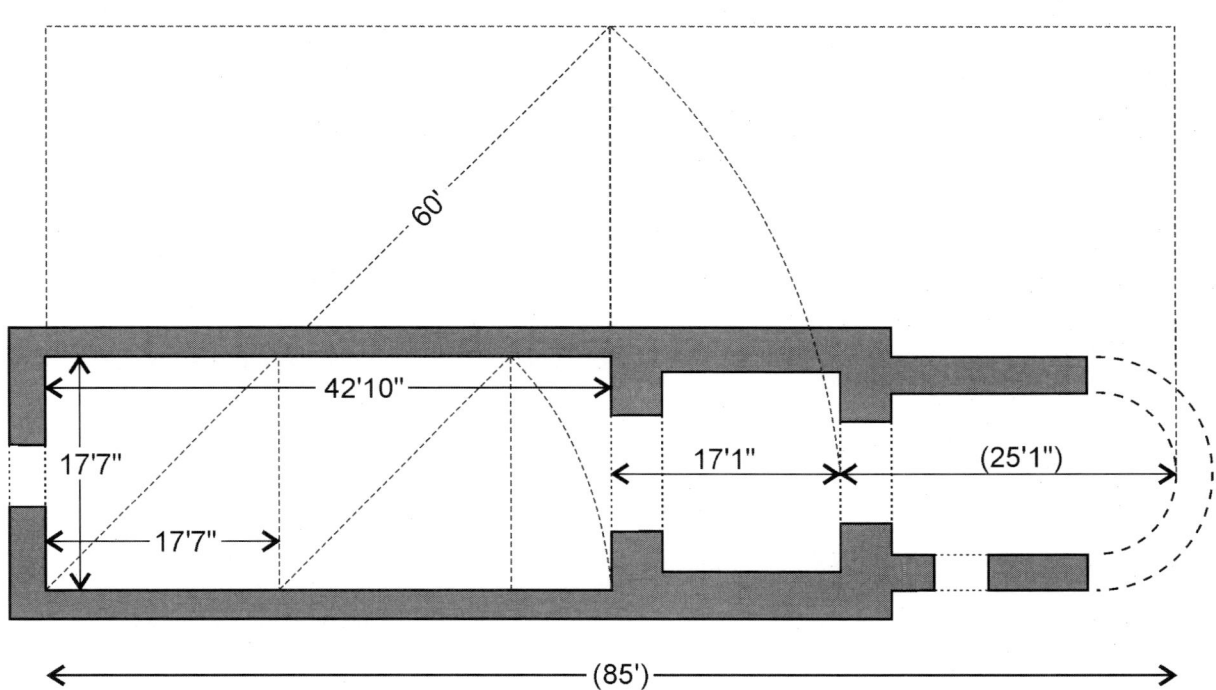

FIG. 3 SCHEMATIC PLAN OF GREAT DUNHAM CHURCH, SHOWING THE MEASUREMENTS AND PROPORTIONAL SYSTEM USED IN LAYING OUT THE FOUNDATIONS (DIGITAL DRAWING BY ANDREW HALL)

---

[7] Fernie 1983, pp. 55-56 for Escomb (8th century) and 146-48 for Bradford-on-Avon (10th century), and Fernie 2000, pp. 288-90 and passim

[8] Taylor and Taylor 1965, p. 221 for the tower height. If the southern boundary of the churchyard included the present lane alongside Great Dunham Primary School, that too would have been 60 feet from the nave. The likely original eastern boundary is unfortunately difficult to determine but if that were 120 feet from the apse the site would be half a furlong (330 feet) east to west and about two chains north to south.

---

[9] Rogerson and Williams 1987, pp. 67-80
[10] Williams 1925, p. 116

the length of the nave. Many Anglo-Saxon representations of the crucifixion show the hand of God emerging from cloud at this point, again suggesting that the measurements of the building highlighted those points of interconnection between the earthly and the divine.[11]

There are many other aspects of the building that indicate its sophistication. So, for example, the tower arch measures 7'7"x 15'9" but the chancel arch to the east is smaller, 6'8" x 14'9". This has several effects. One is the visual prompt to think of the space under the tower as part of the nave and the chancel beyond as separate. Another is channelling or funnelling the line of sight of those in the nave towards the high altar. It also changes the perspective by implying that the distance from the tower arch to the chancel arch is greater than it actually is. A further advantage is that it brings into view the decoration surrounding the chancel arch: the double-framing of cut stone, the impost blocks carved with steps and cable moulding and the semicircular shafts to either side (Fig. 2). So far as is known, the tower arch was always plainer. That however does highlight another distinction, for whereas the double-framing stonework of the chancel arch is concentric with the soffit of the arch itself, the single stone arch above facing the nave must once have been 'bulbous', extending upwards into something like a horseshoe shape. This was clearly deliberate, though its purpose is less clear. Perhaps it served to raise the foot of the Cross as upon the hill of Calvary.

The building of Dunham church was an ambitious enterprise in several respects. To give some idea of the scale of this operation, at a rough estimate it has 600 cubic metres of rubble walling, comprising flint and mortar. All the cut stone was brought from Northamptonshire, probably from Barnack, a distance of some 70 miles involving transport by land and water.[12] There are currently about 200 pieces of this shelly limestone to be found in the building, the vast majority of them used for the quoins of the nave and tower which are constructed in 'long and short' work. In this instance the uprights alternate with flat stones laid horizontally into the thickness of the wall. The 'long' stones can be up to four feet tall, though the vast majority are only about two feet, and they are very roughly square in section (typically from about 6-10 inches). The 'short' stones by contrast are usually between 4-8 inches deep and up to about 2 feet square.[13] In addition to these there are 'slabs' which are suitable for the bases and impost blocks of the main arches, and are also used at Dunham for the two sides of the triangular-headed west doorway. Then there are smaller carved impost stones placed at the springing point of the blind arcading that decorates the nave walls internally (Figs. 4 and 5). The number of stones needed was obviously carefully calculated: an alternating system of 'long and short' quoins requires equal numbers of uprights and horizontals. The height of the tower multiplied by four gave the total length of quoining required, about 240 feet. It is readily apparent that largest of the 'long' stones are used close to ground level. They would be very difficult to lift to any height without some kind of crane, which no doubt explains why there are not many of them. Perhaps only six large flat slabs were required but each was as heavy as the largest 'long' stone. Also of Barnack are the columns and cushion capitals of the original belfry openings.

The weight of all of these comes to about 20 tons, so a considerable number of cart and barge trips would have been needed to bring them to the site. The route was most likely down the River Welland, across what is now the Wash and the lower reaches of the Great Ouse. From there they would have travelled up the River Nar (from near where King's Lynn was soon to be founded) as far as it was navigable, to Castle Acre and perhaps even up to Litcham, which is only two miles from Dunham. A barge of shallow draught might be able to carry three tons of stone, requiring six or seven journeys in total. Using accounts from the later Middle Ages, Salzman calculated an average cost of 2d per ton per mile while noting that travel by water was cheaper.[14] All the same, factoring in the cost of extracting the stone in the first place, the cost of the material and its transportation will have come close to the annual value of Payne's estate. Overall it is probably a fair calculation that the outlay on materials, including the acquisition and transportation of locally-sourced flints and material to make mortar, will have accounted for considerably more than one year's income (or the labour equivalent) for the likely patrons. Spread over five or even ten years, it signals a remarkable and sustained commitment in terms of money and/or labour of 10% or 20% per annum.

Several of the slab stones are embellished with carving on the edges, and these were reserved for, indeed always intended for key positions in the church: the west door, the tower arch, the chancel arch and the impost blocks down the nave (Figs 4 and 5). The repertoire of designs is limited and largely geometrical, as is generally characteristic of early Anglo-Norman as opposed to late Anglo-Saxon architectural sculpture. The motifs include a kind of square billet moulding for the west doorway, 'chip-carved' rectangles on the tower arch and step and cable moulding on the chancel arch. The impost blocks on the blind arcading of the nave add a few even simpler designs including incised Xs and Vs.[15] It remains an open question whether the carving was done at the quarry or the building site. On the one hand it might seem safer to decide how to enrich these elements as the church was being constructed, and it would require less organisation than sending drawings or written descriptions to the quarry. On the other hand, the men at the quarry were experts at working the stone which

---

[11] Raw 1990, illustrates 12 representations with the Hand of God and 7 without
[12] Purcell 1967, 'Barnack' pp. 29-34
[13] See Taylor and Taylor 1965, II, pp. 519-20 for a similar consignment of stones at Rockland All Saints in Norfolk

[14] Salzman 1952, p. 119 and further especially chapters VII Stone: Quarries and XXII Carriage
[15] Thurlby 1996, at pp. 154-55 suggests that the blind arcading derives from the gallery level of Norwich cathedral but that would necessitate dating Dunham to the twelfth century

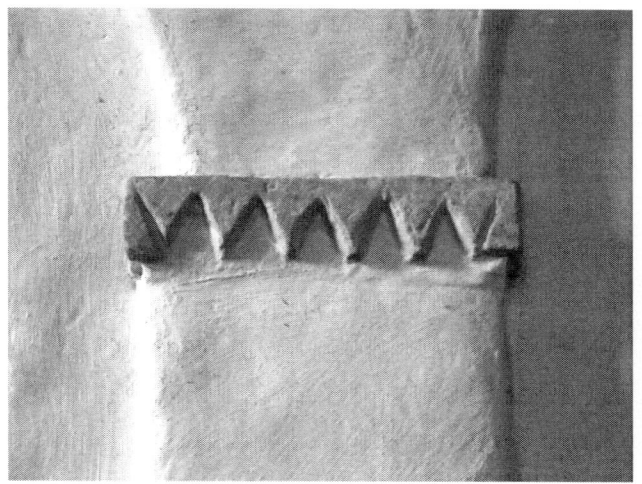

FIG. 4 GREAT DUNHAM CHURCH, IMPOST BLOCK IN THE BLIND ARCADING OF THE NAVE (1)

FIG. 5 GREAT DUNHAM CHURCH, IMPOST BLOCK IN THE BLIND ARCADING OF THE NAVE (2)

was more easily done when it was fresh.[16] An alternative is that one or two masons travelled to Norfolk in order to supervise construction and help make final adjustments to stones that needed alterations or decoration.

That might help explain why the repertoire of motifs, simple as it is, finds good parallels elsewhere in the east Midlands rather than in Norfolk. Thus for example, a combination of flat 'chequer' billet and chip carving can be seen on the eastern impost of the north door at Little Abington in Cambridgeshire.[17] There are other factors that suggest St Andrew's Great Dunham should not be seen as a purely local creation. Perhaps the most striking is the central tower which, most unusually, is externally the same width as the nave and in plan is rectangular rather than square. This arrangement can also be found at Barton Seagrave in Northamptonshire, a church probably constructed around 1100,[18] but is not known elsewhere in Norfolk.

Within the larger Domesday landscape there are churches, or surviving parts of churches, which were built at much the same time as St Andrew's at Dunham, and analysing them provides a set of comparisons which help to throw into relief the scale and ambition of Dunham. These include fragmentary remains such as the single surviving double-splay nave window at nearby Kempstone a mile to the north,[19] and the more complete buildings at Houghton-on-the-Hill, now famous for the late eleventh-century wall paintings in its nave, East Lexham with its early round tower, and Newton-by-Castle Acre, like Dunham a three-cell church with an axial central tower.[20]

Houghton-on-the-Hill lies some six miles south, close to the point at which the Roman road running through Dunham forked off from the Peddars Way. Perhaps not surprisingly, therefore, Roman bricks and tiles feature largely in the construction at Houghton, being used for the chancel arch and window heads and for much of the quoining on the north side of the nave as well as, here and there, in the wall fabric (Fig. 6).[21] There are only five slabs of shelly limestone extant, though there may once have been a few more as the quoins of the south side of the nave were destroyed in the thirteenth century. All in all, this modest church with small nave (25' 5" x 18' 8") and chancel seems to have relied on locally available materials, including flint mined from chalk. It is quite likely that the patron intended from the outset that its principal feature would be the paintings covering the nave walls.[22] The small chancel arch would thus be a way of maximising the area of the east wall available for paint. In 1086, Houghton was recorded as a sixteen acre estate held by Herlewin and worth a mere 16d, so it is perhaps not surprising that the church is not more lavish.[23]

Three miles to the north west of Dunham is Lexham, where a church is recorded in Domesday Book associated with the estate of Fathir, elsewhere called 'a thane of King Edward's'. This seems to have been at West Lexham and unfortunately has been almost entirely rebuilt, though the core of the round tower, now obscured by render, is probably original.[24] At East Lexham however the body

---

[16] For discussion of evidence for cutting at the quarry and cutting on site see Fernie 2000, pp. 290-91
[17] Taylor and Taylor 1965, I, pp. 17-18. Unfortunately their drawing does not show the chequer billet. The use of some Caen stone in the church implies a post-Conquest date
[18] *The History of the County of Northampton*, III Page (ed.) 1930, pp. 178-79; Zarnecki 1951, p. 28
[19] Batcock 1991, pp. 97-101
[20] Taylor and Taylor 1965, I, pp. 325-26, 388-89 and 460-62 respectively

[21] http://www.hoh.org.uk/Docs/Conservation-Plan.pdf
[22] Park and Heywood 1997, pp. 8-9
[23] Brown 1984, II (fol. 232a) 21.15; the small 16 acre estate of Houghton is entered under the lands of Reynold son of Ivo, and held by Herlewin. Herlewin held two other larger estates from Reynold at Haveringland and Thurton
[24] Ibid. (fol. 226b) 20.8; the larger estate at Lexham was of 3.5 carucates and held by Fathir before 1066; thereafter its value declined. Of his four Norfolk estates three are recorded as having churches, at Wilby with ten acres, and at Lexham and Banham with thirty. His status as king's thane is noted for his estate at Bircham, ibid. (fol. 226a) 20.2

Fig. 6 Houghton-on-the-Hill church, exterior from the north

Fig. 7 East Lexham church, exterior from the south west

Fig. 8 Newton-by-Castle Acre church, exterior from the south

of the church and round west tower do seem to date from the years around 1060 (Fig. 7), when it was in the hands of Ulketel as part of a two carucate estate. Immediately after the Conquest it came to Frederic, and after his death in 1070 to his relative William de Warenne. Around 1100, the church was given to Castle Acre priory by Wimer, steward to the Warennes.[25] At East Lexham there is substantial use of imported masonry, not only for the western quoins of the nave where fifteen of the long and short stones survive, but also two of the belfry openings of the round tower. The eastern one is a slab cut with four openings leaving a splayed cross of solid stone at the centre. The north-western belfry opening is also carved from a single slab, cut through in the form of a central column framed by two slender arched openings. It would no doubt have been cheaper to construct two openings off a central column than to carve the composition out of one large block, so the advantage of this solution must have been that it did not rely on constructional experience being available on site. These ambitious set pieces were thus part of a simplified 'kit of parts' that could be easily assembled; they must have been especially requested. Overall, however, the church is modest, the nave walls apparently not much more than ten feet high originally, and without any indication of an architectural division between nave and chancel. The internal width was consistent throughout the whole length of the church, a pattern of church layout seen quite widely in Norfolk in the late eleventh century.[26]

Due west of Dunham is Newton-by-Castle Acre which preserves a good deal of its early fabric including, like Dunham, an axial central tower (Fig. 8). It is in many respects a reduced version of Dunham, though there are some noteworthy differences: the tower is square not rectangular in plan and matches the chancel in width rather than the nave. The extent of the chancel seems to be original, for at the base of the east wall is a long row of large pieces of so-called pudding stone (ferruginous conglomerate or ferricrete) which matches the row in the west wall.[27] Another factor is that the present length of the whole interior, 68 feet long, is twice the length of the nave to the western face of the tower arch.[28] The nave is a double square (17' x 33'10"), and the chancel arch is 47'7" from the west wall of the nave, so the proportion is 1: root 2 as at Dunham. Taken together, these observations imply that the foundations of the whole church were set out and the lowest few feet of the walls built in one campaign. Above that level however, once scaffolding was needed, it seems that the church progressed from east to west. The north-east quoin of the chancel is entirely of shelly limestone disposed in rather random fashion (the south-east quoin is a later replacement). There is not the conscious use of alternating long and short, as at Dunham, and it seems that the consignment comprised an assortment of cut stones for quoins. The only extant set piece

---

[25] Ibid. (fol. 165a) 8.63; for the manor, Blomefield, 1805-10, X, pp. 5-6
[26] Taylor 1978, p. 988 (fig. 727) for Lexham, and compare Beachamwell and Thornage: ibid. p. 977 (and fig. 722) and p. 994 (and fig. 729), respectively 10 miles south west and 18 miles north east of Lexham
[27] Harris 1990, at pp. 210-11
[28] The plan in Taylor and Taylor 1965, I, p. 461 (fig. 220) suggests that the east wall is later, but there is no discussion of any evidence for this in the main text

is the remains of what may be an original window frame in the north chancel wall nearby.[29] Although now obscured by paint, the impost blocks of the chancel arch are probably also slabs of Northamptonshire stone acquired expressly for that position. At the west end of the nave, by contrast, only the lowest seven or eight stones of the north and south quoins are made of this imported material to a height of about eight feet above the probable eleventh-century ground level. Higher up, the quoins are of locally available carstone, and more pieces of it are cut as surrounds for the original windows in the nave, including one arch-headed lintel in situ. The material was apparently not well suited to this role and has cracked, leading to the windows being blocked.[30] Carstone is also employed on all four corners of the axial tower as it rises above the roof level of the original nave and chancel. It is even pressed into service for the central shafts of the belfry openings (two originals survive). Hypothetically, then, after a phase in which cut stone was brought from Northamptonshire, an acceptable local alternative was found which was probably considerably cheaper, given the cost of transport. Similar behaviour is implied by the appearance of mined flints here and there in the walling. Only a few hundred yards south of the church a large, flint-bearing chalk pit is still in active use today. It is a tempting thought that it might originally have been opened up in the late eleventh century. It is likely enough that the exploitation of local resources was a recent development brought about by a competitive market and the rapidly developing need for rubble and cut stone for church building. This same combination of materials is also found nearby in the eastern arm of Castle Acre priory, and it seems possible that the materials used at Newton were in some sense a spin-off from that grand project. If so it implies a date close to 1100, around the time that the priory was moved from the precincts of the castle to a virgin site some half a mile to the west.

Conclusions

There is a remarkable density of churches built in the period c.1060-1100 surviving around Great Dunham. They show considerable variety in their conception of what a church should be like.[31] Dunham itself is long, with high walls and a tall central tower. East Lexham had a round west tower, and a plain rectangular main space containing both nave and chancel. The walls were only half the height of Dunham's and overall the effect is, and must always have been, more domestic in scale and less hierarchical as an architectural experience. Houghton apparently had no tower, only a small nave and a compact chancel. Whereas Dunham and Newton are similar in broad terms, Newton is on a noticeably reduced scale, the tower is square in plan and the width of the chancel rather than of the nave, and it has a flat east end rather than an apse, as Dunham originally had. Overall, Dunham is beyond comparison as regards the sophistication of its proportions and sculptural elaboration. One has to conclude that there was a degree of committed patronage, expertise and money behind the building of Great Dunham church that was not evident elsewhere in the locality.

As regards the availability of building materials, one possible analysis of the evidence would be that as it became increasingly important for cultural reasons to replace wooden churches with stone ones it also became imperative to find local sources of ashlar to supplement or replace the dwindling sources of (reused) Roman brick and the expensive importation of Northamptonshire limestone. Even the vastly wealthy Warennes chose to mix carstone and some clunch with Barnack in the eastern parts of Castle Acre priory rather than rely solely on the Northamptonshire quarries. One possibility is thus that, as more patrons sought to build in stone but were daunted by the price of acquiring ashlar from outside the region, entrepreneurial locals (probably post-Conquest lords) found nearby equivalents and exploited them. If that interpretation is correct, then it should be possible to date the buildings around Great Dunham by looking at the materials used in them. So, those with expensive Northamptonshire stone (for want of any alternative), reused Roman brick and flints picked up on fields would be early. Those using carstone and mined flint from a local quarry would be later. This of course depends on those paying for churches not wishing to spend money unnecessarily in order to show off their wealth, but instead making expeditious use of newly available resources in order to support the local economy. On either count the church at Great Dunham is impressive: one scenario would see it built using large quantities of imported material because there was no alternative, the other – even more remarkable – using imported material even though there was a local alternative.

So much of how the buildings themselves can be understood depends on their chronology, and yet their relative and absolute chronology can only be imagined using hypotheses such as those outlined above. The result of both processes would thus seem to be a circular argument. But if it is treated as a hypothesis for testing, using a wider data set and subject to more detailed analysis, it could prove substantial enough. A difficulty, though perhaps not an insuperable one, would be determining how extensive the study area should be, just west Norfolk, all of East Anglia (factoring in the influx of Caen stone from Normandy along the eastern seaboard and inland up the rivers) and how broad a time frame to consider. Those issues are too large to be dealt with here. What I trust has been established in this paper is that, for some reason, the late eleventh-century church at Great Dunham shows a remarkable and quite individual commitment to ecclesiastical architecture. I hope it has also shown that proper attention to such apparently prosaic matters as the materials used, their availability, quantity and likely cost, has the potential to reveal much about the priorities of patrons and the available means to demonstrate and display those priorities at a crucial period in the history of England both culturally and economically.

---

[29] Discussed and illustrated, ibid
[30] Taylor and Taylor 1965 do not mention the nave windows. For carstone see Harris 1990, 'Building stone', pp. 208-10, also Clifton-Taylor and Ireson 1983, p.35
[31] For the broader distribution of church types in 11th- and 12th-century Norfolk see Heywood 2005, pp. 60-61

Bibliography

Batcock, N. 1991, *The Ruined and Disused Churches of Norfolk*, East Anglian Archaeology 51

Blomefield, F. (and Parkin C.) 1805-10 (2nd edn.), *An Essay towards a Topographical History of the County of Norfolk*, 11 vols. (London)

Brown, P. (ed.) 1984, *Norfolk*, in J. Morris (series ed.) *Domesday Book*, 2 vols. (Chichester)

Carthew, G.A. 1847, 'Notices of the Saxon or early-Norman church of Great Dunham', *Norfolk Archaeology* 1, pp. 91-7

Clifton-Taylor, A., and Ireson, A.S. 1983, *English Stone Building* (London)

Fernie, E. 1983, *The Architecture of the Anglo-Saxons* (London)

Fernie, E. 2000, *The Architecture of Norman England* (Oxford)

Gurney, D. 2005 (3rd edn.), 'Roman Norfolk' in T. Ashwin and A. Davison (eds.) *An Historical Atlas of Norfolk* (Chichester) pp. 28-29

Harris, A.P. 1990, 'Building Stone in Norfolk', in D. Parsons (ed.) *Stone: Quarrying and Building in England AD 43-1525*, (Chichester), pp. 207-16

Heywood, S. 2005 (3rd edn.), 'Round-Towered Churches', in T. Ashwin and A. Davison (eds.) *Historical Atlas of Norfolk* (Chichester), pp. 60-61

Macnair, A., and Williamson, T. 2010, *William Faden and Norfolk's 18th-Century Landscape* (Oxford)

Margary, I.D. 1973 (3rd edn.), *Roman Roads in Britain* (London)

Page, W. (ed.) 1930, *The History of the County of Northampton*, III (London)

Park, D., and Heywood, S. 1997 'Romanesque wall paintings discovered in Norfolk', *Minerva: The international review of ancient arts and archaeology*, March/April Vol. 8 No. 2, pp. 8-9

Purcell, D. 1967, *Cambridge Stone* (London)

Raw, B. 1990, *Anglo-Saxon Crucifixion Iconography* (Cambridge)

Rogerson, A., and Williams, P. 1987, 'The Late Eleventh Century Church of St Peter, Guestwick', in A. Rogerson, S.J. Ashley, P. Williams, and A. Harris, *Three Norman Churches in Norfolk*, East Anglian Archaeology 32, pp. 67-80

Salzman, L.F. 1952, *Building in England down to 1540: a documentary history* (Oxford)

Taylor, H.M., and Taylor, J. 1965, *Anglo-Saxon Architecture*, 2 vols. (Cambridge)

Taylor, H.M., 1978, *Anglo-Saxon Architecture*, vol. 3 (Cambridge)

Thurlby, M. 1996, 'The Influence of the Cathedral on Romanesque Architecture', in I. Atherton, et al. *Norwich Cathedral: Church, City and Diocese 1096-1996* (London and Rio Grande), pp. 136-57

Williams, J.F. 1925 'Great Dunham church', *Journal of the British Archaeological Association*, 2nd ser, 31, pp. 114-18

Zarnecki, G. 1951, *English Romanesque Sculpture 1066-1140* (London)

Recent finds of late twelfth or early thirteenth-century sword and dagger pommels associated with the Crusades

Steven Ashley and Martin Biddle

Abstract: A group of finds of unusual sword and dagger pommels, from England, Holland and the Holy Land, are identified and considered in the light of a recent publication and presented here. They are related to 'a rare group of pommels that can be associated with the Crusades' most of which were collected in the Holy Land over a number of years and are now in the Metropolitan Museum, New York. These were thought to be of French manufacture and to belong to the late twelfth or early thirteenth centuries.[1]

The majority of the pommels listed below were reported to either, the Identification and Recording Section of the Norfolk Historic Environment service, or the Portable Antiquities Scheme. Five of the pommels were illustrated in a price guide for the antiquities trade, with minimal description and one view of each object.[2] However, the author of the guide has subsequently provided additional information, incorporated herein. They include an example of particular interest, an exceptional pommel that carries an enamelled depiction of the Church of the Holy Sepulchre in Jerusalem.

Descriptions of the pommels

1. Copper alloy sword or dagger pommel found in Highnam, Gloucestershire[3] in 2007. Cast in the form of a scalloped disc with twelve lobes or foils. Both faces display a shield *Paly Azure and ?Or/?Argent* set between foliate decoration within a circular bordering line of red enamel and with an engraved trefoil on each of the outer lobes. There are traces of a transverse notch and possible oblique and longitudinal notches to one side of the basal perforation for the missing tang, which may represent assembly marks. Length 34mm. Width 34mm. Thickness 9.5mm. Weighs 49.9g. (Fig. 1).

2. Copper alloy sword or dagger pommel found in Little Wilbraham, Cambridgeshire[4] in 2006. Cast in the form of a scalloped disc with twelve lobes or foils. Both faces are worn and damaged and appear to be undecorated. One face is broken at the foot of the perforation for the missing tang. The base was not photographed and no possible assembly marks were noted. Length 32.96mm. Width 34.26mm. Thickness 14.70mm. Weighs 39.87g. (Fig. 1).

3. Copper alloy sword pommel, said to have been found in Northern Israel.[5] Cast in the form of a scalloped disc with twelve lobes or foils. One face bears a blue enamelled lion passant guardant on a circular field of scrolling foliate decoration. On the other face is an enamelled shield (enamel partly decayed) which may be blazoned [?] *a lion rampant contourné ?Or/?Argent impaling ?Or/?Argent five bends within a border Azure*. Both faces have a series of linked trefoils or fleurs-de-lis, each reserved on blue enamel on each of the outer lobes. Length 51mm. Width 51mm. Thickness tapering from 19mm at the base to 16mm at the top. (Fig. 1).

4. Copper alloy sword or dagger pommel (probably the latter) found in Cliffe and Cliff Woods, Kent[6] in 2003. Cast in a tri-lobed form, each arm with a trefoil terminal. There are traces of a longitudinal notch in the end of one foil, flanking the perforation for the missing tang, which may represent assembly marks. Length 29mm. Width 29mm. Thickness 11mm. (Fig. 1).

5. Copper alloy sword or dagger pommel found in Ashwellthorpe, Norfolk[7] in 2000. Cast in the form of an equal-armed cross flory, decorated with red and blue enamel on both faces. One face bears a fleur-de-lis reserved on a blue-enamelled lozengiform field; the other face has a red enamelled curled-leaf motif. The foliate arms of the cross have red and blue enamelled detail on both faces. There are traces of two longitudinal notches at one end of the rectangular basal perforation for the missing tang which may represent assembly marks. Length 37mm. Width 38mm. Thickness 15mm. (Fig. 4).

6. Copper alloy dagger pommel found in Ashwellthorpe, Norfolk[8] in 1993. Cast in the form of an equal-armed cross flory. Undecorated. The base was not photographed and no possible assembly marks were noted. Length 36mm. Width 31mm. (Fig. 1).

7. Copper alloy sword or dagger pommel, find spot unknown.[9] Cast in the form of an equal-armed cross flory, decorated with a red enamelled curled leaf motif and red and blue enamel on the foils. Width 40mm. (Fig. 1).

---

[1] La Rocca 2011, pp. 133-144
[2] Murawski 2003
[3] Portable Antiquities Scheme (PAS hereafter) database GLO-96A5B8, *Portable Antiquities and Treasure: Annual Report 2008*, pp. 134 and 325, no. 243
[4] PAS database SF-191047
[5] Bought before April 2009 and the details supplied by the present owner, Roger Dundas, via Timothy Duke, Chester Herald
[6] PAS Database KENT-1062C7
[7] Norfolk Historic Environment Record (HER hereafter) 30205
[8] HER 30205
[9] Murawski p. 347, MO4-0308

Fig. 1 Sword pommels, nos. **1 – 4** and **6 – 8**. Scale 1:1

8. Copper alloy sword or dagger pommel (probably the latter) found in Tilbrook, Cambridgeshire[10] in 2008. Cast in the form of an equal-armed cross flory, with traces of engraved decoration on both faces. There is a longitudinal notch at both ends of the rectangular basal perforation containing the corroded remains of the iron tang and iron corrosion on the base. Length 35.4mm. Width 33.4mm. Thickness 12.7mm. Weighs 42.62g. (Fig. 1).

9. Copper alloy sword pommel in the form of an elaborate trefoil, with the remains of the tapering rectangular-sectioned iron tang, found in Lyng, Norfolk[11] in 2013. In the centre of both faces a circular depression is engraved with a cross, each arm formed by four lines. Between moulded ribs and grooves both faces are engraved with pairs of engraved oblique lines, and the upper sides of the two large flanking foils and both sides of the central foil have engraved vertical lines (three sets of six and one of five). Iron corrosion obscures the base. Length (excluding tang) 37mm. Width 38mm. Thickness 14.5mm. Weighs 74g. (Figs. 2 and 4).

10. Copper alloy sword pommel in the form of an elaborate trefoil found in Chilcomb, Hampshire[12] in 2001. In the centre of both faces a circular depression is engraved with a cross, the arms formed by radiating lines. Between moulded ribs and grooves both faces are engraved with pairs of engraved oblique lines, and the upper sides of the two large flanking foils and both sides of the central foil have engraved vertical lines. There is a tapering rectangular perforation for the missing tang. Length 35mm. Width 37.5mm. Thickness 13.5mm. (Fig. 2).

11. Copper alloy sword or dagger pommel 'Found in East Anglia'.[13] Cast sub-lozengiform bearing stamped and engraved decoration, comprising an elaborate foliate motif on one face and a probable Tree of Life on the other. Width 58mm. (Fig. 2).

12. Copper alloy sword or dagger pommel 'Found in the Netherlands'.[14] Cast lozengiform, modified recently and assembled with other parts of uncertain date to form a pastiche of a medieval dagger. The visible face of the pommel has an incised linear depiction of the standing figures of a man and a woman.[15] No dimensions given for the pommel. (Fig. 2).

13. Copper alloy sword or dagger pommel 'Found in the Netherlands'.[16] Cast lozengiform, decorated with an engraved crowned lion passant guardant.[17] Width 45mm. (Fig. 2).

14. Copper alloy sword or dagger pommel 'Found in the Netherlands'.[18] Cast lozengiform, decorated with a champlevé-enamelled masonry building surmounted by a small dome with a dove descending from on high into its apex. The dome is set between a cross at both outer angles. The façade has a central arched double door between slightly lower flanking arches. The dove and both crosses contain white enamel. The masonry blocks contain the remains of blue enamel. Three of the blocks and the two flanking arches on the visible face are partly perforated through to the vertical perforation for the tang, either through miscasting or damage. The building is placed on a field of scrolling vegetation.[19] Width 50mm. (Figs. 2 and 5).

15. Copper alloy sword or dagger pommel found in Cantley, Norfolk[20] in 2009. It comprises a cast crescent-shaped rectangular-sectioned body with the horns pointing upwards, with an oval perforation in the base tapering upwards to become sub-rectangular on the upper (inner) surface of the crescent. One face is decorated with an engraved fleur-de-lis, the other face with a damaged elaborate engraving comprising a shield-shape bearing an eight-pointed star with two crescents in chief and two in base (points downward) perhaps representing an escarbuncle. Vegetal curvilinear lines flank the shield. Length 30mm. Width 36mm. Thickness 13.5mm. (Figs. 3 and 4).

16. Copper alloy sword or dagger pommel found in West Stafford, Dorset[21] in 2013. It comprises a cast crescent-shaped rectangular-sectioned body with the horns pointing upwards, one damaged. The curved lower edge is scalloped. Both faces are undecorated. There is a tapering rectangular perforation for the missing tang. There are no obvious assembly marks on the base. Length 28.08mm. Width 39.91mm. Thickness 14.15mm. Weighs 41.18g. (Fig. 3).

17. Copper alloy dagger pommel comprising a W-shaped arrangement of a central trefoil with flat a base and flanked by two upward and inward curved arms with outward-curled terminals, found in Heveningham, Suffolk[22] in 1997. Both faces are decorated with a

---

[10] PAS Database BH-314918
[11] HER 56922, PAS Database NMS-0707C3
[12] PAS Database HAMP1003
[13] Shown inverted in Murawski p. 346, MO4-0304
[14] Murawski p. 341, MO4-0104. Purchased from a Dutch dealer in antiquities and likely to have been found in the Netherlands: personal communication Paul Murawski
[15] The design is repeated on the other face, personal communication Paul Murawski
[16] Murawski p. 347, MO4-0307. Purchased from a Dutch dealer in antiquities and likely to have been found in the Netherlands: personal communication Paul Murawski
[17] The other face is undecorated, personal communication Paul Murawski
[18] Murawski p. 347, MO4-0306. Purchased from a Dutch dealer in antiquities and likely to have been found in the Netherlands: personal communication Paul Murawski
[19] The design is repeated on the other face, personal communication Paul Murawski
[20] HER 51311, PAS Database NMS-42F552
[21] PAS Database DOR-324BC6
[22] Polaroid photograph in the Norfolk HER

Fig. 2 Sword pommels, nos. **9 – 14**. Scale 1:1, except no.**12**, scale uncertain

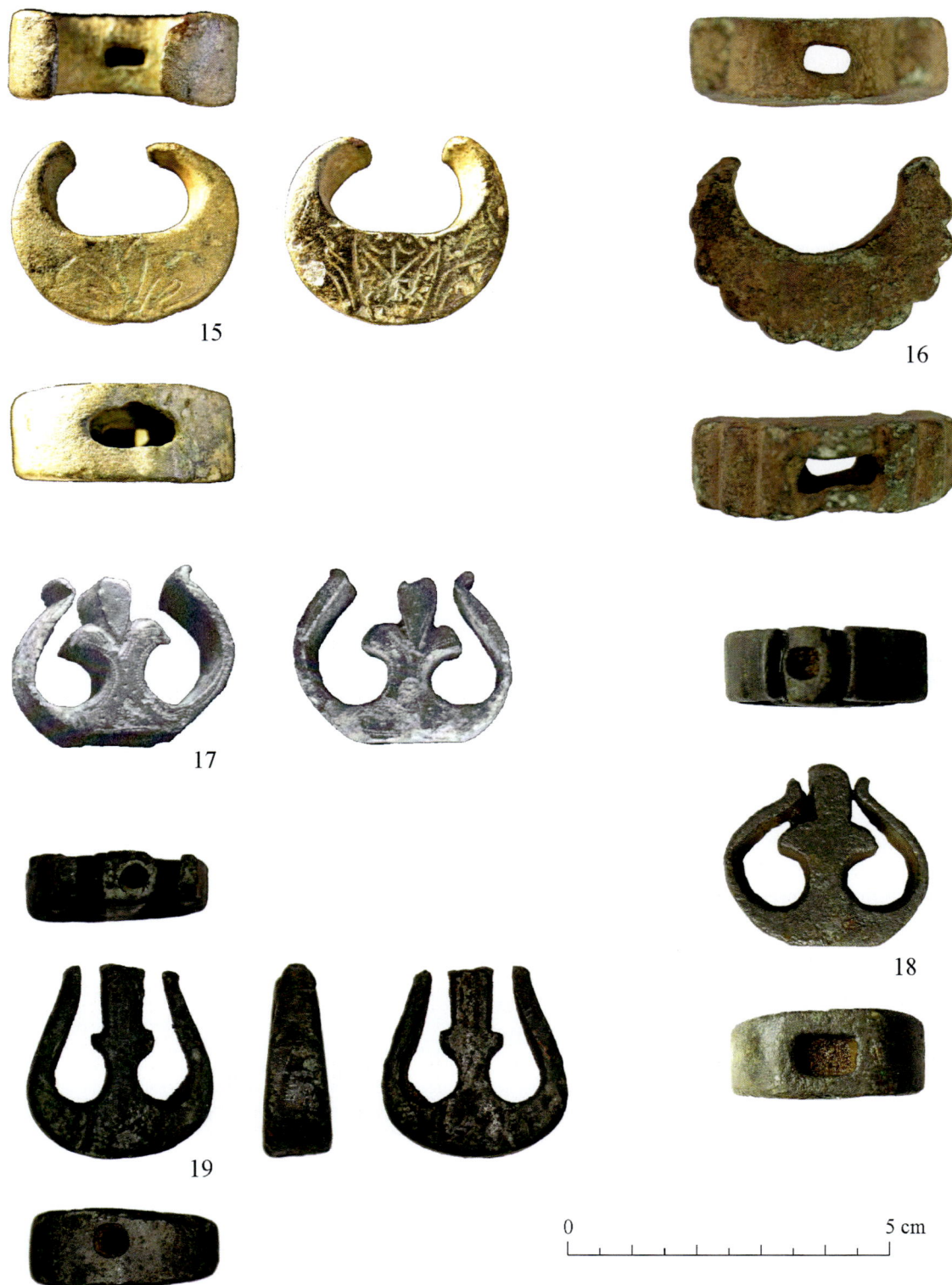

Fig. 3 Sword pommels, nos. **15 – 19**. Scale 1:1

double border of tiny triangular punch marks with larger punch marks between. The base was not photographed and no possible assembly marks were noted. Length 25mm. Width 32mm. (Fig. 3).

18. Copper alloy dagger pommel comprising a W-shaped arrangement of a central trefoil with a flat base and flanked by two upward and inward curved arms with outward-curled terminals, found in Asgarby and Howell, Lincolnshire[23] in 2008. There is a tapering rectangular perforation for the missing tang. There are no assembly marks on the base. Length 27mm. Width 32mm. Thickness 13mm. (Fig. 3).

19. Copper alloy dagger pommel comprising a W-shaped arrangement of a central trefoil with a flat base and flanked by two upward and inward curved arms with slight outward curve at both terminals, found in Barrowby, Lincolnshire[24] in 2010. There is a tapering circular perforation for the missing tang. There are no assembly marks on the base. Length 29.87mm. Width 28.06mm. Thickness 11.23mm. Weighs 25g. (Fig. 3).

Discussion

The pommel from Cantley (**15**) was first published in a round-up of Norfolk finds, where, described as abnormal and oddly-shaped, it was given a possible sixteenth century date.[25] No parallel was noted. However, a recent paper published in the *Metropolitan Museum Journal*[26] has thrown light on the dating and possible origin of this pommel and other pommels described herein.

The paper, by Donald La Rocca,[27] discusses a group of twenty-seven sword or dagger pommels (including one still attached to its iron dagger) from the collections of the Metropolitan Museum.[28] All are of cast and engraved copper alloy and most retain traces of enamelling. A variety of forms is represented, the most numerous of which is discoidal with a scalloped outside edge, either forming an octofoil (thirteen examples) or a multifoil of twelve lobes or foils (five examples). Other forms include lozengiform (three examples), cross flory (two examples), pointed oval (one example), crescentic (one example), fleur-de-lis[29] (one example) and an openwork crown-shape (one example). Simple arms, charges and possible armorial devices are represented on most if not all of the pommels. The cross on the obverse of one of the large group of scalloped disc pommels has been identified as that of the counts of Toulouse, who were rulers of the county of Tripoli from 1109 to 1289.[30] The shield on the reverse (*[?Or/?Argent] a chevron Azure between in chief two mullets of six points in base a ?pinecone ?Gules*) awaits an attribution. The obverse of seven of the other scalloped discoidal examples bears a crowned lion passant guardant, none of which is placed on a shield, but is combined with an armorial shield on the reverse. Of these shields, three are bendy, one chevronny, one has a triple-branched tree, one a lion passant guardant on a bend and the last a triple-towered castle. A further three scalloped discoidal pommels display a triple-towered castle in combination with a tree, a curled vine-leaf on a shield and a griffin passant.

The three scalloped discoidal pommels illustrated herein are all of the twelve-lobed type.[31] The enamelled find from Highnam, Gloucestershire (**1**), with a shield bearing *Paly Azure and ?Or/?Argent*, is closely paralleled by the only English example in the Metropolitan Museum assemblage, which is said to have been found in Bristol.[32] One face of the fine elaborately enamelled pommel from Northern Israel (**3**) has a lion passant guardant on a circular foliate field similar to the lions in La Rocca, described above. However, unlike them, this lion is not crowned. The other face bears distinctive impaled arms, which, as yet, remain unidentified.

The pommel from Cliffe and Cliff Woods in Kent (**4**) is cast in a unique tri-partite form, each arm with a trefoil terminal.

Of four pommels in the form of an equal-armed cross flory, two are from the same site in Ashwellthorpe, Norfolk[33] (**5** and **6**), and may be from a matching set of sword and dagger. The larger possible sword pommel has a fleur-de-lis reserved on a blue-enamelled lozengiform field on one face. The curled-leaf motif on its other face (also present on **7**) can be found on a shield on one of the scalloped discoidal multifoil pommels, in combination with a triple-towered castle,[34] and on three of the octofoil pommels.[35] The cross flory pommel still attached to an iron dagger appears to carry a 'descending bird'.[36] The bird is likely to

---

[23] PAS Database LIN-A493C3
[24] PAS Database DENO-DBCC13
[25] Rogerson and Ashley 2010, at pp. 133-4, Fig. 9, no. 66
[26] La Rocca 2011
[27] Curator, Arms and Armor, The Metropolitan Museum of Art, New York
[28] The majority of the pommels at the Metropolitan Museum discussed by La Rocca are on long-term loan to the museum from Laird and Kathleen Landmann
[29] Described as 'heart-shaped'
[30] La Rocca, p. 137, no. 6

[31] Similar lobed pommels are discussed by Boas (1999, p. 174) citing Clermont-Ganneau (1896, pp. 321-2), who saw a twelve-lobed pommel in a goldsmiths shop in Jerusalem. It was decorated with a 'three-turreted fort' with a gate on one face, and a shield on the other face. Clermont-Ganneau listed a further three pommels; one ten-lobed, also with a turreted fort, and a griffin on the other face, another with eight lobes and a 'floral' design; the last is not described. Boas also notes an example on display in the Rockerfeller Museum in Jerusalem. Twelve-lobed, it bears a crowned lion passant guardant on one face and a shield with seven diagonal lines (? bendy of seven) on the other face, each lobe containing a trefoil or fleur-de-lis reserved on an enamelled field (Raphael 1999, p. 151, fig. 4, and Rozenberg 1999, p. 320, cat. no. 161). Photographs and brief descriptions of two eight-lobed pommels appear in a recent Jerusalem auction catalogue (Ben-Ami Endres Auctions, Auction 212, part D: Charms, Amulets and Talismans, 30 October 2012, p. 52, nos. 188-9). The first has a cross on one face and a triple-towered castle on the other face. The second also bears a cross, its other face is damaged and not shown
[32] La Rocca, p. 140, no. 19
[33] HER 30205
[34] La Rocca, p. 139, no. 14
[35] La Rocca, p. 140, nos. 22 (two examples) and 23 (one example)
[36] La Rocca, p. 142, no. 30

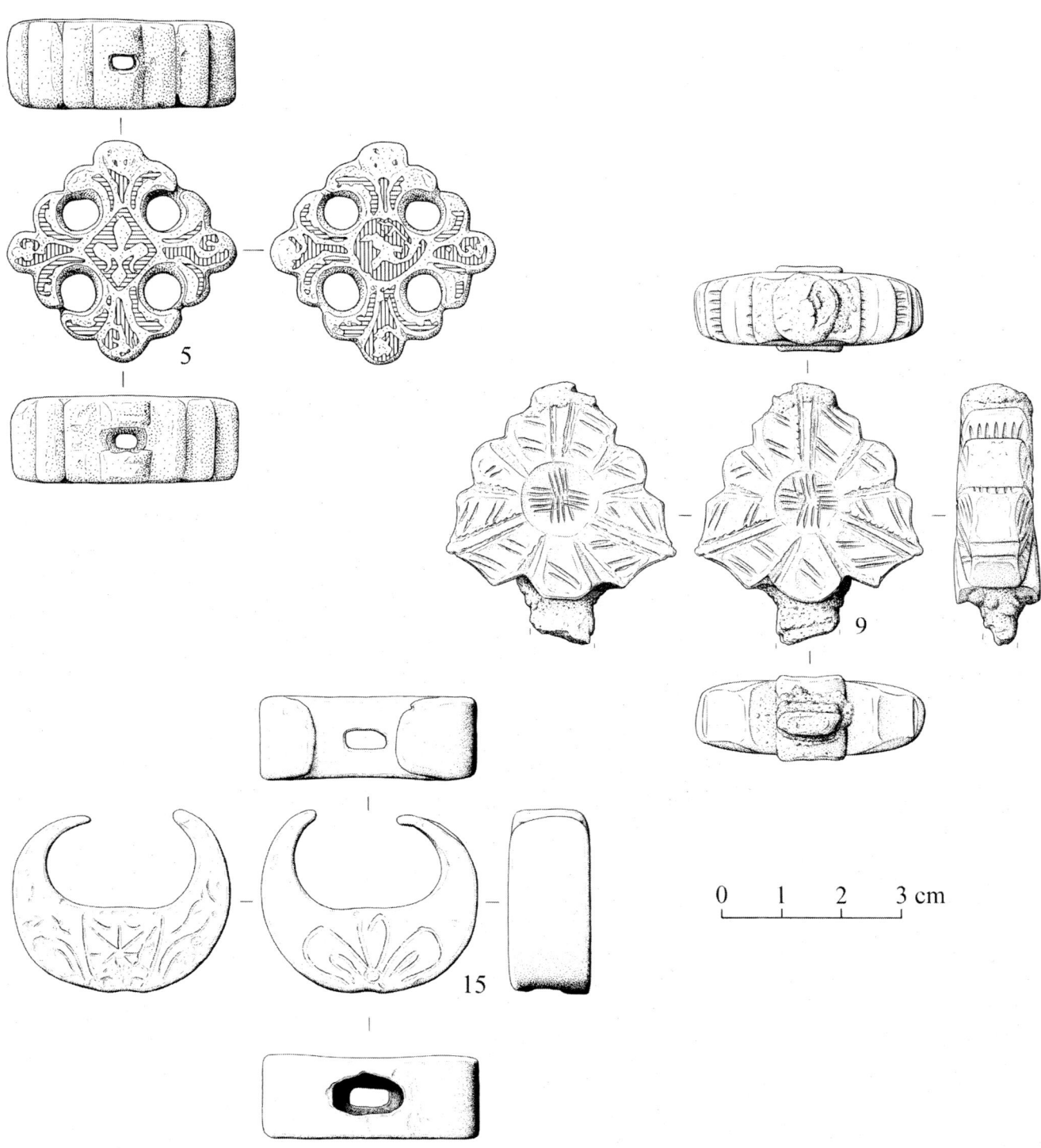

Fig. 4 Sword pommels, nos. **5**, **9** and **15**. Scale 1:1

be a dove, signifying the Holy Spirit. This motif is present on three more examples of scallop-shaped pommels, sometimes with a tree (with which it can be easily confused) shown on the other face.[37] The dove appears, most notably, on pommel **14** (see below).

The elaborate trefoil pommel with the remains of the iron tang found in Lyng, Norfolk (**9**) and another (without tang) from Chilcomb, Hampshire (**10**), have no parallel in the recently published group. However, their trefoil form, solidity of casting and 'feel' suggests a variant type related to the published cross flory examples.

The sub-lozengiform pommel (**11**) has no parallel in the Metropolitan Museum collection. It has decoration comprising two lines of offset opposed triangles with a small gap between,[38] similar to that on pommel **17**.

Of the three lozengiform pommels the scene on pommel **12**, although not enamelled, is otherwise closely related to that on the obverse of a pommel illustrated in la Rocca.[39] The lion on **13** is close to that on the reverse of another pommel in the Metropolitan collection.[40] The decoration on **14** is unparalleled and is discussed below.

The crescent-shaped pommel from Cantley, Norfolk (**15**) is similar to an incomplete example in the Metropolitan collection which is decorated with a scrolling vine motif on one face and a possible griffin passant on the other face.[41] The undecorated scalloped crescent from West Stafford, Dorset (**16**) is an interesting variant type.

The three W-shaped pommels with central trefoil and curved flanking arms, from Heveningham, Suffolk (**17**), Asgarby and Howell, Lincolnshire (**18**) and Barrowby, Lincolnshire (**19**) may be of slightly later date than the other forms. They bear some resemblance to the openwork crown-shaped pommel from the Metropolitan Museum, which has a central trefoil with its side foils joined to flanking uprights.[42] However the English finds are less heavily cast and two of the three examples bear stamped or incised decoration too insubstantial to have been filled with enamel.[43]

Conclusions

The group of pommels from the Metropolitan Museum was dated to c.1175-c.1225 on stylistic, heraldic and technical[44] grounds. A French origin was also suggested. There is nothing amongst the finds presented here to contradict the posited date range for manufacture of the pommels. However, the steady trickle of finds being discovered in England, and perhaps Holland, as evidenced in this note, prompts alternative suggestions for the place of production. The possibility of an English origin is reinforced by the presence of a crowned lion as a charge on many of the examples recovered from the Holy Land.[45] Lions have had an association with kings of England from at least the reign of Henry II,[46] which was strengthened from 1198 when three lions passant guardant were adopted as the English royal arms. Thereafter lions abstracted from, or referring to, the royal arms were commonly employed on a wide variety of personal possessions.[47]

That said, given that the majority of the pommels (mostly those in the Metropolitan Museum) appear to have been found in *Outremer*,[48] it is entirely possible that they were manufactured there, and those finds with European provenance represent swords and daggers (or their pommels at least) brought back by knights on their return from the Crusades.

The most intriguing of the pommels presented herein (**14**) has, unfortunately, disappeared into the antiquities market (Figs. 2 and 5). The image on the one visible face of this pommel shows a building surrounded on all four sides by a pattern of leaves and tendrils. The pattern is more complicated above the building, towards the top of the pommel, where other elements are present, including perhaps a pedimented structure with, to the left, a ?bird, its head marked with an eye, possibly suggesting the derivation of the pattern from an inhabited scroll, animal-like elements of which appear elsewhere among the tendrils.

The building is represented by a rectangular outline, a little taller than wide, consisting of three or four levels, perhaps storeys, topped by a dome. The design is set out in champlevé panels filled with blue glass-like enamel within slightly raised borders.

The lower half of the building consists of three arched fields. The central arch, wider and taller, is apparently closed by double doors below a substantial horizontal entablature. There is a large lunette above the central arch and possible smaller lunettes above the lower arches to either side. The two upper levels are formed of two sets of three square or rectangular shapes. The rectangular building supports a dome filled with blue enamel, flanked to either side by expanding-armed crosses containing white enamel. A bird, also of white enamel, its wings swept back, is diving vertically down through an opening in the top of the dome.

---

[37] La Rocca, p. 139, nos. 17, 18 and 23
[38] The triangles may have been stamped, or alternatively, produced by the use of a two-pronged engraver to form lines of 'interrupted rocker-arm'. These techniques appear on English copper alloy dress accessories and fittings from the late twelfth to late fourteenth centuries, see Egan and Pritchard 1991, pp. 30-1
[39] La Rocca, p. 141, no. 25
[40] La Rocca, p. 141, no. 24 right
[41] La Rocca, p. 141, no. 27
[42] La Rocca, p. 142, no. 28
[43] See above, footnote 38
[44] Dandridge and Wypyski 2011, pp. 145-152
[45] La Rocca, pp. 137-8, nos. 7-13
[46] Ailes 1982
[47] See Shenton 2002, pp. 69-81
[48] 'Overseas' (French: outre-mer), the general name given to the Crusader states established after the First Crusade

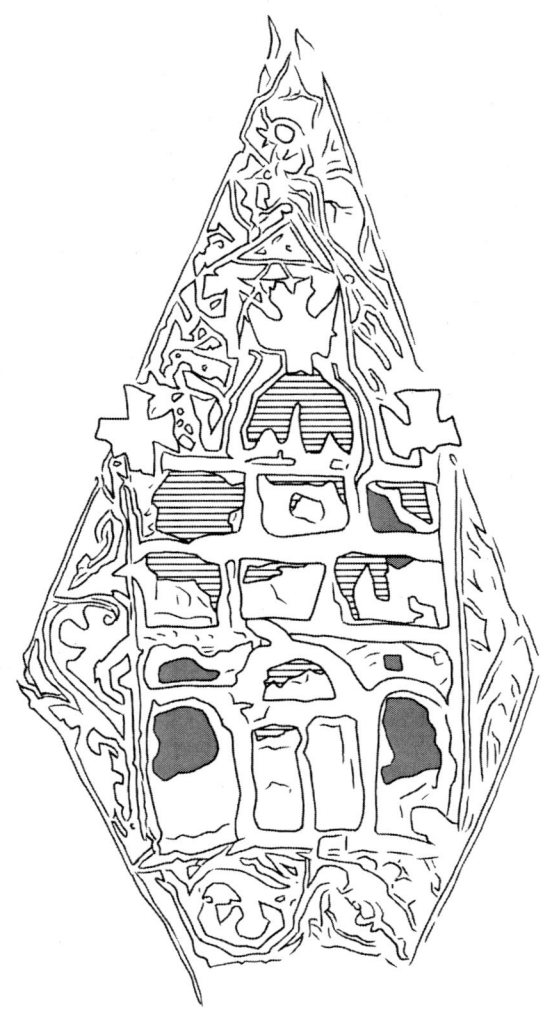

FIG. 5 SIMPLIFIED DRAWING OF THE ENGRAVED AND ENAMELLED DEPICTION OF THE CHURCH OF THE HOLY SEPULCHRE ON SWORD POMMEL NO. **14**. HORIZONTAL HATCHING INDICATES AREAS OF SURVIVING BLUE ENAMEL. GREY TONE SHOWS WHERE THE FACE IS PERFORATED BY MISCASTING OR DAMAGE THROUGH TO THE VERTICAL PERFORATION FOR THE SWORD TANG. THE WHITE ENAMELLED HOLY DOVE AND FLANKING CROSSES ARE LEFT BLANK

FIG. 6 ANONYMOUS INK DRAWING OF (ABOVE) THE CHURCH OF THE HOLY SEPULCHRE SEEN FROM THE SOUTH AND (BELOW) THE EDICULE SEEN FROM THE NORTH-EAST, SHOWING THE HOLY DOVE DESCENDING FROM GOD THROUGH THE OCULUS OF THE DOME OF THE ROTUNDA AND THENCE THROUGH THE CUPOLA OF THE EDICULE, 14TH CENTURY (BIBLIOTECA APOSTOLICA VATICANA, COD. URB. LAT. 1362, F. 1ᵛ)

The design appears to show the Dove sent from God passing through the dome of the rotunda of the Church of the Holy Sepulchre in Jerusalem (Figs. 5 and 6). In its passage down into the Rotunda of the Anastasis, the Resurrection, on Holy Saturday, the Dove was believed to bring the Holy Fire to light a lamp set on the burial slab in the Tomb of Christ below.

If this is correct, the storied image below the dome would be the royal south façade of the Crusader church, as seen from the courtyard known as the Parvis, simplified to show a single doorway beneath the (two) massive decorated stone lintels, which still survive in the Rockerfeller Museum.[49]

No design could be more suitable for the pommel of a sword wielded by a Crusader.

Norwich and Oxford, February 2014

---

[49] Kenaan-Kedar 1999

Acknowledgements

We are most grateful to Helmut Nickel, Donald J. La Rocca, Melanie Rolfe and Adrian Marsden for commenting on the text. The drawings are by Jason Gibbons (Fig. 4, nos. 9 and 15) and Steven Ashley (Fig. 4, no. 5 and fig. 5). The photographs are taken from the Norfolk Historic Environment Record at Gressenhall (Fig. 1, no. 6; Fig. 2, no. 9 and Fig. 3, nos. 15 and 17) and the Portable Antiquities Scheme (Fig. 1, nos. 1, 2, 4 and 8; Fig. 2, no. 10 and Fig. 3, nos. 16, 18 and 19). Photographs of nos. 7, 11, 12, 13 and 14 were kindly supplied by Paul Murawski via Adrian Marsden. The photograph of pommel no. 3 was provided by Roger Dundas, via Timothy Duke, Chester Herald. Digital versions of Figs. 1 – 3 were prepared by Andy Hall. Figs. 4 and 5 were scanned by Mary Chester-Kadwell. We would also like to thank Helen Geake for her help during the preparation of this note.

This paper is dedicated to Andrew Rogerson, who, in more than three decades of sharing an office and the occasional site hut, has taught Steven Ashley much of what he knows about finds, excavation, fieldwork, and how to chilli sprouts.

Bibliography

Ailes, A. 1982, *The Origins of the Royal Arms of England: Their Development to 1199* Reading Medieval Studies Monograph no.2 (Reading)

Boas, A.J. 1999, *Crusader Archaeology: The Material Culture of the Latin East* (London)

Clermont-Ganneau, C. 1896, 'The Depository of Ancient Arrows in the Castle of David – Archaeological or Epigraphic Notes on Palestine' *Palestine Exploration Fund Quarterly Statement*, pp. 136-7

Dandridge, P., and Wypyski, M.T. 2011, 'Sword and Dagger Pommels Associated with the Crusades, Part II: A Technical Study' *Metropolitan Museum Journal* 46, pp. 145-152

Egan, G., and Pritchard, F., 1991, *Medieval Finds from Excavations in London: 3. Dress Accessories c.1150-c.1450* (London)

Kenaan-Kedar, N., 1999, 'The Two Lintels of the Church of the Holy Sepulcher in Jerusalem' in S. Rozenberg (ed.) *Knights of the Holy Land: The Crusader Kingdom of Jerusalem* (Jerusalem), pp. 176-185

La Rocca, D.J. 2011, 'Sword and Dagger Pommels Associated with the Crusades, Part I' *Metropolitan Museum Journal* 46, pp. 133-144

Murawski, P.G. 2003, *Benet's Artefacts* (Ely)

Portable Antiquities and Treasure: Annual Report 2008 (London)

Raphael, K. 1999, 'Crusader Arms and Armor' in S. Rozenberg (ed.) *Knights of the Holy Land: The Crusader Kingdom of Jerusalem* (Jerusalem), pp. 148-159

Rogerson, A., and Ashley, S. 2010, 'A Selection of Finds from Norfolk Recorded in 2010 and Earlier' *Norfolk Archaeology* 46, pp. 121-135

Rozenberg, S., (ed.) 1999, *Knights of the Holy Land: The Crusader Kingdom of Jerusalem* (Jerusalem)

Shenton, C. 2002, 'Edward III and the symbol of the leopard' in P. Coss and M. Keen (eds.) *Heraldry, Pageantry and Social Display in Medieval England* (Woodbridge), pp. 69-81

Too many churches:
the enigma of a Norwich chapel of St Ann

Elizabeth Rutledge

Abstract: Medieval Norwich was a city of churches and chapels. Most of these are well-documented, but an exception is the putative early chapel of St Ann in St Ann Lane. This paper aims to examine the available evidence and in so doing suggests an alternative date and position for the chapel. This involves explaining the possible origin of the name 'St Ann Lane'.

Medieval Norwich was a city of churches. Figure 1 shows the forty-eight late-medieval parishes. In addition, there were parishes that had disappeared by the fifteenth century, such as that of St Margaret Newbridge, which was added to St George Colegate, and St Michael Conesford, that became part of the parish of St Peter Parmentergate.[1] There were also non-parochial churches and chapels, including the great churches of the four Norwich friaries.

One of these is believed to have been the chapel of St Ann in St Ann Lane. Francis Blomefield, writing on the parish of St Clement Conesford in King Street, refers to the chapel in these terms:

> ... and in 1456 Edmund abbot of Wendlyng and the convent released all their right in the advowson [of St Clement], stathe and houses to the city for 100 marks, to be paid by 20 marks a year. And the advowson of the chapel of St Anne, which stood by St Ann's stathe, and had been demolished and united to St Clement about 1370, was particularly conveyed along with it...[2]

This places the chapel in the south-eastern sector of the city, then known as Conesford, and east of King Street (which ran south parallel to the River Wensum), and just south of the river bend. St Ann's staithe, now St Ann Lane, lay on the boundary between the parishes of St Peter Parmentergate and St Julian as shown on Figure 1. On the map of 1746 produced to illustrate his history Blomefield marks 'St Anne's stathe and demolished chapel by it' at the east end of St Ann Lane, beside the river.

Most later writers, understandably, have followed Blomefield's lead, sometimes elevating the chapel of St Ann to a parish church. The 25-inch Ordnance Survey map of 1885 marks 'St Ann's chapel, site of' on the north side of St Ann Lane (then called Staithe Lane), close to the river. James Campbell lists St Ann's among the other parish churches and shows its position at the river end of St Ann Lane.[3] He does, however, point out both that this location is approximate and that it is doubtful whether St Ann's had full parochial status. Brian Ayers includes St Ann's among his list of Norwich parishes that disappeared in the wake of the Black Death,[4] and Carole Hill refers to the chapel as a former parish church in her discussion of Norwich female devotion to St Ann.[5] William Hudson, alone, expresses serious misgivings over the position of an early chapel in St Ann Lane.[6]

St Ann's is not the only church or chapel in King Street that is believed to have disappeared by the fifteenth century, at least three others being in the same position. Working from the south, the one nearest to the city walls was the chapel of St Olaf.[7] Dedicated to a Norwegian saint who was martyred in 1030, the chapel was in the hands of the abbey of St Benet of Holm by the end of the twelfth century.[8] St Olaf's is not among the Norwich churches included in the Norwich Taxation of 1254, but it appears in a late thirteenth-century addition, listing churches not wealthy enough to be taxed in 1254, as 'the chapel of St Olaf in the parish of St Peter [Southgate]'.[9] According to Blomefield St Olaf's was pulled down before 1345.[10] This statement was probably based on the fact that by 1346 Henry le Spicer was paying the city 6d. rent for St Olaf's quay, without mention of the chapel.[11] It might be supposed that the building had disappeared even earlier, as it is not mentioned at all as an abuttal in the detailed Norwich Survey reconstruction plans based primarily on deeds enrolled in the city court from 1285 to 1340.[12] It is clear, however, that these have their limitations. The Norwich antiquary John Kirkpatrick records two deeds for the parish of St Peter Southgate of 1326/7 and of 1366/7 that mention the chapel of St Olaf lying north of the property conveyed, between King Street and the river.[13] One reason for its not appearing more often may be that it lay near the river on the staithe, and so was not always an obvious abuttal. On the other hand, no institution to St Olaf's appears in Tanner's index to the

---

[1] Campbell 1975, p. 24
[2] Blomefield 1805-10, iv, p. 78. This section was first published in 1745
[3] Campbell 1975, p. 23, map 2
[4] Ayers 2003, p. 109
[5] Hill 2010, p. 48
[6] Hudson 1889, pp. 51-2
[7] This should not be confused with the parish church of St Olave, which lay north of the river
[8] West 1932, p. 174
[9] Hudson 1910, pp. 106-7. The addition can be dated between 1272, as it mentions the destruction of the Norwich church of St Ethelbert at that date (Hudson 1910, p. 49), and 1292/3 when William Sessons sold his messuage (see below under St John the Evangelist)
[10] Blomefield 1805-10, iv, p. 65
[11] Hudson and Tingey 1910, p. 365
[12] Norfolk Record Office (NRO), MC 146/52 684X5, plans 134-5
[13] NRO, NCR 21f (98). The earlier of the two, a grant from John to Robert Pillecrow, also survives among the city enrolled deeds (NRO, NCR 1/12 m.1)

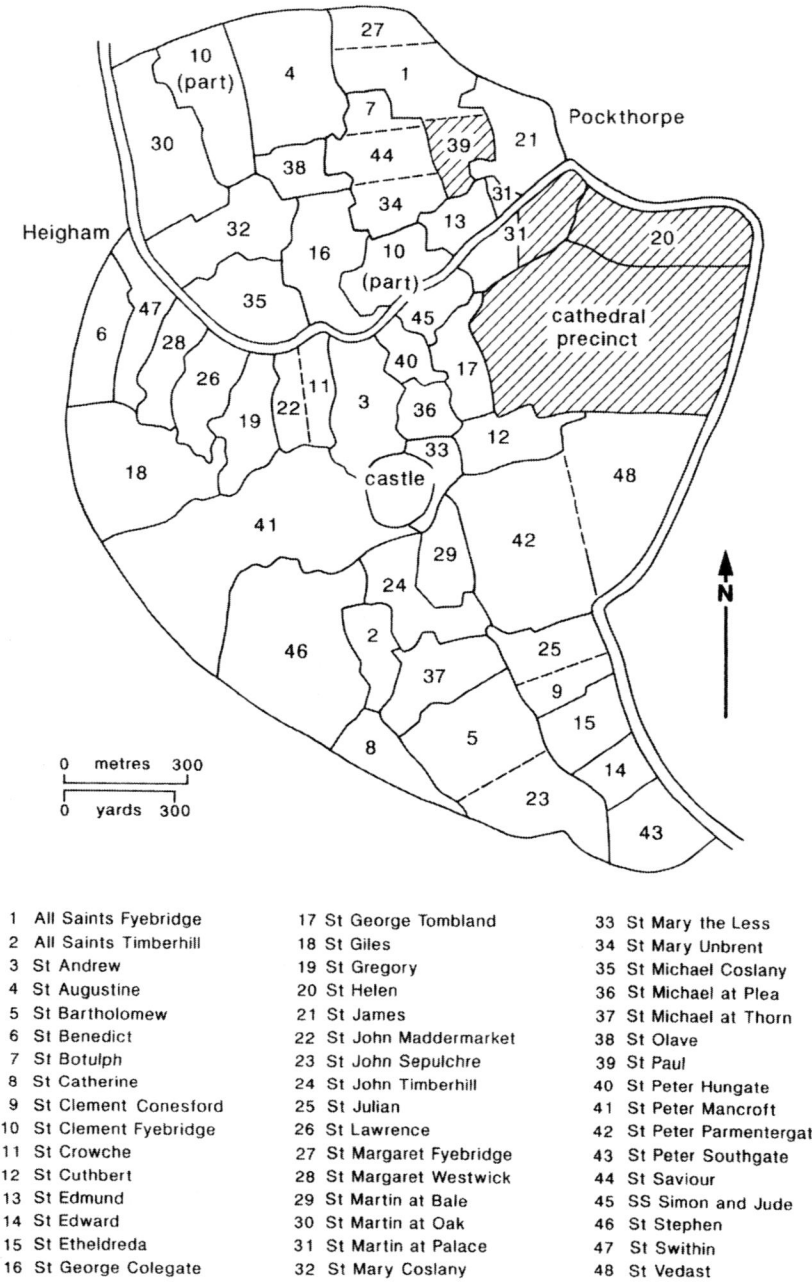

FIG. 1 THE PARISHES OF LATE MEDIEVAL NORWICH (PHILLIP JUDGE)

1 All Saints Fyebridge	17 St George Tombland	33 St Mary the Less
2 All Saints Timberhill	18 St Giles	34 St Mary Unbrent
3 St Andrew	19 St Gregory	35 St Michael Coslany
4 St Augustine	20 St Helen	36 St Michael at Plea
5 St Bartholomew	21 St James	37 St Michael at Thorn
6 St Benedict	22 St John Maddermarket	38 St Olave
7 St Botulph	23 St John Sepulchre	39 St Paul
8 St Catherine	24 St John Timberhill	40 St Peter Hungate
9 St Clement Conesford	25 St Julian	41 St Peter Mancroft
10 St Clement Fyebridge	26 St Lawrence	42 St Peter Parmentergate
11 St Crowche	27 St Margaret Fyebridge	43 St Peter Southgate
12 St Cuthbert	28 St Margaret Westwick	44 St Saviour
13 St Edmund	29 St Martin at Bale	45 SS Simon and Jude
14 St Edward	30 St Martin at Oak	46 St Stephen
15 St Etheldreda	31 St Martin at Palace	47 St Swithin
16 St George Colegate	32 St Mary Coslany	48 St Vedast

Norwich Bishop's Registers, which begin in 1299.[14] What is certain is that the chapel disappeared before 1400. In an inventory of church goods of 1368 (compiled during an archidiaconal visitation) it is described as having lain in past times (*antiquis temporibus*) in the parish of St Peter Southgate, whose church now held its possessions.[15] There is no evidence that St Olaf's was ever of parochial status.

Further up the street lay the church of St Michael Conesford. Its advowson was confirmed to St Benet's abbey in 1147-9 and St Michael's is listed in the post-1272 addition to the Norwich Taxation of 1254.[16] This was definitely a parish church. It appears as a parish in the Taxation of Pope Nicholas in 1291; institutions to the rectory are known from between 1301 and 1351; and the Norwich Survey reconstructions record regular conveyances of property within the parish of St Michael as taking place well into the fourteenth century.[17] The church, itself, however, does not appear as an abuttal on the reconstructions, probably because it was already surrounded by land belonging to the Augustinian friary; by the mid fourteenth century the friars (generally known as the Austin friars) had taken over the

---

[14] NRO, DN/REG 30
[15] Watkin 1947, p. 23. The document is undated but assigned by the editor to 1368 (Watkin 1947, xii)
[16] West 1932, pp. 36-7; Hudson 1910, p. 107
[17] *Taxatio* 1812, pp. 90-1; Blomefield 1805-10, iv, p. 84; NRO, MC 146/52 684X5, plans 118-19

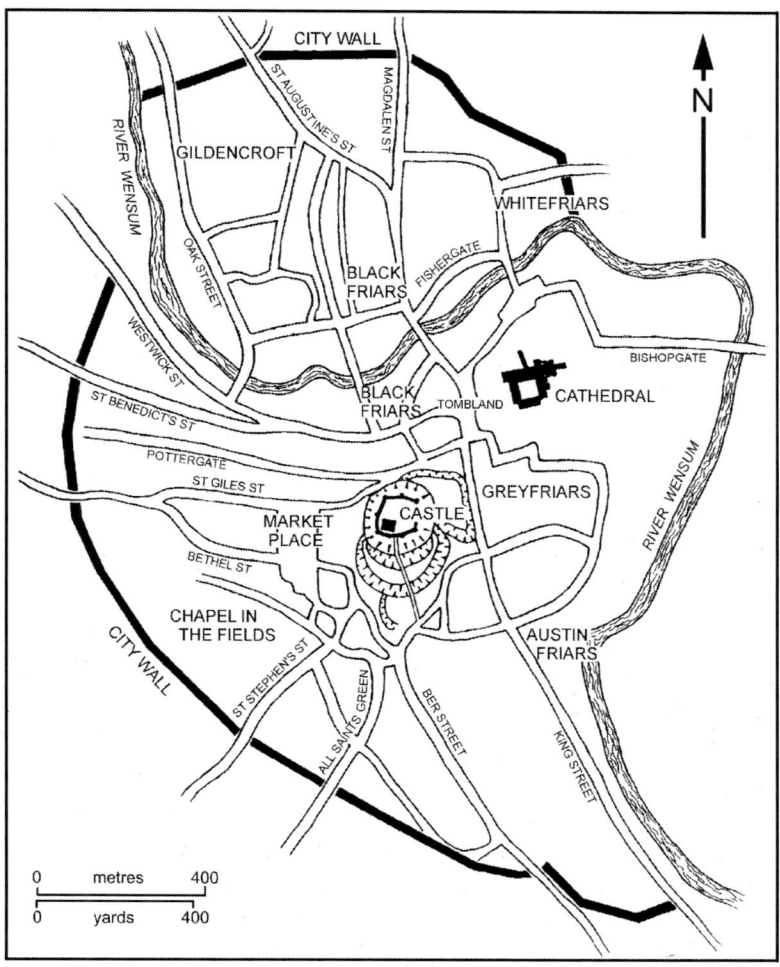

FIG. 2 MEDIEVAL NORWICH (PHILLIP JUDGE)

whole of the parish east of King Street. By 1348 the friary had acquired the advowson of the church and the parish of St Michael was subsequently united to that of St Peter Parmentergate.[18] In the 1368 inventory of church goods the Austin friars are said to have the church of St Michael Conesford within their precinct, having apparently appropriated it in the same year. During his visitation the archdeacon of Norwich had handed over the church goods to Peter Dall a parishioner (*parochiano*) for safe keeping.[19]

The most northerly of the three was the church of St John the Evangelist. This lay on the corner of King Street and Rose Lane, south of the later precinct of the Franciscan friars (Greyfriars), and its churchyard appears as an abuttal in a mid thirteenth-century deed. However neither church nor churchyard can have lasted much longer, as soon after 1272 they are described in the addition to the Norwich Taxation as the place 'where is the tavern of William Seysun'.[20] William Sessons' messuage, described as within the parish of St Peter Parmentergate, appears on the Norwich Survey reconstructions from 1287; he sold the property in 1292/3.[21] Blomefield implies that the site was taken over quite early by the Franciscans, but it was not part of the friars' original precinct and was only owned by them for a comparatively short time in the late fifteenth and early sixteenth centuries.[22] The church was united to that of St Peter Parmentergate and, despite its early disappearance, its possessions are included among those of St Peter in the inventory of 1368.[23]

What is noticeable about the chapel of St Ann in King Street is the complete absence of any early record.[24] Unlike the other churches and chapel discussed above, it is not listed in the taxation of Norwich of 1254 or in the addition of *post* 1272, and it is not a Norwich parish mentioned in the Taxation of Pope Nicholas in 1291. The chapel of St Ann does not appear on the Norwich Survey reconstructions, and, although, as we have seen, this is not necessarily conclusive, nor are there earlier or later title deeds referring to it. Nothing early is known of its advowson and, significantly (again, unlike the other three), it is not mentioned, either on its own or under the heading of St Clement Conesford, in the inventory of church goods of 1368. It was probably this non-appearance in the 1368

---

[18] Kirkpatrick 1845, pp. 136-8; Blomefield 1805-10, iv, p. 85
[19] Watkin 1947, pp. 24-5
[20] NRO, DCN 45/40/20; Hudson 1910, p. 107; Emery 2007, pp. 10-11
[21] NRO, MC 146/52 684X5, plan 115
[22] Blomefield 1805-10, iv, p. 102; Emery 2007, pp. 50, 52-3
[23] Watkin 1947, p. 25
[24] A point also made in Hudson 1889, p. 51

inventory that led Blomefield to believe that the chapel had gone by 1370.

There is another problem in relation to Blomefield's description of the early chapel of St Ann. Unless it was a later foundation than Blomefield suggests, it cannot have been sited at the river end of St Ann Lane, for the simple reason that until at least the end of the fourteenth century there is no evidence of a public right of way to the river at this point.[25] The precursor to the lane first appears in 1285, when the abbot of Woburn granted to John Page part of his holding next to the street. This later became part of the present Dragon Hall complex. At the time of the grant the abbot retained the width of 10ft for cart access between the property granted and the wall of Bartholomew de Acre to the north. This property of Bartholomew de Acre later passed to the Austin friars, probably in 1325.[26] Public access to the water in this area lay about 45 metres to the north, coming out just on the bend of the river where a little stream ran down the east side of the friary. The northerly lane was described as the common way to the water in 1290 and 1291[27] and as a common way in 1329,[28] and may be the closed lane for which the friars paid the king 1d in 1357.[29] Alternatively the northerly lane may not have been closed until 1429/30 when the Austin friars purchased a lane from the city of Norwich for £20.[30] It may even have survived within the precinct of the Augustinian friary, and the later 'My Lord's Garden', as a path or open area in this position is shown on Hochstetter's map of 1789, Millard and Manning's map of 1830 and the Ordnance Survey map of 1885. The first possible mention of the more southerly route as a public right of way comes in 1390/91, when Nicholas de Berford was fined because his servants had lain muck in a lane next to the Austin friars, much of which fell into the river. The reference here, however, may be to the northern way and the first definite documentation of St Ann Lane (though unnamed) comes in 1421, when Robert Clerk, wright, and others were licensed to make a staithe in the common lane on the south side of the Austin friars.[31] Another point bothering Hudson was that by placing the chapel north of St Ann Lane, Blomefield had put it in an area taken over by the Augustinian friary, without there being any evidence of their enclosing it.[32]

None of this is intended to suggest that there was no chapel of St Ann connected with the King Street church of St Clement. Indeed, two late fourteenth-century wills mention one. In 1391 Thomas de Birkeley, rector of the church of St Clement Conesford, left his body to be buried by the altar of St Ann in the church of St Peter Mancroft, if he died in that parish, but in other circumstances to be buried in the chapel of St Ann in the parish of St Clement.

In the same year Thomas Halle of Bramerton left the income from the great tithes of St Clement for the repair of the vestments there, and for the repair of the chapel of St Ann.[33] In 1458 Katherine Marshall bequeathed to St Ann in the church of St Clement Conesford, presumably for an image there, a tablet with a silver chain (*Item lego Sancte Anne in dicta ecclesia 1 tabelet cum cathena argenti*).[34]

The other piece of evidence for the chapel is the record of the transfer of the staithe and the advowson of the adjoining church of St Clement to the city in 1456, as given by Blomefield above. The advowson and the adjoining land were acquired by William de Wendling, the founder of Wendling abbey, in 1266.[35] In 1398 the abbey of Wendling leased the property with the advowson to the city of Norwich for 600 years, for an annual payment of 13s 4d.[36] Neither of these transactions mentioned the chapel of St Ann. The 1456 agreement was for the purchase of the reversion. Although Blomefield gives no reference, his source was the city chamberlains' account for 1456/7, which records the payment of the first instalment of £13 6s 8d (20 marks) to the abbey of Wendling, and what it was paid for.[37] Blomefield's other two references to the chapel being annexed to the church of St Clement may be disregarded.[38] In the first he maintains that John Boor was instituted to the united rectories of St Julian, St Edward and St Clement Conesford with the chapel of St Ann annexed in 1482, and in the second that St Julian with St Edward and St Clement and the chapel of St Ann annexed were consolidated to All Saints in Berstreet in 1737. Neither statement is supported by the Norwich bishops' registers, where the record of the institutions in question makes no mention of the chapel of St Ann, although referring to the other churches as united and annexed.[39]

So what sort of chapel was this chapel of St Ann? First it is clear that it was never a parish church, and its complete absence from the record suggests that it is unlikely to have been in existence as a separate entity before 1368.[40] There is another reason for suggesting a later date. The cult of St Ann developed in the later middle ages with the growth of the veneration of her daughter, the Virgin Mary. Her feast day was not recognised by the pope until 1378, followed in 1382 by an order, as a compliment to Richard II's wife, Anne of Bohemia, to observe the feast throughout the English Church. The popularity of the cult in Norwich may have been increased by the visit of Richard and Anne to the city in 1381. This is not an argument that can be taken too far, as Walter Suffield made St Ann one of the dedicatees of the hospital that he founded in Norwich in 1249, and Norwich cathedral had a chapel of St Ann by

---

[25] This was another of Hudson's concerns: Hudson 1889, p. 51
[26] Shelley 2005, p. 49
[27] Shelley 2005, p. 49 fig. 38
[28] NRO, MC 146/52 684X5, plan 119. However, the plan is misleading as it assumes the lane to be St Ann Lane and places it too far south
[29] Hudson and Tingey 1910, p. 42
[30] NRO, NCR 18a, chamberlains' account book 1384-1448, fol 170d
[31] Kirkpatrick 1889, p. 8
[32] Hudson 1889, pp. 51-2
[33] NRO, NCC Harsyk fols 141d, p. 151
[34] NRO, NCC Brosyard fol 99
[35] NRO, NCR 4a, St Clement Conesford private deeds
[36] NRO, NCR 17b, *Liber Albus*, fols 9d-10
[37] NRO, NCR 17d, Apprenticeship indentures 1548-61 (*sic*), fol xxxi
[38] Blomefield 1805-10, iv, pp. 78, 81
[39] NRO, DN/REG 7, bk 12, fol 97d; DN/REG 22, bk 30A, fol 91
[40] Taylor says that William de Wendling gave the chapel to Wendling abbey on its foundation [*c* 1266]: Taylor 1821, p. 70. No evidence is given and this is probably mere supposition

c 1329.⁴¹ However it reduces the likelihood of an early chapel dedicated to this saint. On the more practical side, only a late foundation could have been sited on St Ann's staithe, and, apart from the lack of evidence and potential problems with the Augustinian friary, there seems no reason at all why a chapel founded here should have been in the hands of the abbey of Wendling. The dates suggest the slight possibility that St Ann's was a chapel at the river end of the more northerly lane, subsequently annexed to the church of St Clement Conesford when the lane was purchased by the Austin friars in 1429/30. This would account for it not being mentioned in earlier transfers of the church of St Clement but appearing in 1456, but, again, does not explain the abbey of Wendling's interest. All the evidence, however, connects the chapel with the parish of St Clement and it seems reasonable to suggest that this is where it lay. It might have been a free-standing chapel on the quay owned by the abbey of Wendling, an explanation possibly compatable with Thomas de Birkeley's desire to be buried in the chapel of St Ann in the parish (rather than the church) of St Clement in 1391,⁴² but not explaining the complete failure to mention the chapel before 1456 whenever the staithe was conveyed, or the reference in 1456 to it being annexed to the church (*eidem ecclesie annex'*). A more satisfactory explanation is that the chapel of St Ann was a later fourteenth-century addition⁴³ actually sited within the churchyard of St Clement. As such it would not appear in abuttals and the 'annexed' could refer not to it being annexed in an ecclesiastical sense but as being physically attached to the church.

What this suggestion does not explain is why, in that case, St Ann Lane and St Ann staithe are so called. That Blomefield, believing as he did in a free-standing chapel of St Ann, should have positioned it on the lane he knew as St Ann's staithe, is not surprising. He may even have seen ruins there which he interpreted as the remains of the chapel, as the Ordnance Survey seems to have done. After all, there may have been the remains of Augustinian friary buildings beside the river, quite apart from ruins of earlier stone houses, such as le Stonhous recorded in a position just north of St Ann Lane in 1329.⁴⁴ Neither 'St Ann staithe' nor 'St Ann lane', however, were early names or appear before the dissolution of the Austin friary in 1538. From the first reference to the staithe in 1421 the lane is described either in relation to the friary to the north or just as a 'common lane',⁴⁵ and 'the common lane' remains the usual terminology used in title deeds up to the end of the seventeenth century.⁴⁶ In fact there was clearly some confusion over its proper name, as both the first detailed map of Norwich in 1696 (by Thomas Cleer) and the James Corbridge map of 1727 mark it as St Anthony's Lane.⁴⁷ However, the term 'St Ann's staithe' occurs regularly in the city records from 1546/7, when it appears in the city chamberlains' accounts.⁴⁸ 'St Ann's lane' is slightly later, being first mentioned in 1695 when the city chamberlain was fined £2 for not repairing the staithe there.⁴⁹ Nevertheless the name was presumably in common currency by *c* 1720, when Kirkpatrick uses it. The question, therefore, is why, if there was no chapel of St Ann sited there, did these names come into use? The simplest explanation is that 'St Ann' originated as an abbreviation. In the same way that Augustinian came to be regularly abbreviated to Austin, so Austin in its turn might be written for brevity as 'Au' or 'An'. Once the Augustinian friary had been dissolved, there would no longer have been the incentive to extend the name.

---

⁴¹ Hill 2010, pp. 18, 45, 173
⁴² This may be just a matter of terminology as in his will Thomas de Birkeley also refers to chapels 'in the parish' of St Peter Mancroft: NRO, NCC Harsyk fol 141
⁴³ Though early enough to be in need of repair or alteration by 1391

⁴⁴ Shelley 2005, p. 48
⁴⁵ Kirkpatrick 1889, p. 8
⁴⁶ For example, NRO, COL/1/115, 1664
⁴⁷ The version of Cleer's map used as a frontispiece to Kirkpatrick 1889 has been altered to give 'St Ann's Lane'
⁴⁸ Kirkpatrick 1889, p. 8
⁴⁹ NRO, NCR 5d/25, 1695

Bibliography

Ayers, B., 2003, *Norwich 'A Fine City'* (Stroud)

Blomefield, F., 1805-10, *An Essay towards a Topographical History of the County of Norfolk*

Campbell, J., 1975, 'Norwich', in M.D. Lobel (ed.), *Atlas of Historic Towns*

Emery, P.A., 2007, *Norwich Greyfriars: Pre-Conquest Town and Medieval Friary* East Anglian Archaeology 120

Hudson, W., 1889, *History of the Parish of St Peter Permountergate, Norwich* (Norwich)

Hudson, W., 1910, 'The Norwich Taxation of 1254', *Norfolk Archaeology* xvii, pp. 46-158

Hudson, W. and Tingey, J.C. (eds.), 1910, *The Records of the City of Norwich* vol. ii (Norwich)

Hill, C., 2010, *Women and Religion in Late Medieval Norwich* (Woodbridge)

Kirkpatrick, J., 1845, *History of the Religious Orders and Communities, Hospitals and Castle, of Norwich*

Kirkpatrick, J., 1889, *The Streets and Lanes of the City of Norwich* (Norwich)

Shelley, A., 2005, *Dragon Hall, King Street, Norwich: Excavation and Survey of a Late Medieval Merchant's Trading Complex* East Anglian Archaeology 112

Taxatio, 1812, *Taxatio Ecclesiastica Anglie et Walliae auctoritate P. Nicholai IV circa A.D.1291*

Taylor, R.C., 1821, *Index Monasticus* (Norwich)

Watkin, Dom. A. (ed.), 1947, *Inventory of Church Goods temp. Edward III* (Norfolk Record Society xix pt 1)

West, J.R. (ed.), 1932, *St Benet of Holm 1020-1210. The eleventh and twelfth century sections of Cott. Ms. Galba Eii* (Norfolk Record Society ii)

Thomas Badeslade:
his life and career from eastern England to north Wales

Bob Silvester

Abstract: A study of Thomas Badeslade reveals a varied career, as copyist, topographical draughtsman, estate surveyor, drainage engineer and atlas compiler. Born probably in Surrey towards the end of the seventeenth century, he surfaced first in Kent illustrating a county history with drawings primarily of the homes of the gentry, before moving to Norfolk where, under the patronage of Robert Walpole, he surveyed the Houghton Hall estates and assessed the drainage problems presented by the Great Ouse in the southern Fens. Falling out with Walpole, his professional life became more peripatetic, but in the mid-1730s he moved westwards to survey lands for some of the big landowners in Cheshire and north Wales, the Grosvenor, Mostyn and Wynn families. Short of work perhaps, he prepared a pocket atlas in 1741-2 and was about to start work for an unknown landowner in mid-Wales when he died at Llandinam in Montgomeryshire in 1744.

Many years ago in the early 1980s I arrived in East Dereham a dedicated late prehistorian and left after seven years of tramping the Norfolk Fens a reasonably resolute medievalist. It wouldn't be correct to infer from this that the forward shift in my chronological interests was fundamentally influenced by the recipient of this *festschrift*, but I have few doubts that his perennial good humour and dedicated approach to the subject even when confronted with numerous bags of small, indeterminate pottery fragments collected from plough-damaged settlements on the silts of the Norfolk Marshland, did influence my thinking. Fieldwalking trips were memorable, less for what was found but more perhaps for the raw garlic sandwiches consumed by AR at lunchtime, an impression indelibly imprinted in my mind thirty years on.

The medieval siltlands bordering the Wash cannot be fully understood solely from documents and archaeology as H.C. Darby inadvertently demonstrated many years ago, and the Fenland Survey fostered in the present writer a deep interest in the work of early surveyors and map-makers who had produced surveys of the southern Fens in the late sixteenth and seventeenth centuries, throwing light on the development of the fenland topography in one of its more transformative eras. Chief amongst these were William Haiwarde's surveys in the last years of Elizabeth's reign and those of the early Stuarts, and full use was made of his maps in unravelling the complexities of the Marshland landscape. Less immediately important at the time was Thomas Badeslade who operated a century later and who seemed to be little more than a copyist of earlier mapmakers creating an invaluable facsimile of Haiwarde's great map of the southern fens which is now lost.

Within a couple of years of moving to north Wales, I was contacted by the late Alec Skempton who was then editing as well compiling parts of the first volume of the *Biographical Dictionary of Civil Engineers*. I was of little help to him in his quest for information on Badeslade whom he knew as a fenland engineer, and when the dictionary appeared in 2002 it was I who learnt more about Badeslade's work in the fens. I encountered Badeslade again in my studies of the limestone plateaux landscapes of north-east Wales and gradually accumulated information on a man who, to use modern jargon, wore different hats at different times during his relatively short career. So I offer this contribution to AR in his *festschrift*, a case of a piece of research that was initiated in a few salient references back in the 1980s and only now thirty years on has materialised into what I hope is a more mature consideration of an accomplished surveyor and draughtsman who made the move from Norfolk to north Wales, nearly three hundred years before I did. I hope he enjoys reading it as much as I have enjoyed researching it.

Thomas Badeslade: perceptions

It is probably the diverse tangents of Badeslade's career that have hindered until now a full statement on the man and his work. This diversity is clearly exposed in the sometimes exclusive descriptions alluding to Badeslade that appear in a number of authoritative dictionaries (though he hasn't made it into the *Dictionary of National Biography*). Repeating what these have to say about the man requires no apology for they set the scene for a career considerably more varied than many of his eighteenth-century contemporaries.

From a Victorian viewpoint Samuel Redgrave in his *Dictionary of Artists of the English School* (1878) stated:

'Thomas Badeslade, topographical draftsman. He practised in London, 1720-1750. He drew many of the seats of the nobility and gentry, which were engraved by Toms and Harris, and made drawings for Dr John Harris's 'History of Kent' published in 1719, and some other publications'.

Almost a century later, E.G.R. Taylor in *The Mathematical Practitioners of Hanoverian England 1714-1840* (1966) wrote:

'Badeslade, Thomas, Engineer, Marine- and Land-surveyor (1724-42). One of the group of surveyors specializing in drainage and navigation canals, Badeslade re-drew and republished John Hayward's [sic] map of the Fens (1604) in 1724. In 1735 he mapped the River Dee etc in relation to a proposed canal to Chester, and published: 1736. The new-cut Canal... and in 1741 *Chorographia Britanniae*'.

In 1982 in his list of major producers of British maps David Smith opined:

> 'Badeslade, Thomas. fl. 1719-45. Engineer and surveyor. Badeslade was basically an engineer interested in the development of waterways and he produced several important works on the subject, particularly concerning land reclamation in the Fens. However, he also drew a set of small county maps of 'Chorographia Britanniae' which was compiled for a tour by the king'.

In the *Dictionary of Land Surveyors and Local Mapmakers* (1997, ii, 19) Sarah Bendall listed the counties Badeslade worked in and classed him as:

> 'Cartographer, engineer, topographical draughtsman, professor of mathematics'.

The fullest biography is in the *Dictionary of Civil Engineers* where Sir Alec Skempton emphasised his fenland work, introducing it in the following terms:

> 'Badeslade, Thomas (fl. 1712-1745), land surveyor, topographical draughtsman and author of a book on fen drainage'.

Badeslade the topographical draughtsman

In the year of his death, 1719, a certain John Harris published the first (and only) volume in what was proposed as a multi-volume county history of Kent.[1] Though Harris lacked the 'scholarship necessary to undertake [such a work]... the published volume is now valuable chiefly for the superb engravings of country houses with which it is illustrated'.[2] Badeslade was responsible for preparing those drawings which comprised elevated views or prospects of some thirty-four country houses and their surroundings in a style that had been developed in the late seventeenth century by Dutch artists who had moved to Britain, the best known being Leonard Knyff.[3] It was a style that emphasised the gardens and designed landscapes with the country house prominent as the centrepiece. The 1719 volume also contained two views of towns, Rochester and Chatham together, and Tunbridge Wells, the latter of interest for the depiction of visitors taking the waters, a well-established practice that had developed from the time the chalybeate springs were discovered early in the seventeenth century.[4] Three further Badeslade drawings – 'the west prospect of the cathedral church of Rochester', 'Howland Great Dock near Deptford' (to which a date of 1717 has sometimes been erroneously attributed) and 'Bromley College' – are extant and appear to have been earmarked for Harris's unpublished second volume.[5]

None of these drawings is dated, but they must be earlier than 1719, possibly by several years, for Colin Flight has noted that the book's publication was delayed by several years after Harris issued his prospectus in 1713. They mark, in as far as can be established, Badeslade's first substantive work and reveal that contrary to what is conventionally assumed he was initially a topographical draughtsman and illustrator. It seems unlikely that we shall ever find out where he learnt these skills or why John Harris employed him.

Over the next twenty years Badeslade put his drawing skills to use on an occasional basis, with some of his later prints being engraved by his long-term collaborator, the London-based W.H. Toms. Within George III's private collection, now in the British Library, are views of Wentworth Castle and Stainborough in Yorkshire (1730), at least two views of Belvoir Castle in Rutland (1731), Averham Park in Nottinghamshire (1731) and from 1735, Mount Edgcumbe near Plymouth in Devon (Fig. 1). Additionally there is a raft of undated drawings of other aristocratic piles such as Belton and Hather Thorpe (Lincs), Exton Park (Rutland) which other evidence suggests was probably prepared in 1730, Keveton House and Ravenfield (both Yorks), Southill (Beds), Shardeloes (Bucks), Tring (Herts) and Boughton (Northants). Many of these were published in 1739.

From 1735 dated topographical drawings reveal Badeslade's move westwards, to north-east Wales and Cheshire, more readily witnessed through his extant estate surveys. There are two prospects of Chirk Castle (Denbs) from that year (Fig. 2), one of Erddig (Flints) from 1739, and from the following year Hawarden Castle (Flints) and Eaton Hall (Ches). These are individual productions, and the inference that we might draw, at least for Badeslade, was that the market in landscape prospects was drying up. Whether he was specifically commissioned to produce these views of stately homes in the 1730s or prepared them in anticipation of subsequent commissions may well remain a mystery other than where household accounts survive. Thus it is reported that documents in the Belvoir archives confirm that Badelslade was employed in 1731, the results seemingly being several drawings of Belvoir and an oil painting of the castle set against the backdrop of the Vale of Belvoir.[6] And it is revealing too that in his testament of 1744 Badeslade noted that Lord Gainsborough of Exton Park near Stamford owed him £100, which might reflect

---

[1] The first edition was produced by D. Midwinter of St Paul's churchyard, London. The plates by Badeslade were later republished as a collection by Henry Chapelle at a date unknown, though possibly around 1740 or 1750 according to the British Library catalogue (Flight 2011, see footnote 5)
[2] Yates 1994, p. 210
[3] Harris 1995, p. 8
[4] Lynam 1953, p. 24
[5] The illustrations have been listed and an invaluable commentary prepared by Colin Flight dated March 2011 at www.kentarchaeology.ac/topographicaltradition/1719-badeslade
[6] Reproduced in Harris 1995, p. 60. As John Harris points out, an oil painting would be a departure, even for Badeslade with his range of specialisms. Harris has suggested that perhaps only part of the painting was by Badeslade, but possibly he did the initial drafting leaving someone else to produce the painting. Alternatively the records which Harris had not had a chance to examine, refer not to the painting but to the prospects referred to above

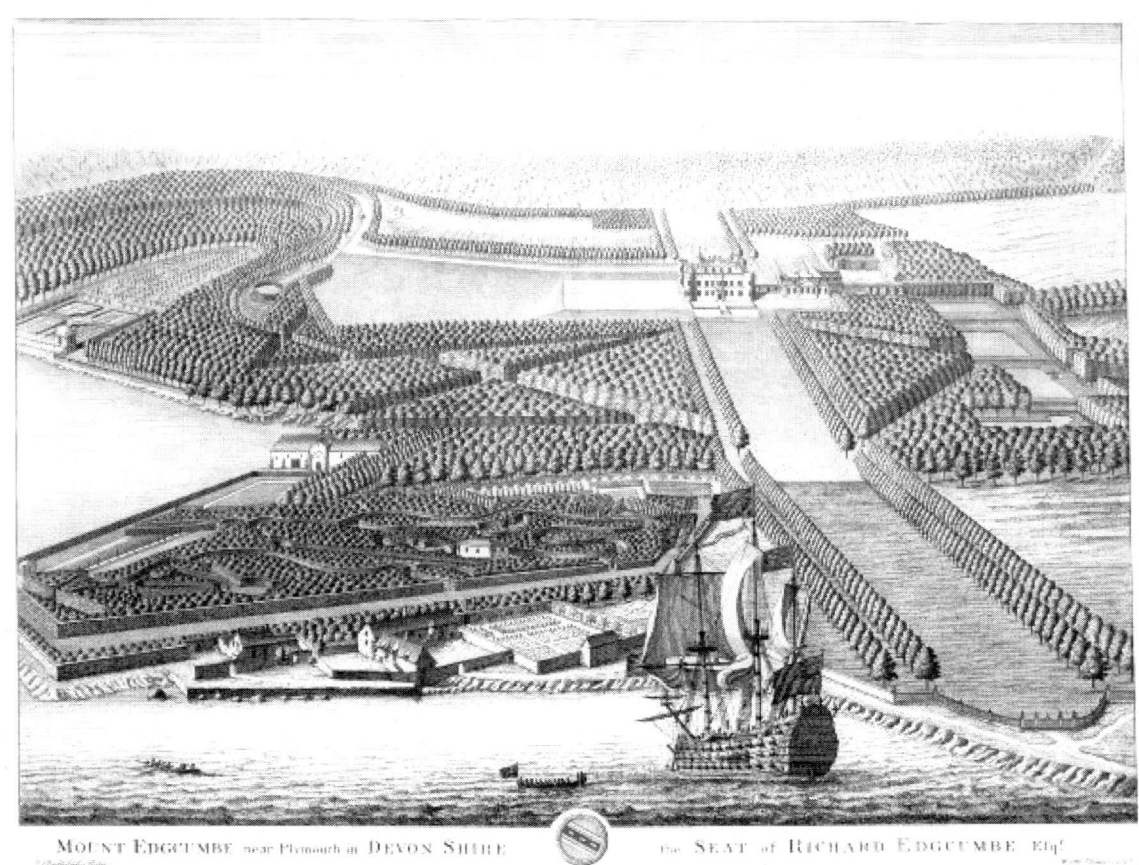

Fig 1 Mount Edgcumbe in Devon, drawn in 1735

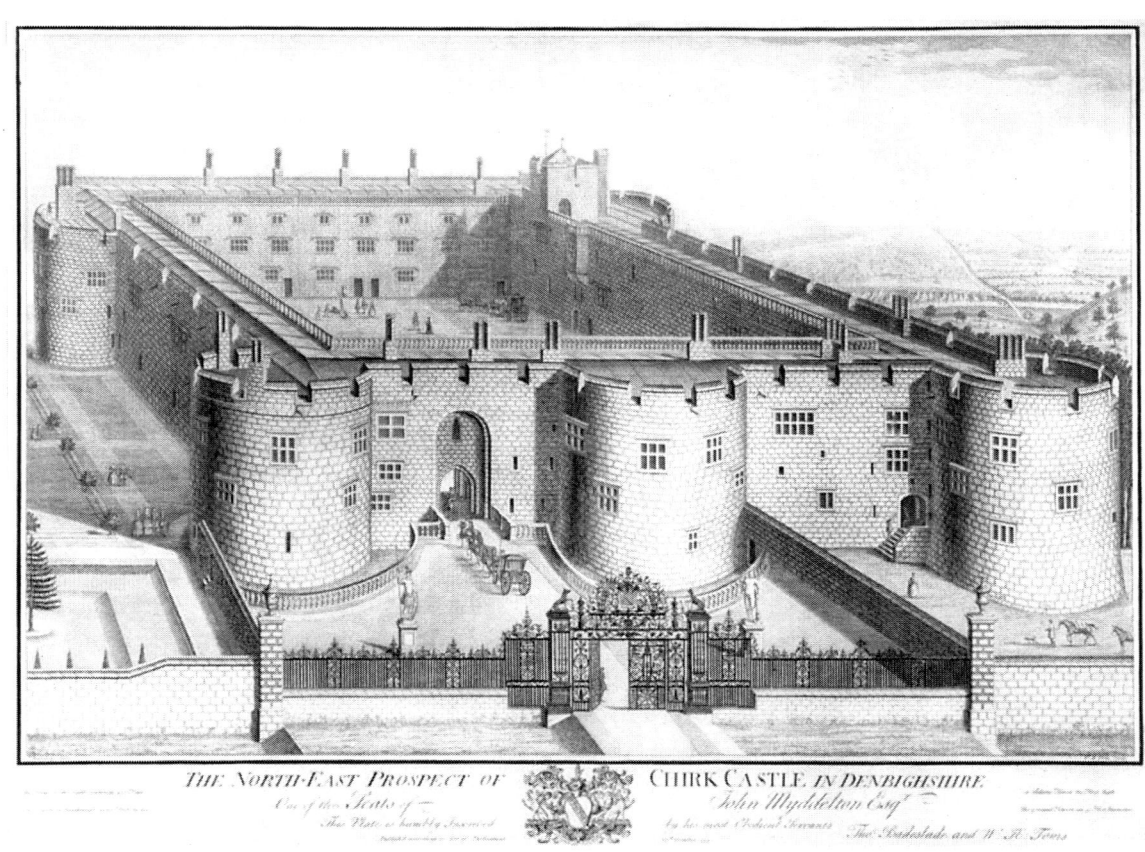

Fig. 2 The north-east prospect of Chirk Castle, Denbighshire, engraved in 1735. This is an atypical drawing by Badeslade in as much as the castle fills almost the entire frame. By contrast Mount Edgcumbe (Fig 1) from the same year is much more typical of his perspective drawings

in part an unpaid charge for the drawing of the house noted above, although it is perhaps more likely to relate to the engineering works that he had undertaken for the aristocrat more than a decade earlier.

A late attempt to capitalise on his topographical drawing skills came with the publication of *Vitruvius Britannicus* (1739). Sub-titled 'a collection of plans, elevations and perspective view of the royal palaces, noblemen [sic], and gentlemen's seats in Great Britain not exhibited in any collection of this nature hitherto published', this was the fourth volume in a series that is inextricably linked with the Scottish architect Colen Campbell (1676-1729) who had published the first three volumes between 1715 and 1725.[7] Modern scholarship has deemed the fourth volume a poor collection compared with its three predecessors, presumably on the basis of the quality of the drawings.[8] The volume was designed according to the title page by J. Badeslade and J. Rocque, the latter immediately recognisable as Badeslade's better known but younger contemporary, John Rocque, while the former appears to be Thomas himself, disguised through a typographical error by the engraver of the 1739 title page. It is conceivable but unlikely that the designer was his brother, John, and that Badeslade himself was responsible only for providing some of the views, effectively drawing on his back catalogue.[9] However, it can be inferred from Badeslade's testament in 1744 that his brother was not at all familiar with his 'engravings of gentlemen's seats', making it unlikely that John had had a hand in the *Vitruvius Britannicus* compilation. Of just over fifty plates, Badeslade drew twenty of them and Rocque contributed most though not all of the remainder. Badeslade's engravers included Toms, Van der Gucht, Thomas Bowles and an otherwise unidentified I. (or J.) Harris. Included from the previous decade were his drawings of Averham Park (1731), Belvoir Castle (1731), Wentworth Castle (1730) and Mount Edgcumbe (1735), while the inclusion of Heanton Satchville Hall at Petrockstowe in Devon, acquired through marriage by Robert Walpole's son, also Robert and later the second earl of Orford, might go back to the 1720s, and there are also the undated prospects of houses in the Home Counties such as Southill and Tring.

There is a single anomaly in this corpus of Badeslade's drawings. In the Natural History Museum are two prints from a copper plate engraving of 1737 entitled *To Sir R. Grosvenor. This plate of the Great American Aloe that blow'd in his gardens at Eaton Hall in Cheshire is dedicated by J. Fossey, T. Badeslade delin*, both bound into a volume entitled *Agave Americana* by John Fossey.

It is as far as I have been able to establish the only non-topographical drawing by Badeslade.

Badeslade the engineer

A key to understanding various aspects of Badeslade's early working life was his relationship with Robert Walpole of Houghton Hall in Norfolk. Walpole was 'prime minister' between 1721 and 1742, and died in 1745. It is likely that Badeslade was initially brought to Houghton to draw the old house and was then employed to survey Walpole's estate (see below). But his emergence as a drainage specialist can also be attributed to Robert Walpole. In his capacity as MP for King's Lynn, Walpole was approached by the Corporation in the early 1720s at a time when they were concerned about the silting of the Great Ouse and its outfall into the Wash and the decay of Lynn Harbour. After taking advice Walpole encouraged Badeslade to collect authentic records about drainage in the Fens and compile observations on the tides at the river's outfall below Lynn. The results, after three years of research, were published as *The History of the Ancient and Present State of the Navigation of the Port of King's-Lyn and of Cambridge* (1725) and contained a long discourse on how the problems of silting might be solved. There was too a series of maps, almost all derivative, but no less important for that. Badeslade produced *inter alia* the copy of William Haiwarde's lost map of the Fens, his own map of the Bedford Level showing the drainage works of past adventurers, original plans and elevations of Denver Sluice,[10] and maps of the Thames and Humber Estuaries.

He was not alone in considering the problems caused by the sluggish flow of the fenland rivers and various reports from other 'experts' appeared during the next few years which led to a further publication from him in 1729, *A Scheme for Draining the Great Level of the Fens, called Bedford Level, and of Improving the Navigation of Lyn-Regis*. H.C. Darby pointed out that Badeslade's second volume criticised the various proposals put forward by a succession of experts from Vermuyden in the 1630s onwards and it concluded with his own design 'founded upon philosophical and mathematical truths'.[11] In due course his 'suggestions became to his successors but one more scheme to criticise and to replace. For, like his predecessors Badeslade had failed to realise that the lowering of the peat surface was the greatest single factor that underlay the evils of the time'.[12] His designs to improve the drainage of that part of the black fen lying north-east of Peterborough and known as the North Level, by improving the outfall of the Shire Drain, were put forward in 1724 and a plan published two years later, but came to nothing.[13]

In the four years separating his two publications Badeslade appears to have been gaining practical experience in

---

[7] A link between Campbell and Badeslade is provided by Houghton Hall, where Sir Robert Walpole appointed Campbell as architect in the early 1720s, a time when Badeslade was still patronised by Walpole
[8] Clayton 1998, p. 48
[9] While the title page indisputably carries the names J. Badeslade and J. Rocque, individual plans are inscribed 'T. Badeslade delin' and in some instances 'W. H. Toms Sculp', referring to Badeslade's long-term collaborator. However, others were engraved by a John Harris, not to be confused with the author of the *History of Kent*

---

[10] Reproduced in Darby 1983, figs. 32, 63 and 65
[11] Badeslade 1729, preface; Darby 1983, p. 115
[12] Darby 1940, p. 122
[13] Skempton et al. 2002, p. 28

drainage matters. He ranged beyond East Anglia, claiming in 1729 to have been at work supervising the cleaning of the harbour at Bideford in north Devon, and later he carried out some 'waterworks' for Lord Gainsborough at Exton Park (Rutland) in 1730,[14] the nature of which remain a mystery.

We may assume that the collapse of his relationship with Robert Walpole brought an end to his interest in the Fens. Having clashed with another fenland drainage engineer Nathaniel Kinderley over the Great Ouse, Badeslade locked horns with him again in 1735 over a ship canal that Kinderley was constructing beside the Dee Estuary below Chester. This led to the emergence of a further set of pamphlets with his adversary in this instance being the engineer John Grundy. In 1735 came Badelsade's *Reasons......Shewing How the Works now Executing.... to Recover and Preserve the Navigation of the River Dee will Destroy the Navigation* and in the following year *The New Cut Canal, Intended for Improving the Navigation off the City of Chester...Compared with the Welland... and Deeping Fens* (1736). In spite of his reservations the excavation of the canal continued, effectively silencing his voice. Badeslade's only other contribution to drainage and rivers came in incidental fashion in 1740 when with the assistance of the young John Boydell who was later to establish a significant reputation as an engraver and printseller,[15] Badeslade prepared a plan of the old and new Dee rivers seemingly for a court case related to the manor of Hawarden which had suffered some loss of land through the construction of the new cut. True to form Badeslade recognised a commercial opportunity for the map was engraved to allow multiple copies to be made: the copper plate itself survives in the Flintshire archives (*D/DM/191*).

Badeslade the estate surveyor

Badeslade's earliest original survey on present evidence is from 1719, of tenements in Leadenhall Street, London leased from the warders and assistants of Rochester Bridge, though this is not his earliest map. Seven years earlier, he had copied a 1657 map of an estate extending across the Kentish parishes of Chatham, Gillingham, Bredhurst, Boxley and Hartlip which had come into the possession of the Dean and Chapter of Rochester Cathedral.[16] There is no explanation as to the purpose of the copy, and it remains an isolated and anonymous marker to the start of his career.

Leadenhall Street was followed by surveys of Sir Robert Walpole's estates in Norfolk. There are eight of these at Houghton Hall, covering parts of Houghton and neighbouring parishes, and five of the maps exist in both draft and final forms. As far as can be established most date to 1720, although the work probably commenced in 1719 for Badeslade's invoice from April 1720 reveals that he had surveyed over 9,400 acres, no mean achievement for an inexperienced land surveyor. His novice status is reinforced by a reference to him being paid 5s by Walpole for the purchase of a surveyor's chain, a standard piece of equipment in the eighteenth-century surveyor's toolbox and one that an experienced surveyor would already have owned.[17] Two of the maps are atypical. For whatever reason the survey of Walpole's Great Massingham estate was conducted in 1730, ten years after the others. More intriguing is the map of Harpley, the parish immediately to the south of Houghton. It too is dated to 1720 but in its decorative details – the title cartouche, scale bar compass rose and monochromed coat-of-arms – and the appearance of Badeslade's autograph, it is entirely different from the remaining maps. The most likely explanation, to my mind, is that Harpley was a trial survey, commissioned by Walpole who was content with the mapping style for the landscape but objected to the heavy decorative embellishments initially employed by Badeslade which were replaced by less elaborate forms on subsequent surveys, although the Walpole arms were emphasised in colour.

The next extant maps expose Badeslade's peripatetic activity in the years after 1729. There are two stray Norfolk surveys, of Wiggenhall on the edge of the Fens in 1729 and of Congham in 1732. It is reasonably clear from the sparse evidence that he was not going to make a living from estate surveying in East Anglia. Whilst working for the Earl of Gainsborough at Exton Hall (Leics) he surveyed the lord's landholding at Cottesmore and Barrow.[18] A fragment of a map of an unknown part of the Exton estate and a survey of the lordship of Exton and Horn,[19] specifically dated to 1730, signify that the Cottesmore survey, the best known, may have been part of a set of surveys. In 1734 he surveyed Epperstone in Nottinghamshire for Lord Howe, and from this time too there may have been a map of the manor of Barnston, known only from its surviving terrier in the Derbyshire Archives (S. Bendall: *pers. comm.*). In the following year Badeslade surveyed a farm called Edmunds at Shere in Surrey for Sir John Evelyn, as far as can be established a solitary commission. There is little doubt that other maps, perhaps unsigned, yet remain to be identified. Every county archive office holds unattributed maps and where a surveyor moved around the country the correlation of a survey with a particular surveyor is likely to be happenstance. The picture that emerges in the earlier 1730s is of a surveyor who took what work he could get regardless of what part of the country it was in.

---

[14] Skempton et al. 2002, p. 28
[15] Boydell (1720-1804) according to his autobiography discovered his vocation when he saw Badeslade's drawing of Hawarden Castle which had been engraved by W.H. Toms (1740). A year later he was taken on as an apprentice by Toms in London (www.oxforddnb.com/view/article/3120)
[16] Bergess 1992, p. 97
[17] Eden 1973, p. 480
[18] Together with a commentary, portions of this map are accessible on the internet at www.leics.gov.uk/index/leisure_tourism/local_history/recordoffice/recordoffice_exhibitions/record_office_exton_project/record_office_exton_project-feature.htm
[19] It is not clear from the Leicestershire Record Office catalogue whether the lordship map is a written survey or a map (DE3214/4535). At this time, the latter seems more likely

By 1737 Badeslade was surveying lands for Sir Robert Grosvenor of Eaton Hall, south of Chester and close to the border separating Cheshire from Wales. Initially the surveys focussed on lowland estates around Chester, but at some point a grander plan was devised to map all of the Grosvenor land holdings, including the commons that constituted significant tracts of upland within the manors and lordships acquired by the family in northeast Wales. He mapped Halkyn Mountain in 1738, one of the great metalliferous areas in Flintshire, together with other wastes in the hundreds of Rhuddlan and Coleshill, and two years later the mountain lands of Bromfield and Yale, further south in Denbighshire. Some of these surveys were straightforward, the mapping of the arable lowlands around Eaton Hall and the Dee being the standard fare of most seventeenth- and eighteenth-century estate surveyors (Fig. 3). But the mapping of the upland commons was a very different matter. These can be classed as extensive surveys rather than the intensive surveys epitomised by open fields and small enclosures in lowland Cheshire and will have involved considerable travel and physical effort.

The extent of the commons was on an altogether different scale from the enclosed lands. Badeslade himself wrote that his map of the hundreds of Rhuddlan and Coleshill was '10 feet long and 5 feet broad, though done by the smallest scale I could use'. Both commons maps were drawn to a scale of 8 inches to the mile (Flintshire Archives GR/332). The upland maps did not depict the fieldscapes of the parishes, but only the open hill pastures, yet their boundaries are shown in some detail and look to be reasonably accurate, as do the intakes enclosed on them. While ostensibly the surveys of the commons represented simply the final strand in the complete depiction of the Grosvenor estate, there were specific purposes to these maps, explained by Badeslade in his title to the later 1740 survey which read: A map of mountain land in the two hundreds of Bromfield and Yale in the county of Denbigh in the Principality of Wales. Done for Sr Robert Grosvenor Baronet. This map sheweth the Lead Works and Coal Works on the mountains; also the Incroachments or Land Inclosed from the Mountains. Surveyed by Thomas Badeslade 1740.

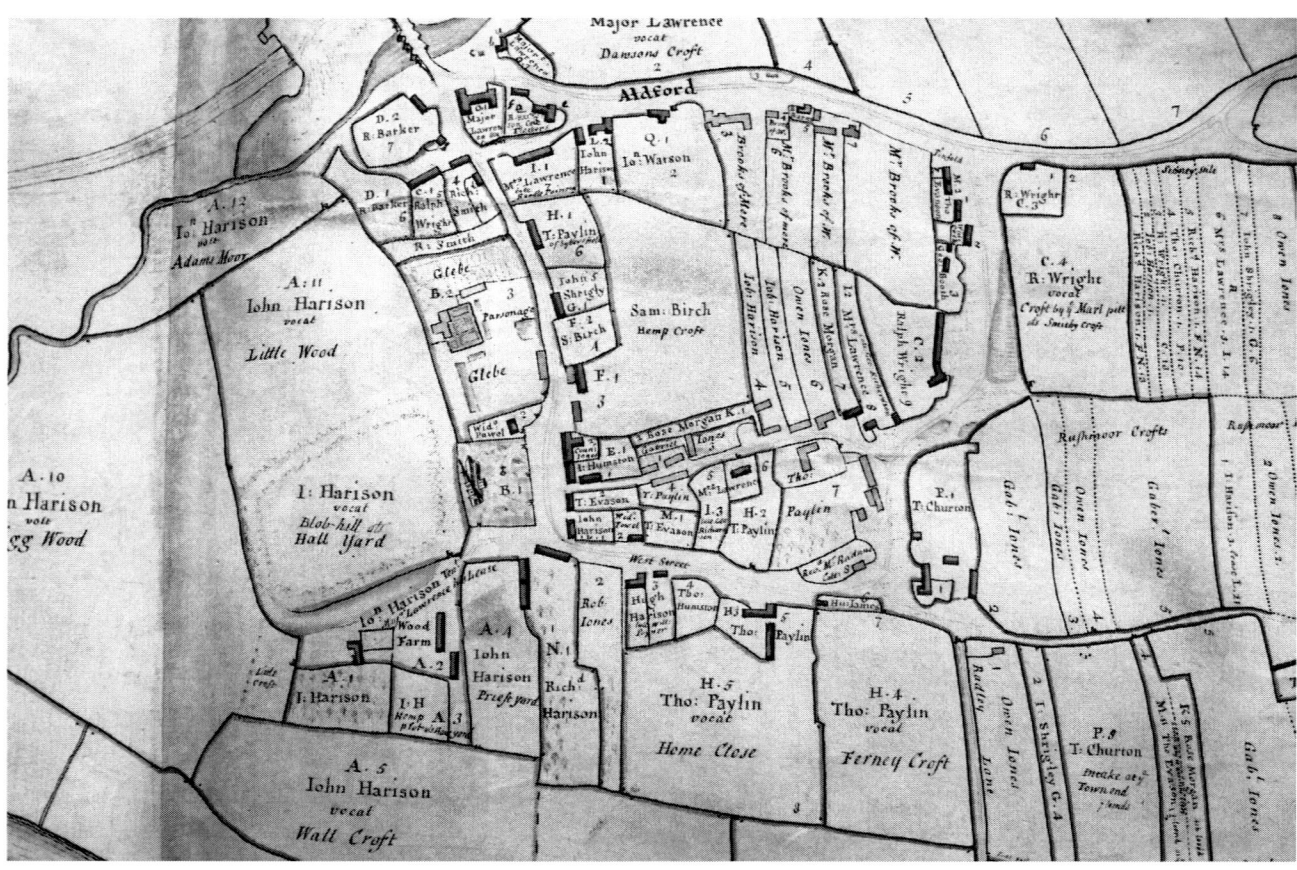

FIG. 3 ALDFORD, CHESHIRE SURVEYED IN 1738, SHOWING THE CHURCH IN PERSPECTIVE, THE ADJACENT MOATED SITE AND SURVIVING STRIP FIELDS. REPRODUCED BY PERMISSION OF THE DUKE OF WESTMINSTER AND THE TRUSTEES OF THE 4TH DUKE OF WESTMINSTER'S SETTLEMENT

Badeslade's ambition was the production of a volume containing all the surveys that he undertook for Grosvenor. His letter of 30 December 1738 notes that 'if the fair drafts are to be put into the book of maps, I would propose drawing Halkyn Mountain by itself, and Soughton, and the rest make a third map. Am I to cast up the contents of each mountain?'. This did not happen. The oversized maps of Rhuddlan and Coleshill (1738) and Bromfield and Yale (1740) are rolled maps, while the other estate plans remain as individual maps in the Eaton Hall archives. One draft map – for Stockton Hall, Malpas – survives in the Flintshire Record Office.

As well as creating the individual maps of the landholdings, seven in total together with the two much larger commons maps, Badeslade reduced each survey to a common size for integration in a general map which provided a geographical perspective of the entire Grosvenor estate. He termed this the index map to 'the book of mapps', presumably the unrealised precursor of the surviving bound volume which contains the terrier listing the details of all tenanted and demesne lands surveyed 'in the years 1737-8-9'. The Bromfield and Yale map lies a little apart from the rest, for it carries the date 1740. Like its Halkyn Mountain counterpart it shows newly enclosed intakes, but it is not cited in the bound terrier, and unlike the Halkyn area, the index map is not cross-referenced to the pages of a prototype schedule. Evidently the Bromfield survey was an afterthought, following the completion of the Cheshire and Flintshire surveys, but soon enough after for a reduced version to be added by Badeslade to the index map.

During the later 1730s Badeslade did not work exclusively for Grosvenor. As is evident from a letter of December 1738 cited below he was also employed by another of the great landowners in the north-east of Wales, Sir Thomas Mostyn of Mostyn Hall in Flintshire. In 1738 he surveyed the hall and park and part of the demesne at Mostyn, and during the following three to four years other Mostyn holdings that included land on the edge of the lower Conwy Valley (1741), around Llangollen in the upper Dee Valley (1742 and in rough draft only), as well as the Gloddaeth Estate near Llandudno (1742). Undated maps of Mostyn's several estates in Cheshire must also date to these years.

Towards the end of his career he was employed by another of the great north Walian landowners, Sir Watkin Williams Wynn, whose main residence and landholdings at Wynnstay near Wrexham were supplemented by other properties across the north of the country and extended into Shropshire. There was no established tradition of estate mapping at Wynnstay in the eighteenth century and different portions of Wynn's extensive landholdings were mapped on a piecemeal basis over many years.[20] Badeslade appears to have been amongst the first to have served Wynn, employed in 1741 to survey several of his demesne holdings including Wynnstay, the year after Wynn inherited the estates from his father. As far as can be determined only one of his maps is now extant, that of Llangedwyn in Denbighshire, but quite remarkably Badeslade also produced a 'pocket book' containing the maps with their schedules reduced to a smaller and more manageable size, a little larger than foolscap. The title page displays various cameo views of Wynnstay and the front views of Llangedwyn and Llanvorda, each set in a foliated cartouche. This was clearly a product for Sir Watkin's own delectation, focussing solely on his string of demesnes and gardens, and was meant no doubt to impress his friends and fellow gentry.

It is evident, too, that there are surveys of which we know nothing. Badeslade's testament in 1744 records that he had produced a survey for the late Lord Howe (possibly though not certainly that of Epperstone compiled ten years earlier) for which he had yet to be reimbursed, that Sir Peter Warburton at Arley Hall near Northwich (Ches) owed him for a survey, as did John Wynne (d.1749) of Gop in Flintshire for a recently produced map, probably of land within the parish of Trelawnyd. Neither of the latter two can be recognised in Badeslade's surviving works.

Some surveyors have a mapping style that is immediately recognisable. Thomas Badeslade's is amongst the more distinctive that I have encountered. His lettering is neat and slightly 'blocky', and changed relatively little over the twenty and more years that he prepared surveys. The format is such that a Badeslade map never appears cluttered, even where a considerable amount of labelling is included on the map, as with the tenants of open-field strips. But over time there were refinements in the presentation, more to do with the labelling of outlying areas where large and rather intrusive lettering gave way to more restrained forms, and where the colours that he used became more subdued. Noticeable too at a time when elaborate and often highly decorated cartouches were popular, where every mapmaker perpetuated a style of his own, mapping conventions showed considerable variety and accurate depictions cannot be relied on, Badeslade's later maps exhibit a consistent appearance that lack elaborate embellishments. Cartouches were frequently eschewed, a map's title typically being given in plain print at the top or bottom of the sheet; and north points and scale bars were similarly plain in comparison with many that were employed by his contemporaries. A further modification that materialised around 1738 was the inclusion of a lettered grid on each map, presumably a mechanism for the identification of specific fields or features; the inclusion of such a grid is not unique but nor is it common. Badeslade signed relatively few of his early maps – of the Houghton Hall collection only Harpley carries his name though as we have seen this was an atypical product. By 1730 appending his autograph was becoming the norm.

---

[20] Silvester 2009, p. 54

Badeslade, the atlas compiler

It was late in his career that Badeslade turned his hand to a new project, the *Chorographia Britanniae,* a small-sized atlas of county maps. It has been suggested that it was produced for George II in advance of an intended royal tour of England and Wales but this is belied by the introduction to the volume which reveals that the maps were drawn by order of 'his late majesty King George I'. The first Hanoverian king had died in 1728 so we can assume that Badeslade had started this compilation while still in favour with Walpole, and had put it to one side when the king died or the royal tour did not materialise, only to pick it up again years later when he identified a niche market and was short of other work.

Engraved by W.H. Toms, some of the maps in the set carry the date 1741 but *Chorographia Britanniae* was not published until the following year. It was the earliest eighteenth-century county atlas of pocket-book size and proved to be a success, soon being distributed by twenty-six booksellers and going through three editions and eight printings.[21] Significantly, 1741 was also the year that Badeslade produced the pocket book of Sir Watkin Williams Wynn's five demesnes in north Wales. One of these projects surely inspired the other, and assuming that the pocket-book maps for George I had progressed beyond the initial planning stage it seems probable that these gave him the idea for the demesne booklet. The atlas contained four general maps showing among other things the coastline of southern Britain with its harbours and docks, a general map of England and Wales defining the counties, a map of the roads leading out of London, and a map of roads linking major towns and cities with the distances between them. Each county map was accompanied by a column of topographical notes on the major towns with their market days, fair dates, the number of MPs returned to parliament, and the main rivers (Fig. 4). Contrary to his claims, Badeslade did not publish individual maps for the counties of Wales – instead there were two maps of north and south Wales, mirroring the approach to the Principality adopted by Christopher Saxton a century and a half previously. All the drawings were prepared by Badeslade and were undoubtedly derived from the county maps of earlier mapmakers, while the road maps can only have had their origin in Ogilby's *Britannia* (1675). Close 'textual' analysis would perhaps clarify whether Badeslade relied on Saxton, Speed or Morden or a combination of these for his source material.

New editions came out after Badeslade's death. In April 1752, it was being touted in the London Gazette as 'the cheapest and most correct sett of maps ever yet published', at a price of 12s for a bound and coloured volume.

Thomas Badeslade – the anatomy of a career

Impossible though it has been to trace either his date of birth or his origins, we can assume that Thomas Badeslade was probably born in the 1690s or perhaps a little earlier, though certainly in the closing years of the seventeenth century. The likelihood is that the family home was in the southern home counties just outside London, and the most precise location yet given is Godalming in Surrey.[22] With such a distinctive and rare surname, we might ponder, though without a solitary scrap of supporting evidence, that like Knyff, Kip, Rocque, Scalé and perhaps others who achieved prominence in the eighteenth century for their drawing and surveying skills, he had a west European background and that the surname was an anglicised version of a continental original.

From these anonymous beginnings, he surfaced as a skilled topographical draughtsman by the second decade of the eighteenth century, although he commenced his career as a copyist, producing a duplicate of an estate map of the modest landholding of a Kentish yeoman, Thomas Long. Broadly speaking his career is mapped out through the finished products that have come down to us. In this respect, though, he is little different from numerous other surveyors who operated in the eighteenth century. He will not have developed his skills overnight and we should assume that John Harris would not have commissioned a complete novice to prepare the plates for his projected history of Kent. But where Badeslade learnt his trade is at present unknown, though there can be little doubt that the works of Leonard Knyff (1650–1722) and Jan Kip (1652-1722), the Dutch team of draughtsman and engraver responsible for the grand volume of elevated perspective drawings of aristocratic houses known as *Britannia Illustrata* (1707) must have been highly influential.

It was presumably the publication of Harris's county history that drew Robert Walpole's attention to Badeslade, leading to an invitation to attend Walpole, soon to become the First Lord of the Treasury, at Houghton Hall. No drawing now survives of Houghton in the topographical drafting tradition in which Badeslade had already demonstrated his abilities, but significantly the Houghton archives preserve Badeslade's account from 1720 for his estate surveys and also allude to a 'perspective draught of the house' which has not survived. It was in 1720 that Walpole decided to rebuild Houghton having perhaps contemplated the idea for some time, so it is not surprising that a drawing of the old house, now seen as outmoded and soon after demolished, has not survived. Almost certainly the view was an original drawing that never progressed to a stage where it could be engraved and more widely distributed. His sojourn in Norfolk led to some other commissions as with a drawing of Walsingham Priory from 1720, prepared for the Society of Antiquaries.[23] There is too

---

[21] Batten and Bennett 1996, p. 56

[22] Worms and Bayton-Williams 2011, p. 35
[23] British Museum 1829, p. 454. Only two copies are recorded, one in the British Library where it came from the Royal Collection of George

FIG. 4 BADESLADE'S POCKET-SIZED MAP OF NORFOLK FROM *CHOROGRAPHIA BRITANNIAE* PUBLISHED IN 1742

the drawing of Heanton Satchville Hall at Petrockstowe in Devon the family home of the heiress who married Walpole's son, also Robert. This has cautiously been given a date of around 1720 in the Houghton Archives catalogue but its appearance, undated, in the collection that made up *Vitruvius Britannicus* (1739) and engraved by Toms whose collaboration with Badeslade cannot at present be pushed back further than 1731, make such an early date questionable. What is unusual is that up to six of Badeslade's preliminary pencil drawings for Heanton Satchville survive at Houghton Hall.

We are left with the estate surveys that were produced of Walpole's lands in the parishes around Houghton Hall, all but Great Massingham from 1720, and then the shift to the fenlands and their drainage, which seems to have started in 1723 as a result of Walpole's recommendation to the Corporation of King's Lynn. Badeslade evidently committed himself wholeheartedly to this project on the drainage of the Bedford Level and the outfall of the Great Ouse over the next few years, yet it is difficult to envisage his entire time taken up with this, and there must be similar queries for the period around 1725 when he expanded

---

III, the other in the Society of Antiquaries Library where it is plate 6 in Volume I of *Vetusta Monumenta*. The importance of patronage and the lengths that Badeslade went to obtain it may be seen at Walsingham. Colin Flight has noted that Badeslade's additional drawing of Bromley College, Kent carries the legend that it was 'founded and Endowed by Iohn Warner late Bp. of Rochester for Twenty Clergymens Widdows and a Chaplaine A.D. 1672. This Plate is Humbly inscrib'd to Lee Warner Esq. of Walsingham in the County of Norfolk 1720.' Lee Warner owned the abbey ruins at Walsingham

his work to other major rivers along the east coast – the Humber and Thames – and different parts of the Fens, particularly the North Level. Whichever the direction of his career in the second half of the 1720s we are likely (at least for the present) to remain in ignorance of it.

Badeslade's appearance at Exton Hall in Leicestershire in c.1730 enables us to pick up the threads again. He combined working for the Earl of Gainsborough on what were termed 'waterworks', presumably in the gardens of Exton, with at least one but probably more surveys of the estate holdings of the aristocrat. This excursion into Leicestershire presages or may have been part of a phase when Badeslade was active in the more northerly areas of England. From 1730 too there are drawings of mansions in Leicestershire, Rutland, Nottinghamshire and Yorkshire and surveys from Nottinghamshire and perhaps Derbyshire. But enquiries have failed to locate any autographed estate surveys in Yorkshire. There are also the topographical drawings from the Home Counties, all of which suggest that Badeslade toured extensively, though whether he was actively commissioned by aristocrats and gentry or was touting for work and patronage remains unclear. The preparation of these works can only account for a small part of those years, and it seems that his professional interests in drainage continued through the early 1730s. Skempton noted that in 1730 Badeslade assisted a fellow drainage specialist, John Perry, who was working on the Welland at Spalding (Lincs), by sending a gang of men to help and in the summer of 1731 he spent several days with Perry at the time of the opening of the great sluice at Spalding.[24] The publication in 1736 of a critical report on Nathaniel Kinderley's work on the Dee Estuary and John Grundy's in Deeping Fen, Lincolnshire reveals his continuing interest in drainage, but marks too the end of his sustained work on outfalls and civil engineering.

All this tells us little of what he had involved himself in over the previous few years. As yet it has not been possible to determine whether an otherwise unremarked trip to Ireland 'where business calls me'[25] was the culmination or the beginning of work in that country. In or around 1735 Badeslade's relationship with Walpole came to an acrimonious end, with Badeslade apportioning full blame to the prime minister. The latter had failed to get the Corporation of King's Lynn to pay for the surveys and the preparation of the 1725 volume on the navigation of the port of Lynn, and additionally Badeslade believed that Walpole had reneged on a promise to provide a permanent base for him. They quarrelled and Badeslade lost not only Walpole's patronage but also access to the circle of courtiers who surrounded the king. Without doubt losing Walpole's good will was a severe blow.

Throughout his career his base remained in London. He had married Letitia Gamble in 1719 at St Margaret's in Westminster, and his children, Thomas William and Katherine were baptised respectively at St John the Evangelist's in Smith Square in June 1732 and at St Dunstan's in west London in July 1735.

During 1735 Badeslade relocated himself to north Wales. In that year he produced the two prospects of Chirk Castle in southern Denbighshire, using his skills in house drawing. As far as can be established he was not employed by John Myddelton, the lord of Chirk and Tory MP for Denbigh Boroughs, to prepare any estate surveys, and the relationship was almost certainly soured in 1740 when W.H. Toms, Badeslade's engraver, was forced to write a grovelling apology to Myddelton for disrespectful remarks about Myddelton's family which according to a third party Toms had purportedly made in London. Nevertheless Badeslade's presence at Chirk in 1735 must have been catalytic in establishing contacts with other members of the gentry in north-east Wales, and he began to find patrons amongst the great families of the region – Grosvenor, Mostyn and Wynn.

It was Sir Robert Grosvenor at Eaton Hall in western Cheshire who from Badeslade's own testimony was effectively Walpole's successor as patron. Based on the dated maps that he produced, Badeslade's professional association with Sir Robert Grosvenor lasted to 1740, and the maps that he prepared represent the culmination of his surveying career. Badeslade's maps of commons and wastes for Grosvenor take their place amongst other manorial and lordship maps from various parts of Wales as early examples of an identifiable trend in the production of large-scale surveys that went beyond the straightforward mapping of the enclosures and fields on single estates to the creation of single maps that revealed the ownership (or lordship) of entire landscapes. John Rocque was to map the manor of Deythur with its former open fields and commons on the border of Montgomeryshire and Shropshire in 1747, two years earlier Lewis Morris had surveyed the largely unenclosed, metal-rich manor of Cwmwd y Perfedd in Cardiganshire for the Crown,[26] and towards the end of the eighteenth century the great lordship of Chirk was mapped for the Myddeltons by an unknown surveyor (thought by the National Library of Wales to have been another surveyor in the Welsh borderlands, William Pain).

It is worth digressing here to consider the thinking behind these upland maps, for they represent something of an innovative departure from the traditional estate surveys in the hilly regions of the west. The first half of the eighteenth century saw an increasing tension between the great landowners and the poorest classes of society. Encroachments onto the commons and waste by the landless had been a regular if occasional feature from the late medieval period onwards, while the total areas involved were certainly outstripped by farmers who simply extended and enlarged their holdings by enclosing tracts of contiguous open hill land.[27] Where challenged by the landowner, frequently the lord of the

---

[24] Skempton et al 2002, p. 27
[25] Badeslade 1735

[26] Bick and Davies 1994
[27] Silvester 2007

manor, the enclosers were forced to pay an annual rent, but many escaped attention and any form of penalty. But as the eighteenth century progressed the trickle of the landless onto the waste became a flood; some of the great landowners railed against the invasion of the commons as was the case with Sir John Vaughan of Crosswood in Cardiganshire who claimed his commons had been 'colonized by the very scum of the earth', costing him £200 per annum.[28] Others (or perhaps their stewards and agents) recognised a financial opportunity in the rents that could be charged, the map offering an ideal record of the geographic locations of existing encroachments and a baseline that could be utilised in the future for pinpointing the new ones that had emerged. Badeslade's upland surveys of around 1738 and 1740 for Grosvenor (and perhaps also for Mostyn) will not have been the first to target illicit encroachments, but they are relatively early compared with most.

We are fortunate to have surviving documents penned by Badeslade regarding his upland work. In a letter dated 30 December 1738 he reported to Robert Grosvenor that the 'survey of Halkyn Mountain and Soughton and their branches took from 4 September to 25th. Went to Caerwys on 26th and was about the other mountains around Caerwys until 4 November. Doing business for Mr Mostyn at Mostyn till 21st and afterwards to ye 29th getting in names on the mountains. The man who assisted me at Caerwys, Mr Kendal, had been steward to Mr Mostyn at Maesmynan and clerk to the justices at the sessions, and had been concerned with gathering waifs (i.e. stray animals) on the mountains so knew the boundaries. He had last kept shop in Caerwys so knew most of the country people, but its market being lost [to] Holywell he was at leisure to go with me every day and under covert [sic] of lighting his pipe got what information he was wanting about the encroachments' (Flintshire Archives GR/332). In passing it might be noted that a further insight into the eighteenth-century surveyor's task is also found on an endorsement on the map of Epperstone (Notts) in 1734 mentioned above. This states that 'a jury of the tenants went over all the fields with me and owned their lands and saw their names wrote upon their pieces of land in the mapp'.[29]

The second motive behind the upland maps was to identify the mineral resources within the wastes at a time when great landowners were increasingly seeking to exploit what they owned, either directly or by lease. Halkyn Mountain had long been a source of lead, probably first mined by the Romans under military control. Badeslade's maps showed the lead rakes of more recent times, old and current mine workings, and coal pits, revealing to the Grosvenor family the extent of their mineral resources. Of all Badeslade's surveys these maps probably had the longest use; copies were commissioned for practical purposes in the second half of the nineteenth century, and the Grosvenor estate office was still citing the map in correspondence regarding mineral rights as late as 1938.[30]

Concurrently with his work for Grosvenor he prepared surveys for the Mostyn family of Mostyn Hall (Flints), whose lands spread across the top of Wales from Gloddaeth in Caernarvonshire through Denbighshire and Flintshire into Cheshire. His dated maps tie this down to the years between 1738 and 1742 or perhaps 1743. In 1741 he started working for one of north Wales' biggest landowners, Sir Watkin Williams Wynn, but the emergence of *Chorographica Britannia* in 1742 hints at another downturn in the amount of work that was coming his way, and the need to diversify is seemingly confirmed by the fact that nothing in the way of fresh survey work can be certainly attributed to 1743, other than a copied map of the manor of Mostyn in legal papers.

Even more frustrating are any pointers to his progress in 1744. On June 3rd of that year Badeslade wrote out his testament addressed to his brother John, focussing on his disposable possessions, and noted that he was going to Montgomeryshire to survey land which would bring in at least £500 and keep him occupied until winter. Reading between the lines the phraseology suggests that he was glad of the work and from the sum involved it was a sizeable commission, in a region of Wales that was new to him. The testament reveals that over the years he had accumulated a stock of drawings and books, run off from existing copper plates which presumably he anticipated would be sold on an occasional basis. A Mr Wright, probably to be identified with the successful bookseller who operated from 132 The Strand in the 1730s[31] held 'near three hundred books of the history of the navigation of the port of Lyn [sic] and draining the fens in Lincolnshire; they sell for a guinea a book in his keeping; and five hundred sets of prints of the gentlemen's seats of the county Kent not bound into books and worth about three half-crowns a set. Mr Wright also has several copper plates with engravings of gentlemen's seats which cost engraving about £150. Mr Toms at no 19 Union Court Holborn has several plates of gentlemen's seats which cost about £150', and Toms had also agreed to deliver 260 copies of *Chorographia Britanniae* carrying Badeslade's autograph and worth £30. There was also a King's Lynn bookseller, Charles Hardwick, then on the verge of bankruptcy, who had 150 copies of the Lynn Navigation.

Badeslade struggled with bad debts. He recorded for his brother's benefit that Lord Gainsborough at Exton Park still owed him £100, a debt which seemingly stretched back more than a decade, while the executor for the late Lord Howe owed £60. Badeslade, it appears, was using the services of an eighteenth-century debt collector for 'Mr Andrews in Grosvenor Street knows of and is employed to get in £30'.

The fact that he felt it wise to write a testament implies that he was not in good health and probably sensed that he might not recover. He was staying at a farm called Ffinnant in Llandinam (Monts), but it not been possible to identify

---

[28] Davies 1976, p. 105
[29] Nichols 1987, p. 47
[30] In 1865 the estate paid George Bellis, a surveyor from Mold (Flints), £40 for copies of the two maps. The original receipts are held in the Flintshire Record Office

[31] Timperley 1839, p. 664

who he was working for or which areas he was being commissioned to survey. His fears were rapidly realised for the parish register for Llandinam records that Thomas Badishall [sic], a gent thought to have come from Surrey was buried in the churchyard there less than a month later, on 2 July 1744. His grave cannot now be located.

Not that this was quite the last we hear of him. Other documents preserved in the National Archives reveal that the testament which effectively cited his brothers John and Charles as executors of his estate was contested by his widow Letitia, and the case came before John Bettesworth of the Prerogative Court of Canterbury on 3 September 1745. The documentation adds the minor detail that Badeslade's home parish was St Clement Danes, now in central London but then in the county of Middlesex.

Badeslade was as we have seen a man of many parts. In this there are similarities with his much better known contemporary, the Huguenot John Rocque (d.1762) mentioned above, and at least two other Welsh surveyors working around the same time, William Williams and Lewis Morris. Rocque's initial drawings were of parks and gardens, and from those he moved to urban mapping (Exeter, Shrewsbury and an exceptional map of London) and estate surveying and later to county maps, the detail and innovative features of his cartography drawing the attention and admiration of modern commentators.[32] He was also an engraver and publisher and in 1751 described himself as Topographer to the Prince of Wales.[33]

William Williams was in his later years based in Cheshire, but is best known for his map of Denbighshire and Flintshire published in 1720 at the beginning of his career and representing the earliest large-scale map of Welsh counties.[34] After this Williams fell back on estate surveys to make a living but is also credited with a book of architectural drawings of Oxford colleges entitled *Oxonia Depicta*, which apparently he had started work on in the early 1720s though it was not published until 1732-3. Of interest here is that while Williams engraved many of the 66 plates, several were done by W.H. Toms.

Lewis Morris (1701-1764) contrived an even more varied career. Back in 1987 Adrian Robinson claimed that 'for a brief period lasting only a decade [1737-48] Morris, through his efforts, could claim to be the most active and the foremost cartographer in Britain. His work on estate mapping in Anglesey and more particularly his survey of the coast of Wales from the Great Ormes Head in the north to Tenby in the south, give him a stature far above that of his contemporaries working elsewhere in Britain at that time'.[35] Bold words indeed, not least in the era of John Rocque. Morris initially practiced as a land surveyor on Anglesey, became a customs officer at Holyhead, set up a printing business, surveyed the coast of Wales, became a mining adventurer and then deputy steward of the Crown Estate in Cardiganshire, and ended as an antiquary.[36]

What is marked about Badeslade's career is his dependence on patronage, first Harris, then Walpole, Grosvenor and finally Mostyn. Other surveyors in the eighteenth century of course depended on the support of great or wealthy men, but Badeslade appears exceptional in the degree to which he was able to attach himself to landowners who provided both work and a base, fitting other commissions in and around these.

Perceptions of Badeslade have changed over time: Peter Eden[37] believed that estate surveying become a subordinate interest for Badeslade as he became increasingly involved in the preparation of topographical views and county maps for publication. This is to overlook the ups and downs in an estate surveyor's career, and if one thing is clear, Badeslade contrived a varied career taking whatever opportunities were presented to him.

Acknowledgements

Researching Badeslade has taken me, metaphorically, to various regions of England and Wales, and it is a pleasure to acknowledge the help and advice of various people, some of whom have gone out of their way to provide assistance: Sarah Bendall at Emmanuel College, Cambridge for providing background information from the data assembled for the *Dictionary of Land Surveyors;* Colin Flight for information on Badeslade's contribution to Harris' *History of Kent*; the Duke of Westminster and the Trustees of the 4th Duke of Westminster's Settlement for access to the Grosvenor Family Archive, and to Louise Martin the archivist for the Grosvenor Estate at Eaton Hall; David Yaxley, the honorary archivist at Houghton Hall in Norfolk; my erstwhile colleague at the Norfolk Archaeological Unit, Ken Penn, who collected information for me on the Badeslade maps in the Norfolk Archives; and archivists in Leicestershire, Cheshire, Flintshire, and at the Society of Antiquaries and the Natural History Museum for answering my queries.

---

[32] Delano-Smith and Kain 1999, p. 88
[33] Varley 1948, p. 87
[34] Walters 1968, p. 138
[35] Morris 1987
[36] Bick and Davies 1994, pp. 1-4
[37] 1973, p. 481

Bibliography

Badeslade, J., and Rocque, J. 1739, *Vitruvius Britannicus, Second Series* (Mineola, New York: Dover Publications Inc. 2009)

Badeslade, T. 1725, *The History of the Ancient and Present State of the Navigation of the Port of King's-Lyn and of Cambridge* (London: J. Roberts)

Badeslade, T. 1729, *A Scheme for Draining the Great Level of the Fens, called Bedford Level, and of Improving the Navigation of Lyn-Regis* (London: J. Roberts)

Badeslade, T. 1735, *Reasons Humbly Offer'd to the Cconsideration of the Publick; Shewing how the Works ... to Recover and Preserve the Navigation of the River Dee, will Destroy the Navigation; and Occasion the Drowning of all the Low Lands Adjacent ...*, (Chester: R Adams)

Badeslade, T. 1736, *The New Cut Canal, Intended for Improving the Navigation of the City of Chester, ... Compared with the Welland, alias Spalding River, now Silted up, and Deeping-Fens Adjacent, now Drowned* (Chester: R Adams)

Batten, K., and Bennett, F. 1996, *The Printed Maps of Devon. County maps 1575-1837* (Tiverton: Devon Books)

Bendall, S. 1997, *Dictionary of Land Surveyors and Local Mapmakers of Great Britain and Ireland, 1530-1850* (London: British Library)

Bergess, W. 1992, *Kent Maps and Plans in the Libraries of Kent and the Adjoining London Boroughs. A finding list* (London: The Library Association)

Bick, D., and Davies, P.W. 1994, *Lewis Morris and the Cardiganshire Mines* (Aberystwyth: National Library of Wales)

British Museum, 1829, *Catalogue of Maps, Prints, Drawings etc forming the Geographical and Topographical Collection attached to The Library of His Late Majesty King George the Third and presented by His Majesty King George the Fourth to the British Museum. Volume II* (London: Trustees of the British Museum)

Clayton, T. 1998, 'Publishing houses; prints of country seats', in D. Arnold (ed.), *The Georgian Country House. Architecture, landscape and society* (Stroud, Gloucestershire: Sutton Publishing Ltd) pp. 43-60

Darby, H.C. 1940, *The Draining of the Fens* (Cambridge: Cambridge University Press)

Darby, H.C. 1983, *The Changing Fenland* (Cambridge: Cambridge University Press)

Davies, A.E. 1976, 'Enclosures in Cardiganshire, 1750-1850', *Ceredigion* 7.1, pp. 100-40

Delano-Smith, C., and Kain, R.J.P. 1999, *English Maps. A history* (London: the British Library)

Eden, P. 1973, 'Land surveyors in Norfolk 1550-1850. Part I: the estate surveyors', *Norfolk Archaeology* 35.4, pp. 471-82

Harris, J. 1995, *The Artist and the Country House from the Fifteenth Century to the Present Day* (London: Sotheby's Institute)

Lynam, E. 1953, *The Mapmaker's Art* (London: The Batchworth Press)

Macartney, M. 1908, *English Houses and Gardens in the 17th and 18th Centuries. A Series of Bird's-eye Views reproduced from Contemporary Engravings by Kip, Badeslade, Harris and Others* (London: B.T. Batsford)

Morris, L. 1987, *Lewis Morris. Plans in St George's Channel – 1748* (Beaumaris: Lewis Morris Productions)

Nichols, H. 1987, *Local Maps of Nottinghamshire to 1800. An Inventory* (Nottingham: Nottinghamshire County Council)

Redgrave S. 1878, *A Dictionary of Artists of the English School* (London: George Bell & Sons)

Silvester, R.J. 2007, 'Landscapes of the poor: encroachment in Wales in the post-medieval centuries', in P. S. Barnwell and M. Palmer (eds), *Post-Medieval Landscapes. Landscape history after Hoskins. Volume III* (Oxford: Windgather Press) pp. 55-67

Silvester, R.J. 2009, 'John Probert of Copthorne; A Georgian land agent', *Trans Shropshire Archaeol. Hist. Soc.* 84, pp. 51-71

Skempton, A.W., Rennison, R.W. and Cox, R.C. (eds) 2002, *A Biographical Dictionary of Civil Engineers, Volume 1, 1500-1830* (London: Thomas Telford on behalf of the Institution of Civil Engineers)

Smith, D. 1982, *Antique Maps of the British Isles* (London: B. T. Batsford Ltd)

Taylor E.G.R. 1966, *The Mathematical Practitioners of Hanoverian England* (London: Methuen and Co Ltd)

Timperley, H.C. 1839, *A Dictionary of Printers and Printing* (London: H. Johnson)

Varley, J. 1948, 'John Rocque. Engraver, surveyor, cartographer and map-seller', *Imago Mundi* 5, pp. 83-91

Walters, G. 1968, 'Themes in the large scale mapping of Wales in the eighteenth century', *Cartographical Journal* pp. 135-46

Williams, W. 1733, *Oxonia Depicta sive Collegiorum et Aularum in Ipclyta Academia Oxoniensi Ichnographica, Orthographica & Scenographica...* (Oxford and London)

Worms, L., and Bayton-Williams, A. 2011, *British Map Engravers. A Dictionary of Engravers, Lithogravers and their Principal Employers to 1850* (London: Rare Book Society)

Yates, N. 1994, 'Kent', in C.R.J. Currie and C.P. Lewis (eds.), *English County Histories. A Guide* (Stroud: Alan Sutton Publishing Ltd) pp. 208-15

New Buckenham in 1820

Paul Rutledge

Abstract: New Buckenham market cross is still recognisable, but a recently-discovered anonymous painting of 1820 shows other timber-framed buildings now hidden behind brick fronts or demolished, the prominently-placed stocks and the appalling mud and slush.

New Buckenham is a place of contrasts. Measuring only 146ha. of which nearly one third is stinted and grazed common land, it is one of the very smallest rural parishes in Norfolk. A chartered town, it is so tiny that the nearby castle is in fact in Old Buckenham. A mesne, that is to say non-royal, borough, it was established between about 1145 and his death in 1176 by the powerful baron William D'Albini or Daubigny II beside his castle, itself an innovation as probably the earliest round keep in England. Moated, the town was tied into the castle's defences.[1] D'Albini's son, William III, refers to burgesses at Buckenham in his father's time in a charter dated between 1176 and 1192 that is confirmed and expanded by his son, the fourth William, between 1192 and 1221.[2] In an already settled landscape D'Albini II was able or willing to endow his new town only very modestly and he was in fact obliged to acquire an outlier of the bishop's estate at Eccles to create a town field, Bishop's Haugh, of about 73ha. As a chartered borough, in Norfolk it is second in date only to Norwich, preceding Lynn (1204) and Yarmouth (1208), though other town charters, notably for D'Albini's other Norfolk borough at Castle Rising, may have been lost. The generous size of the market place and the lack of arable soil indicate that D'Albini II planned it as a service town and supply centre for his castle and it remained a place of tradesmen rather than farmers and workshops rather than barns. Between 1500 and 1699 thirty-three different trades are recorded within the town, including cloth finishing and sale, with some cloth manufacture, haberdashery, butchering, tanning and leather-working, brewing, malting and innkeeping and the linked trades of grocer and apothecary. Especially butchering; in 1542 there were no fewer than twelve butchers' stalls on the market place.[3] Other trades included the making and sale of hats, pins, points (decorative dress tags), tobacco pipes and wigs and there was a silk merchant and, briefly in the 1570s, a book binder. Detailed records are sparse before the mid sixteenth century, but evidence from wills and the grandeur of the church and the larger of the two guildhalls indicate late-medieval prosperity, and mercantile needs encouraged house plans that allowed bulk storage. The prosperity was nevertheless modest and the effect on the housing stock was repair and adaptation rather than replacement, with a fashion for rather dull brick fronts added in the late nineteenth century. Otherwise, it has kept almost unaltered its planned layout, its semi-urban character and many of its vernacular buildings.

New Buckenham is ill-served by maps and topographical drawings. Never enclosed and so without an enclosure award, and almost tithe-free and lacking a comprehensive tithe apportionment, the earliest measured survey is in the large-scale Ordnance Survey sheets of the 1880s.[4] However, we now have in a recently-discovered painting a vision of an earlier New Buckenham on a cold day in 1820 (Fig. 1). The anonymous artist was standing on the south-west corner of the market place by the then timber-framed King's Head Inn, (Fig 2, A on the key), looking east and north. Starting on the left-hand side of the picture, he could see first, partly obscured by the King's Head sign, the former village stores (B), once an inn called the Crown in 1596 and the White Hart in 1637.[5] It had ceased trading by 1750. Then, in front of it (though this is not entirely clear in the painting) the George Inn (D) sprawling over the northern part of the market place. This is recorded probably in 1495[6] and certainly from 1542 and it was demolished about 1872. A new inn on a nearby site then took its name only itself to be recently rechristened the Inn on the Green. Next, on the edge of the market place, a major town house (E), gabled and with close studding. Documented from 1501,[7] it was cleared away about 1848 to make space for the village school. Beyond it the timber framing of a medieval wealden-type house (G) can be glimpsed, one of the very few in Norfolk using this essentially Home Counties method of construction. Then, on the market place itself, a kiln-like structure (F), probably the hearth and chimney of an open-air forge. Next, the prominently-placed stocks (H) and the market cross (I) with its red-painted loft. Despite its antique appearance it was moved to its present site only in 1715, making use of largely second-hand materials. Behind it a sophisticated two-storied shop with awning, corner braces and oriel window (J). On its roof (K) is what may be the housing of a public clock, purchased by the town in 1568.[8] Nos J and L are part of a complex of shops, workshops and stables dividing the market place, that originated as butchers' and other stalls, which by 1542 had become permanent and now form two houses only. The kerbed structure (M) in the lower corner is unexplained. Another puzzle is the church tower (C), lacking its huge pinnacles, certainly *in situ* by this date and shown in the background of an engraving of 1818 of the castle by John Sell Cotman. Is the picture unfinished, or had they been removed for repair?

---

[1] For New Buckenham generally see: Blomefield 1805-10, i, pp. 395-405; Beresford and St Joseph 1979; Rutledge 2003; and Longcroft (ed.) 2005. Unreferenced documents are held by the parish, only the parish registers having as yet been deposited in the Norfolk Record Office
[2] The text of William's charter survives, as does a confirmation by his son. See Rutledge 1999
[3] Rutledge 2007, p. 230

[4] Sheets XCVI.5 and XCVI. 9
[5] NRO, PD 254/172 and will of Simon Reinouldes, NRO, Norf. Arch. wills 1637, OW 16
[6] Will of John Colman, NRO, Norf. Arch. wills 15 Shaw, 1495
[7] Will of Geoffrey Brown, NRO, Norf. Arch. wills 6 Davy, 1501
[8] High Bailiff's account, held by the parish

LANDSCAPES AND ARTEFACTS

Fig. 1 Anonymous watercolour of New Buckenham in 1820 (photograph: Charles Oxley)

Fig. 2 Key to the 1820 watercolour (Catherine D'Alton)

232

Bibliography

Beresford, M.W., and St Joseph, J.K. 1979, *Medieval England, an Aerial Survey*

Blomefield, F. 1805-10, *An Essay towards a Topographical History of the County of Norfolk*

Longcroft, A., (ed.) 2005, *The Historic Buildings of New Buckenham* (Journal of the Norfolk Historic Buildings Group vol ii)

Rutledge, P. 1999, 'New Buckenham, Two Borough Charters', *Norfolk Archaeology* 43, pp. 313-17

Rutledge, P. 2003, *New Buckenham, a Planned Town at Work 1530-1780* (Norfolk Archaeological and Historical Research Group, reissue)

Rutledge, P. 2007, 'New Buckenham in 1542', *Norfolk Archaeology* 45, pp. 222-31

An experiment in conservation: the early years of the Norfolk Archaeological Trust

Peter Wade-Martins

Why Norfolk?

Why is Norfolk the only county in England to have a charitable trust devoted to the acquisition and care of a selection of our most important archaeological sites? Why was Norfolk the first to have a wildlife trust, which is still the largest and most successful such county conservation trust in England, with over 35,000 members? There must be something special about the place, which might well be connected to Andrew's decision to devote his working life to the area, as indeed many of us have done. It is good that he stayed with us, and our knowledge of Norfolk's archaeology has been greatly enhanced by his research over the last 40 years.

Conserving our archaeology

'Conservation, not excavation, is the need of the day' (O.G.S. Crawford, *Editorial* in *Antiquity* 3 (1929).

FIG. 1 PORTRAIT OF BASIL COZENS-HARDY.

The Norfolk Archaeological Trust was started in 1923 by a Norwich solicitor, Basil Cozens-Hardy (1885-1976) (Fig. 1), who was convinced that there was a need for a body committed to the ownership and care of monuments and buildings, and he saw that role as quite separate from the academic activities of the Norfolk and Norwich Archaeological Society.[1] In the early years the Trust's work was focused primarily on historic buildings because they were most easily recognised as being of archaeological importance. The full appreciation of earthwork sites and field monuments came later, particularly with the advent of air photography after the Second World War.

Professional and amateur archaeologists usually spend their time digging, carrying out fieldwork or researching in various ways, and there has never been the same groundswell of interest in conservation management, as there is amongst wildlife enthusiasts. Indeed, so few people have even heard of the Norfolk Archaeological Trust, that the story of its early days seems a good topic for this volume. The Trust was particularly active in the 1920s and 1930s, but after the war it went into a gradual retreat, selling off its properties, and not reviewing its vision for the future until 1982. This chapter mainly concerns its very active inter-war years, while the more recent developments of the Trust up to 2008 can be found in *Conservation Land Management* for November 2008.[2]

Basil Cozens-Hardy's visionary efforts did not stop with the Archaeological Trust and he used the same model to help Dr Sydney Long establish the Norfolk Naturalists' Trust (later re-named the Norfolk Wildlife Trust) in 1926. This was to be independent of the Norfolk and Norwich Naturalist Society, as the Archaeological Trust was to the Archaeological Society. That year 407 acres of the Cley Marshes, a wetland of international importance for bird conservation, had come up for sale and had been purchased by Sydney Long, a Norwich doctor, to prevent them being drained and cultivated. Dr Long then invited friends for lunch at the George Hotel in Cley to discuss the possibility of setting up a county trust, when it became clear that the National Trust was reluctant to take on the marshes. He then gave the marshes to the Naturalists' Trust at its first meeting.

Basil devised both trusts as companies limited by guarantee, and their early Council meetings were held in the offices of Cozens-Hardy & Jewson near Castle Meadow in Norwich. We owe much to him for all that

---
[1] Cresswell 1977.
[2] Wade-Martins 2008

he achieved in those early years when local conservation trusts were otherwise almost unknown.

Basil had joined the Norfolk and Norwich Archaeological Society in 1919 and became their Excursion Secretary three years later and was General Secretary from 1928. He was also Secretary of the Caistor Excavations Committee for the Roman town excavations which ran from 1929. His work as Excursion Secretary enabled him to become familiar with historic buildings and archaeological sites in need of protection throughout the county. As a result of that he compiled a list of 188 which had been scheduled, or he could recommend for scheduling to the Ancient Monuments Board as their chief correspondent, under the 1913 Ancient Monuments Act. He published the full list in *Norfolk Archaeology* in 1926.[3] While the first monuments to be scheduled had tended to be the obvious castles and abbeys, he could see beyond them to a range of places of equal, or often greater, significance also in need of protection. These included the Neolithic flint mines at Grimes Graves (1924), the Dark Age linear earthwork known as High Banks at Ashill (1924), the bishop's chapel on the site of the Anglo-Saxon cathedral at North Elmham (1924), the defended interior of Caistor St Edmund Roman town (1925) and the Roman Saxon Shore fort at Burgh Castle (1929). These list may not be entirely accurate because the original paperwork is often undated. He wrote in his introduction to his 1926 list that 'It may be of interest to remark that with the possible exception of Wiltshire, Norfolk is head of the list in respect of the number of ancient monuments scheduled'. No doubt it was his legal mind, combined with his interest in antiquarian matters which drove him to work so hard to give protection to the county's monuments.

In those early days the information available was often not sufficient to define the limits of the scheduled areas with any precision, and boundaries on the maps which accompanied the scheduling forms were particularly vague. Nevertheless, scheduling gave the sites some legal status for the first time, and then after the 1931 Act owners were required to give three months' notice of their intention to disturb or destroy a monument. The list grew, although the details are now very difficult to find in the archives of English Heritage. The County Council's Development Plan in 1951 shows that by then a further 40 sites had been added, including the Roman Saxon Shore fort at Brancaster.[4] Others, like the more subtle and less obvious earthworks of deserted medieval villages, came much later.

The aims of the Archaeological Trust were set out in its 1923 Memorandum of Articles:

> To promote and foster the discovery, excavation, preservation, recording and study of sites and objects of archaeological and/or historical importance within the County of Norfolk for the public benefit.

Under these aims the Trust could acquire, manage, excavate and 'lay bare' sites and historic buildings, issue appeals, hold public meetings and 'take such other steps as may be required for the purpose of procuring contributions to the funds of the Trust' in furtherance of its objectives. This was all a truly inspired and far-sighted concept.

The first open meeting of the Trust was held in the Norfolk and Norwich Library in Norwich on 2 March 1923. It was agreed that the governing Council should consist of not less than ten and not more than twenty members. It was resolved that the draft Memorandum and Articles of Association of the Trust be approved, and these were subsequently signed on 31 May by eight people including such well known antiquarians as Harry Bradfer-Lawrence and Leonard Bolingbroke, and of course Basil himself. Unlike the Naturalists' Trust three years later, there was no obvious site which required quick action and it took a while before properties were identified and acquired.

National initiatives

Meanwhile, the National Trust had bought some land at Wicken Fen in Cambridgeshire in 1899, but its first Norfolk properties were Blakeney Point acquired in 1912 and Scolt Head in 1923.[5] The Ministry of Works started to take castles and abbeys into voluntary guardianship in Norfolk under the 1883 Act with the first being Castle Acre Priory in 1929.[6] This was followed by the Binham Priory cloisters after the area south and east of Binham church was purchased by the Norfolk Archaeological Trust in 1932 (see below). Guardianship left sites nominally in private ownership but all responsibility for them, except for ownership of finds, passed to the Ministry of Works. There was then a bonanza of 'clearance' and conservation of these ruins by highly skilled gangs employed through a series of local offices. By the outbreak of war 147 sites had been taken into Guardianship in England.[7] Each office had a team of experienced superintendents, foremen, craftsmen and labourers able to clear the newly acquired ruins and consolidate them to a very high standard. The quality of their workmanship still shows today where the ruins they consolidated seldom show much need for major repairs, unless new major faults have developed. Sites chosen were those suitable for public access, and neat lawns were laid out between the freshly repaired walls. The monuments were placed under the day to day control of uniformed custodians, wearing smart peaked caps decorated with gold crowns, sitting in wooden huts at the entrance. The custodians usually had guidebooks or leaflets for sale, although by today's standards these publications are unattractive and not particularly informative to the layman. The various parts of monuments were labelled with cast

---

[3] Cozens-Hardy 1926
[4] Norfolk County Council 1994, pp. 20-21
[5] Waterson 1994, pp. 39-55; Fowler 1976, p. 15
[6] Impey 2008, p. 48
[7] Thurley 2013, pp. 99-161; 122

aluminium signs using words such as *garderobe* which must have left the average visitor baffled. My favourite is one in Binham Priory which simply says MONKS' DORTER ABOVE (Fig. 15).

So, while the quality of monument care was exceptionally good and the consolidation of the structures has survived well, the Ministry's education and interpretation skills were far below what can reasonably be expected today. Their aluminium signs have themselves become period pieces and can now be regarded as a part of the archaeology, although VISITORS ARE FORBIDDEN TO CLIMB ON THE WALLS, MINISTRY OF WORKS (Fig. 14), the first sign you see when entering Binham Priory cloisters, seems unfriendly. In those days the public, no doubt, did as they were told!

Guardianship was seen as an opportunity to give the public more access to the past, but some sites were rejected as being insufficiently accessible. This certainly applied to the extraordinarily evocative St Benet's Abbey in Horning surrounded by marshes in a remote location on the River Bure. The old Ministry of Works site file in the National Archives records that the abbey ruins were offered by the Church Commissioners to the Ministry on three occasions between 1937 and 1954 but rejected each time on the grounds that the ruins were not sufficient, that they were in good repair and too isolated to attract visitors.[8] St Benet's has recently been acquired by the Norfolk Archaeological Trust.

The Trust in its early years

It must have been recognised, even in the 1930s, that this view of the past, as represented mainly by castles and abbeys, did not give the public a rounded view of the county's archaeology and did not ensure that a sufficient range of evidence for Norfolk's past was being protected. Scheduling was still of limited value because even after 1931, owners could destroy a monument after just giving three months' notice to the Ministry. Something more was needed. This is where a local property-owning conservation trust could have a role. After all, the best possible way to protect a site is to own it.

The Council of the Norfolk Archaeological Trust has recently resolved to donate all of its papers which are more than five years old to the Norfolk Record Office.[9] So, the evidence for the history of the Trust is now easily accessible. The best way to follow the story in the early years is through the Council's minute books, although meetings were usually just annual events with day-to-day management left to Basil as Secretary. The activities of the Trust were driven at an extraordinary pace up until the outbreak of war. That put a brake on further expansion, and after the war the Trust went through a period of gradually disposing of its properties once their future was assured. The minute books are the main source for this paper.

Details of all properties in current ownership are on line at www.norfarchtrust.org.uk and the newsletters which have been issued since 2002 are also on the website.

The inter-war years

Runton Common (1923-1980). The first property in which the Trust became involved was 'the so-called Roman Camp' or the 'Black Beacon' near the north coast on Runton Common.[10] It was actually a Napoleonic War beacon site on the Cromer Ridge surrounded by an extensive area of Late Saxon or early medieval iron working pits, although at the time these pits were not recognised. At the first Council meeting on 5 July 1923 it was resolved to make a grant of £10 guineas to the Roman Camp Purchase Fund being organised by the Runton Common Society on the understanding that the Trust would be given a mandate to manage the beacon. The Purchase Fund was seeking to acquire the common to protect it as an open space. After the Fund acquired most of the land it was handed over to the National Trust, but the Archaeological Trust retained ownership of some areas until it was all registered as a common in 1968. Once the future of the area was safeguarded the Trust's share of the land was then sold in 1980.

Augustine Steward's House, Tombland, Norwich (1924-1960). The rescuing in 1924 of this fine mid-sixteenth-century timber-framed house adjoining the Samson and Hercules in Tombland and opposite the Erpingham Gate, was the Trust's first real success (Fig. 2).[11] It had apparently been built by Augustine Steward, lord mayor of Norwich in 1534, 1546 and 1556, and was clearly in a poor state. A second building to the rear was bought the following year. These purchases and the subsequent renovations were funded partly from a joint appeal to members of both the Trust and the Archaeological Society and partly from an overdraft initially of up to £500 from Barclays Bank. The buildings were then let for five years at £100 a year. The saving of these buildings was to be commemorated at the time with 'a carved stone tablet' to be placed on the building, still on the wall of the house facing Tombland Alley (Fig. 3). Misfortune later struck when an 'accidental fire' in May 1944 partly destroyed the roof, and a payment of £1,019 was received from the Norwich Union Fire Insurance for repairs in 1945. A further £125 had to be spent in 1947 to make the upper story habitable, but in 1959 it was resolved to open negotiations with the City Corporation to 'take over' the house for a book value of £2,040. In September 1960 the Council decided 'that in the opinion of the meeting the repair and presentation of Augustine Steward's House was beyond the financial capacity of the Trust and for this reason it should be sold.' Clearly, the Trust was finding its obligations a struggle,

---

[8] WORKS 14/1735
[9] Ref SO 300 Acc 2012/259

[10] NHER 6387
[11] Pevsner and Wilson 1997, p. 292

Fig. 2 Augustine Steward's House, Tombland, Norwich.

Fig. 3 Carved stone plaque on the wall of Augustine Steward's house in Tombland Alley.

and they felt that the future of the building would be better safeguarded in the ownership of the city.

The Corporation agreed to purchase for the book value, and the bank mortgage which had risen by then to £600 was cleared. The next year loans from Basil Cozens-Hardy and from a Mr T.W. Hirst were also discharged. This does show how financially demanding the saving of historic buildings could be in an age when few conservation grants were available. It also reveals how much the finance of the Trust's conservation projects depended on the generosity of individual council members. Only £490 from the sale at the end was left to invest after all loans were repaid.

Sprowston Mill. In November 1926 the Secretary 'reported that the preservation of windmills was being much canvassed' and suggested the appointment of a subcommittee to co-operate with the Archaeological Society 'owing to the possibility of a purchase being entertained.' At the subcommittee meeting in January 1927 it was reported that a Mr Harrison would make a gift of the eighteenth-century post mill at Sprowston, provided that the Trust would put the mill in good repair and lease it back to him at a nominal rent (Fig. 4). The meeting resolved to seek the patronage of twenty-two named people and organisations to cover the cost of repairs, but the project was delayed for several years over an access issue. However, the work did go ahead, and in 1932 it was resolved to lease the mill back to Mr Harrison for 99 years. Then, on 24 March 1933 on the day before the mill was due to be handed over to the Trust, it was totally destroyed by fire, caused by sparks from the burning of some adjoining brushwood (Fig. 5).[12] At the annual meeting in October 1933 it was reported that the Trust would receive £79, presumably as compensation for the repairs carried out before purchase was completed. That must have been a great shock, although Council minutes are too clinical to bring out any sense of the deep frustration they must have all felt. The Trust didn't then try for another mill.

Pykerells House, Norwich. (1928-present) Meanwhile, in May 1928 Basil presented a memorandum to Trust Council proposing that it should seek to acquire a late fifteenth-century hall house, then a de-licensed pub known as the Rosemary Tavern on St Mary's Plain belonging to Bullards Brewery.[13] It had a thatched roof, and was one of only seven thatched houses left in the city. It was sub-let to three different tenants and was being considered for slum clearance. The thatch was in a poor state but otherwise the building was in a fair condition. It had been the house of Thomas Pykerell, lord mayor of Norwich in 1525, 1533 and 1538, and contained a fine oriel hall window and a queen post roof with elaborately carved spandrels. It was resolved to offer up to £300 for the purchase and to have it re-thatched at a cost of about £60. In 1929 further funds were allocated for repairs, and in 1938 it was resolved to change the name to Pykerell's House.

The roof then suffered severe bomb damage in the war, and it was only partly repaired by September 1945 with funds from the War Damage Commission, but with 'the roof only being partly covered in' further repairs were needed. It was later converted into one house and in December 1948 was leased for twenty years to the antiquarian and historian, the Rev. J.F.Williams, who published an article about the building in *The Archaeological Journal*.[14] The roof was re-thatched in 1948 and again in 2010. It is now the only building still in Trust ownership (Figs. 6-8).

St Peter Hungate church museum, Norwich (1931-1936). This ambitious project began in December 1931 when it was resolved to take on a sublease of the redundant St Peter Hungate church from the City Corporation, which had in turn leased it from the Ecclesiastical Commissioners. The idea was to set up an independent committee to run the church as an ecclesiastical museum. In January 1932 it was estimated that the cost of putting the church in good repair would not exceed £800 and annual maintenance would not exceed £50, 'the greater part of which would be met by gate money'. In October 1932 it was resolved to seal the sublease, and by October 1933 arrangements were completed and the museum was open to the public. But, it seems that the Trust soon realised that costs were greater than expected, and by June 1936 it was decided to terminate the sublease. The Corporation then took on responsibility for future management, and the church remained under the city's direct control as a museum until the Norfolk Museums Service took over following local government re-organisation in 1974.

Greenland Fishery, Kings Lynn (1932-1998). Following the death of Edward Beloe, a King's Lynn solicitor who had been one of the original signatories to the Trust's 1923 Memorandum and Articles, his executors offered to sell the Greenland Fishery and its contents to the Trust for £1,000. This is an early seventeenth-century timber-framed and jettied merchant's house (Fig. 9).[15] Council accepted this offer at the October 1932 meeting, and the money was raised with £700 from a mortgage plus £100 from subscriptions and £200 from a King's Lynn committee set up to create a museum in the building. With the help of an honorary curator, Mr Cockle, the museum was open by December 1936, and in December 1938 it was reported that the museum was working successfully.

However, the building was also badly bomb-damaged, and in September 1945 the Secretary reported that the building could 'never be used again' after the bomb had demolished the back premises and 'the Corporation were likely to open another museum in another place.' It was resolved to offer the premises for sale to the King's Lynn Corporation and 'a gift of our half share of the exhibits, now stored away.' But in December 1947 it was reported that the Town Clerk had declined to purchase the freehold, so it was decided to look into the possibility of converting the building into

---

[12] Harrison 1949, p. 14
[13] Pevsner and Wilson 1997, p. 286
[14] Williams 1949
[15] Pevsner and Wilson 1999, p. 492

FIG. 4 SPROWSTON MILL BEFORE THE FIRE.

a house. The building was repaired, converted and let in 1951, and the Trust's half share of the museum exhibits was sold to the King's Lynn Corporation for £75. In 1964 a lease was offered to the King's Lynn Preservation Trust for 21 years, but the offer was not taken up. It was then let to others, but by 1995 the building was vacant again and was proving impossible to let without major expenditure. Discussions about its future had by then re-opened with the King's Lynn Preservation Trust, and it was offered to them for sale in 1996, but the Preservation Trust declined to buy. In the end it was given to them for £1 in December 1997.

Binham Priory cloisters (1933-present). In October 1932 it was resolved to purchase part of the meadow adjacent to Binham Priory which contained the earthworks of the priory cloisters and partly upstanding remains of the east end of the priory church.[16] The plan was to raise the funds for the purchase through a public appeal and then pass the site into the guardianship of the Ministry of Works. Purchase was the only way to ensure that the site passed into Guardianship because it was unlikely that it would be made over voluntarily. The deal was that if the Trust could raise the money to buy the land the Ministry would then be responsible for clearance and consolidation and for opening the site to the public. This was, no doubt, inspired by similar activities at Castle Acre Priory where Lord Leicester had given the ruined priory into Ministry of Works guardianship in 1929. The Binham appeal raised sufficient funds for the purchase which went ahead on 3 October 1933. The site was immediately transferred into guardianship on 26 October, and clearance took place every summer from 1934 until 1938 (Figs. 10-15). Work finished just before the outbreak of war.

FIG. 5 SPROWSTON MILL AFTER THE FIRE.

---

[16] Pevsner and Wilson 1997, pp: 389-92

Fig. 6 Pykerell's House, St Mary's Plain, Norwich

Fig. 7 Plaque on the front wall of Pykerell's House.

Fig. 8 Pykerell's House interior view of the medieval hall with part of the oriel window and queen post roof.

Whatever records may have been made did not survive the war or the sudden death of the excavator, Henry Neville of Tasburgh Hall, who was the driving force behind the project. This may have been the last example of old-style 'clearance' in Norfolk. Neville had retired from the Indian Civil Service, and, as far as we can tell, had no archaeological training and he was probably not expected to make records of the medieval and later levels[17]. Indeed, it was not Ministry policy to do so. Their aim was to remove later layers and structures to put the buildings back into their original form.[18] The Ministry's files in the National Archives do, however, contain full details of the costs of clearance and consolidation year by year. Some finds do survive in the collections of the Norfolk Museum and Archaeology Service in Norwich, and the carved stone is held in storage by English Heritage.

The original acquisition did not include the priory gatehouse, which was purchased by the Trust in 2002 along with the adjacent meadow which contains earthworks of other substantial buildings which were not excavated. Again, this followed Ministry policy at the time to focus just on the church and cloisters.[19]

Tudor Cottage, Field Dalling (1938-2008). In December 1938 it was decided to buy for £30 'a picturesque seventeenth-century cottage at Field Dalling', possibly because Basil had seen it on his way to the excavations at Binham Priory (Fig. 16).[20] The Trust then let the cottage to Mrs Page who remained in occupation until 2007! A bathroom was installed for her in 1966 at a cost of £250. After she moved it was clear that the house needed substantial modernisation before it could be let again, so rather then be faced with a bill for the improvements, the cottage was sold at auction in September 2008.

---
[17] Thurley 2013, pp. 140-1
[18] Thurley 2013, pp. 146-7
[19] Thurley 2013, p. 145
[20] Pevsner and Wilson 1997, p. 468

Fig. 9 Greenland Fishery, King's Lynn.

Fig. 10 Binham Priory old Ministry of Works view of the church and the earthworks and upstanding remains of the east end of the church before clearance began.

Fig. 11 Binham Priory during the consolidation of the east range of the cloisters after excavation.

Fig. 12 Binham Priory cloisters today.

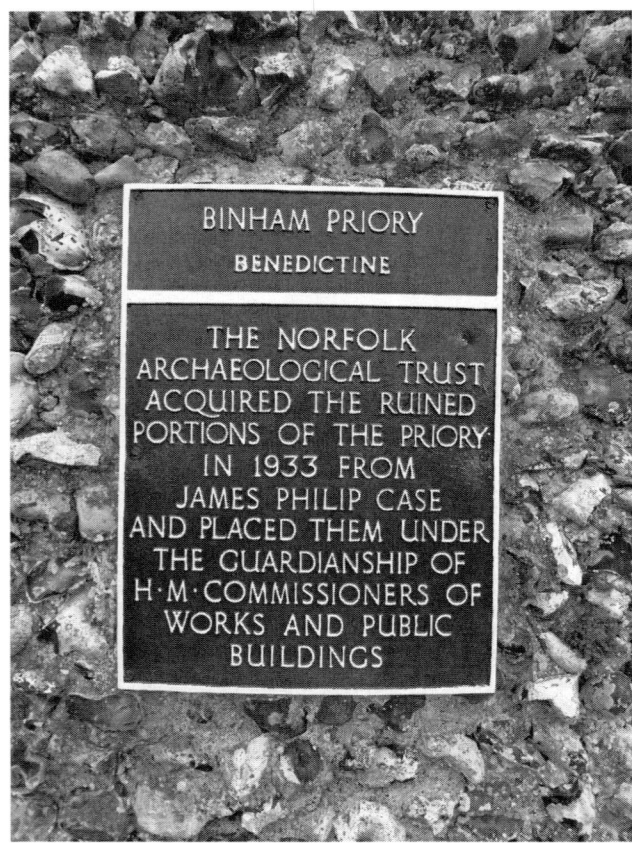

Fig. 13 Binham Priory, cast aluminium sign acknowledging the original purchase by the Trust in 1933.

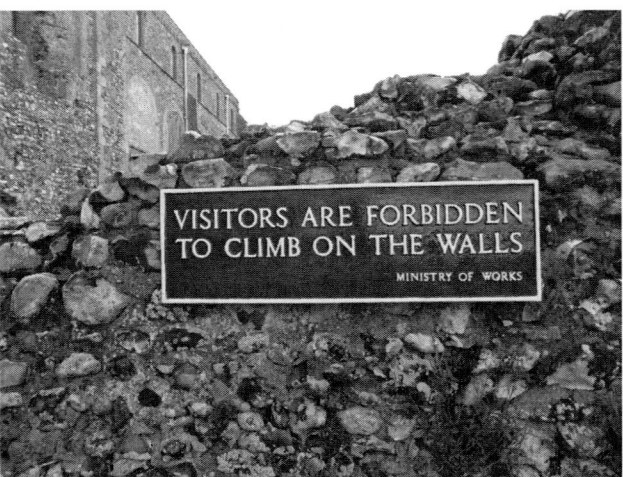

Fig. 14 Binham Priory the cast aluminium sign that greets you at the entrance to the cloisters.

Fig. 15 Binham Priory, a pair of cast aluminium signs in the east range.

Fig. 16 Tudor Cottage, Field Dalling.

Bishop Bonner's cottages, East Dereham (1939-1981). In 1929 it was reported that Walter Rye had secured a 'rent charge' on this row of three seventeenth-century timber-framed cottages in Church Street with a jettied front wall, fine pargeting and a cruck roof (Fig. 17).[21] It was resolved to enquire from the owners if they were prepared to sell, and in 1939 it was reported that a Mr Barton had offered to give the cottages to the Trust, and the property was conveyed into Trust ownership. Without the Trust becoming involved these cottages would probably have been pulled down to widen this dangerous corner of Church Street.

The cottages were re-thatched in 1954 for £253 and leased to the Dereham and District Antiquarian Society for a town museum. Once its future was assured it was sold in 1981 to Dereham Town Council for £5,500 and its occupation by the Dereham Antiquarian Society has continued to this day.

The Great Hall, Oak Street, Norwich (1956-2009). This building, sometimes known as Flowerpot Yard, since it was adjacent to the old Flowerpot public house, was bought in 1931 by Lt. Col. S.E. Glendenning, an active Council member and estate manager for the Trust from 1947, to save it from slum clearance. This, like Pykerell's House, was a rare fifteenth-century hall house with oriel window and a queen post roof, but unlike Pykerell's House the medieval section survived the war almost undamaged, although the front range of the building and almost all the surrounding properties were flattened during the air raids of 1942.[22] Glendenning restored the property, and on his death in 1956 he gave the Trust £775 the buy the building (Figs. 18-19). However, this was really a throwback to the Trust's activities of the 1930s rather than a new surge of enthusiasm in the 1950s.

When the tenancy fell vacant the Trust was unable to re-let the building as an office through selling agents despite carrying out further improvements, and in 2009 it was sold privately to the next-door neighbour who runs a motorbike business.

Garsett House, St Andrew's Plain, Norwich (1997-2005). Garsett House was built by Robert Gartside or Garsett, a Norwich Alderman, dating in part from the first part of the sixteenth century, and a plaque on the front wall before its recent removal recorded that the building was purchased by the Norfolk and Norwich Archaeological Society in 1951 with funds provided by Ernest Kent, who was also a benefactor to the Assembly House. The building sits in a commanding position overlooking St Andrew's Plain and it is an important part of the street scene (Fig. 20).[23] The first floor was used as the Society's library and meetings room, and the ground and second floors were let as barristers' chambers. However, the Archaeological Society found upkeep increasingly difficult and sold it to the Trust for £1 in 1998 on the understanding that if at any time the Trust wanted to sell the building it would sell it back to the Society for the same figure. The Trust, with its previous experience of managing historic buildings, should have understood the problems it was taking on, but there was a wish to help the Society. The first floor continued as the Society's library, and for a while the rest was rented by the Norfolk Archaeological Unit. When the Unit left, no new tenant could be found, and the building was put on the market and sold in 2008 with the sale proceeds going back to the Society.

Two fires, three bombs and a declining membership

With the fires at Sprowston Mill and Augustine Steward's House, and severe bomb damage at Pykerell's House, Greenland Fishery and the Great Hall, the trustees had a run of very bad luck with their acquisitions. In the 1930s Council was also faced with a declining membership. People were joining the Norfolk and Norwich Archaeological Society, but not the Trust, so much of the work had to be funded privately by members of Council. To increase income it was resolved in June 1936 to write to selected members of the Archaeological Society as follows:

> The Norfolk Archaeological Trust asks for the support of all who are interested in the preservation of those properties which have been acquired through the activities of the Norfolk and Norwich Archaeological Society.
>
> The trust was incorporated to hold property for this Society in 1923 by the generosity of a few members who came forward with gifts or loans of money. The membership has declined with the passage of time and fresh support is needed if the properties in our possession are to be maintained adequately and if, as is most desirable, our activities are to be extended. There are ancient sites of great interest which ought to be acquired if they are to be saved from destruction or injury, as without acquisition it is impossible to ensure proper maintenance and excavation. Again, with the rapid development of modern building we are anxious to preserve and keep in good condition typical cottages and buildings of the olden days in various parts of the county.

It was not strictly true to say that the Trust was incorporated to hold property for the Society, but it was, no doubt, intended to promote their fund raising case. The letter listed the properties the Trust had acquired and then went on:

> The income is insufficient for the ordinary costs of administration and maintenance, apart from any question of expansion, and the only solution of the difficulty lies in increased support by members of the Archaeological Society. Membership of the Trust involved an annual subscription of 10/- or a single compound payment of £10, and arrangements have been made for new subscribers to pay their subscriptions by including them with their annual contributions to the Archaeological Society.
>
> May we hope for your help in this important matter?

---

[21] Pevsner and Wilson 1999, pp. 291-2
[22] Barrett 1991; Pevsner and Wilson 1997, p. 290; Ayers 1987
[23] Pevsner and Wilson 1997, p. 294; Smith 1996

Fig. 17 Bishop Bonner's cottages, Church Street, Dereham.

Fig. 18 The Great Hall, Oak Street, Norwich.

Fig. 19 The Great Hall interior view of hall with the top half of the oriel window and queen post roof.

Fig. 20 Garsett House, St Andrew's Plain, Norwich.

The letter was signed by all the officers of the Trust, and a copy is stuck into the Council's minute book. It is not recorded how many members of the Society then joined the Trust, but as the matter wasn't mentioned again, probably very few. Low membership has always been a problem for the Trust, and it still is, for reasons which are always difficult to understand.

Despite its small membership the pre-war achievements of the Trust were very impressive, and indeed it is not now entirely clear where a lot of the money for the acquisitions actually came from since the early accounts do not survive. The wealthier members certainly contributed to Trust funds with loans and mortgages. Despite the problems, they were a dedicated group who deserve to be more widely recognised.

Building maintenance seemed endless

Before the introduction of post-war planning legislation, the Trust undoubtedly saved from demolition most of the buildings it had purchased in the 1930s. The 1944 Town and Country Planning Act gave local authorities the power to draw up 'lists' of historic buildings, and this then became a requirement in 1947. The lists were not completed until 1966, and from 1968 listed building consent was required for the demolition of a grade I or II* building. Although the legislation to protect historic buildings had come in much later than it had for ancient monuments, when it was introduced it was much more effective. After the 1944 Act, Trust Council considered that owning historic buildings was no longer necessary, and it gradually disposed of those it had owned. No further buildings were acquired except for the Great Hall, which it had inherited from an earlier phase, and Garsett House in Norwich.

It would be fair to say that the early energies of the Trust were greatly reduced by the war and by Basil's increasing years. Although he didn't withdraw from participation in the Trust until 1974 (his last Council meeting was in July 1973), the sense of purpose so strong in the 1930s was less obvious by the 1950s. By the 1960s Council meetings were dominated by endless discussions about how to keep their existing properties in good order. For instance, in July 1967 Council were faced with costs as follows:

Bishop Bonners cottages	£91
Greenland Fishery	£225
Pykerells House	£225
Great Hall	£100
Field Dalling cottage	£500
Total	£1,141

With this burden, repeated to some degree year after year, there was little appetite for new initiatives.

The rising threat to archaeology in the countryside

It is interesting that no effort was made to acquire archaeological sites in farmland as diesel tractors grew ever more powerful and bulldozing of earthworks and ploughing became ever more destructive in the 1950s and 1960s. For those of us with an interest in archaeology who were growing up in the Norfolk countryside at the time, watching old meadows, often with earthworks in them, being levelled with government grants was a very distressing experience; 73% of grassland in 1946 had gone by 1973.[24] The flattening, draining and ploughing of the deserted village at Thuxton in 1962/3 was for me the most difficult to comprehend.[25] Why was the archaeological profession not making a big fuss? With hindsight, the simple answer is that there were then still so few working outside museums who were aware of what was going on and able to raise concerns about the devastating damage farming was doing to the historic landscape.

The turning point

The moment when the Trust set itself on a new path can be accurately identified in the minutes as 21 July 1982 when at a Council meeting the Secretary, Jon Skelton who was a senior partner at Cozens-Hardy and Jewson, pointed out that the Trust had sold a number of properties in recent years and had invested the proceeds '..and it was important to take stock of the Trust's future to ensure that the Trust fulfils its objects to the best of its ability.' There was no appetite for more historic buildings, and the writer said that he had been looking for a purchaser for the Roman fort at Brancaster when it had been on the market and wondered whether this sort of project would be suitable for the Trust. It was then agreed to look out for other such suitable sites.

Brancaster had eventually been bought by the National Trust, which then also agreed to acquire a fine and rather vulnerable little motte and bailey castle at Darrow Wood in Denton after it was spotted by the writer for sale in the Small Ads of the *Eastern Daily Press*. But after that an attempt to persuade the National Trust to take on New Buckenham Castle when that was for sale did not succeed. The stage was then set for the Trust to take on a leading role with monument acquisition and conservation in the countryside. So, Jon Skelton's comment that the Trust needed to review its objectives proved timely. Council readily accepted the defended centre of the Roman town at Caistor St Edmund when it was offered as a bequest in 1984. The Trust then went on to acquire the hillfort at Church Field at Tasburgh[26], the Roman fort at Burgh Castle[27], Bloodgate Hill South Creake[28], St Benet's Abbey[29], the motte and bailey castle at Middleton[30] and others, but that is another story.

This programme of acquiring a selection of sites in the countryside in need of better protection was run alongside

---

[24] Norfolk County Council 1994, pp. 20-1
[25] Butler and Wade-Martins 1989
[26] Rogerson and Lawson 1991
[27] Johnson 1983
[28] Penn 2006
[29] Cushion and Davison 2003, pp. 148-9
[30] Ashwin 1999

the Norfolk Monuments Management Project, which the writer initiated and chaired from 1990, to give management advice to farmers of earthwork sites believed to be of schedulable quality[31] and the Norfolk Earthworks Survey from 1994 to make detailed surveys of all significant earthworks in grassland at a scale of 1:1,000.[32] This triple approach has proved to be a model for monument conservation in rural areas, although it is seldom followed elsewhere.

The Trust has all its properties open to the public free of charge, thanks in particular to the generous grants it receives from Natural England under a series of Countryside Stewardship schemes. It must always be remembered, though, that none of this would have happened without the pioneering efforts of those early enthusiasts who did so much to promote conservation of the historic environment despite extraordinary difficulties before conservation grants were available.

August 2013

---

[31] Paterson and Wade-Martins 1999; Robertson and Paterson 2010
[32] Cushion and Davison 2003

Bibliography

Ashwin, T. 1999, 'Middleton Mount: excavations in and around the eastern bailey of Middleton Castle by Andrew Rogerson', *Norfolk Archaeology* 43, pp. 645-56

Ayers, B. 1987, 'Flowerpot Court, Oak Street' *Digging Deeper*, pp. 28-30

Barrett, G.N. 1991, 'The Great Hall, Oak St., Norwich', *Norfolk Archaeology* 41, pp. 202-7

Butler, L., and Wade-Martins, P. 1989, *The Deserted Village of Thuxton, Norfolk*, East Anglian Archaeology 46

Cozens-Hardy, B. 1926, 'Scheduling of the Norfolk Ancient Monuments' *Norfolk Archaeology* 22, pp. 221-6

Cresswell, I. 1977, Obituary to B. Cozens-Hardy, *Norfolk Archaeology* 36, pp. 283-4.

Cushion, B., and Davison, A. 2003, *Earthworks of Norfolk*, East Anglian Archaeology 104

Fowler, E. 1976, 'Some Norfolk Naturalists: a historic survey', *Nature in Norfolk*, pp. 9-17

Harrison, H.C. 1949, *The Story of Sprowston Mill*

Impey, E. 2008, *Castle Acre Priory and Castle*, English Heritage guidebook

Johnson, S. 1983, *Burgh Castle: excavations by Charles Green, 1958-61*, East Anglian Archaeology 20

Norfolk County Council, 1994, *Norfolk Countryside Conservation Strategy*

Paterson, H., and Wade-Martins, P. 1999, 'Monument Conservation in Norfolk: the Monument Management Project and other schemes' in Grenville, J., *Managing the Historic Rural Landscape,* pp. 137-47

Penn, K. 2006, 'Excavations and survey at the Iron Age fort at Bloodgate Hill, South Creake, 2003', *Norfolk Archaeology* 45, pp. 1-27

Pevsner, N., and Wilson, B. 1997, *Norfolk 1: Norwich and north-east*

Pevsner N., and Wilson B. 1999, *Norfolk 2: North-west and south*

Robertson D., and Paterson, H. 2010, 'The Norfolk Monuments Management Project 1990-2010: twenty years conserving the county's rural historic environment', *Norfolk Archaeology* 46, pp. 15-28

Rogerson, A., and Lawson, A. 1991, 'The Earthwork Enclosure at Tasburgh', in Davies, J.A., Gregory, A.K., Lawson, A.J., Rickett, R. and Rogerson, A. *The Iron Age Forts of Norfolk*, East Anglian Archaeology 54, pp. 31-58

Smith, R. 1996, 'Garsett House', *Norfolk Archaeology* 42, pp. 362-73

Thurley, S., 2013, *Men from the Ministry*

Wade-Martins, P. 2008, 'Managing Archaeological Sites in Norfolk', *Conservation Land Management* Vol. 6 (1), pp. 14-18

Waterson, M. 1994, *The National Trust: The First Hundred Years*

Williams, J.F. 1949, 'Pykerell's House, St Mary's Plain, Coslany', *The Archaeological Journal* 106, pp. 82-3